The Theory of Incentives

The Theory of Incentives

THE PRINCIPAL-AGENT MODEL

Jean-Jacques Laffont and
David Martimort

PRINCETON UNIVERSITY PRESS • PRINCETON AND OXFORD

Copyright ©2002 by Princeton University Press

Published by Princeton University Press, 41 William Street, Princeton, New Jersey 08540

In the United Kingdom: Princeton University Press, 3 Market Place, Woodstock, Oxfordshire OX20 1SY

Library of Congress Cataloging-in-Publication Data

Laffont, Jean-Jacques, 1947–

 The theory of incentives: the principal-agent model / Jean-Jacques Laffont and David Martimort.

  p. cm

 Includes bibliographical references and index.

 ISBN 0-691-09183-8 (alk.paper)–ISBN 0-691-09184-6 (pbk.: alk.paper)

  1. Economics. 2. Incentives in industry. I. Martimort, David. II. Title.

 HB171 I22 2002

 338.9–dc2I   2001051039

This book has been composed in Electra

Printed on acid-free paper. ∞

www.pup.princeton.edu

Printed in the United States of America

10 9 8 7 6 5 4 3 2 1

10 9 8 7 6 5 4 3

(Pbk.)

As the economy of incentives as a whole in terms of organization is not usually stressed in economic theory and is certainly not well understood, I shall attempt to indicate the outlines of the theory.

Chester Barnard (1938)

Contents

Foreword

The development of the theory of incentives has been a major advance in economics in the last thirty years. The objective of this book is to provide easy access to this theory for undergraduate and first-year graduate students in economics. Our goal is not to be as complete as possible in covering and surveying the many contributions that have flourished in the realm of incentive theory. Instead, our contribution is methodological and intended to offer students some initial clues for analyzing the issues raised by this theory. As much as possible we have favored the simplest models to explain the core of the theory. The exposition has been divided into three books for methodological clarity. This volume presents the basic principal-agent theory with complete contracts. It allows a first exposition of the transaction costs created by contracting under asymmetric information without having to appeal to sophisticated game theory concepts.

The book allows for two levels of reading. Certain sections in some chapters are marked with a star to the right of the section head. A first reading should concentrate on the non-starred sections. These sections are accessible to readers who have a simple knowledge of maximization with inequality constraints. Most essential economic lessons can be understood from this first level of reading. Covering the starred sections will enable students to manipulate the concepts for better assimilation and will put them in contact with the advanced topics of the field. Going through the text and checking the proofs should provide a good way for students to appropriate the material. Throughout the book we have listed under the heading 📖 the major references that are useful to pursue the study of incentive theory.

We thank our students whose excitement for the topic has led to this enterprise of trying to synthesize what we have learned in incentive theory. We are grateful also to Cécile Aubert, Gary Biglaiser, Xavier Carpentier, Pierre Dubois, Yolande Hiriart, Wu Kai, Fahad Khalil, Claudio Mezzetti, Jérôme Pouyet, and Stéphane Straub, who have offered comments on the first draft and to Marie-Pierre Boé who cheerfully and repeatedly revised our chapters.

The Theory of Incentives

Introduction

It is surprising to find that Schumpeter (1954) does not mention the word "incentives" in his monumental history of economic thought. Today, for many economists, economics is to a large extent a matter of incentives: incentives to work hard, to produce good quality products, to study, to invest, to save, etc. How to design institutions that provide good incentives for economic agents has become a central question of economics.

Maybe Schumpeter's omission arose because, when he was writing, economics was mostly concerned with understanding the theory of value in large economies. For that purpose, neoclassical economics in particular postulates rational individual behavior in the market. In a perfectly competitive market, this assumption translates into profit maximization for firms' owners, which implies cost minimization. In other words, the pressure of competitive markets solves the problem of incentives for cost minimization. Similarly, consumers faced with exogenous prices have the proper incentives for maximizing their utility levels. The major project of understanding how prices are formed in competitive markets can proceed without worrying about incentives.

However, by treating the firm as a black box the theory remains silent on how the owners of firms succeed in aligning the objectives of its various members, such as workers, supervisors, and managers, with profit maximization. When economists began to look more carefully at the firm, either in agricultural or managerial economics, incentives became the central focus of their analysis. Indeed, for various reasons, the owner of the firm must delegate several tasks to the members of the firm. This necessity raises the problem of managing information flows within the firm. The problem of managing information flows was the first research topic for economists, once they mastered behavior under uncertainty, thanks to Von Neumann and Morgenstern (1944). This line of research culminated in the theory of teams (Marschak and Radner [1972]), which recognized the decentralized nature of information but postulated identical objective functions for the members of the firm considered as a "team." How to coordinate actions among the members of the team by the proper management of information was the central focus of this research. Incentive questions were still outside the scope of the analysis.

However, as soon as one acknowledges that the members of a firm may have different objectives, delegation becomes more problematic as recognized early on by Marschak (1955) and also by Arrow when he observes that

> by definition the agent has been selected for his specialized knowledge and the principal can never hope to completely check the agent's performance (1963a).

Delegation of a task to an agent who has different objectives than the principal who delegates this task is problematic when information about the agent is imperfect. This problem is the essence of incentive questions. If the agent had a different objective function but no private information, the principal could propose a contract that perfectly controls the agent and induces the latter's actions to be what he would like to do himself in a world without delegation. Again, incentive issues would disappear.

Conflicting objectives and decentralized information are thus the two basic ingredients of incentive theory. The essential paradigm for the analysis of market behavior by economists is one where economic agents pursue, at least to some extent, their private interests. What is proposed by incentive theory is that this major assumption be maintained in the analysis of organizations, small markets, and any other kind of collective decision-making. This paradigm has its own limits. Social behavior, particularly in small groups, is more complex, and norms of behavior that are culturally inculcated or developed over time play a large role in shaping societies. However, it would be foolish not to recognize the role of private incentives in motivating behavior in addition to these cultural phenomena. The purpose of this book is to synthesize what we have learned from the incentives paradigm.[1] We hope that the step-by-step approach taken here, as well as our attempt to present many different results in a unified framework, will help readers not only to know more about incentive theory, but also to apply this indispensable tool when thinking about society.

The starting point of incentive theory corresponds to the problem of delegating a task to an agent with private information. This private information can be of two types: either the agent can take an action unobserved by the principal, the case of *moral hazard* or *hidden action*; or the agent has some private knowledge about his cost or valuation that is ignored by the principal, the case of *adverse selection* or *hidden knowledge*. Incentive theory considers when this private information is a problem for the principal, and what is the optimal way for the principal to cope with it. Another type of information problem that has been raised in the literature is the case of *nonverifiability*, which occurs when the principal and the agent share ex post the same information but no third party and, in particular, no court of law can observe this information. One can study to what extent the nonverifiability of information is also problematic for contractual design.

We will discover that, in general, these informational problems prevent society from achieving the first-best allocation of resources that could be possible in a world where all information would be common knowledge. The additional costs that must be incurred because of the strategic behavior of privately informed economic agents can be viewed as one category of the transaction costs emphasized by Williamson (1975). They do not exhaust all possible transaction costs, but economists have been rather successful during the last thirty years in modelling and analyzing these types of costs and providing a good understanding of the limits set by these on the allocation of resources. This work shows that the design of proper institutions for successful economic activity is more complex than one could have thought a priori. This line of research also provides a whole set of insights on how to begin to take into account agents' responses to the incentives provided by institutions.

As the next chapter will illustrate, a brief look at the history of economic thought shows that incentive theory was pervasive in many areas of economics, even though it was not central to economic thinking. Before describing how we will present this theory, it may be worth mentioning how the major achievement of economics, namely the general equilibrium theory (GE), met incentives.

General equilibrium theory was capable of producing powerful generalizations and able to deal with uncertainty, time, externalities, and extending the

---

[1]How private incentives interact with cultural norms of behavior might be the next important step of research needed to offer sensible advice on the design of institutions. Nevertheless, it is our conviction that for such a goal the mastering of incentive theory is a must.

validity of the *invisible hand* as long as the appropriate competitive markets could be set up.[2] However, at the beginning of the seventies, works by Akerlof (1970), Spence (1974), and Rothschild and Stiglitz (1976) showed in various ways that asymmetric information was posing a much greater challenge and could not be satisfactorily imbedded in a proper generalization of the Arrow-Debreu theory. The problems encountered were so serious that a whole generation of general equilibrium theorists momentarily gave up the grandiose framework of GE to reconsider the problem of exchange under asymmetric information in its simplest form, i.e., between two traders. In a sense, the theorists went back to basics. They joined another group trained in game theory and in the theory of organizations, and together they built the theory of incentives, which we take as encompassing contract theory and mechanism design.

We will present incentive theory in three progressive steps. This book is the first step; in it we consider the principal-agent model where the principal delegates an action to a single agent through the take-it-or-leave-it offer of a contract. Two implicit assumptions are made here. First, by postulating that it is the principal who makes a take-it-or-leave-it contract offer to the agent, we put aside the bargaining issues that are a topic for game theory.[3] Second, we assume the availability of a benevolent court of law that is able to enforce the contract and impose penalties if one of the contractual partners adopts a behavior that deviates from the one specified in the contract.[4]

Three types of information problems will be considered—adverse selection, moral hazard, and nonverifiability. Each of those informational problems leads to a different paradigm and, possibly, to a different kind of agency cost. On top of the usual technological constraints of neoclassical economics, these agency costs incorporate the informational constraints faced by the principal at the time of designing the contract.

In this book, we will assume that there are no restrictions on the contracts that the principal can offer. As a consequence, the design of the principal's optimal contract reduces to a simple optimization problem.[5] This simple focus will turn out

---

[2]See Mas-Colell, Whinston and Green (1995) for a recent textbook exposition.

[3]See, for example, Osborne and Rubinstein (1994) and Muthoo (1999).

[4]Let us stress here the importance of this assumption, which is apparently innocuous because in equilibrium no penalty is ever paid and the role of the court is minimal in what follows. However, judges must be given proper incentives to enforce contracts. We may rely here on the idea that in repeated relationships the desire to maintain their reputation will provide the appropriate incentives. This latter assumption is a little bit problematic since once could also appeal to the same reputation argument to justify that the principal-agent relationship may achieve allocative efficiency in repeated relationships even in the absence of any contract, with the appropriate cooperative behavior being self-enforcing.

[5]Thus, solving for the optimal contract requires only the simple tools of optimization theory.

to be enough to highlight the various trade-offs between allocative efficiency and the distribution of information rents arising under incomplete information. The mere existence of informational constraints may generally prevent the principal from achieving allocative efficiency. The main objective of the analysis undertaken in this volume is therefore the characterization of the allocative distortions that the principal finds desirable to implement in order to mitigate the impact of informational constraints.

Our next book will be the second step of our analysis. We will consider there, situations with one principal and several agents, still without any restriction on the principal's contracts. Asymmetric information may not only affect the relationship between the principal and each of his agents, but it may also plague the relationships between agents. Moreover, maintaining the hypothesis that agents adopt an individualistic behavior, those organizational contexts require a new equilibrium concept, the Bayesian-Nash equilibrium, which describes the strategic interaction between agents under incomplete information. Three main themes arise in this context. First, the organization may have been built to facilitate a joint decision between the agents. In such a context, the principal must overcome the free-rider problems that may exist among agents when they must undertake a collective decision. Second, the principal may attempt to benefit from the competition between the agents to relax the informational constraints and better reduce the agents' information rents. Auctions, tournaments, yardstick competition, and supervision of one agent by another are all mechanisms designed by the principal with this purpose in mind. Third, the mere attempt by the principal to use competition among agents may also trigger their collusion against the principal. The principal must now worry not only about individual incentives, but also about group incentives in a multiagent organization.

Our third book will be the final step of the analysis and will study the implications of various imperfections in the design of contracts: informed principal, limited commitment, renegotiation, implicit incentives, imperfect coordination among various principals, and incomplete contracting due to the nonverifiability of a parameter relevant for assessing the value of trade. The dynamics of some of these imperfect contractual relationships call for the extensive use of another equilibrium concept, the perfect Bayesian equilibrium. Equipped with this tool, we will be better able to describe the allocation of resources resulting from such imperfect contractual relationships.

In this book we proceed as follows. Chapter 1 gives a brief account of the history of thought concerning incentive theory. It shows that incentives questions have been present in many areas of economics over the last two centuries, even though it is only recently that their importance has been recognized and that economists have undertaken their systematic treatment. Chapter 2 presents the basic rent extraction-efficiency trade-off that arises in principal-agent models with adverse selection. Extensions of this framework to more complex environments are discussed in chapter 3. Chapter 4 presents the two types of agency conflicts under moral hazard: the trade-offs between the extraction of a limited liability rent and efficiency and also between insurance and efficiency. Again, extensions of this basic framework are discussed in chapter 5. Chapter 6 considers the nonverifiability paradigm, which in general does not call for economic distortions. Mixed models with adverse selection, moral hazard, and nonverifiability are the subject of chapter 7. The extension of principal-agent models with adverse selection and moral hazard to dynamic contexts with full commitment is discussed in chapter 8. Finally, chapter 9 discusses a number of simple extensions of the basic framework used throughout the book.

1 Incentives in Economic Thought

Incentive theory[1] emerges with the division of labor and exchange.[2] The division of labor induces the need for delegation. Historically, the first contracts probably appeared in agriculture, when landlords contracted with their tenants. It is no wonder then that Adam Smith encountered incentive problems in his discussion of sharecropping contracts (section 1.1). Delegation was also needed within firms, hence the importance of the topic in the theory of organizations (section 1.2).

For private goods, competitive markets ensure efficiency despite the decentralized nature of the information about individuals' tastes and firms' technologies. Implicitly, yardstick competition solves adverse selection problems and the fixed-price contracts associated with exogenous prices solve moral hazard problems. However, markets fail for pure public goods, and public intervention is thus

---

[1]The reader totally unfamiliar with this topic may benefit from reading Chapters 2 and 4 before Chapter 1 to become acquainted with some basic vocabulary.

[2]Actually, one could also argue that incentive issues arise within the family if one postulates different objective functions for the members of the family.

needed. In this case, the mechanisms used for those collective decisions must solve the incentive problem of acquiring the private information that agents have about their preferences for public goods (section 1.3). Voting mechanisms are particular incentive mechanisms that lack monetary transfers for which the same question of strategic behavior, i.e, not voting according to one's true preferences, can be raised (section 1.4).

For private goods, increasing returns to scale creates a situation of natural monopoly far removed from the world of competitive markets. When the monopoly has private information about its cost or demand, its regulation by a regulatory commission becomes a principal-agent problem (section 1.5).

Exchange raises incentive issues when the commodity that is bought has a value unknown to the buyer but known to the seller. In particular, this issue is the case in insurance markets when the insurance company buys a risk plagued with moral hazard or adverse selection. The insurance company faces a principal-agent problem with each insured agent, but may nevertheless have a statistical knowledge of the distribution of risks (section 1.6). A similar situation occurs when a government attempts to redistribute income between wage earners of different and unknown productive abilities (section 1.7) or when a monopolist looks for the optimal discriminating contract to offer to a population of consumers with heterogeneous tastes for its product (section 1.8). Of course, incentive issues were encountered in managing socialist economies, where profit incentives of managers were suppressed by public ownership of the means of production (section 1.9). The idea that, in noncompetitive economies, it is necessary to design mechanisms taking into account communication and incentive constraints was further developed by theorists dealing with nonconvex economies, and this work led to the mechanism design methodology (section 1.10). The mechanism design methodology is a useful tool for understanding the allocation of resources in multiagent frameworks when information is decentralized. A natural field in which to apply this methodology is the theory of auctions. Auctions are mechanisms used by principals to benefit from the competition among several agents (section 1.11).

1.1 Adam Smith and Incentive Contracts in Agriculture

In his discussion of the determination of wages, Adam Smith (1776, bk. 1, chap. 7) recognized the contractual nature of the relationship between the masters and the workers. He asserted the conflicting interests of those two players and recognized that the bargaining power was not evenly distributed between them; the masters generally had all the bargaining power. In the modern language of the theory of incentives, the masters are principals and the workers, their agents:

> What are the common wages of labour, depends everywhere upon the contract usually made between those two parties, whose interests are not the same. The workmen desire to get as much, the masters to give as little as possible.
>
> —Smith (1776, bk. 1, chap. 7, p. 66)

Smith also stressed one of the basic constraints that we model later on, the agent's participation constraint, which limits what the principal can ask from the agent:

> A man must always live by his work, and his wages must at least be sufficient to maintain him.
>
> —Smith (1776, p. 67)

Smith did not have a vision of economic actors as long-run maximizers of utility. He worried about the consequences of high-power incentives for short-run maximizers:

> Workmen ... when they are liberally paid by the piece, are very apt to overwork themselves, and to ruin their health and constitution in a few years.
>
> —Smith (1776, bk. 1, chap. 8, p. 81)

He stressed the lack of appropriate incentives for slaves:

> [T]he work done by slaves, though it appears to cost only their maintenance, is in the end the dearest of any. A person who can acquire no property, can have no other interest but to eat as much, and to labour as little as possible.
>
> —Smith (1776, bk. 1, chap. 8, p. 365)

To explain the survivance of such highly inefficient contracts, Adam Smith also appealed to noneconomic motives:

> The pride of man makes him love to domineer, and nothing mortifies him so much as to be obliged to condescend to persuade his inferiors.
>
> —Smith (1776, bk. 1, chap. 8, p. 365)

Smith's most precise and famous discussion of incentives appeared in book 3, chapter 2, when he wanted to explain the discouragement of agriculture in Europe after the fall of the Roman Empire. He described the status of metayers (known as *coloni partarii* in ancient times and as steel-bow tenants in Scotland):

The proprietor furnished them with the seed, cattle and instruments of husbandry. The produce was divided equally between the proprietor and the farmer.

—Smith (1776, bk. 3, chap. 2, p. 366)

However, Smith did not conclude that metayers would not exert the appropriate level of effort to maximize social value, as modern incentive theory would claim:

Such tenants, being free men, are capable of acquiring property, and having a certain proportion of the produce of the land, they have a plain interest that the whole produce would be as great as possible, in order that their own proportion may be so.

—Smith (1776, bk. 3, chap. 2, p. 366)

At several places in this volume, we see the fundamental trade-off between incentives and the distribution of the gains from trade. Clearly Smith was not aware of this trade-off. Rather, he saw the most serious incentive problems in the absence of tenants' investment in the land, and in the unobservable misuse of husbandry instruments provided by the proprietor.

It could never, however, be the interest even of this last species of cultivators (the metayers) to lay out, in the further improvement of the land, any part of the little stock they might save from their own share of the produce, because the lord, who laid out nothing, was to get one-half of whatever it produced. ... It *might* be the interest of metayer to make the land produce as much as could be brought out of it by means of the stock furnished by the proprietor; but it could never be in his interest to mix any part of his own with it. In France ... the proprietors complain that their metayers take every opportunity of employing the master's cattle rather in carriage than in cultivation; because in the one case they get the whole profits for themselves, in the other they share them with their landlords.

—Smith (1776, bk. 3, chap. 2, p. 367)

Note the ambiguous *might*, which shows that Smith probably envisioned under-effort but that he considered it secondary compared to the under-investment effect. However, the alternative use of cattle is a typical example of what we will call a hidden action problem or a moral hazard problem.

Smith's criticism of sharecropping has been the point of departure of a large literature in agricultural economics, history of thought, and economic theory trying to understand the characteristics of sharecropping contracts. Following Smith, and until Johnson (1950), economists considered sharecropping to be a "practice which is hurtful to the whole society," an unexplained failure of the invisible hand that should be either discouraged by taxation or improved by appropriate sharing of variable factors.[3] A better understanding of the phenomenon was only achieved when the economists reconsidered the problem in the context of the principal-agent theory.[4]

1.2 Chester Barnard and Incentives in Management

As we saw above, Smith (1776) already discussed the problems associated with piece-rate contracts in the industry. Babbage (1835) went a step further by understanding the need for precise measurement of performances to set up efficient piece-rate or profit-sharing contracts:

> It would, indeed, be of great mutual advantage to the industrious workman, and to the master manufacturer in every trade, if the machines employed in it could register the quantity of work which they perform, in the same manner as a steam-engine does the number of strokes it makes. The introduction of such contrivances gives a greater stimulus to honest industry than can readily be imagined, and removes one of the sources of disagreement between parties.
>
> —Babbage (1835, p. 297)

Also, Babbage proposed various principles to remunerate labor:

> The general principles on which the proposed system is founded, are
>
> 1. That a considerable part of the wages received by each person should depend on the profits made by the establishment; and,
> 2. That every person connected with it should derive more advantage from applying any improvement he might discover than he could by any other course.
>
> (Babbage 1989, Vol. 8, p. 177)

However, Barnard (1938) is the one who can probably be credited with the first attempt to define a general theory of incentives in management, in chapter 11 (the economy of incentives) and chapter 12 (the theory of authority) of his celebrated book *The Functions of the Executive*, which he wrote after a long career in

---

[3]See Schickele (1941) and Heady (1947).
[4]See Stiglitz (1974).

management, most notably as president of the New Jersey Bell Telephone Company:

> [A]n essential element of organizations is the willingness of persons to contribute their individual efforts to the cooperative system. ... Inadequate incentives mean dissolution, or changes of organization purpose, or failure to cooperate. Hence, in all sorts of organizations the affording of adequate incentives becomes the most definitely emphasized task in their existence. It is probably in this aspect of executive work that failure is most pronounced.
>
> —Barnard (1938, p. 139)

Actually, Barnard had a broad view of incentives, involving both what we would now call monetary and nonmonetary incentives:

> An organization can secure the efforts necessary to its existence, then, either by the objective inducements it provides or by changing states of mind. ... We shall call the process of offering objective incentives "the method of incentives"; and the processes of changing subjective attitudes "the method of persuasion."
>
> —Barnard (1938, p. 142)

The incentives may be specific or general:

> The specific inducements that may be offered are of several classes, for example: a) material inducements; b) personal non material opportunities; c) desirable physical conditions; d) ideal benefactions. General incentives afforded are, for example: e) associational attractiveness; f) adaptation of conditions to habitual methods and attitudes; g) opportunity of enlarged participation; h) the condition of communion.
>
> —Barnard (1938, p. 142)

Barnard also stressed the ineffectiveness of material incentives, which at the time were almost exclusively considered by economic theory:

> [E]ven in purely commercial organizations, material incentives are so weak as to be almost negligible except when reinforced by other incentives.
>
> —Barnard (1938, p. 144)

> Persuasion ... includes: a) the creation of coercive conditions (as forced exclusion of indesirables); b) the rationalization of opportunities (if the conviction that material things are worth while ... succeeds in capturing

waste effort and wasted time ... it is clearly advantageous); c) the incul-
cation of motives.[5]

—Barnard (1938, p. 149)

Barnard pointed out the necessary delicate balance of the various types of
incentives for success. Furthermore, such a good balance is highly dependent on
an unstable environment (through competition in particular) and on the internal
evolution of the organization itself (growth, change of personnel). Finally, in his
chapter on authority, Barnard recognized that incentive contracts do not rule all
the activities within an organization. The distribution of authority along communication channels is also necessary to achieve coordination and promote cooperation:

> Authority arises from the technological and social limitations of cooper-
> ative systems on the one hand, and of individuals on the other.
>
> —Barnard (1938, p. 184)

In modern language, Barnard is saying that the incompleteness of contracts
and the bounded rationality of members in the organization require that some
leaders be given authority to make decisions in circumstances not addressed specifically by the contracts. His main point is to stress the need to satisfy ex post participation constraints of members who accept noncontractual orders only if they are
compatible with their own long-run interests:

> A person can and will accept a communication as authoritative only
> when ... at *the time of his decision*, he believes it to be compatible with
> his personal interest as a whole.
>
> —Barnard (1938, p. 165)

Barnard's work emphasized the need to induce appropriate effort levels from
members of the organization—the moral hazard problem—and to create authority
relationships within the organization to deal with the necessary incompleteness
of incentive contracts. Not until a few decades later did Arrow (1963a) introduce into the literature on the control of management, the idea of moral hazard,
borrowed from the world of insurance. This work would be further extended by
Wilson (1968) and Ross (1973), who redefined it explicitly as an *agency problem*.
The chapter on authority written by Barnard directly inspired Simon's (1951) formal theory of the employment relationship. Finally, Williamson (1975) followed
Barnard and Simon to develop his transaction costs theory for the case of symmetric but nonverifiable information between two parties.[6] Grossman and Hart

---

[5]Between parentheses are examples given later in the text.
[6]See Williamson's citation at the beginning of chapter 6.

(1986) modeled this paradigm, which led to the large body of recent literature on incomplete contracts.[7]

1.3 Hume, Wicksell, Groves: The Free-Rider Problem

Hume (1740) may be credited with writing the first explicit statement of the free-rider problem:

> Two neighbours may agree to drain a meadow, which they possess in common; because it is easy for them to know each others mind; and each must perceive, that the immediate consequence of his failing in his part, is the abandoning the whole project. But it is very difficult, and indeed impossible, that a thousand persons shou'd agree in any such action; it being difficult for them to concert so complicated a design, and still more difficult for them to execute it; while each seeks a pretext to free himself of the trouble and expence, and wou'd lay the whole burden on others.
>
> —Hume (1740, p. 538)

At the end of the nineteenth century, a lively debate over public finance took place among European economists about the "benefit" approach and the "ability to pay" approach to taxation. In particular, Mazzola, Pantaleoni, and de Viti de Marco in Italy, and Sax in Austria, used the "modern" concepts of marginal utility and subjective value, extending the benefit approach implicit in the writings of many authors of the eighteenth century, such as Bentham, Locke, and Rousseau. Wicksell (1896), in his discussion of Mazzola's contribution, pointed out what became known later as the free-rider problem, which had been ignored in the benefit approach to taxation:

> If the individual is to spend his money for private and public uses so that his satisfaction is maximized he will obviously pay nothing whatsovever for public purposes. ... Whether he pays much or little will affect the scope of public service so slightly, that for all practical purposes, he himself will not notice it at all. Of course, if everyone were to do the same, the State will soon cease to function.
>
> —Wicksell (1896, p. 81)

Wicksell suggested a solution: the principle of (approximative) unanimity and voluntary consent. Each item in the public budget must be voted simultaneously

---

[7]See Hart (1995) and Tirole (1999) for recent syntheses.

with the determination of its financing and must be accepted only if unanimity (or quasi-unanimity) is obtained.[8] If we could ignore strategic behavior, this process would lead to Pareto optimality. However, which one of the Pareto optima will be reached depends upon the sequential realization of the decision-making process. Indeed, this is the main reason justifying strategic behavior by the participants as they try to manipulate the path of the procedure.

With the exception of Bowen's (1943) voting procedure discussed in the next section, nothing was proposed until the seventies to solve the free-rider problem, which appeared formidable. Nevertheless, in 1971, Drèze and Vallée Poussin extended the literature on the iterative planning procedures of the sixties to public goods. At each step of the procedure, agents announce their marginal rates of substitution between public goods and the private good. They noted that revelation of the true marginal rates of substitution was a maximin strategy, which is a weak incentive property.

Finally, Clarke (1971), Groves (1973) and Groves and Loeb (1975), making strong restrictions on preferences to evade the Gibbard-Satterthwaite Impossibility Theorem,[9] provided mechanisms with monetary transfers inducing truthful revelation of preferences and making the Pareto optimal public good decision. The literature that followed substantially developed incentive theory and mechanism design methodology.[10]

1.4 Borda, Bowen, Vickrey: Incentives in Voting

Since the beginning of the theory on voting, the issue of strategic voting was noticed. Borda (1781) recognized it when he proposed his famous Borda rule:

> My scheme is only intended for honest men.

We have to wait for Bowen (1943) to see a first attempt at addressing the issue of *strategic voting*. For allocating public goods, Bowen (as we mentioned in section 1.3) was searching in voting for an alternative to the missing expression of preferences that exists in markets for private goods. He realized the difficulty of strategic voting:

> At first thought it might be supposed that this information could be obtained from his vote. ... But the individual could not vote intelligently, unless he knew in advance the cost to him of various amounts of the

---

[8]This notion was later formalized by Foley (1967).
[9]See section 1.4 in this chapter.
[10]See Green and Laffont (1979) and Aspremont and Gérard-Varet (1979).

social good, and in any case the results of voting would be unreliable if the individual suspected that his expression of preference would influence the amount of cost to be assessed against him.

—Bowen (1943, p. 45)

Bowen assumed that the distribution of the cost of the public good was exogenously fixed (e.g., equal sharing of cost) and considered successive votes on increments of the public good. He observed that at each step it is in the interest of each voter to vote yes or no according to his true preferences. Such a procedure leads to the optimal level of public good if agents are myopic and consider only their incentives at each step.[11] Black (1948), years after Borda, Condorcet, Laplace, and Dogson, reconsidered the theory of voting and exhibited a wide class of cases (single-peaked preferences) for which majority voting leads to the transitivity of social choice, a solution to the 1785 Condorcet paradox. Black eliminated, by assumption, strategic issues:

When a member values the motions before a committee in a definite order, it is reasonable to assume that, when these motions are put against each other, he votes in accordance with his valuation.

—Black (1948, p. 134), cited in Arrow and Scitovsky (1969)

When Arrow (1951) founded the formal theory of social choice by proving that there is no "reasonable" voting method yielding a nondictatorial social transitive ranking of social alternatives when no restriction is placed on individual preferences, he also abstracted from the gaming issues and noticed that

[t]he point here, broadly speaking, is that, once a machinery for making social choices from individual tastes is established, individuals will find it profitable, from a rational point of view, to misrepresent their tastes by their actions or, more usually, because some other individual will be made so much better off by the first individual's misrepresentation that he could compensate the first individual in such a way that both are better off than if everyone really acted in direct accordance with his tastes."[12]

—Arrow (1951, p. 7)

In a paper that provides a very lucid exposition of Arrow's impossibility theorem, Vickrey (1960) raised the question of strategic misrepresentation of preferences in a social welfare function that associates a social ranking to individual preferences:

---

[11]See Green and Laffont (1979, chap. 14) for a more detailed analysis of this procedure.
[12]Note that the last part of this quotation refers to incentives for groups.

There is another objection to such welfare functions, however, which is
that they are vulnerable to strategy. By this is meant that individuals may
be able to gain by reporting a preference differing from that which they
actually hold.

—Vickrey (1960, p. 517)

and

Such a strategy could, of course, lead to a counterstrategy, and the process
of arriving at a social decision could readily turn into a "game" in the
technical sense.

—Vickrey (1960, p. 518)

Dummett and Farquharson (1961) would indeed pursue the analysis of such
voting games in terms of noncooperative Nash equilibria. Vickrey (1960) further
explained that the social welfare functions that satisfy the assumptions of Arrow's
theorem, in particular the independence assumption, are immune to strategy.
Then comes his conjecture, acknowledged by Gibbard (1973):

It can be plausibly conjectured that the converse is also true, that is, that
if a function is to be immune to strategy and to be defined over a com-
prehensive range of admissible rankings, it must satisfy the independence
criterion, though it is not quite so easy to provide a formal proof of this.

—Vickrey (1960, p. 588)

Therefore, Vickrey is led, through Arrow's theorem, to an impossibility result,
namely the nonexistence of any method of aggregating individual preferences or of
any voting mechanism that is nonmanipulable. The route toward the impossibility
of nonmanipulable and nondictatorial mechanisms via Arrow's theorem was suggested. A complete proof, the greatest achievement of social choice theory since
Arrow's theorem, came thirteen years later in Gibbard (1973).[13] The importance
of Gibbard's theorem for incentive theory lies in showing that with no prior knowledge of preferences, nondictatorial collective decision methods cannot be found
where truthful behavior is a dominant strategy. The positive results of incentive
methods in practice will have to be looked for in restrictions on preferences, as in
the principal-agent theory, or in the relaxation of the required strength of incentives
by giving up dominant strategy implementation.

[13]See also Satterthwaite (1975).

1.5 Léon Walras and the Regulation of Natural Monopolies

Walras (1897) defined a natural monopoly as an industry where monopoly is the efficient market structure and suggested, following Smith (1776), to price the product of the firm by balancing its budget. This led to the Ramsey (1927) and Boiteux (1956) theory of optimal pricing under a budget constraint.

After some price cap regulation attempts in the nineteenth century, the practice of regulation was rate of return regulation, which ensures prices covering costs inclusive of a (higher than the market) cost of capital. This led to the Averch and Johnson (1962) over-capitalization result, which was largely overemphasized.

In 1979, Loeb and Magat finally put the regulation literature in the framework of the principal-agent literature with adverse selection by stressing the lack of information of the regulator. They proposed to use a Groves dominant strategy mechanism, which solves the problem of asymmetric information at no cost when there is no social cost in transfers from the regulator to the firm.

Baron and Myerson (1982) transformed the problem into a second-best problem by weighting the firm's profit with a smaller weight than consumers' surplus in the social welfare function maximized by the regulator. In this scenario, optimal regulation entails a distortion from the first-best (pricing higher than marginal cost) to decrease the information rent of the regulated firm. Laffont and Tirole (1986) used a utilitarian social welfare function with the same weight for profit and consumers' surplus, but introduced a social cost for public funds (due to distortive taxation), which also creates a rent-efficiency trade-off. Their model features both adverse selection and moral hazard, but the ex post observability of cost (commonly used in regulation) makes it technically an adverse selection model.[14] This model was developed in Laffont and Tirole (1993) along many dimensions (dynamics, renegotiation, auctions, political economy, etc.).

1.6 Knight, Arrow, Pauly: Incentives in Insurance

The notion of moral hazard, i.e., the ability of insured agents to affect the probabilities of insured events, was well known in the insurance profession.[15] However,

---

[14]See chapter 7 in this book.
[15]See, for example, Faulkner (1960) and Dickerson (1957).

the insurance writers tended to look upon this phenomenon as a moral or ethical problem affecting their business.

Arrow (1963b) introduced this concept in the economic literature and argued that it led to a market failure because some insurance markets would not emerge due to moral hazard.[16] Arrow was quite influenced by the moral connotation of the concept and looked for solutions involving changes of ethical attitudes. Pauly (1968) rejected this approach, by arguing that it was quite natural for agents to react to zero price—like demanding more health care if treatment was free—and that the noninsurability of some risks did not imply a market failure in that no proof was given of the superiority of public intervention faced with the same informational problems. Pauly (1974) and Helpman and Laffont (1975) showed that competitive insurance markets (with linear prices) were inefficient in the sense that an uninformed government could improve upon the free market outcome.

Spence and Zeckhauser (1971) looked for more sophisticated contracts (nonlinear prices). They solved the maximization of the welfare of a representative agent with a break-even constraint for the insurance company and the moral hazard constraint that each agent chooses his level of self-protection optimally. When the self-protection variable is chosen before nature selects the states of nature (i.e., who has an accident, who does not), they obtained the moral hazard model with a continuum of agents and a break-even constraint. When the self-protection variable is chosen after nature selects the states of nature, they have both moral hazard and adverse selection, making the problem quite close to the Mirrlees optimal income tax problem (as already noted by Zeckhauser 1970).[17]

Ross (1973) expressed the pure principal-agent model with only moral hazard and an individual rationality constraint for the agent before it received its modern treatment in Mirrlees (1975), Guesnerie and Laffont (1979), Holmström (1979), Shavell (1979), and later in Grossman and Hart (1983).

---

[16]LeRoy and Singell (1987) make the claim we share that, by uncertainty, Knight (1921) meant situations in which insurance markets collapse because of moral hazard or adverse selection: "The classification or grouping (necessary for insurance) can only to a limited extent be carried out by any agency outside the person himself who makes the decisions, because of the peculiarly obstinate connection of a moral hazard with this sort of risks" (Knight 1921, p. 251); "We have assumed ... that each man in society knows his own powers as entrepreneur, but that men know nothing about each other in this capacity. ... The presence of true profit, therefore, depends ... on the absence of the requisite organization for combining a sufficient number of instances to secure certainty through consolidation. With men in complete ignorance of the powers of judgement of other men it is hard to see how such organization can be effected" (ibid., 284).

However, Knight did not recognize that problems of moral hazard and adverse selection could be attenuated or eliminated with properly structured contracts.

[17]Spence and Zeckhauser (1971) do not go much beyond writing first-order conditions for this problem, and refer to Mirrlees (1971) when they use the Pontryagin principle. See section 1.7 for a discussion of the Mirrlees model.

The Pareto inefficiency of competitive insurance markets (with linear prices) with adverse selection was shown in Rothschild and Stiglitz (1976),[18] and their successors studied various forms of competition in nonlinear tariffs. As in the case of moral hazard, one can also study the optimal nonlinear tariff, which maximizes the expected welfare of a population of agents having private information about their own risk characteristics.[19] However, this problem was encountered earlier in the literature on price discrimination with quality replacing quantity.[20]

1.7 Sidgwick, Vickrey, Mirrlees: Redistribution and Incentives

The separation of efficiency and redistribution in the second theorem of welfare economics rests on the assumption that lump-sum transfers are feasible. As soon as the bases for taxation can be affected by agents' behavior, dead-weight losses are created. Then raising money for redistributive purposes destroys efficiency. More redistribution requires more inefficiency. A trade-off appears between redistribution and efficiency. When labor income is taxed, the leisure-consumption choices are distorted and the incentives for work are decreased. Sidgwick (1883) in his *Method of Ethics* was apparently the first writer to recognize the incentive problems of redistribution policies:

> It is conceivable that a greater equality in the distribution of products would lead ultimately to a reduction in the total amount to be distributed in consequence of a general preference of leisure to the results of labor.
> —Sidgwick (1883, chap. 7, sec. 2)

The informational difficulty associated with income taxation is that the supply of labor is not observable and therefore not controllable, hence the distortion. However, if the wage was observable, as well as income, the supply of labor would be easily recovered. The next stage in the modelling of the problem was to assume that the wage of an agent equates his innate ability (equal itself to his marginal productivity), which is private information of the agents.[21] Income, the observable variable, is the product of a moral hazard variable—the supply of labor—and of an adverse selection variable—ability.

---

[18]See also Akerlof (1970) and Spence (1973).

[19]See Stiglitz (1977).

[20]See Mussa and Rosen (1978) and Guesnerie and Laffont (1984) for modern treatments.

[21]Note here a difficulty: the wage is paid by the employer who must know the agent's ability. Implicitly, collusion between the employer and the agent is assumed.

A major step was achieved by Vickrey, who was senior economist of the tax research division of the United States Treasury Department and a tax expert for the governor of Puerto Rico. As early as 1945, he used the insights of Von Neumann and Morgenstern to model the optimal income tax problem as a principal-agent problem where the principal is the tax authority and the agents are the taxpayers. In his 1945 article, Vickrey defined the objective function of the government:

> If utility is defined as that quantity the mathematical expression of which is maximized by an individual making choices involving risk, then to maximize the aggregate of such utility over the population is equivalent to choosing that distribution of income which such an individual would select were he asked which of various variants of the economy he would become a member of, assuming that once he selects a given economy with a given distribution of income he has an equal chance of landing in the shoes of each member of it.
>
> —Vickrey (1945, p. 329)

Equipped with this utilitarian social welfare criterion (with, in passing, the Harsanyi [1955] interpretation of expected utility as a justice criterion), Vickrey formulated the fundamental problem of optimal income taxation:[22]

> It is generally considered that if individual incomes were made substantially independent of individual effort, production would suffer and there would be less to divide among the population. Accordingly some degree of inequality is needed in order to provide the required incentives and stimuli to efficient cooperation of individuals in the production process.
>
> —Vickrey (1945, p. 330)

> The question of the ideal distribution of income, and hence of the proper progression of the tax system, becomes a matter of compromise between equality and incentives.
>
> —Vickrey (1945, p. 330)

He then proceeded to a formalization of the problem that is still the current one. The utility function of any individual is made a function of his consumption and of his productive effort. There is a relationship between the amount of output and the amount of effort and unknown productive characteristics of the individual. This leads to an alternative form of the utility function that depends on consumption, output, and the individual's characteristics. Taxation creates a relationship between output and consumption. Adjusting his effort or output optimally,

---

[22]Vickrey viewed his work as a generalization of Edgeworth's (1897) minimum sacrifice principle. Also, Edgeworth's optimal indirect taxation can be viewed as an incentive problem.

the individual obtains his supply of effort characterized by a first-order condition, which is the first-order condition of incentive compatibility for an adverse selection problem. Vickrey stated the government's optimization problem, which is to maximize the sum of individuals' utilities under the incentive compatibility conditions and the budget equation of the government. Recognizing a calculus of variation problem, he wrote the Euler equation and gave up:

> Thus even in this simplified form the problem resists any facile solution.
>
> —Vickrey (1945, p. 332)

The Pontryagin principle was still years away, and it would be twenty-six years before Mirrlees's (1971) neat formulation and solution of the problem.[23]

Note that the problem analyzed here is not in the strict sense a delegation problem as we defined it earlier. The principal is actually delegated by the taxpayers the task of redistributing income, i.e., the choice of a particular public good. The principal observes neither the effort level of a given agent nor his productive characteristics. However, by observing output, which is a function of both, it can reduce the problem to a one-dimensional adverse selection problem. The principal is not facing a single agent over the characteristics of which he has an asymmetry of information, but a continuum of them for which he knows only the distribution of characteristics. Nevertheless, the problem is mathematically identical to a delegation problem with a budget balance equation instead of a participation constraint.[24]

1.8 Dupuit, Edgeworth, Pigou: Price Discrimination

When a monopolist or a government wants to extract consumers' surpluses in the pricing of a commodity, it faces in general the problem of the heterogeneity of consumers' tastes. Even if it knows the distribution of tastes, it does not know the type of any given consumer. By offering different menus of price-quality or price-quantity pairs, i.e., by using second-degree price discrimination, the government or monopolist can increase its objective function. Such an anonymous menu is an incentive mechanism that leads consumers to reveal their type by their self-selection in the menu.

Dupuit (1844) developed the concept of consumer surplus and used it to discuss price discrimination. Dupuit was well aware of the incentive problems faced by the pricing of infrastructures:

---

[23]Zeckhauser (1970) and Wesson (1972) formulated special cases of the optimal incentives-redistribution problem that they solved approximately without being aware of the Vickrey model.

[24]At least when the types of the agents are independently distributed.

The best of all tariffs would be the one which would make pay those
which use a way of communication a price proportional to the utility
they derive from using this service. ... I do not have to say that I do not
believe in the possible application of this voluntary tariff; it would meet
an insurmountable obstacle in the universal dishonesty of passants, but
it is the kind of tariff one must try to approach by a compulsory tariff.

—Dupuit (1849, p. 223)

Edgeworth (1911–13) extended the theory for price discrimination for the
railways industry. Pigou (1920) characterized the different types of price discrimination. Gabor (1955) discussed block tariffs or two-part tariffs that had been recently
introduced in the electricity industry in England and showed that with one type
of consumers two-part tariffs are equivalent to first-degree price discrimination.
Oi (1971) derived an optimal two-part tariff. Mussa and Rosen (1978), Spence
(1977), and Goldman, Leland, and Sibley (1984) provided the general framework
to derive, for a monopolist, an optimal tariff that is nonlinear in prices or qualities,
substantially later than similar work in the income tax or insurance literature.

1.9 Incentives in Planned Economies

We must distinguish between the Soviet practice and the theory of planning developed in the Western countries. As explained by Berliner (1976),

> In the early years of the Soviet period there was some hope that socialist
> society could count on the spirit of public service as a sufficient motiva-
> tion for economic activity. With the intense industrialization drive of the
> thirties, however, that hope was gradually abandoned. In a historic dec-
> laration in 1931, Stalin renounced the egalitarian wage ethic that had
> obliterated "any difference between skilled and unskilled work, between
> heavy and light work" (401).

Following his biting denunciation of "equality mongering," there evolved a new
policy in which personal "material incentives"—primarily money incomes—
became the major instrument for motivating economic activity.

In the Soviet Union, a general set of managerial incentive structures developed during the thirties and lasted for three decades. In this classical period, the
managers' incomes comprised a salary, a basic bonus, and the Enterprise Fund.
This incentive structure had many defects (problems with new products, no proper
incentives for cost minimization, ratchet effect, etc.). It was criticized and under
constant evolution. With the passing of Stalin, the discussion became more intense
and quite open with the 1962 Liberman paper in the *Pravda* and culminated in the

1965 Reform. Among Soviet specialists in the Western world, a literature studying in detail the new Soviet incentive structure developed.[25]

In the famous socialist controversy of the thirties, incentives were largely overlooked. Lange (1936) perceived no problem with imposing rules to managers:

> The decisions of the managers of production are no longer guided by the aim to maximize profit. Instead, there are certain rules imposed on them by the Central Planning Board which aim at satisfying consumers' preferences in the best way possible.
>
> One rule must impose on each production plant the choice of the combination of factors of production and the scale of output which minimizes the average cost of production.
>
> The second rule replaces the free entry of firms into an industry or their exodus from it. This leads to an equality of average cost and the price of the product.
>
> —Lange (1936, p. 62)

Lerner (1934) pointed out the difficulty arising with a small number of firms having increasing returns to scale and reformulated the rules as: Every producer must produce whatever he is producing at the least total cost, and a producer shall produce any output or any increment of output that can be sold for an amount equal to or greater than the marginal cost of that output or increment of output.[26] Even in 1967, Lange did not see any problem of incentives in the working of the socialist economy:

> Were I to rewrite my essay today my task would be much simpler. My answer to Hayek and Robbins would be: so what's the trouble? Let us put the simultaneous equations on an electronic computer and we shall obtain the solution in less than a second. The market process with its cumbersome tâtonnements appears old fashioned.[27]
>
> —Lange (1967, p. 158)

It is therefore not surprising that the voluminous mathematical theory of iterative planning developed in the sixties did not pay any attention to incen-

---

[25]Leeman (1970), Keren (1972), and Weitzman (1976).

[26]Note that Lerner was here simply rediscovering Launhardt's (1885) marginal cost pricing principle that the latter associated with government ownership. This principle was most clearly articulated by Hotelling (1939).

[27]When, at the end of his life, Lange recognized more fully the role of incentives, it was about the innovation process and not the everyday life of the planning system: "What is called optimal allocation is a second-rate matter, what is really of prime importance is that of incentives for the growth of productive forces (accumulation and progress in technology)" (private letters to T. Kowalik 1976).

tives.[28] Such a concern appeared only marginally in Drèze and de la Vallée Poussin (1971), where truthful reporting of private characteristics was shown to be a maximin strategy in a planning procedure for public goods. In 1974 Weitzman, who had participated in the development of the iterative planning literature, made a direct criticism of the implicit idea that planning with prices was good for incentives:

> It seems to me that a careful examination of the mechanisms of successive approximation planning shows that there is no principal informational difference between iteratively finding an optimum by having the center name prices while the firm responds with quantities, or by having the center assign quantities while the firm reveals costs or marginal costs.
>
> —Weitzman (1974, p. 478)

Considering an explicit planning problem with asymmetric information, Weitzman compared price mechanisms and quantity mechanisms. This will be the point of departure of the more general approach in terms of nonlinear prices by Spence (1977). From then on, planning procedures were more systematically studied from the point of view of incentives.[29] However, by then, the lack of interest for iterative planning was fairly general.

1.10 Leonid Hurwicz and Mechanism Design

When general equilibrium theorists attempted to extend the resource allocation mechanisms to nonconvex environments they realized that new issues of communication and incentives arose:

> In a broader perspective, these findings suggest the possibility of a more systematic study of resource allocation mechanisms. In such a study, unlike in the more traditional approach, the mechanism becomes the unknown of the problem rather than a datum. ... The members of such a domain (of mechanisms) can then be appraised in terms of their various "performance characteristics" and, in particular, of their (static and dynamic) optimality properties, their informational efficiency, and the compatibility of their postulated behavior with self-interest (or other motivational variables).
>
> —Hurwicz (1960, p. 28)

---

[28] See Heal (1973) for a synthesis.
[29] See Laffont (1985) for a survey.

Hurwicz (1960) dedicated his paper to Jacob Marschak. Marschak was the only major economist aware of incentive problems in the fifties, problems that he chose not to study:

> This raises the problem of incentives. Organization rules can be devised in such a way that, if every member pursues his own goal, the goal of the organization is served. This is exemplified in practice by bonuses to executives and the promises of loot to besieging soldiers; and in theory, by the (idealized) model of the laisser-faire economy. And there exist, of course, also negative incentives (punishments). I shall have to leave the problem of incentives aside.
>
> —Marschak (1955, p. 128)

Marschak was familiar with the literature of statisticians who became aware of incentive problems quite early. The problem of moral hazard arose in sampling theory for quality control. Whittle (1954) and Hill (1960) understood that the distributions of quality were endogenous and dependent on the care taken in the production process. They studied how to take into account this noncontrollable effort level in their analysis of quality from a sample. Adverse selection appeared when forecasting probabilities of some events. Good (1952), McCarthy (1956), and later Savage (1971) looked for payment formulas leading forecasters to announce their true estimated probabilities and discovered the incentive constraints for the revelation of information.

Economists working with Hurwicz developed a general framework, the mechanism design approach, which treated the competitive markets as just one particular institution in a much more general family of mechanisms run by benevolent planners. During the sixties the emphasis of the research was on the communication costs required by nonconventional environments, until Groves (1973), influenced by Schultze (1969),[30] called for considering incentives in public policy and constructed incentive-compatible mechanisms in a team problem.

The next major step was the understanding of the Revelation Principle,[31] which shows that, with adverse selection and moral hazard, any mechanism for organizing society is equivalent to an incentive-compatible mechanism by which all informed agents reveal their private information to a planner who recommends

---

[30]Schultze (1969) wrote, "public action need not be simply the provision of public facilities ... to offset the economic losses caused by private actions. Rather the objectives of public policy, in such cases, should include a modification of the 'signals' given and incentives provided by the market place so as to induce private actions consistent with public policy" (p. 151).

[31]See Gibbard (1973), Green and Laffont (1977), Dasgupta, Hammond, and Maskin (1979) and Myerson (1979).

actions. The Revelation Principle provided the appropriate framework for the normative analysis of economies with asymmetric information and contracts that can be written on all observable variables. It delivered a neat methodology to study incentive theory that we will use in most of this book.[32]

1.11 Auctions

Auctions are mechanisms by which principals attempt to use the competition among agents to decrease the information rents they have to give up to the agent they are contracting with. It requires a modelling of the relationship between bidders (the agents) who bid under incomplete information about the other agents' valuations for the auctioned good or contract.

Even though auctions have been used at least as far back as 500 B.C. in Babylon, the first academic work on auctions seems to date from 1954 with a thesis on competitive bidding for securities in which Friedman (1956) presented a method to determine optimal bids in a first-price, sealed-bid auction. In this operations-research approach he assumed that there was a single strategic bidder. In a monumental paper, Vickrey (1961) provided the first equilibrium theoretic analysis of the first-price auction that he compared to the second-price auction, often called the Vickrey auction.

It is only after the clarification of the Bayesian-Nash equilibrium concept by Harsanyi (1967–68) that the theory of auctions was massively developed. Three major models were particularly developed: the independent value model credited to Vickrey (1961), the symmetric common value model to Rothkopf (1969) and Wilson (1969; 1977), and the asymmetric common value model to Wilson (1967; 1969). In a major synthetic paper Milgrom and Weber (1982) showed that most of these models are special cases of the affiliated value paradigm, and they clarified the winner's curse developed during empirical work about auctions for oil drilling rights in the Gulf of Mexico (Capen, Clapp, and Campbell 1971). Myerson (1981) used the general mechanism approach to characterize the optimal auctions in models with private values or independent common values.

---

[32]Maskin's (1999, first draft 1977) Nash implementation theorem is the major result when a principal designs a mechanism to be played by agents who know their respective characteristics.

2 The Rent Extraction-Efficiency Trade-Off

Incentive problems arise when a principal wants to delegate a task to an agent. Delegation can be motivated either by the possibility of benefitting from some increasing returns associated with the division of tasks, which is at the root of economic progress, or by the principal's lack of time or lack of any ability to perform the task himself, or by any other form of the principal's bounded rationality when facing complex problems. However, by the mere fact of this delegation, the agent may get access to *information* that is not available to the principal. The exact opportunity cost of this task, the precise technology used, and how good the matching is between the agent's intrinsic ability and this technology are all examples of pieces of information that may become *private knowledge* of the agent. In such cases, we will say that there is *adverse selection*.[1]

---

[1] It is sometimes said that there is *hidden knowledge*, probably a better expression for describing this situation of asymmetric information. Adverse selection is rather a possible consequence of this

The agency model analyzed in this chapter, as well as in most of the book, will be cast in terms of a manager-worker relationship. Examples of such agency relationships under adverse selection abound both in terms of their scope and their economic significance. Both private and public transactions provide examples of contracting situations plagued with informational problems of the adverse selection type. The landlord delegates the cultivation of his land to a tenant, who will be the only one to observe the exact local weather conditions. A client delegates his defense to an attorney who will be the only one to know the difficulty of the case. An investor delegates the management of his portfolio to a broker, who will privately know the prospects of the possible investments. A stockholder delegates the firm's day-to-day decisions to a manager, who will be the only one to know the business conditions. An insurance company provides insurance to agents who privately know how good a driver they are. The Department of Defense procures a good from the military industry without knowing its exact cost structure. A regulatory agency contracts for service with a Public Utility without having complete information about its technology...

The key common aspect of all those contracting settings is that the information gap between the principal and the agent has some fundamental implications for the design of the bilateral contract they sign. In order to reach an efficient use of economic resources, this contract must *elicit* the agent's private information. This can only be done by giving up some *information rent* to the privately informed agent. Generally, this rent is costly to the principal. This information cost just adds up to the standard technological cost of performing the task and justifies distortions in the volume of trade achieved under asymmetric information. The allocative and the informational roles of the contract generally interfere. At the optimal second-best contract, the principal trades off his desire to reach allocative efficiency against the costly information rent given up to the agent to induce information revelation. Under adverse selection, the characterization of the volume of trade cannot be disentangled from the distribution of the gains from trade.

This chapter analyzes the contractual difficulties that appear when this delegation of task takes place in a one-shot relationship. The fact that the relationship is one-shot means that the principal and the agent cannot rely on its repetition to achieve efficient trades.[2] In this case, the bilateral short-term relationship between

---

asymmetric information. However, we will keep the by now classic expression of adverse selection to describe a principal-agent problem in which the agent has private information about a parameter of his optimization problem.

[2] See Fudenberg and Tirole (1991), Myerson (1991), and Osborne and Rubinstein (1994) for analyses of these repeated relationships and applications of the so-called Folk Theorem, which guarantees that, under complete information, almost Pareto optimal trades can be achieved through repeated relationships when agents have a common discount factor close enough to one.

the principal and the agent can be regulated only by a contract. Implicit here is the idea that there exists a legal framework for this contractual relationship. The contract can be *enforced* by a benevolent court of law, and the agents are bound by the terms of the contract. This implicit assumption on the legal framework of trades is not peculiar to contract theory but prevails in most traditional studies of market economies.

The main objective of this chapter is to characterize the optimal rent extraction-efficiency trade-off faced by the principal when designing his contractual offer to the agent. This characterization proceeds through two steps. First, we describe the set of allocations that the principal can achieve despite the information gap from which he suffers. An allocation is an output to be produced and a distribution of the gains from trade. Even under adverse selection, those allocations can be easily characterized once one has described a set of *incentive compatibility constraints* that are only due to asymmetric information. In addition to those constraints, the conditions for voluntary trade require that some *participation constraints* also be satisfied to ensure that the agent wants to participate in the contract. Incentive and participation constraints define the set of *incentive feasible allocations*. Second, once this characterization is achieved, we can proceed to a normative analysis and optimize the principal's objective function within the set of incentive feasible allocations. In general, incentive constraints are binding at the optimum, showing that adverse selection clearly impedes the efficiency of trade. The main lessons of this optimization are that the optimal second-best contract calls for a distortion in the volume of trade away from the first-best and for giving up some strictly positive information rents to the most efficient agents.

Implicit in this optimization are a number of assumptions worth stressing. First, we assume that the principal and the agent both adopt an optimizing behavior and maximize their individual utility. In other words, they are both fully rational individualistic agents. Given the contract he receives from the principal, the agent maximizes his utility and chooses output accordingly. Second, the principal does not know the agent's private information, but the probability distribution of this information is *common knowledge*. There exists an objective distribution for the possible types of the agent that is known by both the agent and the principal, and this fact itself is known by the two players.[3] Third, the principal is a Bayesian expected utility maximizer. In designing the agent's payoff rule, the principal moves first as a Stackelberg leader under asymmetric information anticipating the agent's subsequent behavior and optimizing accordingly within the set of available contracts.

---

[3]More generally, they both know that they know that ...

Section 2.1 describes the adverse selection canonical model that we use in most of this book. For the sake of simplicity, we assume that the agent's type, i.e., his cost parameter, can only take two possible values. The discrete type model turns out to be sufficient to highlight the main phenomena arising under adverse selection without having to deal with the technicalities of a continuum of types.[4] In section 2.2, we provide the benchmark solution corresponding to the case where the principal knows perfectly the agent's cost function. Section 2.3 describes the set of allocations that the principal can achieve despite the information gap from which he suffers. Section 2.4 explains why the principal is generally obliged to give up an information rent to the agent because of the latter's informational advantage. The optimization program of the principal who wants to maximize his expected utility under the constraints of incentive compatibility and voluntary trade is described in section 2.5. The optimal contract of the principal is obtained and discussed in section 2.6. Two major illustrations are given in sections 2.7 and 2.8. Section 2.9 proves the revelation principle in the principal-agent setup. This principle guarantees that there is no loss of generality in restricting the analysis to menus of two contrats when the agent's private cost information takes only two possible values. The analysis of the previous sections is then extended to more general cost and revenue functions in section 2.10. This allows us to illustrate new features of the rent extraction-efficiency trade-off. So far, the analysis assumed risk neutrality of the agent and an *interim* timing of contracting, i.e., the principal offers a contract to an agent once the latter has already learned his type. Section 2.11 considers the more symmetric case where the contract can be offered at the *ex ante* stage, i.e., before the agent learns his type. We perform this analysis under various assumptions on the degrees of risk aversion of the principal and the agent. Implicit in our whole analysis of this chapter is the assumption that the agent and the principal can *commit* to the terms of the contract. This assumption is discussed in section 2.12. Section 2.13 gives a closer look at the set of incentive feasible allocations and in particular at the convexity of this set. We show there the conditions under which stochastic mechanisms can be useful for the principal. Given that the principal suffers from an information gap with the agent, informative signals can be useful for improving contracting and the terms of the rent extraction-efficiency trade-off. Section 2.14 studies the added value of these informative signals. Finally, in section 2.15, we present many examples of contracting relationships highlighting the generality of the framework provided in this chapter.

---

[4]Nevertheless, Appendix 3.1 generalizes the results to the more technical case, often found in the literature, where the agent's type is drawn from a continuous and positive distribution on a compact and convex set of possible types.

2.1 The Basic Model

2.1.1 Technology, Preferences, and Information

Consider a consumer or a firm (the principal) who wants to delegate to an agent the production of q units of a good. The value for the principal of these q units is $S(q)$ where $S' > 0$, $S'' < 0$ and $S(0) = 0$. The marginal value of the good is thus positive and strictly decreasing with the number of units bought by the principal.

The production cost of the agent is unobservable to the principal, but it is common knowledge that the fixed cost is F and that the marginal cost θ belongs to the set $\Theta = \{\underline{\theta}, \bar{\theta}\}$. The agent can be either efficient ($\underline{\theta}$) or inefficient ($\bar{\theta}$) with respective probabilities ν and $1 - \nu$. In other words, he has the cost function

$$C(q, \underline{\theta}) = \underline{\theta}q + F \quad \text{with probability } \nu \tag{2.1}$$

or

$$C(q, \bar{\theta}) = \bar{\theta}q + F \quad \text{with probability } 1 - \nu. \tag{2.2}$$

We denote by $\Delta\theta = \bar{\theta} - \underline{\theta} > 0$ the spread of uncertainty on the agent's marginal cost. When taking his production decision the agent is informed about his type θ. We stress that this information structure is exogenously given to the players.[5]

2.1.2 Contracting Variables

The economic variables of the problem we consider thereafter are the quantity produced q and the transfer t received by the agent. Let $\mathscr{A}$ be the set of feasible allocations. Formally, we have

$$\mathscr{A} = \{(q, t) : q \in \mathbb{R}_+, t \in \mathbb{R}\}. \tag{2.3}$$

These variables are both *observable and verifiable* by a third party such as a benevolent court of law. They can thus be included in a contract which can be enforced with appropriate out-of-equilibrium penalties if either the principal or the agent deviates from the requested output and transfer.

2.1.3 Timing

For most of the book, unless explicitly stated, we will maintain the timing defined in figure 2.1, where A denotes the agent and P the principal.

---

[5]We will discuss the endogeneity of the information structure in chapter 9.

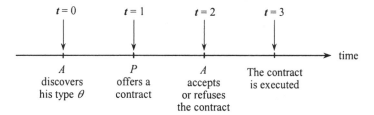

FIGURE 2.1: Timing of Contracting Under Adverse Selection

Note that contracts are offered at the *interim stage*; there is already asymmetric information between the contracting parties when the principal makes his offer.[6]

2.2 The Complete Information Optimal Contract

2.2.1 First-Best Production Levels

First suppose that there is no asymmetry of information between the principal and the agent. The efficient production levels are obtained by equating the principal's marginal value and the agent's marginal cost. Hence, first-best outputs are given by the following first-order conditions

$$S'(\underline{q}^*) = \underline{\theta} \tag{2.4}$$

and

$$S'(\bar{q}^*) = \bar{\theta}. \tag{2.5}$$

The complete information efficient production levels $\underline{q}^*$ and $\bar{q}^*$ should be both carried out if their social values, respectively $\underline{W}^* = S(\underline{q}^*) - \underline{\theta}\underline{q}^* - F$ and $\overline{W}^* = S(\bar{q}^*) - \bar{\theta}\bar{q}^* - F$, are non-negative. The social value of production when the agent is efficient, $\underline{W}^*$, is greater than when he is inefficient, namely $\overline{W}^*$. Indeed, we have $S(\underline{q}^*) - \underline{\theta}\underline{q}^* \geq S(\bar{q}^*) - \underline{\theta}\bar{q}^*$ by definition of $\underline{q}^*$, which maximizes $S(q) - \underline{\theta}q$ and $S(\bar{q}^*) - \underline{\theta}\bar{q}^* \geq S(\bar{q}^*) - \bar{\theta}\bar{q}^*$ because $\bar{\theta} > \underline{\theta}$. For trade to be always carried out, it is thus enough that production be socially valuable for the least efficient type, i.e., the following condition must be satisfied

$$\overline{W}^* = S(\bar{q}^*) - \bar{\theta}\bar{q}^* - F \geq 0, \tag{2.6}$$

[6]For reasons that we do not discuss now, the principal did not have the opportunity to offer a contract to the agent before $t = 0$. We return to this issue later, in section 2.11, where we also analyze the case of *ex ante* contracting.

a hypothesis that we will maintain throughout this chapter. As the fixed cost F plays no role other than justifying the existence of a single agent, it is set to zero from now on in order to simplify notations.[7]

Note that, since the principal's marginal value of output is decreasing, the optimal production levels defined by (2.4) and (2.5) are such that $\underline{q}^* > \bar{q}^*$, i.e., the optimal production of an efficient agent is greater than that of an inefficient agent.

2.2.2 Implementation of the First-Best

For a successful delegation of the task, the principal must offer the agent a utility level that is at least as high as the utility level that the agent obtains outside the relationship (for each value of the cost parameter). We refer to these constraints as the *agent's participation constraints*. If we normalize to zero the agent's outside opportunity utility level (sometimes called his status quo utility level),[8] these participation constraints are written as

$$\underline{t} - \underline{\theta}\underline{q} \geq 0, \tag{2.7}$$

$$\bar{t} - \bar{\theta}\bar{q} \geq 0. \tag{2.8}$$

To implement the first-best production levels, the principal can make the following *take-it-or-leave-it offers* to the agent: If $\theta = \bar{\theta}$ (resp. $\underline{\theta}$), the principal offers the transfer $\bar{t}^*$ (resp. $\underline{t}^*$) for the production level $\bar{q}^*$ (resp. $\underline{q}^*$) with $\bar{t}^* = \bar{\theta}\bar{q}^*$ (resp. $\underline{t}^* = \underline{\theta}\underline{q}^*$). Whatever his type, the agent accepts the offer and makes zero profit. The complete information optimal contracts are thus $(\underline{t}^*, \underline{q}^*)$ if $\theta = \underline{\theta}$ and $(\bar{t}^*, \bar{q}^*)$ if $\theta = \bar{\theta}$.

Importantly, under complete information delegation is costless for the principal, who achieves the same utility level that he would get if he was carrying out the task himself (with the same cost function as the agent).

2.2.3 A Graphical Representation of the Complete Information Optimal Contract

In figure 2.2, we draw the indifference curves of a $\underline{\theta}$-agent (heavy curves) and of a $\bar{\theta}$-agent (light curves) in the (q, t) space. The isoutility curves of both types cor-

---

[7]We come back to another possible role of the fixed cost in section 2.6.3.
[8]This debatable assumption is relaxed in section 3.3.

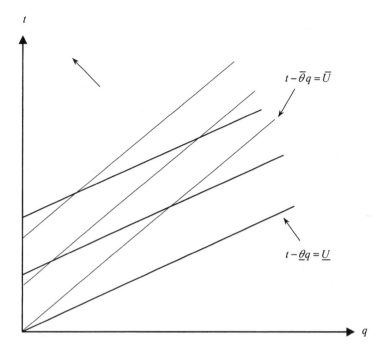

FIGURE 2.2: Indifference Curves of Both Types

respond to increasing levels of utility when one moves in the northwest direction. These indifference curves are straight lines with a slope θ corresponding to the agent's type. Since $\bar{\theta} > \underline{\theta}$, the isoutility curves of the inefficient agent $\bar{\theta}$ have a greater slope than those of the efficient agent. Thus, the isoutility curves for different types cross only once. Throughout this chapter and the next one we will come back several times to this important property called the *single-crossing* or *Spence-Mirrlees* property.

The complete information optimal contract is finally represented in figure 2.3 by the pair of points (A^*, B^*). For each of those two points, the strictly concave indifference curve of the principal is tangent to the zero rent isoutility curve of the corresponding type. Note that the isoutility curves of the principal correspond to increasing levels of utility when one moves in the southeast direction. Thus the principal reaches a higher profit when dealing with the efficient type. We denote by $\bar{V}^*$ (resp. $\underline{V}^*$) the principal's level of utility when he faces the $\bar{\theta}$- (resp. $\underline{\theta}$-) type. Because the principal has all the bargaining power in designing the contract, we have $\bar{V}^* = \bar{W}^*$ (resp. $\underline{V}^* = \underline{W}^*$) under complete information.

Remark: In Figure 2.3, the payment $\underline{t}^*$ is greater than $\bar{t}^*$, but we note that $\underline{t}^*$ can be greater or smaller than $\bar{t}^*$ depending on the curvature of the function $S(\cdot)$, as it can be easily seen graphically. ∎

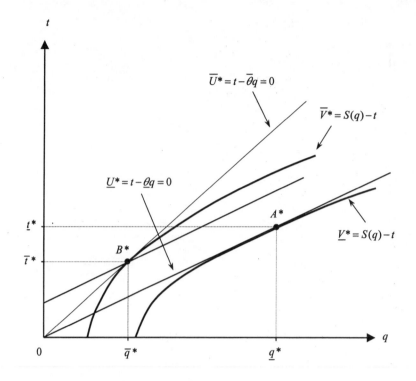

FIGURE 2.3: First-Best Contracts

2.3 Incentive Feasible Menu of Contracts

2.3.1 Incentive Compatibility and Participation

Suppose now that the marginal cost θ is the agent's private information and let us consider the case where the principal offers the menu of contracts $\{(\underline{t}^*, \underline{q}^*); (\bar{t}^*, \bar{q}^*)\}$ hoping that an agent with type $\underline{\theta}$ will select $(\underline{t}^*, \underline{q}^*)$ and an agent with type $\bar{\theta}$ will select instead $(\bar{t}^*, \bar{q}^*)$.

From Figure 2.3, we see that B^* is preferred to A^* by both types of agents. Indeed, the $\underline{\theta}$-agent's isoutility curve that passes through B^* corresponds to a positive utility level instead of a zero utility level at A^*. The $\bar{\theta}$-agent's isoutility curve that passes through A^* corresponds to a negative utility level, which is less than the zero utility level this type gets by choosing B^*. Offering the menu (A^*, B^*) fails to have the agents self-selecting properly within this menu. The efficient type mimics the inefficient one and selects also contract B^*. The complete information optimal contracts can no longer be implemented under asymmetric information. We will thus say that the menu of contracts $\{(\underline{t}^*, \underline{q}^*); (\bar{t}^*, \bar{q}^*)\}$ is *not incentive compatible*. This leads us to definition 2.1:

Definition 2.1: *A menu of contracts* $\{(\underline{t}, \underline{q}); (\bar{t}, \bar{q})\}$ *is incentive compatible when* $(\underline{t}, \underline{q})$ *is weakly*[9] *preferred to* $(\bar{t}, \bar{q})$ *by agent* $\underline{\theta}$ *and* $(\bar{t}, \bar{q})$ *is weakly preferred to* $(\underline{t}, \underline{q})$ *by agent* $\bar{\theta}$.

Mathematically, these requirements amount to the fact that the allocations must satisfy the following *incentive compatibility constraints*

$$\underline{t} - \underline{\theta}\underline{q} \geq \bar{t} - \underline{\theta}\bar{q} \tag{2.9}$$

and

$$\bar{t} - \bar{\theta}\bar{q} \geq \underline{t} - \bar{\theta}\underline{q}. \tag{2.10}$$

> **Remark:** Importantly, we do not presume the existence of any communication between the principal and the agent. We will address the issue of communication more fully in section 2.9. Incentive compatibility constraints should be mainly understood as constraints on final allocations, i.e., on the agent's choices. At a general level, those constraints are thus similar to the simple *revealed preference* arguments used in standard consumption theory.[10] ∎

Furthermore, for a menu to be accepted, it must yield to each type at least his outside opportunity level. The following two *participation constraints* must be satisfied:

$$\underline{t} - \underline{\theta}\underline{q} \geq 0, \tag{2.11}$$

$$\bar{t} - \bar{\theta}\bar{q} \geq 0. \tag{2.12}$$

Together, incentive and participation constraints define a set of *incentive feasible allocations* achievable through a menu of contracts. This leads us to definition 2.2:

Definition 2.2: *A menu of contracts is incentive feasible if it satisfies both incentive and participation constraints* (2.9) *through* (2.12).

The inequalities (2.9) through (2.12) fully *characterize* the set of incentive feasible menus of contracts. The restrictions embodied in this set express additional constraints imposed on the allocation of resources by asymmetric information between the principal and the agent.[11, 12]

---

[9]In order to define incentive compatibility, it is common to impose weak rather than strong preference. At an ε cost for the principal, strict preference is easily obtained.

[10]See Varian (1992, chap. 3) for instance.

[11]It is straightforward to check that the set of incentive feasible contracts is nonempty.

[12]We show in section 2.9 that there is no loss of generality in considering menus of two contracts. Accordingly, inequalities (2.9) through (2.12) characterize those constraints.

2.3.2 Special Cases

- **Bunching or Pooling Contracts:** A first special case of incentive feasible menu of contracts is obtained when the contracts targeted for each type coincide, i.e., when $\underline{t} = \bar{t} = t^p$, $\underline{q} = \bar{q} = q^p$ and both types of agent accept this contract. For those contracts, we say that there is *bunching* or *pooling* of types.

  The incentive constraints are all trivially satisfied by these contracts. Incentive compatibility is thus easy to satisfy, but at the cost of an obvious loss of flexibility in allocations that are no longer dependent on the state of nature. Only the participation constraints matter now. However, the hardest participation constraint to satisfy is that of the inefficient agent since inequality (2.12) implies inequality (2.11) for a pooling contract.

- **Shutdown of the Least Efficient Type:** Another particular case occurs when one of the contracts is the null contract $(0, 0)$ and the nonzero contract (t^s, q^s) is only accepted by the efficient type. Then, (2.9) and (2.11) both reduce to

$$t^s - \underline{\theta} q^s \geq 0. \tag{2.13}$$

The incentive constraint of the bad type reduces to

$$0 \geq t^s - \bar{\theta} q^s. \tag{2.14}$$

If the inequality (2.14) is strict, only the efficient type accepts the contract. With such a contract, the principal gives up production if the agent is a $\bar{\theta}$-type. We will say that it is a *contract with shutdown* of the least efficient type.

As with the pooling contract just seen above, the benefit of the $(0, 0)$ option is that it somewhat reduces the number of constraints since the incentive (2.9) and the participation (2.11) constraints take the same form. Of course, the cost of such a contract may be an excessive screening of types. Here, the screening of types takes the rather extreme form of excluding the least efficient type.

2.3.3 Monotonicity Constraints

Incentive compatibility constraints reduce the set of feasible allocations. Moreover, in well-behaved incentive problems these constraints put lots of structure on the set of feasible profiles of quantities. These quantities must generally satisfy a *monotonicity constraint* which does not exist under complete information. In our simple model, adding (2.9) and (2.10) immediately yields

$$\underline{q} \geq \bar{q}. \tag{2.15}$$

Independently of the principal's preferences, incentive compatibility alone implies that the production level requested from a $\bar{\theta}$-agent cannot be higher than the one requested from a $\underline{\theta}$-agent. We will call condition (2.15) *an implementability condition.* Any pair of outputs $(\underline{q}, \bar{q})$ that is *implementable*, i.e., that can be reached by an incentive compatible contract, must satisfy this condition which is here necessary and sufficient for implementability.

Indeed, suppose that (2.15) holds; it is clear that there exists transfers $\bar{t}$ and $\underline{t}$ such that the incentive constraints (2.9) and (2.10) both hold. It is enough to take those transfers such that

$$\bar{\theta}(\bar{q} - \underline{q}) \leq \bar{t} - \underline{t} \leq \underline{\theta}(\bar{q} - \underline{q}). \tag{2.16}$$

> **Remark:** In our two-type model, the conditions for implementability take a simple form. More generally, with more than two types (or with a continuum), the characterization of these conditions might get harder, as we demonstrate in appendix 3.1 and in section 3.1. The conditions for implementability are also more difficult to characterize when the agent performs several tasks on behalf of the principal (see section 2.10). ∎

2.4 Information Rents

To understand the structure of the optimal contract it is useful to introduce the concept of *information rent.*

We saw in section 2.2 that, under complete information, the principal (who has all the bargaining power by assumption) is able to maintain all types of agents at their zero status quo utility level. Their respective utility levels $\underline{U}^*$ and $\overline{U}^*$ at the first-best satisfy

$$\underline{U}^* = \underline{t}^* - \underline{\theta}\underline{q}^* = 0 \tag{2.17}$$

and

$$\overline{U}^* = \bar{t}^* - \bar{\theta}\bar{q}^* = 0. \tag{2.18}$$

Generally this will not be possible anymore under incomplete information, at least when the principal wants both types of agents to be active.

Take any menu $\{(\bar{t}, \bar{q}); (\underline{t}, \underline{q})\}$ of incentive feasible contracts and consider the utility level that a $\underline{\theta}$-agent would get by mimicking a $\bar{\theta}$-agent. By doing so, he would get

$$\bar{t} - \underline{\theta}\bar{q} = \bar{t} - \bar{\theta}\bar{q} + \Delta\theta\bar{q} = \bar{U} + \Delta\theta\bar{q}. \qquad (2.19)$$

Even if the $\bar{\theta}$-agent utility level is reduced to its lowest utility level fixed at zero, i.e., $\bar{U} = \bar{t} - \bar{\theta}\bar{q} = 0$, the $\underline{\theta}$-agent benefits from an information rent $\Delta\theta\bar{q}$ coming from his ability to possibly mimic the less efficient type. So, as long as the principal insists on a positive output for the inefficient type, $\bar{q} > 0$, the principal must give up a positive rent to a $\underline{\theta}$-agent. This information rent is generated by the informational advantage of the agent over the principal. The principal's problem is to determine the smartest way to give up the rent provided by any given incentive feasible contract.

In what follows, we use the notations $\underline{U} = \underline{t} - \underline{\theta}\underline{q}$ and $\bar{U} = \bar{t} - \bar{\theta}\bar{q}$ to denote the respective information rent of each type.

2.5 The Optimization Program of the Principal

According to our timing of the contractual game, the principal must offer a menu of contracts before knowing which type of agent he is facing. Therefore, he will compute the benefit of any menu of contracts $\{(\underline{t}, \underline{q}); (\bar{t}, \bar{q})\}$ in expected terms. The principal's problem writes as

(P):
$$\max_{\{(\bar{t}, \bar{q}); (\underline{t}, \underline{q})\}} \nu\left(S(\underline{q}) - \underline{t}\right) + (1 - \nu)\left(S(\bar{q}) - \bar{t}\right)$$

subject to (2.9) to (2.12).

Using the definition of the information rents $\underline{U} = \underline{t} - \underline{\theta}\underline{q}$ and $\bar{U} = \bar{t} - \bar{\theta}\bar{q}$, we can replace transfers in the principal's objective function as functions of information rents and outputs so that the new optimization variables are now $\{(\underline{U}, \underline{q}); (\bar{U}, \bar{q})\}$. This change of variables will sharpen our economic interpretations all along the book. The focus on information rents enables us to assess the distributive impact of asymmetric information. The focus on outputs allows us to analyze its impact on allocative efficiency and the overall gains from trade. Instead of viewing allocations as transfer-output pairs, this change of variable stresses that those allocations can be considered as information rent-output pairs. Thus an allocation corresponds to a volume of trade and a distribution of the gains from trade between the principal and the agent.

With this change of variables, the principal's objective function can then be rewritten as

$$\underbrace{\nu\big(S(\underline{q}) - \underline{\theta}\underline{q}\big) + (1 - \nu)\big(S(\bar{q}) - \bar{\theta}\bar{q}\big)}_{\text{Expected Allocative Efficiency}} - \underbrace{\big(\nu\underline{U} + (1 - \nu)\overline{U}\big)}_{\text{Expected Information Rent}}. \qquad (2.20)$$

This new expression clearly shows that the principal wishes to maximize the expected social value of trade *minus* the expected rent of the agent.[13] The principal is ready to accept some distortions away from efficiency in order to decrease the agent's information rent. We see below precisely how.

The incentive constraints (2.9) and (2.10), written in terms of information rents and outputs, are respectively

$$\underline{U} \geq \overline{U} + \Delta\theta\bar{q}, \qquad (2.21)$$

$$\overline{U} \geq \underline{U} - \Delta\theta\underline{q}. \qquad (2.22)$$

The participation constraints (2.11) and (2.12) become respectively

$$\underline{U} \geq 0, \qquad (2.23)$$

$$\overline{U} \geq 0. \qquad (2.24)$$

The principal wishes to solve problem (P) below:

(P): $\displaystyle \max_{\{(\underline{U}, \underline{q});(\overline{U}, \bar{q})\}} \nu(S(\underline{q}) - \underline{\theta}\underline{q}) + (1 - \nu)(S(\bar{q}) - \bar{\theta}\bar{q}) - (\nu\underline{U} + (1 - \nu)\overline{U})$

subject to (2.21) to (2.24).

We index the solution to this problem with a superscript *SB*, meaning *second-best*.

2.6 The Rent Extraction-Efficiency Trade-Off

2.6.1 The Optimal Contract Under Asymmetric Information

The major technical difficulty of problem (P), and more generally of incentive theory, is to determine which of the many constraints imposed by incentive compatibility and participation are the relevant ones, i.e., the binding ones at the optimum of the principal's problem.

---

[13]Note that a social utility maximizer putting an equal weight on the principal's and the agent's expected utility in his objective function would be interested in maximizing expected allocative efficiency only, without any concern for the distribution of information rents between the principal and the agent. In this case, the first-best outputs would be also chosen. Asymmetric information then would have no impact on allocative efficiency.

A first approach could be to apply the Lagrangian techniques to problem (P), once one has checked that the problem is concave. Even in this two-type model the number of constraints calls for a more practical route, where the modeler first guesses which are the binding constraints and checks *ex post* that the omitted constraints are indeed strictly satisfied. In a well-behaved incentive problem, this route is certainly more fruitful. In our very simple model, such a strategy provides a quick solution to the optimization problem. Moreover, it turns out to be more useful to build the economic intuition behind this model.

Let us first consider contracts without shutdown, i.e., such that $\underline{q} > 0$. The ability of the $\underline{\theta}$-agent to mimic the $\bar{\theta}$-agent implies that the $\underline{\theta}$-agent's participation constraint (2.23) is always strictly satisfied. Indeed, (2.24) and (2.21) immediately imply (2.23). If a menu of contracts enables an inefficient agent to reach his status quo utility level, it will also be the case for an efficient agent who can produce at a lower cost. Second, (2.22) also seems irrelevant because, as guessed from Section 2.3, the difficulty comes from a $\underline{\theta}$-agent willing to claim that he is inefficient rather than the reverse.

This simplification in the number of relevant constraints leaves us with only two remaining constraints, the $\underline{\theta}$-agent's incentive constraint (2.21) and the $\bar{\theta}$-agent's participation constraint (2.24). Of course, both constraints must be binding at the optimum of the principal's problem (P). Suppose it is not so. Assume first that $\bar{U} = \varepsilon > 0$. Then the principal can decrease $\bar{U}$ by ε and consequently also (from (2.21)) $\underline{U}$ by ε and gain ε. Therefore, $\bar{U} = 0$ is optimal. Also if $\underline{U} = \Delta\theta\bar{q} + \varepsilon$, $\varepsilon > 0$, the principal can decrease $\underline{U}$ by ε and gain $\nu\varepsilon$. $\underline{U} = \Delta\theta\bar{q}$ is also optimal. Hence, we must have

$$\underline{U} = \Delta\theta\bar{q} \tag{2.25}$$

and

$$\bar{U} = 0. \tag{2.26}$$

Substituting (2.25) and (2.26) into (2.20), we obtain a reduced program (P') with outputs as the only choice variables

(P'): $$\max_{\{(\underline{q}, \bar{q})\}} \nu\left(S(\underline{q}) - \underline{\theta}\underline{q}\right) + (1 - \nu)\left(S(\bar{q}) - \bar{\theta}\bar{q}\right) - \nu\Delta\theta\bar{q}.$$

Compared with the full information setting, asymmetric information alters the principal's optimization simply by the subtraction of the expected rent that has to be given up to the efficient type. The inefficient type gets no rent, but the efficient type $\underline{\theta}$ gets the information rent that he could obtain by mimicking the inefficient type $\bar{\theta}$. This rent depends only on the level of production requested from this inefficient type.

Since the expected rent given up *does not* depend on the production level $\underline{q}$ of the efficient type, the maximization of (P') calls for no distortion away from the first-best for the efficient type's output, namely

$$S'(\underline{q}^{SB}) = \underline{\theta} \text{ or } \underline{q}^{SB} = \underline{q}^*. \tag{2.27}$$

However, maximization with respect to $\bar{q}$ yields

$$(1 - \nu)\left(S'(\bar{q}^{SB}) - \bar{\theta}\right) = \nu\Delta\theta. \tag{2.28}$$

Increasing the inefficient agent's output by an infinitesimal amount dq increases allocative efficiency in this state of nature. The principal's expected payoff is improved by a term equal to the left-hand side of (2.28) times dq. At the same time, this infinitesimal change in output also increases the efficient agent's information rent, and the principal's expected payoff is diminished by a term equal to the right-hand side above times dq.

At the second-best optimum, the principal is neither willing to increase nor to decrease the inefficient agent's output, and (2.28) expresses the important *trade-off between efficiency and rent extraction* which arises under asymmetric information. The expected marginal efficiency gain (resp. cost) and the expected marginal cost (resp. gain) of the rent brought about by an infinitesimal increase (resp. decrease) of the inefficient type's output are equated.

To validate our approach based on the sole consideration of the efficient type's incentive constraint, it is necessary to check that the omitted incentive constraint of an inefficient agent is satisfied, i.e., $0 \geq \Delta\theta\bar{q}^{SB} - \Delta\theta\underline{q}^{SB}$. This latter inequality follows from the monotonicity of the second-best schedule of outputs since we have $\underline{q}^{SB} = \underline{q}^* > \bar{q}^* > \bar{q}^{SB}$.

For further references, it is useful to summarize the main features of the optimal contract (assuming that it is a contract without shutdown).

Proposition 2.1: *Under asymmetric information, the optimal menu of contracts entails:*

- *No output distortion for the efficient type with respect to the first-best, $\underline{q}^{SB} = \underline{q}^*$. A downward output distortion for the inefficient type, $\bar{q}^{SB} < \bar{q}^*$ with*

$$S'(\bar{q}^{SB}) = \bar{\theta} + \frac{\nu}{1 - \nu}\Delta\theta. \tag{2.29}$$

- *Only the efficient type gets a positive information rent given by*

$$\underline{U}^{SB} = \Delta\theta\bar{q}^{SB}. \tag{2.30}$$

- *The second-best transfers are respectively given by $\underline{t}^{SB} = \underline{\theta}\underline{q}^* + \Delta\theta\bar{q}^{SB}$ and $\bar{t}^{SB} = \bar{\theta}\bar{q}^{SB}$.*

2.6.2 A Graphical Representation of the Second-Best Outcome

Starting from the complete information optimal contract (A^*, B^*) that is not incentive compatible, we can construct an incentive compatible contract (B^*, C) with the same production levels by giving a higher transfer to the agent producing $\underline{q}^*$ (figure 2.4). The contract C is on the $\underline{\theta}$-agent's indifference curve passing through B^*. Hence, the $\underline{\theta}$-agent is now indifferent between B^* and C. (B^*, C) becomes an incentive-compatible menu of contracts. The rent that is given up to the $\underline{\theta}$-firm is now $\Delta\theta\bar{q}^*$.

Rather than insisting on the first-best production level $\bar{q}^*$ for an inefficient type, the principal prefers to slightly decrease $\bar{q}$ by an amount dq. By doing so, expected efficiency is just diminished by a second-order term $(\frac{1}{2}|S''(\bar{q}^*)|(dq)^2)$ since $\bar{q}^*$ is the first-best output that maximizes efficiency when the agent is inefficient. Instead, the information rent left to the efficient type diminishes to the first-order $(\Delta\theta dq)$. Of course, the principal stops reducing the inefficient type's output when a further decrease would have a greater efficiency cost than the gain in reducing the information rent it would bring about. The optimal trade-off finally occurs at (A^{SB}, B^{SB}) as shown in figure 2.5.

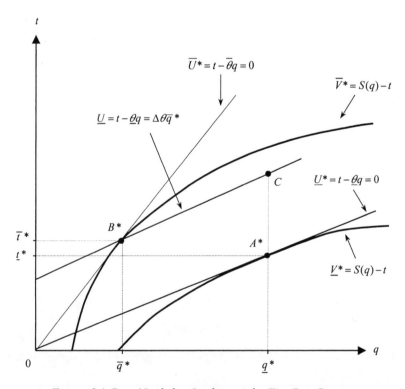

FIGURE 2.4: Rent Needed to Implement the First-Best Outputs

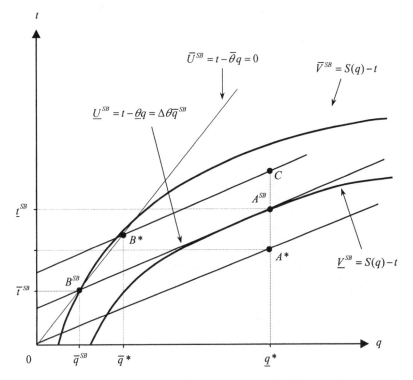

FIGURE 2.5: Optimal Second-Best Contracts A^{SB} and B^{SB}

2.6.3 Shutdown Policy

If the first-order condition in (2.29) has no positive solution, $\bar{q}^{SB}$ should be set at zero. We are in the special case of a contract with *shutdown*. B^{SB} coincides with 0 and A^{SB} with A^* in figure 2.5. No rent is given up to the $\underline{\theta}$-firm by the unique non-null contract $(\underline{t}^*, \underline{q}^*)$ offered and selected only by agent $\underline{\theta}$. The shutdown of the agent occurs when $\theta = \bar{\theta}$. With such a policy, a significant inefficiency emerges because the inefficient type does not produce. The benefit of such a policy is that no rent is given up to the efficient type.

More generally, such a shutdown policy is optimal when

$$\nu\left(S(\underline{q}^*) - \underline{\theta}\underline{q}^*\right) \geq \nu\left(S(\underline{q}^{SB}) - \underline{\theta}\underline{q}^{SB} - \Delta\theta\bar{q}^{SB}\right) + (1 - \nu)\left(S(\bar{q}^{SB}) - \bar{\theta}\bar{q}^{SB}\right) \quad (2.31)$$

or, noting that $\underline{q}^* = \underline{q}^{SB}$, when

$$\nu\Delta\theta\bar{q}^{SB} \geq (1 - \nu)\left(S(\bar{q}^{SB}) - \bar{\theta}\bar{q}^{SB}\right). \quad (2.32)$$

The left-hand side of (2.32) represents the expected cost of the efficient type's rent due to the presence of the inefficient one when the latter produces a positive amount $\bar{q}^{SB}$. The right-hand side of (2.32) represents instead the expected benefit from transacting with the inefficient type at the second-best level of output. Shutdown of the inefficient type is optimal when this expected benefit is lower than the expected cost.

> **Remark:** Looking again at the condition (2.29), we see that shutdown is never desirable when the Inada condition $S'(0) = +\infty$ is satisfied and $\lim_{q \to 0} S'(q)q = 0$. First, $\bar{q}^{SB}$ defined by (2.29) is necessarily strictly positive. Second, note that we can rewrite $S(\bar{q}^{SB}) - (\bar{\theta} + \frac{\nu}{1-\nu}\Delta\theta)\bar{q}^{SB}$ as $S(\bar{q}^{SB}) - S'(\bar{q}^{SB})\bar{q}^{SB}$, which is strictly positive since $S(q) - S'(q)q$ is strictly increasing with q when $S'' < 0$ and is equal to zero for $q = 0$. Hence, $S(\bar{q}^{SB}) - (\bar{\theta} + \frac{\nu}{1-\nu}\Delta\theta)\bar{q}^{SB} > 0$ and shut-down of the least efficient type does not occur.
>
> The shutdown policy is also dependent on the status quo utility levels. Suppose that, for both types, the status quo utility level is $U_0 > 0$. Then (2.32) becomes (dividing by $1 - \nu$)
>
> $$\frac{\nu}{1-\nu}\Delta\theta\bar{q}^{SB} + U_0 \geq S(\bar{q}^{SB}) - \bar{\theta}\bar{q}^{SB}. \tag{2.33}$$
>
> Therefore, for ν large enough, shutdown occurs[14] even if the Inada condition $S'(0) = +\infty$ is satisfied. Note that this case also occurs when the agent has a strictly positive fixed cost $F > 0$ (to see that, just set $U_0 = F$). ∎

Coming back to the principal's problem (P), the occurrence of shutdown can also be interpreted as saying that the principal has, on top of the agent's production, another choice variable to solve the screening problem. This extra variable is the *subset of types*, which are induced to produce a positive amount. Reducing the subset of producing agents obviously reduces the rent of the most efficient type. In our two-type model, exclusion of the least efficient type may thus be optimal.

2.7 The Theory of the Firm Under Asymmetric Information

When the delegation of task occurs within the firm, a major conclusion of the above analysis is that, because of asymmetric information, the firm does not maximize the social value of trade, or more precisely its profit—a maintained assumption of most economic theory. This lack of allocative efficiency should not be

---

[14]Suppose on the contrary that (2.33) does not hold. Then $\bar{q}^{SB}$ goes to zero as ν goes to one and $S(\bar{q}^{SB}) - \bar{\theta}\bar{q}^{SB}$ as well as $\frac{\nu}{1-\nu}\Delta\theta\bar{q}^{SB}$ go to zero. But then (2.33) must hold strictly for ν close enough to one, a contradiction.

considered as a failure in the rational use of resources within the firm. Indeed, the point is that allocative efficiency is only one part of the principal's objective. The allocation of resources within the firm remains *constrained optimal* once informational constraints are fully taken into account.

This systematic deviation away from profit maximization can be interpreted as an *X-inefficiency* à la Leibenstein (1966), who has stressed the management failures that take place within the largest firms, i.e., those that are the most likely to suffer from significant internal informational problems.

Williamson (1975) has also advanced the view that various transaction costs may impede the achievement of economic transactions. Among the many origins of these costs, Williamson stresses *informational impactedness* as an important source of inefficiency. Clearly, even in a world with a costless enforcement of contracts, a major source of allocative inefficiency is the existence of asymmetric information between trading partners. Of course, another important insight of Williamson's analysis is that transaction costs may be mitigated by the choice of convenient organizational forms. This point does not contradict our interpretation of transaction costs as coming from informational problems if one is ready to accept the view that various organizational forms generate different degrees and costs of asymmetric information between partners, an issue which is clearly high on the current research agenda of organization theory.[15]

The idea that various organizational forms are associated with different information structures has been used by some authors to provide a theory of vertical integration. Arrow (1975) suggested that an upstream firm may want to integrate backward and acquire a downstream supplier to reduce the extent of asymmetric information between those two units. An obvious limitation of this approach is that it takes as exogenous the fact that vertical integration improves information. This exogeneity has led to an important debate over the last fifteen years between proponents of this idea (for instance, Williamson 1985) and opponents (such as Grossman and Hart 1986).

One last point is worth stressing. Even though asymmetric information generates allocative inefficiencies, those inefficiencies *do not call* for any public policy motivated by reasons of pure efficiency. Indeed, any benevolent policymaker in charge of correcting these inefficiencies would face the same informational constraints as the principal. The allocation obtained above is Pareto optimal in the set of incentive feasible allocations or incentive Pareto optimal. Nevertheless, the policymaker might want to implement different trade-offs between efficiency and rent

---

[15] See Aghion and Tirole (1997).

extraction, as we will see in section 2.15.1 in the archetypical case of regulatory intervention. In this case redistribution would be the motivation for public policy.

2.8 Asymmetric Information and Marginal Cost Pricing

Let us view the principal as acting for a set of consumers and the agent as a firm producing a consumption good. The first-best rules defined by (2.4) and (2.5) can be interpreted as *price equal to marginal cost* since consumers on the market will equate their marginal utility of consumption to price.

Under asymmetric information, price equates marginal cost only when the producing firm is efficient ($\theta = \underline{\theta}$). Using (2.29), we immediately get the expression of the price $p(\bar{\theta})$ for the inefficient type's output

$$p(\bar{\theta}) = \bar{\theta} + \frac{\nu}{1 - \nu}\Delta\theta. \qquad (2.34)$$

Price is higher than marginal cost in order to decrease the quantity $\bar{q}$ produced by the inefficient firm and reduce the efficient firm's information rent. Alternatively, we can say that price is equal to a *generalized (or virtual[16]) marginal cost* that includes, in addition to the traditional marginal cost of the inefficient type $\bar{\theta}$, an information cost that is worth $\frac{\nu}{1-\nu}\Delta\theta$. What is required is to generalize the concept of cost to include the *information cost* imposed by asymmetric information.

2.9 The Revelation Principle

In the above analysis, we have restricted the principal to offer a menu of contracts, one for each possible type. First, one may wonder if a better outcome could be achieved with a more complex contract allowing the agent possibly to choose among more options. Second, one may also wonder whether some sort of communication device between the agent and the principal could be used to transmit information to the principal so that the latter can recommend outputs and payments as a function of transmitted information. The *revelation principle* ensures that there is no loss of generality in restricting the principal to offer simple menus having at most as many options as the cardinality of the type space. Those simple menus are actually examples of *direct revelation mechanisms* for which we now give a couple of definitions.

---

[16]To use the expression coined by Myerson (1979).

Definition 2.3: A *direct revelation mechanism is a mapping g(·) from* Θ *to* $\mathscr{A}$ *which writes as* $g(\theta) = (q(\theta), t(\theta))$ *for all* θ *belonging to* Θ. *The principal commits to offer the transfer* $t(\tilde{\theta})$ *and the production level* $q(\tilde{\theta})$ *if the agent announces the value* $\tilde{\theta}$ *for any* $\tilde{\theta}$ *belonging to* Θ.

Definition 2.4: A *direct revelation mechanism g(·) is truthful if it is incentive compatible for the agent to announce his true type for any type, i.e., if the direct revelation mechanism satisfies the following incentive compatibility constraints:*

$$t(\underline{\theta}) - \underline{\theta}q(\underline{\theta}) \geq t(\bar{\theta}) - \underline{\theta}q(\bar{\theta}), \tag{2.35}$$

$$t(\bar{\theta}) - \bar{\theta}q(\bar{\theta}) \geq t(\underline{\theta}) - \bar{\theta}q(\underline{\theta}). \tag{2.36}$$

Denoting transfer and output for each possible report respectively as $t(\underline{\theta}) = \underline{t}$, $q(\underline{\theta}) = \underline{q}$, $t(\bar{\theta}) = \bar{t}$ and $q(\bar{\theta}) = \bar{q}$, we get back to the notations of the previous sections and in particular to the incentive constraints (2.9) and (2.10).

A more general *mechanism* can be obtained when communication between the principal and the agent is more complex than simply having the agent report his type to the principal. Let $\mathscr{M}$ be the message space offered to the agent by a more general mechanism. This message space can be very complex. Conditionally, on a given message m received from the agent, the principal requests a production level $\tilde{q}(m)$ and provides a corresponding payment $\tilde{t}(m)$.

Definition 2.5: A *mechanism is a message space* $\mathscr{M}$ *and a mapping* $\tilde{g}(·)$ *from* $\mathscr{M}$ *to* $\mathscr{A}$ *which writes as* $\tilde{g}(m) = (\tilde{q}(m), \tilde{t}(m))$ *for all* m *belonging to* $\mathscr{M}$.

When facing such a mechanism, the agent with type θ chooses a best message $m^*(\theta)$ that[17] is implicitly defined as

$$\tilde{t}(m^*(\theta)) - \theta\tilde{q}(m^*(\theta)) \geq \tilde{t}(\tilde{m}) - \theta\tilde{q}(\tilde{m}) \quad \text{for all } \tilde{m} \text{ in } \mathscr{M}. \tag{2.37}$$

The mechanism $(\mathscr{M}, \tilde{g}(·))$ induces therefore an *allocation rule* $a(\theta) = (\tilde{q}(m^*(\theta)), \tilde{t}(m^*(\theta)))$ mapping the set of types Θ into the set of allocations $\mathscr{A}$. Then we are ready to state the revelation principle in the one agent case.

Proposition 2.2: The Revelation Principle. *Any allocation rule* $a(\theta)$ *obtained with a mechanism* $(\mathscr{M}, \tilde{g}(·))$ *can also be implemented with a truthful direct revelation mechanism.*

---

[17]Possibly, the agent's best response can be a correspondence without changing anything below; just pick one of the possible maximizers and call it $m^*(\theta)$. The agent being indifferent between those maximizers, one generally assumes that the allocation most preferred by the principal is selected.

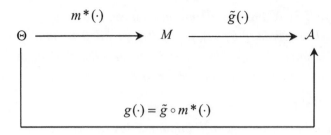

FIGURE 2.6: The Revelation Principle

Proof: The indirect mechanism $(\mathcal{M}, \tilde{g}(\cdot))$ induces an allocation rule $a(\theta) = (\tilde{q}(m^*(\theta)), \tilde{t}(m^*(\theta)))$ from Θ into $\mathcal{A}$. By composition of $\tilde{g}(\cdot)$ and $m^*(\cdot)$, we can construct a direct revelation mechanism $g(\cdot)$ mapping Θ into $\mathcal{A}$, namely $g = \tilde{g} \circ m^*$, or more precisely $g(\theta) = (q(\theta), t(\theta)) \equiv \tilde{g}(m^*(\theta)) = (\tilde{q}(m^*(\theta)), \tilde{t}(m^*(\theta)))$ for all θ in Θ.

Figure 2.6 illustrates this construction, which is at the core of the revelation principle.

We check now that the direct revelation mechanism $g(\cdot)$ is truthful. Indeed, since (2.37) is true for all $\tilde{m}$, it holds in particular for $\tilde{m} = m^*(\theta')$ for all θ' in Θ. Thus we have

$$\tilde{t}(m^*(\theta)) - \theta \tilde{q}(m^*(\theta)) \geq \tilde{t}(m^*(\theta')) - \theta \tilde{q}(m^*(\theta')) \quad \text{for all } (\theta, \theta') \text{ in } \Theta^2. \quad (2.38)$$

Finally, using the definition of $g(\cdot)$, we get

$$t(\theta) - \theta q(\theta) \geq t(\theta') - \theta q(\theta') \quad \text{for all } (\theta, \theta') \text{ in } \Theta^2. \quad (2.39)$$

Hence, the direct revelation mechanism $g(\cdot)$ is truthful. ∎

Importantly, the revelation principle provides a considerable simplification of contract theory. It enables us to restrict the analysis to a simple and well-defined family of functions, the truthful direct revelation mechanisms.

> Earlier analyses of the set of incentive compatible mechanisms took place in multiagent environments because their focus was the provision of public good, bargaining, or voting problems. It is out of the scope of this volume to discuss multiagent models, but let us briefly mention that dominant strategy implementation requires that each agent's best strategy is to reveal his type truthfully whatever the reports made by the other agents. Gibbard (1973) characterized the dominant strategy (nonrandom) mechanisms (mappings from arbitrary strategy spaces into allocations) when feasible allocations belong to a finite set and when there is no a priori information

on the players' preferences (which are strict orderings). He showed that such mechanisms had to be dictatorial, i.e., they had to correspond to the optimal choice of a single agent. As a corollary he showed that any voting mechanism (i.e., direct revelation mechanism) for which the truth was a dominant strategy was also dictatorial. In this environment, anything achievable by a dominant strategy mechanism can also be achieved by a truthful direct revelation mechanism. So, Gibbard proved one version of the revelation principle indirectly. For the case of quasi-linear preferences, Green and Laffont (1977) defined dominant-strategy, truthful direct revelation mechanisms and proved directly that, for any other dominant strategy mechanism, there is an equivalent truthful direct revelation mechanism (and they characterized the class of these mechanisms). Dasgupta, Hammond, and Maskin (1979) extended this direct proof to any family of preferences. The revelation principle can be extended to settings where several agents are privately informed about their own types with the less demanding concept of Bayesian-Nash equilibrium. In such a Bayesian context, the revelation principle requires that each agent's truthful report of his own type is a Bayesian-Nash equilibrium (Myerson 1979). The expression "the revelation principle" finally appeared in Myerson (1981). ∎

2.10 A More General Utility Function for the Agent

Still keeping quasi-linear utility functions, let $U = t - C(q, \theta)$ now be the agent's objective function with the assumptions: $C_q > 0$, $C_\theta > 0$, $C_{qq} > 0$ and $C_{qq\theta} > 0$. The generalization of the Spence-Mirrlees property used so far is now $C_{q\theta} > 0$. This latter condition still ensures that the different types of the agent have indifference curves which cross each other at most once. It is obviously satisfied in the linear case $C(q, \theta) = \theta q$ that was analyzed before. Economically, this Spence-Mirrlees property is quite clear; it simply says that a more efficient type is also more efficient at the margin.

The analysis of the set of implementable allocations proceeds closely, as was done previously. Incentive feasible allocations satisfy the following incentive and participation constraints:

$$\underline{U} = \underline{t} - C(\underline{q}, \underline{\theta}) \geq \bar{t} - C(\bar{q}, \underline{\theta}), \tag{2.40}$$

$$\bar{U} = \bar{t} - C(\bar{q}, \bar{\theta}) \geq \underline{t} - C(\underline{q}, \bar{\theta}), \tag{2.41}$$

$$\underline{U} = \underline{t} - C(\underline{q}, \underline{\theta}) \geq 0, \tag{2.42}$$

$$\bar{U} = \bar{t} - C(\bar{q}, \bar{\theta}) \geq 0. \tag{2.43}$$

2.10.1 The Optimal Contract

Following the same steps as in section 2.5, the incentive constraint of an efficient type in (2.40) and the participation constraint for the inefficient type in (2.43) are the two relevant constraints for optimization. These constraints rewrite respectively as

$$\underline{U} \geq \overline{U} + \Phi(\bar{q}) \tag{2.44}$$

where $\Phi(\bar{q}) = C(\bar{q}, \bar{\theta}) - C(\bar{q}, \underline{\theta})$ (with $\Phi' > 0$ and $\Phi'' > 0$ from the assumptions made on $C(\cdot)$) and

$$\overline{U} \geq 0. \tag{2.45}$$

Those constraints are both binding at the second-best optimum, which leads to the following expression of the efficient type's rent

$$\underline{U} = \Phi(\bar{q}). \tag{2.46}$$

Since $\Phi' > 0$, reducing the inefficient agent's output also reduces, as in Section 2.6, the efficient agent's information rent.

With the assumptions made on $C(\cdot)$, one can also check that the principal's objective function is strictly concave with respect to outputs. The solution of the principal's program can finally be summarized as follows:

Proposition 2.3: *With general preferences satisfying the Spence-Mirrlees property, $C_{q\theta} > 0$, the optimal menu of contracts entails:*

- *No output distortion with respect to the first-best outcome for the efficient type, $\underline{q}^{SB} = \underline{q}^*$ with*

$$S'(\underline{q}^*) = C_q(\underline{q}^*, \underline{\theta}). \tag{2.47}$$

A downward output distortion for the inefficient type, $\bar{q}^{SB} < \bar{q}^*$ with

$$S'(\bar{q}^*) = C_q(\bar{q}^*, \bar{\theta}) \tag{2.48}$$

and

$$S'(\bar{q}^{SB}) = C_q(\bar{q}^{SB}, \bar{\theta}) + \frac{\nu}{1 - \nu}\Phi'(\bar{q}^{SB}). \tag{2.49}$$

- *Only the efficient type gets a positive information rent given by $\underline{U}^{SB} = \Phi(\bar{q}^{SB})$.*
- *The second-best transfers are respectively given by $\underline{t}^{SB} = C(\underline{q}^*, \underline{\theta}) + \Phi(\bar{q}^{SB})$ and $\bar{t}^{SB} = C(\bar{q}^{SB}, \bar{\theta})$.*

The first-order conditions (2.47) and (2.49) characterize the optimal solution if the neglected incentive constraint (2.41) is satisfied. For this to be true, we need to have

$$\bar{t}^{SB} - C(\bar{q}^{SB}, \bar{\theta}) \geq \underline{t}^{SB} - C(\underline{q}^{SB}, \underline{\theta}) + C(\underline{q}^{SB}, \underline{\theta}) - C(\underline{q}^{SB}, \bar{\theta}), \qquad (2.50)$$

which amounts to

$$0 \geq \Phi(\bar{q}^{SB}) - \Phi(\underline{q}^{SB}). \qquad (2.51)$$

We have $\Phi' > 0$ from the Spence-Mirrlees property, hence (2.51) is equivalent to $\bar{q}^{SB} \leq \underline{q}^{SB}$. But from our assumptions we easily derive that $\underline{q}^{SB} = \underline{q}^* > \bar{q}^* > \bar{q}^{SB}$.[18] So the Spence-Mirrlees property guarantees that only the efficient type's incentive constraint has to be taken into account.

The critical role played by the Spence-Mirrlees property in simplifying the problem will appear more clearly in models with more than two types.[19]

> **Remark:** The Spence-Mirrlees property is more generally a *constant sign condition*[20] on $C_{q\theta}$. If $C_{q\theta} < 0$, then Proposition 2.3 is unchanged except that now the inefficient type's output is distorted upwards $\bar{q}^{SB} > \bar{q}^* > \underline{q}^*$. Indeed, in such a model, the first-best production level of the inefficient type is higher than that level for the efficient type. Moreover, the information rent of the efficient type is still $\Phi(\bar{q}) = C(\bar{q}, \bar{\theta}) - C(\bar{q}, \underline{\theta})$, but now an increase of $\bar{q}$ is required to decrease this rent because $C_{q\theta} < 0$. ∎

2.10.2 Nonresponsiveness

Coming back to our linear specification of the agent's cost function, let us assume that the principal's return from contracting depends also directly on θ and is written as $S(q, \theta)$. This is an instance of a *common value* model where the agent's type directly affects the principal's utility function. On top of the usual assumptions of a positive and decreasing marginal value of trade, we also assume that $S_{q\theta} > 1$. This latter assumption simply means that the marginal gross value of trade for the principal increases quickly with the agent's type. For instance, the efficient agent

---

[18]By definition of q^*, $S'(\underline{q}^*) = C_q(\underline{q}^*, \underline{\theta}) < C_q(\underline{q}^*, \bar{\theta})$ because $C_{q\theta} > 0$. Hence, using the fact that $S(q) - C(q, \bar{\theta})$ is concave in q and maximum for $\bar{q}^*$, we have $\underline{q}^* > \bar{q}^*$. Moreover, $\Phi' > 0$ implies that $S'(\bar{q}^{SB}) > C_q(\bar{q}^{SB}, \bar{\theta})$. Thus, we also have $\bar{q}^{SB} < \bar{q}^*$.

[19]See Section 3.1 and Appendix 3.1 below.

[20]In Guesnerie and Laffont (1984), the Spence-Mirrlees property is called the *constant sign* (CS+ or CS−) *assumption*.

produces a lower quality good than the inefficient one, and the principal prefers a high quality good.

The first-best productions are now defined by $S_q(q^*, \underline{\theta}) = \underline{\theta}$ and $S_q(\bar{q}^*, \bar{\theta}) = \bar{\theta}$. With our assumption on $S_{q\theta}$, the first-best production schedule is such that $\underline{q}^* < \bar{q}^*$, i.e., it does not satisfy the monotonicity condition in (2.15) implied by incentive compatibility.[21]

In this case, there exists a strong conflict between the principal's desire to have the $\bar{\theta}$-type produce more than the $\underline{\theta}$-agent for pure efficiency reasons and the monotonicity condition imposed by asymmetric information. This is what Guesnerie and Laffont (1984) call a phenomenon of *nonresponsiveness* in their general analysis of the principal-agent's model with a continuum of types. This phenomenon makes screening of types quite difficult. Indeed, the second-best optimum induces screening only when $\underline{q}^{SB} = \underline{q}^*$ and $\bar{q}^{SB}$ defined by

$$S_q(\bar{q}^{SB}, \bar{\theta}) = \bar{\theta} + \frac{\nu}{1 - \nu} \Delta\theta \tag{2.52}$$

satisfy the monotonicity condition $\underline{q}^{SB} \geq \bar{q}^{SB}$. However, when ν is small enough, $\bar{q}^{SB}$ defined in (2.52) is close to the first-best outcome $\bar{q}^*$. Thus, we have $\bar{q}^{SB} > \underline{q}^{SB}$, and the monotonicity condition (2.15) is violated. Nonresponsiveness forces the principal to use a pooling allocation. Figure 2.7 illustrates this nonresponsiveness.

As in figure 2.4, the pair of first-best contracts (A^*, B^*) is not incentive compatible. But, contrary to the case of section 2.6.2, the contract C, which makes the $\underline{\theta}$-type indifferent to whether he tells the truth or takes contract B^*, is not incentive compatible for the $\bar{\theta}$-type who also strictly prefers C to B^*.

One possibility to restore incentive compatibility would be to distort $\bar{q}$ down to $\underline{q}^*$, which would decrease the $\underline{\theta}$-type's information rent to yield contract D while still preserving incentive compatibility for both types. By this action we would obtain a pooling allocation at D. However, the principal can do better by choosing another pooling allocation, which is obtained by moving along the zero isoutility line of a $\bar{\theta}$-type. Indeed, the best pooling allocation solves problem (P) below:

(P):
$$\max_{\{(q^p, t^p)\}} \nu S(q^p, \underline{\theta}) + (1 - \nu)S(q^p, \bar{\theta}) - t^p$$

subject to

$$t^p - \underline{\theta}q^p \geq 0 \tag{2.53}$$

$$t^p - \bar{\theta}q^p \geq 0. \tag{2.54}$$

---

[21] Differentiating the expression and defining implicitly the first-best $q^*(\theta)$ by $S_q(q^*(\theta), \theta) = \theta$, we get $\frac{dq^*}{d\theta}(\theta) = \frac{1 - S_{q\theta}}{S_{qq}} > 0$.

The harder participation constraint is obviously that of the least efficient type, namely (2.54). Hence, the optimal solution is characterized by

$$vS_q(q^p, \underline{\theta}) + (1 - v)S_q(q^p, \bar{\theta}) = \bar{\theta} \qquad (2.55)$$

and

$$t^p = \bar{\theta}q^p, \qquad (2.56)$$

with $q^p < \bar{q}^*$ because $S_{q\theta} > 0$.

This pooling contract is represented by point E in figure 2.7 (which can be to the left or to the right of D) where the indifference curve (the heavy line through E) of the principal corresponds to the "average" utility function $\widehat{S}(q) - t = vS(q, \underline{\theta}) + (1 - v)S(q, \bar{\theta}) - t$.

In summary, when nonresponsiveness occurs, the sharp conflict between the principal's preferences and the incentive constraints (which reflect the agent's preferences) makes it impossible to use any information transmitted by the agent about his type.

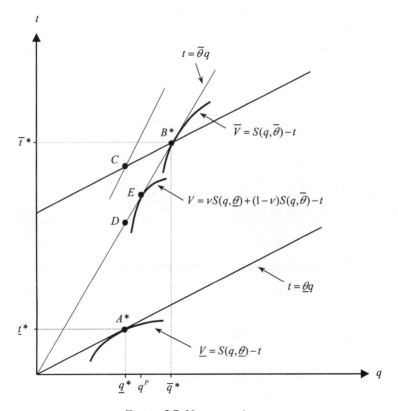

FIGURE 2.7: Nonresponsiveness

2.10.3 More than Two Goods

Let us now assume that the agent is producing a whole vector of goods $q = (q_1, \ldots, q_n)$ for the principal. The agent's cost function becomes $C(q, \theta)$ with $C(\cdot)$ being strictly convex in q. The value for the principal of consuming this whole bundle is now $S(q)$ with $S(\cdot)$ being strictly concave in q.

In this *multi-output* incentive problem, the principal is interested in a whole set of activities carried out simultaneously by the agent. It is straightforward to check that the efficient agent's information rent is now written as $\underline{U} = \Phi(q)$ with $\Phi(q) = C(q, \bar{\theta}) - C(q, \underline{\theta})$.

This leads to second-best optimal outputs. The efficient type produces the first-best vector of outputs $\underline{q}^{SB} = \underline{q}^*$ with

$$S_{q_i}(\underline{q}^*) = C_{q_i}(\underline{q}^*, \underline{\theta}) \quad \text{for all } i \text{ in } \{1, \ldots, n\}. \tag{2.57}$$

The inefficient type's vector of outputs $\bar{q}^{SB}$ is instead characterized by the first-order conditions

$$S_{q_i}(\bar{q}^{SB}) = C_{q_i}(\bar{q}^{SB}, \bar{\theta}) + \frac{\nu}{1 - \nu} \Phi_{q_i}(\bar{q}^{SB}) \quad \text{for all } i \text{ in } \{1, \ldots, n\}, \tag{2.58}$$

which generalizes the distortion of models with a single good.

Without further specifying the value and cost functions, it is hard to compare the second-best outputs a priori with the first-best outputs defined by the following n first-order conditions:

$$S_{q_i}(\bar{q}^*) = C_{q_i}(\bar{q}^*, \bar{\theta}), \quad \text{for all } i \text{ in } \{1, \ldots, n\}. \tag{2.59}$$

Indeed, it may well be the case that the n first-order conditions (2.58) define a vector of outputs with some components $\bar{q}_i^{SB}$ above $\bar{q}_i^*$ for a subset of indices i.

Turning now to incentive compatibility, summing the incentive constraints $\underline{U} \geq \bar{U} + \Phi(\bar{q})$ and $\bar{U} \geq \underline{U} - \Phi(\underline{q})$ for any incentive feasible contract yields

$$\Phi(\underline{q}) = C(\underline{q}, \bar{\theta}) - C(\bar{q}, \bar{\theta})$$

$$\geq C(\underline{q}, \underline{\theta}) - C(\bar{q}, \underline{\theta})$$

$$= \Phi(\bar{q}) \quad \text{for all implementable pairs } (\bar{q}, \underline{q}). \tag{2.60}$$

Obviously, this condition is satisfied if the Spence-Mirrlees property $C_{q_i \theta} > 0$ holds for each output i and if the monotonicity conditions $\bar{q}_i < \underline{q}_i$ for all i are satisfied. Inequality (2.60) is indeed satisfied for the second-best solution (2.58), because then $\bar{q}_i^{SB} < \bar{q}_i^* < \underline{q}_i^* = \underline{q}_i^{SB}$ for all i. However, the reverse is not true. It might well be the case that $\bar{q}_i^{SB} > \underline{q}_i^{SB} = \underline{q}_i^*$ for some output i and the condition (2.60), which is a condition on the whole vector of outputs, nevertheless still holds for the second-best vector of outputs $\underline{q}^*$ and $\bar{q}^{SB}$.

So, in general, the implementability condition (2.60) in a multi-output environment is more complex than the simple monotonicity condition found in a single-good setting.

2.11 *Ex Ante* versus *Ex Post* Participation Constraints

As we have already mentioned, in most of our discussion dealing with the case of adverse selection, we consider the case of contracts offered at the interim stage, i.e., once the agent already knows his type. However, sometimes the principal and the agent can contract at the *ex ante* stage, i.e., before the agent discovers his type. For instance, the contours of the firm may be designed before the agent receives any piece of information on his productivity. In this section, we characterize the optimal contract for this alternative timing under various assumptions about the risk aversion of the two players.

2.11.1 Risk Neutrality

Suppose that, instead of contracting after the agent has discovered θ, the principal and the agent meet and contract *ex ante*, i.e., before the agent obtains information. If the agent is risk neutral, his *ex ante participation constraint* is now written as

$$\nu \underline{U} + (1 - \nu)\overline{U} \geq 0. \tag{2.61}$$

This *ex ante* participation constraint replaces the two *interim participation constraints* (2.23) and (2.24) in problem (P). What matters now to ensure participation is that the agent's expected information rent remains non-negative.

From (2.20), we see that the principal's objective function is decreasing in the agent's expected information rent. Ideally, the principal wants to impose a zero expected rent to the agent and have (2.61) be binding.

Moreover, the principal must structure the rents $\underline{U}$ and $\overline{U}$ to ensure that the wedge between those two levels is such that the incentive constraints (2.21) and (2.22) remain satisfied. An example of such a rent distribution that is both incentive compatible and satisfies the *ex ante* participation constraint with an equality is

$$\underline{U}^* = (1 - \nu)\Delta\theta\bar{q}^* > 0 \quad \text{and} \quad \overline{U}^* = -\nu\Delta\theta\bar{q}^* < 0. \tag{2.62}$$

With such a rent distribution, the optimal contract implements the first-best outputs without cost from the principal's point of view as long as the first-best is monotonic as requested by the implementability condition. This may not be the case, for instance, when the nonresponsiveness property holds, as in section 2.10.2. In that case, even under *ex ante* contracting and risk neutrality some inefficiency still arises.[22]

In the contract defined by (2.62), the agent is rewarded when he is efficient and punished when he turns out to be inefficient. There must be some risk in the distribution of information rents to induce information revelation, but this risk is costless for the principal because of the agent's risk neutrality. However, to be feasible, such an *ex ante* contract requires a strong ability of the court of law to enforce contracts that could possibly lead to a negative payoff when a bad state of nature realizes.[23]

Proposition 2.4: *When the agent is risk neutral and contracting takes place* ex ante, *the optimal incentive contract implements the first-best outcome.*

Remark: The principal has in fact much more leeway in structuring the rents $\underline{U}$ and $\overline{U}$ in such a way that the incentive constraints (2.21) and (2.22) hold and the *ex ante* participation constraint (2.61) is an equality. Consider the following contracts $\{(\underline{t}^*, \underline{q}^*); (\overline{t}^*, \overline{q}^*)\}$ where $\underline{t}^* = S(\underline{q}^*) - T^*$ and $\overline{t}^* = S(\overline{q}^*) - T^*$, with T^* being a lump-sum payment to be defined below. This contract is incentive compatible since

$$\underline{t}^* - \underline{\theta}\underline{q}^* = S(\underline{q}^*) - \underline{\theta}\underline{q}^* - T^* > \overline{t}^* - \underline{\theta}\overline{q}^* = S(\overline{q}^*) - \underline{\theta}\overline{q}^* - T^* \quad (2.63)$$

by definition of $\underline{q}^*$, and

$$\overline{t}^* - \overline{\theta}\overline{q}^* = S(\overline{q}^*) - \overline{\theta}\overline{q}^* - T^* > \underline{t}^* - \overline{\theta}\underline{q}^* = S(\underline{q}^*) - \overline{\theta}\underline{q}^* - T^* \quad (2.64)$$

by definition of $\overline{q}^*$.

Note that the incentive compatibility constraints are now strict inequalities. Moreover, the fixed-fee T^* can be used to satisfy the agent's *ex ante* participation constraint with an equality by choosing $T^* = \nu(S(\underline{q}^*) - \underline{\theta}\underline{q}^*) + (1 - \nu)(S(\overline{q}^*) - \overline{\theta}\overline{q}^*)$.

This implementation of the first-best outcome amounts to having the principal selling the benefit of the relationship to the risk-neutral agent for a fixed up-front payment T^*. The agent benefits from the full value of the good and trades off the value of any production against its cost just as if he was an efficiency maximizer. We will say that the agent is *residual claimant* for the firm's profit.[24] ∎

---

[22] So, one cannot conclude that the distortions imposed by incentive compatibility in the model of section 2.1 are only due to the inability to contract before θ is revealed to the agent, i.e., to some sort of *contractual incompleteness*. Some distortions may still arise with *ex ante* contracting.

[23] See section 9.2 for a weakening of this enforceability condition.

[24] We will obtain a similar first-best implementation under moral hazard in chapter 4.

Harris and Raviv (1979) proposed a theory of the firm as a mechanism allocating resources at the *ex ante* stage. The first best allocation remains implementable when the firm has a strong ability to enforce contracts. ∎

2.11.2 Risk Aversion

A Risk-Averse Agent

The previous section has shown us that the implementation of the first-best is feasible with risk neutrality. The counterpart of this implementation is that the agent is subject to a significant amount of risk. Such a risk is obviously costly if the agent is risk-averse.

Consider now a risk-averse agent with a Von Neumann–Morgenstern utility function $u(\cdot)$ defined on his monetary gains $t - \theta q$, such that $u' > 0$, $u'' < 0$ and $u(0) = 0$. We suppose, as in section 2.11.1, that the contract between the principal and the agent is signed before the agent discovers his type.[25] The incentive constraints are unchanged but the agent's *ex ante* participation constraint is now written as

$$\nu u(\underline{U}) + (1 - \nu)u(\overline{U}) \geq 0. \tag{2.65}$$

As usual, we guess a solution such that (2.22) is slack at the optimum, and we let the reader check this *ex post*. The principal's program reduces now to

$$(P): \qquad \max_{\{(\overline{U}, \bar{q}); (\underline{U}, \underline{q})\}} \nu(S(\underline{q}) - \underline{\theta}\underline{q} - \underline{U}) + (1 - \nu)(S(\bar{q}) - \bar{\theta}\bar{q} - \overline{U}),$$

$$\text{subject to (2.21) and (2.65).}$$

We summarize the solution in the next proposition.[26]

> **Proposition 2.5:** *When the agent is risk-averse and contracting takes place ex ante, the optimal menu of contracts entails:*
>
> - *No output distortion for the efficient type $\underline{q}^{SB} = \underline{q}^*$. A downward output distortion for the inefficient type $\bar{q}^{SB} < \bar{q}^*$, with*
>
> $$S'(\bar{q}^{SB}) = \bar{\theta} + \frac{\nu(u'(\overline{U}^{SB}) - u'(\underline{U}^{SB}))}{\nu u'(\underline{U}^{SB}) + (1 - \nu)u'(\overline{U}^{SB})} \Delta\theta. \tag{2.66}$$

---

[25] If the contract is signed after the risk-averse agent discovers his type, the solution is the same as with risk neutrality (proposition 2.1) since interim participation and incentive constraints take the same form as with risk neutrality.

[26] See appendix 2.1 for the proof.

- *Both (2.21) and (2.65) are the only binding constraints. The efficient (resp. inefficient) type gets a strictly positive (resp. negative) ex post information rent, $\underline{U}^{SB} > 0 > \overline{U}^{SB}$.*

With risk aversion, the principal can no longer costlessly structure the agent's information rents to ensure the efficient type's incentive compatibility constraint, contrary to section 2.11.1. Creating a wedge between $\underline{U}$ and $\overline{U}$ to satisfy (2.21) makes the risk-averse agent bear some risk. To guarantee the participation of the risk-averse agent, the principal must now pay a risk premium. Reducing this premium calls for a downward reduction in the inefficient type's output so that the risk borne by the agent is lower. As expected, the agent's risk aversion leads the principal to weaken the incentives.

For the constant absolute risk aversion utility function $u(x) = \frac{1-\exp(-rx)}{r}$, (2.66) leads to a closed-form expression for output:

$$S'(\bar{q}^{SB}) = \bar{\theta} + \frac{\nu}{1-\nu}\Delta\theta\left(1 - \frac{1}{\nu + (1-\nu)\exp(r\Delta\theta\bar{q}^{SB})}\right). \qquad (2.67)$$

Also, the efficient agent's *ex post* utility writes as

$$\underline{U}^{SB} = \Delta\theta\bar{q}^{SB} + \frac{1}{r}\ln(1 - \nu + \nu\exp(-r\Delta\theta\bar{q}^{SB})) > 0 \qquad (2.68)$$

and the inefficient agent's *ex post* utility is

$$\overline{U}^{SB} = \frac{1}{r}\ln(1 - \nu + \nu\exp(-r\Delta\theta\bar{q}^{SB})) < 0. \qquad (2.69)$$

Incentives (and outputs) decrease with risk aversion. If risk aversion goes to zero ($r \to 0$), $\bar{q}^{SB}$ converges towards the first-best value $\bar{q}^*$. Indeed, we know from Section 2.11.1 that, with risk neutrality and an *ex ante* participation constraint, the optimal contract induces an efficient outcome. Moreover, the utility levels of both types converge toward those described in (2.62).

When the agent becomes infinitely risk averse, everything happens as if he had an *ex post* individual rationality constraint for the worst state of the world given by (2.24). In the limit, the inefficient agent's output $\bar{q}^{SB}$ and the utility levels $\underline{U}^{SB}$ and $\overline{U}^{SB}$ all converge toward the same solution as in proposition 2.1. So, the model of section 2.1 can also be interpreted as a model with *ex ante* contracting but with an infinitely risk-averse agent at the zero utility level.

Salanié (1990) analyzed the case of a continuum of types. Pooling for the least efficient types always occurs when risk aversion is large enough. Laffont and Rochet (1998) showed a similar phenomenon with interim participation constraints when a regulator (the principal) max-imizes *ex ante* social welfare and deals with a risk-averse regulated firm (the agent). ∎

A Risk-Averse Principal

Consider now a risk-averse principal with a Von Neumann–Morgenstern utility function $v(\cdot)$ defined on his monetary gains from trade $S(q) - t$ such that $v' > 0$, $v'' < 0$ and $v(0) = 0$. Again, the contract between the principal and the risk-neutral agent is signed before the agent knows his type.

In this context, the first-best contract obviously calls for the first-best output $\underline{q}^*$ and $\bar{q}^*$ being produced. It also calls for the principal to be fully insured between both states of nature and for the agent's *ex ante* participation constraint to be binding. This leads us to the following two conditions that must be satisfied by the agent's rents $\underline{U}^*$ and $\overline{U}^*$:

$$S(\underline{q}^*) - \underline{\theta}\underline{q}^* - \underline{U}^* = S(\bar{q}^*) - \bar{\theta}\bar{q}^* - \overline{U}^* \tag{2.70}$$

and

$$\nu\underline{U}^* + (1 - \nu)\overline{U}^* = 0. \tag{2.71}$$

Solving this system of two equations with two unknowns $(\underline{U}^*, \overline{U}^*)$ yields

$$\underline{U}^* = (1 - \nu)\big(S(\underline{q}^*) - \underline{\theta}\underline{q}^* - (S(\bar{q}^*) - \bar{\theta}\bar{q}^*)\big) \tag{2.72}$$

and

$$\overline{U}^* = -\nu\big(S(\underline{q}^*) - \underline{\theta}\underline{q}^* - (S(\bar{q}^*) - \bar{\theta}\bar{q}^*)\big). \tag{2.73}$$

Note that the first-best profile of information rents satisfies both types' incentive compatibility constraints since

$$\underline{U}^* - \overline{U}^* = S(\underline{q}^*) - \underline{\theta}\underline{q}^* - (S(\bar{q}^*) - \bar{\theta}\bar{q}^*) > \Delta\theta\bar{q}^* \tag{2.74}$$

(from the definition of $\underline{q}^*$) and

$$\overline{U}^* - \underline{U}^* = S(\bar{q}^*) - \bar{\theta}\bar{q}^* - (S(\underline{q}^*) - \underline{\theta}\underline{q}^*) > -\Delta\theta\underline{q}^*, \tag{2.75}$$

(from the definition of $\bar{q}^*$). Hence, the profile of rents $(\underline{U}^*, \overline{U}^*)$ is incentive compatible and the first-best allocation is easily implemented in this framework. We can thus generalize proposition 2.4 as follows:

Proposition 2.6: *When the principal is risk-averse over the monetary gains $S(q) - t$, the agent is risk-neutral, and contracting takes place* ex ante, *the optimal incentive contract implements the first-best outcome.*

It is interesting to note that $\underline{U}^*$ and $\overline{U}^*$ obtained in (2.72) and (2.73) are also the levels of rent obtained in (2.63) and (2.64). Indeed, the lump-sum payment $T^* = v(S(\underline{q}^*) - \underline{\theta}\underline{q}^*) + (1 - v)(S(\overline{q}^*) - \overline{\theta}\overline{q}^*)$, which allows the principal to make the risk-neutral agent residual claimant for the hierarchy's profit, also provides full insurance to the principal. By making the risk-neutral agent the residual claimant for the value of trade, *ex ante* contracting allows the risk-averse principal to get full insurance and implement the first-best outcome despite the informational problem.

Of course this result does not hold anymore if the agent's interim participation constraints must be satisfied. In this case, we still guess a solution such that (2.22) is slack at the optimum. The principal's program now reduces to

(P):
$$\max_{\{(\overline{U},\overline{q}),(\underline{U},\underline{q})\}} vv\big(S(\underline{q}) - \underline{\theta}\underline{q} - \underline{U}\big) + (1 - v)v\big(S(\overline{q}) - \overline{\theta}\overline{q} - \overline{U}\big)$$

subject to (2.21) and (2.24).

Inserting the values of $\underline{U}$ and $\overline{U}$ that were obtained from the binding constraints in (2.21) and (2.24) into the principal's objective function and optimizing with respect to outputs leads to $\underline{q}^{SB} = \underline{q}^*$, i.e., no distortion for the efficient type, just as in the case of risk neutrality and a downward distortion of the inefficient type's output $\overline{q}^{SB} < \overline{q}^*$ given by

$$S'(\overline{q}^{SB}) = \overline{\theta} + \frac{vv'(\underline{V}^{SB})}{(1 - v)v'(\overline{V}^{SB})}\Delta\theta, \qquad (2.76)$$

where $\underline{V}^{SB} = S(\underline{q}^*) - \underline{\theta}\underline{q}^* - \Delta\theta\overline{q}^{SB}$ and $\overline{V}^{SB} = S(\overline{q}^{SB}) - \overline{\theta}\overline{q}^{SB}$ are the principal's payoffs in both states of nature. We can check that $\overline{V}^{SB} < \underline{V}^{SB}$ since $S(\overline{q}^{SB}) - \overline{\theta}\overline{q}^{SB} < S(\underline{q}^*) - \underline{\theta}\underline{q}^*$ from the definition of $\underline{q}^*$. In particular, we observe that the distortion in the right-hand side of (2.76) is always lower than $\frac{v}{1-v}\Delta\theta$, its value with a risk-neutral principal. The intuition is straightforward. By increasing $\overline{q}$ above its value with risk neutrality, the risk-averse principal reduces the difference between $\underline{V}^{SB}$ and $\overline{V}^{SB}$. This gives the principal some insurance and increases his *ex ante* payoff.

For example, if $v(x) = \frac{1 - e^{-rx}}{r}$, (2.76) becomes $S'(\overline{q}^{SB}) = \overline{\theta} + \frac{v}{1-v}e^{r(\overline{V}^{SB} - \underline{V}^{SB})}\Delta\theta$. If $r = 0$, we get back the distortion obtained in section 2.6 with a risk-neutral principal and interim participation constraints for the agent. Since $\overline{V}^{SB} < \underline{V}^{SB}$, we observe that the first-best is implemented when r goes to infinity. In the limit, the infinitely risk-averse principal is only interested in the inefficient state of nature for which he wants to maximize the surplus, since there is no rent for the inefficient agent. Moreover, giving a rent to the efficient agent is now without cost for the principal.

📖 Risk aversion on the side of the principal is quite natural in some contexts. A local regulator with a limited budget or a specialized bank dealing with relatively correlated projects may be insufficiently diversified to become completely risk neutral. See Lewis and Sappington (1995) for an application to the regulation of public utilities. ∎

2.12 Commitment

To solve our incentive problem, we have implicitly assumed that the principal has a strong ability to commit himself not only to a distribution of rents that will induce information revelation but also to some allocative inefficiency designed to reduce the cost of this revelation. Alternatively, this assumption also means that the court of law can perfectly enforce the contract and that neither *renegotiating* nor *reneging* on the contract is a feasible alternative for the agent and (or) the principal. What can happen when either of those two assumptions is relaxed?

2.12.1 Renegotiating a Contract

A first source of *limited commitment* occurs when the principal can renegotiate the contract offered to the agent along the course of actions. Renegotiation is a voluntary act that should benefit both the principal and the agent. It should be contrasted with a breach of contract, which can hurt one of the contracting parties. One should view a renegotiation procedure as the ability of the contracting partners to achieve a Pareto improving trade if any becomes incentive feasible along the course of actions.

Once the different types have revealed themselves to the principal by selecting the contracts $(\underline{t}^{SB}, \underline{q}^{SB})$ for the efficient type and $(\bar{t}^{SB}, \bar{q}^{SB})$ for the inefficient type, the principal may propose a renegotiation to get around the allocative inefficiency he has imposed on the inefficient agent's output. The gain from this renegotiation comes from raising allocative efficiency for the inefficient type and moving output from $\bar{q}^{SB}$ to $\bar{q}^*$. To share these new gains from trade with the inefficient agent, the principal must at least offer him the same utility level as before renegotiation. The participation constraint of the inefficient agent can still be kept at zero when the transfer of this type is raised from $\bar{t}^{SB} = \bar{\theta}\bar{q}^{SB}$ to $\bar{t}^* = \bar{\theta}\bar{q}^*$. However, raising this transfer also hardens the *ex ante* incentive compatibility constraint of the efficient type. Indeed, it becomes more valuable for an efficient type to hide his type so that he can obtain this larger transfer, and truthful revelation by the efficient type is no longer obtained in equilibrium. There is a fundamental trade-off between raising efficiency *ex post* and hardening *ex ante* incentives when renegotiation is an issue.

The ability to commit to a menu of contracts may not be too problematic in some instances. Producing a quantity q may require building capacity up to that level.[27] Raising production as requested by the renegotiation procedure asks for increasing the productive capacity and this can be excessively costly compared to the allocative gains coming from a larger volume of trade. Moreover, this commitment issue seems highly dependent on the use of a direct revelation mechanism since renegotiation takes place after the agent has revealed his type but before the principal imposes an output target.[28] Therefore let us consider the simple and equivalent *indirect mechanism* where the principal offers the same menu to the agent but lets the agent choose the output himself (as we did in section 2.9). This alternative mechanism does not require any communication from the agent to the principal before production takes place. The agent makes the choice of an output and, if this choice is irreversible, there is no scope for renegotiation since the one-shot relationship ends. The commitment issue becomes much more problematic in truly dynamic contexts where different actions take place at various dates.[29]

2.12.2 Reneging on a Contract

A second source of imperfection arises when either the principal or the agent causes a breach in the contract and thus reneges on their previous contractual obligation. Let us take the case of the principal reneging on the contract.[30] Indeed, once the agent has revealed himself to the principal by selecting the contract within the menu offered by the principal, the latter, having learned the agent's type, might propose the complete information contract which extracts all rents without inducing any allocative inefficiency. Of course, this breach of contract should be anticipated by the agent and the agent's anticipation of the breach will interfere with his truthful revelation in the first place. Additionally, the agent may want to renege on a contract which gives him a negative *ex post* utility level as we mentioned in section 2.11.1. In this case, the threat of the agent reneging a contract signed at the *ex ante* stage forces the agent's participation constraints to

---

[27]See Beaudry and Poitevin (1994) for a model along these lines.

[28]Beaudry and Poitevin (1993) and Wambach (1999) have analyzed such a timing of the renegotiation game.

[29]We will return to the difficult issues raised by the renegotiation of contracts in section 9.3.

[30]See section 8.2.4 and section 9.3 for other models where the agent may renege on the contract.

be written in interim terms. Such a setting justifies the focus of this chapter on the case of interim contracting.[31]

2.13 Stochastic Mechanisms ⋆

We consider here the framework of section 2.10 with a general cost function $C(q, \theta)$. Let us rewrite the principal's problem as

$$(P): \quad \max_{\{(\underline{q}, \underline{U}); (\bar{q}, \overline{U})\}} \nu\big(S(\underline{q}) - C(\underline{q}, \underline{\theta})\big) + (1 - \nu)\big(S(\bar{q}) - C(\bar{q}, \bar{\theta})\big) - \nu\underline{U} - (1 - \nu)\overline{U},$$

subject to

$$\underline{U} - \overline{U} - \Phi(\bar{q}) \geq 0, \tag{2.77}$$

$$\overline{U} - \underline{U} + \Phi(\underline{q}) \geq 0, \tag{2.78}$$

$$\underline{U} \geq 0, \tag{2.79}$$

$$\overline{U} \geq 0. \tag{2.80}$$

When $S(\cdot)$ is concave and $C(\cdot)$ is convex, the principal's objective function is concave in $(\underline{q}, \bar{q}, \underline{U}, \overline{U})$. Neglecting constraints (2.78) and (2.79) as usual, the remaining constraints (2.77) and (2.80) define a convex set in $(\underline{q}, \bar{q}, \underline{U}, \overline{U})$ if $\Phi(\cdot)$ is convex in q. Then the optimal mechanism cannot be stochastic. To show this result suppose, on the contrary, that this mechanism is stochastic. A *random direct revelation mechanism* is then a probability measure on the set of possible transfers and outputs, which is conditional on the agent's report of his type. Let $\{(\tilde{\underline{q}}, \tilde{\underline{U}}); (\tilde{\bar{q}}, \tilde{\overline{U}})\}$ be such a *random stochastic mechanism*. We can replace this stochastic mechanism by the deterministic mechanism constructed with the expectations of those variables, namely $E(\tilde{\bar{q}})$, $E(\tilde{\underline{q}})$, $E(\tilde{\underline{U}})$, and $E(\tilde{\overline{U}})$, where $E(\cdot)$ denotes the expectation operator. Since the principal's objective function is strictly concave in q, this new mechanism gives a higher expected utility to the principal by Jensen's inequality.[32] Similarly, when $\Phi(\cdot)$ is convex, Jensen's inequality also implies that $-\Phi(E\tilde{\bar{q}}) \geq -E(\Phi(\tilde{\bar{q}}))$, so that the new deterministic mechanism expands the feasible set defined by the constraints in (2.77) and (2.80). The principal could thus achieve a higher utility level with the new deterministic mechanism, which is a contra-

---

[31]In section 9.2, we will discuss further the issue of enforcement in such a context.

[32]Jensen's inequality says that for any concave function $f(\cdot)$ and any random variable $\tilde{x}$: $E(f(\tilde{x})) \leq f(E(\tilde{x}))$, when $E(\cdot)$ denotes the expectation operator, with a strict inequality if $f(\cdot)$ is strictly concave.

diction. Therefore, a *sufficient* condition to ensure the deterministic nature of the optimal contract is $\Phi(\cdot)$ convex or, equivalently, $C_{qq\theta} > 0$.

Let us explore briefly what happens if the assumption $C_{qq\theta} > 0$ is no longer satisfied everywhere. Substituting (2.77) and (2.80) into the principal's objective function, and taking into account that $\underline{q}^{SB} = \underline{q}^*$ (where again $S'(\underline{q}^*) = C_q(\underline{q}^*, \underline{\theta})$), the principal's problem amounts to maximizing an objective function

$$(1 - \nu)\big(S(\bar{q}) - C(\bar{q}, \bar{\theta})\big) - \nu\Phi(\bar{q}), \tag{2.81}$$

which may no longer be strictly concave in $\bar{q}$ everywhere.

When this strict concavity is not satisfied, (2.81) may have several maximizers among which the principal can randomize.[33] Note that the randomness of contracts only affects outputs. From risk neutrality, with the principal and the agent's objective functions being linear in transfers, the randomness of transfers is useless because any lottery of transfers can be replaced by its expected value without changing the principal and the agent's payoffs in any state of nature.

The lack of concavity of (2.81) in fact captures a deeper property: the possible lack of convexity of the set of incentive feasible allocations. To illustrate this phenomenon, note that, for contracts such that (2.80) is binding and such that $\underline{q} = \underline{q}^*$, (2.77) can then be written as

$$\underline{U} \geq \Phi(\bar{q}). \tag{2.82}$$

Figure 2.8 represents the set of implementable allocations in the $(\underline{U}, \bar{q})$ space and shows that this set may not be convex when $\Phi(\cdot)$ is nonconvex. Points A and B are two possible deterministic maximizers of the principal's (reduced) objective function,[34]

$$(1 - \nu)(S(\bar{q}) - C(\bar{q}, \bar{\theta})) - \nu\underline{U}. \tag{2.83}$$

However, the principal can obtain a greater payoff by committing himself to randomize among incentive feasible allocations. Using such random direct revelation mechanisms leads indeed to a convexification of the set of incentive feasible allocations as shown in figure 2.9.[35] With the objective function (2.83) being strictly concave in $(\underline{U}, \bar{q})$, a unique maximizer to the principal's problem exists, and it is now given by point C.

---

[33] This randomization is, in this case, not uniquely defined.

[34] Note that this function is strictly concave in the space $(\underline{U}, \bar{q})$.

[35] The convexification adds to the set of incentive feasible allocations the crossed area in figure 2.9.

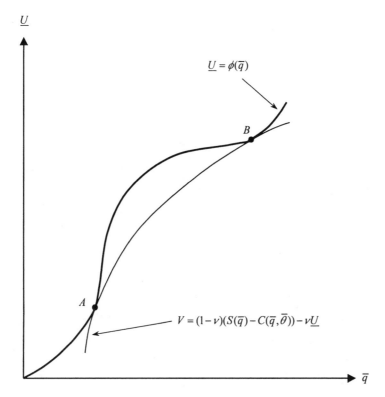

FIGURE 2.8: Multiple Maximizers

By being able to commit to a randomization through a stochastic mechanism, the principal can achieve a payoff that is strictly greater than what he obtains with deterministic mechanisms. Of course, the difficulty may come from the fact that this randomization has to be verifiable by a court of law before it can be employed in contracting. Ensuring this verifiability is a more difficult problem than ensuring that a deterministic mechanism is enforced, because any deviation away from a given randomization can only be statistically detected once a sufficient number of realizations of the contracts have been observed. This suggests that such a deviation can only be detected in a repeated relationship framework or when the principal is involved in many bilateral one-shot principal-agent relationships and always deviates in the same way. The enforcement of such stochastic mechanisms in a bilateral one-shot relationship is thus particularly problematic. This has led scholars to give up those random mechanisms or, at least, to focus on economic settings where they are not optimal.

Stochastic mechanisms have been sometimes suggested in the insurance, nonlinear pricing, and optimal taxation literatures (see Stiglitz 1987, Arnott and Stiglitz 1988, and Maskin and Riley 1984). ∎

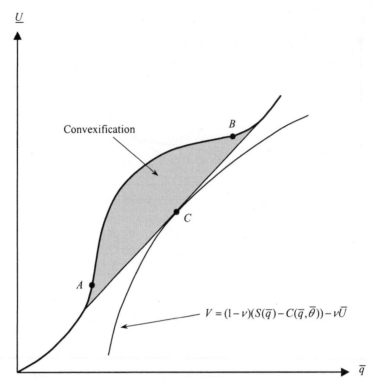

FIGURE 2.9: Unique Maximizer with Randomization

2.14 Informative Signals to Improve Contracting ★

In this section, we investigate the impacts of various improvements of the principal's information system on the optimal contract. The idea here is to see how signals that are exogenous to the relationship can be used by the principal to better design the contract with the agent. The simple observation of performances in similar principal-agent relationships and the choice of monitoring structures are examples of devices used to improve the agent's control by mitigating the information gap between the principal and his agent.

2.14.1 *Ex Post* Verifiable Signal

Suppose that the principal, the agent and the court of law observe *ex post* a verifiable signal σ which is correlated with θ. This signal is observed after the agent's choice of production (or alternatively after the agent's report to the principal in a direct revelation mechanism). The contract can then be conditioned on both the agent's report and the observed signal that provides useful information on the underlying state of nature.

For simplicity, we assume that this signal may take only two values, σ_1 and σ_2. Let the conditional probabilities of these respective realizations of the signal be $\mu_1 = \Pr(\sigma = \sigma_1/\theta = \underline{\theta}) \geq 1/2$ and $\mu_2 = \Pr(\sigma = \sigma_2/\theta = \bar{\theta}) \geq 1/2$. Note that, if $\mu_1 = \mu_2 = 1/2$, the signal σ is uninformative. Otherwise, σ_1 brings *good news*—the fact that the agent is efficient—and σ_2 brings *bad news*, since it is more likely that the agent is inefficient in this case.

Let us adopt the following notations for the *ex post* information rents: $u_{11} = t(\underline{\theta}, \sigma_1) - \underline{\theta}q(\underline{\theta}, \sigma_1)$, $u_{12} = t(\underline{\theta}, \sigma_2) - \underline{\theta}q(\underline{\theta}, \sigma_2)$, $u_{21} = t(\bar{\theta}, \sigma_1) - \bar{\theta}q(\bar{\theta}, \sigma_1)$, and $u_{22} = t(\bar{\theta}, \sigma_2) - \bar{\theta}q(\bar{\theta}, \sigma_2)$. Similar notations are used for the outputs q_{ij}. The agent discovers his type and plays the mechanism before the signal σ realizes. Then the incentive and participation constraints must be written in expectation over the realization of σ. Incentive constraints for both types write respectively as

$$\mu_1 u_{11} + (1 - \mu_1)u_{12} \geq \mu_1(u_{21} + \Delta\theta q_{21}) + (1 - \mu_1)(u_{22} + \Delta\theta q_{22}) \quad (2.84)$$

$$(1 - \mu_2)u_{21} + \mu_2 u_{22} \geq (1 - \mu_2)(u_{11} - \Delta\theta q_{11}) + \mu_2(u_{12} - \Delta\theta q_{12}). \quad (2.85)$$

Participation constraints for both types are written as

$$\mu_1 u_{11} + (1 - \mu_1)u_{12} \geq 0, \quad (2.86)$$

$$(1 - \mu_2)u_{21} + \mu_2 u_{22} \geq 0. \quad (2.87)$$

Note that, for a given schedule of output q_{ij}, the system (2.84) through (2.87) has as many equations as unknowns u_{ij}. When the determinant of the system (2.84) to (2.87) is nonzero, it is possible to find *ex post* rents u_{ij} (or equivalent transfers) such that all these constraints are binding:[36] In this case, the agent receives no rent whatever his type. Moreover, any choice of production levels, in particular the complete information optimal ones, can be implemented this way. The determinant of the system is nonzero when

$$1 - \mu_1 - \mu_2 \neq 0. \quad (2.88)$$

Importantly, the condition (2.88) holds generically. It fails only if $\mu_1 = \mu_2 = \frac{1}{2}$, which corresponds to the case of an uninformative and useless signal.

Riordan and Sappington (1988) introduced the condition (2.88) in a single-agent environment. Crémer and McLean (1988) generalized this use of correlated information in their analysis of multiagent models. We will cover the important topic of yardstick competition for multiagent organizations in our next book. ∎

---

[36]In fact, using Farkas's lemma, one can even ensure that incentive constraints are strict inequalities (see Crémer and McLean 1988 for details in a multiagent setting).

2.14.2 *Ex Ante* Nonverifiable Signal

We keep the same informational structure as in section 2.14.1, but now we suppose that a *nonverifiable* binary signal σ about θ is available to the principal at the *ex ante* stage. Before offering an incentive contract, the principal computes, using the Bayes law, his posterior belief that the agent is efficient for each value of this signal, namely

$$\hat{\nu}_1 = \Pr(\theta = \underline{\theta}/\sigma = \sigma_1) = \frac{\nu\mu_1}{\nu\mu_1 + (1-\nu)(1-\mu_2)}, \tag{2.89}$$

$$\hat{\nu}_2 = \Pr(\theta = \underline{\theta}/\sigma = \sigma_2) = \frac{\nu(1-\mu_1)}{\nu(1-\mu_1) + (1-\nu)\mu_2}. \tag{2.90}$$

Then the optimal contract entails a downward distortion of the inefficient agent's production $\bar{q}^{SB}(\sigma_i)$, which is for signals σ_1 and σ_2 respectively:

$$S'(\bar{q}^{SB}(\sigma_1)) = \bar{\theta} + \frac{\hat{\nu}_1}{1 - \hat{\nu}_1}\Delta\theta = \bar{\theta} + \frac{\nu\mu_1}{(1-\nu)(1-\mu_2)}\Delta\theta \tag{2.91}$$

$$S'(\bar{q}^{SB}(\sigma_2)) = \bar{\theta} + \frac{\hat{\nu}_2}{1 - \hat{\nu}_2}\Delta\theta = \bar{\theta} + \frac{\nu(1-\mu_1)}{(1-\nu)\mu_2}\Delta\theta. \tag{2.92}$$

In the case where $\mu_1 = \mu_2 = \mu > \frac{1}{2}$, we can interpret μ as an index of the *informativeness of the signal*. Observing σ_1, the principal thinks that it is more likely that the agent is efficient. A stronger reduction in $\bar{q}^{SB}$, and thus in the efficient type's information rent, is called for after σ_1. (2.91) shows that incentives decrease with respect to the case without informative signal since ($\frac{\mu}{1-\mu} > 1$). In particular, if μ is large enough, the principal shuts down the inefficient firm after having observed σ_1. The principal offers a high-powered incentive contract only to the efficient agent, which leaves him with no rent. On the contrary, because he is less likely to face an efficient type after having observed σ_2, the principal reduces less of the information rent than in the case without informative signal since ($\frac{1-\mu}{\mu} < 1$). Incentives are stronger.

> Boyer and Laffont (2000) provided a comparative statics analysis of the effect of a more competitive environment on the optimal contract in an adverse selection framework. In their analysis, the competitiveness of the environment is linked to the informativeness of the signal σ. ∎

2.14.3 More or Less Favorable Distribution of Types

In the last two sections, 2.14.1 and 2.14.2, we considered "improvements" in the information structure. More generally, even in the basic model of this chapter, one may wonder how information structures can be ranked by the principal and the agent in an adverse selection framework.[37]

We will say that a distribution $(\tilde{\nu}, 1 - \tilde{\nu})$ is *more favorable* than a distribution $(\nu, 1 - \nu)$ if and only if $\tilde{\nu} > \nu$. Then the expected utility of the principal is higher with a more favorable distribution. Indeed, we can define this expected utility as

$$V(\nu) = \nu(S(\underline{q}^*) - \underline{\theta}\underline{q}^* - \Delta\theta\bar{q}^{SB}(\nu)) + (1 - \nu)(S(\bar{q}^{SB}(\nu)) - \bar{\theta}\bar{q}^{SB}(\nu)), \qquad (2.93)$$

where we make explicit the dependence of V and $\bar{q}^{SB}$ on ν.

Using the Envelope Theorem, we obtain

$$\begin{aligned}\frac{dV(\nu)}{d\nu} &= (S(\underline{q}^*) - \underline{\theta}\underline{q}^* - \Delta\theta\bar{q}^{SB}) - (S(\bar{q}^{SB}) - \bar{\theta}\bar{q}^{SB}) \\ &= (S(\underline{q}^*) - \underline{\theta}\underline{q}^*) - (S(\bar{q}^{SB}) - \underline{\theta}\bar{q}^{SB}), \end{aligned} \qquad (2.94)$$

which is strictly positive by definition of $\underline{q}^*$.

The rent of the efficient type, $\Delta\theta\bar{q}^{SB}$, is clearly lower when the distribution is more favorable. As can be seen by differentiating (2.29), $\bar{q}^{SB}(\nu)$ is a decreasing function of ν. Incentives decrease as the distribution becomes more favorable. The perspective of a more likely efficient type leads the principal to a trade-off that is tilted against information rents, i.e., a trade-off that is less favorable to allocative efficiency. For the *ex ante* rent of the agent, $U(\nu) = \nu\Delta\theta\bar{q}^{SB}(\nu)$, we have instead

$$\frac{dU(\nu)}{d\nu} = \Delta\theta\bar{q}^{SB}(\nu) + \nu\Delta\theta\frac{d\bar{q}^{SB}(\nu)}{d\nu} \qquad (2.95)$$

or, using (2.29),

$$\frac{dU(\nu)}{d\nu} = \underbrace{\Delta\theta\bar{q}^{SB}(\nu)}_{>0} + \underbrace{\frac{\nu(\Delta\theta)^2}{(1 - \nu)^2 S''(\bar{q}^{SB}(\nu))}}_{<0}. \qquad (2.96)$$

Therefore, for $\Delta\theta$ small enough, the expected rent increases when the distribution is more favorable, but it decreases when $\Delta\theta$ is rather large. Note that if there is shutdown when ν becomes larger, the expected rent decreases necessarily.

---

[37]An improvement of the information structure in the sense of Blackwell (1951) (see section 4.6.2 for a definition) does not necessarily increase the principal's welfare. The reason is that, in addition to its usual statistical effect, a better information structure affects the information rents and therefore affects directly the principal's objective function.

The most interesting result is that, for $\Delta\theta$ small, both the principal and the agent gain from a more favorable distribution. There is no conflict of interests on the choice of the information structure.

> See Laffont and Tirole (1993, chap. 1) for a similar analysis in the case of a continuum of types. ∎

2.15 Contract Theory at Work

This section proposes several classical settings where the basic model of this chapter is useful. Introducing adverse selection in each of these contexts has proved to be a significative improvement of standard microeconomic analysis.

2.15.1 Regulation

In the Baron and Myerson (1982) regulation model, the principal is a regulator who maximizes a weighted average of the consumers' surplus $S(q) - t$ and of a regulated monopoly's profit $U = t - \theta q$, with a weight $\alpha < 1$ for the firm's profit. The principal's objective function writes now as $V = S(q) - \theta q - (1 - \alpha)U$. Because $\alpha < 1$ it is socially costly to give up a rent to the firm. Maximizing expected social welfare under incentive and participation constraints leads to $q^{SB} = q^*$ for the efficient type and a downward distortion for the inefficient type, $\bar{q}^{SB} < \bar{q}^*$, which is given by

$$S'(\bar{q}^{SB}) = \bar{\theta} + \frac{\nu}{1 - \nu}(1 - \alpha)\Delta\theta. \tag{2.97}$$

Note that a higher value of α reduces the output distortion, because the regulator is less concerned by the distribution of rents within society as α increases. If $\alpha = 1$, the firm's rent is no longer costly and the regulator behaves as a pure efficiency maximizer implementing the first-best output in all states of nature.

> The regulation literature of the last fifteen years has greatly improved our understanding of government intervention under asymmetric information. We refer to Laffont and Tirole (1993) for a comprehensive view of this theory and its various implications for the design of real world regulatory institutions. ∎

2.15.2 Nonlinear Pricing by a Monopoly

In Maskin and Riley (1984), the principal is the seller of a private good with production cost cq who faces a continuum of buyers. The principal has thus a utility function $V = t - cq$. The tastes of a buyer for the private good are such that his utility function is $U = \theta u(q) - t$, where q is the quantity consumed and t his payment to the principal. Suppose that the parameter θ of each buyer is drawn independently from the same distribution on $\Theta = \{\underline{\theta}, \bar{\theta}\}$ with respective probabilities $1 - \nu$ and ν.

We are now in a setting with a continuum of agents. However, it is mathematically equivalent to the framework of section 2.5 with a single agent. Now the distribution of θ to be considered is the actual distribution of types, i.e., ν is the frequency of type $\bar{\theta}$ by the Law of Large Numbers. It is important to stress this interpretation because it considerably enlarges the relevance of the principal-agent model analyzed before.

Incentive and participation constraints can as usual be written directly in terms of the information rents $\underline{U} = \underline{\theta} u(\underline{q}) - \underline{t}$ and $\bar{U} = \bar{\theta} u(\bar{q}) - \bar{t}$ as

$$\underline{U} \geq \bar{U} - \Delta\theta u(\bar{q}), \tag{2.98}$$

$$\bar{U} \geq \underline{U} + \Delta\theta u(\underline{q}), \tag{2.99}$$

$$\underline{U} \geq 0, \tag{2.100}$$

$$\bar{U} \geq 0. \tag{2.101}$$

The principal's program now takes the following form:

$$(P): \max_{\{(\bar{U}, \bar{q}); (\underline{U}, \underline{q})\}} \nu\left(\bar{\theta} u(\bar{q}) - c\bar{q}\right) + (1 - \nu)\left(\underline{\theta} u(\underline{q}) - c\underline{q}\right) - \left(\nu\bar{U} + (1 - \nu)\underline{U}\right)$$

$$\text{subject to (2.98) to (2.101).}$$

The analysis is the mirror image of that of section 2.5, where now the *efficient type* is the one with the highest valuation for the good $\bar{\theta}$. Hence, (2.99) and (2.100) are the two binding constraints. As a result, there is no output distortion with respect to the first-best outcome for the high valuation type and $\bar{q}^{SB} = \bar{q}^*$, where $\bar{\theta} u'(\bar{q}^*) = c$.

However, there exists a downward distortion of the low valuation agent's output with respect to the first-best outcome. We have $\underline{q}^{SB} < \underline{q}^*$, where

$$\left(\underline{\theta} - \frac{\nu}{1 - \nu}\Delta\theta\right) u'(\underline{q}^{SB}) = c \quad \text{and} \quad \underline{\theta} u'(\underline{q}^*) = c. \tag{2.102}$$

So the unit price is not the same if the buyers demand $\bar{q}^*$ or $\underline{q}^{SB}$, hence the expression of nonlinear prices.

The literature on nonlinear pricing is huge. The interested reader will find in Tirole (1988), Varian (1988), and Wilson (1993) excellent reviews of this topic. In chapter 9, we discuss the link between direct revelation mechanisms and nonlinear prices, and in particular how and when the optimal direct mechanism can be implemented with a menu of simple linear prices in the case of a continuum of types that has been the focus of most of the nonlinear pricing literature. ∎

2.15.3 Quality and Price Discrimination

Mussa and Rosen (1978) studied a very similar problem to the one in section 2.15.2, where agents buy one unit of a commodity with quality q but are vertically differentiated with respect to their preferences for the good. The marginal cost (and average cost) of producing one unit of quality q is $C(q)$ and the principal has the utility function $V = t - C(q)$. The utility function of an agent is now $U = \theta q - t$ with θ in $\Theta = \{\underline{\theta}, \bar{\theta}\}$, with respective probabilities $1 - \nu$ and ν.

Incentive and participation constraints can still be written directly in terms of the information rents $\underline{U} = \underline{\theta}\underline{q} - \underline{t}$ and $\bar{U} = \bar{\theta}\bar{q} - \bar{t}$ as

$$\underline{U} \geq \bar{U} - \Delta\theta\bar{q}, \tag{2.103}$$

$$\bar{U} \geq \underline{U} + \Delta\theta\underline{q}, \tag{2.104}$$

$$\underline{U} \geq 0, \tag{2.105}$$

$$\bar{U} \geq 0. \tag{2.106}$$

The principal solves now:

(P): $\quad \max_{\{(\underline{U},\underline{q});(\bar{U},\bar{q})\}} \nu(\bar{\theta}\bar{q} - C(\bar{q})) + (1 - \nu)(\underline{\theta}\underline{q} - C(\underline{q})) - (\nu\bar{U} + (1 - \nu)\underline{U})$

subject to (2.103) to (2.106).

Following procedures similar to what we have done so far, only (2.104) and (2.105) are binding constraints. Finally, we find that the high valuation agent receives the first-best quality $\bar{q}^{SB} = \bar{q}^*$ where $\bar{\theta} = C'(\bar{q}^*)$. However, quality is now reduced below the first-best for the low valuation agent. We have $\underline{q}^{SB} < \underline{q}^*$, where

$$\underline{\theta} = C'(\underline{q}^{SB}) + \frac{\nu}{1 - \nu}\Delta\theta \quad \text{and} \quad \underline{\theta} = C'(\underline{q}^*). \tag{2.107}$$

Interestingly, the spectrum of qualities (defined as the difference of qualities between what is obtained respectively by the high valuation and by the low valuation agent) is larger under asymmetric information than under complete information. This incentive of the seller to put a low quality good on the market is a well-documented phenomenon in the industrial organization literature. Some authors have even argued that damaging its own goods may be part of the firm's optimal selling strategy when screening the consumers' willingness to pay for quality is an important issue.

2.15.4 Financial Contracts

Asymmetric information significantly affects the financial markets. For instance, in Freixas and Laffont (1990) the principal is a lender who provides a loan of size k to a borrower. Capital costs Rk to the lender since it could be invested elsewhere in the economy to earn the risk-free interest rate R. The lender has thus a utility function $V = t - Rk$. The borrower makes a profit $U = \theta f(k) - t$ where $\theta f(k)$ is the production with k units of capital and t is the borrower's repayment to the lender. We assume that $f' > 0$ and $f'' < 0$. The parameter θ is a productivity shock drawn from $\Theta = \{\underline{\theta}, \bar{\theta}\}$ with respective probabilities $1 - \nu$ and ν.

Incentive and participation constraints can again be written directly in terms of the borrower's information rents $\underline{U} = \underline{\theta} f(\underline{k}) - \underline{t}$ and $\bar{U} = \bar{\theta} f(\bar{k}) - \bar{t}$ as

$$\underline{U} \geq \bar{U} - \Delta\theta f(\bar{k}), \qquad (2.108)$$

$$\bar{U} \geq \underline{U} + \Delta\theta f(\underline{k}), \qquad (2.109)$$

$$\underline{U} \geq 0, \qquad (2.110)$$

$$\bar{U} \geq 0. \qquad (2.111)$$

The principal's program takes now the following form:

$$(P): \quad \max_{\{(\underline{U},\underline{k});(\bar{U},\bar{k})\}} \nu\big(\bar{\theta} f(\bar{k}) - R\bar{k}\big) + (1 - \nu)\big(\underline{\theta} f(\underline{k}) - R\underline{k}\big) - \big(\nu\bar{U} + (1 - \nu)\underline{U}\big)$$

$$\text{subject to (2.108) to (2.111)}.$$

We let the reader check that (2.109) and (2.110) are now the two binding constraints. As a result, there is no capital distortion with respect to the first-best outcome for the high productivity type and $\bar{k}^{SB} = \bar{k}^*$ where $\bar{\theta} f'(\bar{k}^*) = R$. In this case, the return on capital is equal to the risk-free interest rate. However, there also exists a downward distortion in the size of the loan given to a low productivity borrower with respect to the first-best outcome. We have $\underline{k}^{SB} < \underline{k}^*$, where

$$\left(\underline{\theta} - \frac{\nu}{1 - \nu}\Delta\theta\right) f'(\underline{k}^{SB}) = R \quad \text{and} \quad \underline{\theta} f'(\underline{k}^*) = R. \qquad (2.112)$$

Screening borrowers according to the size of their loans amounts to some kind of rationing for the low productivity firms. This phenomenon is well documented in the finance literature, and we refer to Freixas and Rochet (1999, chap. 5) for a more complete analysis and further references on screening in financial contracts. We will see in section 3.6 that instead of using the loan size the lender may also rely on other screening devices, like auditing or the threat of termination, to get valuable information about the firm requesting financing. ∎

2.15.5 Labor Contracts ★

Asymmetric information also undermines the relationship between a worker and the firm for which he works. In Green and Kahn (1983) and Hart (1983b) among others, the principal is a union (or a set of workers) providing its labor force l to a firm. To simplify the analysis, we assume that the union has full bargaining power in determining the labor contract with the firm and that the latter has a zero reservation utility.

The firm makes a profit $\theta f(l) - t$, where $f(l)$ is the return on labor and t is the worker's payment. We assume that $f' > 0$ and $f'' < 0$. The parameter θ is a productivity shock drawn from $\Theta = \{\underline{\theta}, \bar{\theta}\}$ with respective probabilities $1 - \nu$ and ν. In the labor contracting literature, the firm knows the realization of the shock and the union ignores its value. The firm's objective is to maximize its profit $U = \theta f(l) - t$. Workers have a utility function defined on consumption and labor. If their disutility of labor is counted in monetary terms and all revenues from the firm are consumed, they get $V = v(t - l)$ where l is their disutility of providing l units of labor and $v(\cdot)$ is increasing and concave ($v' > 0$, $v'' < 0$).

In this context, the firm's boundaries are determined before the realization of the shock and contracting takes place *ex ante*. The *ex ante* participation constraint is written in a way similar to (2.71). It should be clear that the model is similar to that of section 2.11.2 with a risk-averse principal and a risk-neutral agent.

Using the results of that section, we know that the risk-averse union will propose a contract to the risk-neutral firm which provides full insurance and implements the first-best levels of employments $\bar{l}^*$ and $\underline{l}^*$, defined respectively by $\bar{\theta} f'(\bar{l}^*) = 1$ and $\underline{\theta} f'(\underline{l}^*) = 1$.

Let us now turn to the more difficult case where workers have a utility function exhibiting an income effect, and let us assume, to simplify, that $V = v(t) - l$.

The first-best optimal contract would still require efficient employment in both states of nature. Moreover, it would also call for equating the worker's marginal utility of income across states:

$$\underline{t}^* = \bar{t}^*, \tag{2.113}$$

and making the firm's expected utility equal to zero:

$$\nu(\bar{\theta}f(\bar{l}^*) - \bar{t}^*) + (1 - \nu)(\underline{\theta}f(\underline{l}^*) - \underline{t}^*) = 0. \tag{2.114}$$

Solving those latter two equations for the pair of transfers $(\bar{t}^*, \underline{t}^*)$ immediately yields $\bar{t}^* = \underline{t}^* = \nu\bar{\theta}f(\bar{l}^*) + (1 - \nu)\underline{\theta}f(\underline{l}^*) = E(\theta f(l^*))$, where $E(\cdot)$ denotes the expectation operator with respect to θ and $\tilde{\theta}$ is the random effect.

Inserting this value of the transfer into the union's objective function, the principal chooses the levels of employment that are obtained as solutions to

(P): $$\max_{\{(\bar{l},\underline{l})\}} \nu\left(\nu\bar{\theta}f(\bar{l}) + (1 - \nu)\underline{\theta}f(\underline{l})\right) - \nu\bar{l} - (1 - \nu)\underline{l}.$$

We immediately find the first-best levels of labor,

$$\bar{\theta}f'(\bar{l}^*) = \frac{1}{\nu'(E(\theta f(l^*)))} \tag{2.115}$$

and

$$\underline{\theta}f'(\underline{l}^*) = \frac{1}{\nu'(E(\theta f(l^*)))}. \tag{2.116}$$

It follows that $\bar{\theta}f'(\bar{l}^*) = \underline{\theta}f'(\underline{l}^*)$. Using the fact that $f'' < 0$, we finally obtain that $\bar{l}^* > \underline{l}^*$. The firm uses more labor when the productivity shock is larger.

Let us now consider the case of asymmetric information. The firm's incentive compatibility constraints in both states of nature are written as

$$\bar{\theta}f(\bar{l}) - \bar{t} \geq \bar{\theta}f(\underline{l}) - \underline{t} \tag{2.117}$$

in the good state $\bar{\theta}$, and

$$\underline{\theta}f(\underline{l}) - \underline{t} \geq \underline{\theta}f(\bar{l}) - \bar{t} \tag{2.118}$$

in the bad state $\underline{\theta}$.

Summing (2.117) and (2.118), we immediately obtain the implementability condition

$$\bar{l} \geq \underline{l}. \tag{2.119}$$

Note that the first-best menu $\{(\underline{t}^*, \underline{l}^*); (\bar{t}^*, \bar{l}^*)\}$ satisfies (2.117) but violates (2.118). Therefore, let us look for an optimal incentive feasible contract where the binding incentive constraint prevents the firm from claiming that a high shock $\bar{\theta}$ has realized when, in fact, a low shock $\underline{\theta}$ has realized. In this example,

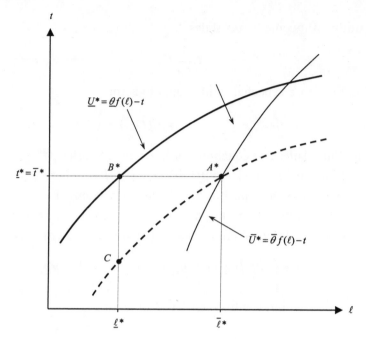

FIGURE 2.10: First-Best Labor Contracts

the *bad* type $\underline{\theta}$ wants to mimic the *good* type $\bar{\theta}$. This may be surprising in view of the previous analysis carried out in this chapter. To understand this result, it is useful to look at figure 2.10 where we have represented the first-best contracts A^* and B^* of the $\bar{\theta}$-firm and the $\underline{\theta}$-firm respectively.

The indifference curves of the firm are concave in the (l, t) space with higher levels of utility obtained as one moves towards the southeast. The $\bar{\theta}$-indifference curve has a greater slope than the $\underline{\theta}$-one so that the single crossing property still holds in our context.

At the first-best, the union requests a constant wage because it is averse to monetary risk. A^* and B^* are thus on the same horizontal line. If the union offers this pair of contracts under asymmetric information, the firm has an incentive to always claim that state $\bar{\theta}$ realized and obtain more labor. To avoid this, the union may propose the incentive compatible menu (A^*, C). The firm is then indifferent between A^* and C in state $\underline{\theta}$ and strictly prefers A^* to C in state $\bar{\theta}$. This menu is good from an allocative point of view, because the levels of employment are still equal to their first-best values. However, this contract makes the union bear an excessive risk in monetary transfers. This risk can be reduced by decreasing the gap between $\bar{l}$ and $\underline{l}$. Because of the impact of asymmetric information on the marginal utility of income of the union members in both states of nature, it is hard to assess graphically how the second-best optimal contract should be chosen.

Let us move therefore to a formal derivation of this second-best contract. The union's problem writes now as

(P):
$$\max_{\{(\bar{t},\bar{l});(\underline{t},\underline{l})\}} \nu(v(\bar{t}) - \bar{l}) + (1 - \nu)(v(\underline{t}) - \underline{l})$$

subject to (2.118), and

$$\nu\bar{t} + (1 - \nu)\underline{t} \leq \nu\bar{\theta}f(\bar{l}) + (1 - \nu)\underline{\theta}f(\underline{l}), \tag{2.120}$$

where (2.120) is the firm's *ex ante* participation constraint.

Let us denote the respective multipliers of these constraints with λ and μ. Optimizing with respect to $\bar{t}$ and $\underline{t}$ leads to

$$\nu v'(\bar{t}^{SB}) + \lambda - \mu\nu = 0 \tag{2.121}$$

$$(1 - \nu)v'(\underline{t}^{SB}) - \lambda - \mu(1 - \nu) = 0. \tag{2.122}$$

Summing (2.121) and (2.122), we immediately obtain that $\mu = \nu v'(\bar{t}^{SB}) + (1 - \nu)v'(\underline{t}^{SB}) > 0$. As expected, the firm's participation constraint (2.120) is binding. Using (2.121) and (2.122), we also get $\lambda = \nu(1 - \nu)(v'(\underline{t}^{SB}) - v'(\bar{t}^{SB}))$. To satisfy (2.118) and (2.119), it must be that $\bar{t}^{SB} \geq \underline{t}^{SB}$. Moreover, the equality holds only if we have bunching and $\bar{l} = \underline{l}$. For $\bar{l} > \underline{l}$, the inequality is strict. In this case, $\lambda > 0$ and the incentive constraint (2.118) is also binding. This allows us to finally express the optimal second-best transfers as

$$\bar{t}^{SB} = \nu\bar{\theta}f(\bar{l}^{SB}) + (1 - \nu)\underline{\theta}f(\underline{l}^{SB}) + (1 - \nu)\underline{\theta}(f(\bar{l}^{SB}) - f(\underline{l}^{SB})) \tag{2.123}$$

$$\underline{t}^{SB} = \nu\bar{\theta}f(\bar{l}^{SB}) + (1 - \nu)\underline{\theta}f(\underline{l}^{SB}) - \nu\underline{\theta}(f(\bar{l}^{SB}) - f(\underline{l}^{SB})). \tag{2.124}$$

Substituting the transfers into the principal's objective function and optimizing with respect to $\bar{l}$ and $\underline{l}$, we finally obtain

$$-\nu + \mu\nu\bar{\theta}f'(\bar{l}^{SB}) - \lambda\underline{\theta}f'(\bar{l}^{SB}) = 0 \tag{2.125}$$

$$-(1 - \nu) + \mu(1 - \nu)\underline{\theta}f'(\underline{l}^{SB}) + \lambda\underline{\theta}f'(\underline{l}^{SB}) = 0. \tag{2.126}$$

Or, to put it differently:

$$\bar{\theta}f'(\bar{l}^{SB}) = \frac{1}{\mu} + \frac{\lambda\underline{\theta}}{\mu\nu}f'(\bar{l}^{SB}), \tag{2.127}$$

$$\underline{\theta}f'(\underline{l}^{SB}) = \frac{1}{\mu} - \frac{\lambda\underline{\theta}}{\mu(1 - \nu)}f'(\underline{l}^{SB}); \tag{2.128}$$

where

$$\mu = \nu v'\left(E(\tilde{\theta}f(\tilde{l}^{SB})) + (1 - \nu)\underline{\theta}(f(\bar{l}^{SB}) - f(\underline{l}^{SB}))\right)$$
$$+ (1 - \nu)v'\left(E(\tilde{\theta}f(\tilde{l}^{SB})) - \nu\underline{\theta}(f(\bar{l}^{SB}) - f(\underline{l}^{SB}))\right), \tag{2.129}$$

and

$$\lambda = \nu(1 - \nu)\big(v'\big(E(\tilde{\theta}f(\tilde{l}^{SB}))\big) - \nu\underline{\theta}\,(f(\bar{l}^{SB}) - f(\underline{l}^{SB}))\big)$$
$$- v'\big(E(\tilde{\theta}f(\tilde{l}^{SB})) + (1 - \nu)\underline{\theta}\,(f(\bar{l}^{SB}) - f(\underline{l}^{SB}))\big)\big). \qquad (2.130)$$

The system of four nonlinear equations (2.127) through (2.130) is quite hard to solve. One reason for this difficulty is that one cannot immediately deduce from (2.127) and (2.128) that $\bar{l}^{SB}$ is smaller and $\underline{l}^{SB}$ is larger than the corresponding first-best values. Indeed, the marginal utility of income μ changes between both settings.

Nevertheless, one point is worth making. Assume that $v''' > 0$;[38] then, by Jensen's inequality

$$\mu > v'(E(\tilde{\theta}f(\tilde{l}^{SB}))). \qquad (2.131)$$

Using (2.128), we observe that

$$\underline{\theta}f'(\underline{l}^{SB}) < \frac{1}{v'(E(\tilde{\theta}f(\tilde{l}^{SB})))}. \qquad (2.132)$$

Conditionally on the level of labor $\bar{l}^{SB}$ in state $\bar{\theta}$ (which, keep in mind, is no longer equal to the first-best level $\bar{l}^*$) the inequality (2.132) shows that there is an incentive to expand output in state $\underline{\theta}$ above what would be optimal under complete information. This can be interpreted as a source of overemployment in the model.

In state $\bar{\theta}$, things are less clear. To reduce the costly incentive constraint (2.118), the union wants $\bar{l}^{SB}$ to be chosen closer to $\underline{l}^{SB}$ than at the first-best. However, because $\underline{l}^{SB}$ has a priori been shifted upward, this does not imply that $\bar{l}^{SB}$ is below its first-best value. The complete comparison with the first-best levels of employment depends on the utility function.

This section has illustrated how income effects make the analysis much harder even in two-type models. Those income effects were avoided in the standard model of this chapter since the principal's marginal utility of income was one under complete and asymmetric information. Doing so may be justified in partial equilibrium settings where income effects may be negligible.

Green and Kahn (1983) and Chari (1983) have also highlighted the incentives for overemployment in similar models but with a continuum of types. Neglecting the impact on the marginal utility of income, all types are induced to expand outputs when the local incentive constraints have a positive multiplier. The normality of leisure can be shown to be a sufficient

---

[38]This assumption is ensured when $v(\cdot)$ has decreasing absolute risk aversion.

condition for this property. For further references on this topic, the interested reader can look at Hart and Holmström (1987) and the references therein. ∎

Appendix 2.1: Proof of Proposition 2.5

Let us form the following Lagrangian for the principal's problem

$$L(\underline{q}, \bar{q}, \underline{U}, \overline{U}, \lambda, \mu) = \nu(S(\underline{q}) - \underline{\theta}\underline{q} - \underline{U}) + (1 - \nu)(S(\bar{q}) - \bar{\theta}\bar{q} - \overline{U})$$
$$+ \lambda(\underline{U} - \overline{U} - \Delta\theta\bar{q}) + \mu(\nu u(\underline{U}) + (1 - \nu)u(\overline{U})), \quad (2.133)$$

where λ is the multiplier of (2.21) and μ is the multiplier of (2.65).

Optimizing w.r.t. $\underline{U}$ and $\overline{U}$ yields respectively

$$-\nu + \lambda + \mu\nu u'(\underline{U}^{SB}) = 0 \quad (2.134)$$

$$-(1 - \nu) - \lambda + \mu(1 - \nu)u'(\overline{U}^{SB}) = 0. \quad (2.135)$$

Summing (2.134) and (2.135), we obtain

$$\mu(\nu u'(\underline{U}^{SB}) + (1 - \nu)u'(\overline{U}^{SB})) = 1, \quad (2.136)$$

and thus $\mu > 0$. Using (2.136) and inserting it into (2.134) yields

$$\lambda = \frac{\nu(1 - \nu)(u'(\overline{U}^{SB}) - u'(\underline{U}^{SB}))}{\nu u'(\underline{U}^{SB}) + (1 - \nu)u'(\overline{U}^{SB})}. \quad (2.137)$$

Moreover, (2.21) implies that $\underline{U}^{SB} \geq \overline{U}^{SB}$ and thus $\lambda \geq 0$, with $\lambda > 0$ for a positive output $\underline{y}$.

Optimizing with respect to outputs yields respectively

$$S'(\underline{q}^{SB}) = \underline{\theta} \quad (2.138)$$

and

$$S'(\bar{q}^{SB}) = \bar{\theta} + \frac{\lambda}{1 - \nu}\Delta\theta. \quad (2.139)$$

Simplifying by using (2.137) yields (2.66).

3 Incentive and Participation Constraints with Adverse Selection ★

The main theme of chapter 2 was to determine how the fundamental conflict between rent extraction and efficiency could be solved in a principal-agent relationship with adverse selection. In the models presented in chapter 2, this conflict was relatively easy to understand because it resulted from the simple interaction of a *single* incentive constraint with a *single* participation constraint. A major difficulty of incentive theory in general, and adverse selection models in particular, lies in the numerous constraints imposed by incentive compatibility when one moves away from the simple models of chapter 2.[1]

In this chapter, we consider more complex contractual environments that have in common the fact that they raise further difficulties for the determination

---

[1]Even in those simple models, the optimal solution is only derived by first guessing which are the binding incentive and participation constraints and then checking *ex post* that the remaining constraints are really satisfied by the solution of the relaxed problem.

of the binding incentive and participation constraints. Those difficulties are not only purely technical ones due to the increased mathematical complexity of the models, but they are also deeply rooted in the economics of the problems under scrutiny. They often lead to a quite novel analysis of the rent extraction-efficiency trade-off, sometimes challenging its main insights, but always offering sharp and interesting economic conclusions.

We can roughly classify the features of the new contractual settings analyzed in this chapter into three broad categories. Each of these categories yields a particular perturbation of the standard rent extraction-efficiency trade-off. Let us briefly describe these three categories.

• **Conflict between several of the agent's incentive constraints:** In environments that are more complex than the bare-bones model of chapter 2, the agent may have more than two possible types. These models include the relatively straightforward three-type extensions of the basic set up of chapter 2, the case of a continuum of types often found in the literature, and also the less easy-to-handle *multidimensional modelling of adverse selection*. In the case of multidimensional modelling, new conflicts arise between several of the agent's incentive constraints of the agent.

In a unidimensional model with three types, the *Spence-Mirrlees property* enables us to simplify the analysis considerably, because it suggests that only local incentive constraints need to be taken into account. However, the sole consideration of upward incentive compatibility constraints may be misleading, and the optimal contract may call for some downward incentive compatibility constraints to be binding as well. *Bunching* of different types on the same contract arises quite naturally when the distribution of types does not satisfy the *monotone hazard rate property*. Three-type models alone are enough to highlight this bunching phenomenon. However, for the sake of completeness, appendices 3.1 and 3.2 at the end of this chapter are entirely devoted to the case of a continuum of types. We solve there for the optimal contract with a continuum of types. Also, we present the techniques needed to replace the infinite number of incentive constraints with a *local incentive constraint*, and we show the validity of this approach when the Spence-Mirrless property holds. Then, we move on to solve for the optimal contract with a continuum of types in the presence of bunching.

In practice, the agent's private information is often multidimensional. A regulator is ignorant of both the marginal cost and the fixed cost of a regulated firm. A bank is ignorant of both the quality of an investment and the risk aversion of the investor. A monopolistic seller knows neither the willingness to pay nor the marginal utility of income of the buyer. By the mere multidimensionality of the type space, different types of agents cannot be unambiguously ordered, and multidimensional models are still characterized by some conflicts between various incentive constraints. Nothing like the monotone hazard rate property guarantees the full separation of types on different allocations in the multidimensional model. However, at least in two by two discrete models, some analogies with the unidimensional model of chapter 2 can still be drawn.

• **Conflict between the agent's incentive and type-dependent participation constraints:** Another significant simplification made in chapter 2 was to assume that the status quo utility level of the agent was independent of his type (and normalized to zero). Quite often, outside his relationship with the principal an efficient agent has better opportunities than an inefficient agent. To model those valuable opportunities, we assume that the agent gets an exogenous type-dependent utility level when he is not trading with the principal. When the efficient type's status quo utility level becomes high enough, the principal finds that it is no longer useful to reduce allocative efficiency to decrease the agent's information rent, which is bounded below by this outside opportunity. Keeping the efficient agent within the relationship may even lead the principal to give him such a great deal that the inefficient agent is also willing to take this offer, i.e., to mimic the efficient type. The inefficient agent's incentive constraint is then binding, a case of so called *countervailing incentives.*

Instead of being deterministic, the agent's outside opportunities may also be random. This leads to *random participation constraints* and thus to a probabilistic participation of some types. In a two-type model where only the inefficient type's participation is random, the contract must not only induce information revelation by the efficient type but must also arbitrate between the benefit of trading more often with an inefficient type and the cost of providing that inefficient type with enough incentives to participate.

• **Constraints on transfers:** So far we have assumed that the monetary transfers between the principal and the agent were unlimited. Several kinds of constraints can be imposed on these transfers.

Under *ex ante* contracting and with a risk-neutral agent, we showed in section 2.11.1 that the first-best allocation was implementable provided that the agent receives a negative payoff in the bad state of nature. However, agents are often financially constrained and have limited liability. When such penalties are restricted by different kinds of *limited liability constraints*, it becomes harder to induce information revelation. The conflict between incentive compatibility and *ex ante* participation constraints is no longer costless to solve. Second-best volumes of trade are then distorted away from their first-best values. Nevertheless, the direction of the distortion depends on the nature of the limited liability constraints.

In section 2.14.1 we have already seen how informative signals on the agent's type enabled the principal to improve the terms of the rent extraction-efficiency trade-off. *Auditing* is an endogenous way to obtain such signals. Audit allows a costly enlargement of the principal's tools that are available to screen the agent's types.[2] At some cost, the principal may be able to verify with some probability the agent's message on his type. In cases where a lie is detected, the agent is punished and has to pay a penalty, which again can be limited in different ways either by the agent's assets or his gains from trade with the principal. Of course, this threat of an audit relaxes the incentive compatibility constraint. But the trade-off between incentive compatibility and participation constraints is again dependent on the particular constraints imposed on punishments.

Most of this book is concerned with principal-agent relationships where the conflict between the principal and the agent is quite obvious and leads to binding participation constraints. However, when the principal is a benevolent government willing to redistribute income between heterogeneous agents, the agency conflict comes from the interaction between the principal's *budget balance constraint* and the agent's incentive constraint. Solving such problems requires slightly different methods than those we have used so far. Indeed, for such models one cannot determine, sequentially, the distribution of information rents that implement a given output profile at a minimal cost and then the second-best outputs. Instead, the technical difficulties of such models come from the simultaneous characterization of the second-best outputs and the profile of information rents. Those taxation models highlight a new trade-off between allocative efficiency and redistribution.

Section 3.1 presents the straightforward three-type extension of the standard model of chapter 2. In this section we discuss the Spence-Mirrlees property and the monotone hazard rate property, which together ensure monotonicity of the optimal schedule of outputs and the absence of any bunching of types. Section 3.2 deals with a bidimensional adverse selection model—solving it for the optimal outputs and comparing it with a standard unidimensional model. Section 3.3 offers a careful analysis of a two-type model with type-dependent reservation utilities, discussing all possible regimes of the solution. We also discuss several instances where this modelling has turned out to be useful for understanding various economic phenomena. Section 3.4 introduces random participation constraints. In section 3.5, we look at the impacts that different limited liability constraints, on either transfers or rents, may have on the allocation of resources under *ex ante* contracting. The first constraints increase the volume of trade whereas the second ones reduce it. In section 3.6, we analyze audit models and derive optimal audit policies for punishments satisfying various constraints. Audit models are then compared to models where incentives for truthful revelation are based on the threat of

---

[2]Another tool available to the principal to improve screening is the threat of terminating his relationship with the agent. As we will show, one can draw some analogy between those latter models and models with audit.

terminating, with some probability, the relationship between the principal and the agent. Finally, section 3.7 analyzes the trade-off between efficiency and redistribution. It shows how to optimize such an efficiency-equity trade-off. Appendices 3.1 and 3.2 deal with the case of a continuum of types for the basic model of section 2, which exhibits a simple rent-efficiency trade-off.

3.1 More than Two Types

Suppose that θ may take three possible values, i.e., $\Theta = \{\underline{\theta}, \hat{\theta}, \bar{\theta}\}$, with $\bar{\theta} - \hat{\theta} = \hat{\theta} - \underline{\theta} = \Delta\theta$ for simplicity, and with respective probabilities $\underline{\nu}$, $\hat{\nu}$, and $\bar{\nu}$ such that $\underline{\nu} + \hat{\nu} + \bar{\nu} = 1$. We denote a truthful direct revelation mechanism in this three-type environment by $\{(\underline{t}, \underline{q}); (\hat{t}, \hat{q}); (\bar{t}, \bar{q})\}$. Using similar notations, information rents write respectively as $\underline{U} = \underline{t} - \underline{\theta}\underline{q}$, $\widehat{U} = \hat{t} - \hat{\theta}\hat{q}$, and $\overline{U} = \bar{t} - \bar{\theta}\bar{q}$. As a benchmark, note that the first-best outputs are respectively given by $S'(\underline{q}^*) = \underline{\theta}$, $S'(\hat{q}^*) = \hat{\theta}$ and $S'(\bar{q}^*) = \bar{\theta}$.

3.1.1 Incentive Feasible Contracts

For each of the three possible types, we now have the following incentive constraints: For the most efficient type $\underline{\theta}$,

$$\underline{U} \geq \widehat{U} + \Delta\theta\hat{q}, \tag{3.1}$$

$$\underline{U} \geq \overline{U} + 2\Delta\theta\bar{q}; \tag{3.2}$$

for the intermediate type $\hat{\theta}$,

$$\widehat{U} \geq \overline{U} + \Delta\theta\bar{q}, \tag{3.3}$$

$$\widehat{U} \geq \underline{U} - \Delta\theta\underline{q}; \tag{3.4}$$

for the least efficient type $\bar{\theta}$,

$$\overline{U} \geq \widehat{U} - \Delta\theta\hat{q}, \tag{3.5}$$

$$\overline{U} \geq \underline{U} - 2\Delta\theta\underline{q}. \tag{3.6}$$

As an example, let us show how (3.1) and (3.2) are obtained. We want that a $\underline{\theta}$-agent does not announce $\hat{\theta}$. This requires

$$\underline{U} = \underline{t} - \underline{\theta}\underline{q} \geq \hat{t} - \underline{\theta}\hat{q} = \hat{t} - \hat{\theta}\hat{q} + (\hat{\theta} - \underline{\theta})\hat{q} \tag{3.7}$$

or

$$\underline{U} \geq \widehat{U} + \Delta\theta\widehat{q}. \tag{3.8}$$

Additionally, we want a $\underline{\theta}$-agent that does not pretend to be $\bar{\theta}$. This requires

$$\underline{U} = \underline{t} - \underline{\theta}\underline{q} \geq \bar{t} - \underline{\theta}\bar{q} = \bar{t} - \bar{\theta}\bar{q} + (\bar{\theta} - \underline{\theta})\bar{q} \tag{3.9}$$

or

$$\underline{U} \geq \bar{U} + 2\Delta\theta\bar{q}. \tag{3.10}$$

The six incentive constraints (3.1) to (3.6) can be classified into two categories: *local* and *global* incentive constraints. Local incentive constraints involve adjacent types, such as the upward incentive constraints (3.1) and (3.3) or the downward incentive constraints (3.5) and (3.4). Global incentive constraints involve nonadjacent types, such as the upward incentive constraint (3.2) or the downward incentive constraint (3.6).

To simplify the analysis and find the relevant binding constraints, we proceed in two steps. First, as in chapter 2, intuition suggests that the most efficient types want to lie upward and claim they are less efficient. Therefore, we can momentarily ignore the downward incentive constraints, as we did in chapter 2. We are left with the remaining upward incentive constraints (3.1), (3.2), and (3.3).

Second, the incentive constraints (3.1) to (3.6) also imply some *implementability conditions* on the schedule of outputs. Indeed, adding the incentive constraints for two adjacent types yields $\underline{q} \geq \widehat{q}$ (use (3.1) and (3.4)) and $\widehat{q} \geq \bar{q}$ (use (3.3) and (3.5)). Therefore, we get the monotonicity constraints

$$\underline{q} \geq \widehat{q} \geq \bar{q}. \tag{3.11}$$

This monotonicity helps to further simplify the set of relevant incentive constraints by getting rid of the global incentive constraint (3.2). Indeed, adding (3.1) and (3.3) yields

$$\underline{U} \geq \bar{U} + \Delta\theta(\widehat{q} + \bar{q}). \tag{3.12}$$

But, using $\widehat{q} \geq \bar{q}$, the second term of the right-hand side above is greater than $2\Delta\theta\bar{q}$. Therefore, the global incentive constraint (3.2) is implied by the two local incentive constraints (3.1) and (3.3) when the monotonicity constraint holds.

Finally, to obtain the optimal contract we will only consider the two upward local incentive constraints with the monotonicity constraint on outputs (implying the global upward constraint), and we will check *ex post* that the downward incentive constraints are also satisfied.

3.1.2 The Optimal Contract

When this huge simplification in the set of incentive constraints is made, all relevant constraints for the principal are reduced to the incentive constraints (3.1) and (3.3), the implementability condition (3.11) and the least efficient type's participation constraint

$$\bar{U} \geq 0. \tag{3.13}$$

The optimal contract thus solves the program (P) below:

$$(P): \quad \max_{\{(\underline{U}, \underline{q}); (\widehat{U}, \hat{q}); (\bar{U}, \bar{q})\}} \underline{\nu}(S(\underline{q}) - \underline{\theta}\underline{q} - \underline{U}) + \hat{\nu}(S(\hat{q}) - \hat{\theta}\hat{q} - \widehat{U}) + \bar{\nu}(S(\bar{q}) - \bar{\theta}\bar{q} - \bar{U}),$$

subject to (3.1), (3.3), (3.11), and (3.13).

It should be clear that constraints (3.1), (3.3), and (3.13) are all binding at the optimal contract. This leads to the following expressions of the information rents, $\underline{U} = \Delta\theta(\hat{q} + \bar{q})$, $\widehat{U} = \Delta\theta\bar{q}$, and $\bar{U} = 0$. Substituting the rents into the objective function of problem (P), the principal must finally solve program (P') below:

$$(P'): \max_{\{(\underline{q}, \hat{q}, \bar{q})\}} \underline{\nu}(S(\underline{q}) - \underline{\theta}\underline{q} - \Delta\theta(\hat{q} + \bar{q})) + \hat{\nu}(S(\hat{q}) - \hat{\theta}\hat{q} - \Delta\theta\bar{q}) + \bar{\nu}(S(\bar{q}) - \bar{\theta}\bar{q}),$$

subject to (3.11).

Proposition 3.1 summarizes the solution of the principal's problem.[3]

Proposition 3.1: *In a three-type adverse selection model, the optimal contract entails the following:*

- *Constraints (3.1), (3.3), and (3.13) are all binding.*
- *When $\hat{\nu} > \bar{\nu}\underline{\nu}$, the monotonicity conditions (3.11) are strictly satisfied. Optimal outputs are given by $\underline{q}^{SB} = \underline{q}^*$, $\hat{q}^{SB} < \hat{q}^*$, and $\bar{q}^{SB} < \bar{q}^*$ with*

$$S'(\hat{q}^{SB}) = \hat{\theta} + \frac{\underline{\nu}}{\hat{\nu}}\Delta\theta, \tag{3.14}$$

$$S'(\bar{q}^{SB}) = \bar{\theta} + \frac{\underline{\nu} + \hat{\nu}}{\bar{\nu}}\Delta\theta. \tag{3.15}$$

- *When $\hat{\nu} \leq \bar{\nu}\underline{\nu}$, some bunching emerges. We still have $\underline{q}^{SB} = \underline{q}^*$, but now $\hat{q}^{SB} = \bar{q}^{SB} = q^P < \underline{q}^*$, with*

$$S'(q^P) = \bar{\theta} + \frac{2\underline{\nu}}{\hat{\nu} + \bar{\nu}}\Delta\theta. \tag{3.16}$$

---

[3]The proof is left to the reader as an exercise.

When $\hat{\nu} > \bar{\nu}\underline{\nu}$, we have a straightforward extension of proposition 2.1. The most efficient type's production level is not distorted. Since his information rent, namely $\underline{U} = \Delta\theta(\hat{q} + \bar{q})$, depends now on the production levels of all the types who are less efficient than the efficient type, those production levels must be distorted downward to reach the optimal rent extraction-efficiency trade-off. The reason for this expression of the θ-agent's rent is that all the local upward incentive constraints, and only those constraints, are binding. The $\hat{\theta}$-agent also has an information rent, $\widehat{U} = \Delta\theta\bar{q}$, because he can pretend to be a $\bar{\theta}$-agent. This justifies a second downward distortion of $\bar{q}$. Only the least efficient agent gets a zero rent $\overline{U} = 0$.[4]

If the profile of production levels obtained strictly satisfies the monotonicity conditions (3.11), all of the other incentive constraints also hold strictly. If not, some bunching emerges, as described in the second part of proposition 3.1. Bunching now arises from the conflict between the desire of the principal to implement a schedule of outputs, which is increasing over an interval when only upward incentive constraints are taken into account, namely $\hat{q} < \bar{q}$, and the implementability condition, which requires the opposite monotonicity, namely $\hat{q} \geq \bar{q}$. Indeed, when $\hat{\nu}$ is rather small and $\underline{\nu}$ is rather large, the information rent of the $\hat{\theta}$-type is not too costly for the principal but that of a $\underline{\theta}$-type is much more. Reducing those information rents calls for strongly reducing $\hat{q}$, but a reduction in $\bar{q}$ is much less necessary. In this case, the implementability condition limits the ability of the principal to reduce the agent's information rent and bunching emerges.

> **Remark:** This source of bunching in a three-type model can be compared to the one arising in the case of nonresponsiveness, seen in section 2.10.2. There, the dependency of the gross surplus on θ (namely $S(q, \theta)$ with $S_{q\theta} > 1$) introduced a conflict between the desire of the principal to have an output increasing in θ for pure efficiency reasons and the need to satisfy the implementability condition, even in a simple two-type model. In the present three-type model, the principal's gross surplus does not depend on θ, but the probability distribution of θ is such that the *virtual surplus*, which is defined as $S(q) - (\theta + \frac{\sum_{\theta' < \theta}\Pr(\theta')}{\Pr(\theta)})q$ and should be maximized by the principal if only upward incentive constraints mattered, is maximized by a schedule of outputs that increases over an interval. It appears again a conflict between efficiency considerations and the implementability conditions. ∎

[4]All these features of the optimal contract are more general and hold for any number of types.

Such bunching occurs in the basic model only when there are more than two types, or with a continuum.[5] Remember, indeed, that it never holds in the standard two type model of section 2.3. To avoid bunching, modelers often chose to impose a sufficient condition on the distribution of types, the *monotonicity of the hazard rate*.

Definition 3.1: A *distribution of types satisfies the monotone hazard rate property if and only if*

$$\frac{\Pr(\theta < \hat{\theta})}{\Pr(\theta = \hat{\theta})} = \frac{\nu}{\hat{\nu}} < \frac{\Pr(\theta < \bar{\theta})}{\Pr(\theta = \bar{\theta})} = \frac{\nu + \hat{\nu}}{\bar{\nu}}. \tag{3.17}$$

This sufficient condition ensures that the incentive distortions on the right-hand sides of (3.14) and (3.15) are increasing with the agent's type. The *virtual costs* of the different types, namely $\underline{\theta}$, $\hat{\theta} + \frac{\nu}{\hat{\nu}}\Delta\theta$, and $\bar{\theta} + \frac{\nu+\hat{\nu}}{\bar{\nu}}\Delta\theta$, are thus ranked exactly as the true physical costs. The virtual surplus is maximized by a decreasing schedule of outputs. Asymmetric information does not perturb the ranking of types.

> **Remark:** With n types, i.e., $\Theta = \{\theta_1, \dots, \theta_n\}$, and a distribution of types such that $\Pr(\theta_i) = \nu_i > 0$ for all i, the monotonicity of the hazard rate property says that $\frac{\Pr(\theta < \theta_i)}{\Pr(\theta = \theta_i)} = \frac{\sum_{k=1}^{i-1} \nu_k}{\nu_i}$ is increasing in i. In appendix 3.1, we provide the corresponding condition in the case of a continuum of types. ∎

3.1.3 The Spence-Mirrlees Property with More than Two Types

When the local incentive constraints imply the global ones, it is sufficient to check that the agent does not want to *lie locally* to be sure that he does not want to *lie globally*. The incentive problem is then well behaved since there is a huge simplification in the number of relevant constraints. It is precisely this simplification that yielded the clear analysis in the last section. This huge simplification holds for any number of types, or even for a continuum[6] if the agent's utility function satisfies the so-called Spence-Mirrlees property. Let us expand the scope of our previous analysis and assume that the agent's utility function, which is defined over allo-

---

[5] See appendix 3.2 for an analysis of bunching in the case of a continuum of types.
[6] See appendix 3.3.

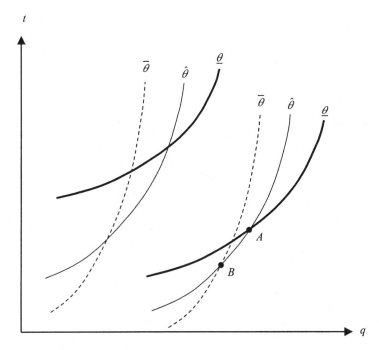

FIGURE 3.1: The Spence-Mirrlees Property

cations (q, t) in $\mathcal{A}$ and types θ in Θ, writes as $U(q, t, \theta)$.[7] In this framework, the Spence-Mirrlees property tells us that the marginal rates of substitution between output and money can be ranked in a monotonic way. The following property must thus be satisfied:

$$\frac{\partial}{\partial \theta}\left(\frac{U_q}{U_t}\right) \begin{array}{c} > 0 \\ (\text{or} < 0) \end{array} \qquad \text{for any } (t, q, \theta) \text{ in } \mathcal{A} \times \Theta. \qquad (3.18)$$

Economically, this property means that the indifference curves always move in the same direction as θ changes. In figure 3.1 we have drawn the case where the marginal rates of substitution $\frac{U_q}{U_t}$, which are also the slopes of the agent's indifference curves, are increasing with the agent's type. At point A, where the indifference curves of a $\underline{\theta}$- and a $\bar{\theta}$-type cross each other, the indifference curve of the $\hat{\theta}$-type has the greater slope; and at point B, where the indifference curves of a $\hat{\theta}$-type and a $\bar{\theta}$-type cross each other, the indifference curve of the $\bar{\theta}$-type has a greater slope.

Of course, the particular objective function used in chapter 2 and section 3.1.1, namely $U = t - \theta q$, satisfies the Spence-Mirrlees property, because $\frac{\partial}{\partial \theta}(\frac{U_q}{U_t}) = -1$. Also, the objective function used in section 2.10, $U = t - C(q, \theta)$, satisfies this condition if $C_{q\theta} > 0$ (or $C_{q\theta} < 0$), because $\frac{\partial}{\partial \theta}(\frac{U_q}{U_t}) = -C_{q\theta}$.

[7]Working with non-quasi-linear utility functions turns out to be necessary when we analyze adverse selection in the insurance market, as in section 3.3.2.

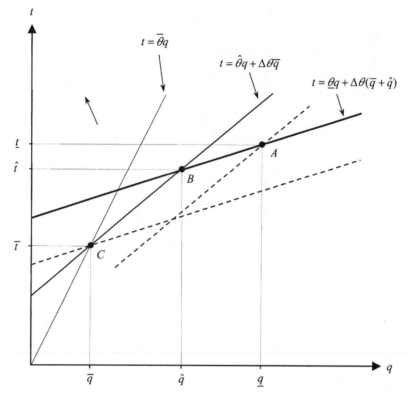

FIGURE 3.2: Indifference Curves with Three Types and Where $U = t - \theta q$

Figure 3.2 illustrates why the Spence-Mirrlees property ensures that, when upward local incentive constraints are binding, global ones and downward ones are strictly satisfied. Suppose the agent is offered a menu $\{A, B, C\}$ for which all the upward local incentive constraints are binding. As can be easily seen in the figure, the efficient type is indifferent between telling the truth and lying upward to $\hat{\theta}$, i.e., he is indifferent between contracts A and B. However, lying upward up to $\bar{\theta}$ would significantly reduce his utility level, because contract C is on an indifference curve with a lower level of utility than what a $\underline{\theta}$-type gets by choosing A. Hence, the $\underline{\theta}$-type's global incentive constraint is satisfied. Similarly, consider an agent with type $\hat{\theta}$. This agent is indifferent between telling the truth and lying upward up to $\bar{\theta}$, i.e., he is indifferent between choosing B and C. However, by lying downward, type $\hat{\theta}$ would get contract A, which yields him a strictly lower utility level. The downward incentive constraint is strictly satisfied.

The Spence-Mirrless property makes the incentive problem well behaved in the sense that only local incentive constraints need to be considered. At a rough level, it is similar to a concavity condition in the usual maximization problems. As for a concavity condition, the optimization of the agent's problem is obtained by looking at the benefits of *local* changes away from his truthful report strategy as *global* changes are certainly dominated. The analysis of incentive problems satisfying this property is very similar to that developed in chapter 2.

When the Spence-Mirrlees property holds, the analysis of chapter 2 can also be easily extended[8] to the case of a continuum of types $[\underline{\theta}, \bar{\theta}]$, which is what we do in appendices 3.1 and 3.2. If it is not satisfied, the analysis of the continuum case becomes quickly untractable, and the study of the finite-type case requires that we consider all combinations of binding constraints and calls very quickly for numerical methods.

Spence (1973) introduced the single-crossing assumption in his theory of signaling on the labor market. Similarly, Mirrlees (1971) also used a single-crossing assumption in his theory of optimal income taxation. It was called the *constant sign assumption* in Guesnerie and Laffont (1984). Araujo and Moreira (2000) provided an analysis of optimal contracts in which the Spence-Mirrlees property may not be satisfied and types are distributed continuously. Matthews and Moore (1987) provided an extensive study of the set of incentive constraints in the case where this Spence-Mirrlees property may not hold. They also solved an example. ∎

3.2 Multidimensional Asymmetric Information

Another important limitation of our analysis of adverse selection in chapter 2 is that the adverse selection parameter θ was modeled as a unidimensional parameter. In many instances, the agent simultaneously knows several pieces of information that are payoff relevant and affect the optimal trade. For instance, a tax authority would like to know both the elasticity of an agent's labor supply and his productivity before fixing his tax liability. Similarly, an insurance company would like to know both the probability of accident for an insurer and his degree of risk aversion before fixing the risk premium that the agent should pay. The producer of a good knows not only the marginal cost of producing the good but also the associated fixed cost. In all these situations, the unidimensional paradigm must be given up in order to assess the full consequences of asymmetric information on the rent extraction-efficiency trade-off.

[8]See Guesnerie and Laffont (1984).

3.2.1 A Discrete Bare-Bones Model

We now extend the analysis of chapter 2 to the case of bidimensional asymmetric information. The simplest way to do so is to have the agent accomplish two activities for the principal. Each of those activities is performed by the agent at a marginal cost which is private information. Let us assume that the agent produces two goods in respective quantities q_1 and q_2 with a utility function $U = t - (\theta_1 q_1 + \theta_2 q_2)$, with θ_i in $\{\underline{\theta}, \bar{\theta}\}$ for $i = 1, 2$. We also assume that there is no externality between the two tasks for the principal, so that the surpluses associated with both tasks add up in the latter's objective function, which becomes $V = S(q_1) + S(q_2) - t$.

The probability distribution of the adverse selection vector $\theta = (\theta_1, \theta_2)$ is now defined by $\underline{\nu} = \Pr(\theta_1 = \underline{\theta}, \theta_2 = \underline{\theta})$, $\frac{\hat{\nu}}{2} = \Pr(\theta_1 = \underline{\theta}, \theta_2 = \bar{\theta}) = \Pr(\theta_1 = \bar{\theta}, \theta_2 = \underline{\theta})$, $\bar{\nu} = \Pr(\theta_1 = \bar{\theta}, \theta_2 = \bar{\theta})$ with a *positive correlation* among types arising when $\rho = \underline{\nu}\bar{\nu} - \frac{\hat{\nu}^2}{4} > 0$. As usual, this distribution is common knowledge.

The components of the direct revelation mechanism are respectively denoted by (t_{11}, q_{11}, q_{11}) if $(\theta_1 = \underline{\theta}, \theta_2 = \underline{\theta})$, (t_{12}, q_{12}, q_{21}) if $(\theta_1 = \underline{\theta}, \theta_2 = \bar{\theta})$, (t_{12}, q_{21}, q_{12}) if $(\theta_1 = \bar{\theta}, \theta_2 = \underline{\theta})$, and (t_{22}, q_{22}, q_{22}) if $(\theta_1 = \bar{\theta}, \theta_2 = \bar{\theta})$, where we impose (without a loss of generality) a symmetry restriction on transfers. Similar notations are used for the information rents U_{ij}. Because of the symmetry of the model, there are only three relevant levels of information rents, $\underline{U} = U_{11}$, $\hat{U} = U_{12} = U_{21}$, and $\bar{U} = U_{22}$. Similarly, we denote outputs by $q_{11} = \underline{q}$, $q_{12} = \hat{q}_2$, $q_{21} = \hat{q}_1$, and $q_{22} = \bar{q}$, and transfers by $t_{11} = \underline{t}$, $t_{21} = t_{12} = \hat{t}$, and $t_{22} = \bar{t}$. These notations, even though they look quite cumbersome, unify the present multidimensional modelling with that of section 3.1.1 above.

Again, following the logic of the unidimensional model, we may guess that only the upward incentive constraints matter. The three following incentive constraints then become relevant:

$$\underline{U} = \underline{t} - 2\underline{\theta}\underline{q} \geq \hat{t} - \underline{\theta}(\hat{q}_1 + \hat{q}_2) = \hat{U} + \Delta\theta\hat{q}_1, \tag{3.19}$$

$$\underline{U} \geq \bar{t} - 2\underline{\theta}\bar{q} = \bar{U} + 2\Delta\theta\bar{q}, \tag{3.20}$$

$$\hat{U} = \hat{t} - \underline{\theta}\hat{q}_2 - \bar{\theta}\hat{q}_1 \geq \bar{t} - (\underline{\theta} + \bar{\theta})\bar{q} = \bar{U} + \Delta\theta\bar{q}. \tag{3.21}$$

We can also expect the participation constraint of an agent who is inefficient on both dimensions ($\theta_1 = \bar{\theta}$ and $\theta_2 = \bar{\theta}$) to be binding, i.e.,

$$\bar{U} = 0. \tag{3.22}$$

We leave it to the reader to check that adding incentive constraints for types taken two by two yields the following impementability conditions:

$$\underline{q} \geq \max(\hat{q}_1, \bar{q}) \tag{3.23}$$

and

$$\hat{q}_2 \geq \max(\hat{q}_1, \bar{q}). \tag{3.24}$$

3.2.2 The Optimal Contract

We can expect (3.21) and (3.22) to be binding at the optimum. Then (3.19) and (3.20) can be summarized as

$$\underline{U} \geq \Delta\theta \max(2\bar{q}, \bar{q} + \hat{q}_1), \tag{3.25}$$

which should also be binding at the optimum to reduce the efficient agent's information rent.

After the substitution of the information rents as functions of outputs, the principal's optimization program can be reduced to:

$$(P'): \quad \max_{\{(\underline{q}, \hat{q}_1, \hat{q}_2, \bar{q})\}} \nu(2S(\underline{q}) - 2\underline{\theta}\underline{q} - \Delta\theta \max(2\bar{q}, \bar{q} + \hat{q}_1))$$

$$+ \hat{\nu}(S(\hat{q}_1) + S(\hat{q}_2) - \underline{\theta}\hat{q}_2 - \bar{\theta}\hat{q}_1 - \Delta\theta\bar{q}) + \bar{\nu}(2S(\bar{q}) - 2\bar{\theta}\bar{q}).$$

We must distinguish two cases depending on the level of correlation ρ between both dimensions of adverse selection.

CASE 1: Weak Correlation

Let us first assume that the solution is such that $\bar{q} \leq \hat{q}_1$. In this case, $\max(2\bar{q}, \hat{q}_1 + \bar{q}) = \hat{q}_1 + \bar{q}$ and optimizing (P') yields the following second-best outputs:

$$S'(\underline{q}^{SB}) = S'(\hat{q}_2^{SB}) = \underline{\theta}, \tag{3.26}$$

$$S'(\hat{q}_1^{SB}) = \bar{\theta} + \frac{\nu}{\hat{\nu}}\Delta\theta, \tag{3.27}$$

$$S'(\bar{q}^{SB}) = \bar{\theta} + \frac{\nu + \hat{\nu}}{2\bar{\nu}}\Delta\theta. \tag{3.28}$$

This latter schedule of outputs is the solution when the posited monotonicity condition $\bar{q}^{SB} \leq \hat{q}_1^{SB}$ holds, i.e., when

$$\frac{\nu}{\hat{\nu}} \leq \frac{\nu + \hat{\nu}}{2\bar{\nu}}, \tag{3.29}$$

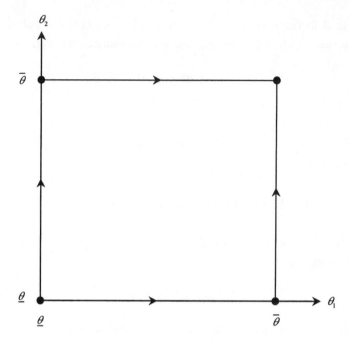

FIGURE 3.3: Binding Incentive Constraints with Weak Correlation

or, to put it differently, when $\rho \leq \frac{\hat{\nu}}{4}(2\underline{\nu} + \hat{\nu})$. This condition obviously holds in the case where θ_1 and θ_2 are independently drawn, since the correlation is then zero and $\rho = 0$. We leave it to the reader to check that all of the neglected incentive and participation constraints are satisfied when (3.29) holds.

In the case of weak correlation, the binding constraints are only the local ones. In figure 3.3, an arrow from a point in the type space, say A, to another one, say B, means that A is *attracted* by B,[9] i.e., the corresponding incentive constraint is binding at the optimum.

CASE 2: Strong Correlation

If we had perfect correlation, $\hat{\nu} = 0$, the binding incentive constraint would obviously be from $(\underline{\theta}, \underline{\theta})$ to $(\bar{\theta}, \bar{\theta})$, as shown in figure 3.4. Then we would be back to the usual unidimensional model along the diagonal.

More generally, for a strong positive correlation we may expect an intermediary case with the upward incentive constraints being binding as in figure 3.5.

Indeed, consider the case where the condition (3.29) does not hold. In this case the outputs, defined by (3.27) and (3.28), are such that $\max(2\bar{q}, \hat{q}_1 + \bar{q}) = 2\bar{q}$, a contradiction with our starting assumption $\bar{q} \leq \hat{q}_1$. Let us assume that instead we have $\bar{q} > \hat{q}_1$. In this case, $\max(2\bar{q}, \hat{q}_1 + \bar{q}) = 2\bar{q}$ and optimizing (P') leads to

[9]Border and Sobel (1987) coined this expression.

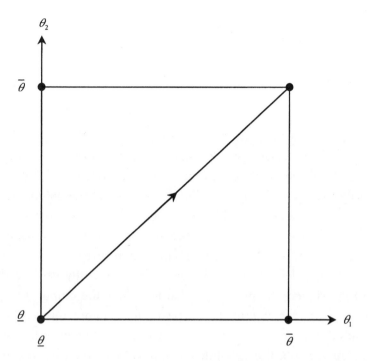

FIGURE 3.4: Binding Incentive Constraint with Perfect Correlation

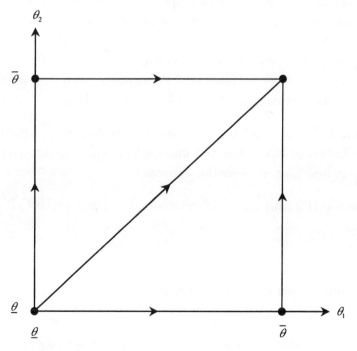

FIGURE 3.5: Binding Incentive Constraints with Strong Correlation

(3.27) and (3.28) being respectively replaced by

$$S'(\hat{q}_1) = \bar{\theta} \tag{3.30}$$

and

$$S'(\bar{q}) = \bar{\theta} + \frac{2\nu + \hat{\nu}}{2\bar{\nu}}\Delta\theta. \tag{3.31}$$

However, we immediately observe that $\bar{q} < \hat{q}_1$ for those outputs. Again, this is a contradiction with our starting assumption $\bar{q} > \hat{q}_1$. When (3.29) does not hold, we necessarily have $\hat{q}_1 = \bar{q} = q^P$, and bunching arises at the optimal contract.

To understand the origin of this bunching, let us first consider the case where the principal is concerned only with the upward incentive compatibility constraints (3.19) and (3.21). With a strong correlation of types, the principal finds the information rent left to the $(\underline{\theta}, \underline{\theta})$-type to be very costly because this type is relatively likely. Hence, the principal is led to reduce the output $\hat{q}_1$ significantly. On the other hand, the intermediate type $(\underline{\theta}, \bar{\theta})$ is rather unlikely. Hence, the principal finds it not very useful to reduce the output $\bar{q}$ to reduce the latter's information rent. As a result, the schedule of outputs that would be implemented by the principal, had he taken into account only the downward incentive constraints, would be such that $\bar{q} > \hat{q}_1$. The high output $\bar{q}$ requested from a $(\bar{\theta}, \bar{\theta})$-type makes the $(\underline{\theta}, \underline{\theta})$-type willing to mimic the $(\bar{\theta}, \bar{\theta})$-type rather than the intermediate type $(\underline{\theta}, \bar{\theta})$. With a strong correlation it is no longer correct to neglect the global incentive constraint (3.2). Both the local incentive constraints (3.19) and the global incentive constraints (3.2) are binding at the optimum, and this situation is only possible when the optimal allocation entails some bunching.

> **Remark:** Just as in the three-type model of section 3.1.2, a probability distribution of types such that intermediate types are rather unlikely creates bunching at the optimal contract. ∎

Optimizing (P') with the added constraint $\bar{q} = \hat{q}_1$ still yields (3.26) but also

$$S'(q^P) = \bar{\theta} + \frac{2\nu + \hat{\nu}}{\hat{\nu} + 2\bar{\nu}}\Delta\theta. \tag{3.32}$$

We summarize our findings in proposition 3.2.

Proposition 3.2: *In a symmetric bidimensional adverse selection setting, the optimal contract with a weak correlation of types keeps many features of the unidimensional case with two types; only upward incentive constraints are binding. With a strong correlation, the optimal contract* *may instead entail some bunching; a global incentive constraint becomes binding.*

Finally, note that more complex situations arise when the correlation is negative, asymmetric distributions are postulated, or when the dimensionality of actions is not the same as the dimensionality of the asymmetry of information.

We now describe two examples where modelling adverse selection with multidimensional types has proved to be useful.

EXAMPLE 1: Unknown Fixed Cost

Let us suppose that the agent has a cost function $C(\theta, q) = \theta_1 q + \theta_2$ where both the marginal cost θ_1 and the fixed cost θ_2 are unknown. As shown in Baron and Myerson (1982) and Rochet (1984), stochastic mechanisms, where the decision to produce or not produce is used as a screening device, are useful in this context. To explain why, let us introduce x in $[0, 1]$ as the probability of a positive production. As a function of the contracting variables q and x, the agent's utility function now writes as $U = t - (\theta_1 q x + \theta_2 x)$. This expression almost takes the same form as what we have analyzed above. It is easy to show that the shutdown of some types is also a valuable screening device to learn the value of the fixed cost θ_2.

EXAMPLE 2: Unknown Cost and Demand

Let us assume that the agent is a retailer who serves a market with a linear inverse demand $P(q) = a - \theta_1 - q$, where θ_1 is an intercept parameter, which is the first piece of private information of the agent. This agent has also a cost function $C(q) = \theta_2 q$, where the marginal cost θ_2 is the second piece of private information of the agent. The latter's utility function writes finally as $U = \tilde{t} + (a - \theta_1 - q)q - \theta_2 q$, where $\tilde{t}$ is the transfer received from the principal, here a manufacturer. To simplify, we also assume that the manufacturer incurs no production cost for the intermediate good he provides to the agent. Introducing a new variable $t = \tilde{t} + aq - q^2$, the agent's utility function rewrites as $U = t - (\theta_1 + \theta_2)q$. On the other hand, the principal's objective becomes $V = aq - q^2 - t$. In this example the bidimensional adverse selection model amounts to a unidimensional model, where $\theta = \theta_1 + \theta_2$ is a sufficient statistic for all information known by the agent. If each type θ_i belongs to $\Theta = \{\underline{\theta}, \bar{\theta}\}$, θ may take three possible values, $2\underline{\theta}$, $\bar{\theta} + \underline{\theta}$, or $2\bar{\theta}$. The framework of section 3.1 can then be used to derive the optimal contract.

> **Remark:** The dimensionality of the type space plays a crucial role in determining the binding participation constraints. To understand this point remember that, in a unidimensional case, the least efficient type's participation constraint is the only binding participation constraint (at

least as long as shutdown is not optimal) and the same result holds for a continuum of types (see appendix 3.1). Now suppose that it holds also with a continuum of bidimensional types, i.e., only the *least* efficient type on dimensions θ_1 and θ_2 is put at its reservation utility. Let us imagine that the principal slightly uniformly decreases the whole transfer schedule he offers to the agent by ε. Of course, a whole subset of types around $(\bar{\theta}, \bar{\theta})$ prefers to stop producing. The efficiency loss for the principal is roughly of the order ε^2. However, by uniformly reducing the whole transfer schedule, the principal reduces all information rents of the remaining types by ε, which means he makes a gain of the order $\varepsilon(1 - \varepsilon^2) \approx \varepsilon$. Therefore, the shutdown of a subset of types with nonzero measure is always optimal. ∎

Armstrong and Rochet (1999) provided a complete analysis of the two-type model. The case of a continuum of types was first analyzed by McAfee and McMillan (1988), who attempted to generalize the Spence-Mirrlees assumption to a multidimensional case, and Laffont, Maskin, and Rochet (1987), who explicitly solved an example in the case where the principal has only one output and one transfer with which to screen a bidimensional adverse selection parameter (see also Sibley and Srinagesh 1997). The result, that a shutdown of a nonzero measure of types is always optimal for a continuum of types, is due to Armstrong (1996), who also offered some closed-form solutions for the optimal contract when the set of types includes the origin. See also Wilson (1993) on this point. The analysis of Rochet and Choné (1998) is the most general. They showed that bunching of types is always found in these bidimensional models, and they also provided the so-called *ironing and sweeping* techniques designed to analyze this bunching issue. These techniques are difficult and outside the scope of this book. Rochet and Choné (1998) also show that bunching implies that a whole set of types with nonzero measure exists, such that $q_1 = q_2$ at the optimal contract. They interpret this as a bundling requirement imposed by incentive compatibility. Finally, Armstrong (1999) pushed the idea that multidimensional adverse selection problems may introduce a significant simplification in the optimal contract between a seller (the principal) and a buyer (the agent) who is privately informed of his type. Instead of explicitly computing this contract, Amstrong provides a lower boundary on what can be achieved with simple two-part tariffs and, using the Law of Large Numbers, shows that these contracts can approximate the first-best when the number of products sold to this buyer is large enough. ∎

3.3 Type-Dependent Participation Constraint and Countervailing Incentives

The models in sections 3.1 and 3.2 have already illustrated the difficulties that the modeler faces when there is no obvious order between the various incentive constraints. The same kind of difficulties arise when the agent's participation constraint is type-dependent. Indeed, those participation constraints may also perturb the natural ordering of the incentive and participation constraints that was discussed in chapter 2. Determining which participation and incentive constraints are binding becomes a more difficult task. To analyze those issues, we now come back to our two-type model. In chapter 2, we made a simple and debatable assumption by postulating that the outside opportunities of the two types of agents were identical (and without loss of generality normalized to zero). Then we proved that the binding incentive constraint is always the efficient type's constraint. However, in many cases there is a correlation (in general a positive one) between the agent's productivity in a given principal-agent relationship and his outside opportunity. We now assume that the efficient agent's outside utility level is $U_0 > 0$, and we still normalize the inefficient agent's outside utility level to zero. The efficient- and inefficient-type participation constraints are now written, respectively, as

$$\underline{U} \geq U_0, \tag{3.33}$$

$$\overline{U} \geq 0. \tag{3.34}$$

3.3.1 The Optimal Contract with Type-Dependent Status Quo

The principal's problem is to optimize the expression (2.20), subject to the relevant upward incentive compatibility constraints (IC) (2.21) and (2.22) and the new type-dependent participation constraints (PC) (3.33) and (3.34). The solution to this problem exhibits five different regimes, depending on the value of U_0.

CASE 1: Irrelevance of the Outside Opportunity Utility Level
This case arises when $U_0 < \Delta\theta\bar{q}^{SB}$. Then the optimal second-best solution (2.27), (2.29), and (2.30), obtained in section 2.6, remains valid since the neglected participation constraint (3.33) is satisfied by the solution discussed in proposition 2.1. When the outside option does not provide a level of utility to the efficient agent that is high enough, it does not affect the second-best contract.

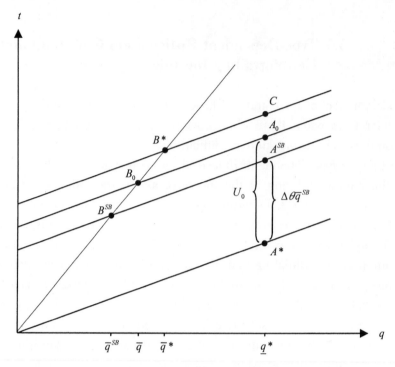

FIGURE 3.6: Type-Dependent Participation Constraint: Case 2

CASE 2: Both PCs and the Efficient Agent's IC Are Binding

This case arises when $\Delta\theta\bar{q}^* > U_0 > \Delta\theta\bar{q}^{SB}$. The former solution is now no longer valid. To induce the efficient type's participation, he must receive a higher level of utility than the information rent obtained in the optimal second-best contract corresponding to $U_0 = 0$. Then, one can afford less distortion in the inefficient type's production level and choose $\bar{q}$ such that $U_0 = \Delta\theta\bar{q}$. As long as U_0 belongs to $[\Delta\theta\bar{q}^{SB}, \Delta\theta\bar{q}^*]$, the incentive constraint of the efficient type and both participation constraints are simultaneously binding (see, for example, the pair of contracts (A_0, B_0) in figure 3.6).

CASE 3: Both PCs Are Binding

This case arises when $\Delta\theta\underline{q}^* > U_0 > \Delta\theta\bar{q}^*$. Still raising U_0, the principal finds that it is no longer optimal to use the inefficient type's output to raise the efficient agent's information rent and induce his participation. Because output is already at its first-best level, the remaining tool available to the principal to raise the efficient agent's rent is the transfer $\underline{t}$, and we now have $\underline{t} = \underline{\theta}\underline{q}^* + U_0$. This solution is valid as long as the inefficient agent's incentive constraint is not binding, i.e., as long as $0 = \overline{U} > U_0 - \Delta\theta\underline{q}^*$ (see the pair of contracts (A_0, B_0) in figure 3.7; this case remains valid as long as A_0 is between C and D). In that region, both production levels are the efficient ones.

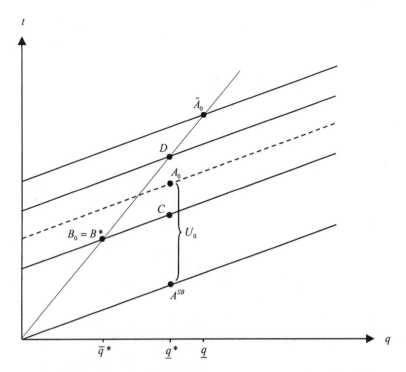

FIGURE 3.7: Type-Dependent Participation Constraint: Cases 3 and 4

CASE 4: Both PCs and the Inefficient Agent's IC Are Binding

This case arises when $\Delta\theta \underline{q}^{CI} > U_0 \geq \Delta\theta q^*$, where $\underline{q}^{CI}$ is given by

$$S'(\underline{q}^{CI}) = \underline{\theta} - \frac{1-\nu}{\nu}\Delta\theta, \tag{3.35}$$

with the superscript "CI" meaning *countervailing incentives*.[10]

When U_0 continues to increase (A_0 is now above D), the inefficient type is now attracted by the allocation given to the efficient type, but the constraints (3.33) and (3.34) remain binding. As a result, the efficient agent's output is distorted upwards to reach a value $\underline{q}$, defined by $U_0 = \Delta\theta \underline{q}$ (corresponding to the point $\tilde{A}_0$ above D in Figure 3.7).

CASE 5: The Efficient Type's PC and the Inefficient Type's IC Are both Binding

This case arises when $U_0 > \Delta\theta \underline{q}^{CI}$. Let us maximize (2.20) under the constraints (3.33) and (2.22). Assuming that those two constraints are binding, we obtain $\underline{U} = U_0$ and $\bar{U} = U_0 - \Delta\theta \underline{q}$. When we insert those expressions into the principal's objective function, we get a reduced-form program given by:

$$(P'): \quad \max_{\{\underline{q}, \bar{q}\}} \nu(S(\underline{q}) - \underline{\theta}\underline{q}) + (1-\nu)(S(\bar{q}) - \bar{\theta}\bar{q}) + (1-\nu)\Delta\theta \underline{q} - U_0.$$

---

[10]We will come back to the meaning of this term when we analyze case 5.

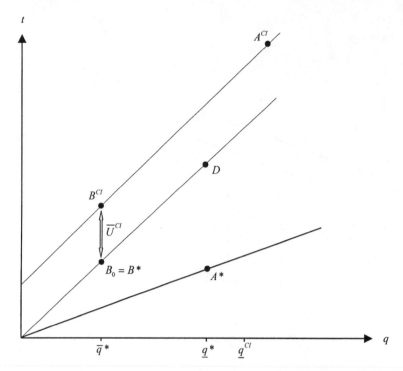

FIGURE 3.8: Type-Dependent Participation Constraint: Case 5

Optimizing with respect to outputs yields no distortion for the inefficient type who produces efficiently, $\bar{q}^{CI} = \bar{q}^*$, and now yields an *upward* distortion characterized in equation (3.35) for the efficient type, $\underline{q}^{CI} > \underline{q}^*$. As U_0 becomes greater than $\Delta\theta\underline{q}^{CI}$, a rent $\bar{\bar{U}}^{CI} = U_0 - \Delta\theta\underline{q}^{CI}$ must now be given up to the inefficient type (see the pair of contracts $(A^{CI}, \bar{B}^{CI})$ in figure 3.8).

Figure 3.9 summarizes the profiles of production levels as functions of the efficient type's outside opportunity utility level U_0. For U_0 higher than $\Delta\theta\underline{q}^*$, we are in the case of *countervailing incentives*. In order to attract the efficient type who has such profitable outside opportunities, it is necessary to offer him a very high transfer. However, then this contract becomes attractive for the inefficient type. The production level of the efficient type is distorted upward to satisfy the inefficient type's incentive constraint. For $U_0 > \Delta\theta\underline{q}^{CI}$, even a positive rent must be given up to the inefficient type to satisfy this constraint at the lowest cost.

Type-dependent utilities with interesting economic implications have appeared successively in Kahn (1985) and Moore (1985) for models of labor contracts with type-dependent reservation wages, in Lewis and Sappington (1989) for an extension of the Baron and Myerson (1982) regulation model with fixed costs, in Laffont and Tirole (1990a) for the regulation of bypass, in Feenstra and Lewis (1991) and Brainard and Martimort (1996) for a model of international trade, in Jeon and Laffont (1999) for a model of downsizing the public sector, and in Saha (2001) for a model of corruption. Jullien (2000) provided a general theory of type-dependent reservation utility with a continuum of types. Biglaiser and Mezzetti (1993, 2000) endogenized the agent's reservation utility by explicitly modelling competition between several principals. On this, see also Champsaur and Rochet (1989) and Stole (1995). ∎

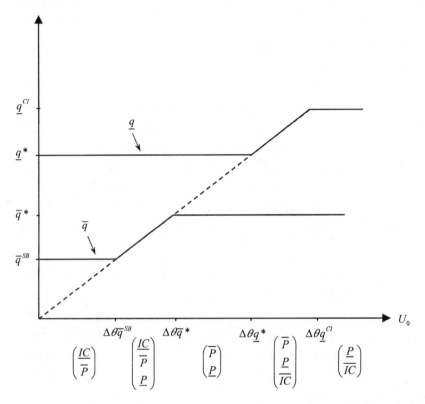

FIGURE 3.9: Type-Dependent Participation Constraint: Output Distortions and Binding Constraints

3.3.2 Examples

State Dependent Fixed Costs

Lewis and Sappington (1989), who coined the expression *countervailing incentives*, reconsidered the Baron-Myerson model with a firm having a fixed cost negatively correlated with its marginal cost. The firm's cost function is $C(\theta, q) = \theta q + F(\theta)$, where θ belongs to $\{\underline{\theta}, \bar{\theta}\}$ with respective probabilities ν and $1 - \nu$. The fixed costs are such that $F(\underline{\theta}) > F(\bar{\theta})$, i.e., high marginal costs are associated with low fixed costs and vice versa.

In this model, incentive constraints are still expressed as (2.21) and (2.22). The participation constraints instead become

$$\underline{U} \geq F(\underline{\theta}) = F(\bar{\theta}) + (F(\underline{\theta}) - F(\bar{\theta})) \tag{3.36}$$

and

$$\bar{U} \geq F(\bar{\theta}). \tag{3.37}$$

It should be clear that, up to a constant term $F(\bar{\theta})$, the model is identical to the one in section 3.3.1. The difference $F(\underline{\theta}) - F(\bar{\theta}) > 0$ plays the role of U_0 and may lead to countervailing incentives if it is large enough.

> **Remark:** With more than two types, or with a continuum, countervailing incentives may create some pooling for intermediate types. When the agent's status quo utility level is decreasing with the type θ, those intermediate agents are indeed torn between their desire to pretend to be less efficient to save on their cost and their desire to pretend to be more efficient to justify higher status quo utility levels and receive higher transfers from the principal. In a related context, the optimal contract has been interpreted by Lewis and Sappington (1991) as an *inflexible rule* coming from the existence of countervailing incentives. ∎

Lewis and Sappington (1989) studied a model with a continuum of types and emphasized the bunching region they obtain in the transition from upward to downward binding incentive constraints. Maggi and Rodriguez-Clare (1995a) showed that bunching is due to the concavity that Lewis and Sappington assume for the $F(\cdot)$ function. If $F(\cdot)$ is convex, countervailing incentives are compatible with fully separating contracts. ∎

Bypass

Laffont and Tirole (1990a) considered consumers of a network technology such as electricity. Consumers are of two possible types, $\underline{\theta}$ and $\bar{\theta}$, having utility function $U = \theta v(q) - t$. They can either consume the good produced by the network technology, which offers a menu of contracts, $\{(\underline{t}, \underline{q}); (\bar{t}, \bar{q})\}$, or they can use an alternative bypass technology which has a fixed cost σ and a marginal cost d. By choosing this latter option, consumers obtain the utility levels $\underline{S} = \max_q \{\underline{\theta} v(q) - \sigma - dq\}$ and $\bar{S} = \max_q \{\bar{\theta} v(q) - \sigma - dq\}$. The consumers' participation constraints become

$$\underline{U} = \underline{\theta} v(\underline{q}) - \underline{t} \geq \underline{S}, \tag{3.38}$$

$$\bar{U} = \bar{\theta} v(\bar{q}) - \bar{t} \geq \bar{S} = \underline{S} + \bar{S} - \underline{S}. \tag{3.39}$$

Up to a change in the definition of the *efficient* and the *inefficient* type, $\bar{S} - \underline{S}$ here plays the role that U_0 plays in section 3.3.1 and can again give rise to countervailing incentives.

When the network industry is very efficient, a regulated or profit-maximizing network attracts all consumers with a discriminating menu of contracts. As its efficiency deteriorates, it must distort the pricing scheme to maintain the high-valuation consumers in the network, and the good deal made to these consumers may attract low-valuation consumers and create countervailing incentives. Finally, as the network efficiency deteriorates further, the profit-maximizing network lets the high valuation consumers leave the network.

Downsizing the Public Sector

An inefficient public sector exhibits sometimes considerable labor redundancy. Hence, downsizing constitutes a natural step for every public sector reform. However, downsizing is subject to adverse selection. To model this issue, Jeon and Laffont (1999) assumed that a worker of the public firm has a private cost θ in $\{\underline{\theta}, \bar{\theta}\}$ when working in that firm. Let $U^p(\theta)$ be the rent obtained by a θ-worker in the public firm and $U^m(\theta)$ be the rent he would obtain in the private sector with the normalization $U^m(\bar{\theta}) = 0$.

A (voluntary) downsizing mechanism for a continuum $[0, 1]$ of workers is a pair of transfers and probabilities[11] of being maintained in the firm, $\{(\underline{t}, \underline{p}); (\bar{t}, \bar{p})\}$, which must satisfy the participation constraints

$$\underline{U} = \underline{t} - \underline{p}\underline{\theta} + (1 - \underline{p})U^m(\underline{\theta}) \geq U^p(\underline{\theta}), \tag{3.40}$$

$$\bar{U} = \bar{t} - \bar{p}\bar{\theta} \geq U^p(\bar{\theta}), \tag{3.41}$$

and the incentive constraints

$$\underline{U} = \underline{t} - \underline{p}\underline{\theta} + (1 - \underline{p})U^m(\underline{\theta}) \geq \bar{t} - \bar{p}\underline{\theta} + (1 - \bar{p})U^m(\underline{\theta}), \tag{3.42}$$

$$\bar{U} = \bar{t} - \bar{p}\bar{\theta} \geq \underline{t} - \underline{p}\bar{\theta}. \tag{3.43}$$

If we define the worker's full cost θ^f as the sum of the production cost and his rent in the private sector, $\theta^f = \theta + U^m(\theta)$, these equations can be rewritten as

$$\underline{t} - \underline{p}\underline{\theta}^f \geq U^p(\underline{\theta}) - U^m(\underline{\theta}), \tag{3.44}$$

$$\bar{t} - \bar{p}\bar{\theta}^f \geq U^p(\bar{\theta}), \tag{3.45}$$

$$\underline{t} - \underline{p}\underline{\theta}^f \geq \bar{t} - \bar{p}\underline{\theta}^f, \tag{3.46}$$

[11]These probabilities can also be interpreted as part-time work in the public firm.

$$\bar{t} - \bar{p}\bar{\theta}^f \geq \underline{t} - \underline{p}\bar{\theta}^f. \tag{3.47}$$

We can reduce the problem to the one treated in section 3.3 if we rewrite the participation constraints in the following manner:

$$\bar{t} - \bar{p}\bar{\theta}^f \geq U^p(\bar{\theta}), \tag{3.48}$$

$$\underline{t} - \underline{p}\underline{\theta}^f \geq U^p(\bar{\theta}) + U^p(\underline{\theta}) - U^p(\bar{\theta}) - U^m(\underline{\theta}). \tag{3.49}$$

Defining $U_0 = U^p(\underline{\theta}) - U^p(\bar{\theta}) - U^m(\underline{\theta})$, we could proceed as in section 3.3.

If $\bar{\theta}^f > \underline{\theta}^f$, i.e., $\Delta\theta > U^m(\underline{\theta})$, the worker with production cost $\underline{\theta}$ remains the low full-cost worker. Furthermore, if $U^p(\underline{\theta}) - U^p(\bar{\theta}) = \Delta\theta$, i.e., the discrimination in the public firm fits the productivity difference, then $U_0 = \Delta\theta^f$ and we have necessarily countervailing incentives. Indeed, the difference of status quo payoffs is larger than the largest information rent which can be given to the efficient type $\bar{p}\Delta\theta^f \leq \Delta\theta^f$. The rent of the high full cost is then $U^p(\underline{\theta}) - U^m(\underline{\theta}) - \underline{p}\Delta\theta^f$ and, to decrease this information rent, $\underline{p}$ is increased. This means that down-sizing decreases under asymmetric information. This situation is illustrated in figure 3.10.

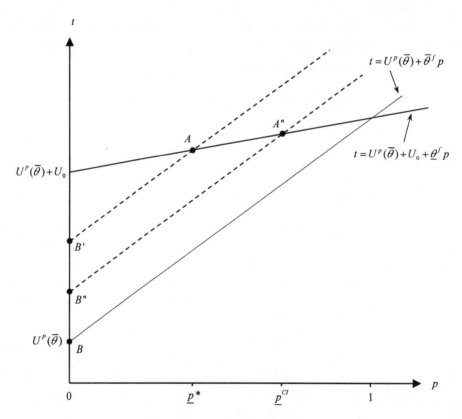

FIGURE 3.10: Downsizing the Public Sector

Consider a case where downsizing is large and the complete information downsizing entails excluding all the inefficient workers (contract B) and a proportion p^* of efficient ones (contract A). Under incomplete information this requires giving up a rent BB' to the inefficient type and creates countervailing incentives. In order to decrease this rent, $\underline{p}$ is increased to $\underline{p}^{CI}$ (contracts (A'', B'')).

If $\bar{\theta}^f < \underline{\theta}^f$, the high full cost is the worker with low production cost. But we have again countervailing incentives and the rent of the high full cost is $\bar{p}\Delta\theta^f + U^p(\bar{\theta})$. Now $\Delta\theta^f < 0$ and $\bar{p}$ is decreased. Downsizing increases again under incomplete information, but now the workers with low production costs are excluded first.

International Trade and Protection

Private industries subject to international competition often obtain some protection from their national government to avoid delocalization. The goal of public intervention is first to provide domestic firms with at least their profits when they delocalize and, second, as in domestic regulation, to correct any market power.

To model such issues, let us consider a variation of the Baron-Myerson model discussed in section 2.15.1. The domestic firm's utility function is $U = t - \theta C(q)$, with $C(q) = \frac{q^2}{2}$. The domestic regulator maximizes $S(q + q_f) - p_w q_f - \theta C(q) - (1 - \alpha)U$, where q_f is foreign production imported at the world price p_w. Decreasing returns are necessary here so that the national consumption is split in a nontrivial way between national and foreign productions. Again, the efficiency parameter θ can take values in $\Theta = \{\underline{\theta}, \bar{\theta}\}$ with respective probabilities ν and $1 - \nu$.

It is clear that the first-best outcome is such that the domestic firm produces at the world price and the residual domestic demand is imported at this price. This leads to $p_w = \underline{\theta}\underline{q}^*$ and $p_w = \bar{\theta}\bar{q}^*$.

Under asymmetric information, and if regulation applies to a national public enterprise that has no outside option, the second best policy becomes $\underline{q}^{SB} = \underline{q}^*$, and $\bar{q}^{SB}$ given by

$$p_w = \left(\bar{\theta} + \frac{\nu}{1 - \nu}(1 - \alpha)\Delta\theta\right)\bar{q}^{SB}. \tag{3.50}$$

Consider now a private enterprise that could take all its assets away from the national country and behave competitively in the world market. Participation constraints for type $\underline{\theta}$ and $\bar{\theta}$ become, respectively,

$$\underline{U} \geq \underline{U}_0 = \max_q p_w q - \underline{\theta}C(q) = \frac{p_w^2}{2\underline{\theta}} \tag{3.51}$$

and

$$\bar{U} \geq \bar{U}_0 = \max_q p_w q - \bar{\theta}C(q) = \frac{p_w^2}{2\bar{\theta}}. \tag{3.52}$$

In this model, we can redefine U_0 as $U_0 = \underline{U}_0 - \overline{U}_0 = \frac{b_w^2 \Delta\theta}{2\overline{\theta}\underline{\theta}}$. The information rents corresponding to the first-best outputs $\underline{q}^*$ and $\bar{q}^*$ are now $\frac{\Delta\theta \underline{q}^{*2}}{2}$ and $\frac{\Delta\theta \bar{q}^{*2}}{2}$. Hence $\frac{\Delta\theta \underline{q}^{*2}}{2} > U_0 > \frac{\Delta\theta \bar{q}^{*2}}{2}$, and we are (up to a change in the cost function) in case 3 above, leading to no countervailing incentives and with the participation constraints of both types now binding.

Insurance Contracts Under Monopoly

In this example, we analyze an insurance problem where the agent's reservation utility is type-dependent. Another important feature of this environment is that we have common values, i.e., the agent's type directly affects the principal's utility. As we will see below, the type-dependent participation constraint makes the implementation of the first-best full insurance policy impossible.

Standard microeconomic analysis shows that, under complete information, all agents subject to some diversifiable risk should receive complete insurance against this risk from a risk neutral insurance company. This conclusion fails under asymmetric information. Let us consider a risk-averse agent with utility function $u(\cdot)$, which is increasing and concave ($u' > 0$, $u'' < 0$ with $u(0) = 0$). The agent's initial wealth is w, but with probability θ the agent suffers from a damage that has value d. The agent is a low risk $\underline{\theta} < 1$ (resp. high risk $\bar{\theta}$, such that $\underline{\theta} < \bar{\theta} < 1$) with probability $1 - \nu$ (resp. ν). The agent knows his probability of accident, which remains unknown to the insurance company. The agent's wealth level is common knowledge. The agent's expected utility writes thus as $U = \theta u(w - d + t_a) + (1 - \theta)u(w - t_n)$, where t_a is the agent's reimbursement in case of a damage and t_n is what he pays to the insurance company when there is no accident. Many of the technical difficulties encountered with this model come from the nonlinearity of the agent's utility function with respect to transfers. Nevertheless, note that the Spence-Mirrlees property (3.18) is satisfied, because $\frac{U_{t_a}}{U_{t_n}} = -\left(\frac{\theta}{1-\theta}\right)\frac{u'(w-d+t_a)}{u'(w-t_n)}$ is a monotonically decreasing function of θ.

To make things simpler, we assume that the risk-neutral insurance company is a monopoly and maximizes the expectation of its profit $V = -\theta t_a + (1 - \theta)t_n$.[12] In this model where the quasi-linearity of the agent's objective function is lost, it is useful for the moment to keep incentive and participation constraints as functions of transfers. This leads to the following expressions:

$$\underline{U} = \underline{\theta}u(w - d + \underline{t}_a) + (1 - \underline{\theta})u(w - \underline{t}_n) \geq \underline{\theta}u(w - d + \bar{t}_a)$$
$$+ (1 - \underline{\theta})u(w - \bar{t}_n), \tag{3.53}$$

---

[12] Because θ enters the principal's utility function, we are in a common value environment.

$$\bar{U} = \bar{\theta}u(w - d + \bar{t}_a) + (1 - \bar{\theta})u(w - \bar{t}_n) \geq \bar{\theta}u(w - d + \underline{t}_a)$$
$$+ (1 - \bar{\theta})u(w - \underline{t}_n), \tag{3.54}$$

$$\underline{U} \geq \underline{U}_0, \tag{3.55}$$

$$\bar{U} \geq \bar{U}_0, \tag{3.56}$$

where $\underline{U}_0$ (resp. $\bar{U}_0$) is the reservation utility of the low- (resp. high-) risk agent. These reservation utilities are given by the expected utility that the agent gets in the absence of any insurance, i.e., $\underline{U}_0 = \underline{\theta}u(w - d) + (1 - \underline{\theta})u(w) \equiv u(\underline{w})$ and $\bar{U}_0 = \bar{\theta}u(w - d) + (1 - \bar{\theta})u(w) \equiv u(\bar{w})$, where $\underline{w}$ denote the certainty income-equivalent for types $\underline{\theta}$ and $\bar{\theta}$, respectively. Note that $\bar{\theta} > \underline{\theta}$ implies that $\bar{U}_0 < \underline{U}_0$ and thus that $\bar{w} < \underline{w}$. The low-risk agent thus has a higher reservation utility than the high-risk agent.

Under complete information, the insurance company would provide full insurance against damage for both types. In that case, we would have $w - d + \underline{t}_a^* = w - \underline{t}_n^* = \underline{w}$, and $w - d + \bar{t}_a^* = w - \bar{t}_n^* = \bar{w}$. Note that the pair of insurance contracts $\{(\underline{t}_a^*, \underline{t}_n^*); (\bar{t}_a^*, \bar{t}_n^*)\}$ is not incentive compatible. Indeed, since $\bar{w} < \underline{w}$, the high-risk agent is willing to take the insurance contract of the low-risk agent. By doing so, the $\bar{\theta}$-agent gets $u(\underline{w})$ instead of $u(\bar{w})$ for sure. This situation is represented in figure 3.11. A* (resp. B*) is the complete information contract of the agent with a low (resp. high) probability of accident. A* and B* both provide full insurance. Indifference curves correspond to higher levels of utility when one moves in the northeast direction in figure 3.11, thus the $\bar{\theta}$-agent prefers contract A* to contract B*.

Under asymmetric information, the principal's program takes now the following form:

(P): $$\max_{\{(\bar{t}_a, \bar{t}_n); (\underline{t}_a, \underline{t}_n)\}} (1 - v)(-\underline{\theta}\underline{t}_a + (1 - \underline{\theta})\underline{t}_n) + v(-\bar{\theta}\bar{t}_a + (1 - \bar{\theta})\bar{t}_n)$$

subject to (3.53) to (3.56).

Because the reservation utilities are type-dependent, we are looking for a solution with countervailing incentives where the high-risk type is attracted by the low-risk one. We first assume that (3.53) and (3.56) are the two nonbinding constraints of the program above. We will check *ex post* that this conjecture is in fact true. Because of the nonlinearity of the model, this will be a slightly harder task than usual.

It is now useful to rewrite the program using the following change of variables: $u(w - d + t_a) = u_a$ and $u(w - t_n) = u_n$. These new variables are the agent's utility levels whenever an accident occurs or not. Denoting the inverse function of $u(\cdot)$

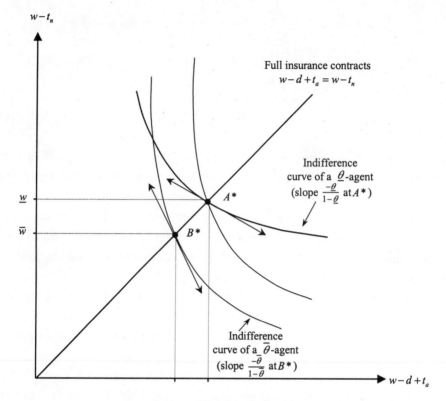

FIGURE 3.11: Full Insurance Contracts

by $h = u^{-1}$ and observing that it is an increasing and strictly convex function ($h' > 0$, $h'' > 0$ with $h(0) = 0$), one can check that the principal's objective function is strictly concave, with a set of linear constraints, and the principal's problem can be rewritten as

(P):
$$\max_{\{(\bar{u}_a, \bar{u}_n); (\underline{u}_a, \underline{u}_n)\}} (1 - \nu)(-\underline{\theta}d + w - \underline{\theta}h(\underline{u}_a) - (1 - \underline{\theta})h(\underline{u}_n))$$
$$+ \nu(-\bar{\theta}d + w - \bar{\theta}h(\bar{u}_a) - (1 - \bar{\theta})h(\bar{u}_n)),$$

subject to

$$\bar{\theta}\bar{u}_a + (1 - \bar{\theta})\bar{u}_n \geq \bar{\theta}\underline{u}_a + (1 - \bar{\theta})\underline{u}_n, \tag{3.57}$$

$$\underline{\theta}\underline{u}_a + (1 - \underline{\theta})\underline{u}_n \geq u(\underline{w}). \tag{3.58}$$

Let us denote the respective multipliers of (3.57) and (3.58) with λ and μ. Optimizing the Lagrangian of the principal's problem with respect to $\underline{u}_a$ and $\underline{u}_n$ yields, respectively,

$$-\underline{\theta}(1 - \nu)h'(\underline{u}_a) - \bar{\theta}\lambda + \mu\underline{\theta} = 0, \tag{3.59}$$

$$-(1 - \underline{\theta})(1 - \nu)h'(\underline{u}_n) - (1 - \bar{\theta})\lambda + \mu(1 - \underline{\theta}) = 0. \tag{3.60}$$

Optimizing with respect to $\bar{u}_a$ and $\bar{u}_n$ also yields

$$-\bar{\theta}\nu h'(\bar{u}_a) + \bar{\theta}\lambda = 0, \tag{3.61}$$

$$-(1 - \bar{\theta})\nu h'(\bar{u}_n) + (1 - \bar{\theta})\lambda = 0. \tag{3.62}$$

Using (3.61) and (3.62), it is immediately apparent that the high-risk agent receives full insurance at the optimum:

$$\bar{u}_a = \bar{u}_n = \bar{u}. \tag{3.63}$$

From (3.61), we get $\lambda = \nu h'(\bar{u}) > 0$, and therefore (3.57) is binding. More-over, summing (3.59) to (3.62), we get $\mu = \nu h'(\bar{u}) + (1 - \nu)(\underline{\theta}h'(\underline{u}_a) + (1 - \underline{\theta})h'(\underline{u}_n)) > 0$, and thus (3.58) is also binding. Knowing that (3.57) and (3.58) are both binding, we also obtain:

$$\bar{u} = -\Delta\theta\Delta u + u(\underline{w}), \tag{3.64}$$

where $\underline{u}_n - \underline{u}_a = \Delta u$ is the difference of utilities of a low-risk agent between not having and having an accident. The fact that (3.58) is binding also implies that one can write $\underline{u}_a = u(\underline{w}) - (1 - \underline{\theta})\Delta u$ and $\underline{u}_n = u(\underline{w}) + \underline{\theta}\Delta u$. Inserting the expressions of $\underline{u}_a$, $\bar{u}_a$, $\underline{u}_n$, and $\bar{u}_n$ into the principal's objective function and optimizing with respect to Δu,[13] we obtain that the second-best value Δu^{SB} is defined implicitly as a solution to

$$\frac{\nu\Delta\theta}{(1-\nu)\underline{\theta}(1-\underline{\theta})}h'(-\Delta\theta\Delta u^{SB} + u(\underline{w}))$$
$$= h'(u(\underline{w}) + \underline{\theta}\Delta u^{SB}) - h'(u(\underline{w}) - (1 - \underline{\theta})\Delta u^{SB}). \tag{3.65}$$

The left-hand side of (3.65) is positive, and thus we have $h'(u(\underline{w}) + \underline{\theta}\Delta u^{SB}) > h'(u(\underline{w}) - (1 - \underline{\theta})\Delta u^{SB})$. Because $h'(\cdot)$ is increasing, we finally get

$$\underline{u}_n^{SB} - \underline{u}_a^{SB} = \Delta u^{SB} > 0. \tag{3.66}$$

To reduce the incentives of the high-risk agent to pretend that he is a low-risk one, the insurance company let this latter agent bear some risk. Imperfect insurance arises as a second-best optimum.

> **Remark:** When $\Delta\theta$ is small enough, a simple Taylor expansion shows that the right-hand side of (3.65) is close to $h''(u(\underline{w}))\Delta u^{SB}$, and we get the following approximation:
>
> $$\Delta u^{SB} = \frac{\nu}{1 - \nu}\Delta\theta\frac{h'(u(\underline{w}))}{h''(u(\underline{w}))} > 0. \tag{3.67}$$

[13] It is easy to prove that the principal's objective function is strictly concave with respect to Δu.

The neglected participation constraint of the high risk agent amounts to $\overline{U}^{SB} = \bar{u}^{SB} = -\Delta\theta\Delta u^{SB} + u(\underline{w}) > u(\bar{w})$, which is now automatically satisfied because, when $\Delta\theta$ is small enough, $u(\underline{w}) - u(\bar{w})$ is positive and of order $\Delta\theta$, while $\Delta\theta\Delta u^{SB}$ is of order $(\Delta\theta)^2$. ∎

More generally, the high risk agent's participation constraint is not binding as long as $\Delta\theta\Delta u^{SB} < u(\underline{w}) - u(\bar{w}) = \Delta\theta(u(w) - u(w - d))$, or $\Delta u^{SB} < u(w) - u(w - d)$, where Δu^{SB} is defined implicitly by (3.65). Using the strict concavity of the principal's objective function with respect to Δu, this latter condition rewrites as

$$\frac{\nu\Delta\theta}{(1 - \nu)\underline{\theta}(1 - \underline{\theta})}h'(\bar{\theta}u(w - d) + (1 - \bar{\theta})u(w))$$
$$< h'(u(w)) - h'(u(w - d)), \tag{3.68}$$

and holds, for instance, when d is large enough.

When this latter condition does not hold, the high risk agent's participation constraint is also binding. We are then in a case where the participation constraints of both types are binding. This is the equivalent of case 3 in section 3.3.1, with the specific features imposed by the nonlinearity of the agent's utility function. As long as both participation constraints (3.55) and (3.56) are the only binding ones, we have $\Delta u^{SB} = u(w) - u(w - d)$.

Figure 3.12 illustrates the optimal second-best solution in the (u_a, u_n) plane when only the low risk agent's participation constraint is binding.

The contracts A^* and B^* are respectively offered to a $\underline{\theta}$- and a $\bar{\theta}$-agent under complete information. Instead, A^{SB} and B^{SB} are now offered to those agents under asymmetric information. The $\bar{\theta}$-agent is indifferent between A^{SB} and B^{SB} and thus weakly prefers the full insurance contract B^{SB}. The $\underline{\theta}$-agent strictly prefers A^{SB} to B^{SB} but gets no information rent.

📖 Stiglitz (1997) treated the case of a monopoly providing insurance to risk-averse agents differentiated with respect to their probability of an accident in the same manner as in the model above. Generally, the analysis of the insurance market starts by supposing that this market is competitive. Screening takes place in a competitive environment that is more complex than the monopolistic screening enviornment we analyzed here (Rothschild and Stiglitz 1976). An important feature of the analysis is that a pure strategy contract equilibrium may fail to exist in such a context. Two different routes were taken by researchers vis-à-vis this problem. Some argued that one should change the equilibrium concept to ensure the existence of pure strat-

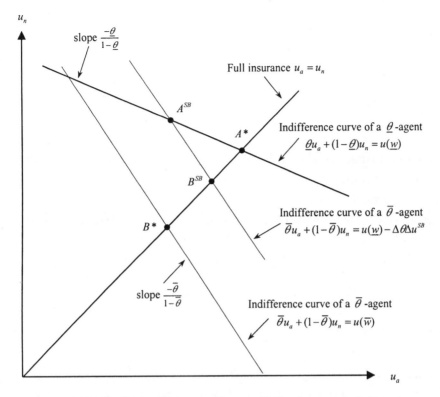

FIGURE 3.12: The Optimal Insurance Contract Under Asymmetric Information

egy equilibria (Wilson 1977, Riley 1979, and Hellwig 1987). Others preferred to prove the existence of mixed-strategy equilibria and derived their properties (Dasgupta and Maskin 1986, and Rosenthal and Weiss 1984). ∎

3.4 Random Participation Constraint

The previous section has shown how a deterministic but type-dependent participation constraint could perturb the standard results on the optimal rent extraction-efficiency trade-off. We now perturb the agent's participation constraint in another direction, by allowing some randomness in the decision to participate. Instead of the agent's reservation utility being perfectly known, let us consider a risk-neutral agent with a *random* participation constraint,

$$\underline{U} \geq \tilde{\varepsilon} \tag{3.69}$$

and

$$\overline{U} \geq \tilde{\varepsilon}. \tag{3.70}$$

We assume that $\tilde{\varepsilon}$ is drawn from the interval $[-\bar{\varepsilon}, \bar{\varepsilon}]$, centered at zero with a cumulative distribution function $G(\varepsilon)$. We denote by $g(\varepsilon) = G'(\varepsilon)$ the density of this random variable.

The motivation for such a stochastic specification of the reservation utility levels is that the agent might have some random opportunity cost of accepting the contract proposed by the principal and that this cost is already revealed to the agent at the time of contracting, even if the principal has no ability to screen this information.[14] Alternatively, the agent may be facing a whole set of possible trading opportunities outside of his relationship with a given principal. Those trading opportunities yield a random profit $\tilde{\varepsilon}$ to the agent. Implicit here is the idea that the principal competes with other principals who have unknown characteristics. However, this competition is still modeled as an exogenous black box.

In this model, the incentive constraints for both types remain, as usual,

$$\underline{U} \geq \overline{U} + \Delta\theta\bar{q}, \tag{3.71}$$

and

$$\overline{U} \geq \underline{U} - \Delta\theta\underline{q}. \tag{3.72}$$

A deterministic incentive-feasible contract $\{(\underline{U}, \underline{q}); (\overline{U}, \bar{q})\}$ is accepted by both types if and only if (3.69) and (3.70) both hold. Acceptance is now a random event. A priori, both types only accept the contract with some probability, which is $G(\underline{U})$ for the $\underline{\theta}$-type and $G(\overline{U})$ for the $\bar{\theta}$-type. To simplify the analysis, we will assume that $\tilde{\varepsilon}$ is small with respect to $\Delta\theta\bar{q}$. This assumption will imply that $G(\underline{U}) = 1$, and only the inefficient agent might not participate with some strictly positive probability $1 - G(\overline{U})$. The optimal contract must solve the program below:

$$(P): \quad \max_{\{(\overline{U}, \bar{q}); (\underline{U}, \underline{q})\}} \nu(S(\underline{q}) - \underline{\theta}\underline{q} - \underline{U}) + (1 - \nu)G(\overline{U})(S(\bar{q}) - \bar{\theta}\bar{q} - \overline{U}),$$

subject to (3.71) and (3.72).

On top of the usual concavity of $S(\cdot)$, assuming that $\frac{\nu + (1-\nu)G(\varepsilon)}{g(\varepsilon)}$ is increasing with ε ensures the quasi-concavity of this program. Its solution is then described in the next proposition. It is indexed by a superscript R that means *random participation*.

Proposition 3.3: *Assume random participation constraints, but also that $\tilde{\varepsilon}$ is small enough. Then the optimal contract entails:*

- *The incentive constraint of the efficient agent (3.71) is binding.*

---

[14]It is assumed implicitly that the principal does not attempt to elicit the value taken by the random variable $\tilde{\varepsilon}$ with a stochastic mechanism.

- *The rent $\overline{U}^R$ and the output $\bar{q}^R$ of an inefficient agent are determined together as the solutions to*

$$S'(\bar{q}^R) = \bar{\theta} + \frac{\nu \Delta \theta}{(1-\nu)G(\overline{U}^R)} \qquad (3.73)$$

and

$$S(\bar{q}^R) - \bar{\theta}\bar{q}^R = \overline{U}^R + \frac{\nu + (1-\nu)G(\overline{U}^R)}{(1-\nu)g(\overline{U}^R)}. \qquad (3.74)$$

Two important remarks should be made at this point. First, since an inefficient agent trades with the principal with a probability of less than one (i.e., $G(\overline{U}^R) < 1$), the principal finds it relatively more likely that he will face an efficient agent on the condition that trade is being carried on. Hence, the principal is more willing to distort the inefficient agent's output downward to reduce the relatively high expected cost of the efficient agent's information rent. Indeed, $\bar{q}^R$ defined by (3.73) is more distorted than the usual second-best distortion $\bar{q}^{SB}$ obtained with an exogenously given zero participation constraint.

Second, the principal chooses a level of the inefficient agent's rent $\overline{U}^R$ that trades off the marginal gain of inducing slightly more participation by this type against the marginal cost of this extra participation. The marginal gain of increasing the rent by $d\overline{U}^R$ is precisely the net total surplus $S(\bar{q}^R) - \bar{\theta}\bar{q}^R - \overline{U}^R$ times the increase in probability that the inefficient agent chooses to participate, namely $(1-\nu)g(\overline{U}^R)d\overline{U}^R$. The marginal cost takes into account the fact that this extra rent $d\overline{U}^R$ has to be given to all participating agents, i.e., both the efficient one who trades with probability of one and also the inefficient one who contracts with a probability of only $G(\overline{U}^R)$ less than one. The cost is thus $(\nu + (1-\nu)G(\overline{U}^R))d\overline{U}^R$. The marginal benefit is equal to the marginal cost when (3.74) holds.

It is interesting to note that the output $\bar{q}^R$ converges towards $\bar{q}^{SB}$ defined in (2.28) as $\bar{\varepsilon}$ goes to zero. In this case the random participation constraint almost becomes the usual deterministic participation constraint with zero reservation value.

Finally, the *generalized* monotone hazard rate property, namely $\frac{\nu + (1-\nu)G(\varepsilon)}{(1-\nu)g(\varepsilon)}$ increasing in ε, guarantees that $\overline{U}^R$ is strictly positive when $S(\bar{q}^R) - \bar{\theta}\bar{q}^R > 0$.[15] To induce a relatively more likely participation, the principal must a priori give to the inefficient agent a *strictly* positive rent. Lastly, the probability that the inefficient type participates is strictly lower than one when $S(\bar{q}^{SB}) - \bar{\theta}\bar{q}^{SB} > \bar{\varepsilon} + \frac{1}{(1-\nu)g(\bar{\varepsilon})}$, where $\bar{q}^{SB}$ is the second-best optimal output with a deterministic participation constraint.

---

[15]This latter condition always holds when $S(\cdot)$ satisfies the Inada condition $S'(0) = +\infty$.

Rochet and Stole (2000) provided a complete analysis of a model with random participation constraints and a continuum of types. In such a setting, they also looked at the interesting case of competition among principals. ∎

3.5 Limited Liability

Sometimes the set of incentive-feasible contracts is constrained by some exogenous limits on the feasible transfers between the principal and the agent. These exogenous financial constraints could reveal the existence of previous financial contracts that the agent might have already signed. Those constraints will of course affect the usual rent-efficiency trade-off.

A first possible limit is that the net transfer of the agent, taking into account his own asset holding l, should not be lower than zero. This leads to the following *limited liability constraints on transfers*:

$$\underline{t} \geq -l \tag{3.75}$$

and

$$\bar{t} \geq -l. \tag{3.76}$$

A possible motivation for this type of constraint is that the agent can use the transfer received from the principal to cover a debt of level $-l$. The production cost θq being already sunk, it does not enter into the left-hand sides of (3.75) and (3.76).

A second limit on transfers arises when the agent's information rent itself must be greater than an exogenous value $-l$. This leads to the following *limited liability constraints on rents*:

$$\underline{U} \geq -l, \tag{3.77}$$

$$\bar{U} \geq -l. \tag{3.78}$$

The production cost θq is now incurred when the transfer t takes place. Again, the interpretation is that contracting with the principal may involve negative rents $\underline{U}$ or $\bar{U}$ as long as those losses can be covered by the agent's own liabilities l. To assess the impact of these limited liability constraints, let us go back to the framework of section 2.11. When contracting takes place *ex ante*, we have seen that the first-best outcome can still be obtained provided that the inefficient risk-neutral agent receives a negative payoff, $\bar{U}^* < 0$. Obviously this negative payoff may conflict with the constraint (3.78).

With *ex ante* contracting, we have already seen that the relevant incentive and participation constraints are, respectively,[16]

$$\underline{U} \geq \overline{U} + \Delta\theta\bar{q} \tag{3.79}$$

and

$$\nu\underline{U} + (1 - \nu)\overline{U} \geq 0. \tag{3.80}$$

Adding the limited liability constraints, the principal's program is written as

(P): $$\max_{\{(\overline{U}, \bar{q}); (\underline{U}, \underline{q})\}} \nu(S(\underline{q}) - \underline{\theta}\underline{q} - \underline{U}) + (1 - \nu)(S(\bar{q}) - \bar{\theta}\bar{q} - \overline{U}),$$

subject to (3.79), (3.80), and either {(3.75), (3.76)} or {(3.77), (3.78)},

where limited liability constraints are either on transfers or on rents.[17]

The next two propositions summarize the features of the optimal contract with a limited liability constraint on rents and transfers, respectively.[18] We index with a superscript L, meaning *limited liability*, the second-best optimal contracts in these environments. We first focus on limited liability constraints on rents.

Proposition 3.4: *Assume* ex ante *contracting and limited liability on rents. Then, the optimal contract entails*

- *For $l > \nu\Delta\theta\bar{q}^*$, only (3.79) and (3.80) are binding and the first-best outcome of section 2.11.1 remains optimal.*
- *For $\nu\Delta\theta\bar{q}^{SB} \leq l \leq \nu\Delta\theta\bar{q}^*$, (3.79), (3.80), and (3.78) are all binding. The efficient agent produces efficiently $q^L = q^*$, and the inefficient agent's production is distorted downward from the first-best $\bar{q}^L \leq \bar{q}^*$, with $\bar{q}^L \geq \bar{q}^{SB}$ and*

$$l = \nu\Delta\theta\bar{q}^L. \tag{3.81}$$

- *For $l < \nu\Delta\theta\bar{q}^{SB}$, only (3.79) and (3.78) are binding. The efficient agent produces efficiently $q^L = q^*$, and the inefficient agent's production is equal to the second-best output with the ex post participation constraints, $\bar{q}^L = \bar{q}^{SB}$, defined in (2.28).*

A limited liability constraint on *ex post* rents may reduce the efficiency of *ex ante* contracting. If the limited liability constraint on the inefficient type is stringent enough, the principal must reduce the inefficient agent's output to keep

---

[16]We leave it to the reader to check that the inefficient agent's incentive constraint is slack at the optimum.

[17]Here we have analyzed the case where the two sets of constraints are mutually exclusive.

[18]The proofs of these propositions are in appendix 3.4.

the limited liability constraint satisfied. The agent is then subject to less risk on the allocation of *ex post* rents. When the limited liability constraint is even harder, the principal must give up his desire to hold the *ex ante* participation constraint binding. The limited liability constraint then implies an *ex ante* information rent. Indeed, when l is small enough, the agent's expected utility becomes $U = -l + \nu \Delta \theta \bar{q}^{SB}$, which is then strictly positive.

> **Remark:** Note the similarity of the solution obtained in Proposition 3.4 with that obtained when the agent is risk averse in section 2.11.2 (proposition 2.5). The limited liability constraint on rents plays a similar role as the agent's risk aversion. Indeed, in both cases, the principal finds it costly to create a wedge between $\underline{U}$ and $\bar{U}$, and reducing this cost calls for incentives that are lower powered than one would find with risk neutrality and unlimited transfers. More precisely, with a limited liability constraint on rents, everything happens as if the agent has an infinite risk aversion below a wealth of $-l$.[19] ∎

Let us now turn to the case of limited liability constraints on transfers. Restricting the analysis to a few particular cases, we have the following characterization of the optimal contract.

Proposition 3.5: *Assume* ex ante *contracting and limited liability on transfers. Then the optimal contract entails:*

- *For $l \geq -(\nu \underline{\theta} + (1-\nu)\bar{\theta})q^*$, only (3.80) is binding and the first-best outcome of section 2.11.1 remains optimal.*
- *For $-(\nu \underline{\theta} + (1-\nu)\bar{\theta})q^* \leq l \leq -(\nu \underline{\theta} + (1-\nu)\bar{\theta})\bar{q}^*$, (3.79), (3.80), and (3.76) are all binding. The efficient agent produces efficiently $\underline{q}^L = q^*$, and the inefficient agent's production is distorted upwards from the first-best, with $\underline{q}^* > \bar{q}^L > \bar{q}^*$, and*

$$l = -(\nu \underline{\theta} + (1-\nu)\bar{\theta})\bar{q}^L. \tag{3.82}$$

- *For $l < -(\nu \underline{\theta} + (1-\nu)\bar{\theta})q^*$, there is bunching such that both types produce the same output q^L and (3.75), (3.76), (3.79), and (3.80) are all binding. The constant output target q^L is given by*

$$l = -(\nu \underline{\theta} + (1-\nu)\bar{\theta})q^L. \tag{3.83}$$

---

[19]The same kind of analysis comparing the effects of limited liability and risk aversion will be applied in chapter 4 to the case of moral hazard.

The limited liability constraints on transfers give rise to allocative distortions that are rather different from those highlighted in proposition 3.4. As the limited liability constraint (3.76) is more stringent, it becomes quite difficult to create the wedge between $\underline{U}$ and $\overline{U}$ that is necessary to ensure incentive compatibility. However, to relax the limited liability constraint (3.76), the principal now *increases* the inefficient type's output. Indeed, using the information rent to rewrite (3.76), we obtain

$$\overline{U} \geq -l - \bar{\theta}\bar{q}. \tag{3.84}$$

Therefore, distorting the inefficient type's output *upward* relaxes this limited liability constraint. A limited liability constraint on transfers implies higher-powered incentives for the agent. It is almost the same as what we would obtain by assuming that the agent is a *risk lover*. The limited liability constraint on transfers somewhat *convexifies* the agent's utility function.

Of course, the principal cannot indefinitively raise the inefficient agent's output without conflicting with the implementability condition. Hence, some bunching emerges. In this case, the agent receives a fixed payment that covers their cost in expectation. This transfer also satisfies the limited liability constraints (3.75) and (3.76), which both take the same form.

It is interesting to note that the limited liability constraints on transfers can only be binding when l is negative. This arises, for instance, when the transfer received by the agent from the principal must be used to reimburse a loan contract worth l.

Sappington (1983) derived the optimal contract under adverse selection and limited liability constraints. Lewis and Sappington (2000) also provided a model involving moral hazard elements. Che and Gale (2000) and Lewis and Sappington (2001) analyzed models where the agent is privately informed both of his ability and of his wealth. These latter papers showed that the wealth level and the agent's ability are complements in determining the probability that trade occurs with the agent. ∎

3.6 Audit Mechanisms and Costly State Verification

Sometimes the principal would like to relax the efficient type's incentive constraint by making it somewhat costly for him to lie and claim that he is inefficient. One important way to do so is by using an *audit technology* that can detect the agent's nontruthful report and allows for some punishment when a false report is detected. This audit technology allows the principal, at a cost, to verify the state of nature announced by the agent. Of course, the mere fact that this technology is costly may prevent its systematic use by the principal.

Let us assume that the principal owns an audit technology and that the agent's true type can be observed with probability p if the principal incurs a cost $c(p)$, with $c(0) = 0$, $c' > 0$, and $c'' > 0$. To ensure interior solutions, we assume that the following Inada conditions $c'(0) = 0$ and $c'(1) = +\infty$ both hold.

3.6.1 Incentive-Feasible Audit Mechanisms

The possibility of an audit significantly enlarges the set of incentive-feasible mechanisms. An incentive mechanism includes not only the transfer $t(\tilde{\theta})$ and the output target $q(\tilde{\theta})$ but also a probability of audit $p(\tilde{\theta})$ and a punishment $P(\theta, \tilde{\theta})$ if the agent's announcement $\tilde{\theta}$ differs from its observed true type θ. We denote thereafter by $\{(\underline{U}, \underline{q}, \underline{p}, \underline{P}); (\overline{U}, \bar{q}, \bar{p}, \overline{P})\}$ this audit mechanism with the obvious notations $\underline{P} = P(\underline{\theta}, \bar{\theta})$ and $\overline{P} = P(\bar{\theta}, \underline{\theta})$. In equilibrium, the Revelation Principle applies and reports are truthful. Therefore, those punishments are never used. They will nevertheless significantly affect the incentive constraints.

> **Remark:** We stress that the principal has the ability to commit to this mechanism. We will comment on the importance of this assumption later on. Furthermore, we do not allow rewards when audit reveals that the agent has revealed truthfully. ∎

The Revelation Principle still applies in this context, and there is no loss of generality in focusing on truthful direct mechanisms satisfying the following incentive constraints:

$$\underline{U} = \underline{t} - \underline{\theta}\underline{q} \geq \bar{t} - \underline{\theta}\bar{q} - \bar{p}\underline{P}, \tag{3.85}$$

$$\overline{U} = \bar{t} - \bar{\theta}\bar{q} \geq \underline{t} - \bar{\theta}\underline{q} - \underline{p}\overline{P}. \tag{3.86}$$

Note that the positive punishments $\underline{P}$ and $\overline{P}$ relax those incentive constraints if the audit is performed with a strictly positive probability.

Let us now turn to a description of those punishments. Punishments used in the literature can be classified into two subsets:

- **Exogenous Punishments:** $\underline{P}$ (resp. $\overline{P}$) cannot be greater than some exogenous threshold l, so that

$$\underline{P} \leq l, \tag{3.87}$$

$$\overline{P} \leq l. \tag{3.88}$$

These exogenous punishments can be viewed as the maximal amount of the agents' assets that can be seized in the case of a detected lie.

- **Endogenous Punishments:** $\underline{P}$ (resp. $\overline{P}$) cannot be greater than the lying agent's benefit from his false announcement:

$$\underline{P} \leq \bar{t} - \underline{\theta}\bar{q}, \tag{3.89}$$

$$\overline{P} \leq \underline{t} - \bar{\theta}\underline{q}. \tag{3.90}$$

In this case, the agent may have no asset to be seized by the principal. Only his profit from the relationship can now be taken back.

Of course, these two sets of constraints on punishments are mutually exclusive.

On top of the constraints (3.85) through (3.90), the usual participation constraints,

$$\underline{U} \geq 0, \tag{3.91}$$

$$\overline{U} \geq 0, \tag{3.92}$$

still must be satisfied by any incentive-feasible audit mechanism.

3.6.2 Optimal Audit Mechanism

The principal's problem is now written as

$$(P): \quad \max_{\{(\overline{U}, \bar{q}, \bar{p}, \overline{P}); \ (\underline{U}, \underline{q}, \underline{p}, \underline{P})\}} \nu(S(\underline{q}) - \underline{\theta}\underline{q} - \underline{U} - c(\underline{p})) + (1-\nu)(S(\bar{q}) - \bar{\theta}\bar{q} - \overline{U} - c(\bar{p})),$$

subject to (3.85), (3.86), (3.91), (3.92), and either $\{(3.87), (3.88)\}$ or $\{(3.89), (3.90)\}$.

A preliminary remark should be made. Although punishments help to relax incentive constraints, they do not enter directly into the principal's objective function since the Revelation Principle tells us that the agent's reports are truthful and lies never occur.

As usual, we conjecture that only the upward incentive constraint (3.85) and the least efficient type's participation constraint (3.92) are relevant.[20]

Let us now turn to the value of the punishments. Both with endogenous and exogenous punishments, the constraint (3.87) and the constraint (3.89) should be binding, respectively. Indeed, by raising the punishment as much as possible in case of a detected lie by the efficient type, the principal can reduce the right-hand

---

[20]As an exercise, we leave it to the reader to find the conditions under which this statement is true.

side of the efficient agent's incentive constraint as much as possible, making it easier to satisfy. This is the so-called *Maximal Punishment Principle*.

Another important remark should be made at this point: there is no need to audit an agent claiming that he is efficient, because the inefficient type's incentive constraint (3.86) is slack anyway and auditing is costly. Hence, we necessarily have $\underline{p} = 0$ at the optimum. Similarly, the value of $\overline{P}$ is irrelevant when (3.86) holds strictly.

Once (3.85) and (3.92) are both binding, we can also rewrite (3.89) as

$$\underline{U} = \Delta\theta\bar{q} - \bar{p}\underline{P} \geq 0 \quad \text{or} \quad \underline{P} \leq \Delta\theta\bar{q}. \tag{3.93}$$

We are thus led to optimize a reduced-form problem, which is written as

(P'): $\quad \max_{\{(\bar{q}, \underline{q}, \bar{p}, \underline{P})\}} \nu(S(\underline{q}) - \underline{\theta}\underline{q} - \Delta\theta\bar{q} + \bar{p}\underline{P}) + (1 - \nu)(S(\bar{q}) - \bar{\theta}\bar{q} - c(\bar{p}))$

subject to either (3.87) or (3.93).

Proposition 3.6 summarizes the solution. The superscript A means *audit*.

Proposition 3.6: *With audit, the optimal contract entails:*

- *Maximal punishments and either (3.87) (with exogenous punishments) or (3.93) (with endogenous punishments) is binding.*
- *No output distortion with respect to the first-best outcome for the efficient type, $\underline{q}^A = \underline{q}^*$, and a downward distortion for the less efficient type,*

$$S'(\bar{q}^A) = \bar{\theta} + \frac{\nu}{1 - \nu}\Delta\theta, \tag{3.94}$$

with exogenous punishment, and

$$S'(\bar{q}^A) = \bar{\theta} + \frac{\nu}{1 - \nu}(1 - \bar{p}^A)\Delta\theta, \tag{3.95}$$

with endogenous punishment.

- *Only the inefficient type is audited with a strictly positive probability $\bar{p}^A$, such that*

$$c'(\bar{p}^A) = \frac{\nu}{1 - \nu}l, \tag{3.96}$$

with exogenous punishment;

$$c'(\bar{p}^A) = \frac{\nu}{1 - \nu}\Delta\theta\bar{q}^A, \tag{3.97}$$

with endogenous punishment.

A comparison of the results obtained with endogenous and with exogenous punishments shows that, in both cases, a strictly positive probability of auditing the least efficient type is obtained. This probability trades off the physical cost of an audit against its benefit in diminishing the efficient type's information rent. In the case of an exogenous punishment, increasing the probability of audit of the inefficient agent by a small amount $d\bar{p}$ allows the principal to reduce the transfer $\underline{t}$ of the efficient type by an amount $Pd\bar{p}$, where P is the exogenous maximal punishment. There is no distortion of production, which is still equal to the second-best optimal output without audit. We have $\bar{q}^A = \bar{q}^{SB}$, where $\bar{q}^{SB}$ is defined in (2.28). Audit is only useful in reducing the incentive transfer, but it has no impact on allocative efficiency.

With an endogenous punishment, the small increase $d\bar{p}$ in the probability of auditing allows the principal to reduce the transfer $\underline{t}$ to the efficient type by an amount $\Delta\theta\bar{q}d\bar{p}$. Output distortions become less valuable as a means of reducing the efficient type's information rent, and the audit becomes a substitute for high-powered incentives shifting output upwards towards the first-best. We have now $\bar{q}^A > \bar{q}^{SB}$. Audit now has an allocative impact.

Finally, note that the solution exhibited in proposition 3.6 in the case of an exogenous punishment is really the solution as long as the efficient type's participation constraint (3.91) is slack, i.e., when $l\bar{p}^A < \Delta\theta\bar{q}^A$. Otherwise, the constraint $\Delta\theta\bar{q} - l\bar{p} \geq 0$ must be taken into account in the principal's organization. The production distortion is then smaller, and the probability of audit $\bar{p}$ lower.

> **Remark:** Let us briefly comment on the commitment assumption. The key lesson of these audit models is that the principal must commit to auditing an inefficient firm with some probability in order to relax the efficient type's incentive constraint. Of course, such commitment is *ex post* inefficient. Indeed, once the principal knows that only the inefficient firm claims, in equilibrium, that it is inefficient, he has no longer any incentive to incur the audit cost. However, if he does not audit, the efficient agent anticipates this. This efficient agent will not tell the truth anymore. Quite naturally, the lack of commitment to an audit strategy generates a mixed strategy equilibrium, where the efficient agent mixes between telling the truth or not and the principal mixes between auditing or not auditing an inefficient report. ∎

The Maximal Punishment Principle is a term coined by Baron and Besanko (1984a). Border and Sobel (1987) provide a careful analysis of the set of binding incentive constraints with a finite number of types. The fundamental difficulty is that those models lose the Spence-Mirrlees property, and so the incentive problem with more than two types is badly behaved and quickly becomes intractable as the number of types grows. Mookherjee and P'ng (1989) analyzed an audit problem in an insurance setting. The specificity of their model comes from the fact that the agent is no longer risk neutral. A random audit significantly helps in relaxing the incentive constraint. Risk aversion gives another reason for using a stochastic audit mechanism, namely, increasing the risk exposure of an efficient agent if he lies and mimics an inefficient one. Khalil (1997) offered a nice treatment of the case without commitment. On this issue, see also Gale and Hellwig (1989). Reinganum and Wilde (1985) and Scotchmer (1987) provide two noticeable contributions to analyzing audit in the framework of the optimal taxation literature.   ∎

3.6.3 Financial Contracting

Audit models have been mainly developed in the financial contracting and optimal taxation literature.[21] These models are different from the model we just discussed because of their focus on a continuum of types (profit levels) for the agent (for convenience, think of the agent as a borrower), and because the only screening instrument for the principal (a lender) is the probability of audit. In our model of section 3.6.2, the screening instruments are less crude since the principal can use the agent's production even in the absence of an audit. Let us sketch this type of a financial contracting model. If the profit θ can take two possible values in $\{\underline{\theta}, \bar{\theta}\}$ with respective probabilities $1 - \nu$ and ν, the incentive contract is written as $\{(\underline{t}, \underline{p}, \underline{P}); (\bar{t}, \bar{p}, \bar{P})\}$. Note that, again, there is no point in auditing the high-profit agent, and $\bar{p} = 0$ at the optimum. The high-profit agent's incentive constraint thus becomes

$$\bar{\theta} - \bar{t} \geq \bar{\theta} - \underline{t} - \underline{p}\underline{P}, \tag{3.98}$$

and the low-profit agent's participation constraint is written as

$$\underline{\theta} - \underline{t} \geq 0. \tag{3.99}$$

In general, the financial contracting literature assumes endogenous punishments, so that

$$\bar{P} \leq \bar{\theta} - \underline{t}. \tag{3.100}$$

The justification of this assumption comes from the interpretation of the audit model, which is generally made by the financial contracting literature. The audit is

---

[21] See Townsend (1978), Gale and Hellwig (1985), and Williamson (1987).

often viewed as a costly bankruptcy procedure following a strategic announcement of default by the manager of the indebted firm. In this case, the debtholders reap all possible profits from the firm following a default. The lender's problem is written as follows:

(P):
$$\max_{\{\bar{t}, \underline{t}, p\}} v\bar{t} + (1 - v)(\underline{t} - c(\underline{p})),$$

subject to (3.98) to (3.100).

It is readily apparent that all of those constraints are binding at the optimum. This leads to the transfers $\underline{t}^A = \underline{\theta}$, $\bar{t}^A = \bar{\theta} - (1 - p^A)\Delta\theta$, and the maximal punishment $\underline{P}^A = \Delta\theta$ and an optimal probability of auditing an inefficient firm that is now given by $c'(p^A) = \frac{v}{1-v}\Delta\theta$, where $\Delta\theta$ is again the high-profit firm's information rent when it is not audited by the principal.

In order to clarify the role of asymmetric information in constraining financing, let us consider the case where the lender provides an amount of cash I to finance the borrower's project. First-best efficiency calls for financing as long as the venture's expected profits cover the investment, i.e., as long as

$$V^* = v\bar{\theta} + (1 - v)\underline{\theta} - I > 0. \tag{3.101}$$

Under asymmetric information, the lender's net profit is written as

$$V^{SB} = v\bar{\theta} + (1 - v)\underline{\theta} - v(1 - p^A)\Delta\theta - (1 - v)c(p^A) - I, \tag{3.102}$$

or, using the definition of p^A,

$$V^{SB} = V^* - (1 - v)\big(c(p^A) + (1 - p^A)c'(p^A)\big). \tag{3.103}$$

When the Inada condition $c'(0) = 0$ holds, $p^A > 0$, and $c(p^A) + (1 - p^A) \cdot c'(p^A) > 0$. Hence, the set of values of the investment such that the lender makes a positive profit is reduced under asymmetric information. This can be interpreted as the source of some credit rationing.

In a model with a continuum of types, Gale and Hellwig (1985) show that the optimal contract *with a deterministic audit* involves two different regions. In the first one, there is verification of announced low profits if they are below a threshold R and of a full repayment if they are over this region. In the second region, there is no verification and a fixed repayment R. This optimal contract can be interpreted as a debt contract. ∎

3.6.4 The Threat of Termination

In the audit model of the finance literature, the lender has only one tool with which to screen the borrower's type: the probability of an audit. When an audit technology is not available, the lender may have to find other devices to induce information revelation. One such device is the threat of terminating financing.

In a model with two levels of profit, Bolton and Scharfstein (1990) argue that the threat of termination of a long-term relationship between a lender and his borrower may play the same role as an audit and also relaxes the efficient agent's incentive constraint. They interpret their model as a debt contract where the probability of refinancing is contingent on the agent's past performance. To understand the analogy between the Bolton and Scharfstein (1990) model and the costly state verification literature discussed above, let us consider the following bare-bones model that stresses the threat of termination as an incentive device.

A cashless agent requires an amount of funds I to start a project. With probability ν (resp. $1 - \nu$), this project yields profit $\bar{\theta}$ (resp. $\underline{\theta}$). We will assume that the project is socially valuable, $\nu\bar{\theta} + (1 - \nu)\underline{\theta} > I$. Moreover, the worst profit is already enough to finance the project, $\underline{\theta} > I$. As in the literature on costly state verification, the level of profit is nonobservable by the lender. The lender will have to rely on the agent's announcement of the realized profit to fix a repayment. However, a payment alone is not enough to screen the agent's type: the threat of termination is the complementary screening device needed by the principal. Moreover, we assume that the agent is protected by limited liability and can never get a negative payoff.

Suppose now that the contractual relationship lasts for two periods with independently and identically distributed types or profits θ and without any discounting. Then, the lender can use the threat of terminating financing to induce information revelation in the first period as we will see later.

In the second period, it is still true that the maximal repayment that can be obtained by the lender is $\underline{\theta}$ since this period ends the relationship and the principal does not have enough instruments to induce information revelation in this last period. Note that such a repayment yields an expected information rent $\nu\Delta\theta$ to the borrower if the relationship continues for the second period.

We denote a first period direct mechanism by $\{(\bar{t}, \bar{p}); (\underline{t}, \underline{p})\}$. The probability of not refinancing the firm (resp. the borrower's payment) is now $\bar{p}$ (resp. $\bar{t}$) when the agent reports having a high profit $\bar{\theta}$ in the first period. A similar definition applies to $\underline{p}$ (resp. $\underline{t}$).

The first period incentive compatibility constraints for both types are therefore written as

$$\bar{\theta} - \bar{t} + (1 - \bar{p})\nu\Delta\theta \geq \bar{\theta} - \underline{t} + (1 - \underline{p})\nu\Delta\theta \tag{3.104}$$

and

$$\underline{\theta} - \underline{t} + (1 - \underline{p})\nu\Delta\theta \geq \underline{\theta} - \bar{t} + (1 - \bar{p})\nu\Delta\theta. \tag{3.105}$$

The intertemporal participation constraints for both types are also written as

$$\bar{\theta} - \bar{t} + (1 - \bar{p})\nu\Delta\theta \geq 0 \tag{3.106}$$

and

$$\underline{\theta} - \underline{t} + (1 - \underline{p})\nu\Delta\theta \geq 0. \tag{3.107}$$

Finally, because the agent is cashless to start with, the following first period limited liability constraints must be satisfied:

$$\bar{\theta} - \bar{t} \geq 0 \tag{3.108}$$

and

$$\underline{\theta} - \underline{t} \geq 0. \tag{3.109}$$

Knowing that the repayment he gets in the second period is always $\underline{\theta}$, the principal's program is thus

(P): $\quad \max_{\{(\bar{t},\bar{p});(\underline{t},\underline{p})\}} \nu(\bar{t} + (1 - \bar{p})(\underline{\theta} - I)) + (1 - \nu)(\underline{t} + (1 - \underline{p})(\underline{\theta} - I)) - I$

$\quad\quad\quad\quad$ subject to (3.104) to (3.109).

We leave it to the reader to check that (3.104) and (3.109) are the only two constraints that are binding at the optimum. Hence, we obtain the following values of the first-period payments: $\underline{t} = \underline{\theta}$ and $\bar{t} = \underline{\theta} + (p - \bar{p})\nu\Delta\theta$. Inserting these expressions into the principal's objective function yields a reduced program that depends only on the probabilities of refinancing $\bar{p}$ and $\underline{p}$:

(P'): $\quad \max_{\{(\bar{p},\underline{p})\}} \nu(\underline{\theta} + (1 - \bar{p})(\nu\bar{\theta} + (1 - \nu)\underline{\theta} - I) - (1 - \underline{p})\nu\Delta\theta)$

$\quad\quad\quad\quad + (1 - \nu)(\underline{\theta} + (1 - \underline{p})(\underline{\theta} - I)) - I.$

We index this optimal contract with a superscript R meaning *refinancing*. Because the project is valuable in expectation, it would be costly for the principal not to refinance the project following a high first-period profit, and therefore we have $\bar{p}^R = 0$. Following a high first-period profit, the project is therefore always refinanced with probability one.

Even if $\underline{\theta} > I$, it may well be that the fixed investment I is large enough so that

$$\underline{\theta} - \frac{\nu^2}{1 - \nu} \Delta\theta - I < 0. \tag{3.110}$$

In this case, it is never optimal to refinance a project following a low first-period profit and $\underline{p}^R = 1$, as can be seen from (P') by looking at the coefficient of $\underline{p}$ in the principal's objective function. There exists a whole set of values for the cost of the project I, namely I in $[\underline{\theta} - \frac{\nu^2}{1-\nu}\Delta\theta, \underline{\theta}]$, which are such that it is efficient to finance the project, under complete information, but asymmetric information implies that those projects are nevertheless not renewed following that announcement of a low first-period profit. It is interesting to note that the probability of not refinancing the project plays the same role as the probability of audit in a Townsend-Gale-Hellwig model. First, it relaxes the high-profit agent's incentive constraint. Second, like auditing, not renewing finance is also costly for the principal, because projects are always socially valuable.

Finally, note that the lender's intertemporal profit under asymmetric information becomes $V^{SB} = \nu\bar{\theta} + (1 - \nu)\underline{\theta} - I + \underline{\theta} - I$. It is obviously lower than the intertemporal profit when profit is verifiable $V^* = 2(\nu\bar{\theta} + (1 - \nu)\underline{\theta} - I)$, but it is greater than realizing the project each period and asking for a payment $\underline{\theta}$ that yields $2(\underline{\theta} - I)$.

The idea that the threat of termination of a relationship is a powerful incentive device in an adverse selection framework is used in many areas of incentive economics. An earlier contribution to the finance and the labor literatures was made by Stiglitz and Weiss (1983). In the case of sovereign debt, it has often been argued that the threat of not refinancing a country could be used to foster debt repayment (see Allen 1983, and Eaton and Gersovitz 1981).

3.7 Redistributive Concerns and the Efficiency-Equity Trade-Off

In the rent extraction-efficiency trade-off analyzed so far, the principal wants to minimize the information rent left to the agent for a given level of output. The principal has no redistributive concerns vis-à-vis the agent. In the optimal taxation literature, starting with the seminal paper of Mirrlees (1971),[22] the principal (generally a government or a tax authority) wants to redistribute wealth among members of society according to a particular social objective function $G(\cdot)$, which we will assume is increasing and strictly concave ($G' > 0$ and $G'' < 0$). Of course, for the redistribution problem to be nontrivial, agents have to be heterogeneous. We will thus assume that with probability ν (resp. $1 - \nu$) an agent is a high- (resp. low-) productivity one having a cost of production $\underline{\theta}$ (resp. $\bar{\theta}$). An agent's utility function is thus written as usual as $U = t - \theta q$. The principal's objective is instead $V = \nu G(\underline{U}) + (1 - \nu)G(\bar{U})$, where $\underline{U} = \underline{t} - \underline{\theta}\underline{q}$ and $\bar{U} = \bar{t} - \bar{\theta}\bar{q}$.

This redistributive objective of the government is limited by the government's *budget constraint*. Typically, if the return from production of each type is $S(q)$, the budget constraint requires that the government cannot redistribute more that what is actually produced, i.e.,

$$\nu S(\underline{q}) + (1 - \nu)S(\bar{q}) \geq \nu \underline{t} + (1 - \nu)\bar{t}. \tag{3.111}$$

Using the definition of the information rents $\underline{U}$ and $\bar{U}$, the budget constraint can be rewritten as

$$\nu(S(\underline{q}) - \underline{\theta}\underline{q}) + (1 - \nu)(S(\bar{q}) - \bar{\theta}\bar{q}) \geq \nu\underline{U} + (1 - \nu)\bar{U}.^{23} \tag{3.112}$$

Under complete information, the principal can distinguish between high and low productivity agents. The optimal redistribution scheme must solve the following problem:

(P):
$$\max_{\{(\underline{U},\underline{q});(\bar{U},\bar{q})\}} \nu G(\underline{U}) + (1 - \nu)G(\bar{U})$$

subject to (3.112).

The problem is concave and the first-order conditions are necessary and sufficient for optimality. Optimizing with respect to $\underline{U}$ and $\bar{U}$ respectively yields

$$\mu = G'(\underline{U}^*) = G'(\bar{U}^*), \tag{3.113}$$

where μ is the positive multiplier of (3.112).

When $G(\cdot)$ is strictly concave, the full information policy calls for *complete redistribution*, so that $\underline{U}^* = \bar{U}^* = U^*$.

---

[22]We will cover this paper more extensively in chapter 7.

[23] If the government must also cover a fixed spending B out of the society's production, B must be added on the right-hand side above. The only impact of this spending is that all transfers are increased by a fixed amount B.

Optimizing with respect to outputs yields the usual first-best productions q^* and $\bar{q}^*$. Hence, any agent, whatever his type, gets

$$U^* = \nu(S(\underline{q}^*) - \underline{\theta}\underline{q}^*) + (1 - \nu)(S(\bar{q}^*) - \bar{\theta}\bar{q}^*). \tag{3.114}$$

Under complete information, the government chooses to maximize the "size of the cake" before redistributing equal shares of it to everybody. There is no conflict between efficiency and equality.

Let us now turn to the more realistic case where the agent's productivity is nonobservable. An incentive-feasible redistribution policy must now satisfy not only the budget constraint (3.112) but also the following incentive constraints:

$$\underline{U} - \bar{U} \geq \Delta\theta\bar{q} \tag{3.115}$$

and

$$\bar{U} - \underline{U} \geq -\Delta\theta\underline{q}. \tag{3.116}$$

First, note that the optimal first-best policy is such that $\underline{U}^* - \bar{U}^* = 0 < \Delta\theta\bar{q}^{FB}$, i.e., the high-productivity agent's incentive constraint is violated. Hence, we suspect (3.115) to be binding under asymmetric information, and we look for an optimal second-best policy as a solution to the following program:

(P): $$\max_{\{(\underline{U},\underline{q});(\bar{U},\bar{q})\}} \nu G(\underline{U}) + (1 - \nu)G(\bar{U}),$$

subject to (3.112) and (3.115).[24]

Denoting the respective multipliers of (3.112) and (3.115) by μ and λ, the first-order conditions for optimality with respect to $\underline{U}$ and $\bar{U}$ yield, respectively,

$$\nu G'(\underline{U}^{SB}) = \mu\nu - \lambda \tag{3.117}$$

and

$$(1 - \nu)G'(\bar{U}^{SB}) = \mu(1 - \nu) + \lambda. \tag{3.118}$$

Summing those last two equations, we obtain

$$\mu = \nu G'(\underline{U}^{SB}) + (1 - \nu)G'(\bar{U}^{SB}) > 0, \tag{3.119}$$

and the budget constraint is again binding. Also, we compute

$$\lambda = \nu(1 - \nu)(G'(\bar{U}^{SB}) - G'(\underline{U}^{SB})). \tag{3.120}$$

---

[24] We leave it to the reader to check that the inefficient agent's incentive constraint is slack at the optimum.

Because $G(\cdot)$ is concave and $\overline{U}^{SB} < \underline{U}^{SB}$ is necessary to satisfy the incentive constraint (3.115) if $\bar{q} > 0$, we have $\lambda > 0$, and the incentive compatibility constraint is also binding.

Optimizing with respect to outputs immediately yields $\underline{q}^{SB} = \underline{q}^*$, i.e., no distortion of the high-productivity agent's output and a downward distortion of the low-productivity agent's output. Indeed, we have $\bar{q}^{SB} < \bar{q}^*$, where

$$S'(\bar{q}^{SB}) = \bar{\theta} + \frac{\lambda}{(1 - \nu)\mu}\Delta\theta. \qquad (3.121)$$

Using the definitions of λ and μ given above, we finally obtain

$$S'(\bar{q}^{SB}) = \bar{\theta} + \nu\left(\frac{G'(\overline{U}^{SB}) - G'(\underline{U}^{SB})}{\nu G'(\underline{U}^{SB}) + (1 - \nu)G'(\overline{U}^{SB})}\right)\Delta\theta. \qquad (3.122)$$

We summarize all those results in proposition 3.7.

Proposition 3.7: *Under asymmetric information, the optimal redistributive policy calls for a downward distortion of the low-productivity agent's output, $\bar{q}^{SB} < \bar{q}^*$, and a positive wedge between the low- and the high-productivity agents' utilities, $\underline{U}^{SB} > \overline{U}^{SB}$.*

To induce information revelation by the high-productivity type, the principal raises his after-tax utility level and reduces that of the low-productivity type. Introducing this unequal distribution of utilities is costly for the principal, who maximizes a strictly concave social objective. To reduce this cost, and thereby to reduce inequality, the principal decreases the low-productivity agent's output. Under asymmetric information, there exists a true trade-off between equity and efficiency.

Remark: It is interesting to give an approximation of the distortion described in (3.122) when $\Delta\theta$ is small enough. Using simple Taylor expansions, we get $G'(\overline{U}^{SB}) - G'(\underline{U}^{SB}) \approx -G''(U^*)(\underline{U}^{SB} - \overline{U}^{SB}) = -G''(U^*)\Delta\theta\bar{q}^{SB}$, and $\nu G'(\underline{U}^{SB}) + (1 - \nu)G'(\overline{U}^{SB}) \approx G'(U^*)$. Hence, we finally obtain

$$S'(\bar{q}^{SB}) \approx \bar{\theta} - \nu\frac{G''(U^*)}{G'(U^*)}(\Delta\theta)^2\bar{q}^{SB}. \qquad (3.123)$$

As the degree of the government's inequality aversion $-\frac{G''(U^*)}{G'(U^*)}$ increases, the principal becomes more averse to inequality, and he must more significantly reduce the low-productivity agent's output. ∎

The taxation literature has been mostly developed, following Mirrlees (1971), in the case of a continuum of productivity shocks. As our two-type model has already shown, the technical difficulties of such models come from the impossibility to proceed in two steps as usual, i.e., first, find the distribution of utilities and, second, optimize with respect to output. Those two steps must be performed simultaneously by relying on complex optimization techniques (calculus of variations or Pontryagin Principle). This makes the analysis quite difficult, and explicit solutions are generally not available (see Atkinson and Stiglitz 1980, Stiglitz 1987, and Myles 1997 for the techniques needed to solve this problem in the case of a continuum of types). A second peculiarity of the optimal solution with a continuum of types is that both the lowest and the highest productivity agents produce the first-best output, provided that second-order conditions are satisfied (Lollivier and Rochet 1983). Otherwise, it may sometimes be optimal to have the least productive agents producing zero output. For all other types, the production is downward distorted as in our two-type example. The clear advantage of the continuum model is that it gives realistic predictions on the taxation schedule. This allows discussion of the progressivity or regressivity of this schedule. The fact that high-productivity agents produce efficiently also implies that the marginal tax rate faced by the highest productivity agents should be zero in the optimal taxation literature. This seems nevertheless to contradict most empirical observations. ∎

Appendix 3.1: The Optimal Contract with a Continuum of Types

Despite the fact that few new economic insights can be obtained in the continuum case, we give a brief account of this case here, because most of the principal-agent literature is written within this framework.

Reconsider the model of section 2.1 with θ in $\Theta = [\underline{\theta}, \bar{\theta}]$, with a cumulative distribution function $F(\theta)$ and a density function $f(\theta) > 0$ on $[\underline{\theta}, \bar{\theta}]$. Nothing in the proof of proposition 2.1 is specific to the discrete case. Hence, the revelation principle is still valid with a continuum of types, and we can restrict our analysis to direct revelation mechanisms $\{(q(\tilde{\theta}), t(\tilde{\theta}))\}$, which are truthful, i.e., such that

$$t(\theta) - \theta q(\theta) \geq t(\tilde{\theta}) - \theta q(\tilde{\theta}) \qquad \text{for any } (\theta, \tilde{\theta}) \text{ in } \Theta^2. \qquad (3.124)$$

In particular, (3.124) implies

$$t(\theta) - \theta q(\theta) \geq t(\theta') - \theta q(\theta'), \tag{3.125}$$

$$t(\theta') - \theta' q(\theta') \geq t(\theta) - \theta' q(\theta) \qquad \text{for all pairs } (\theta, \theta') \text{ in } \Theta^2. \tag{3.126}$$

Adding (3.125) and (3.126) we obtain

$$(\theta - \theta')(q(\theta') - q(\theta)) \geq 0. \tag{3.127}$$

Incentive compatibility alone requires that the schedule of output $q(\cdot)$ has to be nonincreasing. This implies that $q(\cdot)$ is differentiable almost everywhere (a.e.), from which we can derive that $t(\cdot)$ is also differentiable with the same points of nondifferentiability. The most general class of direct revelation mechanisms to consider is therefore the class of a.e. differentiable functions. In practice, we use piecewise differentiable functions and in most cases differentiable functions. Here, we will restrict the analysis to differentiable functions, but it can be immediately extended to piecewise differentiable functions.[25]

(3.124) implies that the following first-order condition for the optimal response $\tilde{\theta}$ chosen by type θ is satisfied:

$$\dot{t}(\tilde{\theta}) - \theta\dot{q}(\tilde{\theta}) = 0. \tag{3.128}$$

For the truth to be an optimal response for all θ, it must be the case that

$$\dot{t}(\theta) - \theta\dot{q}(\theta) = 0, \tag{3.129}$$

and (3.129) must hold for all θ in Θ since θ is unknown to the principal.

It is also necessary to satisfy the local second-order condition,

$$\ddot{t}(\tilde{\theta})\big|_{\tilde{\theta}=\theta} - \theta\ddot{q}(\tilde{\theta})\big|_{\tilde{\theta}=\theta} \leq 0 \tag{3.130}$$

or

$$\ddot{t}(\theta) - \theta\ddot{q}(\theta) \leq 0. \tag{3.131}$$

But differentiating (3.129), (3.131) can be written more simply as

$$-\dot{q}(\theta) \geq 0. \tag{3.132}$$

---

[25]Laffont and Tirole (1993, chap. 6) provide an example of an optimal discontinuous direct revelation mechanism. See also Guesnerie and Laffont (1984).

(3.129) and (3.132) constitute the local incentive constraints, which ensure that the agent does not want to lie locally. Now we need to check that he does not want to lie globally either, therefore the following constraints must be satisfied:

$$t(\theta) - \theta q(\theta) \geq t(\tilde{\theta}) - \theta q(\tilde{\theta}) \qquad \text{for any } (\theta, \tilde{\theta}) \text{ in } \Theta^2. \qquad (3.133)$$

From (3.129) we have

$$t(\theta) - t(\tilde{\theta}) = \int_{\tilde{\theta}}^{\theta} \tau \dot{q}(\tau) \, d\tau = \theta q(\theta) - \tilde{\theta} q(\tilde{\theta}) - \int_{\tilde{\theta}}^{\theta} q(\tau) \, d\tau \qquad (3.134)$$

or

$$t(\theta) - \theta q(\theta) = t(\tilde{\theta}) - \theta q(\tilde{\theta}) + (\theta - \tilde{\theta}) q(\tilde{\theta}) - \int_{\tilde{\theta}}^{\theta} q(\tau) \, d\tau, \qquad (3.135)$$

where $(\theta - \tilde{\theta}) q(\tilde{\theta}) - \int_{\tilde{\theta}}^{\theta} q(\tau) d\tau \geq 0$, because $q(\cdot)$ is nonincreasing.

So, it turns out that the local incentive constraints (3.128) also imply the global incentive constraints.[26]

In such circumstances, the infinity of incentive constraints (3.133) reduces to a differential equation and to a monotonicity constraint. Local analysis of incentives is enough. Truthful revelation mechanisms are then *characterized* by the two conditions (3.129) and (3.132).

Let us use the rent variable $U(\theta) = t(\theta) - \theta q(\theta)$, instead of the transfer as we did in the text of chapter 2. The local incentive constraint is now written as[27] (by using (3.129))

$$\dot{U}(\theta) = -q(\theta). \qquad (3.136)$$

The optimization program of the principal becomes

(P): $$\max_{\{(U(\cdot), q(\cdot))\}} \int_{\underline{\theta}}^{\bar{\theta}} (S(q(\theta)) - \theta q(\theta) - U(\theta)) f(\theta) \, d\theta,$$

subject to

$$\dot{U}(\theta) = -q(\theta), \qquad (3.137)$$

$$\dot{q}(\theta) \leq 0, \qquad (3.138)$$

$$U(\theta) \geq 0. \qquad (3.139)$$

---

[26]This is due to the fact that the Spence-Mirrlees property holds. See section 3.1.3 for a general definition of this property.

[27]$\dot{U}(\theta) = -q(\theta) + (\dot{t}(\theta) - \theta \dot{q}(\theta))$, but the term in parentheses is zero from the first-order condition (3.129). By employing the Envelope Theorem, the incentive constraint reduces to (3.136).

Using (3.136), the participation constraint (3.139) simplifies to $U(\bar{\theta}) \geq 0$. As in the discrete case, incentive compatibility implies that only the participation constraint of the most inefficient type can be binding. Furthermore, it is clear from the above program that it will be binding, i.e., $U(\bar{\theta}) = 0$.

Momentarily ignoring (3.138), we can solve (3.137)

$$U(\bar{\theta}) - U(\theta) = - \int_\theta^{\bar{\theta}} q(\tau)\, d\tau \qquad (3.140)$$

or, since $U(\bar{\theta}) = 0$,

$$U(\theta) = \int_\theta^{\bar{\theta}} q(\tau)\, d\tau. \qquad (3.141)$$

The principal's objective function becomes

$$\int_{\underline{\theta}}^{\bar{\theta}} \left(S(q(\theta)) - \theta q(\theta) - \int_\theta^{\bar{\theta}} q(\tau)\, d\tau \right) f(\theta)\, d\theta, \qquad (3.142)$$

which, by an integration of parts, gives

$$\int_{\underline{\theta}}^{\bar{\theta}} \left(S(q(\theta)) - \left(\theta + \frac{F(\theta)}{f(\theta)} \right) q(\theta) \right) f(\theta)\, d\theta. \qquad (3.143)$$

Maximizing pointwise (3.143), we get the second-best optimal outputs

$$S'(q^{SB}(\theta)) = \theta + \frac{F(\theta)}{f(\theta)}, \qquad (3.144)$$

which generalizes (2.27) and (2.29) to the case of a continuum of types.

If the monotone hazard rate property $\frac{d}{d\theta}\left(\frac{F(\theta)}{f(\theta)}\right) \geq 0$ holds,[28] the solution $q^{SB}(\theta)$ of (3.144) is clearly decreasing, and the neglected constraint (3.138) is satisfied.[29] All types choose therefore different allocations and there is no bunching in the optimal contract.

From (3.144), we note that there is no distortion for the most efficient type (since $F(\underline{\theta}) = 0$) and a downward distortion for all the other types.

---

[28]This sufficient condition is satisfied by most parametric single-peak densities (see Bagnoli and Bergstrom 1989).

[29]If $q^{SB}(\theta)$ is increasing, it is not the solution. The solution, which involves bunching in some intervals (i.e., $q^{SB}(\theta)$ constant on some intervals), can be easily obtained by the Pontryagin principle (see appendix 3.2 and Guesnerie and Laffont 1984).

All types, except the least efficient one, obtain a positive information rent at the optimal contract

$$U^{SB}(\theta) = \int_{\theta}^{\bar{\theta}} q^{SB}(\tau) \, d\tau. \qquad (3.145)$$

Finally, one could also allow for some shutdown of types. The virtual surplus $S(q) - \left(\theta + \frac{F(\theta)}{f(\theta)}\right)q$ decreases with θ when the monotone hazard rate property holds, and shutdown (if any) occurs on an interval $[\theta^*, \bar{\theta}]$. θ^* is obtained as a solution to

$$\max_{\{\theta^*\}} \int_{\underline{\theta}}^{\theta^*} \left(S(q^{SB}(\theta)) - \left(\theta + \frac{F(\theta)}{f(\theta)}\right) q^{SB}(\theta) \right) f(\theta) \, d\theta.$$

For an interior optimum, we find that

$$S(q^{SB}(\theta^*)) = \left(\theta^* + \frac{F(\theta^*)}{f(\theta^*)}\right) q^{SB}(\theta^*).$$

As in the discrete case, we leave it to the reader to check that the Inada condition $S'(0) = +\infty$ and the condition $\lim_{q \to 0} S'(q)q = 0$ ensure the corner solution $\theta^* = \bar{\theta}$.

> **Remark:** The optimal solution above can be also derived by using the Pontryagin principle.[30] The Hamiltonian is then
>
> $$H(q, U, \mu, \theta) = (S(q) - \theta q - U)f(\theta) - \mu q, \qquad (3.146)$$
>
> where μ is the co-state variable, U the state variable and q the control variable.
>
> From the Pontryagin principle,
>
> $$\dot{\mu}(\theta) = -\frac{\partial H}{\partial U} = f(\theta). \qquad (3.147)$$
>
> From the transversality condition (since there is no constraint on $U(\cdot)$ at $\underline{\theta}$),
>
> $$\mu(\underline{\theta}) = 0. \qquad (3.148)$$
>
> Integrating (3.147) using (3.148), we get
>
> $$\mu(\theta) = F(\theta). \qquad (3.149)$$

---

[30] See Kamien and Schwartz (1981) for an introduction to dynamic programming.

Optimizing with respect to $q(\cdot)$ also yields

$$S'(q^{SB}(\theta)) = \theta + \frac{\mu(\theta)}{f(\theta)}, \qquad (3.150)$$

and inserting the value of $\mu(\theta)$ obtained from (3.149) again yields (3.144). ∎

We have derived, in three steps (through the use of the revelation principle, characterization of truthful direct revelation mechanisms, and optimization of the principal's expected welfare in the class of truthful direct revelation mechanisms), the optimal truthful direct revelation mechanism $\{(q^{SB}(\theta), U^{SB}(\theta))\}$, or $\{(q^{SB}(\theta), t^{SB}(\theta))\}$. It remains to be investigated if there is a simple implementation of this mechanism. Since $q^{SB}(\cdot)$ is decreasing,[31] we can invert this function and obtain $\theta^{SB}(q)$. Then,

$$t^{SB}(\theta) = U^{SB}(\theta) + \theta q^{SB}(\theta) \qquad (3.151)$$

becomes

$$T(q) = t^{SB}(\theta^{SB}(q)) = \int_{\theta(q)}^{\bar{\theta}} q^{SB}(\tau)\, d\tau + \theta(q)q. \qquad (3.152)$$

To the optimal truthful direct revelation mechanism we have associated a nonlinear transfer $T(q)$. We can check that the agent confronted with this nonlinear transfer chooses the same allocation as when he is faced with the optimal revelation mechanism. Indeed, we have $\frac{d}{dq}(T(q) - \theta q) = T'(q) - \theta = \frac{dt^{SB}}{d\theta} \cdot \frac{d\theta^{SB}}{dq} - \theta = 0$, since $\frac{dt^{SB}}{d\theta} - \theta\frac{dq^{SB}}{d\theta} = 0$.

> **Remark:** In chapter 9, we will give one more result that is specific to the continuum case, namely the possibility to implement (sometimes) the optimal contract by a menu of linear contracts. ∎

To conclude, the economic insights obtained in the continuum case are not different from those obtained in the two-state case studied in this chapter. The case of partial bunching where a whole set of types with nonzero measure choose the same allocation is discussed in appendix 3.2.

The differentiable method was used in Mirrlees (1971) and Mussa Rosen (1978), but the systematic approach of differentiable direct revelation mechanisms was provided in Laffont and Maskin (1980), in the more

---

[31]When $q^{SB}(\cdot)$ is not strictly decreasing, some care must be exerted in the writing below. A "flat" in $q(\cdot)$ is associated with nondifferentiability of $T(\cdot)$.

general case of dominant strategy mechanisms for multiagent frameworks. Baron and Myerson (1982) and Guesnerie and Laffont (1984) extended the analysis to cases where the monotonicity condition may be binding. Milgrom and Segal (2000) discussed the conditions under which (3.140) holds. They showed that imposing piecewise continuously differentiability may be excessive, and they offered less stringent conditions on the primitives (the agent's utility function) validating (3.140). ∎

Appendix 3.2: Bunching in the Case of a Continuum of Types

In this appendix we analyze the bunching problem in the case of a continuum of types. The framework is that of appendix 3.1.

In the case of a continuum of types, the principal's optimization program is written (see appendix 3.1):

(P):
$$\max_{\{(U(\theta),q(\theta))\}} \int_{\underline{\theta}}^{\bar{\theta}} (S(q(\theta)) - \theta q(\theta) - U(\theta))f(\theta)\, d\theta$$

subject to

$$\dot{U}(\theta) = -q(\theta), \tag{3.153}$$

$$\dot{q}(\theta) \leq 0, \tag{3.154}$$

$$U(\theta) \geq 0, \qquad \text{for all } \theta \text{ in } \Theta, \tag{3.155}$$

where (3.154) is the local second-order condition of the agent's problem.

We can solve (3.153) for $U(\theta)$ and, using $U(\bar{\theta}) = 0$, substitute in the principal's objective program. Then we define $q(\theta)$ as the new state variable and $y(\theta) = \dot{q}(\theta)$ as the control variable. (P) reduces to

(P'):
$$\max_{\{(q(\theta),y(\theta))\}} \int_{\underline{\theta}}^{\bar{\theta}} \left(S(q(\theta)) - \theta q(\theta) - \frac{F(\theta)}{f(\theta)} q(\theta) \right) f(\theta)\, d\theta$$

$$\dot{q}(\theta) = y(\theta) \tag{3.156}$$

$$y(\theta) \leq 0. \tag{3.157}$$

We denote by $\mu(\theta)$ the multiplier of (3.156).

The Hamiltonian is then

$$H(q, y, \mu, \theta) = \left(S(q) - \left(\theta + \frac{F(\theta)}{f(\theta)} \right) q \right) f(\theta) + \mu y. \qquad (3.158)$$

From the Pontryagin principle, we have

$$\dot{\mu}(\theta) = -\frac{\partial H}{\partial q} = -\left(S'(q(\theta)) - \left(\theta + \frac{F(\theta)}{f(\theta)} \right) \right) f(\theta). \qquad (3.159)$$

Maximizing with respect to $y(\cdot)$ with the constraint (3.157) yields $\mu(\theta) \geq 0$, with $y(\theta) = 0$ if $\mu(\theta) > 0$.

Consider an interval where the monotonicity constraint (3.157) is not binding. Then, $\mu(\theta)$ is zero on this interval (and therefore $\dot{\mu}(\theta) = 0$ also on this interval). Maximizing with respect to $q(\cdot)$, we find the second-best solution characterized by

$$S'(q^{SB}(\theta)) = \theta + \frac{F(\theta)}{f(\theta)}. \qquad (3.160)$$

So, when the monotonicity constraint is not binding, the optimal solution coincides with the second-best solution.

Consider now an interval $[\theta_0, \theta_1]$ where the monotonicity constraint is binding. Then $q(\cdot)$ is constant in the interval. Denote this value by $\bar{q}$. Because (3.157) is not binding to the left of θ_0 and to the right of θ_1, from the continuity of the Pontryagin multiplier $\mu(\theta)$ we have $\mu(\theta_0) = \mu(\theta_1) = 0$. Integrating (3.159) between θ_0 and θ_1, we obtain

$$\int_{\theta_0}^{\theta_1} \left(S'(\bar{q}) - \left(\theta + \frac{F(\theta)}{f(\theta)} \right) \right) f(\theta) \, d\theta = 0, \qquad (3.161)$$

or, putting it differently,

$$S'(\bar{q}) = \frac{\int_{\theta_0}^{\theta_1} (\theta f(\theta) + F(\theta)) \, d\theta}{\int_{\theta_0}^{\theta_1} f(\theta) \, d\theta}. \qquad (3.162)$$

Integrating the numerator of (3.162) by parts, we get

$$S'(\bar{q}) = \frac{\theta_1 F(\theta_1) - \theta_0 F(\theta_0)}{F(\theta_1) - F(\theta_0)}. \qquad (3.163)$$

To determine the three unknowns θ_0, θ_1 and $\bar{q}$, we have three equations, namely (3.163) and $\bar{q} = q^{SB}(\theta_0) = q^{SB}(\theta_1)$ from (3.160) at $\theta = \theta_0$ and $\theta = \theta_1$ (see figure 3.13).

There is bunching in the interval $[\theta_0, \theta_1]$.

 See Guesnerie and Laffont (1984) for more general solutions with several possible intervals of bunching. ∎

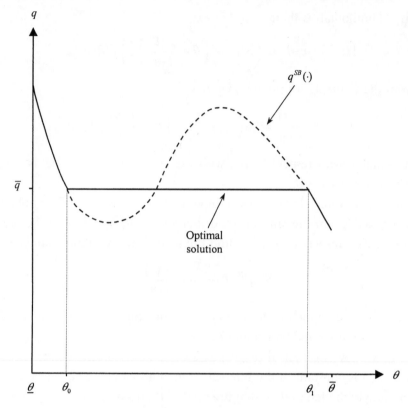

FIGURE 3.13: Bunching

Appendix 3.3: The Spence-Mirrlees Property

The goal of this appendix is to see the importance of the Spence-Mirrlees property in a general incentive problem.

Consider the general utility function $U(q, t, \theta)$ for the agent with $U_t > 0$. Local incentive compatibility for the direct revelation mechanism $\{(q(\tilde{\theta}), t(\tilde{\theta}))\}$ is written as

$$U_q(q(\theta), t(\theta), \theta)\dot{q}(\theta) + U_t(q(\theta), t(\theta), \theta)\dot{t}(\theta) = 0, \qquad (3.164)$$

The local second-order condition is written as (after using the first-order condition)

$$U_{q\theta}(q(\theta), t(\theta), \theta)\dot{q}(\theta) + U_{t\theta}(q(\theta), t(\theta), \theta)\dot{t}(\theta) \geq 0, \qquad (3.165)$$

or, using the first-order condition,

$$\dot{q}(\theta)\left(U_{q\theta}(q(\theta), t(\theta), \theta) - U_{t\theta}(q(\theta), t(\theta), \theta) \cdot \frac{U_q(q(\theta), t(\theta), \theta)}{U_t(q(\theta), t(\theta), \theta)}\right) \geq 0,$$

or, finally,

$$\dot{q}(\theta) \cdot U_t(q(\theta), t(\theta), \theta) \cdot \frac{\partial}{\partial \tilde{\theta}} \left(\frac{U_q(q(\theta), t(\theta), \tilde{\theta})}{U_t(q(\theta), t(\theta), \tilde{\theta})} \right) \Bigg|_{\tilde{\theta}=\theta} \geq 0. \tag{3.166}$$

Using the Spence-Mirrlees property at $\tilde{\theta} = \theta$,

$$\frac{\partial}{\partial \theta} \left(\frac{U_q}{U_t} \right) < 0, \tag{3.167}$$

and $U_t > 0$, we conclude that $\dot{q}(\theta) \leq 0$.

Global incentive compatibility requires

$$U(q(\theta), t(\theta), \theta) \geq U(q(\tilde{\theta}), t(\tilde{\theta}), \theta) \quad \text{for all } (\theta, \tilde{\theta}) \text{ in } \Theta^2. \tag{3.168}$$

(3.168) can be rewritten as

$$\int_{\tilde{\theta}}^{\theta} (U_q(q(\tau), t(\tau), \theta)\dot{q}(\tau) + U_t(q(\tau), t(\tau), \theta)\dot{t}(\tau)) \, d\tau \geq 0. \tag{3.169}$$

or, using again the first-order condition to express $\dot{t}(\tau)$,

$$\int_{\tilde{\theta}}^{\theta} \dot{q}(\tau) U_t(q(\tau), t(\tau), \theta) \left(\frac{U_q(q(\tau), t(\tau), \theta)}{U_t(q(\tau), t(\tau), \theta)} - \frac{U_q(q(\tau), t(\tau), \tau)}{U_t(q(\tau), t(\tau), \tau)} \right) d\tau \geq 0. \tag{3.170}$$

Because $\dot{q}(\tau) \leq 0$, $U_t > 0$, and using the Spence-Mirrlees property with $\tau < \theta$, we can conclude that

$$\int_{\tilde{\theta}}^{\theta} \dot{q}(\tau) U_t(q(\tau), t(\tau), \theta) \left(\frac{U_q(q(\tau), t(\tau), \theta)}{U_t(q(\tau), t(\tau), \theta)} - \frac{U_q(q(\tau), t(\tau), \tau)}{U_t(q(\tau), t(\tau), \tau)} \right) d\tau$$

$$\geq \int_{\tilde{\theta}}^{\theta} \dot{q}(\tau) U_t(q(\tau), t(\tau), \theta) \left(\frac{U_q(q(\tau), t(\tau), \tau)}{U_t(q(\tau), t(\tau), \tau)} - \frac{U_q(q(\tau), t(\tau), \tau)}{U_t(q(\tau), t(\tau), \tau)} \right) d\tau = 0. \tag{3.171}$$

Hence, the local second-order condition $\dot{q}(\tau) \leq 0$ also implies global optimality of the truth-telling strategy when the Spence-Mirrlees property (3.168) holds.

> **Remark:** It is important to notice that, for reducing the second-order condition to $\dot{q}(\theta) \leq 0$, we need only use the Spence-Mirrlees property at $(q(\theta), t(\theta), \theta)$. However, to reach global incentive compatibility we need this condition at $(q(\tau), t(\tau), \theta)$ for any (τ, θ), i.e., for any (q, t, θ), which is a *much stronger requirement*.
> For models linear in θ, such as $t - \theta C(q)$, the "local Spence-Mirrlees property" $\frac{\partial}{\partial \tilde{\theta}}(-\theta C'(q(\tilde{\theta})))_{\tilde{\theta}=\theta} < 0$ for all θ implies the "global Spence-Mirrlees property" $\frac{\partial}{\partial \theta}(-\theta C'(q(\tau)))$ for all (θ, τ). ∎

Appendix 3.4: Proofs of Propositions 3.4 and 3.5

We start with proposition 3.4. Suppose first that $l < \nu\Delta\theta\bar{q}^{SB}$; we conjecture that the relevant constraints are (3.79) and (3.78). Those constraints are obviously binding to minimize the expected rent $\nu\underline{U} + (1 - \nu)\overline{U}$ left to the agent. Hence, $\overline{U}^L = -l$ and $\underline{U}^L = -l + \Delta\theta\bar{q}$. Inserting these values into the principal's objective function and optimizing with respect to $\underline{q}$ and $\bar{q}$ yields $\underline{q}^L = q^*$ and $\bar{q}^L = \bar{q}^{SB}$.

This solution is valid as long as the agent's *ex ante* participation constraint is strictly satisfied, i.e., $\nu\underline{U}^L + (1 - \nu)\overline{U}^L = -l + \nu\Delta\theta\bar{q}^{SB} > 0$.

Note that the $\bar{\theta}$-agent's incentive constraint and the limited liability constraint (3.77) are both slack. Supposing that $\nu\Delta\theta\bar{q}^{SB} \le l \le \nu\Delta\theta\bar{q}^*$, we then conjecture that (3.80) is also binding. In this case we obtain that $\nu\underline{U}^L + (1 - \nu)\overline{U}^L = -l + \nu\Delta\theta\bar{q}^L = 0$, and thus the output distortion is explicitly defined by (3.81). This distortion continues to hold as long as $\bar{q} \le \bar{q}^*$. For $l > \nu\Delta\theta\bar{q}^*$, the principal implements the first-best outcome by fixing $\underline{U}^L = (1 - \nu)\Delta\theta\bar{q}^*$ and $\overline{U}^L = -\nu\Delta\theta\bar{q}^*$. These rents satisfy (3.79) and (3.80) with an equality. Moreover, the limited liability constraints (3.77) and (3.78) also hold.

We now turn to the proof of proposition 3.5. Note first that we can rewrite (3.75) and (3.76) respectively as

$$\underline{U} \ge -l - \underline{\theta}\underline{q}, \tag{3.172}$$

$$\overline{U} \ge -l - \bar{\theta}\bar{q}. \tag{3.173}$$

Incentive compatibility still requires $\underline{q} \ge \bar{q}$. In the optimal contract without limited liability constraint, the contract with the highest value of $\overline{U}$ is such that $\overline{U} = -\nu\Delta\theta\bar{q}^*$. The constraint is not binding if $\overline{U} \ge -l - \bar{\theta}\bar{q}^*$ or if $l \ge -(\nu\underline{\theta} + (1 - \nu)\bar{\theta})\bar{q}^*$, in which case the first-best is still implemented. When l becomes lower, the constraint (3.173) becomes binding and $\bar{q}$ must be adjusted upward so that $l = -(\nu\underline{\theta} + (1 - \nu)\bar{\theta})\bar{q}$.

When l reaches $-(\nu\underline{\theta} + (1 - \nu)\bar{\theta})q^*$, the implementability condition becomes binding, and bunching occurs with $\underline{q} = \bar{q} = q^L$ and $l = -(\nu\underline{\theta} + (1 - \nu)\bar{\theta})q^L$.

The contract is valuable as long as q^L is lower than q^{max}, defined by $S(q^{max}) = (\nu\underline{\theta} + (1 - \nu)\bar{\theta})q^{max}$, so that the principal makes a positive profit.

4 Moral Hazard: The Basic Trade-Offs

In chapter 2, we stressed that the delegation of tasks creates an information gap between the principal and his agent when the latter learns some piece of information relevant to determining the efficient volume of trade. Adverse selection is not the only informational problem one can imagine. Agents to whom a task has been delegated by a principal may also choose *actions* that affect the value of trade or, more generally, the agent's performance. By the mere fact of delegation, the principal often loses any ability to control those actions that are no longer observable, either by the principal who offers the contract or by the court of law that enforces it. Those actions cannot be contracted upon because no one can verify their value. In such cases we will say that there is *moral hazard*.[1]

The leading candidates for such moral hazard actions are effort variables, which positively influence the agent's level of production but also create a disutility for the agent. For instance, the yield of a field depends on the amount of time that the tenant has spent selecting the best crops, or the quality of their harvesting.

---

[1]This situation is sometimes also referred to as *hidden action*. See section 1.6 for the origin of the expression "moral hazard."

Similarly, the probability that a driver has a car crash depends on how safely he drives, which also affects his demand for insurance. Also, a regulated firm may have to perform a costly and nonobservable investment to reduce its cost of producing a socially valuable good. The agent's action may be a more complex array of decisions that define the agent's task or his job attributes. The agent may sometimes choose among various projects to be carried out on behalf of the principal, each project being associated with a particular stream of profit for the principal and a particular nontransferable private benefit that the agent may get if this project is selected. For example, the manager of a large corporation may divert the firm's resources into perks rather than in hiring new engineers for the firm's research lab.

It is important to stress that, as with adverse selection, moral hazard would not be an issue if the principal and the agent had the same objective function. Crucial to the agency cost arising under moral hazard is the *conflict* between the principal and the agent over which action should be carried out. The nonobservability of the agent's action may then prevent an efficient resolution of this conflict of interest, because no enforceable contract can ever stipulate which action should be taken by the agent.

As in the case of adverse selection, asymmetric information also plays a crucial role in the design of the optimal incentive contract under moral hazard. However, instead of being an exogenous uncertainty for the principal, uncertainty is now endogenous. The probabilities of the different states of nature, and thus the expected volume of trade, now depend explicitly on the agent's effort. In other words, the realized production level is only a noisy signal of the agent's action. This uncertainty is key to understanding the contractual problem under moral hazard. If the mapping between effort and performance were completely deterministic, the principal and the court of law would have no difficulty in inferring the agent's effort from the observed output. Even if the agent's effort was not observable directly, it could be indirectly contracted upon, since output would itself be observable and verifiable. The nonobservability of the effort would not put any real constraint on the principal's ability to contract with the agent, and their conflict of interests would be costless to solve.

In a moral hazard context, the random output aggregates the agent's effort and the realization of pure luck. However, the principal can only design a contract based on the agent's observable performance. Through this contract the principal wants to induce, at a reasonable cost, a high effort from the agent despite the impossibility of directly conditioning the agent's reward on his action. In general, the nonobservability of the agent's effort affects the cost of implementing a given action. To illustrate this point we present a simple 2×2 model, where a risk-averse agent can choose a binary effort and the production level can be either high or low. A first step of the analysis in this chapter is to study the properties of incentive schemes that induce a positive and costly effort. Such schemes must thus satisfy an *incentive constraint*. Also, inducing the agent's voluntary participation imposes a standard *participation constraint*. *Incentive feasible contracts* are those satisfying those two constraints. Among such schemes, the principal prefers the one that implements the positive level of effort *at minimal cost*. This cost minimization yields the characterization of the second-best cost of implementing this effort. In general, this second-best cost is *greater* than the first-best cost that would be obtained by assuming that effort is observable. The reason is that the incentive constraint is generally binding for the incentive scheme implementing a positive effort at minimal cost.

Once this first step of the analysis is performed, we can characterize the second-best effort chosen by the principal. This second-best effort trades off the principal's benefit of inducing a given effort against the second-best cost of implementing this effort, The main lesson of this second step of the analysis is that the second-best effort may differ from the first-best one. An allocative inefficiency emerges as the result of the conflict of interests between the principal and the agent.

Let us now see in more detail the terms of the moral hazard trade-offs. When the agent is risk neutral, the nonobservability of effort has no effect on the efficiency of trade. Moral hazard does not create any transaction cost. The principal can achieve the same utility level as if he could directly control the agent's effort. This first-best outcome is obtained through a contract that is contingent on the level of production. The agent is "incentivized" by being rewarded for good production levels and penalized otherwise. Since the agent is risk neutral, he is ready to accept penalties and rewards as long as the expected payment he receives satisfies his *ex ante* participation constraint. Transfers can be structured to make the agent's participation constraint binding while inducing the desirable effort level. One way of doing so is to make the agent *residual claimant* for the gains from trade and to grasp all these expected gains by means of an *ex ante* lump-sum transfer.

If the risk-neutral agent has no wealth and cannot be punished, a new limited liability constraint must be satisfied on top of the usual incentive and participation constraints. In this case there is a conflict between the limited liability and the incentive constraints. Indeed, punishment being now infeasible, the principal is restricted to use only rewards to induce effort. This restriction of the principal's instruments implies that he must give up some *ex ante* rent to the agent. This *limited liability rent* is costly for the principal, who then distorts the second-best effort level below its first-best value to reduce the cost of this rent. As in the case of adverse selection and the interim participation constraints of chapter 2, we have a similar rent extraction-efficiency trade-off leading to a downward distortion in the expected volume of trade.

If the agent is risk averse, a constant wage provides full insurance but induces no effort provision. Inducing effort requires the principal to let the agent bear some risk. To accept such a risky contract, the agent must receive a risk premium. There is now a conflict between the incentive and the participation constraints of the agent. This leads to an *insurance-efficiency trade-off*. To solve this trade-off the principal must distort the complete information risk-sharing agreement between him and the agent to induce effort provision. As we will see in chapter 5, there is no general lesson on how the second-best and the first-best efforts can be compared in a moral hazard environment. However, in the model presented in this chapter, which involves two levels of effort, one can still easily show that a high effort is less often implemented by the principal than under complete information.

In section 4.1 we present the general moral hazard model highlighting the stochastic nature of the production process in a 2×2 (i.e., two-effort/two-outcome) setting. We also describe the set of *incentive feasible contracts* that induce a high level of effort, and we derive the first-best decision rule as a benchmark. In section 4.2, we show that moral hazard imposes no real transaction cost on the efficiency of contracting when the agent is risk neutral. Section 4.3 focuses on the trade-off between extraction of the limited liability rent and allocative efficiency under risk neutrality. Section 4.4 deals with the trade-off between insurance and efficiency under risk aversion. These latter two sections are the core of the chapter. We then extend the basic framework to provide various comparative statics results on the optimal contract. In section 4.5, we generalize our previous insights to the case of more than two levels of performance. This extension is worth pursuing to analyze the conditions on the information structures that ensure the monotonicity of the agent's compensation schedule in the observed performance. In section 4.6, we investigate the properties of various information systems from an agency point of view. Here we prove an important property: any signal that informs the principal of the agent's effort should be included as an argument of his compensation payment. Section 4.7 proposes a brief overview of the insights obtained from the moral hazard paradigm to understand the theory of the firm. Section 4.8 develops a number of bare-bones examples where the moral hazard paradigm has proved to be extremely useful. Finally, section 4.9 briefly discusses the assumption of commitment.

4.1 The Model

4.1.1 Effort and Production

We consider an agent who can exert a costly effort e. Two possible values can be taken by e, which we normalize as a zero effort level and a positive effort of one:

e in $\{0, 1\}$. Exerting effort e implies a disutility for the agent that is equal to $\psi(e)$ with the normalizations $\psi(0) = \psi_0 = 0$ and $\psi(1) = \psi_1 = \psi$.

The agent receives a transfer t from the principal. We assume that his utility function is separable between money and effort,[2] $U = u(t) - \psi(e)$, with $u(\cdot)$ increasing and concave ($u' > 0$, $u'' < 0$) and normalized so that $u(0) = 0$. Sometimes we will use the function $h = u^{-1}$, the inverse function of $u(\cdot)$, which is increasing and convex ($h' > 0$, $h'' > 0$).

Production is stochastic, and effort affects the production level as follows: the stochastic production level $\tilde{q}$ can only take two values $\{\underline{q}, \bar{q}\}$, with $\bar{q} - \underline{q} = \Delta q > 0$, and the stochastic influence of effort on production is characterized by the probabilities $\Pr(\tilde{q} = \bar{q}|e = 0) = \pi_0$, and $\Pr(\tilde{q} = \bar{q}|e = 1) = \pi_1$, with $\pi_1 > \pi_0$. We will denote the difference between these two probabilities by $\Delta\pi = \pi_1 - \pi_0$.

Note that effort improves production in the sense of *first-order stochastic dominance*, i.e., $\Pr(\tilde{q} \leq q^*|e)$ is decreasing with e for any given production q^*. Indeed, we have $\Pr(\tilde{q} \leq \underline{q}|e = 1) = 1 - \pi_1 < 1 - \pi_0 = \Pr(\tilde{q} \leq \underline{q}|e = 0)$, and $\Pr(\tilde{q} \leq \bar{q}|e = 1) = 1 = \Pr(\tilde{q} \leq \bar{q}|e = 0)$. This property implies that any principal who has a utility function $v(\cdot)$ that is increasing in production prefers the stochastic distribution of production induced by the positive effort level $e = 1$ to that induced by the null effort level $e = 0$. Indeed, we have $\pi_1 v(\bar{q}) + (1 - \pi_1)v(\underline{q}) = \pi_0 v(\bar{q}) + (1 - \pi_0)v(\underline{q}) + (\pi_1 - \pi_0)(v(\bar{q}) - v(\underline{q}))$, which is greater than $\pi_0 v(\bar{q}) + (1 - \pi_0)v(\underline{q})$ if $v(\cdot)$ is increasing. An increase in effort improves production in a strong sense in this model with two possible levels of performance.

4.1.2 Incentive Feasible Contracts

Mimicking what we did in chapters 2 and 3, we start by describing incentive feasible contracts in a moral hazard environment. In such an environment, the agent's action is not directly observable by the principal. The principal can only offer a contract based on the observable and verifiable production level, i.e., a function $\{t(\tilde{q})\}$ linking the agent's compensation to the random output $\tilde{q}$. With two possible outcomes $\bar{q}$ and $\underline{q}$, the contract can be defined equivalently by a pair of transfers $\bar{t}$ and $\underline{t}$. Transfer $\bar{t}$ (resp. $\underline{t}$) is the payment received by the agent if the production $\bar{q}$ (resp. $\underline{q}$) is realized. Keeping the same notations as in chapter 2, the

---

[2]This assumption facilitates notations and is irrelevant in this chapter. See chapter 5 for the case of nonseparability and its possible impact on the main features of the optimal contract.

risk-neutral[3] principal's expected utility is now written as

$$V_1 = \pi_1(S(\bar{q}) - \bar{t}) + (1 - \pi_1)(S(\underline{q}) - \underline{t}) \tag{4.1}$$

if the agent makes a positive effort ($e = 1$), and

$$V_0 = \pi_0(S(\bar{q}) - \bar{t}) + (1 - \pi_0)(S(\underline{q}) - \underline{t}) \tag{4.2}$$

if the agent makes no effort ($e = 0$). For notational simplicity, throughout this chapter we will denote the principal's benefits in each state of nature by $S(\bar{q}) = \bar{S}$ and $S(\underline{q}) = \underline{S}$.

The problem of the principal is now to decide whether to induce the agent to exert effort or not and, if he chooses to do so, then to decide which incentive contract should be used.

Each level of effort that the principal wishes to induce corresponds to a set of contracts ensuring participation and incentive compatibility. In our model with two possible levels of effort, we will say that a contract is *incentive feasible* if it induces a positive effort and ensures the agent's participation. The corresponding *moral hazard incentive constraint* is thus written as

$$\pi_1 u(\bar{t}) + (1 - \pi_1)u(\underline{t}) - \psi \geq \pi_0 u(\bar{t}) + (1 - \pi_0)u(\underline{t}). \tag{4.3}$$

(4.3) is the incentive constraint that imposes upon the agent to prefer to exert a positive effort. If he exerts effort, the agent faces the lottery that gives $\bar{t}$ (resp. $\underline{t}$) with probability π_1 (resp. $1 - \pi_1$) and not the lottery that yields $\bar{t}$ (resp. $\underline{t}$) with probability π_0 (resp. $1 - \pi_0$). However, when he does not exert effort, the agent incurs no disutility of effort and saves an amount ψ.

Still normalizing the agent's reservation utility at zero, the agent's participation constraint is now written as

$$\pi_1 u(\bar{t}) + (1 - \pi_1)u(\underline{t}) - \psi \geq 0. \tag{4.4}$$

(4.4) is the agent's participation constraint that ensures that if the agent exerts effort, it will yield at least his outside opportunity utility level. Note that this participation constraint is ensured at the *ex ante* stage, i.e., before the realization of the production shock.[4]

---

[3]We will restrict our analysis to risk-neutral principals. The risk aversion of the principal creates a different benchmark for the complete information case in which the principal and the agent share risk rather than having the principal insure completely the agent. With moral hazard most results we provide can be extended at the cost of greater complexity.

[4]See section 2.11 for a similar timing in the case of *ex ante* contracting under adverse selection.

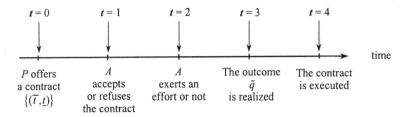

FIGURE 4.1: Timing of Contracting Under Moral Hazard

Definition 4.1: *An incentive feasible contract satisfies the incentive and participation constraints (4.3) and (4.4).*

The timing of the contracting game under moral hazard is summarized in figure 4.1.

4.1.3 The Complete Information Optimal Contract

As a benchmark, let us first assume that the principal and a benevolent court of law can both observe effort. This variable is now *verifiable* and can thus be included into a contract enforced by the court of law. Then, if he wants to induce effort, the principal's problem becomes

(P): $$\max_{\{(\bar{t}, \underline{t})\}} \pi_1(\bar{S} - \bar{t}) + (1 - \pi_1)(\underline{S} - \underline{t})$$

subject to (4.4).

Indeed, only the agent's participation constraint matters for the principal, because the agent can be forced to exert a positive level of effort. If the agent were not choosing this level of effort, his deviation could be perfectly detected by both the principal and the court of law. The agent could be heavily punished, and the court could commit to enforce such a punishment.

Denoting the multiplier of this participation constraint by μ and optimizing with respect to $\bar{t}$ and $\underline{t}$ yields, respectively, the following first-order conditions:

$$-\pi_1 + \mu\pi_1 u'(\bar{t}^*) = 0, \tag{4.5}$$

$$-(1 - \pi_1) + \mu(1 - \pi_1)u'(\underline{t}^*) = 0, \tag{4.6}$$

where $\bar{t}^*$ and $\underline{t}^*$ are the first-best transfers.

From (4.5) and (4.6) we immediately derive that $\mu = \frac{1}{u'(\underline{t}^*)} = \frac{1}{u'(\bar{t}^*)} > 0$, and finally that $\underline{t}^* = \bar{t}^* = t^*$.

With a verifiable effort, the agent obtains *full insurance* from the risk-neutral principal, and the transfer t^* he receives is the same whatever the state of nature. Because the participation constraint is binding we also obtain the value of this transfer, which is just enough to cover the disutility of effort, namely $t^* = h(\psi)$. This is also the expected payment made by the principal to the agent, or the *first-best cost* C^{FB} of implementing the positive effort level. For the principal, inducing effort yields an expected payoff equal to

$$V_1 = \pi_1 \overline{S} + (1 - \pi_1)\underline{S} - h(\psi). \tag{4.7}$$

Had the principal decided to let the agent exert no effort, $e = 0$, he would make a zero payment to the agent whatever the realization of output. In this scenario, the principal would instead obtain a payoff equal to

$$V_0 = \pi_0 \overline{S} + (1 - \pi_0)\underline{S}. \tag{4.8}$$

Inducing effort is thus optimal from the principal's point of view when $V_1 \geq V_0$, i.e., $\pi_1 \overline{S} + (1 - \pi_1)\underline{S} - h(\psi) \geq \pi_0 \overline{S} + (1 - \pi_0)\underline{S}$, or to put it differently, when

$$\underbrace{\Delta\pi\Delta S}_{\substack{\text{Expected} \\ \text{gain} \\ \text{of effort}}} \geq \underbrace{h(\psi)}_{\substack{\text{First-best cost} \\ \text{of inducing} \\ \text{effort}}}, \tag{4.9}$$

where $\Delta S = \overline{S} - \underline{S} > 0$.

The left-hand side of (4.9) captures the gain of increasing effort from $e = 0$ to $e = 1$. This gain comes from the fact that the return $\overline{S}$, which is greater than $\underline{S}$, arises more often when a positive effort is exerted. The right-hand side of (4.9) is instead the first-best cost of inducing the agent's acceptance when he exerts a positive effort.

Denoting the benefit of inducing a strictly positive effort level by $B = \Delta\pi\Delta S$, the first-best outcome calls for $e^* = 1$ if and only if $B \geq h(\psi)$, as shown in figure 4.2.

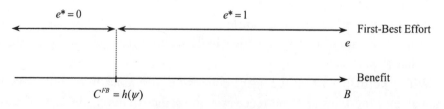

FIGURE 4.2: First-Best Level of Effort

4.2 Risk Neutrality and First-Best Implementation

If the agent is risk-neutral, we can assume that (up to an affine transformation) $u(t) = t$ for all t and $h(u) = u$ for all u. The principal who wants to induce effort must thus choose the contract that solves the following problem:

(P):
$$\max_{\{(\bar{t}, \underline{t})\}} \pi_1(\overline{S} - \bar{t}) + (1 - \pi_1)(\underline{S} - \underline{t})$$

$$\pi_1 \bar{t} + (1 - \pi_1)\underline{t} - \psi \geq \pi_0 \bar{t} + (1 - \pi_0)\underline{t} \qquad (4.10)$$

$$\pi_1 \bar{t} + (1 - \pi_1)\underline{t} - \psi \geq 0. \qquad (4.11)$$

With risk neutrality the principal can, for instance, choose incentive compatible transfers $\bar{t}$ and $\underline{t}$, which make the agent's participation constraint binding and leave no rent to the agent. Indeed, solving (4.10) and (4.11) with equalities, we immediately obtain

$$\underline{t}^* = -\frac{\pi_0}{\Delta\pi}\psi \qquad (4.12)$$

and

$$\bar{t}^* = \frac{1 - \pi_0}{\Delta\pi}\psi. \qquad (4.13)$$

The agent is rewarded if production is high. His net utility in this state of nature $\overline{U}^* = \bar{t}^* - \psi$ is $\overline{U}^* = \frac{1-\pi_1}{\Delta\pi}\psi > 0$. Conversely, the agent is punished if production is low. His corresponding net utility $\underline{U}^* = \underline{t}^* - \psi$ is $\underline{U}^* = -\frac{\pi_1}{\Delta\pi}\psi < 0$.

The principal (who is risk-neutral with respect to transfers) makes an expected payment $\pi_1 \bar{t}^* + (1 - \pi_1)\underline{t}^* = \psi$, which is equal to the disutility of effort he would incur if he could control the effort level perfectly or if he was carrying the agent's task himself. The principal can costlessly structure the agent's payment so that the latter has the right incentives to exert effort. Indeed, by increasing effort from $e = 0$ to $e = 1$, the agent receives the transfer $\bar{t}^*$ more often than the transfer $\underline{t}^*$. Using (4.12) and (4.13), his expected gain from exerting effort is thus $\Delta\pi(\bar{t}^* - \underline{t}^*) = \psi$, i.e., it exactly compensates the agent for the extra disutility of effort that he incurs when increasing his effort from $e = 0$ to $e = 1$.

Here delegation is *costless* to the principal. Therefore, if effort is socially valuable in the first-best world, it will also be implemented by the principal with the incentive scheme $\{(\bar{t}^*, \underline{t}^*)\}$ when effort is no longer observed by the principal and the agent is risk-neutral. Proposition 4.1 summarizes this result.

Proposition 4.1: *Moral hazard is not an issue with a risk-neutral agent despite the nonobservability of effort. The first-best level of effort is still implemented.*

> **Remark 1:** The reader will have recognized the similarity of these results with those described in section 2.11. In both cases, when contracting takes place *ex ante*, i.e., before the realization of the state of nature, the incentive constraint, under either adverse selection or moral hazard, does not conflict with the *ex ante* participation constraint with a risk-neutral agent, and the first-best outcome is still implemented. ∎

> **Remark 2:** The transfers $(\bar{t}^*, \underline{t}^*)$ defined in (4.12) and (4.13) yield only one possible implementation of the first-best outcome, an implementation such that the incentive constraint (4.10) is exactly binding. Other pairs of transfers can be used, which may induce a strict preference of the agent for exerting effort. Let us consider the following transfers $\bar{t}^{*'} = \overline{S} - T^*$ and $\underline{t}^{*'} = \underline{S} - T^*$, where T^* is an up-front payment made by the agent before output realizes. These transfers satisfy the agent's incentive constraint since:
>
> $$\Delta\pi(\bar{t}^{*'} - \underline{t}^{*'}) = \Delta\pi\Delta S > h(\psi) = \psi, \qquad (4.14)$$

where the inequality comes from the fact that effort is socially optimal in a first-best world. Moreover, the up-front payment T^* can be adjusted by the principal to have the agent's participation constraint be binding. The corresponding value of this transfer is $T^* = \pi_1\overline{S} + (1 - \pi_1)\underline{S} - \psi$. With the transfers $\bar{t}^{*'}$ and $\underline{t}^{*'}$ above, the agent becomes residual claimant for the profit of the firm. The up-front payment T^* is thus precisely equal to this expected profit. The principal chooses this *ex ante* payment to reap all gains from delegation.

Making the risk-neutral agent residual claimant for the hierarchy's profit is an optimal response to the moral hazard problem. In other words, the principal then sells the property rights over the firm to the agent. Indeed, a proper allocation of property rights is sufficient to induce efficiency.[5] ∎

---

[5] See Tirole (1999) for a more general discussion that demonstrates how a proper allocation of property rights implements the optimal contract. See also section 5.2.5.

On the contrary, inefficiencies in effort provision due to moral hazard will arise when the agent is no longer risk-neutral. There are two alternative ways to model these transaction costs. One is to maintain risk neutrality for positive income levels but to impose a limited liability constraint, which requires transfers not to be too negative. The other is to let the agent be strictly *risk-averse*. In sections 4.3 and 4.4 we analyze these two contractual environments and the different trade-offs they imply.

4.3 The Trade-Off Between Limited Liability Rent Extraction and Efficiency

Let us consider a risk-neutral agent. As we have already seen, (4.3) and (4.4) now take the following forms:

$$\pi_1 \bar{t} + (1 - \pi_1)\underline{t} - \psi \geq \pi_0 \bar{t} + (1 - \pi_0)\underline{t} \tag{4.15}$$

and

$$\pi_1 \bar{t} + (1 - \pi_1)\underline{t} - \psi \geq 0. \tag{4.16}$$

Let us also assume that the agent's transfer must always be greater than some exogenous level $-l$, with $l \geq 0$. The framework is quite similar to that of section 3.5, and we refer the reader to that section for some motivations and discussions of the origins of such limited liability constraints on transfers. Limited liability constraints in both states of nature are thus written as

$$\bar{t} \geq -l \tag{4.17}$$

and

$$\underline{t} \geq -l. \tag{4.18}$$

These constraints obviously reduce the set of incentive feasible allocations and may prevent the principal from implementing the first-best level of effort even if the agent is risk-neutral. Indeed, when he wants to induce a high effort, the principal's program is written as

$(P):$ $\qquad \displaystyle\max_{\{(\bar{t},\,\underline{t})\}} \pi_1(\bar{S} - \bar{t}) + (1 - \pi_1)(\underline{S} - \underline{t})$

$\qquad\qquad$ subject to (4.15) to (4.18).

A first observation is that the transfers (4.12) and (4.13), allowing the implementation of the first-best, may not satisfy the newly added limited liability constraints. Proposition 4.2 summarizes the solution to (P).[6]

Proposition 4.2: *With limited liability, the optimal contract inducing effort from the agent entails:*

- *For $l > \frac{\pi_0}{\Delta\pi}\psi$, only (4.15) and (4.16) are binding. Optimal transfers are given by (4.12) and (4.13). The agent has no expected limited liability rent; $EU^{SB} = 0$.*
- *For $0 \leq l \leq \frac{\pi_0}{\Delta\pi}\psi$, (4.15) and (4.18) are binding. Optimal transfers are then given by:*

$$\underline{t}^{SB} = -l, \tag{4.19}$$

$$\bar{t}^{SB} = -l + \frac{\psi}{\Delta\pi}. \tag{4.20}$$

Moreover, the agent's expected limited liability rent EU^{SB} is non-negative:

$$EU^{SB} = \pi_1\bar{t}^{SB} + (1 - \pi_1)\underline{t}^{SB} - \psi = -l + \frac{\pi_0}{\Delta\pi}\psi \geq 0. \tag{4.21}$$

First, we note that only the limited liability constraint in the bad state of nature may be binding. Indeed, since inducing effort requires the creation of a positive wedge between $\bar{t}$ and $\underline{t}$, (4.18) necessarily implies (4.17). When the limited liability constraint (4.18) is binding, the principal is limited in his punishments to induce effort. The risk-neutral agent does not have enough assets to cover the punishment requested by the principal if $\underline{q}$ is realized in order to induce effort provision. The principal uses rewards when a good state of nature $\bar{q}$ is realized. As a result, the agent receives a non-negative *ex ante* limited liability rent described by (4.21). Compared with the case without limited liability, this rent is actually the additional payment that the principal must incur because of the conjunction of moral hazard and limited liability.

As the agent is endowed with more assets, i.e., as l gets larger, the conflict between moral hazard and limited liability diminishes and then disappears whenever l is large enough. In this case, the agent avoids bankruptcy even when he has to pay the optimal penalty to the principal in the bad state of nature.

Let us now assume that $l = 0$ so that only non-negative transfers are feasible. Therefore, we model a contractual environment in which the agent owns no asset

---

[6]The proof is in appendix 4.1.

at the time of starting the relationship with the principal. When the principal induces effort from the agent, the principal's expected utility can be computed as

$$V_1^{SB} = \pi_1 \overline{S} + (1 - \pi_1)\underline{S} - \frac{\pi_1 \psi}{\Delta \pi}. \tag{4.22}$$

If the principal gives up the goal of inducing effort from the agent, he can choose $\underline{t} = \overline{t} = 0$ and instead obtain the expected utility level (4.8). It is worth inducing effort if V_1^{SB} is greater than V_0, i.e., when

$$\Delta \pi \Delta S \geq \frac{\pi_1 \psi}{\Delta \pi} = \psi + \frac{\pi_0 \psi}{\Delta \pi}. \tag{4.23}$$

The left-hand side of (4.23) is the gain of inducing effort, i.e., the gain of increasing the probability of a high production level. The right-hand side is instead the *second-best cost* C^{SB} of inducing effort, which is the disutility of effort ψ plus the limited liability rent $\frac{\pi_0 \psi}{\Delta \pi}$. This second-best cost of implementing effort obviously exceeds the first-best cost. As it can easily been seen by comparing (4.23) and the right-hand side of (4.9) (taken for the case of risk neutrality, i.e., for $h(\psi) = \psi$), limited liability and moral hazard together make it more costly to induce effort.

Figure 4.3 describes the reduced subset of values of B, justifying a high effort from the agent when limited liability and moral hazard interact.

Moral hazard justifies an underprovision of effort when the benefit $B = \Delta \pi \Delta S$ of a strictly positive effort lies between ψ and $\frac{\pi_1}{\Delta \pi}\psi$. Our analysis is summarized in proposition 4.3.

Proposition 4.3: *With moral hazard and limited liability, there is a trade-off between inducing effort and giving up an* ex ante *limited liability rent to the agent. The principal chooses to induce a high effort from the agent less often.*

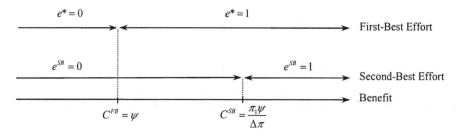

FIGURE 4.3: First-Best and Second-Best Efforts with Moral Hazard and Limited Liability

4.4 The Trade-Off Between Insurance and Efficiency

Let us now turn to the second source of inefficiency in a moral hazard context—the agent's risk aversion. When the agent is risk-averse, the principal's program is written as:

(P):
$$\max_{\{(\bar{t},\, \underline{t})\}} \pi_1(\bar{S} - \bar{t}) + (1 - \pi_1)(\underline{S} - \underline{t})$$
subject to (4.3) and (4.4).

It is not obvious that (P) is a concave program for which the first-order Kuhn and Tucker conditions are necessary and sufficient. The reason for this possible lack of concavity is that the concave function $u(\cdot)$ appears on both sides of the incentive compatibility constraint (4.3). However, the following change of variables shows that concavity of the program is ensured. Let us define $\bar{u} = u(\bar{t})$ and $\underline{u} = u(\underline{t})$, or equivalently let $\bar{t} = h(\bar{u})$ and $\underline{t} = h(\underline{u})$. These new variables are the levels of *ex post* utility obtained by the agent in both states of nature. The set of incentive feasible contracts can now be described by two *linear* constraints:

$$\pi_1\bar{u} + (1 - \pi_1)\underline{u} - \psi \geq \pi_0\bar{u} + (1 - \pi_0)\underline{u}, \tag{4.24}$$

which replaces the incentive constraint (4.3), and also

$$\pi_1\bar{u} + (1 - \pi_1)\underline{u} - \psi \geq 0, \tag{4.25}$$

which replaces the participation constraint (4.4).

Program (P) can now be replaced by the new program (P'), which writes as

(P'):
$$\max_{\{(\bar{u},\, \underline{u})\}} \pi_1(\bar{S} - h(\bar{u})) + (1 - \pi_1)(\underline{S} - h(\underline{u}))$$
subject to (4.24) and (4.25).

Note that the principal's objective function is now strictly concave in $(\bar{u}, \underline{u})$ because $h(\cdot)$ is strictly convex. The constraints are now linear and the interior of the constrained set is obviously nonempty, and therefore (P') is a concave problem, with the Kuhn and Tucker conditions being sufficient and necessary for characterizing optimality.

4.4.1 Optimal Transfers

Letting λ and μ be the non-negative multipliers associated respectively with the constraints (4.24) and (4.25), the first-order conditions of this program can be expressed as

$$-\pi_1 h'(\bar{u}^{SB}) + \lambda \Delta \pi + \mu \pi_1 = -\frac{\pi_1}{u'(\bar{t}^{SB})} + \lambda \Delta \pi + \mu \pi_1 = 0, \quad (4.26)$$

$$-(1-\pi_1)h'(\underline{u}^{SB}) - \lambda \Delta \pi + \mu(1-\pi_1) = -\frac{(1-\pi_1)}{u'(\underline{t}^{SB})} - \lambda \Delta \pi + \mu(1-\pi_1) = 0, \quad (4.27)$$

where $\bar{t}^{SB}$ and $\underline{t}^{SB}$ are the second-best optimal transfers. Rearranging terms, we get

$$\frac{1}{u'(\bar{t}^{SB})} = \mu + \lambda \frac{\Delta \pi}{\pi_1}, \quad (4.28)$$

$$\frac{1}{u'(\underline{t}^{SB})} = \mu - \lambda \frac{\Delta \pi}{1-\pi_1}. \quad (4.29)$$

The four variables $(\underline{t}^{SB}, \bar{t}^{SB}, \lambda, \mu)$ are simultaneously obtained as the solutions to the system of four equations (4.24), (4.25), (4.28), and (4.29). Multiplying (4.28) by π_1 and (4.29) by $1 - \pi_1$, and then adding those two modified equations, we obtain

$$\mu = \frac{\pi_1}{u'(\bar{t}^{SB})} + \frac{1-\pi_1}{u'(\underline{t}^{SB})} > 0. \quad (4.30)$$

Hence, the participation constraint (4.25) is necessarily binding.
Using (4.30) and (4.28), we also obtain

$$\lambda = \frac{\pi_1(1-\pi_1)}{\Delta \pi} \left(\frac{1}{u'(\bar{t}^{SB})} - \frac{1}{u'(\underline{t}^{SB})} \right), \quad (4.31)$$

where λ must also be strictly positive. Indeed, from (4.24) we have $\bar{u}^{SB} - \underline{u}^{SB} \geq \frac{\psi}{\Delta \pi} > 0$ and thus $\bar{t}^{SB} > \underline{t}^{SB}$, implying that the right-hand side of (4.31) is strictly positive since $u'' < 0$. Using that (4.24) and (4.25) are both binding, we can immediately obtain the values of $u(\bar{t}^{SB})$ and $u(\underline{t}^{SB})$ by solving a system of two equations with two unknowns.

Note that the risk-averse agent does not receive full insurance anymore. This result must be contrasted with what we have seen under complete information in section 4.1.3. Indeed, with full insurance, the incentive compatibility constraint

(4.3) can no longer be satisfied. Inducing effort requires the agent to bear some risk. Proposition 4.4 provides a summary.

Proposition 4.4: *When the agent is strictly risk-averse, the optimal contract that induces effort makes both the agent's participation and incentive constraints binding. This contract does not provide full insurance. Moreover, second-best transfers are given by*

$$\bar{t}^{SB} = h\left(\psi + (1 - \pi_1)\frac{\psi}{\Delta\pi}\right) \tag{4.32}$$

and

$$\underline{t}^{SB} = h\left(\psi - \pi_1\frac{\psi}{\Delta\pi}\right). \tag{4.33}$$

It is also worth noting that the agent receives more than the complete information transfer when a high output is realized, $\bar{t}^{SB} > h(\psi)$. When a low output is realized, the agent instead receives less than the complete information transfer, $\underline{t}^{SB} < h(\psi)$. A risk premium must be paid to the risk-averse agent to induce his participation since he now incurs a risk by the fact that $\underline{t}^{SB} < \bar{t}^{SB}$. Indeed, when (4.4) is binding we have

$$\psi = \pi_1 u(\bar{t}^{SB}) + (1 - \pi_1)u(\underline{t}^{SB}) < u\left(\pi_1\bar{t}^{SB} + (1 - \pi_1)\underline{t}^{SB}\right), \tag{4.34}$$

where the right-hand side inequality in (4.34) follows from Jensen's inequality. The expected payment $\pi_1\bar{t}^{SB} + (1 - \pi_1)\underline{t}^{SB}$ given by the principal is thus larger than the first-best cost $C^{FB} = h(\psi)$, which is incurred by the principal when effort is observable (as we have seen in section 4.1.3).

4.4.2 The Optimal Second-Best Effort

Let us now turn to the question of the second-best optimality of inducing a high effort, from the principal's point of view. The second-best cost C^{SB} of inducing effort under moral hazard is the expected payment made to the agent $C^{SB} = \pi_1\bar{t}^{SB} + (1 - \pi_1)\underline{t}^{SB}$. Using (4.32) and (4.33), this cost is rewritten as

$$C^{SB} = \pi_1 h\left(\psi + (1 - \pi_1)\frac{\psi}{\Delta\pi}\right) + (1 - \pi_1)h\left(\psi - \frac{\pi_1\psi}{\Delta\pi}\right). \tag{4.35}$$

The benefit of inducing effort is still $B = \Delta\pi\Delta S$, and a positive effort $e^* = 1$ is the optimal choice of the principal whenever

$$\Delta\pi\Delta S \geq C^{SB} = \pi_1 h\left(\psi + (1 - \pi_1)\frac{\psi}{\Delta\pi}\right) + (1 - \pi_1)h\left(\psi - \frac{\pi_1\psi}{\Delta\pi}\right). \tag{4.36}$$

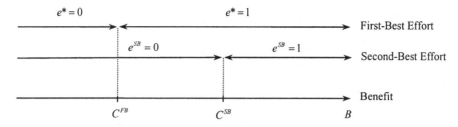

FIGURE 4.4: Second-Best Level of Effort with Moral Hazard and Risk Aversion

With $h(\cdot)$ being strictly convex, Jensen's inequality implies that the right-hand side of (4.36) is strictly greater than the first-best cost of implementing effort $C^{FB} = h(\psi)$. Therefore, inducing a higher effort occurs less often with moral hazard than when effort is observable. Figure 4.4 represents this phenomenon graphically.

For B belonging to the interval $[C^{FB}, C^{SB}]$, the second-best level of effort is zero and is thus strictly below its first-best value. There is now an under-provision of effort because of moral hazard and risk aversion.

Proposition 4.5: *With moral hazard and risk aversion, there is a trade-off between inducing effort and providing insurance to the agent. In a model with two possible levels of effort, the principal induces a positive effort from the agent less often than when effort is observable.*

In order to get further insights on the dependency of the second-best cost of implementation on various parameters, we can specialize the model and assume that $h(u) = u + \frac{ru^2}{2}$, where $r > 0$ and $u \geq -\frac{1}{r}$.[7] Equivalently, $u(x) = \frac{-1+\sqrt{1+2rx}}{r}$ for $x \geq -\frac{1}{2r}$. For this quadratic expression of $h(\cdot)$, we have

$$C^{SB} = E\left(\tilde{u}^{SB} + \frac{r}{2}(\tilde{u}^{SB})^2 \right), \tag{4.37}$$

where $E(\cdot)$ denotes the expectation operator and $\tilde{u}^{SB}$ is the random utility level that the agent gets in the different states of nature. More precisely, we have

$$C^{SB} = E(\tilde{u}^{SB}) + \frac{r}{2}(E(\tilde{u}^{SB}))^2 + \frac{r}{2}\,\mathrm{var}(\tilde{u}^{SB}), \tag{4.38}$$

taking into account that (4.25) is binding at the optimal contract $E(\tilde{u}^{SB}) = \pi_1 \bar{u}^{SB} + (1 - \pi_1)\underline{u}^{SB} = \psi$. Moreover,

$$\bar{u}^{SB} = \psi + \frac{(1 - \pi_1)\psi}{\Delta \pi} \tag{4.39}$$

---

[7]This quadratic specification can be viewed as an approximation of any inverse function $h(u)$ whenever u is small enough. Note that r can then be considered as the agent's degree of absolute risk aversion at zero, $\frac{-u''(x)}{u'(x)}\big|_{x=0} = r$.

and

$$\underline{u}^{SB} = \psi - \frac{\pi_1 \psi}{\Delta \pi}.$$ (4.40)

The agent receives a premium of $\frac{(1-\pi_1)\psi}{\Delta\pi}$ (in utility terms) when production is high and suffers a penalty $\frac{\pi_1\psi}{\Delta\pi}$ (in utility terms) when production is low. This risky payoff has a variance $\text{var}(\tilde{u}^{SB}) = \frac{\pi_1(1-\pi_1)\psi^2}{(\Delta\pi)^2}$.

Gathering everything, we finally have the following expression of C^{SB}:

$$C^{SB} = \psi + \frac{r\psi^2}{2} + \frac{r\psi^2 \pi_1(1-\pi_1)}{2(\Delta\pi)^2}.$$ (4.41)

The first-best cost of implementing effort with such a utility function would instead be

$$C^{FB} = \psi + \frac{r\psi^2}{2}.$$ (4.42)

Hence, the agency cost AC, which is also the principal's loss between his first-best and second-best expected profit when he implements a positive effort, can be defined as

$$AC = C^{SB} - C^{FB} = \frac{r\psi^2 \pi_1(1-\pi_1)}{2(\Delta\pi)^2}.$$ (4.43)

This agency cost increases with r, a measure of the agent's degree of risk aversion, with ψ, the cost of one unit of effort, and with $\eta = \frac{\pi_1(1-\pi_1)}{(\Delta\pi)^2}$, which is a measure of the informational problem for the principal. Everything else being kept equal, it becomes harder and less often optimal for the principal to induce a high effort as η increases. When π_1 is close to $\frac{1}{2}$, η is larger. In this case, the variance of the measured performance $\tilde{q}$ is the greatest possible one: the observable output is a rather poor indicator of the agent's effort. Therefore, more noisy measures of the agent's effort will more often call for inducing a low effort at the optimum and for a fixed wage without any incentives being provided. Finally, note that η is also larger when $\Delta\pi$ is small, i.e., when the difference in utilities $u(\bar{t}^{SB}) - u(\underline{t}^{SB})$ necessary to incentivize the agent gets larger. More generally, the agency cost's dependence on η shows that the informational content of the observable output plays a crucial role in the design of the optimal contract. This is a general theme of agency theory that we will cover more extensively in section 4.6.

4.5 More than Two Levels of Performance

We now extend our previous 2×2 model to allow for more than two levels of performance.[8] We consider a production process where n possible outcomes can be realized. Those performances can be ordered so that $q_1 < q_2 < \cdots < q_i < \cdots < q_n$. We denote the principal's return in each of those states of nature by $S_i = S(q_i)$. In this context, a contract is a n-uple of payments $\{(t_1, \ldots, t_n)\}$. Also, let π_{ik} be the probability that production q_i takes place when the effort level is e_k. We assume that $\pi_{ik} > 0$ for all pairs[9] (i, k) with $\sum_{i=1}^{n} \pi_{ik} = 1$. Finally, we keep the assumption that only two levels of effort are feasible, i.e., e_k in $\{0, 1\}$. We still denote $\Delta \pi_i = \pi_{i1} - \pi_{i0}$.

4.5.1 Limited Liability

Consider first the limited liability model of section 4.4. If the optimal contract induces a positive effort, it solves the following program:

$$(P): \qquad \max_{\{(t_1, \ldots, t_n)\}} \sum_{i=1}^{n} \pi_{i1}(S_i - t_i),$$

subject to

$$\sum_{i=1}^{n} \pi_{i1} t_i - \psi \geq 0, \tag{4.44}$$

$$\sum_{i=1}^{n} (\pi_{i1} - \pi_{i0}) t_i \geq \psi, \tag{4.45}$$

$$t_i \geq 0, \qquad \text{for all } i \text{ in } \{1, \ldots, n\}. \tag{4.46}$$

(4.44) is the agent's participation constraint. (4.45) is his incentive constraint. (4.46) are all the limited liability constraints that we simplify, with respect to section 4.3, by assuming that the agent cannot be given a negative payment. i.e., the agent has no asset of his own before starting the relationship with the principal.

---

[8]See appendix 4.2 for the case of a continuum of performances.
[9]Mirrlees (1975) has shown that if the support of probabilities varies with the level of effort, then the first-best can be achieved. This is because there is a nonzero probability that the agent's performance reveals that he has not taken the postulated effort level, and he can be punished strongly in that case.

First, note that the participation constraint (4.44) is implied by the incentive (4.45) and the limited liability (4.46) constraints. Indeed, we have

$$\sum_{i=1}^{n} \pi_{i1} t_i - \psi \geq \underbrace{\sum_{i=1}^{n} (\pi_{i1} - \pi_{i0}) t_i - \psi}_{\geq 0 \ \text{from (4.45)}} + \underbrace{\sum_{i=1}^{n} \pi_{i0} t_i}_{\geq 0 \ \text{from (4.46)}} .$$

Hence, we can neglect the participation constraint (4.44) in the optimization of problem (P).

Denoting the multiplier of (4.45) by λ and the respective multipliers of (4.46), by ξ_i the first-order conditions of program (P) lead to

$$-\pi_{i1} + \lambda \Delta \pi_i + \xi_i = 0, \tag{4.47}$$

with the slackness conditions $\xi_i t_i = 0$ for each i in $\{1, \ldots, n\}$.

For i such that the second-best transfer t_i^{SB} is strictly positive, $\xi_i = 0$, and we must have $\lambda = \frac{\pi_{i1}}{\pi_{i1} - \pi_{i0}}$ for any such i. If the ratios $\frac{\pi_{i1} - \pi_{i0}}{\pi_{i1}}$ are all different, there exists a single index j such that $\frac{\pi_{j1} - \pi_{j0}}{\pi_{j1}}$ is the highest possible ratio. Then, the structure of the optimal payments is *bang-bang*. The agent receives a strictly positive transfer only in this particular state of nature j, and this payment is such that the incentive constraint (4.45) is binding, i.e., $t_j^{SB} = \frac{\psi}{\pi_{j1} - \pi_{j0}}$. In all other states, the agent receives no transfer and $t_i^{SB} = 0$ for all $i \neq j$. Finally, the agent gets a strictly positive *ex ante* limited liability rent that is worth $EU^{SB} = \frac{\pi_{j0} \psi}{\pi_{j1} - \pi_{j0}}$.

The important point here is that the agent is rewarded in the state of nature that is the most informative about the fact that he has exerted a positive effort. Indeed, $\frac{\pi_{i1} - \pi_{i0}}{\pi_{i1}}$ can be interpreted as a *likelihood ratio*. The principal therefore uses a *maximum likelihood ratio criterion* to reward the agent. The agent is only rewarded when this likelihood ratio is maximum. Like an econometrician, the principal tries to infer from the observed output what has been the *parameter* (effort) underlying this distribution. But here the *parameter* is endogenous and affected by the incentive contract.[10]

Definition 4.2: *The probabilities of success satisfy the monotone likelihood ratio property[11] (MLRP) if $\frac{\pi_{i1} - \pi_{i0}}{\pi_{i1}}$ is nondecreasing in i.*

---

[10]Once he has observed that q_i has realized, the principal wants to infer the most likely effort from this sample. A statistician will infer that $e = 1$ (rather than $e = 0$) is the best estimate if the likelihood ratio $\frac{\pi_{i1}}{\pi_{i0}}$ is larger than one or if $\frac{\pi_{i1} - \pi_{i0}}{\pi_{i1}} > 0$. The linearity in transfers of the utility function leads to putting all the weight in the reward function on the state of nature that has the highest likelihood ratio.

[11]If $i = 2$, this property reduces to the assumption made in section 4.1 $\pi_1 > \pi_0$.

When this monotonicity property holds, the structure of the agent's rewards is quite intuitive and is described in proposition 4.6.[12]

Proposition 4.6: *If the probability of success satisfies MLRP, the second-best payment t_i^{SB} received by the agent may be chosen to be nondecreasing with the level of production q_i.*

To understand this result intuitively, let us consider the case of $n = 3$. Then, MLRP means

$$\frac{\pi_{11} - \pi_{10}}{\pi_{11}} \leq \frac{\pi_{21} - \pi_{20}}{\pi_{21}} \leq \frac{\pi_{31} - \pi_{30}}{\pi_{31}}. \tag{4.48}$$

Observe that MLRP is stronger than first-order stochastic dominance, which amounts here to

$$\pi_{10} \geq \pi_{11} \tag{4.49}$$

$$\pi_{10} + \pi_{20} \geq \pi_{11} + \pi_{21}. \tag{4.50}$$

Suppose (4.49) is false when MLRP holds. Then $\pi_{11} > \pi_{10}$, which implies $\pi_{21} + \pi_{31} < \pi_{20} + \pi_{30}$. Then, we necessarily have either $\pi_{21} - \pi_{20} < 0$ or $\pi_{31} - \pi_{30} < 0$, which contradicts (4.48)

Suppose (4.50) is false when MLRP holds and $\pi_{10} \geq \pi_{11}$. Then $\pi_{10} + \pi_{20} < \pi_{11} + \pi_{21}$, which implies $\pi_{30} > \pi_{31}$ and $\pi_{21} - \pi_{20} > 0$. Again, it contradicts (4.48).

First-order stochastic dominance ensures that an increase of effort is good for the principal in a very strong sense, namely that any principal with a utility function increasing in q favors a higher effort level. However, this is not enough to reward the agent with a transfer increasing in q. It must also be the case that a higher production level is clear evidence that the agent has made a higher effort. MLRP provides this additional information. As (4.48) shows, a higher effort level increases the likelihood of a high production level *more* than the likelihood of a low production level.

Innes (1990) characterizes optimal contracts in a model with a risk-neutral principal and a risk-neutral agent, both with limited liability constraints, using the first order approach described below for concave utility functions (see also Park 1995). Milgrom (1981) proposes an extensive discussion of the MLRP assumption. ∎

---

[12]See appendix 4.3 for the proof.

4.5.2 Risk Aversion

Suppose now that the agent is strictly risk-averse. The optimal contract that induces effort must solve the program below:

(P):
$$\max_{\{(t_1,\dots,t_n)\}} \sum_{i=1}^{n} \pi_{i1}(S_i - t_i),$$

subject to

$$\sum_{i=1}^{n} \pi_{i1} u(t_i) - \psi \geq \sum_{i=1}^{n} \pi_{i0} u(t_i) \tag{4.51}$$

and

$$\sum_{i=1}^{n} \pi_{i1} u(t_i) - \psi \geq 0, \tag{4.52}$$

where the latter constraint is the agent's participation constraint.

Using the same change of variables as in section 4.4, it should be clear that (P) is again a concave problem with respect to the new variables $u_i = u(t_i)$. Using the same notations as in section 4.4, the first-order conditions of program (P) are written as:

$$\frac{1}{u'(t_i^{SB})} = \mu + \lambda\left(\frac{\pi_{i1} - \pi_{i0}}{\pi_{i1}}\right) \qquad \text{for all } i \text{ in } \{1,\dots,n\}. \tag{4.53}$$

Multiplying each of these equations by π_{i1} and summing over i yields $\mu = E_q(\frac{1}{u'(t_i^{SB})}) > 0$, where $E_q(\cdot)$ denotes the expectation operator with respect to the distribution of outputs induced by effort $e = 1$.

Multiplying (4.53) by $\pi_{i1} u(t_i^{SB})$, summing all these equations over i, and taking into account the expression of μ obtained above yields

$$\lambda\left(\sum_{i=1}^{n} (\pi_{i1} - \pi_{i0}) u(t_i^{SB})\right) = E_q\left(u(\tilde{t}_i^{SB})\left(\frac{1}{u'(\tilde{t}_i^{SB})} - E\left(\frac{1}{u'(\tilde{t}_i^{SB})}\right)\right)\right). \tag{4.54}$$

Using the slackness condition $\lambda(\sum_{i=1}^{n}(\pi_{i1} - \pi_{i0})u(t_i^{SB}) - \psi) = 0$ to simplify the left-hand side of (4.54), we finally get

$$\lambda\psi = \text{cov}\left(u(\tilde{t}_i^{SB}), \frac{1}{u'(\tilde{t}_i^{SB})}\right). \tag{4.55}$$

By assumption, $u(\cdot)$ and $u'(\cdot)$ covary in opposite directions. Moreover, a constant wage $t_i^{SB} = t^{SB}$ for all i does not satisfy the incentive constraint, and thus t_i^{SB} cannot be constant everywhere. Hence, the right-hand side of (4.55) is necessarily strictly positive. Thus we have $\lambda > 0$, and the incentive constraint (4.51) is binding.

Coming back to (4.53), we observe that the left-hand side is increasing in t_i^{SB} since $u(\cdot)$ is concave. For t_i^{SB} to be nondecreasing with i, MLRP must again hold. Then higher outputs are also those that are the more informative ones about the realization of a high effort. Hence, the agent should be more rewarded as output increases.

The benefit of offering a schedule of rewards to the agent that increases with the level of production is that such a scheme does not create any incentive for the agent to sabotage or destroy production to increase his payment.[13] However, only the rather strong assumption of a monotone likelihood ratio ensures this intuitive property. To show why, consider a simple example where MLRP does not hold. Let the probabilities in the different states of nature be $\pi_{10} = \pi_{30} = \frac{1}{6}$, $\pi_{20} = \frac{2}{3}$ when the agent exerts no effort and $\pi_{11} = \pi_{21} = \pi_{31} = \frac{1}{3}$ when he exerts an effort. Then we have

$$\frac{\pi_{11} - \pi_{10}}{\pi_{11}} = \frac{\pi_{31} - \pi_{30}}{\pi_{31}} = \frac{1}{2} > \frac{\pi_{21} - \pi_{20}}{\pi_{21}} = -1, \tag{4.56}$$

and thus MLRP fails. Of course, when the principal's benefits are such that S_3 is much larger than S_2 and S_1 (with $q_3 > q_2 > q_1$ and $S_3 > S_2 > S_1$), the principal would like to implement a positive effort in order to increase the probability that the state of nature 3 is realized. Since outputs q_1 and q_3 are equally informative of the fact that the agent has exerted a positive effort, the agent must receive the same transfers in both states 1 and 3 from (4.53). Since output q_2 is also particularly informative of the fact that the agent has exerted no effort, the second-best payment should be lower in this state of nature. Hence, the non-monotonic schedule reduces the agent's incentives to shirk and therefore reduces the probability that state 2, which is bad from the principal's point of view, is realized.

4.6 Informative Signals to Improve Contracting

As in the case of adverse selection analyzed in section 2.14, various verifiable signals can be used by the principal to improve the provision of incentives to the agent in a moral hazard framework. These pieces of information can be gathered by different kinds of information systems that are internal to the organization in the case of monitoring and supervision, or that are obtained by comparing the agent's performances with those of other related agents in the market place if such public information is available. Those practices are sometimes called "benchmarking" or "yardstick competition."

---

[13]Implicit here is the idea that the principal does not observe the production q but that the agent can show hard evidence that he has produced an amount q. This evidence can always be hidden from the principal by destroying production. "Lying upward" and pretending to have produced more than what has really been done is impossible.

4.6.1 Informativeness of Signals

The framework of section 4.5, with multiple levels of performance, is extremely useful when assessing the principal's benefit from sources of information other than the agent's sole performance. To assess the role of improved information structures, let us still assume that there are only two levels of production $\bar{q}$ and $\underline{q}$, and that the principal also learns a binary signal $\tilde{\sigma}$ belonging to the set $\Sigma = \{\sigma_0, \sigma_1\}$, which depends directly on the agent's effort. More precisely, the matrix in figure 4.5 gives the probabilities of each signal σ_i for i in $\{0,1\}$ as a function of the agent's effort.

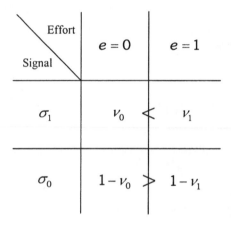

FIGURE 4.5: Information Structure

Note that the signal σ_1 (resp. σ_0) is *good news* (resp. *bad news*), that the agent has exerted a high level of effort. The signal is uninformative on the agent's effort when $\nu_0 = \nu_1$.

The signal $\tilde{\sigma}$ being verifiable, the principal now has the ability to condition the agent's performance on four possible different states of nature, y_i, for i in $\{1, \ldots, 4\}$. Each of these states is defined in table 4.1.

TABLE 4.1

State of nature	Probability when e_0	Probability when e_1
$y_1 = \{\bar{q}, \sigma_1\}$	$\pi_{10} = \pi_0 \nu_0$	$\pi_{11} = \pi_1 \nu_1$
$y_2 = \{\bar{q}, \sigma_0\}$	$\pi_{20} = \pi_0(1 - \nu_0)$	$\pi_{21} = \pi_1(1 - \nu_1)$
$y_3 = \{\underline{q}, \sigma_1\}$	$\pi_{30} = (1 - \pi_0)\nu_0$	$\pi_{31} = (1 - \pi_1)\nu_1$
$y_4 = \{\underline{q}, \sigma_0\}$	$\pi_{40} = (1 - \pi_0)(1 - \nu_0)$	$\pi_{41} = (1 - \pi_1)(1 - \nu_1)$

The signal $\tilde{\sigma}$ is not related to output, but only to effort. We assume that it does not affect the principal's return from the relationship, and we have $S^1 = S^2 = \overline{S}$ and $S^3 = S^4 = \underline{S}$.[14]

Denoting the respective multipliers of the agent's incentive and participation constraints by λ and μ, the first-order conditions (4.53) now become

$$\frac{1}{u'(t_1^{SB})} = \mu + \lambda\left(\frac{\pi_1 \nu_1 - \pi_0 \nu_0}{\pi_1 \nu_1}\right), \tag{4.57}$$

$$\frac{1}{u'(t_2^{SB})} = \mu + \lambda\left(\frac{\pi_1(1 - \nu_1) - \pi_0(1 - \nu_0)}{\pi_1(1 - \nu_1)}\right), \tag{4.58}$$

$$\frac{1}{u'(t_3^{SB})} = \mu + \lambda\left(\frac{(1 - \pi_1)\nu_1 - (1 - \pi_0)\nu_0}{(1 - \pi_1)\nu_1}\right), \tag{4.59}$$

$$\frac{1}{u'(t_4^{SB})} = \mu + \lambda\left(\frac{(1 - \pi_1)(1 - \nu_1) - (1 - \pi_0)(1 - \nu_0)}{(1 - \pi_1)(1 - \nu_1)}\right). \tag{4.60}$$

Note that $t_1^{SB} = t_2^{SB}$ and $t_3^{SB} = t_4^{SB}$ only when $\nu_1 = \nu_0$, i.e., when $\tilde{\sigma}$ is not informative of the agent's effort. In this case, conditioning the agent's contribution on a risk $\tilde{\sigma}$ unrelated to the agent's effort is of no value to the principal. This situation can only increase the risk borne by the agent without any incentive benefit. Indeed, any compensation $t(\tilde{\sigma}, \tilde{q})$ yielding utility $u(t(\tilde{\sigma}, \tilde{q}))$ to the agent can be replaced by a new scheme $\hat{t}(\tilde{q})$ that is independent of $\tilde{\sigma}$, such that $u(\hat{t}(\tilde{q})) = E_{\tilde{\sigma}} u(t(\tilde{\sigma}, \tilde{q}))$ for any $\tilde{q}$ without changing the agent's incentive and participation constraints. Furthermore, this new scheme is also *less costly* to the principal, because $E_{\tilde{q}}(\hat{t}(\tilde{q})) < E_{(\tilde{\sigma}, \tilde{q})} t(\tilde{\sigma}, \tilde{q})$. As proof of this latter inequality, note that, using the definition of $\hat{t}(q)$, we have $\hat{t}(q) = h(E_{\tilde{\sigma}}(u(t(\tilde{\sigma}, q))))$, and thus

$$E_{\tilde{q}}(\hat{t}(\tilde{q})) = E_{\tilde{q}}\left(h(E_{\tilde{\sigma}}(u(t(\tilde{\sigma}, \tilde{q}))))\right) < E_{\tilde{q}}\left(E_{\tilde{\sigma}}(h \circ u(t(\tilde{\sigma}, \tilde{q})))\right)$$

$$= E_{(\tilde{\sigma}, \tilde{q})}(t(\tilde{\sigma}, \tilde{q})), \tag{4.61}$$

where the first inequality comes from using Jensen's inequality for $h(\cdot)$ convex,[15] and the second equality is the Law of Iterated Expectations.

Instead, when $\tilde{\sigma}$ is informative of the agent's effort, conditioning the agent's reward on the realization of $\tilde{\sigma}$ has some positive incentive value as shown in equations (4.57) through (4.60). We state this as a proposition:

---

[14]In fact, we could allow for some differences in the values of those surpluses in a more general model, where the principal's surplus would be written as $S(\tilde{q}, \tilde{\sigma})$.

[15]The inequality is strict as soon as $E(u(t(\sigma_0, \tilde{q}))) \neq E(u(t(\sigma_1, \tilde{q})))$.

Proposition 4.7: *Any signal $\tilde{\sigma}$ that is informative of the agent's effort should be used to condition the agent's compensation scheme.*

This result is known as Holmström's *Sufficient Statistic Theorem* (1979). It was initially proved in a model with a continuum of outcomes and a continuum of effort levels, but its logic is the same as above. The most spectacular applications of the Sufficient Statistic Theorem arise in multiagent environments. In such environments, it has been shown that the performance of an agent can be used to incentivize another agent if their performances are correlated, even if their efforts are technologically unrelated. On this, see Mookherjee (1984) and the tournament literature (Nalebuff and Stiglitz 1983, and Green and Stockey 1983). ∎

4.6.2 More Comparisons Among Information Structures ★

The previous section has shown how the principal can strictly prefer a given information structure $\{\tilde{q}, \tilde{\sigma}\}$ to another structure $\{\tilde{q}\}$ as soon as the signal $\tilde{\sigma}$ is informative of the agent's effort. More generally, the choice between various information structures will trade off the costs and benefits of these systems. The costs may increase as the principal uses signals on the agent's performance which are more informative. The possible benefits come from reducing the agency costs.

Let us thus define an *information structure* $\pi(e)$ as a n-uple $\{\pi_i(e)\}_{i\in\{1,\dots,n\}}$ such that $\pi_i(e) \geq 0$ for all i and $\sum_{i=1}^n \pi_i(e) = 1$ for each value of e. Again, we assume that e can be either 0 or 1, and to simplify we denote $\pi(1) = \pi$.

A natural ordering of information systems is provided by *Blackwell's condition* stated in definition 4.3.

Definition 4.3: *The information structure $\pi(e)$ is sufficient, in the sense of Blackwell, for the information structure $\hat{\pi}(e)$ if and only if there exists a transition matrix[16] $P = (p_{ij})$, $(i, j) \in \{1, \dots, n\}^2$, that is independent of e and that is such that $\hat{\pi}_i(e) = \sum_{i=1}^n p_{ij}\pi_j(e)$, for all e in $\{0, 1\}$.*

An intuitive example of this ordering is given by the *garbling* of an information structure. Then, each signal of the information structure 1 is transformed by a purely random information mechanism (independent of the signal considered) into a vector of final signals. The new information, say structure 2, is such that the information structure 1 is sufficient for the information structure 2. The

---

[16] A transition matrix is such that $p_{ij} \geq 0$ for all i, and $\sum_{i=1}^n p_{ij} = 1$ for all j.

ordering implied by the Blackwell condition is an interesting expression of dominance, because it is a necessary and sufficient condition for any decision-maker to prefer information structure 1 to information structure 2.[17] We want to understand whether this natural statistical ordering among information structures also ranks the agency costs in the incentive problems associated with these information structures.[18] To see that, let us define $C^{SB}(\pi)$ as the second-best cost of implementing a positive effort when the information structure is π. By definition, we have $C^{SB}(\pi) = \sum_{i=1}^{n} \pi_{i1} t_i^{SB}(\pi) = \sum_{i=1}^{n} \pi_{i1} h(u_i^{SB}(\pi))$, where $t_i^{SB}(\pi)$ is given by (4.53). Note that we make the dependence of these transfers on the information system explicit, because different information systems certainly do not yield the same second-best transfers and implementation costs.

We are interested in comparing information structures according to their agency costs. Let us first state definition 4.4.

Definition 4.4: *The information structure π is weakly more efficient than the information structure $\hat{\pi}$ if and only if $C^{SB}(\pi) \leq C^{SB}(\hat{\pi})$.*

We can then obtain the comparison outlined in proposition 4.8.

Proposition 4.8: *If the information structure π is sufficient for the information structure $\hat{\pi}$ in the sense of Blackwell, then π is weakly more efficient than $\hat{\pi}$.*

Proof: To prove this result, note first that the definition of the information system $\hat{\pi}$ implies that

$$C^{SB}(\hat{\pi}) = \sum_{i=1}^{n} \hat{\pi}_{i1} h(u_i^{SB}(\hat{\pi})) = \sum_{i=1}^{n} \left(\sum_{k=1}^{n} p_{ik} \pi_{k1} \right) h(u_i^{SB}(\hat{\pi}))$$

$$= \sum_{k=1}^{n} \pi_{k1} \left(\sum_{i=1}^{n} p_{ik} h(u_i^{SB}(\hat{\pi})) \right)$$

$$\geq \sum_{k=1}^{n} \pi_{k1} h \left(\sum_{i=1}^{n} p_{ik} u_i^{SB}(\hat{\pi}) \right), \qquad (4.62)$$

where the second equality uses the definition of $\hat{\pi}$ and the last line is obtained from Jensen's inequality.

However, $u_i^{SB}(\hat{\pi})$ implements a positive effort at a minimal cost when the information structure is $\hat{\pi}$. Hence, the agent's incentive compatibility constraint $\sum_{i=1}^{n} (\hat{\pi}_{i1} - \hat{\pi}_{i0}) u_i^{SB}(\hat{\pi}) = \psi$, and his participation constraint $\sum_{i=1}^{n} \hat{\pi}_{i1} u_i^{SB}(\hat{\pi}) = \psi$

---

[17] See Blackwell (1951) and (1953).
[18] If the principal wants to induce zero effort, he does so by offering a wage that is identically null whatever the information system.

are both binding. Using the definition of $\hat{\pi}$ again, those two last equations are written, respectively, as

$$\sum_{i=1}^{n}\left(\sum_{k=1}^{n}p_{ik}(\pi_{k1}-\pi_{k0})\right)u_i^{SB}(\hat{\pi}) = \sum_{k=1}^{n}\left((\pi_{k1}-\pi_{k0})\left(\sum_{i=1}^{n}p_{ik}u_i^{SB}(\hat{\pi})\right)\right) = \psi \quad (4.63)$$

and

$$\sum_{i=1}^{n}\left(\sum_{k=1}^{n}p_{ik}\pi_{k1}\right)u_i^{SB}(\hat{\pi}) = \sum_{k=1}^{n}\pi_{k1}\left(\sum_{i=1}^{n}p_{ik}u_i^{SB}(\hat{\pi})\right) = \psi. \quad (4.64)$$

Let us now define the *ex post* utility levels $\tilde{u}_k = \sum_{i=1}^{n}p_{ik}u_i^{SB}(\hat{\pi})$. These new utility levels implement the high level of effort for the information structure π (from the right-hand equality of (4.63)) and make the agent's participation constraint binding (from (4.64)). By definition of $C^{SB}(\pi)$, we have $\sum_{k=1}^{n}\pi_{k1}h(\tilde{u}_k) \geq C^{SB}(\pi)$.

Finally, using (4.62) we obtain $C^{SB}(\hat{\pi}) \geq \sum_{k=1}^{n}\pi_{k1}h(\tilde{u}_k) \geq C^{SB}(\pi)$. ∎

Proposition 4.8 is due to Gjesdal (1982) and Grossman and Hart (1983). Blackwell's dominance between two information structures implies a ranking between the agency costs of the two agency problems associated with these information structures. However, the reverse is not true. Indeed, Kim (1995) showed that an information structure π is more efficient than an information structure $\hat{\pi}$ if the likelihood ratio of $\hat{\pi}$ is a mean preserving spread of that of π, i.e., if $\frac{\hat{\pi}_{i1}-\hat{\pi}_{i0}}{\hat{\pi}_{i1}} = \frac{\pi_{i1}-\pi_{i0}}{\pi_{i1}} + z_i$, for all i in $\{1, \dots, n\}$ where $\sum_{i=1}^{n}z_i = 0$. It can be shown that this latter property is not implied by Blackwell's dominance. Jewitt (2000) generalized Kim's results. Demougin and Fluet (1999) endogenized the precision of the signal used by the principal to control the agent's performance by explicitly allowing the principal to detect mistakes made by the agent and by having the agent's effort affect the probability distribution of those mistakes. ∎

4.7 Moral Hazard and the Theory of the Firm

The trade-off between risk and incentives provides one possible explanation of the wage compensations used in firms.[19] The widespread use of stock options for

---

[19]See Prendergast (1999) for a critical assessment of this trade-off through the light of some recent empirical works trying to test the negative relationship between risk and incentives that is predicted by the standard moral hazard model.

CEOs can be seen as a result of the desire of the firm's owners to let these agents bear more risk so that they are better incentivized.[20] Similarly, the use of low-powered incentives for workers within the firm can, according to the paradigm, be viewed as evidence that the firm's owners have only imperfect measures of the workers' performances or that the workers are much more risk-averse than the top management of the firm.

The moral hazard paradigm is not only useful for understanding the internal structure of the firm, but it also provides insights on the relationship of the firm with many of its possible stakeholders: equity-owners, debtholders, regulators, and consumers. The corporate finance literature has advanced the view that the capital structure of the firm is not irrelevant[21] once agency conflicts are explicitly taken into account.[22] For instance, Jensen and Meckling (1976) argued that a conflict exists between equity-owners and managers because the managers only get a fraction of the firm's profit but bear the full cost of their own effort in enhancing the firm's profitability. Later on, Jensen (1986) stressed that debt contracts have significant value in this context because they force managers to pay out cash. By paying cash, the amount of *free-cash flows* available to engage in perks and other profit-reducing activities diminishes, and this strategy relaxes the agency problem. Simultaneously, the debt contract also introduces a conflict of interests between debtholders and equity-owners who fail to invest optimally at the *ex ante* stage because they only get a fraction of the firm's return. More generally, the corporate finance literature has shown how the capital structure of the firm may be used as a powerful incentive device.

Moral hazard within the firm may be also affected by the economic environment in which the firm evolves. The general idea here is that markets may complement the formal incentives that contracts offer. Fama (1980) was an earlier contribution arguing that the labor market may provide enough *implicit incentives* for the managers to exert effort. Managers are willing to build a reputation as being efficient, and to do so they should exert the first-best level of effort even in the absence of formal contracts. Holmström (1999a) formalized this idea in a model where the manager's talent is unknown and his past performances are affected by effort, talent, and random noise.[23] He showed that reputation generally fails to provide enough incentives to the agent.

---

[20] Jensen and Murphy (1990) is an earlier paper arguing that top managers are hardly responsive to incentives. Since then, several other studies have found much more evidence for this responsiveness. See Chiappori and Salanié (2000) for a survey.

[21] Modigliani and Miller (1958) proved the irrelevance of the firm's capital structure in a general equilibrium framework with complete markets.

[22] See Harris and Raviv (1992) for a survey.

[23] See section 8.3 for a model along these lines.

Since Leibenstein (1966), it has often been suggested that market discipline might also tend to remove inefficiencies within the firm. Hart (1983b) argued that the price mechanism may reduce the manager's incentives to shirk. However, the feedback between competition and the power of incentive contracts within the firm is complex and highly dependent on the specifications made both on preferences and on the nature of competition as it was later on argued by Scharfstein (1988a) and Schmidt (1997).

Finally, it has also been argued that financial markets might play a role in disciplining management. In a case where the firm performs too badly, outsiders may take over the firm and replace its management to implement profit-enhancing actions. The threat of a takeover may thus appear as a substitute to an inefficient provision of incentives. However, this simple argument fails to explain why those profit-enhancing actions cannot be implemented by the initial owners of the firm by changing the managers' incentive schemes themselves. Two possible explanations are that the raider may have acquired private information on the firm's technology[24] or that synergies become possible once the raider has acquired the firm.[25]

4.8 Contract Theory at Work

This section elaborates on the moral hazard paradigm discussed so far in a number of settings that have been discussed extensively in the contracting literature.

4.8.1 Efficiency Wage

Let us consider a risk-neutral agent working for a firm, the principal. By exerting effort e in $\{0, 1\}$, the firm's added value is $\overline{V}$ (resp. $\underline{V}$) with probability $\pi(e)$ (resp. $1 - \pi(e)$). The agent can only be rewarded for a good performance and cannot be punished for a bad outcome, since they are protected by limited liability.

To induce effort, the principal must find an optimal compensation scheme $\{(\underline{t}, \bar{t})\}$ that is the solution to the program below:

(P): $$\max_{\{(\underline{t}, \bar{t})\}} \pi_1(\overline{V} - \bar{t}) + (1 - \pi_1)(\underline{V} - \underline{t}),$$

subject to

$$\pi_1 \bar{t} + (1 - \pi_1)\underline{t} - \psi \geq \pi_0 \bar{t} + (1 - \pi_0)\underline{t}, \qquad (4.65)$$

---

[24] On this see Scharfstein (1988b).
[25] Holmström and Tirole (1988) provided an overview of the literature on takeovers.

$$\pi_1 \bar{t} + (1 - \pi_1)\underline{t} - \psi \geq 0, \tag{4.66}$$

$$\underline{t} \geq 0. \tag{4.67}$$

The problem is completely isomorphic to that analyzed in section 4.3. The limited liability constraint is binding at the optimum, and the firm chooses to induce a high effort when $\Delta\pi\Delta V \geq \frac{\pi_1\psi}{\Delta\pi}$. At the optimum, $\underline{t}^{SB} = 0$ and $\bar{t}^{SB} > 0$. The positive wage $\bar{t}^{SB} = \frac{\psi}{\Delta\pi}$, is often called an *efficiency wage* because it induces the agent to exert a high (efficient) level of effort. To induce production, the principal must give up a positive share of the firm's profit to the agent.

The macroeconomic literature on efficiency wages started with Solow (1979) and Salop (1979) and was best developed by Shapiro and Stiglitz (1984), who presented a treatment of the dynamic incentive issues. When the performance of an agent is not easily verifiable, contracts cannot promise a share of profit to the agent and must use the threat of termination as a disciplinary device. Shapiro and Stiglitz (1984) argued that this results in voluntary unemployment. Firms offer high real-wages to prevent shirking by their workers. If any shirking is detected, agents are fired and return to the unemployment pool. See Saint-Paul (1996) for a survey. Carmichael (1985) and McLeod and Malcomson (1987) analyzed the efficiency wage model using a more microeconomic perspective on the self-enforceability of labor contracts in a dynamic context. ∎

4.8.2 Sharecropping

The moral hazard paradigm has been one of the leading tools used by development economists to analyze agrarian economies. In the sharecropping example, the principal is now a landlord and the agent is the landlord's tenant. By exerting an effort e in $\{0, 1\}$, the tenant increases (resp. decreases) the probability $\pi(e)$ (resp. $1 - \pi(e)$) that a large $\bar{q}$ (resp. small $\underline{q}$) quantity of an agricultural product is produced. The price of this good is normalized to one so that the principal's stochastic return on the activity is also $\bar{q}$ or $\underline{q}$, depending on the state of nature.

It is often the case that peasants in developing countries are subject to strong financial constraints. To model such a setting we assume that the agent is risk neutral and protected by limited liability. When he wants to induce effort, the principal's optimal contract must solve

(P):

$$\max_{\{(\underline{t}, \bar{t})\}} \pi_1(\bar{q} - \bar{t}) + (1 - \pi_1)(\underline{q} - \underline{t})$$

subject to (4.65) to (4.67).

The optimal contract therefore satisfies $\underline{t}^{SB} = 0$ and $\bar{t}^{SB} = \frac{\psi}{\Delta\pi}$. This is again akin to an efficiency wage. The expected utilities obtained respectively by the principal and the agent are given by

$$EV^{SB} = \pi_1\bar{q} + (1 - \pi_1)\underline{q} - \frac{\pi_1\psi}{\Delta\pi},\tag{4.68}$$

and

$$EU^{SB} = \frac{\pi_0\psi}{\Delta\pi}.\tag{4.69}$$

The flexible second-best contract described above has sometimes been criticized as not corresponding to the contractual arrangements observed in most agrarian economies. Contracts often take the form of simple linear schedules linking the tenant's production to his compensation. As an exercise, let us now analyze a simple *linear sharing rule* between the landlord and his tenant, with the landlord offering the agent a fixed share α of the realized production. Such a sharing rule automatically satisfies the agent's limited liability constraint, which can therefore be omitted in what follows. Formally, the optimal linear rule inducing effort must solve

(P): $$\max_\alpha (1 - \alpha)(\pi_1\bar{q} + (1 - \pi_1)\underline{q})$$

subject to

$$\alpha(\pi_1\bar{q} + (1 - \pi_1)\underline{q}) - \psi \geq \alpha(\pi_0\bar{q} + (1 - \pi_0)\underline{q}),\tag{4.70}$$

$$\alpha(\pi_1\bar{q} + (1 - \pi_1)\underline{q}) - \psi \geq 0\tag{4.71}$$

Obviously, only (4.70) is binding at the optimum. One finds the optimal linear sharing rule to be

$$\alpha^{SB} = \frac{\psi}{\Delta\pi\Delta q}.\tag{4.72}$$

Note that $\alpha^{SB} < 1$ because, for the agricultural activity to be a valuable venture in the first-best world, we must have $\Delta\pi\Delta q > \psi$. Hence, the return on the agricultural activity is shared between the principal and the agent, with high-powered incentives (α close to one) being provided when the disutility of effort ψ is large or when the principal's gain from an increase in effort $\Delta\pi\Delta q$ is small.

This sharing rule also yields the following expected utilities to the principal and the agent, respectively

$$EV_\alpha = \pi_1\bar{q} + (1 - \pi_1)\underline{q} - \left(\frac{\pi_1\bar{q} + (1 - \pi_1)\underline{q}}{\Delta q}\right)\frac{\psi}{\Delta\pi}\tag{4.73}$$

and

$$EU_\alpha = \left(\frac{\pi_1 \bar{q} + (1 - \pi_1)\underline{q}}{\Delta q}\right)\frac{\psi}{\Delta\pi} - \psi. \qquad (4.74)$$

Comparing (4.68) and (4.73) on the one hand and (4.69) and (4.74) on the other hand, we observe that the constant sharing rule benefits the agent but not the principal. A linear contract is less powerful than the optimal second-best contract. The former contract is an inefficient way to extract rent from the agent even if it still provides sufficient incentives to exert effort. Indeed, with a linear sharing rule, the agent always benefits from a positive return on his production, even in the worst state of nature. This positive return yields to the agent more than what is requested by the optimal second-best contract in the worst state of nature, namely zero. Punishing the agent for a bad performance is thus found to be rather difficult with a linear sharing rule.

A linear sharing rule allows the agent to keep some strictly positive rent EU_α. If the space of available contracts is extended to allow for fixed fees β, the principal can nevertheless bring the agent down to the level of his outside opportunity by setting a fixed fee β^{SB} equal to $(\frac{\pi_1 \bar{q} + (1-\pi_1)\underline{q}}{\Delta q})\frac{\psi}{\Delta\pi} - \psi$.

The literature on sharecropping, in its desire to be as close as possible to real world practices, has often assumed at the outset that contracts are linear (see Stiglitz 1974, Eswaran and Kotwal 1985, and Laffont and Matoussi 1995 for an empirical analysis). As we will see in Section 9.5.2, this linearity can be derived from more fundamental assumptions on contracting abilities and preferences. ∎

4.8.3 Wholesale Contracts

Let us now consider a manufacturer-retailer relationship. The manufacturer supplies at constant marginal cost c an intermediate good to the risk-averse retailer, who sells this good on a final market. Demand on this market is high (resp. low) $\bar{D}(p)$ (resp. $\underline{D}(p)$) with probability $\pi(e)$ where, again, e is in $\{0, 1\}$ and p denotes the price for the final good. Effort e is exerted by the retailer, who can increase the probability that demand is high if after-sales services are efficiently performed. The wholesale contract consists of a retail price maintenance agreement specifying the prices $\bar{p}$ and $\underline{p}$ on the final market with a sharing of the profits, namely $\{(\underline{t}, \underline{p}); (\bar{t}, \bar{p})\}$. When he wants to induce effort, the optimal contract offered by the manufacturer solves the following problem:

(P): $$\max_{\{(\underline{t},\,\underline{p});\,(\bar{t},\,\bar{p})\}} \pi_1((\bar{p}-c)\overline{D}(\bar{p})-\bar{t})+(1-\pi_1)((\underline{p}-c)\underline{D}(\underline{p})-\underline{t})$$

subject to (4.3) and (4.4).

The solution to this problem is obtained by appending the following expressions of the retail prices to the transfers given in (4.32) and (4.33): $\bar{p}^*+\frac{\overline{D}(\bar{p}^*)}{\overline{D}'(\bar{p}^*)}=c$, and $\underline{p}^*+\frac{\underline{D}(\underline{p}^*)}{\underline{D}'(\underline{p}^*)}=c$. Note that these prices are the same as those that would be chosen under complete information. The pricing rule is not affected by the incentive problem, an example of what Laffont and Tirole (1993) called a *dichotomy* property in another context.

4.8.4 Financial Contracts

Moral hazard is a very important issue in financial markets. Let us now assume that a risk-averse entrepreneur wants to start a project that requires an initial investment worth an amount I. The entrepreneur has no cash of his own and must raise money from a bank or any other financial intermediary. The return on the project is random and equal to $\overline{V}$ (resp. $\underline{V}$), with probability $\pi(e)$ (resp. $1-\pi(e)$), where the effort exerted by the entrepreneur e belongs to $\{0, 1\}$. We denote the spread of profits by $\Delta V = \overline{V} - \underline{V} > 0$. The financial contract consists of repayments $\{(\bar{z}, \underline{z})\}$, depending upon whether the project is successful or not.

To induce effort from the borrower, the risk-neutral lender's program is written as

(P): $$\max_{\{(\underline{z},\bar{z})\}} \pi_1\bar{z} + (1-\pi_1)\underline{z} - I$$

subject to

$$\pi_1 u(\overline{V}-\bar{z}) + (1-\pi_1)u(\underline{V}-\underline{z}) - \psi$$

$$\geq \pi_0 u(\overline{V}-\bar{z}) + (1-\pi_0)u(\underline{V}-\underline{z}), \qquad (4.75)$$

$$\pi_1 u(\overline{V}-\bar{z}) + (1-\pi_1)u(\underline{V}-\underline{z}) - \psi \geq 0, \qquad (4.76)$$

where (4.75) and (4.76) are respectively the agent's incentive and participation constraints. Note that the project is a valuable venture if it provides the bank with a positive expected profit.

With the change of variables, $\bar{t} = \overline{V} - \bar{z}$ and $\underline{t} = \underline{V} - \underline{z}$, the principal's program takes its usual form. This change of variables also highlights the fact that everything happens as if the lender was benefitting directly from the return of the project, and then paying the agent only a fraction of the returns in the different states of nature.

Let us define the second-best cost of implementing a positive effort C^{SB} as we did in section 4.4, and let us assume that $\Delta\pi\Delta V \geq C^{SB}$, so that the lender wants to induce a positive effort level even in a second-best environment. The lender's expected profit is worth

$$V_1 = \pi_1\overline{V} + (1 - \pi_1)\underline{V} - C^{SB} - I. \tag{4.77}$$

Let us now parameterize projects according to the size of the investment I. Only the projects with positive value $V_1 > 0$ will be financed. This requires the investment to be low enough, and typically we must have

$$I < I^{SB} = \pi_1\overline{V} + (1 - \pi_1)\underline{V} - C^{SB}. \tag{4.78}$$

Under complete information and no moral hazard, the project would instead be financed as soon as

$$I < I^* = \pi_1\overline{V} + (1 - \pi_1)\underline{V}. \tag{4.79}$$

For intermediary values of the investment, i.e., for I in $[I^{SB}, I^*]$, moral hazard implies that some projects are financed under complete information but no longer under moral hazard. This is akin to some form of credit rationing.[26]

Finally, note that the optimal financial contract offered to the risk-averse and cashless entrepreneur does not satisfy the limited liability constraint $\underline{t} \geq 0$. Indeed, we have $\underline{t}^{SB} = h(\psi - \frac{\pi_1\psi}{\Delta\pi}) < 0$. To be induced to make an effort, the agent must bear some risk, which implies a negative payoff in the bad state of nature. Adding the limited liability constraint, the optimal contract would instead entail $\underline{t}^{LL} = 0$ and $\bar{t}^{LL} = h(\frac{\psi}{\Delta\pi})$. Interestingly, this contract has sometimes been interpreted in the corporate finance literature as a *debt contract*, with no money being left to the borrower in the bad state of nature and the residual being pocketed by the lender in the good state of nature.

Finally, note that

$$\bar{t}^{LL} - \underline{t}^{LL} = h\left(\frac{\psi}{\Delta\pi}\right) < \bar{t}^{SB} - \underline{t}^{SB} = h\left(\psi + (1 - \pi_1)\frac{\psi}{\Delta\pi}\right)$$
$$- h\left(\psi - \frac{\pi_1\psi}{\Delta\pi}\right), \tag{4.80}$$

since $h(\cdot)$ is strictly convex and $h(0) = 0$. This inequality shows that the debt contract has less incentive power than the optimal incentive contract. Indeed, it becomes harder to spread the agent's payments between both states of nature to induce effort if the agent is protected by limited liability. To the agent, who is interested only in his payoff in the high state of nature, only rewards are attractive.

[26]The reader will recognize the similarity of this result with that of section 3.6.3.

Remark: The corporate finance literature, starting with Jensen and Meckling (1976), has stressed that moral hazard within the firm may not be due to the desire of the manager to avoid costly effort, but instead might be due to his desire to choose projects with *private benefits*. Those private benefits arise, for instance, when the manager devotes the resources of the firm to consume perquisites.

The modelling of these private benefits is very similar to that of the standard moral hazard problem viewed so far.[27] Let us consider that the risk-neutral manager can choose between a *good* and a *bad* project. The shareholders' return of the good project is $\overline{V}$, with probability π_1 and π_0 otherwise. However, by choosing the bad project, the manager gets a private benefit B that is strictly positive. A contract is again a pair of transfers $\{(\bar{t}, \underline{t})\}$ where, assuming limited liability, $\underline{t} = 0$.

The manager chooses the good project when the following incentive constraint is satisfied:

$$\pi_1 \bar{t} \geq \pi_0 \bar{t} + B, \tag{4.81}$$

which amounts to

$$\bar{t} \geq \frac{B}{\Delta \pi}. \tag{4.82}$$

This constraint is obviously binding at the optimum of the financier's problem, and the financier gets an expected payoff V_1 such that

$$V_1 = \pi_1 \left(\overline{V} - \frac{B}{\Delta \pi} \right) - I, \tag{4.83}$$

where I is the investment cost that the financier has incurred. Obviously, compared with complete information, the set of valuable investments is reduced under moral hazard because of the agency cost incurred to avoid private benefits. ∎

Holmström and Tirole (1994) presented a theory of credit rationing based on a similar model with private benefits. Two differences come from the fact that there is a competitive market of lenders and that the agent may finance part of the project with equity. One conclusion of their model is that wealthier agents find financing more easily. ∎

---

[27] The private benefit is an *output* that is not observed by the principal, while effort is an unobserved *input*.

4.8.5 Insurance Contracts ★

Moral hazard also undermines the functioning of insurance markets. We consider now a risk-averse agent with utility function $u(\cdot)$ and initial wealth w. With probability $\pi(e)$ (resp. $1 - \pi(e)$) the agent has no (resp. an) accident and pays an amount $\bar{z}$ (resp. $\underline{z}$) to an insurance company. The damage incurred by the agent is worth d. Effort e in $\{0, 1\}$ can now be interpreted as a level of safety care.

Monopoly

To make things simpler, and as in section 3.3.2, the insurance company is first assumed to be a monopoly and to have all of the bargaining power when offering the insurance contract to the insuree. To induce effort from the insuree, the optimal insurance contract must solve

(P):
$$\max_{\{(\underline{z},\bar{z})\}} \pi_1 \bar{z} + (1 - \pi_1)\underline{z}$$

subject to

$$\pi_1 u(w - \bar{z}) + (1 - \pi_1)u(w - d - \underline{z}) - \psi$$
$$\geq \pi_0 u(w - \bar{z}) + (1 - \pi_0)u(w - d - \underline{z}), \tag{4.84}$$

$$\pi_1 u(w - \bar{z}) + (1 - \pi_1)u(w - d - \underline{z}) - \psi \geq u(\hat{w}), \tag{4.85}$$

where $\hat{w}$ is the certainty equivalent of the agent's wealth when he does not purchase any insurance and when he exerts an effort. The certainty equivalent $\hat{w}$ is implicity defined as $u(\hat{w}) = \pi_1 u(w) + (1 - \pi_1)u(w - d) - \psi.$[28]

Note that the right-hand side of (4.85) is not zero. Except for this nonzero reservation value, the problem is very close to that of section 4.5 after having replaced variables so that the net transfers received by the agent are $\bar{t} = w - \bar{z}$ and $\underline{t} = w - d - \underline{z}$ and having noticed that $\overline{S} = w$ and $\underline{S} = w - d$.

Both constraints (4.84) and (4.85) are again binding at the optimum, and the second-best cost of inducing effort is now written as

$$C^{SB}(\hat{w}) = \pi_1 h\left(\psi + u(\hat{w}) + (1 - \pi_1)\frac{\psi}{\Delta\pi}\right)$$
$$+ (1 - \pi_1)h\left(\psi + u(\hat{w}) - \frac{\pi_1\psi}{\Delta\pi}\right). \tag{4.86}$$

---

[28]We assume that the agent wants to exert an effort in the absence of an insurance contract, i.e., $u(w) - u(w - d) > \frac{\psi}{\Delta\pi}$. One could assume instead that he does not want to exert effort when he is not insured. In this case, his status quo utility level would be $\pi_0 u(w) + (1 - \pi_0)u(w - d) = u(\hat{w}')$.

Without moral hazard this cost of inducing effort would instead be

$$C^{FB}(\hat{w}) = h(\psi + u(\hat{w})). \tag{4.87}$$

Let us thus use $AC(\hat{w}) = C^{SB}(\hat{w}) - C^{FB}(\hat{w})$ to denote the agency cost due to moral hazard incurred by the principal, i.e., the difference between the second-best and the first-best cost of inducing effort. Differentiating with respect to $\hat{w}$, we have

$$AC'(\hat{w}) = u'(\hat{w})\left(\pi_1 h'\left(\psi + u(\hat{w}) + (1 - \pi_1)\frac{\psi}{\Delta\pi} \right) \right.$$

$$\left. + (1 - \pi_1)h'\left(\psi + u(\hat{w}) - \frac{\pi_1 \psi}{\Delta\pi} \right) - h'(\psi + u(\hat{w})) \right) > 0, \quad (4.88)$$

if $h'(\cdot)$ is convex. In fact, we let the reader check that this latter convexity is ensured when $p_u(x) < 3r_u(x)$, where $p_u(x) = -\frac{u'''(x)}{u''(x)}$ is the agent's degree of absolute prudence and $r_u(x) = -\frac{u''(x)}{u'(x)}$ is his degree of absolute risk aversion.[29]

The fact that $AC(\hat{w})$ is monotonically increasing with $\hat{w}$ can be interpreted as saying that, as the agent's wealth increases, there is more distortion due to moral hazard in the decision of the insurance company to induce effort or not. However, the sufficient condition on $h(\cdot)$ needed to obtain this result is somewhat intricate. This highlights the important difficulties that modellers often face when they want to derive comparative statics results from even a simple agency problem.

Competitive Market

The insurance market is often viewed as an archetypical example of a perfectly competitive market where insurers' profits are driven to zero. Without entering too much into the difficult issues of competitive markets plagued by agency problems, it is nevertheless useful to characterize the equilibrium contract inducing a positive effort. Because of perfect competition among insurance companies, this contract should maximize the agent's expected utility subject to the standard incentive compatibility constraint (written with our usual change of variables)

$$\bar{u} - \underline{u} \geq \frac{\psi}{\Delta\pi}, \tag{4.89}$$

and subject to the constraint of non-negative profit for the insurance company

$$\pi_1(w - h(\bar{u})) + (1 - \pi_1)(w - d - h(\underline{u})) \geq 0. \tag{4.90}$$

---

[29]This latter property holds when $u(\cdot)$ is CARA. See also Thiele and Wambach (1999) for similar comparative statics.

The equilibrium contract must therefore solve the following problem:

(P): $$\max_{\{(\bar{u},\, \underline{u})\}} \pi_1 \bar{u} + (1 - \pi_1)\underline{u} - \psi$$

subject to (4.89) and (4.90).

Denoting by $\hat{\lambda}$ and $\hat{\mu}$ the respective multipliers of those two constraints, the necessary and sufficient first-order conditions for this concave problem are written, respectively, as (with the superscript M for market equilibrium)

$$\pi_1 + \hat{\lambda} = \hat{\mu}\pi_1 h'(\bar{u}^M) \tag{4.91}$$

and

$$1 - \pi_1 - \hat{\lambda} = \hat{\mu}(1 - \pi_1)h'(\underline{u}^M). \tag{4.92}$$

Summing those two equations immediately yields

$$\hat{\mu} = \frac{1}{\pi_1 h'(\bar{u}^M) + (1 - \pi_1)h'(\underline{u}^M)} > 0. \tag{4.93}$$

Hence, the zero profit constraint of the firm is automatically satisfied by this equilibrium contract. Similarly, we also find that

$$\hat{\lambda} = \pi_1(1 - \pi_1)\frac{(h'(\bar{u}^M) - h'(\underline{u}^M))}{\pi_1 h'(\bar{u}^M) + (1 - \pi_1)h'(\underline{u}^M)} > 0, \tag{4.94}$$

because $h(\cdot)$ is convex and $\bar{u}^M > \underline{u}^M$ is necessary to guarantee that (4.89) holds. The incentive compatibility constraint is thus also binding at the equilibrium contract.

Denoting by U^M the agent's expected utility when exerting a positive effort, the binding non-negative profit constraint of the insurance company can be rewritten as:

$$\pi_1 h\left(U^M + \psi + (1 - \pi_1)\frac{\psi}{\Delta\pi}\right) + (1 - \pi_1)h\left(U^M + \psi - \pi_1\frac{\psi}{\Delta\pi}\right)$$
$$= w - d(1 - \pi_1). \tag{4.95}$$

The market does not break down as long as (4.95) defines implicity a value U^M, which is greater than what the agent gets by not taking any insurance contract, i.e., $u(\hat{w}) = \pi_1 u(w) + (1 - \pi_1)u(w - d) - \psi$. In fact, $U^M > u(\hat{w})$ amounts to

$$\pi_1 h\left(u(\hat{w}) + \psi + (1 - \pi_1)\frac{\psi}{\Delta\pi}\right) + (1 - \pi_1)h\left(u(\hat{w}) + \psi - \pi_1\frac{\psi}{\Delta\pi}\right)$$
$$< w - d(1 - \pi_1). \tag{4.96}$$

Under complete information the agent would be perfectly insured and would exert a positive effort. He would then get a positive expected utility U^*, such that $h(U^* + \psi) = w - d(1 - \pi_1)$. Again, the market does not break down as long as $U^* > u(\hat{w})$, which amounts to

$$h(u(\hat{w}) + \psi) < w - d(1 - \pi_1). \tag{4.97}$$

Note that (4.97) always holds when $u(\hat{w}) = \pi_1 u(w) + (1 - \pi_1)u(w - d) - \psi$, because then $\pi_1 u(w) + (1 - \pi_1)u(w - d) < u(w - d(1 - \pi_1))$ by Jensen's inequality. Hence, the market never breaks down under complete information. Because $h(\cdot)$ is convex, Jensen's inequality also implies that the left-hand side of (4.96) is greater than $h(u(\hat{w}) + \psi)$. Hence, the condition (4.96) may not hold even if (4.97) always holds. Moral hazard may induce a market breakdown.

4.9 Commitment Under Moral Hazard ★

The assumption of full commitment to an incentive scheme was already discussed in section 2.12 in the case of adverse selection. This issue is also quite important under moral hazard. For instance, to induce a positive effort level the principal must let the risk-averse agent bear some risk. However, once this effort is sunk, and before uncertainty is resolved, the principal would like to offer more insurance to the agent to avoid paying an excessive agency cost. For this reinsurance stage to have any impact, the principal must be aware, maybe through direct observation of the effort itself or by indirectly getting a signal correlated with the effort, that effort has already been performed. Of course, the renegotiation stage would be perfectly anticipated by the rational agent at the time of exerting effort. Renegotiation is unlikely to lead to complete insurance *ex post*, because the agent would then have no incentive to exert effort in the first place.

Fudenberg and Tirole (1990) showed how the possibility of renegotiation induced a mixed strategy in the effort provision of the agent. The complexity of the model comes from the fact that the agent's actual choice of effort becomes an endogenous adverse selection variable at the renegotiation stage. This creates an inefficiency. This inefficiency can be avoided if the informed party makes the renegotiation offer, as in Matthews (1995), who allowed renegotiation on the equilibrium path, or Ma (1994), who focused on renegotiation-proof contracts. Finally, Hermalin and Katz (1991) showed that the first-best outcome could be implemented when the principal observes the nonverifiable effort of the agent before renegotiation, because then renegotiation takes place under complete information. ∎

Appendix 4.1: Proof of Proposition 4.2

- First suppose that $0 \leq l \leq \frac{\pi_0}{\Delta \pi} \psi$. We conjecture that (4.15) and (4.18) are the only relevant constraints. Of course, since the principal is willing to minimize the payments made to the agent, both constraints must be binding. Hence, $\underline{t}^{SB} = -l$ and $\bar{t}^{SB} = -l + \frac{\psi}{\Delta \pi}$. We check that (4.17) is satisfied since $-l + \frac{\psi}{\Delta \pi} > -l$. We also check that (4.16) is satisfied since $\pi_1 \bar{t}^{SB} + (1 - \pi_1)\underline{t}^{SB} - \psi = -l + \frac{\pi_0}{\Delta \pi} \psi \geq 0$.

- For $l > \frac{\pi_0}{\Delta \pi} \psi$, note that the transfers $\underline{t}^* = -\frac{\pi_0}{\Delta \pi} \psi$ and $\bar{t}^* = \psi + \frac{(1-\pi_1)}{\Delta \pi} \psi > \underline{t}^*$ are such that both limited liability constraints (4.17) and (4.18) are strictly satisfied, and (4.15) and (4.16) are both binding. In this case, it is costless to induce a positive effort by the agent, and the first-best outcome can be implemented.

Appendix 4.2: A Continuum of Performances

Let us now assume that the level of performance $\tilde{q}$ is drawn from a continuous distribution with a cumulative function $F(\cdot|e)$ on the support $[\underline{q}, \bar{q}]$. This distribution is conditional on the agent's level of effort, which still takes two possible values e in $\{0, 1\}$. We denote by $f(\cdot|e)$ the density corresponding to the above distributions. A contract $t(q)$ inducing a positive effort in this context must satisfy the incentive constraint

$$\int_{\underline{q}}^{\bar{q}} u(t(q))f(q|1)dq - \psi \geq \int_{\underline{q}}^{\bar{q}} u(t(q))f(q|0)dq, \qquad (4.98)$$

and the participation constraint

$$\int_{\underline{q}}^{\bar{q}} u(t(q))f(q|1)dq - \psi \geq 0. \qquad (4.99)$$

The risk-neutral principal's problem is thus written as

(P):
$$\max_{\{t(q)\}} \int_{\underline{q}}^{\bar{q}} (S(q) - t(q))f(q|1)dq,$$
$$\text{subject to (4.98) and (4.99).}$$

Denoting the multipliers of (4.98) and (4.99) by λ and μ, respectively, the Lagrangian of (P) writes as $L(q, t) = (S(q) - t)f(q|1) + \lambda(u(t)(f(q|1) - f(q|0)) - \psi) + \mu(u(t)f(q|1) - \psi)$.

Optimizing pointwise with respect to t yields

$$\frac{1}{u'(t^{SB}(q))} = \mu + \lambda\left(\frac{f(q|1) - f(q|0)}{f(q|1)}\right). \tag{4.100}$$

Multiplying (4.100) by $f_1(q)$ and taking expectations,[30] we obtain, as in the main text,

$$\mu = E_{\bar{q}}\left(\frac{1}{u'(t^{SB}(\tilde{q}))}\right) > 0, \tag{4.101}$$

where $E_{\bar{q}}(\cdot)$ is the expectation operator with respect to the probability distribution of output induced by an effort e^{SB}. Finally, using this expression of μ, inserting it into (4.100), and multiplying it by $f(q|1)u(t^{SB}(q))$, we obtain

$$\lambda(f(q|1) - f(q|0))u(t^{SB}(q))$$
$$= f(q|1)u(t^{SB}(q))\left(\frac{1}{u'(t^{SB}(q))} - E_{\bar{q}}\left(\frac{1}{u'(t^{SB}(\tilde{q}))}\right)\right). \tag{4.102}$$

Integrating over $[\underline{q}, \bar{q}]$ and taking into account the slackness condition $\lambda(\int_{\underline{q}}^{\bar{q}}(f(q|1) - f(q|0))u(t^{SB}(q))dq - \psi) = 0$ yields $\lambda\psi = \text{cov}(u(t^{SB}(\tilde{q})), \frac{1}{u'(t^{SB}(\tilde{q}))}) \geq 0$.

Hence, $\lambda \geq 0$ because $u(\cdot)$ and $u'(\cdot)$ vary in opposite directions. Also, $\lambda = 0$ only if $t^{SB}(q)$ is a constant, but in this case the incentive constraint is necessarily violated. As a result, we have $\lambda > 0$. Finally, $t^{SB}(\pi)$ is monotonically increasing in π when the *monotone likelihood property* $\frac{d}{dq}(\frac{f(q|1)-f(q|0)}{f(q|1)}) \geq 0$ is satisfied.

Appendix 4.3: Proof of Proposition 4.6

Indeed, let J be the set of indices j, such that $\frac{\pi_{j1}-\pi_{j0}}{\pi_{j1}} = \max_i\{\frac{\pi_{i1}-\pi_{i0}}{\pi_{i1}}\}$. If $J = \{n\}$, then we have $t_n = \frac{\psi}{\pi_{n1}-\pi_{n0}}$ and $t_i = 0$ for $i < n$. Otherwise $t_i = 0$ if $i \notin J$, and for $i \in J$ the transfer t_i must satisfy the incentive constraint as an equality. Thus, $\sum_{i \in J}(\pi_{i1} - \pi_{i0})t_i = \psi$, and the principal (and the agent) are indifferent to the profiles of positive transfers. For example, they can be chosen positive and increasing.

---

[30]Note that $\int_{\underline{q}}^{\bar{q}} f(q|e)dq = 1$ for e in $\{0,1\}$.

5 Incentive and Participation Constraints with Moral Hazard ★

In chapter 4, we stressed the various conflicts that may appear in a moral hazard environment. The analysis of these conflicts, under both limited liability and risk aversion, was made easy because of our focus on a simple 2×2 environment with a binary effort and two levels of performance. The simple interaction between a *single* incentive constraint with either a limited liability constraint or a participation constraint was quite straightforward.

However, moral hazard models also inherit the major difficulties of Incentive Theory, which we have already encountered in our investigation of complex adverse selection models carried out in chapter 3. Indeed, when one moves away from the 2×2 (by far too simplistic) model of chapter 4, numerous incentive constraints have to be taken into account in complex moral hazard environments. The analysis becomes much harder, and characterizing the optimal incentive contract is a difficult task. Examples of such complex contracting environments abound.

Effort may no longer be binary but, instead, may be better characterized as a continuous variable. A manager may no longer choose between working or not working on a project but may be able to fine-tune the exact effort spent on this project. Even worse, the agent's actions may no longer be summarized by a one-dimensional parameter but may be better described by a whole array of control variables that are technologically linked. For instance, the manager of a firm may have to choose how to allocate his effort between productive activities and monitoring his peers and other workers. The manager's performances, i.e., his profit, may also be better approximated as a continuous variable, a less crude assumption than the one made in chapter 4.[1] Real-world incentive schemes for the manager of the firm are not based on a discrete number of performances but instead on the more continuous level of profit of the firm. Lastly, the agent's preferences over effort and consumption may no longer be separable as we have assumed in chapter 4.

Mirroring the analysis performed in chapter 3 for the case of adverse selection as much as possible, we argue here that complex contractual environments with moral hazard also raise many new difficulties for the characterization of the binding incentive and participation constraints. Again mimicking what was done in chapter 3, we propose a classification of the new contractual settings analyzed in the present chapter. Each of those categories corresponds to a particular perturbation of the standard moral hazard trade-offs analyzed in chapter 2.

• **Conflict between several of the agent's incentive constraints:** Let us consider a first class of models where the agent can exert more than two possible levels of effort. The agent may choose his one-dimensional action within a finite set, or he may be able to fine-tune his effort supply continuously. In both cases, the agent's performance remains a single dimensional vector. Alternatively, the agent may be performing several tasks on the principal's behalf, thus controlling various dimensions of effort and with each of those efforts affecting a particular aspect of the agent's performance. In those complex contracting environments, a major difficulty is to ensure that *local incentive constraints*, which are the easiest ones to handle, still drive the design of incentives.

When the agent's performance has a single dimension, we first derive the *second-best cost* of implementing any given level of effort. This cost is obtained by minimizing the agent's expected payment subject to his incentive and participation constraints. As in chapter 4, it is true that the second-best cost is greater than the first-best cost as soon as one incentive constraint is binding. Second, we generalize the second-best analysis of chapter 4 to find the optimal effort level that the prin-

---

[1] Appendix 4.2 already gives an example of such an analysis with a continuum of performances and two levels of effort.

cipal wants to induce under moral hazard. This analysis already shows that there is no general lesson on the nature of the distortion entailed by moral hazard. The second-best level of effort may be either higher or lower than its first-best value, contrary to our findings in the binary effort model of chapter 4. We then develop the so-called *first-order approach* to moral hazard problems where effort is a continuous variable. This approach replaces the set of possible incentive constraints by a local incentive constraint, a legitimate step provided that the agent's problem is concave. This concavity is in turn obtained under rather stringent assumptions, namely that the cumulative distribution function of the performance level should be a convex function of the agent's effort (CDFC) and MLRP should also be satisfied. As we have already seen in chapter 4, this latter property also implies that the agent's compensation schedule is *nondecreasing* with his performance.

In practice, the agent's effort is often better characterized as a multidimensional variable. For instance, a retailer selling goods on the manufacturer's behalf must reduce retailing costs but also improve after-sales services. A worker is not only involved in productive tasks but also must sometimes monitor his peers. A tenant must simultaneously choose the quality of the crops he seeds and the level of physical investment he makes. A teacher must allocate his time between doing research and supervising students. All of these examples belong to the class of *multitask incentive problems*. In those models, agency costs are significantly affected by the conflicts that may arise when incentivizing the various tasks performed by the agent. The characterization of the optimal contract depends on the *complementarity or substitutability* of the tasks. The technological relationship between tasks thus has strong incentive consequences. Viewing the relationship between the principal and his agent as a cluster of various transactions significantly expands the scope of standard incentive theory. New issues arise in such a framework. For instance, one can study how the distribution of efforts along those different dimensions of the agent's activity or the degrees of informativeness of the different performances affect the power of incentives, deriving rich lessons for organizational design from such an analysis.[2]

---

[2]Even though the relevant literature (see Holmström and Milgrom 1991 and 1994) has been mostly developed in a particular framework (a framework that considers the case of a continuum of possible performances, a continuum of possible effort levels on each task, and a disutility of effort being evaluated in monetary terms with CARA utility functions), we have found it useful to recast the lessons of this literature in a discrete framework that naturally extends the standard model of chapter 4. By doing so, we clearly gain in consistency by offering an integrated framework throughout the book. Moreover, this discrete modelling allows us to discuss the conditions under which nonlocal incentive constraints affect the design of incentives, giving us strong economic intuitions about the economic phenomenon at stake in this multitask environment. Nevertheless, we develop in section 9.6.2 the Holmström-Milgrom model in more detail.

We also present a number of important examples of the multitask principal-agent models. These applications cover a broad range of issues, such as the interlinking of agrarian contracts, the design of incentive schemes based on aggregate performances, and finally the choice of whether to integrate vertically or not a downstream unit and its consequences for the comparison between the power of incentives in market environments and within firms.

• **Strong conflict between the agent's incentive and participation constraints:** One peculiarity of the principal-agent models with risk aversion presented so far is that, even though various incentive constraints might be taken into account by the principal, the separability of the agent's utility function between consumption and effort implies that giving up an *ex ante* rent to the agent is never optimal from the principal's point of view. The conflict between incentives and insurance is not strong enough to leave a rent to the agent. Instead, with a *nonseparability* between consumption and effort in the agent's utility function, the conflict between incentive and participation constraints may become stronger, and it may be better solved by leaving a *positive ex ante rent* to the agent. Leaving such a rent allows the principal to benefit from wealth effects, which may reduce the cost of providing incentives.

• **Constraints on transfers:** Finally, we also replace the conflict between incentive and participation constraints by the conflict between incentive and budget balance constraints that appear in the optimal taxation literature. Again, in a model with a binary level of effort, under-provision of effort appears with moral hazard.

Section 5.1 presents the straightforward extensions of the standard model of chapter 4 to the cases where the agent can perform more than two and possibly a continuum of levels of effort. In this section we discuss there the two-step characterization of the second-best optimum, first with the derivation of the second-best cost of implementing a level of effort, and second with the analysis of the trade-off between the benefit and the cost of implementing any given effort. We prove, by exhibiting an example, that the second-best level of effort in an insurance-efficiency trade-off can be distorted upwards. Therefore, this shows that complex moral hazard models may fail to perpetuate the simple lessons of chapter 4. Nevertheless, we also provide a limited liability rent-efficiency trade-off with a continuum of levels of effort where the basic lessons of section 4.5.1 carry over. There, the trade-off between the extraction of the limited liability rent and allocative efficiency always calls for a reduction in the expected volume of trade. Finally, this section ends with an exposition of the first-order approach. The first-order approach allows the modeler to replace the infinity of incentive constraints, which arise when the agent controls a continuous effort variable, with a simple first-order condition. Section 5.2 deals with a multitask model, solving first for the optimal contracts that induce efforts on both dimensions of the agent's activity and then deriving the second-best level of effort on each of these dimensions. This analysis is first performed in the simple framework of a risk-neutral agent who is protected by limited liability. Then, we turn to the somewhat more complex case of risk aversion. We show the possibility of *diseconomies of scope* in agency costs, and we discuss their precise origins. Several examples of multitask agency models are then presented. Section 5.3 analyzes the case where the agent's utility function is no longer separable between consumption and effort. In this section we discuss the conditions under which the agent's participation constraint may not be binding at the optimum. We also provide a simple example of preferences where the disutility of effort can be expressed in monetary terms for which, despite the nonseparability between effort and consumption, the optimal contract keeps almost the same features as in the case of separability.[3] Finally, section 5.4 analyzes the trade-off between efficiency and redistribution in a moral hazard context.

5.1 More than Two Levels of Effort

5.1.1 A Discrete Model

Let us extend the model of chapter 4 by allowing more than two levels of effort. Consider the more general case, with n levels of production $q_1 < q_2 < \cdots < q_n$ and K levels of effort with $0 = e_0 < e_1 < \cdots < e_{K-1}$ and the disutilities of effort $\psi(e_k) = \psi_k$ for all k in $\{0, \ldots, K-1\}$. We still make the normalization $\psi_0 = 0$ and assume that ψ_k is increasing in k. Let π_{ik} for i in $\{1, \ldots, n\}$ also denote the probability of producing q_i when the effort level is e_k. Let $S_i = S(q_i)$ denote the value for the principal of production q_i for i in $\{1, \ldots, n\}$. The agent still has a separable utility function over monetary transfer and effort $U = u(t) - \psi(e)$, where $u(\cdot)$ is increasing and concave ($u' > 0$ and $u'' \leq 0$) with the normalization $u(0) = 0$. In such an environment, a contract is a set of transfers $\{(t_1, \ldots t_n)\}$ corresponding to all possible output levels. As in chapter 4, we proceed in two steps. First, we compute the second-best cost of inducing effort e_k for the principal. We denote this cost by C_k^{SB}. Second, we find the optimal level of effort from the principal's point of view, taking into account both the costs and benefits of each action e_k.

Let us thus denote by (P_k) the cost minimization problem of a principal willing to implement effort e_k. Using our by now standard change of variables, the important variables are the utility levels in each state of nature, i.e., $u_i = u(t_i)$

---

[3]This example will be useful later on in section 9.5.2, in which we will investigate how optimal contracts may be linear in more structured moral hazard environments.

or alternatively $t_i = h(u_i)$ where $h = u^{-1}$ is increasing and convex ($h' > 0$ and $h'' > 0$). (P_k) is now a convex problem that is written as:

(P_k):
$$\min_{\{(u_1, \ldots, u_n)\}} \sum_{i=1}^{n} \pi_{ik} h(u_i)$$

subject to

$$\sum_{i=1}^{n} (\pi_{ik} - \pi_{ik'}) u_i \geq \psi_k - \psi_{k'} \qquad \text{for all } k' \neq k, \tag{5.1}$$

$$\sum_{i=1}^{n} \pi_{ik} u_i - \psi_k \geq 0. \tag{5.2}$$

(5.1) is the incentive constraint preventing the agent from exerting effort $e_{k'}$, for $k' \neq k$ when the principal wants to implement effort e_k. There are $K - 1$ such constraints. (5.2) is the agent's participation constraint when he exerts effort e_k. We denote the multiplier of (5.1) by $\lambda_k^{k'}$ and still, as in chapter 4, the multiplier of (5.2.) by μ. The value of this problem is the *second-best cost of implementation* C_k^{SB} for effort e_k.

It should be immediately clear that the second-best cost of implementing effort e_k is such that $C_k^{SB} \geq C_k^{FB} = h(\psi_k)$, where C_k^{FB} denotes the first-best cost of implementing effort e_k. This is so because the presence of incentive constraints in problem (P_k) implies that the value of this problem is necessarily not less than under complete information. Note that the inequality above is strict whenever one of the incentive constraints in (5.1) is binding at the optimum of (P_k).

The necessary and sufficient first-order conditions for the optimization of program (P_k) are thus written as

$$\frac{1}{u'(t_{ik})} = \mu + \sum_{k' \neq k} \lambda_k^{k'} \left(\frac{\pi_{ik} - \pi_{ik'}}{\pi_{ik}} \right), \qquad i = 1, \ldots, n, \tag{5.3}$$

where t_{ik} is the transfer given to the agent in state i when the principal wants to implement effort e_k.

The new difficulty coming from more than two levels of effort is that there may be several incentive constraints binding, i.e., several multipliers $\lambda_k^{k'}$ that may be different from zero. Looking only at local incentive constraints may not be enough to characterize the solution to (P_k), and the optimal payments are then the solutions of a complex system of nonlinear equations. However, if the only binding incentive constraint is the local downward incentive constraint, the first-order condition for problem (P_k) is written simply as

$$\frac{1}{u'(t_{ik})} = \mu + \lambda_k^{k-1} \left(\frac{\pi_{ik} - \pi_{i(k-1)}}{\pi_{ik}} \right). \tag{5.4}$$

When the cumulative distribution function of production is a convex function of the level of effort, and when MLRP holds, the local approach described above can be validated, as has been shown by Grossman and Hart (1983). We prove this proposition in section 5.1.3 for the case of a continuum of effort levels and a continuum of performances, but the same kind of proof also applies in this discrete framework.[4]

Even if describing the behavior of the second-best cost of implementation C_k^{SB} is in general a difficult task, one may try to get some insights on how the principal chooses the second-best level of effort. The optimal second-best effort is indeed defined as $e^{SB} = \arg\max_{e_k} \sum_{i=1}^n \pi_{ik} S_i - C_k^{SB}$.[5]

Finding this second-best effort e^{SB} is a rather difficult problem and there is, a priori, no reason to be sure that it is below its first-best value. Under- as well as over-provision of effort may now be obtained at the second-best effort.

Under-provision was obtained in chapter 4. To understand how over-provision may also arise, let us consider the following example with three possible levels of effort e_0, e_1, and e_2, and two possible outcomes yielding $\overline{S}$ and $\underline{S}$ to the principal. The probabilities that $\overline{S}$ is realized are, respectively, π_0, π_1, and π_2, with $\pi_0 < \pi_1 < \pi_2$ and the corresponding disutilities of effort being $\psi_0 = 0 < \psi_1 < \psi_2$. Under complete information, the intermediate effort is chosen when

$$\frac{h(\psi_1)}{\pi_1 - \pi_0} < \overline{S} - \underline{S} < \frac{h(\psi_2) - h(\psi_1)}{\pi_2 - \pi_1}. \tag{5.5}$$

The first inequality means that effort e_1 is preferred to e_0. The second inequality means that e_1 is also preferred to e_2.

Under moral hazard, let us first observe that the first-best effort e_1 may no longer be implementable. Indeed, let us denote by $\bar{u}$ and $\underline{u}$ the levels of utility offered to the agent when $\overline{S}$ and $\underline{S}$ realize. Incentive compatibility requires that

$$\bar{u} - \underline{u} \geq \frac{\psi_1}{\pi_1 - \pi_0}, \tag{5.6}$$

so that the agent prefers exerting effort e_1 rather than e_0. Similarly, we must also have

$$\bar{u} - \underline{u} \leq \frac{\psi_2 - \psi_1}{\pi_2 - \pi_1} \tag{5.7}$$

---

[4]Then, the MLRP condition says that $\frac{\pi_{ik} - \pi_{i(k-1)}}{\pi_{ik}}$ is not decreasing in i for all $k \geq 1$. The cumulative distribution $F_{ik} = \sum_{j=1}^i \pi_{jk}$ is convex in effort whenever $F_{ik} + F_{ik'} \geq 2F_{i(\frac{k+k'}{2})}$ for all (k, k') in K^2 (when $\frac{k+k'}{2}$ is not an integer, one may choose $E[\frac{k+k'}{2}] + 1$ where $E(\cdot)$ denotes the integer part).

[5]If there are several such maximizers, just pick any of them.

to ensure that the agent prefers exerting effort e_1 than e_2. However, when $\frac{\psi_2 - \psi_1}{\pi_2 - \pi_1} < \frac{\psi_1}{\pi_1 - \pi_0}$, the set of payoffs $(\bar{u}, \underline{u})$, such that (5.6) and (5.7) are both satisfied, is empty. Hence, e_1 can no longer be implemented.

Effort e_0 remains obviously implementable with a null payment in each state of nature. Finally, effort e_2 is implemented when the incentive constraint

$$\bar{u} - \underline{u} \geq \max\left\{\frac{\psi_2 - \psi_1}{\pi_2 - \pi_1}; \frac{\psi_2}{\pi_2 - \pi_0}\right\}, \tag{5.8}$$

which ensures that effort e_2 is preferred to both e_1 and e_0, and the participation constraint

$$\pi_2 \bar{u} + (1 - \pi_2)\underline{u} - \psi_2 \geq 0, \tag{5.9}$$

are both satisfied.

When $\frac{\psi_2 - \psi_1}{\pi_2 - \pi_1} < \frac{\psi_2}{\pi_2 - \pi_0}$, the maximand on the right-hand side of (5.8) is $\frac{\psi_2}{\pi_2 - \pi_0}$. Hence, the second-best cost of implementing effort e_2 can easily be computed as

$$C_2^{SB} = \pi_2 h\left(\psi_2 + \frac{(1 - \pi_2)\psi_2}{\pi_2 - \pi_0}\right) + (1 - \pi_2)h\left(\psi_2 - \frac{\pi_2 \psi_2}{\pi_2 - \pi_0}\right). \tag{5.10}$$

Therefore, effort e_2 is second-best optimal when

$$\bar{S} - \underline{S} > \frac{C_2^{SB}}{\pi_2 - \pi_0}. \tag{5.11}$$

It is easy to check that one can find values of $\bar{S} - \underline{S}$, so that (5.5) and (5.11) both hold simultaneously. Our conclusion is in proposition 5.1.

Proposition 5.1: *With more than two levels of effort, the second-best effort level may be greater than the first-best level.*

5.1.2 Two Outcomes with a Continuum of Effort Levels

To reduce the cumbersome difficulty of the discrete case, modellers have often preferred to allow for a continuum of effort levels. With more than two states of nature, one meets the soon-important technical problems analyzed in section 5.1.3. With only two possible levels of performance, the analysis nevertheless remains very tractable as we will demonstrate in this section. To make some progress in this direction, we reparameterize the model by assuming that $\pi(e) = e$, for all e in $[0, 1]$. Hence, the agent's effort level equals the probability of a high performance. The disutility of effort function $\psi(e)$ is increasing and convex in e ($\psi' > 0$ and $\psi'' > 0$) with $\psi(0) = 0$. Moreover, to ensure interior solutions, we assume that the Inada conditions $\psi'(0) = 0$ and $\psi'(1) = +\infty$ both hold. Let us finally consider a risk-neutral agent with zero initial wealth who is protected by the limited liability constraints

$$\underline{t} \geq 0 \tag{5.12}$$

and

$$\bar{t} \geq 0. \tag{5.13}$$

Faced with an incentive contract $\{(\underline{t}, \bar{t})\}$, this agent chooses an effort e, such that

$$e = \arg \max_{\tilde{e} \in [0,1]} \tilde{e}\bar{t} + (1 - \tilde{e})\underline{t} - \psi(\tilde{e}). \tag{5.14}$$

By strict concavity of the agent's objective function, the incentive constraint rewrites with the following necessary and sufficient first-order condition:

$$\bar{t} - \underline{t} = \psi'(e). \tag{5.15}$$

The principal's program becomes

(P): $$\max_{\{(e,\bar{t},\underline{t})\}} e\bar{S} + (1 - e)\underline{S} - e\bar{t} - (1 - e)\underline{t}$$

subject to (5.12), (5.13), and (5.15).

As in the model of section 4.3, the limited liability constraint in (5.12) (resp. (5.13)) is again binding (resp. slack). Replacing $\bar{t}$ with $\psi'(e)$ in the principal's objective function, the principal's reduced program (P′) is written as

(P′): $$\max_{e \in [0,1]} e\bar{S} + (1 - e)\underline{S} - e\psi'(e).$$

When $\psi''' > 0$ the principal's objective function is strictly concave in e, and direct optimization leads to the following equation defining the second-best level of effort e^{SB}:

$$\Delta S = \psi'(e^{SB}) + e^{SB}\psi''(e^{SB}). \tag{5.16}$$

This second-best effort is obviously lower than the first-best effort e^*, which is defined by

$$\Delta S = \psi'(e^*). \tag{5.17}$$

The first-best effort is such that the marginal benefit ΔS of increasing effort by a small amount de is just equal to the marginal disutility of doing so $\psi'(e^*)de$.

Under moral hazard, the marginal benefit $\Delta S de$ must be equal to the marginal cost $\psi'(e^{SB})de$ plus the marginal cost of the agent's limited liability rent $e^{SB}\psi''(e^{SB})de$.

Indeed, with moral hazard the limited liability rent of the agent is strictly positive because this rent is also rewritten as $EU^{SB} = e^{SB}\psi'(e^{SB}) - \psi(e^{SB}) > 0$, where the right-hand side inequality is derived from the convexity of $\psi(\cdot)$, $\psi(0) = 0$, and the fact that $e^{SB} > 0$. Reducing this rent, which is costly from the principal's point view, calls for decreasing effort below the first-best.

> **Remark:** The model with a risk-neutral agent protected by limited liability bears some strong resemblance to the adverse selection model of chapter 2. Indeed, in both models the principal reduces the expected volume of trade with the agent to reduce the latter's information rent. Distortions in effort are now replacing distortions in output to reduce this information rent. ∎

5.1.3 The First-Order Approach

Let us now consider the case where the risk-averse agent may exert a continuous level of effort e in a compact interval $[0, \bar{e}]$ and by doing so incurs a disutility $\psi(e)$ which is increasing and convex ($\psi' > 0$ and $\psi'' > 0$) with $\psi(0) = 0$. To avoid corner solutions, we will also assume that the Inada conditions $\psi'(0) = 0$ and $\psi'(\bar{e}) = +\infty$ are satisfied.

The agent's performance $\tilde{q}$ may take any possible value in the compact interval $Q = [\underline{q}, \bar{q}]$ with the conditional distribution $F(q|e)$ and the everywhere positive density function $f(q|e)$. We assume that $F(\cdot|e)$ is twice differentiable with respect to e and that those distributions all have the same full support Q.

Formally, a contract $\{t(\tilde{q})\}$ that implements a given level of effort e must now satisfy the following incentive constraints:

$$\int_{\underline{q}}^{\bar{q}} u(t(q))f(q|e)\,dq - \psi(e) \geq \int_{\underline{q}}^{\bar{q}} u(t(q))f(q|\tilde{e})\,dq - \psi(\tilde{e}), \quad \text{for all } \tilde{e} \text{ in } [0, \bar{e}]$$

(5.18)

and the participation constraint

$$\int_{\underline{q}}^{\bar{q}} u(t(q))f(q|e)\,dq - \psi(e) \geq 0.$$

(5.19)

The principal's problem is thus

(P): $$\max_{\{(t(\cdot),\, e)\}} \int_{\underline{q}}^{\bar{q}} (S(q) - t(q))f(q|e)\,dq,$$

subject to (5.18) and (5.19).

We denote by $\{(t^{SB}(\cdot), e^{SB})\}$ the solution to (P). The first difficulty with this problem is to ensure that such an optimum exists within the class of all admissible functions $t(\cdot)$. For instance, Mirrlees (1999) has shown that the problem may sometimes have no optimal solution in the class of unbounded sharing rules. The difficulty here comes from the lack of compacity of the set of incentive feasible contracts.[6] We leave aside these technicalities to focus on what we think is the main difficulty of problem (P)—*simplifying* the infinite number of global incentive constraints in (5.18) and replacing those constraints by the simpler *local* incentive constraint:

$$\int_{\underline{q}}^{\bar{q}} u(t(q))f_e(q|e)\, dq - \psi'(e) = 0, \tag{5.20}$$

which is a necessary condition if the optimal effort level is positive.

This constraint simply means that the agent is indifferent about his choice between effort e and increasing (or decreasing) his effort by an amount de when he receives the compensation schedule $\{t(\tilde{q})\}$.

Let us thus define (P^R) as the *relaxed* problem of the principal, where the infinite number of constraints (5.18) have now been replaced by (5.20):

$$(P^R): \qquad \max_{\{(t(\cdot),\, e)\}} \int_{\underline{q}}^{\bar{q}} (S(q) - t(q))f(q|e)\, dq,$$

subject to (5.19) and (5.20).

We denote by $\{(t^R(\cdot), e^R)\}$ the solution to this relaxed problem. We will first characterize this solution. Then we will find sufficient conditions under which the solution of the relaxed problem (P^R) satisfies the constraints of the original problem (P). Hence, we will have obtained a characterization of the solution for problem (P).

Let us first characterize the solution to the relaxed problem (P^R). Denoting the multiplier of (5.20) by λ and the multiplier of (5.19) by μ, we can write the Lagrangian L of this problem as

$$L(t, e) = (S(q) - t)f(q|e) + \lambda(u(t)f_e(q|e) - \psi'(e)) + \mu(u(t)f(q|e) - \psi(e)). \tag{5.21}$$

Pointwise optimization with respect to $t(q)$ yields

$$\frac{1}{u'(t^R(q))} = \mu + \lambda\frac{f_e(q|e^R)}{f(q|e^R)}. \tag{5.22}$$

---

[6]To solve this technical issue, some authors like Holmström (1979) and Page (1987) have put further restrictions on the class of incentive schemes, such as for instance, equicontinuity.

The left-hand side of (5.22) is increasing with respect to $t^R(q)$, because $u'' < 0$. Provided that $\lambda > 0$, MLRP (here in its strict version for simplicity),

$$\frac{\partial}{\partial q}\left(\frac{f_e(q|e)}{f(q|e)}\right) > 0 \qquad \text{for all } q, \tag{5.23}$$

guarantees that the right-hand side of (5.22) is also increasing in q. Hence, under MLRP, $t^R(q)$ is strictly increasing with respect to q.

> **Remark:** Note that the probability that the realized output is greater than a given q when effort e is exerted is $1 - F(q|e)$. Let us check that increasing e raises this probability when MLRP holds. We have
>
> $$F_e(q|e) = \int_{\underline{q}}^{q} \frac{f_e(q|e)}{f(q|e)} f(q|e)\, dq = \int_{\underline{q}}^{q} \alpha(q, e) f(q|e)\, dq, \tag{5.24}$$
>
> where $\alpha(q, e) = \frac{\partial}{\partial e}(\log f(q|e)) = \frac{f_e(q|e)}{f(q|e)}$ is the derivative of the log-likelihood of $f(\cdot)$. But, by MLRP, $\alpha(q, e)$ is increasing in q. $\alpha(q, e)$ cannot be everywhere negative, because by definition $F_e(\bar{q}|e) = 0 = \int_{\underline{q}}^{\bar{q}} f(q|e)\alpha(q, e)\, dq$. Hence, there exists q^* such that: $\alpha(q, e) \leq 0$ if and only if $q \leq q^*$. $F_e(q|e)$ is decreasing in q (resp. increasing) on $[\underline{q}, q^*]$ (resp. $[q^*, \bar{q}]$). Since $F_e(\underline{q}|e) = F_e(\bar{q}|e) = 0$, we necessarily have $F_e(q|e) \leq 0$ for any q in $[\underline{q}, \bar{q}]$. Hence, when the agent exerts an effort e which is greater than e', the distribution of output with e dominates the distribution of output with e' in the sense of first-order stochastic dominance. ∎

We now show that indeed $\lambda > 0$. Let us first denote by e^R the effort level solution of (P^R). Multiplying (5.22) by $f(q|e^R)$ and integrating over $[\underline{q}, \bar{q}]$ yields

$$\mu = \int_{\underline{q}}^{\bar{q}} \frac{1}{u'(t^R(q))} f(q|e^R)\, dq = \underset{\tilde{q}}{E}\left(\frac{1}{u'(t^R(\tilde{q}))}\right),$$

since $\int_{\underline{q}}^{\bar{q}} f_e(q|e^R)\, dq = 0$. The expectation operator with respect to the distribution of output induced by effort e^R is denoted by $\underset{\tilde{q}}{E}(\cdot)$. Because $u' > 0$, we have $\mu > 0$ and the participation constraint in (5.19) is binding.

Using (5.22) again, we also find

$$\frac{\lambda f_e(q|e^R)}{f(q|e^R)} = \frac{1}{u'(t^R(q))} - \underset{\tilde{q}}{E}\left(\frac{1}{u'(t^R(\tilde{q}))}\right). \tag{5.25}$$

Multiplying both sides of (5.25) by $u(t^R(q))f(q|e^R)$ and integrating over $[\underline{q}, \bar{q}]$ yields

$$\lambda \int_{\underline{q}}^{\bar{q}} u(t^R(q))f_e(q|e^R)dq = \text{cov}\left(u(t^R(\tilde{q})), \frac{1}{u'(t^R(\tilde{q}))}\right), \qquad (5.26)$$

where $\text{cov}(\cdot)$ is the covariance operator.

Using the slackness condition associated with (5.20), namely $\lambda(\int_{\underline{q}}^{\bar{q}} u(t^R(q)) \times f_e(q|e)\, dq - \psi'(e)) = 0$, we finally get

$$\lambda \psi'(e^R) = \text{cov}\left(u(t^R(\tilde{q})), \frac{1}{u'(t^R(\tilde{q}))}\right). \qquad (5.27)$$

Since $u(\cdot)$ and $u'(\cdot)$ covary in opposite directions, we necessarily have $\lambda \geq 0$. Moreover, the only case where this covariance is exactly zero is when $t^R(q)$ is a constant for all q. But then the incentive constraint (5.20) can no longer be satisfied at a positive level of effort. Having proved that $\lambda > 0$, we derive the following proposition from above.

Proposition 5.2: *Under MLRP, the solution $t^R(q)$ to the relaxed problem (P^R) is increasing in q.*

We can rewrite the agent's expected utility when he receives the scheme $\{t^R(q)\}$ and exerts an effort e as

$$U(e) = \int_{\underline{q}}^{\bar{q}} u(t^R(q))f(q|e)\, dq - \psi(e),$$

$$= [u(t^R(q))F(q|e)]_{\underline{q}}^{\bar{q}} - \int_{\underline{q}}^{\bar{q}} u'(t^R(q))\frac{dt^R}{dq}(q)F(q|e)\, dq - \psi(e)$$

$$= u(t^R(\bar{q})) - \int_{\underline{q}}^{\bar{q}} u'(t^R(q))\frac{dt^R}{dq}(q)F(q|e)\, dq - \psi(e), \qquad (5.28)$$

where the second line is obtained simply by integrating by parts, and the third line uses the fact that $F(\underline{q}|e) = 0$ and $F(\bar{q}|e) = 1$ for all e.

Since $\psi'' > 0$, $u' > 0$ and $t^R(q)$ is increasing when MLRP holds, $U(e)$ is concave in e as soon as $F_{ee}(q|e) > 0$ for all (q, e). This last property is called the *convexity of the distribution function condition* (CDFC).

> **Remark 1:** Joined to MLRP, CDFC captures the idea that increasing the agent's effort also increases, at a decreasing rate, the probability $1 - F(q|e)$ that the realized output is greater than q. ∎

Remark 2: Note that CDFC may not always hold. Let us assume, for instance, that production is linked to effort as follows: $q = e + \epsilon$ where ϵ is distributed on $]-\infty, +\infty[$ with a cumulative distribution function $G(\cdot)$. Then, CDFC implies that the distribution of ϵ has an increasing density, a rather stringent assumption. ∎

Remark 3: It may seem surprising that such stringent assumptions are needed to prove the simple and intuitive result that the agent's reward increases as his performance increases. However, remember that the dependence of $t^R(\cdot)$ on q (which is bad from the insurance point of view) is interesting only to the extent that it creates incentives for effort. For a higher q to be a signal of a high effort, it must be that an increase of effort increases production unambiguously,[7] but also that the informativeness of q about e increases with q (this is ensured by MLRP). ∎

Since $U(e)$ is concave for a solution of the relaxed problem, the first-order condition (5.20) is sufficient to characterize the incentive constraints. Accordingly, the first-order conditions of problem (P) are the same as those of problem (P^R). Proposition 5.3 provides a summary.

Proposition 5.3: *Assume that both MLRP and CDFC both hold. If the optimal effort level is positive, it is characterized by the solution of a relaxed problem (P^R) using the first-order approach in (5.20). We have* $\{(t^{SB}(\cdot), e^{SB})\} = \{(t^R(\cdot), e^R)\}$.

This solution $\{t^{SB}(\cdot), e^{SB}\}$ is then characterized by the binding participation constraint (5.19), the incentive constraint (5.20), and the two first-order conditions of the principal's problem, namely (5.22) and

$$\int_{\underline{q}}^{\bar{q}} (S(q) - t^{SB}(q)) f_e(q|e^{SB}) dq + \lambda \left(\int_{\underline{q}}^{\bar{q}} u(t^{SB}(q)) f_{ee}(q|e^{SB}) dq - \psi''(e^{SB}) \right) = 0.$$

(5.29)

Given the highly restrictive assumptions imposed to prove proposition 5.3, the validity of the first-order approach is somewhat limited. Furthermore, when the first-order approach is not valid, using it can be very misleading. The true solution may not even be one among the multiple solutions of the first-order conditions for the relaxed problem.[8] As a consequence, most of the applied moral hazard literature adopts the discrete $\{0, 1\}$ formalization outlined in chapter 4.

---

[7] In the sense of first-order stochastic dominance.
[8] Grossman and Hart (1983) offer a graphical illustration of this phenomenon.

An example: Take $S(q) = q$ and the probability distribution of production $f(q|e) = \frac{1}{e}\exp(-q|e)$, $q \geq 0$.

Note that $f_e(q|e) = \frac{(q-e)}{e^3}\exp(-q/e)$ and $\frac{f_e(q|e)}{f(q|e)} = \frac{(q-e)}{e^2}$. This distribution satisfies the MLRP property, since $\frac{\partial}{\partial q}\left(\frac{f_e}{f}\right) = \frac{1}{e^2} > 0$ for all $q \geq 0$.

Moreover, we have $F(q|e) = 1 - \exp(-q/e)$. Hence, $F_e(q|e) = -\frac{q}{e^2}\exp(-q/e) < 0$, i.e., an increase of effort increases production in the first-order stochastic dominance sense. Finally, $F_{ee}(q|e) = \frac{(2e-q)q}{e^4}\exp(-q/e)$, so that CDFC is not satisfied.

The agent has utility function $U = 2\sqrt{t} - e^2$. (5.22) is immediately written as

$$t(q) = \left(\mu + \lambda\frac{(q-e)}{e^2}\right)^2. \tag{5.30}$$

For a high enough status quo utility level U_0 of the agent,[9] one can solve the binding participation constraint of the agent, the first order condition (5.20) of the agent's problem with respect to e, and the first order condition (5.29) of the principal's problem with respect to e, and obtain the optimal values of the parameters λ^{SB}, μ^{SB}, and e^{SB} of the transfer function, which becomes

$$t^{SB}(q) = \left(\left(\mu^{SB} - \frac{\lambda^{SB}}{e^{SB}}\right) + \frac{\lambda^{SB}}{(e^{SB})^2}q\right)^2.$$

Note that the agent's objective function is strictly concave despite the fact that CDFC is not satisfied. Indeed,

$$E\left(2\sqrt{t^{SB}(q)}\right) - e^2 = 2\left(\mu^{SB} - \frac{\lambda^{SB}}{e^{SB}}\right) + 2\frac{\lambda^{SB}}{(e^{SB})^2}e - e^2.$$

Designing by t^{FB} the sure transfer associated with the first-best, figure 5.1 summarizes the analysis.

With respect to the first-best, the agent is punished for $q \leq q^*$ and rewarded for $q > q^*$. The agent bears some risk that induces him to exert some effort e^{SB}, which depends on U.

The first-order approach has been one of the most debated issues in contract theory in the late seventies and early eighties. Mirrlees (1975) was the first to point out the limits of this approach and argued that

---

[9]This is necessary to induce a non-negative value of t so that $\sqrt{t}$ is always well defined. Indeed, with such a utility function the agent cannot be punished with negative transfers, so his expected utility must be positive.

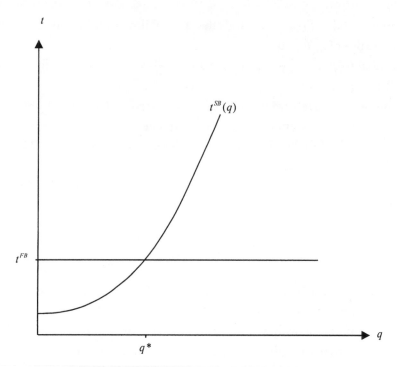

FIGURE 5.1: First-Best and Second-Best Transfers

it is valid only when the agent's problem has a unique maximizer.[10,11] Later he offered a proof for the use of this approach when the conditions MLRP and CDFC both hold. This proof was corrected by Rogerson (1985a). Finally, Jewitt (1988) offered a direct proof that the multiplier of the local incentive constraint was positive.[12] Jewitt also showed that CDFC can be relaxed, provided that the agent's utility function satisfies further fine properties. Brown, Chiang, Ghosh, and Wolfstetter (1986) provided a condition validating the first-order approach independently of restrictions on the information structures. Aloi (1997) extended the first-order approach to nonseparable utility functions for the agent. Sinclair-Desgagné (1994) generalized the first-order approach to the case where the principal observes several dimensions of the agent's performance. Grossman and Hart (1983) gave an exhaustive characterization of the agent's incentive scheme. Their approach is based on a complete description of the incentive and participation constraints when the performances take $n \geq 2$ values and the agent's effort belongs to a finite set. Araujo and Moreira (2001) showed how to solve the moral hazard problem in the absence of a first-order approach. ∎

---

[10]See also Guesnerie and Laffont (1978).
[11]This mimeo was later published in Mirrlees (1999).
[12]We have used his proof in the text.

5.2 The Multitask Incentive Problem

It is often the case that the agent does not exert a single-dimensional effort, particularly when he is involved in many related activities associated with the same job. Such examples abound, as we will see in section 5.2.5 below. When the agent simultaneously performs several tasks for the principal, new issues arise: How does the technological interaction among those tasks affect incentives? What sort of optimal incentive contracts should be provided to the agent? How do incentive considerations affect the optimal mix of efforts along each dimension of the agent's performance?

5.2.1 Technology

To answer the above questions, we now extend the simple model of chapter 4 and let the agent perform two tasks for the principal with respective efforts e^1 and e^2. For simplicity, we first assume that those two tasks are completely symmetric and have the same stochastic returns $S^i = \overline{S}$ or $\underline{S}$, for $i = 1, 2$. Those returns are independently distributed with respective probabilities $\pi(e^1)$ and $\pi(e^2)$. Since there are basically only three possible outcomes, yielding $2\overline{S}, \overline{S} + \underline{S}$, and $2\underline{S}$ to the principal, a contract is in fact a triplet of corresponding payments $(\bar{t}, \hat{t}, \underline{t})$. $\bar{t}$ is given in case of success on both tasks, $\hat{t}$ is given in case of success on only one task and $\underline{t}$ is given when none of the tasks has been successful.[13]

Again, we normalize each effort to belong to $\{0, 1\}$. Note that the model has, by symmetry, three possible levels of *aggregate* effort. The agent can exert a high effort on both tasks, on only one task, or on no task at all. The reader will recognize that the multitask agency model should thus inherit many of the difficulties discussed in section 5.1. However, the multitask problem also has more structure thanks to the technological assumption generally made on these tasks. We will denote by ψ_2, ψ_1, and $\psi_0 = 0$ the agent's disutilities of effort when he exerts, respectively, two high-effort levels, only one, or none. Of course, we have $\psi_2 > \psi_1 > 0$. Moreover, we say that the two tasks are *substitutes* when $\psi_2 > 2\psi_1$, and *complements* when instead $\psi_2 < 2\psi_1$. When tasks are substitutes, it is harder to accomplish the second task at the margin when the first one is already performed. The reverse holds when the two tasks are complements.

---

[13]It is a straightforward extension to allow the principal's payoff to be symmetric and a nonlinear function $S(\tilde{q}^1, \tilde{q}^2)$ of the random outputs $\tilde{q}^1$ and $\tilde{q}^2$. Various asymmetries can also be handled, as we will see in section 5.2.4 below.

5.2.2 The Simple Case of Limited Liability and Substitutability of Tasks

In this section we begin by analyzing a simple example with a risk-neutral agent protected by limited liability.

First-Best Outcome

Let us first assume that the principal performs the tasks himself, or alternatively that he uses a risk-neutral agent to do so and that effort is observable.

Because the performances on each task are independent variables, the principal's net benefit of choosing to let the agent exert a positive effort on both tasks is $V_2^{FB} = 2(\pi_1\overline{S} + (1 - \pi_1)\underline{S}) - \psi_2$. Note also that $C_2^{FB} = \psi_2$ is the first-best cost of implementing both efforts in this case of risk neutrality.

If he chooses to let the agent exert only one positive level of effort, the principal instead gets $V_1^{FB} = \pi_1\overline{S} + (1 - \pi_1)\underline{S} + \pi_0\overline{S} + (1 - \pi_0)\underline{S} - \psi_1$. The first-best cost of implementing only one effort is then $C_1^{FB} = \psi_1$.

Finally, if he chooses to let the agent exert no effort at all, the principal gets $V_0^{FB} = 2(\pi_0\overline{S} + (1 - \pi_0)\underline{S})$.

Hence, exerting both efforts is preferred to any other allocation when $V_2^{FB} \geq \max(V_1^{FB}, V_0^{FB})$, or to put it differently, when

$$\Delta\pi\Delta S \geq \max\left\{\frac{\psi_2}{2}, \psi_2 - \psi_1\right\}. \tag{5.31}$$

When the two tasks are substitutes, we have $\psi_2 - \psi_1 > \frac{\psi_2}{2}$. The more stringent constraint on the right-hand side of (5.31) is obtained when the principal lets the agent exert one positive level of effort.[14] Figure 5.2 summarizes the first-best choices of effort made by the principal as a function of the incremental benefit $\Delta\pi\Delta S$ associated with each task.

When tasks are substitutes a whole range of intermediate values of $\Delta\pi\Delta S$ exist, which are simultaneously large enough to justify a positive effort on one task and small enough to prevent the principal from willing to let the agent exert both efforts.

Moral Hazard

Let us now turn to the case where efforts are nonobservable and the risk-neutral agent is protected by limited liability.

---

[14]In this latter case, given the symmetry of the model, there is no loss of generality in assuming that the only high effort is performed on task 1.

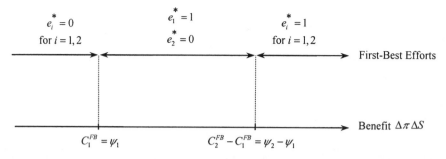

FIGURE 5.2: First-Best Levels of Effort with Substitutes

Suppose first that the principal wants to induce a high effort on both tasks. We leave it to the reader to check that the best way to do so is for the principal to reward the agent only when $\tilde{q}^1 = \tilde{q}^2 = \bar{q}$, i.e., when both tasks are successful. Differently stated, we have $\bar{t} > \hat{t} = \underline{t} = 0$.

The *local incentive constraint* that prevents the agent from exerting only one effort is written as

$$\pi_1^2 \bar{t} - \psi_2 \geq \pi_1 \pi_0 \bar{t} - \psi_1. \tag{5.32}$$

The *global incentive constraint* that prevents the agent from exerting no effort at all is instead written as

$$\pi_1^2 \bar{t} - \psi_2 \geq \pi_0^2 \bar{t}. \tag{5.33}$$

Both incentive constraints (5.32) and (5.33) can finally be summarized as

$$\bar{t} \geq \frac{1}{\Delta\pi} \max\left\{ \frac{\psi_2 - \psi_1}{\pi_1}, \frac{\psi_2}{\pi_1 + \pi_0} \right\}.^{15} \tag{5.34}$$

The principal's problem (P) is thus written as:

(P): $$\max_{\{\bar{t}\}} \pi_1^2 (2\bar{S} - \bar{t}) + 2\pi_1(1 - \pi_1)(\bar{S} + \underline{S}) + 2(1 - \pi_1)^2 \underline{S}$$

subject to (5.34).

The latter constraint is obviously binding at the optimum of (P). The second-best cost of implementing both efforts is thus $C_2^{SB} = \frac{\pi_1}{\Delta\pi} \max\{\psi_2 - \psi_1, \frac{\pi_1 \psi_2}{\pi_1 + \pi_0}\}$. For the principal, the net benefits from inducing a positive effort on both activities is written as

$$V_2^{SB} = 2(\pi_1 \bar{S} + (1 - \pi_1)\underline{S}) - \frac{\pi_1}{\Delta\pi} \max\left\{ \psi_2 - \psi_1, \frac{\pi_1 \psi_2}{\pi_1 + \pi_0} \right\}. \tag{5.35}$$

---

[15]Note that the right-hand side of (5.34) is strictly positive. Hence, the limited liability constraint $\bar{t} \geq 0$ is automatically satisfied.

If the principal chooses to induce only one effort, e.g., on task 1, he instead offers a transfer $\hat{t} = \frac{\psi_1}{\Delta\pi}$ each time that $\tilde{q}_1 = \bar{q}$ and zero otherwise, just as in chapter 4. The second-best cost of implementing effort on a single task is thus $C_1^{SB} = \frac{\pi_1 \psi_1}{\Delta\pi}$. The second-best net benefit for the principal of inducing this single dimension of effort is

$$V_1^{SB} = \pi_1 \overline{S} + (1 - \pi_1)\underline{S} + \pi_0 \overline{S} + (1 - \pi_0)\underline{S} - \frac{\pi_1 \psi_1}{\Delta\pi}. \tag{5.36}$$

Again, there are three possible sets of parameters, characterizing different zones for which the principal wants to induce either zero, one, or two efforts.

It is easy to check that the principal now chooses to exert zero effort more often than under complete information, because

$$C_1^{SB} = \frac{\pi_1 \psi_1}{\Delta\pi} > \psi_1 = C_1^{FB}. \tag{5.37}$$

Let us turn to the determination of whether or not the principal induces two positive efforts under moral hazard less often than under complete information.

We isolate two cases. First, when $\frac{\pi_0 \psi_2}{\pi_1 + \pi_0} \geq \psi_1$, one can check that the local incentive constraint is the more constraining one for a principal willing to induce both efforts from the agent. This means that $\bar{t} = \frac{\psi_2 - \psi_1}{\pi_1 \Delta\pi}$. Then, the inequality $\frac{\pi_0 \psi_2}{\pi_1 + \pi_0} \geq \psi_1$ implies that

$$C_2^{SB} - C_1^{SB} = \frac{\pi_1}{\Delta\pi}(\psi_2 - 2\psi_1) \geq C_2^{FB} - C_1^{FB} = \psi_2 - \psi_1. \tag{5.38}$$

This inequality means that the principal induces those two efforts less often than under complete information (figure 5.3).

The intuition behind this result is the following. Under moral hazard, the cost of implementing either two efforts or one effort is greater than under complete information. Because of the technological substitutability between tasks, what matters for evaluating whether both tasks should be incentivized *less often* than under complete information is how the second-best incremental cost $C_2^{SB} - C_1^{SB}$ can be compared to the first-best incremental cost $C_2^{FB} - C_1^{FB}$. When the local incentive

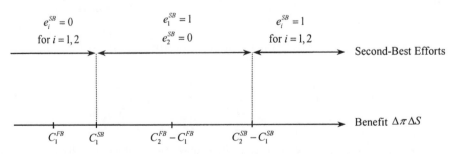

FIGURE 5.3: Second-Best Levels of Effort with Substitutes (for $\frac{\pi_0 \psi_2}{\pi_1 + \pi_0} \geq \psi_1$)

constraint is binding it is harder to incentivize effort on a second task when a positive effort is already implemented on the first one. The second-best cost of inducing effort increases *more* quickly than the first-best cost as one goes from one task to two tasks.

> **Remark:** Note that $\pi_0 < \pi_1$ implies that the condition $\frac{\pi_0 \psi_2}{\pi_1 + \pi_0} > \psi_1$ is more stringent than the condition for task substitutability, namely $\psi_2 > 2\psi_1$. For the second-best cost of implementation to satisfy (5.38), it must be true that efforts are in fact *strong substitutes*. It is then much harder to accomplish the second task at the margin when the first one is already done. ∎

Let us now turn to the case where $\frac{\pi_0 \psi_2}{\pi_1 + \pi_0} < \psi_1 < \frac{\psi_2}{2}$. For such a weak substitutability, the global incentive constraint is now the more constraining one for a principal willing to induce both efforts from the agent. The transfer received by the agent is thus $\bar{t} = \frac{\psi_2}{(\pi_1 + \pi_0)\Delta\pi}$. Then, $\frac{\pi_0 \psi_2}{\pi_1 + \pi_0} < \psi_1$ implies that we also have

$$C_2^{SB} - C_1^{SB} = \frac{\pi_1(\pi_1\psi_2 - (\pi_1 + \pi_0)\psi_1)}{\Delta\pi(\pi_1 + \pi_0)} < C_2^{FB} - C_1^{FB} = \psi_2 - \psi_1. \qquad (5.39)$$

The principal now prefers to induce both efforts rather than only one *more often* than under complete information. The second-best cost of inducing effort increases *less* quickly than the first-best cost as one goes from one task to two tasks. Intuitively, incentives create a complementarity between tasks which goes counter to the technological diseconomies of scope.

We summarize these findings in proposition 5.4.

> **Proposition 5.4:** *Under moral hazard and limited liability, the degree of diseconomies of scope between substitute tasks increases or decreases depending on whether local or global incentive constraints are binding in the principal's problem.*

The Case of Complements

Let us briefly discuss the case where the two tasks are complements. Figure 5.4 describes the values of benefit for which the principal wants to induce both efforts.

Under moral hazard, the global incentive constraint is now *always* binding for a principal willing to induce both efforts. Indeed, the inequality $\frac{\psi_2}{\pi_1 + \pi_0} > \frac{\psi_2 - \psi_1}{\pi_1}$ always holds when $\psi_2 < 2\psi_1$. Hence, we have also $C_2^{SB} = \frac{\pi_1^2 \psi_2}{(\pi_1 + \pi_0)\Delta\pi}$. The principal now finds it harder to induce both efforts than under complete information, as can be seen in figure 5.5.

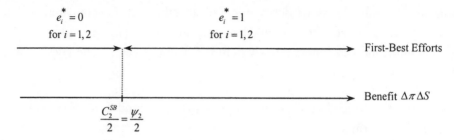

FIGURE 5.4: First-Best Levels of Effort with Complements

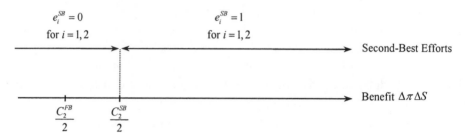

FIGURE 5.5: Second-Best Levels of Effort with Complements

Hence, the principal induces a pair of high efforts under moral hazard less often than under complete information. Intuitively, the case of complementarity is very much like the case of a single activity analyzed in chapter 4.

5.2.3 The Optimal Contract with a Risk-Averse Agent

In this section and the following one we assume that the agent is strictly risk-averse. Because of the symmetry between tasks, there is again no loss of generality in assuming that the principal offers a contract $\{(\bar{t}, \hat{t}, \underline{t})\}$ where $\bar{t}$ is given in case of success on both tasks, $\hat{t}$ is given when only one task is successful, and $\underline{t}$ is given when no task succeeds.

Let us now describe the set of incentive feasible contracts that induce effort on both dimensions of the agent's activity. As usual, it is useful to express these constraints with the agent's utility levels in each state of nature as the new variables. Let us thus define $\bar{u} = u(\bar{t})$, $\hat{u} = u(\hat{t})$ and $\underline{u} = u(\underline{t})$. We have to consider the possibility that the agent could shirk, not only on one dimension of effort but also on both dimensions. The first incentive constraint is a local incentive constraint which is written as

$$(\pi_1)^2\bar{u} + 2\pi_1(1 - \pi_1)\hat{u} + (1 - \pi_1)^2\underline{u} - \psi_2$$
$$\geq \pi_1\pi_0\bar{u} + (\pi_1(1 - \pi_0) + \pi_0(1 - \pi_1))\hat{u} + (1 - \pi_1)(1 - \pi_0)\underline{u} - \psi_1. \quad (5.40)$$

The second incentive constraint is instead a global incentive constraint and is written as

$$(\pi_1)^2 \bar{u} + 2\pi_1(1 - \pi_1)\hat{u} + (1 - \pi_1)^2 \underline{u} - \psi_2$$

$$\geq (\pi_0)^2 \bar{u} + 2\pi_0(1 - \pi_0)\hat{u} + (1 - \pi_0)^2 \underline{u}. \tag{5.41}$$

Finally, the agent's participation constraint is

$$(\pi_1)^2 \bar{u} + 2\pi_1(1 - \pi_1)\hat{u} + (1 - \pi_1)^2 \underline{u} - \psi_2 \geq 0. \tag{5.42}$$

If he wants to induce both efforts, the principal's problem can be stated as:

$$(P): \max_{\{(\bar{u}, \hat{u}, \underline{u})\}} (\pi_1)^2 (2\bar{S} - h(\bar{u})) + 2\pi_1(1 - \pi_1)(\bar{S} + \underline{S} - h(\hat{u})) + (1 - \pi_1)^2 (2\underline{S} - h(\underline{u})),$$

subject to (5.40) through (5.42).

Structure of the Optimal Contract

A priori, the solution to problem (P) may entail that either one or two incentive constraints is binding. Moreover, when there is only one such binding constraint it might be either the local or the global incentive constraint. We derive the full-fledged analysis when the inverse utility function $h = u^{-1}$ is quadratic, i.e., $h(u) = u + \frac{ru^2}{2}$ for some $r > 0$ and $u \geq -\frac{1}{r}$, in appendix 5.1. The next proposition summarizes our findings.

> **Proposition 5.5:** *In the multitask incentive problem (P) with $h(u) = u + \frac{ru^2}{2}$ ($r > 0$), the optimal contract that induces effort on both tasks is such that the participation constraint (5.42) is always binding. Moreover, the binding incentive constraints are:*
>
> - *The local incentive constraint (5.40) in the case of substitute tasks, such that $\psi_2 > 2\psi_1$.*
> - *Both the local and the global incentive constraints (5.40) and (5.41) in the case of weak complement tasks, such that $\left(\frac{(\Delta\pi)^2 + 2\pi_1(1-\pi_1)}{(\Delta\pi)^2 + \pi_1(1-\pi_1)}\right)\psi_1 \leq \psi_2 \leq 2\psi_1$.*
> - *The global incentive constraint (5.41) in the case of strong complement tasks, such that $\psi_2 \leq \left(\frac{(\Delta\pi)^2 + 2\pi_1(1-\pi_1)}{(\Delta\pi)^2 + \pi_1(1-\pi_1)}\right)\psi_1$.*

The incentive problem in a multitask environment with risk aversion has an intuitive structure that is somewhat similar to the one obtained in section 5.2.2. When efforts are substitutes, the principal finds it harder to provide incentives for both tasks simultaneously than it was for only one task. Indeed, the agent is more willing to reduce his effort on task 1 if he already exerts a high effort on task 2. The local incentive constraint is thus binding. On the contrary, with a strong complementarity between tasks, inducing the agent to exert a positive effort on both tasks simultaneously rather than on none becomes the most difficult constraint for the principal. The global incentive constraint is now binding. For intermediary cases, i.e., with weak complements, the situation is less clear. All incentive constraints, both local and global ones, are then binding.

> **Remark:** The reader will have recognized the strong similarity between the structure of the optimal contract in the moral hazard multitask problem and the structure of the optimal contract in the multidimensional adverse selection problem that was discussed in section 3.2. In both cases, it may happen that either local or global incentive constraints bind. A strong complementarity of efforts plays almost the same role as a very strong correlation in the agent's types under adverse selection. It makes it more likely that the global incentive constraint binds. ∎

Optimal Effort

Let us turn now to the characterization of the optimal effort chosen by the principal in this second-best environment. To better understand these choices it is useful to start with the simple case where tasks are technologically unrelated, i.e., $\psi_2 = 2\psi_1$.

Suppose that the principal wants to induce effort on only one task. Under complete information, the expected incremental benefit of doing so, $\Delta\pi\Delta S$, should exceed the first-best cost C_1^{FB} of implementing this effort:

$$\Delta\pi\Delta S \geq C_1^{FB} = h(\psi_1) = \psi_1 + \frac{r\psi_1^2}{2}. \tag{5.43}$$

With two tasks, and still under complete information, the principal prefers to induce effort on both tasks rather than on only one when the incremental expected benefit from implementing one extra unit of effort, which is again $\Delta\pi\Delta S$, exceeds the increase in the cost of doing so, i.e., $C_2^{FB} - C_1^{FB}$, where $C_2^{FB} = h(2\psi_1) = 2\psi_1 + \frac{r}{2}(2\psi_1)^2$ is the first-best cost of implementing two efforts. This leads to the condition

$$\Delta\pi\Delta S \geq C_2^{FB} - C_1^{FB} = \psi_1 + \frac{3r\psi_1^2}{2}. \tag{5.44}$$

It is easy to check that the right-hand side of (5.44) is greater than the right-hand side of (5.43), because $C_2^{FB} > 2C_1^{FB}$ as soon as $r > 0$. When $\Delta\pi\Delta S$ belongs to $[C_1^{FB}, C_2^{FB} - C_1^{FB}]$ only one effort is induced. Note for further reference that this interval has a positive length $C_2^{FB} - 2C_1^{FB}$.

Moreover, the inequality $C_2^{FB} - C_1^{FB} > C_1^{FB}$ means that it is less often valuable for the principal to induce both efforts rather than inducing one effort when effort is verifiable. The latter inequality also means that the first-best cost of implementing efforts exhibits some *diseconomies of scope*. Adding up tasks makes it more costly to induce effort from the agent, even if those tasks are technologically unrelated and contracting takes place under complete information. The point here is that inducing the agent to exert more tasks requires increasing the certainty equivalent income necessary to satisfy his participation constraint. Adding more tasks therefore changes the cost borne by the principal for implementing an extra level of effort. Now that the agent has a decreasing marginal utility of consumption, multiplying the level of effort by two requires multiplying the transfer needed to ensure the agent's participation by more than two. For that reason, the diseconomies of scope isolated above can be viewed as pure *participation diseconomies of scope*.

Now, still with unrelated tasks, let us move to the case of moral hazard. Under moral hazard, we already know from section 4.4 that, with the specification made on the agent's utility function, the second-best cost of implementing a single effort is written as

$$C_1^{SB} = \psi_1 + \frac{r\psi_1^2}{2} + \frac{r\psi_1^2 \pi_1(1-\pi_1)}{2(\Delta\pi)^2}. \tag{5.45}$$

The principal now prefers to induce one effort rather than none when

$$\Delta\pi\Delta S \geq C_1^{SB} = C_1^{FB} + \frac{r\psi_1^2 \pi_1(1-\pi_1)}{2(\Delta\pi)^2}, \tag{5.46}$$

i.e., less often than under complete information.

In appendix 5.2, we also compute C_2^{SB} to be the second-best cost of implementing a positive effort on both tasks. For unrelated tasks this cost writes as

$$C_2^{SB} = 2\psi_1 + \frac{r}{2}(2\psi_1)^2 + \frac{r\psi_1^2 \pi_1(1-\pi_1)}{(\Delta\pi)^2},$$

$$= C_2^{FB} + \frac{r\psi_1^2 \pi_1(1-\pi_1)}{(\Delta\pi)^2}. \tag{5.47}$$

This cost again has an intuitive meaning. Since tasks are technologically unrelated, providing incentives on one of those tasks does not affect the cost of incentives on the other. Just as in chapter 4, the principal must incur an agency cost $\frac{r\psi_1^2 \pi_1(1-\pi_1)}{2(\Delta\pi)^2}$ per task on top of the complete information cost C_2^{FB} that is needed to ensure the agent's participation.

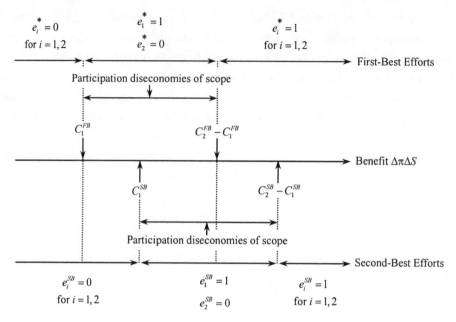

FIGURE 5.6: First-Best and Second-Best Efforts with Unrelated Tasks

Given this agency cost, the principal prefers to induce two positive efforts rather than only one when

$$\Delta\pi\Delta S \geq C_2^{SB} - C_1^{SB} = C_2^{FB} - C_1^{FB} + \frac{r\psi_1^2\pi_1(1-\pi_1)}{2(\Delta\pi)^2}. \tag{5.48}$$

(5.48) is more stringent than (5.46), because $C_2^{SB} > 2C_1^{SB}$.

When $\Delta\pi\Delta S$ belongs to $[C_2^{SB}, C_2^{SB} - C_1^{SB}]$, only one effort is induced under moral hazard and this interval has length $C_2^{SB} - 2C_1^{SB}$. In fact, one can easily observe that the second-best rules (5.48) and (5.46) are respectively "translated" from the first-best rules (5.44) and (5.43) by adding the same term $\frac{r\psi_1^2\pi_1(1-\pi_1)}{2(\Delta\pi)^2}$, which is precisely the extra cost paid by the principal to induce a positive effort on a single dimension of the agent's activities when there is moral hazard.

We conclude from this analysis that, with technologically unrelated tasks, agency problems do not reduce the set of parameters over which the principal induces only one effort from the agent, because $C_2^{SB} - 2C_1^{SB} = C_2^{FB} - 2C_1^{FB}$. This can be seen in figure 5.6.[16]

Let us now turn to the more interesting case where efforts are *substitutes*, i.e., $\psi_2 > 2\psi_1$. On top of the participation diseconomies of scope already seen above, our analysis will highlight the existence of *incentives diseconomies of scope*. To

---

[16]In this figure, we assume that it is task 1 that is performed when incentivizing only one effort is optimal. This is without loss of generality by symmetry.

see their origins, we proceed as before and first analyze the complete information decision rule. The principal still prefers to induce one effort rather than none when (5.43) holds. However, the principal prefers now to induce two efforts rather than only one when

$$\Delta\pi\Delta S \geq C_2^{FB} - C_1^{FB}, \tag{5.49}$$

where $C_2^{FB} = h(\psi_2) = \psi_2 + \frac{r\psi_2^2}{2}$.

Again, we can check that the right-hand side of (5.49) is greater than the right-hand side of (5.43) since

$$C_2^{FB} - 2C_1^{FB} = h(\psi_2) - 2h(\psi_1) > h(2\psi_1) - 2h(\psi_1) > 0, \tag{5.50}$$

where the first inequality uses the facts that $h(\cdot)$ is increasing and that $\psi_2 > 2\psi_1$ and the second inequality uses the convexity of $h(\cdot)$.

Moving now to the case of moral hazard, the principal still prefers to induce one effort rather than none when (5.46) holds. Moreover, the second-best cost of inducing two efforts is now[17]

$$C_2^{SB} = \psi_2 + \frac{r\psi_2^2}{2} + \frac{r(\psi_2 - \psi_1)^2\pi_1(1 - \pi_1)}{(\Delta\pi)^2},$$

$$= C_2^{FB} + \frac{r(\psi_2 - \psi_1)^2\pi_1(1 - \pi_1)}{(\Delta\pi)^2}. \tag{5.51}$$

Again, this expression has an intuitive meaning. In order to induce the agent to exert two efforts that are substitutes, the principal must consider the more constraining local incentive constraint, which prevents the agent from exerting effort on only one dimension of his activities. For each of those two local incentive constraints,[18] the incentive cost that should be added to the first-best cost of implementing both efforts is $\frac{r(\psi_2-\psi_1)^2\pi_1(1-\pi_1)}{2(\Delta\pi)^2}$, where $\psi_2 - \psi_1$ is the incremental disutility of effort when moving from one effort to two efforts.

Hence, the principal prefers to induce both efforts rather than only one when

$$\Delta\pi\Delta S \geq C_2^{SB} - C_1^{SB} = C_2^{FB} - C_1^{FB} + \frac{r\pi_1(1 - \pi_1)}{(\Delta\pi)^2}\left((\psi_2 - \psi_1)^2 - \frac{\psi_1^2}{2}\right). \tag{5.52}$$

In a second-best environment, both efforts are incentivized less often than only one. Indeed, the second-best decision rule to induce both efforts (5.52) is

[17] See appendix 5.2 for a derivation of this formula.
[18] The agent should prefer to exert two tasks instead of only task 1 or task 2.

more stringent than the second-best decision rule (5.46) to induce only one, since

$$
C_2^{FB} - C_1^{FB} + \frac{r\pi_1(1 - \pi_1)}{(\Delta\pi)^2}\left((\psi_2 - \psi_1)^2 - \frac{\psi_1^2}{2}\right)
$$

$$
> C_1^{FB} + \frac{r\pi_1(1 - \pi_1)\psi_1^2}{2(\Delta\pi)^2} = C_1^{SB}. \tag{5.53}
$$

We notice that again there are some diseconomies of scope in implementing both efforts. However, those diseconomies of scope now have a double origin. First, there are the participation diseconomies of scope that ensure that (5.50) holds under complete information. Second, and contrary to the case of technologically unrelated tasks, *incentives diseconomies of scope* now appear, since

$$
\underbrace{\frac{r\pi_1(1 - \pi_1)}{(\Delta\pi)^2}\left((\psi_2 - \psi_1)^2 - \frac{\psi_1^2}{2}\right)}_{(C_2^{SB} - C_1^{SB}) - (C_2^{FB} - C_1^{FB})} > \underbrace{\frac{r\pi_1(1 - \pi_1)\psi_1^2}{2(\Delta\pi)^2}}_{C_1^{SB} - C_1^{FB}} \tag{5.54}
$$

if and only if $\psi_2 > 2\psi_1$.

Moving from the first-best world to the case of moral hazard it becomes even harder to induce effort on both tasks rather than on only one because of these incentives diseconomies of scope. Figure 5.7 graphically shows the impact of these new agency diseconomies of scope on the optimal decision rule followed by the principal.

We also summarize our findings in proposition 5.6.

Proposition 5.6: *When tasks are substitutes and entail moral hazard, the principal must face some new incentives diseconomies of scope that reduce the set of parameters such that inducing both efforts is second-best optimal.*

This proposition highlights the new difficulty faced by the principal when incentivizing the agent on two tasks under moral hazard. Incentives diseconomies of scope imply that the principal will choose to induce effort on only one task more often than under complete information. Task focus may be a response to these agency diseconomies of scope.

> **Remark:** The case of complements could be treated similarly. It would highlight that *incentives economies of scope* exist when an agent performs two tasks that are complements. ∎

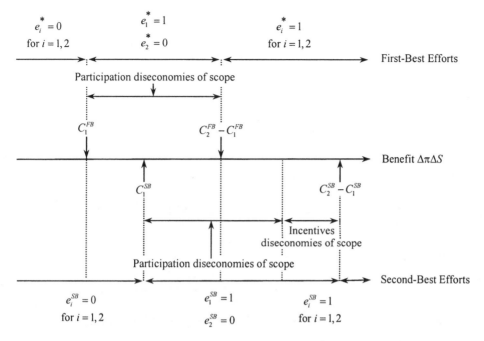

FIGURE 5.7: First-Best and Second-Best Efforts with Substitute Tasks

5.2.4 Asymmetric Tasks

The analysis that we have performed in section 5.2.3 was simplified by our assumption of symmetry between the two tasks. In a real world contracting environment, those tasks are likely to differ along several dimensions, such as the noises in the agent's performances, the expected benefits of those tasks, or the sensitivity of the agent's performance on his effort. The typical example along these lines is that of a university professor who must devote effort to both research and teaching. Those two tasks are substitutes; giving more time to teaching reduces the time spent on research. Moreover, the performances on each of those tasks cannot be measured with the same accuracy. Research records may be viewed as precise measures of the performance along this dimension of the professor's activity. Teaching quality is harder to assess.

To model such settings, we now generalize the multitask framework to the case of asymmetric tasks, which we still index with a superscript i in $\{1, 2\}$. Task i yields a benefit $\overline{S^i}$ to the risk-neutral principal with probability $\pi^i(e_k^i) = \pi_k^i$ and a benefit $\underline{S^i}$ with probability $1 - \pi_k^i$ when the agent exerts effort e_k^i on task i. Effort e_k^i still belongs to $\{0, 1\}$, and we assume the same disutilities of effort as in the symmetric case. Benefits and probabilities distributions may now differ across tasks.

A contract is now a four-uple $\{(\bar{t}, \hat{t}_1, \hat{t}_2, \underline{t})\}$ where $\hat{t}_1$ is offered when the outcome is $(\overline{S}^1, \underline{S}^2)$ and $\hat{t}_2$ is offered when $(\underline{S}^1, \overline{S}^2)$ is realized. We must allow for the possibility that $\hat{t}_1$ is possibly different from $\hat{t}_2$, contrary to our previous assumption in section 5.2.3. Indeed, to take advantage of the asymmetry between tasks, the principal may want to distinguish these two payments.

Let us again use our usual change of variables so that transfers are replaced by utility levels in each state of nature: $\bar{u} = u(\bar{t})$, $\hat{u}_1 = u(\hat{t}_1)$, $\hat{u}_2 = u(\hat{t}_2)$, and $\underline{u} = u(\underline{t})$. An incentive feasible contract inducing a positive effort on both tasks must satisfy two local incentive constraints,

$$\pi_1^1 \pi_1^2 \bar{u} + \pi_1^1(1 - \pi_1^2)\hat{u}_1 + (1 - \pi_1^1)\pi_1^2 \hat{u}_2 + (1 - \pi_1^1)(1 - \pi_1^2)\underline{u} - \psi_2$$
$$\geq \pi_0^1 \pi_1^2 \bar{u} + \pi_0^1(1 - \pi_1^2)\hat{u}_1 + (1 - \pi_0^1)\pi_1^2 \hat{u}_2 + (1 - \pi_0^1)(1 - \pi_1^2)\underline{u} - \psi_1, \quad (5.55)$$

$$\pi_1^1 \pi_1^2 \bar{u} + \pi_1^1(1 - \pi_1^2)\hat{u}_1 + (1 - \pi_1^1)\pi_1^2 \hat{u}_2 + (1 - \pi_1^1)(1 - \pi_1^2)\underline{u} - \psi_2$$
$$\geq \pi_1^1 \pi_0^2 \bar{u} + \pi_1^1(1 - \pi_0^2)\hat{u}_1 + (1 - \pi_1^1)\pi_0^2 \hat{u}_2 + (1 - \pi_1^1)(1 - \pi_0^2)\underline{u} - \psi_1; \quad (5.56)$$

and a global incentive constraint,

$$\pi_1^1 \pi_1^2 \bar{u} + \pi_1^1(1 - \pi_1^2)\hat{u}_1 + (1 - \pi_1^1)\pi_1^2 \hat{u}_2 + (1 - \pi_1^1)(1 - \pi_1^2)\underline{u} - \psi_2$$
$$\geq \pi_0^1 \pi_0^2 \bar{u} + \pi_0^1(1 - \pi_0^2)\hat{u}_1 + (1 - \pi_0^1)\pi_0^2 \hat{u}_2 + (1 - \pi_0^1)(1 - \pi_0^2)\underline{u}. \quad (5.57)$$

Finally, a contract must also satisfy the usual participation constraint,

$$\pi_1^1 \pi_1^2 \bar{u} + \pi_1^1(1 - \pi_1^2)\hat{u}_1 + (1 - \pi_1^1)\pi_1^2 \hat{u}_2 + (1 - \pi_1^1)(1 - \pi_1^2)\underline{u} - \psi_2 \geq 0. \quad (5.58)$$

The principal's problem is thus written as

(P): $\quad \max_{\{(\bar{u}, \hat{u}_1, \hat{u}_2, \underline{u})\}} \pi_1^1 \pi_1^2(\overline{S}^1 + \overline{S}^2 - h(\bar{u})) + \pi_1^1(1 - \pi_1^2)(\overline{S}^1 + \underline{S}^2 - h(\hat{u}_1))$

$$+ (1 - \pi_1^1)\pi_1^2(\underline{S}_1 + \overline{S}^2 - h(\hat{u}_2))$$

$$+ (1 - \pi_1^1)(1 - \pi_1^2)(\underline{S}^1 + \underline{S}^2 - h(\underline{u})),$$

subject to (5.55) to (5.58).

Again, to obtain an explicit solution to (P) we specify a quadratic expression for the inverse utility function so that $h(u) = u + \frac{ru^2}{2}$ for some $r > 0$ and $u \geq -\frac{1}{r}$.

The intuition built in section 5.2.3 suggests that local incentive constraints are the most difficult ones to satisfy in the case where tasks are substitutes, i.e., when $\psi_2 > 2\psi_1$. This is indeed the case as it is confirmed in the next proposition, which generalizes proposition 5.5 to the case of asymmetric tasks.

Proposition 5.7: *When tasks are substitutes, the solution to* (P) *is such that the local incentive constraints* (5.55) *and* (5.56) *and the participation constraint* (5.58) *are all binding. The global incentive constraint* (5.57) *is always slack.*

Using the second-best values of $\bar{u}^{SB}$, $\hat{u}_1^{SB}$, $\hat{u}_2^{SB}$, and $\underline{u}^{SB}$ that we derive in appendix 5.3, we can compute the second-best cost of implementing two positive levels of effort C_2^{SB}. After easy computations, we find that

$$
C_2^{SB} = \underbrace{\psi_2 + \frac{r\psi_2^2}{2}}_{\text{First-Best Cost } C_2^{FB}} + \underbrace{\frac{r(\Delta\psi)^2}{2}\left(\frac{\pi_1^1(1-\pi_1^1)}{(\Delta\pi^1)^2} + \frac{\pi_1^2(1-\pi_1^2)}{(\Delta\pi^2)^2}\right)}_{\text{Incentive Cost.}}, \tag{5.59}
$$

where $\Delta\psi = \psi_2 - \psi_1$, $\Delta\pi^1 = \pi_1^1 - \pi_0^1$, and $\Delta\pi^2 = \pi_1^2 - \pi_0^2$.

This second-best cost can be given an intuitive interpretation. Under complete information, ensuring the agent's participation costs $C_2^{FB} = \psi_2 + \frac{r\psi_2^2}{2}$ to the principal. This is the first term of the right-hand side of (5.59). Under moral hazard and with substitute tasks, each of the tasks i can be incentivized by giving a bonus in utility terms[19] $(1 - \pi_1^i)\frac{\Delta\psi}{\Delta\pi^i}$ when $\widetilde{S}^i = \bar{S}$, i.e., with probability π_1^i, and imposing a punishment $-\pi_1^i\frac{\Delta\psi}{\Delta\pi^i}$ when $\widetilde{S}^i = \underline{S}$, i.e., with probability $1 - \pi_1^i$. Success and failure on each task being independent events, the incentive costs of inducing those two independent risks in the agent's payoff just add up. These costs represent the second bracketed term on (5.59). The above expression of C_2^{SB} will be used throughout the next subsection.

5.2.5 Applications of the Multitask Framework

Aggregate Measures of Performances
Let us suppose that $\bar{S}^1 + \underline{S}^2 = \underline{S}^1 + \bar{S}^2$. In this case, the principal, by simply observing the aggregate benefit of his relationship with the agent, cannot distinguish the successful task from the unsuccessful one. The only contracts that can be written are conditional on the agent's *aggregate performance*. They are thus of the form $\{(\bar{t}, \hat{t}, \underline{t})\}$. With respect to the framework of section 5.2.4, everything happens as if a new constraint $\hat{t} = \hat{t}_1 = \hat{t}_2$ was added. This restriction in the space of available contracts is akin to an *incomplete contract* assumption. To show the consequences of such an incompleteness, it is useful to use the expressions for $\hat{u}_1^{SB}$ and $\hat{u}_2^{SB}$ found in appendix 5.3 to compute the difference of payoffs $\hat{u}_1^{SB} - \hat{u}_2^{SB} = \Delta\psi\left(\frac{1}{\Delta\pi^1} - \frac{1}{\Delta\pi^2}\right)$. Given this value, the only case where the measure of aggregate performance does as well as the measure of individual performances on both tasks is when $\Delta\pi^1 =$

---

[19]See section 4.4.

$\Delta \pi^2$, i.e., in the case of symmetric tasks analyzed in section 5.2.3. Otherwise, there is a welfare loss incurred by the principal from not being able to distinguish between the two intermediate states of nature.

Let us assume now that $\Delta \pi^1 < \Delta \pi^2$. This condition means that task 1 is harder to incentivize than task 2, because an increase of effort has less impact on performances. In this case, $\hat{u}_1^{SB}$ should thus be greater than $\hat{u}_2^{SB}$ if the benefits of each task were observable. With only an aggregate measure of performance, the principal is forced to set $\hat{u}_1 = \hat{u}_2$. Then it becomes more difficult to provide incentives on task 1, which is the more costly task from the incentive point of view, and easier to give incentives on task 2, which is the least costly. Consequently, there may be a misallocation of the agent's efforts, because he prefers to shift his effort towards task 2. Even if task 1 is as valuable as task 2 for the principal, the latter will find it less often optimal to incentivize this first task.

A simple example illustrates this point. Consider a retailer who must allocate his efforts between improving cost and raising demand for the product he sells on behalf of a manufacturer. If the only observable aggregate is profit, the optimal retail contract is a sharing rule that nevertheless might induce the manager to exert effort only on one task, e.g., the one that consists of enhancing demand, if the latter task is easier to incentivize for the principal.

More or Less Informative Performances

Let us thus assume that the principal can still observe the whole vector of performances $(\tilde{S}_1, \tilde{S}_2)$ and offers a fully contingent contract $\{(\bar{t}, \hat{t}_1, \hat{t}_2, \underline{t})\}$. We now turn to the rather difficult question of finding the second-best choice of efforts that the principal would like to implement when tasks are asymmetric.

We have already derived the second-best cost C_2^{SB} of implementing two positive efforts in section 5.2.4. Had the principal chosen to implement a positive effort on task 1 only, the second-best cost of implementing this effort would instead be

$$C^{1SB} = \psi_1 + \frac{r\psi_1^2}{2} + \frac{r\psi_1^2 \pi_1^1 (1 - \pi_1^1)}{2(\Delta \pi^1)^2}.^{[20]} \tag{5.60}$$

Similarly, the second-best cost of implementing a positive effort on task 2 is written as

$$C^{2SB} = \psi_1 + \frac{r\psi_1^2}{2} + \frac{r\psi_1^2 \pi_1^2 (1 - \pi_1^2)}{2(\Delta \pi^2)^2}. \tag{5.61}$$

Let us denote the benefits obtained by the principal on each activity when he induces a high level of effort by $B^1 = \Delta \pi^1 \Delta S^1$ and $B^2 = \Delta \pi^2 \Delta S^2$. The principal

---

[20] See section 4.4.

prefers to induce $e^1 = e^2 = 1$, rather than $e^1 = e^2 = 0$, when $B^1 + B^2 - C_2^{SB} \geq 0$. The principal also prefers to induce $e^1 = e^2 = 1$ rather than $e^1 = 1$ and $e^2 = 0$ when $B^1 + B^2 - C_2^{SB} \geq B^1 - C^{1SB}$. Similarly, $e^1 = e^2 = 1$ is preferred to $e^1 = 0$ and $e^2 = 1$ when $B^1 + B^2 - C_2^{SB} \geq B^2 - C^{2SB}$.

Proceeding similarly, we could determine the set of values of the parameters where inducing the pairs of efforts $(e^1 = 1, e^2 = 0)$ and $(e^1 = 0, e^2 = 1)$ are respectively optimal. Figure 5.8a, b offers a complete characterization of all these areas of dominance where it has been taken into account that some diseconomies of scope exist in implementing a high effort on both tasks (i.e., $C_2^{SB} > C^{1SB} + C^{2SB}$) when those tasks are substitutes.

In these figures all pairs of parameters (B^1, B^2) lying on the northeast quadrant of point B justify the implementation of two positive efforts. On the southwest quadrant of point A, no effort is implemented. On the southeast (resp. northwest) of the line joining A and B, only task 1 (resp. task 2) is incentivized.

When the performance on task 2 becomes more noisy, the variance of output $\tilde{q}^2$, which is $\pi_1^2(1 - \pi_1^2)(\bar{q}^2 - \underline{q}^2)^2$, increases to $\pi_1^{2'}(1 - \pi_1^{2'})(\bar{q}^2 - \underline{q}^2)^2$. Comparing (5.59) and (5.61), we observe that the cost C_2^{SB} increases more quickly than C^{2SB} with this variance. This effect increases the area of parameters (B^1, B^2) where the principal wants to induce $e^1 = 1$ and $e^2 = 0$, since point A is shifted to $\hat{A}$ and point B to $\hat{B}$, as can be seen in figure 5.7.

The intuition behind this phenomenon is clear. When the performance on task 2 becomes a more noisy signal of the corresponding effort, inducing effort along this dimension becomes harder for the principal. By rewarding only the more informative task 1, the principal reduces the agent's incentives to substitute effort e^2 for effort e^1. This relaxes the incentive problem on task 1, making it easier to induce effort on this task. More often the principal chooses to have the agent exert effort only on task 1. Finally, the agent receives higher powered incentives only for the less noisy task, the one that is the most informative on his effort. This can be interpreted as saying that the principal prefers that the agent focuses his attention on the more informative activity.[21]

The Interlinking of Agrarian Contracts

In various contracting environments a principal is not involved in a single transaction with the agent but requires from the latter a bundle of different services or activities. This phenomenon, called the interlinking of contracts, is pervasive in agrarian economies where landlords sometimes offer consumption services, finance, and various inputs to their tenants. This bundling of different contracting

[21] See the seminal paper of Holmström and Milgrom (1991) and the multitask model of section 9.5.2 in this book.

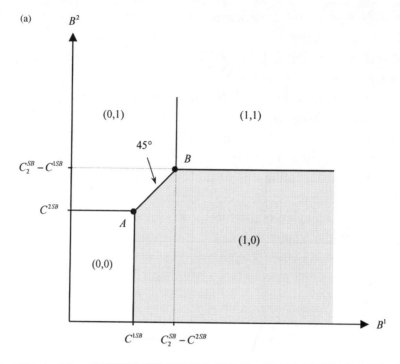

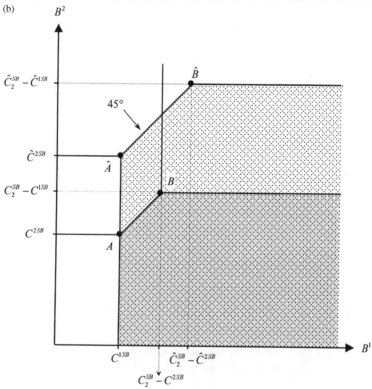

FIGURE 5.8: (a) Optimal Effort Levels, (b) Optimal Effort Levels when Performance on Task 2 Is More Noisy

activities also occurs in more developed economies when input suppliers also offer lines of credit to their customers.

This phenomenon can be easily modelled within a multitask agency framework. To this end, let us consider a relationship between a risk-neutral landlord and a risk-averse tenant similar to that described in section 4.8.2. The landlord and the tenant want to share the production of an agricultural product (the price of which is normalized to one for simplicity). However, and this is the novelty of the multitask framework, the tenant can also make an investment $\tilde{I}$ that, together with his effort, affects the stochastic production process. The probability that $\bar{q}$ is realized now becomes $\pi(e, \tilde{I})$, where effort e belongs to $\{0, 1\}$. We will also assume that $\frac{\partial \pi}{\partial I}(e, \tilde{I}) > 0$, i.e., a greater investment improves the probability that a high output realizes. For simplicity, we will assume that $\tilde{I}$ can only take two values, respectively 0 and $I > 0$. Denoting the interest rate by R, the cost incurred by the agent, when investing I, is thus $(1 + R)I$. If $\tilde{I}$ is not observed by the landlord, the framework is akin to a multitask agency model where the principal would like to control not only the agent's choice of effort e but also his investment $\tilde{I}$.

As a benchmark, let us suppose that the investment I is observable and verifiable at a cost C by the landlord. If the principal wants to make a positive investment, the incentive feasible contract inducing effort must satisfy the following simple incentive constraint:

$$\pi(1, I)u(\bar{t} - (1 + R)I) + (1 - \pi(1, I))u(\underline{t} - (1 + R)I) - \psi$$

$$\geq \pi(0, I)u(\bar{t} - (1 + R)I) + (1 - \pi(0, I))u(\underline{t} - (1 + R)I). \tag{5.62}$$

Similarly, the following participation constraint must be satisfied:

$$\pi(1, I)u(\bar{t} - (1 + R)I) + (1 - \pi(1, I))u(\underline{t} - (1 + R)I) - \psi \geq 0. \tag{5.63}$$

The optimal incentive feasible contract inducing effort is thus a solution to the following problem:

(P):
$$\max_{\{(\bar{t}, \underline{t})\}} \pi(1, I)(\bar{q} - \bar{t}) + (1 - \pi(1, I))(\underline{q} - \underline{t}) - C,$$

subject to (5.62) and (5.63).

Thereafter we will denote the solution to this problem by $\bar{t}^v$ and $\underline{t}^v$.

Let us now assume that the investment is nonobservable by the landlord. The choice of the investment level cannot be included in the contract. An incentive feasible contract must now induce the choice of a positive investment if the principal still finds this investment valuable. Two new incentive constraints must be added to describe the set of incentive feasible contracts. First, the following constraint prevents an agent from *simultaneously* reducing his effort and his investment:

$$\pi(1, I)u(\bar{t} - (1 + R)I) + (1 - \pi(1, I))u(\underline{t} - (1 + R)I) - \psi$$

$$\geq \pi(0, 0)u(\bar{t}) + (1 - \pi(0, 0))u(\underline{t}). \tag{5.64}$$

Second, we must take into account the incentive constraint inducing investment when the agent already exerts an effort:

$$\pi(1, I)u(\bar{t} - (1 + R)I) + (1 - \pi(1, I))u(\underline{t} - (1 + R)I) - \psi$$

$$\geq \pi(1, 0)u(\bar{t}) + (1 - \pi(1, 0))u(\underline{t}) - \psi. \tag{5.65}$$

To simplify the analysis of the possible binding constraints, let us also assume that

$$\Delta\pi(I) = \pi(1, I) - \pi(0, I) > \pi(1, 0) - \pi(0, 0) = \Delta\pi(0). \tag{5.66}$$

This assumption ensures that the investment has more impact on the probability that $\bar{q}$ is realized when the agent already exerts a positive effort. There is thus a *complementarity* between effort and investment.

In this case, any contract-inducing effort at minimal cost when the investment is performed will not induce this effort when no such investment is made. Indeed, to check this assertion, note that

$$u(\bar{t}) - u(\underline{t}) < u(\bar{t} - (1 + R)I) - u(\underline{t} - (1 + R)I) = \frac{\psi}{\Delta\pi(I)} < \frac{\psi}{\Delta\pi(0)}. \tag{5.67}$$

The first inequality uses $\bar{t} > \underline{t}$, and the fact that $u(\cdot)$ is concave. The equality uses the fact that (5.62) is binding if the effort is induced at minimal cost. Finally, the second inequality uses the assumption (5.66). Therefore, (5.64) is more stringent than (5.65). (5.64) may be the more constraining of the incentive constraints when both investment and effort are nonobservable. In this case, the contract offered when $\tilde{I}$ is contractible, namely $\{(\bar{t}^v, \underline{t}^v)\}$, may no longer be optimal. When $\tilde{I}$ is nonobservable, a simultaneous shirking deviation along both the effort and the investment dimensions may occur.[22]

The benefit of controlling the agent's investment comes from the reduction in the agency cost. Of course, this benefit should be traded off against the possible

---

[22]The reader will recognize here the similarity of the analysis with the case of strong complements analyzed in section 5.2.3. The difference comes from the fact that the cost of investment is now in monetary terms.

fixed cost that the principal would incur if he wanted to establish the monitoring system that would make $\tilde{I}$ directly controllable. The interlinking of contracts may thus appear as an institutional response to the technological complementarity between effort and investment in a world where verifying investment is not too costly.

Braverman and Stiglitz (1982) analyzed a model of tenancy-cum-credit contracts, and they show that the landlord may encourage the tenant to get indebted to him when, by altering the terms of the loan contract, he induces the landlord to work harder. Bardhan (1991) reviewed the other justifications for interlinking transactions. In particular, he argued that the interlinking of contracts may help, in nonmonetized economies, by reducing enforcement costs.[23] ∎

Vertical Integration and Incentives

Sometimes it may be hard to contract on the return for some of the agent's activities. A retailer's building up of a good reputation or goodwill and the maintenance of a productive asset are examples of activities that are hard or even impossible to measure. Even though no monetary payments can be used to do so, those activities should still be incentivized. The only feasible contract is then to allocate or not the return of the activity to the agent. Such an allocation is thus akin to a simple *bang-bang* incentive contract. Hence, some authors like Demsetz (1967), Holmström and Milgrom (1991), and Crémer (1995) have argued that ownership of an asset entitles its owner to the returns of this asset. We stick to this definition of ownership in what follows and analyze the interaction between the principal's willingness to induce effort from the agent and the ownership structure.

Let us thus consider a multitask principal-agent relationship that is somewhat similar to that in section 5.2.3. By exerting a maintenance effort e_1 normalized to one, the risk-averse agent can improve the value of an asset by an amount V. This improvement is assumed to take place with probability one to simplify the analysis. We assume that V is large enough so that inducing a maintenance effort is always optimal. The important assumption is that the proceeds V cannot be shared between the principal and the agent. Whoever owns the asset receives all proceeds from the asset. The only feasible incentive contract is the allocation of the returns from the asset between the principal and the agent.

The agent must also perform an unobservable productive effort e_2 in $\{0, 1\}$ whose stochastic return is, on the contrary, contractible. As usual, with probability π_1 (resp. π_0) the return to this activity is $\overline{S}$ and, with probability $1 - \pi_1$ (resp.

---

[23] See chapter 9 for a model of enforcement.

$1 - \pi_0$), this return is $\underline{S}$ when the agent exerts $e_2 = 1$ (resp. $e_2 = 0$). Efforts on production and maintenance are substitutes, so that $\psi_2 > 2\psi_1$. Finally, we assume that the inverse utility function is again quadratic: $h(u) = u + \frac{ru^2}{2}$ for some $r > 0$ and $u \geq -\frac{1}{r}$.

In this context, a contract first entails a remuneration $\{(\bar{t}, \underline{t})\}$ contingent on the realization of the contractible return and, second, an allocation of ownership for the asset. We analyze in turn the two possible ownership structures in the following cases.

CASE 1: The Principal Owns the Asset

When the principal owns the asset, he benefits from any improvement on its value. Since the agent does not benefit from his maintenance effort but bears all the cost of this effort, he exerts no such effort and $e_1 = 0$. Of course, when V is large enough this outcome is never socially optimal. The optimal contract in this case can be derived as usual. The following second-best optimal transfers $\bar{t}^{SBP} = h(\psi_1 + \frac{(1-\pi_1)\psi_1}{\Delta\pi})$ and $\underline{t}^{SBP} = h(\psi_1 - \frac{\pi_1\psi_1}{\Delta\pi})$ implement a positive productive effort.

On the condition that the maintenance effort is null, $e_1 = 0$, inducing effort on the productive task is then optimal when

$$\Delta\pi\Delta S > C_1^{SB} = \psi_1 + \frac{r\psi_1^2}{2} + \frac{r\psi_1^2\pi_1(1 - \pi_1)}{2(\Delta\pi)^2}. \tag{5.68}$$

CASE 2: The Agent Owns the Asset

When V is large enough, the agent is always willing to exert the maintenance effort. Nevertheless, inducing effort on the productive task requires the following incentive constraint to be satisfied:

$$\pi_1 u(\bar{t} + V) + (1 - \pi_1)u(\underline{t} + V) - \psi_2$$
$$\geq \pi_0 u(\bar{t} + V) + (1 - \pi_0)u(\underline{t} + V) - \psi_1, \tag{5.69}$$

as well as the participation constraint

$$\pi_1 u(\bar{t} + V) + (1 - \pi_1)u(\underline{t} + V) - \psi_2 \geq 0. \tag{5.70}$$

As usual, both constraints above are binding at the optimum of the principal's problem. This yields the following expression of the second-best transfers: $\bar{t}^{SBA} = -V + h(\psi_2 + \frac{(1-\pi_1)\Delta\psi}{\Delta\pi})$ and $\underline{t}^{SBA} = -V + h(\psi_2 - \frac{\pi_1\Delta\psi}{\Delta\pi})$, where $\Delta\psi = \psi_2 - \psi_1$.

Under the agent's ownership, the principal gets the following payoff by inducing a productive effort:

$$V_1^A = \pi_1\bar{S} + (1 - \pi_1)\underline{S} + V - C_2^{SB}, \tag{5.71}$$

where

$$C_2^{SB} = \pi_1 h\left(\psi_2 + \frac{(1-\pi_1)\Delta\psi}{\Delta\pi}\right) + (1-\pi_1)h\left(\psi_2 - \frac{\pi_1\Delta\psi}{\Delta\pi}\right)$$

$$= \psi_2 + \frac{r\psi_2^2}{2} + \frac{r(\psi_2 - \psi_1)^2\pi_1(1-\pi_1)}{2(\Delta\pi)^2}. \tag{5.72}$$

By instead offering a fixed wage $\bar{t} = \underline{t} = t$, no productive effort is induced and t is chosen so that the agent's participation constraint $u(t + V) - \psi_1 \geq 0$ is binding.[24] One easily finds that

$$V_0^A = \pi_0 \overline{S} + (1-\pi_0)\underline{S} + V - C_1^{FB}, \tag{5.73}$$

where $C_1^{FB} = \psi_1 + \frac{r\psi_1^2}{2}$.

When V is large enough, the agent should own the asset in order to obtain this socially valuable proceed. The principal then induces a productive effort only when $V_1^A > V_0^A$, i.e., if and only if $\Delta\pi\Delta S \geq C_2^{SB} - C_1^{FB}$.

Under the assumption that tasks are substitutes, it is easy to check that $C_2^{SB} - C_1^{FB} \geq C_1^{SB}$. Hence, when the agent owns the asset, inducing a productive effort becomes more costly for the principal than when the agent does not own it. The principal chooses less often to induce a productive effort than when he owns the asset himself.

However, it is worth noting that, on the condition that inducing effort remains optimal, the agent should be put under a higher powered incentive scheme when he also owns the asset. Indeed, under agent's ownership, we have

$$\bar{t}^{SBA} - \underline{t}^{SBA} = h\left(\psi_2 + (1-\pi_1)\frac{\Delta\psi}{\Delta\pi}\right) - h\left(\psi_2 - \pi_1\frac{\Delta\psi}{\Delta\pi}\right),$$

$$= \frac{\Delta\psi}{\Delta\pi}\left(1 + \frac{r((1-2\pi_0)\psi_2 - (1-2\pi_1)\psi_1)}{2\Delta\pi}\right). \tag{5.74}$$

When the principal owns the asset, the power of incentives is instead given by

$$\bar{t}^{SBP} - \underline{t}^{SBP} = \frac{\psi_1}{\Delta\pi}\left(1 + \frac{r(1-2\pi_0)\psi_1}{2\Delta\pi}\right). \tag{5.75}$$

The comparison of these incentive powers amounts to comparing $\Delta\psi$ and ψ_1. For substitute tasks, the agent is thus given higher powered incentives when he owns the asset.

---

[24]Note that the agent prefers to exert the maintenance effort when $V \geq h(\psi_1)$.

The intuitive explanation is as follows. Under vertical separation, the agent has greater incentives to exert effort on maintenance. The only way for the principal to incentivize the agent along the production dimension is to put him under a high-powered incentive scheme. Otherwise, the agent would systematically substitute away effort on production to improve maintenance. Asset ownership by the agent also comes with high-powered incentives akin to piece-rate contracts. Instead, less powered incentives, i.e., fixed wages, are more likely to occur under the principal's ownership.

Holmström and Milgrom (1994) discussed the strong complementarity between asset ownership and high-powered incentive schemes, arguing in a model along the lines above (but without any wealth effects), that this complementarity comes from some substitutability between efforts in the agent's cost function of effort. They built their theory to fit a number of empirical facts, notably those illustrated by the studies of Anderson (1985) and Anderson and Schmittlein (1984). Those latter authors argued that the key factor explaining the choice between an in-house sales office and an external sales firm is the difficulty of measuring the agent's performance. More costly measurement systems call for the choice of in-house sales. Holmström (1999b) also advanced the idea that measurement costs may be part of an explanation of the firm's boundaries. ∎

5.3 Nonseparability of the Utility Function

The separability in transfer and effort of the agent's utility function simplifies the principal-agent theory with moral hazard by ensuring that the agent's participation constraint is binding. However, it neglects one significant incentive effect, namely that one way to provide incentives is to make the agents richer by decreasing their marginal disutility of effort. The interaction between consumption and effort is clearly important in development economics when one wants to study agrarian contracts. For example, richer agents may be able to have a better diet, which increases their resistance. Then, the optimal compensation may entail a fixed payment whose objective is to bring the agent to a utility level where the marginal disutility of effort is lower. This type of compensation may require leaving him a rent which has a different (even though related) motivation than the limited liability rent exhibited in chapter 4.

In section 5.3.1, we show graphically how nonseparability calls for relaxing the participation constraint. Nevertheless, section 5.3.2 provides an example without wealth effect where the nonseparability is not exploited by the principal to relax the participation constraint.

5.3.1 Nonbinding Participation Constraint

Let us now assume that the agent has a general utility function defined over transfers and effort, namely $U = u(t, e)$. Contrary to the standard framework used so far, we no longer postulate a priori the separability between transfer and effort. Effort can still take either of two values e in $\{0, 1\}$; to simplify notations, let us denote $u_1(t) = u(t, 1)$ and $u_0(t) = u(t, 0)$. Because effort is costly, we obviously have $u_1(t) < u_0(t)$ for all t. Moreover, for i in $\{0, 1\}$, $u_i(\cdot)$ is still increasing and concave in t for all t ($u_i' > 0$, $u_i'' < 0$).

For what follows, it is also interesting to denote the inverse function of $u_0(\cdot)$ by $h_0(\cdot)$, which is increasing and convex ($h_0' > 0$ and $h_0'' > 0$). Consider the case where $u_1(\cdot)$ is a *concave transformation* of $u_0(\cdot)$, i.e., $u_1(\cdot) = g \circ u_0(\cdot)$ with $g(\cdot)$ increasing and concave. Intuitively, this means that exerting effort makes the agent more averse to monetary lotteries.

In this framework, incentive and participation constraints are written respectively as

$$\pi_1 u_1(\bar{t}) + (1 - \pi_1)u_1(\underline{t}) \geq \pi_0 u_0(\bar{t}) + (1 - \pi_0)u_0(\underline{t}) \tag{5.76}$$

and

$$\pi_1 u_1(\bar{t}) + (1 - \pi_1)u_1(\underline{t}) \geq 0. \tag{5.77}$$

Extending the methodology of chapter 4, we now introduce the following change of variables: $\bar{u}_0 = u_0(\bar{t})$, and $\underline{u}_0 = u_0(\underline{t})$. With these new variables, the incentive and participation constraints (5.76) and (5.77) are written respectively as

$$\pi_1 g(\bar{u}_0) + (1 - \pi_1)g(\underline{u}_0) \geq \pi_0 \bar{u}_0 + (1 - \pi_0)\underline{u}_0 \tag{5.78}$$

and

$$\pi_1 g(\bar{u}_0) + (1 - \pi_1)g(\underline{u}_0) \geq 0. \tag{5.79}$$

The risk-neutral principal's problem is thus written as

(P): $$\max_{\{(\bar{u}_0, \underline{u}_0)\}} \pi_1(\overline{S} - h_0(\bar{u}_0)) + (1 - \pi_1)(\underline{S} - h_0(\underline{u}_0))$$

$$\text{subject to (5.78) and (5.79).}$$

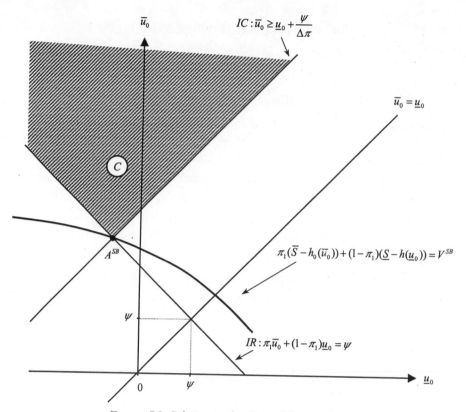

FIGURE 5.9: Solution in the Case of Separability

The fact that $g(\cdot)$ is concave ensures that the constrained set C of incentive feasible contracts $(\bar{u}_0, \underline{u}_0)$ is a nonempty convex set.[25] Since the principal's objective function is strictly concave, the first-order Kuhn and Tucker conditions will again be necessary and sufficient to characterize the solution to this problem.[26]

Instead of proposing a general resolution to this problem, we restrict ourselves to a graphical description of the possible features of the solution for general functions $u_1(\cdot)$ and $u_0(\cdot)$ to satisfy the above properties. As a benchmark, it is useful to represent graphically the usual case of separability where, in fact, we have $u_1(t) = u_0(t) - \psi$ for all t. In this case, we have immediately $g(u) = u - \psi$ for all u, and $u_1(\cdot)$ is simply a linear transformation of $u_0(\cdot)$.

In figure 5.9, we have represented the set C of incentive feasible contracts in the case of a separable utility function. It is a dieder turned downward and lying strictly above the 45° line. The principal's indifference curve V^{SB} is inversely U-shaped. It is graphically obvious that the optimal contract must therefore be on the extremal point A^{SB} of the dieder. We easily recover our analytical result

---

[25]This set is obviously not empty, as it can be easily seen in figure 5.9.
[26]The convexity of C and the concavity of the objective functions ensure that stochastic mechanisms are not useful. See section 2.13 for a related argument in the case of adverse selection.

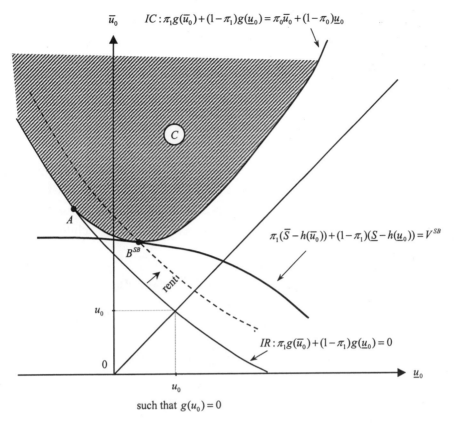

$IC : \pi_1 g(\bar{u}_0) + (1-\pi_1)g(\underline{u}_0) = \pi_0 \bar{u}_0 + (1-\pi_0)\underline{u}_0$

$\pi_1(\bar{S} - h(\bar{u}_0)) + (1-\pi_1)(\underline{S} - h(\underline{u}_0)) = V^{SB}$

$IR : \pi_1 g(\bar{u}_0) + (1-\pi_1)g(\underline{u}_0) = 0$

such that $g(u_0) = 0$

FIGURE 5.10: Solution in the Case of Nonseparability

of section 4.4. The risk-averse agent receives less than full insurance at the optimum, and the agent's participation constraint is also binding.

Let us now turn to the case of nonseparability, which is the focus of this section. Figure 5.10 represents the set C of incentive feasible contracts and the possible second-best optimal contract A.

With a nonseparability, the binding incentive constraint (5.78) defines a locus of contracts that is no longer a straight line but a *strictly convex* curve in the plan $(\underline{u}_0, \bar{u}_0)$.[27]

Similarly, the binding participation constraint (5.79) also defines a convex locus. The set C of incentive feasible contracts is again strictly convex, with an extremal point A still obtained when both constraints are binding. However, the strict convexity of C now leaves some scope for the optimal contract to be at point B^{SB}, where only the incentive constraint is binding. In this case, the best way to solve the incentive problem is to give up a strictly positive *ex ante* rent to the

[27]Moreover, note that this curve is increasing whenever $\frac{1-\pi_0}{1-\pi_1} > g'(\bar{u}_0)$ and $g'(\underline{u}_0) > \frac{\pi_0}{\pi_1}$.

agent. This case is more likely to take place when the *IC* constraint defines a very convex curve, i.e., when $g(\cdot)$ is very concave. This occurs when the agent is much more risk averse when he exerts a positive effort than when he does not. In this case, offering a risky lottery to induce effort and keep the agent's expected utility relatively low is costly for the principal. The principal prefers to raise the agent's expected utility to move toward areas where a risky lottery is much less costly.

> **Remark:** Before closing this section, let us notice that we have already presented in chapter 4 a simple example of a contracting environment where the agent's participation constraint is slack at the optimum, that is when the risk-neutral agent is protected by limited liability. ∎

5.3.2 A Specific Model with No Wealth Effect

Sometimes, even without any separability between transfer and effort in the agent's utility function, the agent receives zero *ex ante* rent. For example, suppose that the agent's cost of effort is counted in monetary terms. The agent's utility function is no longer separable between income and effort, and it is written as $u(t - \psi(e))$, where $u(\cdot)$ is again increasing and concave. With our usual notations, the moral hazard incentive constraint is now written as

$$\pi_1 u(\bar{t} - \psi) + (1 - \pi_1) u(\underline{t} - \psi) \geq \pi_0 u(\bar{t}) + (1 - \pi_0) u(\underline{t}). \tag{5.80}$$

The participation constraint is now

$$\pi_1 u(\bar{t} - \psi) + (1 - \pi_1) u(\underline{t} - \psi) \geq u(0), \tag{5.81}$$

where $u(0)$ is the agent's reservation utility that he obtains when he refuses the contract.

Let us also assume that the agent has a constant risk aversion, namely the constant absolute risk aversion (CARA) utility function $u(x) = -\exp(-rx)$. When facing a binary lottery yielding wealths a and b with respective probabilities π and $1 - \pi$, this agent obtains a certainty equivalent of income, which is defined as

$$w_e = \pi a + (1 - \pi) b - c(\pi, a - b), \tag{5.82}$$

where $c(\pi, x) = \frac{1}{r} \ln(\pi \exp((-r(1-\pi)x)) + (1-\pi) \exp(r\pi x))$ is a risk premium.[28] One can check that $c(\pi, x)$ is increasing with x for all $x \geq 0$.

---

[28] For a risky income $\tilde{x}$ and a Von Neumann Morgenstern utility function $u(\cdot)$, the risk premium ρ is defined as: $E(u(\tilde{x})) = u(E(\tilde{x}) - \rho)$.

Using this formulation based on certainty equivalents, we can now rewrite (5.80) and (5.81) as

$$\pi_1 \bar{t} + (1 - \pi_1)\underline{t} - \psi - c(\pi_1, \bar{t} - \underline{t}) \geq \pi_0 \bar{t} + (1 - \pi_0)\underline{t} - c(\pi_0, \bar{t} - \underline{t}) \qquad (5.83)$$

and

$$\pi_1 \bar{t} + (1 - \pi_1)\underline{t} - \psi - c(\pi_1, \bar{t} - \underline{t}) \geq 0. \qquad (5.84)$$

The principal's problem becomes:

(P): $$\max_{\{(\bar{t},\underline{t})\}} \pi_1 (\overline{S} - \bar{t}) + (1 - \pi_1)(\underline{S} - \underline{t})$$

subject to (5.83) and (5.84).

It is important to note that these constraints depend in a separable way on, first, the average transfer $(\pi_1 \bar{t} + (1 - \pi_1)\underline{t})$ received by the agent and, second, the risk created by these transfers $(\bar{t} - \underline{t})$. More precisely, the principal can ensure that the participation constraint (5.84) is binding by reducing the agent's average transfer without perturbing the power of the incentive contract, i.e., still keeping the incentive constraint (5.83) satisfied. Indeed, this latter constraint can also be written as

$$\Delta\pi\Delta t \geq \psi + c(\pi_1, \Delta t) - c(\pi_0, \Delta t), \qquad (5.85)$$

where $\Delta t = \bar{t} - \underline{t}$ is the incentive power of the contract. We leave it to the reader to check that this incentive constraint must be binding. The second-best power of incentives Δt^{SB} is thus the unique positive solution to

$$\Delta\pi\Delta t^{SB} = \psi + c(\pi_1, \Delta t^{SB}) - c(\pi_0, \Delta t^{SB}). \qquad (5.86)$$

Given that the participation constraint (5.84) is also binding, the optimal second-best transfers are defined by:

$$\bar{t}^{SB} = \psi + c(\pi_1, \Delta t^{SB}) + (1 - \pi_1)\Delta t^{SB} \qquad (5.87)$$

and

$$\underline{t}^{SB} = \psi + c(\pi_1, \Delta t^{SB}) - \pi_1 \Delta t^{SB}. \qquad (5.88)$$

By inducing effort, the principal therefore gets

$$V_1^{SB} = \pi_1 \overline{S} + (1 - \pi_1)\underline{S} - \psi - c(\pi_1, \Delta t^{SB}). \qquad (5.89)$$

If he does not induce effort, the principal can offer $\bar{t} = \underline{t} = 0$. The principal thereby gets an expected payoff $V_0 = \pi_0 \overline{S} + (1 - \pi_0) \underline{S}$. Hence, the principal prefers to induce effort when $\Delta\pi\Delta S \geq \psi + c(\pi_1, \Delta t^{SB})$. Under complete information, the principal induces a first-best effort by offering a constant wage $\bar{t} = \underline{t} = \psi$, and the optimal effort is positive when $\Delta\pi\Delta S \geq \psi$.

Therefore, as in a model with separability between consumption and effort, the principal induces a positive effort less often than in the first-best world, because $c(\pi_1, \Delta t^{SB})$ is strictly positive when $\Delta t^{SB} > 0$.

> **Remark 1:** The fact that the principal can play independently both on the agent's expected transfer to ensure his participation and on the power of incentives to induce him to exert effort is, of course, a direct consequence of the agent having CARA preferences that do not exhibit wealth effects. The agent's average wealth level does not affect incentives. ∎

> **Remark 2:** The second direct consequence of this model is that the power of incentives and the decision to induce effort would be the same if the agent's certainty equivalent from not working with the principal was w instead of zero as we have assumed above. The solution to this new problem is directly translated from the solution in the case where $w = 0$, and we obtain $\bar{t}^{SB}(w) = \bar{t}^{SB} + w$, and $\underline{t}^{SB}(w) = \underline{t}^{SB} + w$. This translation result will be particularly useful in section 9.5.2. ∎

> **Remark 3:** When r is small enough, we have $c(\pi, x) \approx \frac{r\pi(1-\pi)x^2}{2}$. The model is then akin to assuming that the agent has mean-variance preferences $E(\tilde{t}) - \psi - \frac{r}{2} \operatorname{var}(\tilde{t})$ over the monetary payoff $\tilde{t} - \psi$. In this more general case, we can solve (5.86) explicitly for Δt^{SB}, and we find that (provided that $1 - \pi_1 - \pi_0 > 0$ and that ψ is small enough to ensure existence of the solution)
> $$\Delta t^{SB} = \frac{1 - \sqrt{1 - \frac{2r\psi}{\Delta\pi}(1 - \pi_1 - \pi_0)}}{r(1 - \pi_1 - \pi_0)} > 0, \qquad (5.90)$$
> which is approximately equal to $\frac{\psi}{\Delta\pi}$ when r is small. ∎

5.4 Redistribution and Moral Hazard

In chapter 3, we have already seen how the conflict between incentive compatibility and budget balance leads to the under-provision of output in an adverse selection model. The same qualitative result still holds in a moral hazard environment. Expected volume of trade may be reduced by moral hazard. To illustrate this point, we consider a simple model of redistribution and moral hazard. There is a unit mass population of agents who are all *ex ante* identical and have a utility function $U = u(t) - \psi(e)$, where $u(\cdot)$ ($u' > 0$, $u'' < 0$) is defined over monetary gains and $\psi(e)$ is the disutility of effort. Each of those agents exerts an effort e in $\{0, 1\}$, and may be successful or not in producing output. When successful (resp. unsuccessful), i.e., with probability $\pi(e)$ (resp. $1 - \pi(e)$), the return of this effort is $\bar{q}$ (resp. $\underline{q} < \bar{q}$). The agents are all *ex ante* identical, so the government maximizes an objective function $V = U$, which corresponds to the utility of a representative agent.[29]

A *redistributive scheme* is a pair of transfers $\{(\bar{t}, \underline{t})\}$ that depend on whether the agent is successful or not. To be incentive feasible, such a scheme must satisfy the following *budget constraint*:

$$\pi_1(\bar{q} - \bar{t}) + (1 - \pi_1)(\underline{q} - \underline{t}) \geq 0, \qquad (5.91)$$

as well as the usual incentive compatibility constraint,

$$\pi_1 u(\bar{t}) + (1 - \pi_1)u(\underline{t}) - \psi_1 \geq \pi_0 u(\bar{t}) + (1 - \pi_0)u(\underline{t}). \qquad (5.92)$$

Note that (5.91) means that the budget is balanced in expectation over the whole population of agents. Indeed, by the Law of Large Numbers, π_1 can also be viewed as the fraction of successful agents in society.

When effort is verifiable, the government solves the following problem if it wants to implement a high level of effort:

$$\max_{\{(\bar{t},\underline{t})\}} \pi_1 u(\bar{t}) + (1 - \pi_1)u(\underline{t}) - \psi_1,$$

subject to (5.91).

Let us denote the multiplier of the budget constraint (5.91) by μ. The necessary and sufficient Kuhn and Tucker optimality conditions with respect to $\bar{t}$ and $\underline{t}$ then lead to

$$\mu = u'(\bar{t}^{FB}) = u'(\underline{t}^{FB}) > 0. \qquad (5.93)$$

The complete information optimal redistributive scheme calls for complete insurance and the constant transfer received by each agent in both states of nature is

$$t^{FB} = \bar{t}^{FB} = \underline{t}^{FB} = \pi_1 \bar{q} + (1 - \pi_1)\underline{q}, \qquad (5.94)$$

---

[29]Contrary to the model of section 3.8, agents differ now *ex post* by the realization of the income shock and not *ex ante* by their productivity.

i.e., it is equal to the average output. The optimal redistributive scheme amounts to a perfect insurance system. Taxation provides social insurance by transferring income from those agents who have been lucky to those who have been unlucky.

Let us now consider the case where effort is nonobservable by the government. If the government wants to induce zero effort, it still relies on the complete insurance scheme above, and the representative agent gets an expected utility $u(\pi_0 \bar{q} + (1 - \pi_0)\underline{q})$.

If the government wants to induce a high effort, it instead solves the following problem:

$$(P): \qquad \max_{\{(\bar{t}, \underline{t})\}} \pi_1 u(\bar{t}) + (1 - \pi_1)u(\underline{t}) - \psi,$$

subject to (5.91) and (5.92).

Denoting the respective multipliers of those two constraints by μ and λ, the first-order conditions for optimality with respect to $\bar{t}$ and $\underline{t}$ can be written respectively as

$$u'(\bar{t}^{SB})(\pi_1 + \lambda \Delta \pi) = \pi_1 \mu, \tag{5.95}$$

and

$$u'(\underline{t}^{SB})(1 - \pi_1 - \lambda \Delta \pi) = (1 - \pi_1)\mu. \tag{5.96}$$

Dividing (5.95) by $u'(\bar{t}^{SB})$ and (5.96) by $u'(\underline{t}^{SB})$ and summing, we obtain that μ is strictly positive since $\mu = \frac{u'(\bar{t}^{SB})u'(\underline{t}^{SB})}{\pi_1 u'(\underline{t}^{SB}) + (1 - \pi_1)u'(\bar{t}^{SB})} > 0$. Therefore, the budget constraint is binding. Similarly, we also find that $\lambda = \frac{\pi_1(1-\pi_1)}{\Delta \pi}(u'(\underline{t}^{SB}) - u'(\bar{t}^{SB})) > 0$, because $\bar{t}^{SB} > \underline{t}^{SB}$ is necessary to satisfy the incentive compatibility constraint (5.92) and $u(\cdot)$ is concave. Hence, this latter constraint is also binding and both $\bar{t}^{SB}$ and $\underline{t}^{SB}$ are obtained as solutions to the following nonlinear system:

$$\pi_1 \bar{t}^{SB} + (1 - \pi_1)\underline{t}^{SB} = \pi_1 \bar{q} + (1 - \pi_1)\underline{q} \tag{5.97}$$

and

$$u(\bar{t}^{SB}) - u(\underline{t}^{SB}) = \frac{\psi}{\Delta \pi}. \tag{5.98}$$

Under moral hazard complete redistribution is not achieved. Furthermore, it is socially optimal to induce a high effort when

$$\pi_1 u(\bar{t}^{SB}) + (1 - \pi_1)u(\underline{t}^{SB}) - \psi \geq u(\pi_0 \bar{q} + (1 - \pi_0)\underline{q}). \tag{5.99}$$

Because $u(\cdot)$ is strictly concave and $\bar{t}^{SB} > \underline{t}^{SB}$, Jensen's inequality implies that the left-hand side of (5.99) is strictly lower than

$$u(\pi_1 \bar{t}^{SB} + (1 - \pi_1)\underline{t}^{SB}) - \psi = u(\pi_1 \bar{q} + (1 - \pi_1)\underline{q}) - \psi_1. \tag{5.100}$$

Hence, the second-best rule (5.99) is more stringent than the first-best rule, which calls for a positive effort if and only if

$$u(\pi_1 \bar{q} + (1 - \pi_1)\underline{q}) - \psi \geq u(\pi_0 \bar{q} + (1 - \pi_0)\underline{q}). \tag{5.101}$$

A high effort is implemented less often under moral hazard because the benefit of doing so is lower. The reader will have recognized the similarity of this section with section 4.8.5. Indeed, the redistributive scheme analyzed above is akin to the insurance contract that would be offered by a competitive sector.

Appendix 5.1: Proof of Proposition 5.5

We first write the Lagrangian of problem (P):

$$
\begin{aligned}
L(\bar{u}, \hat{u}, \underline{u}) =\ & (\pi_1)^2(2\bar{S} - h(\bar{u})) + 2\pi_1(1 - \pi_1)(\bar{S} + \underline{S} - h(\hat{u})) \\
& + (1 - \pi_1)^2(2\underline{S} - h(\underline{u})) \\
& + \lambda_l \left(\pi_1^2 \bar{u} + 2\pi_1(1 - \pi_1)\hat{u} + (1 - \pi_1)^2 \underline{u} - \psi_2 \right) \\
& - (\pi_1 \pi_0 \bar{u} + (\pi_1(1 - \pi_0) + \pi_0(1 - \pi_1))\hat{u} + (1 - \pi_1)(1 - \pi_0)\underline{u} - \psi_1) \\
& + \lambda_g \left(\pi_1^2 \bar{u} + 2\pi_1(1 - \pi_1)\hat{u} + (1 - \pi_1)^2 \underline{u} - \psi_2 \right. \\
& \left. - (\pi_0^2 \bar{u} + 2\pi_0(1 - \pi_0)\hat{u} + (1 - \pi_0)^2 \underline{u}) \right) \\
& + \mu \left(\pi_1^2 \bar{u} + 2\pi_1(1 - \pi_1)\hat{u} + (1 - \pi_1)^2 \underline{u} - \psi_2 \right), \tag{5.102}
\end{aligned}
$$

where λ_l, λ_g, and μ denote, respectively, the multipliers of (5.40), (5.41), and (5.42).

Optimizing the Lagrangian with respect to $\bar{u}$, $\hat{u}$, and $\underline{u}$ yields, respectively,

$$\pi_1^2 h'(\bar{u}) = \lambda_l \Delta\pi\pi_1 + \lambda_g \Delta\pi(\pi_1 + \pi_0) + \mu\pi_1^2, \tag{5.103}$$

$$2\pi_1(1 - \pi_1)h'(\hat{u}) = \lambda_l \Delta\pi(1 - 2\pi_1) + 2\lambda_g \Delta\pi(1 - \pi_1 - \pi_0)$$
$$+ \mu 2\pi_1(1 - \pi_1), \tag{5.104}$$

$$(1 - \pi_1)^2 h'(\underline{u}) = -\lambda_l \Delta\pi(1 - \pi_1) - \lambda_g \Delta\pi(2 - \pi_1 - \pi_0)$$
$$+ \mu(1 - \pi_1)^2. \tag{5.105}$$

Taking into account that $h'(u) = 1 + ru$ and summing equations (5.103) to (5.105) yields

$$1 + rE(\tilde{u}) = \mu, \tag{5.106}$$

where $E(\cdot)$ denotes the expectation operator with respect to the distribution of $\tilde{q}^1$ and $\tilde{q}^2$ induced by high efforts. Because (5.42) must hold, we have $\mu \geq 1 + r\psi_2 > 0$, and thus (5.42) is binding. Inserting the value of expected utility $E\tilde{u} = \psi_2$ into (5.106), we obtain that $\mu = 1 + r\psi_2$.

We now investigate three classes of solutions to (P) depending on the parameter values ψ_1 and ψ_2.

CASE 1: Only the Local Incentive Constraint Is Binding
Let us first assume that $\lambda_l > 0$ and $\lambda_g = 0$. Using (5.103) to (5.105) allows us to express all utility levels as functions of λ_l:

$$\bar{u} = \psi_2 + \frac{\lambda_l \Delta \pi}{r \pi_1}, \tag{5.107}$$

$$\hat{u} = \psi_2 + \frac{\lambda_l \Delta \pi (1 - 2\pi_1)}{2r\pi_1(1 - \pi_1)}, \tag{5.108}$$

$$\underline{u} = \psi_2 - \frac{\lambda_l \Delta \pi}{r(1 - \pi_1)}. \tag{5.109}$$

Inserting those values of $\bar{u}$, $\hat{u}$, and $\underline{u}$ into the binding local incentive constraint yields the value of λ_l, namely $\lambda_l = \frac{2r(\psi_2 - \psi_1)\pi_1(1 - \pi_1)}{(\Delta \pi)^2}$. Inserting this value into (5.107) through (5.109), we obtain

$$\bar{u} = \psi_2 + \frac{2(\psi_2 - \psi_1)(1 - \pi_1)}{\Delta \pi}, \tag{5.110}$$

$$\hat{u} = \psi_2 + \frac{(\psi_2 - \psi_1)(1 - 2\pi_1)}{\Delta \pi}, \tag{5.111}$$

$$\underline{u} = \psi_2 - \frac{2(\psi_2 - \psi_1)\pi_1}{\Delta \pi}. \tag{5.112}$$

We will assume that parameter values are such that these values of $\bar{u}$, $\hat{u}$, and $\underline{u}$ are all greater than $-\frac{1}{r}$. It holds if ψ_2 is much greater than $-\frac{1}{r}$.

The global incentive constraint (5.41) is strictly satisfied when

$$\pi_0^2 \bar{u} + 2\pi_0(1 - \pi_0)\hat{u} + (1 - \pi_0)^2 \underline{u} < 0. \tag{5.113}$$

Inserting the corresponding values of $\bar{u}$, $\hat{u}$, and $\underline{u}$, given by (5.110) to (5.112) into (5.113) yields (after some computations) the condition $\psi_2 > 2\psi_1$, i.e., tasks are substitutes.

CASE 2: Only the Global Incentive Constraint Is Binding

Let us now assume that $\lambda_l = 0$ and $\lambda_g > 0$. Using (5.103) to (5.105) allows us again to express all utility levels as functions of λ_g:

$$\bar{u} = \psi_2 + \frac{\lambda_g \Delta \pi (\pi_1 + \pi_0)}{r \pi_1^2}, \tag{5.114}$$

$$\hat{u} = \psi_2 + \frac{\lambda_g \Delta \pi (1 - \pi_1 - \pi_0)}{r \pi_1 (1 - \pi_1)}, \tag{5.115}$$

$$\underline{u} = \psi_2 - \frac{\lambda_g \Delta \pi (2 - \pi_1 - \pi_0)}{r (1 - \pi_1)^2}. \tag{5.116}$$

Inserting those latter values of $\bar{u}$, $\hat{u}$, and $\underline{u}$ into the binding global incentive constraint yields $\lambda_g = \frac{r \psi_2 \pi_1^2 (1 - \pi_1)^2}{(\Delta \pi)^2 ((\Delta \pi)^2 + 2 \pi_1 (1 - \pi_1))}$. Inserting this value into (5.114) through (5.116) yields

$$\bar{u} = \psi_2 + \frac{\psi_2 (\pi_1 + \pi_0)(1 - \pi_1)^2}{\Delta \pi ((\Delta \pi)^2 + 2 \pi_1 (1 - \pi_1))}, \tag{5.117}$$

$$\hat{u} = \psi_2 + \frac{\psi_2 (1 - \pi_1 - \pi_0) \pi_1 (1 - \pi_1)}{\Delta \pi ((\Delta \pi)^2 + 2 \pi_1 (1 - \pi_1))}, \tag{5.118}$$

$$\underline{u} = \psi_2 - \frac{\psi_2 (2 - \pi_1 - \pi_0) \pi_1^2}{\Delta \pi ((\Delta \pi)^2 + 2 \pi_1 (1 - \pi_1))}. \tag{5.119}$$

The local incentive constraint (5.40) is strictly satisfied when

$$\pi_1 \bar{u} + (1 - 2 \pi_1) \hat{u} - (1 - \pi_1) \underline{u} > \frac{\psi_2 - \psi_1}{\Delta \pi}. \tag{5.120}$$

Inserting the values of $\bar{u}$, $\hat{u}$, and $\underline{u}$, which were obtained in (5.117) to (5.119), into (5.120) yields the condition $\psi_2 (\frac{\pi_1 (1 - \pi_1) + (\Delta \pi)^2}{2 \pi_1 (1 - \pi_1) + (\Delta \pi)^2}) < \psi_1$.

Note that $\pi_1 > \pi_0$ implies that $\frac{\pi_1 (1 - \pi_1) + (\Delta \pi)^2}{2 \pi_1 (1 - \pi_1) + (\Delta \pi)^2} > \frac{1}{2}$. Hence, the global incentive constraint is the only binding one in the case of a strong complementarity between both tasks.

CASE 3: Both Incentive Constraints Are Binding

For the intermediate case, i.e., $(\frac{2 \pi_1 (1 - \pi_1) + \Delta \pi^2}{\pi_1 (1 - \pi_1) + \Delta \pi^2}) \psi_1 < \psi_2 < 2 \psi_1$, both the local and the global incentive constraints are simultaneously binding. This case is somewhat less interesting. Using (5.103) to (5.105) and the binding constraints (5.40) and (5.41) yields a system of five equations with five unknowns, the solutions of which can be easily computed.

Appendix 5.2: Second-Best Cost of Implementation

We compute the second-best cost C_2^{SB} of implementing two high levels of effort in the case of substitutes:

$$C_2^{SB} = \pi_1^2 h(\bar{u}^{SB}) + 2\pi_1(1 - \pi_1)h(\hat{u}^{SB}) + (1 - \pi_1)^2 h(\underline{u}^{SB}), \tag{5.121}$$

where $\bar{u}^{SB}$, $\hat{u}^{SB}$, and $\underline{u}^{SB}$ are given by equations (5.110) to (5.112). Using the quadratic specification of $h(\cdot)$, we can rewrite

$$C_2^{SB} = E(h(\tilde{u}^{SB})) = E(\tilde{u}^{SB}) + \frac{r}{2}(E(\tilde{u}^{SB}))^2 + \frac{r}{2}\text{var}\,(\tilde{u}^{SB}), \tag{5.122}$$

where $E(\cdot)$ and $\text{var}(\cdot)$ respectively denote the expectation and the variance operators with respect to the joint distribution of output $(\tilde{q}^1, \tilde{q}^2)$ induced by high effort. We finally find $C_2^{SB} = \psi_2 + \frac{r\psi_2^2}{2} + \frac{r}{2}\text{var}(\tilde{u}^{SB})$, where $\text{var}(\tilde{u}^{SB}) = \frac{2(\psi_2 - \psi_1)^2 \pi_1(1-\pi_1)}{\Delta\pi^2}$. Simplifying, we obtain

$$C_2^{SB} = \psi_2 + \frac{r\psi_2^2}{2} + \frac{r(\psi_2 - \psi_1)^2 \pi_1(1 - \pi_1)}{(\Delta\pi)^2}. \tag{5.123}$$

In the case of strong complements, again we have

$$C_2^{SB} = E(u^{SB}) + \frac{r}{2}(E(u^{SB}))^2 + \frac{r}{2}\text{var}(u^{SB}), \tag{5.124}$$

where still $E(u^{SB}) = \psi_2$, and now using (5.117) to (5.119) we get that $\text{var}(\tilde{u}^{SB}) = \frac{\psi_2^2 \pi_1^2(1-\pi_1)^2}{(\Delta\pi)^2((\Delta\pi)^2 + 2\pi_1(1-\pi_1))}$. Finally, using (5.123) we get:

$$C_2^{SB} = \psi_2 + \frac{r\psi_2^2}{2} + \frac{r\psi_2^2 \pi_1^2(1 - \pi_1)^2}{2(\Delta\pi)^2 ((\Delta\pi)^2 + 2\pi_1(1 - \pi_1))}. \tag{5.125}$$

Appendix 5.3: Optimal Contracts with Asymmetric Tasks

Proof of Proposition 5.7
We first denote by λ^1, λ^2, and μ the respective multipliers of (5.55), (5.56), and (5.58). Forming the Lagrangian corresponding to problem (P), where (5.57) has been omitted, and optimizing with respect to $\bar{u}$, $\hat{u}_1$, $\hat{u}_2$, and $\underline{u}$ yields, respectively,

$$\pi_1^1 \pi_1^2 h'(\bar{u}) = \lambda^1 \Delta\pi^1 \pi_1^2 + \lambda^2 \Delta\pi^2 \pi_1^1 + \mu\pi_1^1 \pi_1^2, \tag{5.126}$$

$$\pi_1^1(1 - \pi_1^2)h'(\hat{u}_1) = \lambda^1 \Delta\pi^1(1 - \pi_1^2) - \lambda^2 \Delta\pi^2 \pi_1^1 + \mu\pi_1^1(1 - \pi_1^2), \tag{5.127}$$

$$(1 - \pi_1^1)\pi_1^2 h'(\hat{u}_2) = -\lambda^1 \Delta \pi^1 \pi_1^2 + \lambda^2 \Delta \pi^2 (1 - \pi_1^1) + \mu(1 - \pi_1^1)\pi_1^2, \quad (5.128)$$

$$(1 - \pi_1^1)(1 - \pi_1^2)h'(\underline{u}) = -\lambda^1 \Delta \pi^1 (1 - \pi_1^2) - \lambda^2 \Delta \pi^2 (1 - \pi_1^1)$$
$$+ \mu(1 - \pi_1^1)(1 - \pi_1^2). \quad (5.129)$$

Summing equations (5.126) to (5.129) and taking into account that $h'(u) = 1 + ru$, we obtain $\mu = 1 + rE(\tilde{u}) = 1 + r\psi_2$, where $E(\cdot)$ is the expectation operator with respect to the joint distribution of outputs $(\tilde{q}^1, \tilde{q}^2)$ induced by a positive effort on each task.

We leave it to the reader to check that the linear system (5.126) to (5.129), plus the binding constraints (5.55) and (5.56), admit the following solutions:

$$\lambda^1 = \frac{r\Delta\psi\pi_1^1(1 - \pi_1^1)}{(\Delta\pi^1)^2} > 0, \quad (5.130)$$

$$\lambda^2 = \frac{r\Delta\psi\pi_1^2(1 - \pi_1^2)}{(\Delta\pi^2)^2} > 0, \quad (5.131)$$

and

$$\bar{u}^{SB} = \psi_2 + \Delta\psi\left(\frac{(1 - \pi_1^1)}{\Delta\pi^1} + \frac{(1 - \pi_1^2)}{\Delta\pi^2}\right), \quad (5.132)$$

$$\hat{u}_1^{SB} = \psi_2 + \Delta\psi\left(\frac{(1 - \pi_1^1)}{\Delta\pi^1} - \frac{\pi_1^2}{\Delta\pi^2}\right), \quad (5.133)$$

$$\hat{u}_2^{SB} = \psi_2 + \Delta\psi\left(-\frac{\pi_1^1}{\Delta\pi^1} + \frac{(1 - \pi_1^2)}{\Delta\pi^2}\right), \quad (5.134)$$

$$\underline{u}^{SB} = \psi_2 + \Delta\psi\left(-\frac{\pi_1^1}{\Delta\pi^1} - \frac{\pi_1^2}{\Delta\pi^2}\right), \quad (5.135)$$

where $\Delta\psi = \psi_2 - \psi_1$, $\Delta\pi^1 = \pi_1^1 - \pi_0^1$ and $\Delta\pi^2 = \pi_1^2 - \pi_0^2$. We check that (5.57) is slack at the optimum. For this to be true, we must have

$$\pi_0^1\pi_0^2\bar{u}^{SB} + \pi_0^1(1 - \pi_0^2)\hat{u}_1^{SB} + (1 - \pi_0^1)\pi_0^2\hat{u}_2^{SB} + (1 - \pi_0^1)(1 - \pi_0^2)\underline{u}^{SB} < 0, \quad (5.136)$$

or using equations (5.132) to (5.135) and simplifying, we obtain $\psi_2 > 2\psi_1$.

6   Nonverifiability

When two parties engage in a relationship, it is often the case that they are uncertain about the value of some parameter that will affect their future gains from trade. This uncertainty is represented by assuming that the parameter can take several values, each value corresponding to different states of nature whose probability distribution is common knowledge. In this chapter the parameter will take two values. Even though they will both learn the value of the parameter in the future, the trading partners cannot write *ex ante* contracts contingent on the state of nature, because this state of nature is not verifiable by a third party, a benevolent court of law, that could enforce their contract. As the following quote from Williamson (1975) suggests, such situations might entail transaction costs:

> Both buyer and seller have identical information and assume, further-
> more, that this information is entirely sufficient for the transaction to be
> completed. Such exchanges might nevertheless experience difficulty if,
> despite identical information, one agent makes representations that the
> true state of the world is different than both parties know it to be and if

in addition it is costly for an outside arbiter to determine what the true state of the world is (p. 32).

The goal of this chapter is to assess whether the nonverifiability of the state of nature significantly affects the ability of the contractual partners to realize the full gains from trade. More precisely, we ask whether this nonverifiability has any bite in the realm of complete contract theory, i.e., when the principal has the full ability to commit to a mechanism at the *ex ante* stage and a benevolent court of law is available, as we assume throughout this whole volume. Actually, we show that the nonverifiability of the state of nature alone does not create transaction costs under those assumptions.

Section 6.1 starts with a useful benchmark and considers the case where the principal and the agent do not write any contract *ex ante*. Bargaining over the gains from trade takes place *ex post*, i.e., once the state of nature is commonly known. If the principal has all the bargaining power *ex post*, the first-best allocation is implemented, with the agent being maintained at his status quo utility level.[1] If we had considered a more even distribution of the bargaining power *ex post*, allocative efficiency would still be preserved, but the distribution of the gains from trade would be more egalitarian: the principal (resp. the agent) would obtain a lower (resp. higher) utility level. Hence, if the principal does not expect to have all the bargaining power at the *ex post* stage, he strictly prefers to design a mechanism at the *ex ante* stage when he still has all the bargaining power. Similarly, *ex ante* contracting may also be preferred when the principal is risk averse and thus has an *ex ante* demand for insurance. In section 6.2, we argue that the simple incentive contracts already analyzed in an adverse selection context with *ex ante* contracting in chapter 2 perform quite well in the case of nonverifiability and risk neutrality of the agent. Efficiency is always achieved when the Spence-Mirrlees property is satisfied for the agent's objective function. However, in the case of nonresponsiveness, or when the agent is risk averse, the optimal *ex ante* contract entails inefficiencies.

To circumvent this weakness of *ex ante* contracting, in section 6.3 we elaborate a more complex mechanism that always achieves the first-best with *Nash implementation*.[2] The principal offers a mechanism that is designed to ensure that the noncooperative play of the game by both the principal and the agent yields the desired first-best allocation. In this context, we extend our methodology of

---

[1] In chapter 2, we have assumed that the principal has all the bargaining power both at the *ex ante* stage (before the state of nature realizes) and at the interim stage (after the agent has learned the state of nature).

[2] Furthermore, we will show in section 7.3 that such mechanisms are always needed to achieve first-best efficiency in mixed models with both moral hazard and nonverifiability.

chapter 2 and prove a revelation principle when both the principal and the agent simultaneously report messages over the state of the world to a benevolent court of law. In playing such a two-agent mechanism, the principal and the agent adopt a Nash behavior. An *allocation rule is implementable in Nash equilibrium* if there exists a mechanism and a Nash equilibrium of this mechanism where the agents follow strategies that induce the desired allocation in each state of the world. Then, we show that the standard principal-agent models are such that the first-best is implementable in Nash equilibrium with rather simple mechanisms.

However, Nash implementation may not be sufficient to always ensure that a *unique* equilibrium yielding the desired allocation exists in each state of nature. Multiple equilibria may arise, with some being nontruthful. In other words, an allocation rule may fail to be *uniquely implementable*. We then define the notion of *monotonicity* of an allocation rule and show that unique Nash implementation implies monotonicity. For allocation rules that fail to be monotonic and thus do not allow unique Nash implementation, the important question is whether one can build more complex mechanisms, possibly with sequential instead of simultaneous moves, that still allow unique implementation. In other words, is it possible to design an extensive form game whose subgame-perfect equilibrium uniquely implements a given allocation rule? In section 6.4 instead of providing a full theory of *subgame-perfect implementation*, we construct a simple extensive form that solves the problem in a specific example. Finally, section 6.5 presents some extensions for the case of risk aversion, and section 6.6 offers some concluding remarks about the nonverifiability paradigm.

6.1 No Contract at Date 0 and *Ex Post* Bargaining

With the same model as in chapter 2, we now assume that the parameter θ is unknown at the contracting date (date $t = 0$) but becomes common knowledge between the two parties, the principal and the agent, later on (at date $t = 1$). First we examine the case where no initial contract has been signed at date $t = 0$.

At date $t = 1$, the principal is informed about θ and can make a take-it-or-leave-it offer to the agent at date $t = 2$ under complete information. See figure 6.1 for the timing of the game.

These take-it-or-leave-it offers implement the first-best volumes of trade and obviously leave no rent to the agent since the principal has all the bargaining power at date $t = 2$. For instance, when the agent is efficient, his output q^* satisfies $S'(q^*) = \underline{\theta}$, and the transfer $\underline{t}^*$ he receives from the principal is $\underline{t}^* = \underline{\theta}q^*$. Similarly, the inefficient agent produces $\bar{q}^*$ such that $S'(\bar{q}^*) = \bar{\theta}$, and the transfer $\bar{t}^*$ he receives just covers his cost: $\bar{t}^* = \bar{\theta}\bar{q}^*$.

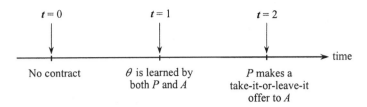

FIGURE 6.1: Timing with No *Ex Ante* Contract

So far we have assumed that the principal was endowed with all the bargaining power both at the *ex ante* and at the interim stages, i.e., before the agent has learned the piece of information θ or just after. In the nonverifiability paradigm, it is frequent to analyze a more even distribution of the bargaining power at date $t = 2$. For example, the principal may have performed an (unmodeled) investment specific to the relationship, so that he finds himself in a position of bilateral monopoly vis-à-vis the agent, thereby justifying a nonzero bargaining power *ex post* for the agent.

Obviously, changing the principal and the agent's bargaining powers at date $t = 2$ does not affect allocative efficiency. To see that, let us assume that the principal and the agent bargain *ex post*, i.e., at date $t = 2$, over the entire gains from trade. See figure 6.2.

To model this bargaining, we use the cooperative Nash bargaining solution with the principal and the agent having now equal weights in the negotiation. In state θ, they agree on a transfer t and production q, which are solutions to the following problem:

$$(P): \qquad \max_{\{(q,\,t)\}} (S(q) - t)(t - \theta q).$$

We easily find that the Nash bargaining solution consists of the first-best output $q^*(\theta)$ and a transfer $t^{NB}(\theta)$, which satisfy

$$t^{NB}(\theta) = \frac{S(q^*(\theta)) + \theta q^*(\theta)}{2} \qquad (6.1)$$

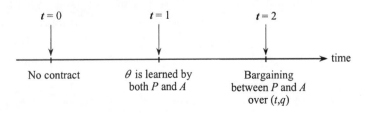

FIGURE 6.2: Timing with No *Ex Ante* Contract and with *Ex Post* Bargaining

and

$$S'(q^*(\theta)) = \theta. \tag{6.2}$$

As a result, both the principal and the agent receive an equal share of the first-best gains from trade. Denoting the principal and the agent's shares of the surplus respectively by $V^{NB}(\theta)$ and $U^{NB}(\theta)$, we have thus

$$V^{NB}(\theta) = U^{NB}(\theta) = \frac{1}{2}(S(q^*(\theta)) - \theta q^*(\theta)) = \frac{1}{2}W^*(\theta), \tag{6.3}$$

where $W^*(\theta)$ is the first-best surplus in state θ.

> **Remark:** Similar results would also hold with any kind of cooperative or noncooperative bargaining solution, for instance, the Rubinstein (1982) alternative offers bargaining game. The particular way of splitting the *ex post* surplus has no allocative impact. The volume of trade remains always at its first-best value. ∎

More generally, the higher the agent's bargaining power in the negotiation over the surplus at date $t = 2$, the lower (resp. the higher) the principal's (resp. the agent's) gains from trade. As a corollary, if the principal expects to be stuck in a bilateral relationship at date $t = 2$ with a lower bargaining power than at the *ex ante* stage, he will prefer to contract with the agent at the *ex ante* stage (date $t = 0$). Next, we study what can then be achieved with such *ex ante* contracting.

6.2 Incentive Compatible Contract

Instead of waiting for the realization of the state of nature, the principal can offer to the agent, at the *ex ante* stage (date $t = 0$), a contract that ensures *ex post* efficiency under some rather weak conditions, as we see in the following.

This contract can only be written in terms of the verifiable variables available to the trading partners, namely the transfer t and the production level q just as in chapter 2. For instance, a contract saying, "If state θ realizes, the agent must produce $q^*(\theta)$ and be paid $t^*(\theta)$ by the principal" cannot be enforced because the state of nature θ is not verifiable at the *ex post* contracting stage and consequently cannot be written into a contract. However, a nonlinear price $t(q)$ or a menu $\{(\underline{t}, \underline{q}); (\bar{t}, \bar{q})\}$ is a feasible instrument at the *ex ante* stage.

When he accepts such a contract, the agent anticipates that his choice of outputs $q(\theta)$ in state θ will satisfy the following interim constraints:

$$t(q(\theta)) - \theta q(\theta) \geq t(\tilde{q}) - \theta \tilde{q} \qquad (6.4)$$

for all $\tilde{q}$ in the domain of $t(\cdot)$ and all θ in Θ.

These constraints are the same as the standard incentive compatibility constraints highlighted in chapter 2 as the reader will have recognized. Hence, there is a formal correspondence between the case where contracting takes place under asymmetric information between the principal and the agent, and the case of *ex ante* contracting when the state of nature is not verifiable. The revelation principle still applies in this context and the class of truthful direct revelation mechanisms of the form $\{(\underline{t}, \underline{q}); (\overline{t}, \overline{q})\}$ is enough to describe all feasible contracts that command trade at date $t = 2$ and that can be signed at date $t = 0$ between the principal and the agent. Pushing this analogy, from now on we call these mechanisms *incentive compatible contracts*.

The fact that the principal knows θ *ex post* is not used in such a mechanism. The benefit of incentive compatible contracts is that there is no need for the principal to act *ex post* (i.e., at date $t = 2$), as shown in figure 6.3. Only the agent reports the state of nature. The mechanism is thus not very demanding on the communication side and could be attractive if those communication costs were explicitly modeled.

We already know from section 2.11.1 that the first-best outcome can still be achieved with *ex ante* contracting, provided that the agent is risk neutral in a two-type environment. Nevertheless, note that the transfers with *ex ante* contracting are different from those obtained with no contract at date $t = 0$, as we can easily observe by comparing the results of sections 2.11.1 and 6.1. The reason for this difference is simple. With no contract at all, the transfers $\underline{t}^* = \underline{\theta} \underline{q}^*$ and $\overline{t}^* = \overline{\theta} \overline{q}^*$, which are offered by the principal at date $t = 2$, are no longer incentive compatible,[3] as is requested with *ex ante* contracting.

However, this first-best implementation generalizes to several types and more general utility functions $V = S(q, \theta) - t$ for the principal and $U = t - C(q, \theta)$ for the agent if the Spence-Mirrlees properties $S_{q\theta} < 0$ and $C_{q\theta} > 0$ are both satisfied. Otherwise, the second-order conditions for incentive compatibility may create some inefficiencies and may require some bunching, as in the case of nonresponsiveness in section 2.10.2. When second-order conditions impose some pooling over several types, there may exist a real trade-off between an *ex ante* inefficient contract and an *ex post* negotiation leaving only a partial bargaining power to the principal.

---

[3] Indeed, we have $0 = \underline{t}^* - \underline{\theta} \underline{q}^* < \overline{t}^* - \underline{\theta} \overline{q}^* = \Delta\theta \overline{q}^*$.

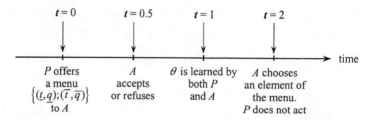

FIGURE 6.3: Timing with *Ex Ante* Contracting and Nonverifiability

An incentive compatible contract may also be useful if the principal is risk-averse and wants to obtain some insurance from the agent. Making the agent residual claimant for the gains from trade and reaping all of his profit with an up-front payment helps the principal to achieve the first-best outcome.[4] However, as is also shown in section 2.11, *ex ante* contracting fails to achieve efficiency when the agent is risk-averse. The nonverifiability of the state of nature may then conflict with the insurance concern of the agent if the principal offers an incentive compatible contract. Therefore, section 2.11.2 also provides an analysis of the efficiency loss incurred when *ex ante* contracting limited to incentive compatible contracts takes place in a world of nonverifiability and risk aversion.

Green and Laffont (1992) characterized the incentive compatible contracts that optimize the principal's expected welfare when *ex post* renegotiation led by the principal takes the utility levels achieved by those contracts as status quo utility payoffs.

6.3 Nash Implementation

In section 6.2, we have just seen how the principal and the agent can achieve *ex post* efficiency through an *ex ante* contract when they are both risk neutral. This contract uses only the agent's message but fails to achieve efficiency when the agent is risk-averse or when nonresponsiveness occurs. We now propose a slightly more complicated implementation of the *ex post* efficient allocation that also works in these cases. The new feature of this implementation comes from the fact that both the principal and the agent must now send a report on the state of nature at date $t = 2$. Requesting both the principal and the agent to report the state of nature moves us somewhat beyond the technics that have been the focus of this volume. This extension is only a small detour into a multiagent setting. It is needed

---

[4]See section 2.11.1 for the case of adverse selection and section 6.5.2 for more on this particular scenario.

to assess the true importance of the nonverifiability constraint in principal-agent models.[5]

The principal now offers to play a game with the agent, the outcome of which is enforced by the uniformed court of law. In this game, the principal is, like the agent, an active player, so that the mechanism to be played is a two-player game. However, as this game is played *ex post* under complete information, the characterization of the optimal two-player mechanism is relatively straightforward.

In this context, a general mechanism should involve two message spaces, one for the principal, say $\mathcal{M}_p$, and one for the agent, $\mathcal{M}_a$. Still denoting by $\mathcal{A}$ the set of feasible allocations, we have the following definition:

Definition 6.1: *A mechanism is a pair of message spaces $\mathcal{M}_a$ and $\mathcal{M}_p$ and a mapping $\tilde{g}(\cdot)$ from $\mathcal{M} = \mathcal{M}_a \times \mathcal{M}_p$ into $\mathcal{A}$, which writes as $\tilde{g}(m_a, m_p) = (\tilde{q}(m_a, m_p), \tilde{t}(m_a, m_p))$ for all pairs (m_a, m_p) belonging to $\mathcal{M}$.*

To fix ideas, let us assume that the principal and the agent have respective utility functions $V = S(q, \theta) - t$ and $U = t - C(q, \theta)$. In this context, the first-best allocation rule $a^*(\theta) = (t^*(\theta), q^*(\theta))$ is such that

$$S_q(q^*(\theta), \theta) = C_q(q^*(\theta), \theta) \tag{6.5}$$

and

$$t^*(\theta) = C(q^*(\theta), \theta). \tag{6.6}$$

We consider that those traders play a Nash equilibrium[6] of the mechanism $(\mathcal{M}, \tilde{g}(\cdot))$.

A Nash equilibrium of the mechanism $(\mathcal{M}, \tilde{g}(\cdot))$ is a pair of message functions $(m_a^*(\cdot), m_p^*(\cdot))$, which satisfy the following incentive conditions: for the principal,

$$S(\tilde{q}(m_a^*(\theta), m_p^*(\theta)), \theta) - \tilde{t}(m_a^*(\theta), m_p^*(\theta)) \geq S(\tilde{q}(m_a^*(\theta), \tilde{m}_p), \theta) - \tilde{t}(m_a^*(\theta), \tilde{m}_p),$$

$$\text{for all } \theta \text{ in } \Theta \text{ and } \tilde{m}_p \text{ in } \mathcal{M}_p; \tag{6.7}$$

and for the agent,

$$\tilde{t}(m_a^*(\theta), m_p^*(\theta)) - C(\tilde{q}(m_a^*(\theta), m_p^*(\theta)), \theta) \geq \tilde{t}(\tilde{m}_a, m_p^*(\theta)) - C(\tilde{q}(\tilde{m}_a, m_p^*(\theta)), \theta),$$

$$\text{for all } \theta \text{ in } \Theta \text{ and } \tilde{m}_a \text{ in } \mathcal{M}_a. \tag{6.8}$$

---

[5] In other words, restricting the analysis of this chapter to incentive compatible contracts could leave the reader with the feeling that some inefficiencies may emerge with nonverifiability. However, the room for those inefficiencies is much more restricted when more general mechanisms are allowed.

[6] We focus on pure-strategy equilibria for the sake of simplicity but without loss of generality.

According to (6.7), when the principal conjectures that the agent's strategy is given by $m_a^*(\theta)$ in state θ, his best response is $m_p^*(\theta)$. Similarly, (6.8) states that the agent's strategy $m_a^*(\theta)$ is a best response to the principal's behavior.

We can now state the definition that follows:

Definition 6.2: *An allocation rule $a(\theta)$ from Θ to $\mathcal{A}$ is implementable in Nash equilibrium by a mechanism $(\mathcal{M}, \tilde{g}(\cdot))$ if there exists a Nash equilibrium $(m_a^*(\cdot), m_p^*(\cdot))$ such that $a(\theta) = (\tilde{q}(m_a^*(\theta), m_p^*(\theta)), \tilde{t}(m_a^*(\theta), m_p^*(\theta)))$ for all θ in Θ.*

When the message spaces $\mathcal{M}_a$ and $\mathcal{M}_p$ are reduced to the set of possible types Θ, we have the following definitions:

Definition 6.3: *A direct revelation mechanism is a mapping $g(\cdot)$ from Θ^2 to $\mathcal{A}$, which writes as $g(\tilde{\theta}_a, \tilde{\theta}_p) = (q(\tilde{\theta}_a, \tilde{\theta}_p), t(\tilde{\theta}_a, \tilde{\theta}_p))$ where $\tilde{\theta}_a$ (resp. $\tilde{\theta}_p$) is the agent's (resp. principal's) report in Θ.*

Definition 6.4: *A direct revelation mechanism $g(\cdot)$ is truthful if it is a Nash equilibrium for the agent and the principal to report truthfully the state of nature.*

Denoting the set of Nash equilibria of the direct revelation mechanism $g(\cdot)$ in state θ by $N_g(\theta)$, we have the following definition:

Definition 6.5: *The allocation $a(\theta)$ is implementable in Nash equilibrium by the direct revelation mechanism $g(\cdot)$ if the pair of truthful reporting strategies of the principal and the agent forms a Nash equilibrium of $g(\cdot)$ ((θ, θ) in $N_g(\theta)$ for all θ in Θ) such that $a(\theta) = g(\theta, \theta)$ for all θ in Θ.*

Truthful direct revelation mechanisms must thus satisfy the following Nash incentive constraints:

$$S(q(\theta, \theta), \theta) - t(\theta, \theta) \geq S(q(\theta, \tilde{\theta}_p), \theta) - t(\theta, \tilde{\theta}_p)$$
$$\text{for all } (\theta, \tilde{\theta}_p) \text{ in } \Theta^2, \tag{6.9}$$

and

$$t(\theta, \theta) - C(q(\theta, \theta), \theta) \geq t(\tilde{\theta}_a, \theta) - C(q(\tilde{\theta}_a, \theta), \theta)$$
$$\text{for all } (\tilde{\theta}_a, \theta) \text{ in } \Theta^2. \tag{6.10}$$

We can now prove a new version of the revelation principle in this complete information environment.

Proposition 6.1: *Any allocation rule $a(\theta)$ that is implemented in Nash equilibrium by a mechanism $(\mathcal{M}, \tilde{g}(\cdot))$ can also be implemented in Nash equilibrium by a truthful direct revelation mechanism.*

Proof: The mechanism $(\mathcal{M}, \tilde{g}(\cdot))$ induces an allocation rule $a(\theta) = (\tilde{q}(m_a^*(\theta),$ $m_p^*(\theta)), \tilde{t}(m_a^*(\theta), m_p^*(\theta)))$, where $(m_a^*(\theta), m_p^*(\theta))$ are the messages of the agent and the principal in state θ at the Nash equilibrium of $(\mathcal{M}, \tilde{g}(\cdot))$ that we consider. Let us define a direct revelation mechanism $g(\cdot)$ from Θ^2 into $\mathcal{A}$, such that $g(\theta, \theta) = \tilde{g} \circ m^*(\theta)$ where $m^*(\theta) = (m_a^*(\theta), m_p^*(\theta))$. For all states of nature θ, we have thus $g(\theta, \theta) = (q(\theta, \theta), t(\theta, \theta)) \equiv \tilde{g}(m^*(\theta)) = (\tilde{q}(m_a^*(\theta), m_p^*(\theta)), \tilde{t}(m_a^*(\theta), m_p^*(\theta)))$. We check that it is a Nash equilibrium for the players to report the truth when they face the direct revelation mechanism $g(\cdot)$. For the principal, we have

$$S(q(\theta, \theta), \theta) - t(\theta, \theta) = S(\tilde{q}(m_a^*(\theta), m_p^*(\theta)), \theta) - \tilde{t}(m_a^*(\theta), m_p^*(\theta))$$
$$\geq S(\tilde{q}(m_a^*(\theta), \tilde{m}_p, \theta) - \tilde{t}(m_a^*(\theta), \tilde{m}_p)$$

for all $\tilde{m}_p$ in $\mathcal{M}_p$ and for all θ in Θ.

Taking $\tilde{m}_p = m_p^*(\theta')$ for any θ' in Θ, we obtain

$$S(q(\theta, \theta), \theta) - t(\theta, \theta) \geq S(\tilde{q}(m_a^*(\theta), m_p^*(\theta')), \theta) - \tilde{t}(m_a^*(\theta), m_p^*(\theta'))$$

for all (θ, θ') in Θ^2.

Finally, we get

$$S(q(\theta, \theta), \theta) - t(\theta, \theta) \geq S(q(\theta, \theta'), \theta) - t(\theta, \theta'),$$

for all (θ, θ') in Θ^2.

Hence, the principal's best response to a truthful reporting strategy by the agent is also to report truthfully.

Proceeding similarly for the agent, we prove that the agent's best response is also to report his type truthfully. Hence, truthful reporting is a Nash equilibrium.

∎

The important question at this point is to determine which restrictions are really put on allocations by the incentive compatibility constraints (6.9) and (6.10). In particular, we would like to know under which conditions the first-best allocation rule $a^*(\theta) = (t^*(\theta), q^*(\theta))$ is implementable as a Nash equilibrium of the direct revelation mechanism played by the principal and the agent. It turns out that incentive compatibility in this multiagent framework imposes very few restrictions on the set of implementable allocations.

To see that, let us first consider the simple case where the principal's utility function does not depend directly on θ, i.e., his utility is given by $V = S(q) - t$.

P's strategy

		$\underline{\theta}$	$\bar{\theta}$
A's strategy	$\underline{\theta}$	$(\underline{t}^*, \underline{q}^*)$	$(0,0)$
	$\bar{\theta}$	$(0,0)$	$(\bar{t}^*, \bar{q}^*)$

FIGURE 6.4: Nash Implementation of the First-Best with the No-Trade Option as Punishment

The agent also has the standard linear cost function of chapter 2, $U = t - \theta q$. We know that the first-best allocation entails producing outputs $q^*(\theta)$, such that $S'(q^*(\theta)) = \theta$. Using transfers $t^*(\theta) = \theta q^*(\theta)$ allows then the principal to extract all of the agent's rent.

A truthful direct revelation mechanism $g(\cdot)$ that implements in Nash equilibrium the first-best allocation rule $a^*(\theta) = (t^*(\theta), q^*(\theta))$ can be summarized by a matrix (Figure 6.4), where the lines (resp. columns) represent the agent's (resp. principal's) possible reports in $\Theta = \{\underline{\theta}, \bar{\theta}\}$. In each box of the matrix, we have represented the transfer-output pair corresponding to the reports made by the principal and the agent.

For instance, when both the principal and the agent report to the court that $\underline{\theta}$ has realized, the contract $(\underline{t}^*, \underline{q}^*)$ is enforced. The principal gets a net surplus $S(\underline{q}^*) - \underline{t}^* = S(\underline{q}^*) - \underline{\theta}\underline{q}^*$, and the agent gets $\underline{t}^* - \underline{\theta}\underline{q}^* = 0$ if the true state of nature is $\underline{\theta}$. If they disagree, the *no-trade* option is enforced, with no output being produced and no transfer being made.

The important point to note is that the *same* game form must be played by the agent and the principal, whatever the true state of nature θ. Indeed, the state of nature being nonverifiable, the transfers and outputs in each box of the matrix cannot be made contingent upon it. The goal of this mechanism is to ensure that there exists a truthful Nash equilibrium in each state θ that implements the first-best allocation $a^*(\theta) = (t^*(\theta), q^*(\theta))$.

Proposition 6.2: *Assume that preferences are given by $V = S(q) - t$ and $U = t - \theta q$, then the first-best allocation rule is Nash-implementable.*

Proof: Let us check that truthtelling is a Nash equilibrium of the direct revelation mechanism $g(\cdot)$ in each state of nature. Consider first state $\underline{\theta}$. Given that the agent reports $\underline{\theta}$, the principal gets $S(\underline{q}^*) - \underline{t}^* = S(\underline{q}^*) - \underline{\theta}\underline{q}^*$ by reporting the truth and zero otherwise. By assumption, trade is valuable when $\underline{\theta}$ realizes $(S(\underline{q}^*) - \underline{\theta}\underline{q}^* > 0)$, and telling the truth is a best response for the principal. The agent is indifferent between telling the truth or not when the principal reports $\underline{\theta}$, because $\underline{t}^* - \underline{\theta}\underline{q}^* = 0$. Hence, he weakly prefers to tell the truth as a best response. Consider now state $\bar{\theta}$. Given that the agent reports $\bar{\theta}$, the principal gets $S(\bar{q}^*) - \bar{t}^* = S(\bar{q}^*) - \bar{\theta}\bar{q}^*$

by reporting the truth and zero otherwise. By assumption, trade is also valuable when $\bar{\theta}$ realizes ($S(\bar{q}^*) - \bar{\theta}\bar{q}^* > 0$). Telling the truth is a best response for the principal. Similarly, the agent is indifferent between telling the truth or not when the principal reports truthfully, because $\bar{t}^* - \bar{\theta}\bar{q}^* = 0$. He weakly prefers to tell the truth. This ends the proof that truthtelling is a Nash equilibrium of $g(\cdot)$. ∎

It is important to note that, when $\underline{\theta}$ realizes, the pair of truthful strategies is not the unique Nash equilibrium of the direct mechanism $g(\cdot)$. Indeed, $(\bar{\theta}, \bar{\theta})$ is another Nash equilibrium in this state of nature. The agent strictly gains from misreporting if the principal does so, because $\bar{t}^* - \underline{\theta}\bar{q}^* = \Delta\theta\bar{q}^* > 0$. Also, the principal prefers to report $\bar{\theta}$ if the agent does so, because he obtains $S(\bar{q}^*) - \bar{t}^* > 0$.

There are two possible attitudes vis-à vis this *multiplicity problem*. First, one may forget about it and argue that truth-telling should be a focal equilibrium. This attitude rests on a relatively shaky argument in the absence of a definitive theory of equilibrium selection. Moreover, some authors have shown in related models that the nontruthful equilibrium may sometimes Pareto dominate the truthful one from the players' point of view.[7] In this case, the focus on the truthful equilibrium is less attractive. This argument is less compelling in our context since the two equilibria cannot be Pareto-ranked: the agent does better in the nontruthful equilibrium, than in the truthful one, but the principal does worse.

The second possible attitude towards the multiplicity of equilibria is to take it seriously and to look for mechanisms that ensure that the first-best allocation is *uniquely implementable*. This second attitude is the route we are going to take now.

Definition 6.6: *The first-best allocation rule $a^*(\theta)$ is uniquely implementable in Nash equilibrium by the mechanism $(\mathcal{M}, \tilde{g}(\cdot))$ if the mechanism has a unique Nash equilibrium for each θ in Θ and it induces the allocation $a^*(\theta)$.*

In the definition above, we do not restrict a priori the mechanism $\tilde{g}(\cdot)$ to be a direct revelation mechanism. It could well be that the cost of obtaining unique implementation is the expansion of the space of messages that the agent and the principal use to communicate with the court. Such extensions are often used in multiagent (three or more) frameworks. In our principal-agent model, those extensions are not needed, provided that one conveniently defines the out-of-equilibrium-path punishments.

For the time being, let us consider a truthful direct revelation mechanism like that shown in figure 6.5.

---

[7] See Demski and Sappington (1984) for such a model.

P's strategy

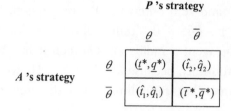

FIGURE 6.5: Nash Implementation of the First-Best with General Punishments

The outcomes $(\hat{t}_1, \hat{q}_1)$ and $(\hat{t}_2, \hat{q}_2)$ may be different from the no-trade option used above, in order to give more flexibility to the court in designing off-the-equilibrium punishments, ensuring both the truthful revelation and the uniqueness of the equilibrium. Let us now see how it is possible to do so.

The conditions for having a truthful Nash equilibrium in state $\underline{\theta}$ are, for the principal,

$$S(\underline{q}^*) - \underline{t}^* > S(\hat{q}_2) - \hat{t}_2, \tag{6.11}$$

and for the agent

$$0 = \underline{t}^* - \underline{\theta}\underline{q}^* > \hat{t}_1 - \underline{\theta}\hat{q}_1. \tag{6.12}$$

Similarly, the conditions for having a truthful Nash equilibrium in state $\bar{\theta}$ are, for the principal,

$$S(\bar{q}^*) - \bar{t}^* > S(\hat{q}_1) - \hat{t}_1, \tag{6.13}$$

and for the agent,

$$0 = \bar{t}^* - \bar{\theta}\bar{q}^* > \hat{t}_2 - \bar{\theta}\hat{q}_2. \tag{6.14}$$

Let us now turn to the conditions ensuring that there is no nontruthful, pure-strategy Nash equilibrium in either state of nature. Consider a possible nontruthful equilibrium $(\bar{\theta}, \bar{\theta})$ when state $\underline{\theta}$ realizes. Given that (6.13) is needed to satisfy the principal's incentive constraint in state $\bar{\theta}$, the only way to break the possible equilibrium is to induce a deviation by the agent. Therefore, we must have

$$\bar{t}^* - \underline{\theta}\bar{q}^* < \hat{t}_2 - \underline{\theta}\hat{q}_2. \tag{6.15}$$

Now consider a possible nontruthful pure-strategy Nash equilibrium $(\underline{\theta}, \underline{\theta})$ when state $\bar{\theta}$ realizes. Given that (6.11) is needed to ensure the principal's incentive constraint in state $\underline{\theta}$, the only way to break the possible equilibrium is again to induce a deviation by the agent:

$$\underline{t}^* - \bar{\theta}\underline{q}^* < \hat{t}_1 - \bar{\theta}\hat{q}_1. \tag{6.16}$$

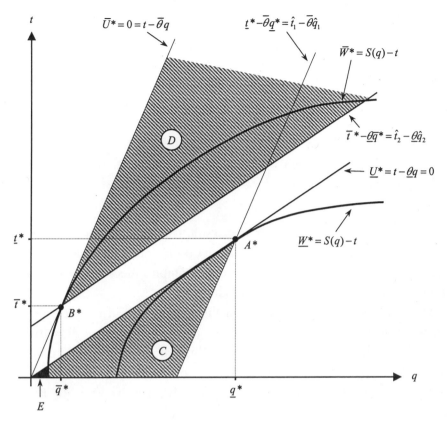

FIGURE 6.6: Off-the-Equilibrium Path Punishments

A truthful direct revelation mechanism $g(\cdot)$, which uniquely implements the first-best as a Nash equilibrium, exists when the conditions (6.11) through (6.16) are all satisfied by a pair of punishment contracts $(\hat{t}_1, \hat{q}_1)$ and $(\hat{t}_2, \hat{q}_2)$. We now have the following proposition:

Proposition 6.3: *Assume preferences are given by* $V = S(q) - t$ *and* $U = t - \theta q$. *A truthful direct revelation mechanism* $g(\cdot)$ *exists that uniquely implements in Nash equilibrium the first-best allocation rule* $a^*(\theta)$.

Proof: The clearest way of doing this proof is to draw a picture. In Figure 6.6, we have represented the first-best allocation $a^*(\theta)$ and the possible punishments $(\hat{t}_1, \hat{q}_1)$ and $(\hat{t}_2, \hat{q}_2)$.

Because the first-best allocation requires that the agent produce efficiently and gets zero rent, the indifference curves of the principal are tangent to the zero-profit lines of the agent in each state of nature at points A^* and B^*. First, the $\underline{\theta}$-agent incentive compatibility constraint (6.12) and the condition (6.16) define a subset C where $(\hat{t}_1, \hat{q}_1)$ may lie (crossed area in figure 6.6). Within this subset, the principal's incentive constraint (6.13) further reduces the set of possible punishments $(\hat{t}_1, \hat{q}_1)$

to the area E close to the origin (shaded area in figure 6.6). This set is nonempty, because the principal's indifference curve $\overline{\overline{W}}^* = S(q) - t$ does not go through the origin when trade is valuable in state $\bar{\theta}$ (namely when $S(\bar{q}^*) - \bar{\theta}\bar{q}^* > 0$).

Similarly, the agent's incentive constraints (6.14) and (6.15) define a subset D of possible values for the punishment $(\hat{t}_2, \hat{q}_2)$ (crossed area in figure 6.6). In figure 6.6, this full set satisfies the principal's incentive compatibility constraint (6.11). More generally, by strict concavity of the principal's indifference curve $\overline{\overline{W}}^* = S(q) - t$ going through B^*, there exists a nonempty subset of D that lies strictly above this indifference curve. All those points obviously lie above the principal's indifference curve $\underline{W}^* = S(q) - t$ going through A^*. ∎

Proposition 6.3 yields a very striking result. It says that direct revelation mechanisms are enough to ensure efficiency always if the court can design punishments in a clever way. There is no need to use more complex mechanisms in this simple and rather structured principal-agent model.

More generally, one may wonder if the requirement of unique Nash implementation imposes some structure on the set of allocation rules $a(\theta) = (t(\theta), q(\theta))$ that can be implemented this way. Indeed, this structure exists. Before describing it, we need another definition, which we cast in the general case where the principal's and the agent's preferences are respectively given by $V = S(q, \theta) - t$ and $U = t - C(q, \theta)$.

Definition 6.7: *An allocation rule $a(\theta) = (t(\theta), q(\theta))$ is monotonic if and only if for any θ in Θ, such that $a(\theta) \neq a(\theta')$ for some θ' in Θ, there exists an allocation $(\hat{t}, \hat{q})$ such that one of the two conditions below is true:*

$$(\mathrm{P}) \begin{cases} S(q(\theta), \theta) - t(\theta) \geq S(\hat{q}, \theta) - \hat{t} \\ \text{and} \\ S(\hat{q}, \theta') - \hat{t} > S(q(\theta), \theta') - t(\theta) \end{cases}$$

or

$$(\mathrm{A}) \begin{cases} t(\theta) - C(q(\theta), \theta) \geq \hat{t} - C(\hat{q}, \theta) \\ \text{and} \\ \hat{t} - C(\hat{q}, \theta') > t(\theta) - C(q(\theta), \theta'). \end{cases}$$

These inequalities have a simple meaning.[8] The allocation rule $a(\cdot)$ selects the pair $a(\theta) = (t(\theta), q(\theta))$ in state θ and not in state θ', if there exists another allocation $(\hat{t}, \hat{q})$ such that either the principal or the agent prefers this allocation to $a(\theta)$ when the state of nature is θ'.

---

[8]An alternative definition that may better explain the expression "monotonicity" goes intuitively as follows. If $a(\theta)$ is selected in state θ, and if the allocation $a(\theta)$ "progresses" in the preferences of both players in another state of nature θ', $a(\theta)$ must also be chosen in state θ'.

Under the assumptions of proposition 6.3, the first-best allocation rule $a^*(\cdot)$ is monotonic. Indeed, first we note that $a^*(\underline{\theta}) \neq a^*(\bar{\theta})$. Second, the principal's utility function being independent of θ, there does not exist any allocation $(\hat{t}, \hat{q})$ such that condition (P) holds. Lastly, there exists $(\hat{t}, \hat{q})$ such that condition (A) holds. In state $\underline{\theta}$, the set of such pairs is the set C in figure 6.6. In state $\bar{\theta}$, it is the set D.

The monotonicity of allocation rules is an important property that follows immediately from unique implementation in Nash equilibrium, as is shown in proposition 6.4.

Proposition 6.4: *Consider an allocation rule $a(\cdot)$, which is uniquely implemented in Nash equilibrium by a mechanism $(\mathcal{M}, \tilde{g}(\cdot))$; then the allocation rule $a(\cdot)$ is monotonic.*

Proof: The mechanism $(\mathcal{M}, \tilde{g}(\cdot))$ uses the message spaces $\mathcal{M}_a$ and $\mathcal{M}_p$. If the allocation rule $a(\cdot)$ is uniquely implementable in Nash equilibrium by $\tilde{g}(\cdot)$, we know that, in state θ, there exists a pair of strategies $(m_a^*(\theta), m_p^*(\theta))$ such that $(q(\theta), t(\theta)) = (\tilde{q}(m_a^*(\theta), m_p^*(\theta)), \tilde{t}(m_a^*(\theta), m_p^*(\theta)))$, and these strategies form a Nash equilibrium

$$S(\tilde{q}(m_a^*(\theta), m_p^*(\theta)), \theta) - \tilde{t}(m_a^*(\theta), m_p^*(\theta)) \geq S(\tilde{q}(m_a^*(\theta), \tilde{m}_p), \theta) - \tilde{t}(m_a^*(\theta), \tilde{m}_p)$$

$$\text{for all } \tilde{m}_p \text{ in } \mathcal{M}_p; \tag{6.17}$$

$$\tilde{t}(m_a^*(\theta), m_p^*(\theta)) - C(\tilde{q}(m_a^*(\theta), m_p^*(\theta)), \theta) \geq \tilde{t}(\tilde{m}_a, m_p^*(\theta)) - C(\tilde{q}(\tilde{m}_a, m_p^*(\theta)), \theta)$$

$$\text{for all } \tilde{m}_a \text{ in } \mathcal{M}_a. \tag{6.18}$$

Moreover, $a(\theta)$ being different from $a(\theta')$ for a θ' different from θ, $a(\theta)$ is not a Nash equilibrium in state θ'. This means that either the principal (or the agent) finds it strictly better to send a message $\tilde{m}_p$ rather than $m_p^*(\theta)$ (or $\tilde{m}_a$ rather than $m_a^*(\theta)$ in the case of the agent). For the principal, this means that

$$S(q(\theta), \theta') - t(\theta) < S(\tilde{q}(m_a^*(\theta), \tilde{m}_p), \theta') - \tilde{t}(m_p^*(\theta), \tilde{m}_p). \tag{6.19}$$

For the agent, this means that

$$t(\theta) - C(q(\theta), \theta') < \tilde{t}(\tilde{m}_a, m_p^*(\theta)) - C(\tilde{q}(\tilde{m}_a, m_p^*(\theta)), \theta'). \tag{6.20}$$

In each case, it is easy to show that the allocation rule $a(\cdot)$ is monotonic. Take $(\hat{t}, \hat{q}) = (\tilde{t}(m_a^*(\theta), \tilde{m}_p), \tilde{q}(m_a^*(\theta), \tilde{m}_p)))$ in the first case (the principal's deviation) and $(\hat{t}, \hat{q}) = (\tilde{t}(\tilde{m}_a, m_p^*(\theta)), \tilde{q}(\tilde{m}_a, m_p^*(\theta)))$ in the second case (the agent's deviation). ∎

The intuitive meaning of proposition 6.4 is rather clear. In order to prevent an allocation implemented in one state of nature θ to be also chosen in another state θ', either the principal or the agent must deviate and choose another message in state θ'. Hence, the mechanism $\tilde{g}(\cdot)$ that uniquely implements the allocation rule $a(\cdot)$ must include an allocation $(\hat{t}, \hat{q})$, which is worse than $(t(\theta), q(\theta))$ for both agents in state θ but better for at least one in state θ'. In this case, the latter player's preferences are reversed between states θ and θ', breaking a possible equilibrium that would also implement $a(\theta)$ in state θ'.

The monotonicity property is a necessary condition satisfied by an allocation rule that is uniquely implementable in Nash equilibrium. The remaining question is to know how far away this property is from sufficiency. With more than two agents $(n \geq 3)$, Maskin (1999)[9] shows that monotonicity plus another property, *no veto power*,[10] is also sufficient for unique Nash implementation. With two agents only, Dutta and Sen (1991) and Moore and Repullo (1990) have provided necessary and sufficient conditions for unique Nash implementation in more general environments than the principal-agent relationship analyzed in this chapter.

6.4 Subgame-Perfect Implementation ★

From proposition 6.4, a necessary condition for unique Nash implementation is that an allocation rule $a(\cdot)$ be monotonic. Any allocation rule that fails to be monotonic will also fail to guarantee unique Nash implementation. Then, one may wonder if refinements of the Nash equilibrium concept can still be used to ensure unique implementation. The natural refinement of subgame perfection will appear when one moves to a game with sequential moves, where the principal and the agent take turns sending messages to the court. An allocation rule $a(\theta)$ is uniquely implementable in subgame-perfect equilibrium by a mechanism $\bar{g}(\cdot)$

---

[9]The first version of this fundamental paper appeared in 1977.

[10]This property says that whenever $n - 1$ agents prefer an allocation to all others in one state of nature the nth agent cannot veto it, and this allocation belongs to the domain of the allocation rule. The no veto power property is a rather innocuous property to fulfill in economic contexts with more than two agents.

provided that its unique subgame-perfect equilibrium yields allocation $a(\theta)$ in any state θ.

Instead of presenting the general theory of subgame-perfect implementation, which is quite complex, we propose a simple example showing the mechanics of the procedure. Let us first single out a principal-agent setting where the first-best allocation rule is nonmonotonic. As we know from the last section, this calls for a more complex modelling of information than what we have used so far if we remain in the context of principal-agent models with quasi-linear objective functions. Consider a principal with utility function $V = S(q) - t$ independent of the state of nature θ. For simplicity, we assume that $S(q) = \mu q - \frac{\lambda q^2}{2}$, where μ and λ are common knowledge. The agent instead has a utility function $U = t - \theta_1 q - \theta_2 \frac{q^2}{2}$, where $\theta = (\theta_1, \theta_2)$ is now a bidimensional state of nature.

The first-best outputs $q^*(\theta_1, \theta_2)$ are given by the first-order conditions $S'(q^*(\theta_1, \theta_2)) = \theta_1 + \theta_2 q^*(\theta_1, \theta_2)$. We immediately find that $q^*(\theta_1, \theta_2) = \frac{\mu - \theta_1}{\lambda + \theta_2}$.

We assume that each parameter θ_i belongs to $\Theta = \{\underline{\theta}, \bar{\theta}\}$. A priori, there are four possible states of nature and four first-best outputs. Assuming that $\frac{\mu - \bar{\theta}}{\lambda + \underline{\theta}} = \frac{\mu - \underline{\theta}}{\lambda + \bar{\theta}}$, i.e., $\mu - \lambda = \underline{\theta} + \bar{\theta}$, we are left with three first-best outputs $\underline{q}^* = \frac{\mu - \underline{\theta}}{\lambda + \underline{\theta}}$, $\hat{q}^* = \frac{\mu - \underline{\theta}}{\lambda + \bar{\theta}} = 1$, and $\bar{q}^* = \frac{\mu - \bar{\theta}}{\lambda + \bar{\theta}}$ that we assume to be all positive.

Of course, even if the production level is the same in states $(\underline{\theta}, \bar{\theta})$ and $(\bar{\theta}, \underline{\theta})$, the agent has different costs and should receive different transfers $\hat{t}_1^*$ and $\hat{t}_2^*$ from the principal in those two states of nature. We denote by $\underline{t}^*$ and $\bar{t}^*$ the transfers in the other states of nature.

In figure 6.7, we have represented the first-best allocations corresponding to the different states of nature.

Importantly, the indifference curve of a $(\underline{\theta}, \bar{\theta})$-agent going through the first-best allocation C^* of a $(\underline{\theta}, \bar{\theta})$-agent (dotted curve in figure 6.7) is tangent to and always above that of a $(\bar{\theta}, \underline{\theta})$-agent.[11] This means that one cannot find any allocation $(\hat{t}, \hat{q})$ such that condition (A) of definition 6.6 holds. In other words, the first-best allocation rule $a^*(\theta)$ is nonmonotonic in this bidimensional example. To see more precisely why it is so, note that any mechanism $\tilde{g}(\cdot)$ implementing the first-best allocation $a^*(\bar{\theta}, \underline{\theta})$ must be such that

$$\tilde{t}(m_a^*(\bar{\theta}, \underline{\theta}), m_p^*(\bar{\theta}, \underline{\theta})) - \bar{\theta}\tilde{q}(m_a^*(\bar{\theta}, \underline{\theta}), m_p^*(\bar{\theta}, \underline{\theta})) - \frac{\underline{\theta}\tilde{q}^2(m_a^*(\bar{\theta}, \underline{\theta}), m_p^*(\bar{\theta}, \underline{\theta}))}{2}$$

$$\geq \tilde{t}(\tilde{m}_a, m_p^*(\bar{\theta}, \underline{\theta})) - \bar{\theta}\tilde{q}(\tilde{m}_a, m_p^*(\bar{\theta}, \underline{\theta})) - \frac{\underline{\theta}\tilde{q}^2(\tilde{m}_a, m_p^*(\bar{\theta}, \underline{\theta}))}{2}, \quad \text{for all } \tilde{m}_a \text{ in } \mathcal{M}_a.$$

[11] Since $\bar{\theta} > \underline{\theta}$, the second derivative of the $(\underline{\theta}, \bar{\theta})$-indifference curve at C^* is greater in absolute value than the second derivative of the $(\bar{\theta}, \underline{\theta})$-indifference curve at C^*.

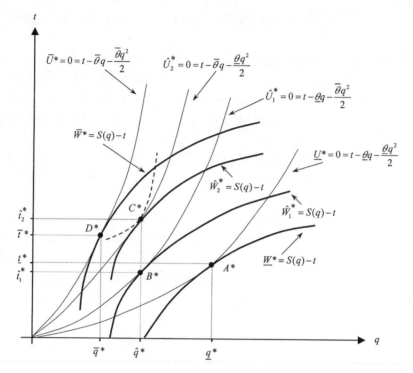

FIGURE 6.7: First-Best Allocations

But, since the indifference curve of a $(\underline{\theta}, \bar{\theta})$-agent through C^* is above the one of a $(\bar{\theta}, \underline{\theta})$-agent, this inequality also implies that

$$\tilde{t}(m_a^*(\bar{\theta}, \underline{\theta}), m_p^*(\bar{\theta}, \underline{\theta})) - \underline{\theta}\tilde{q}(m_a^*(\bar{\theta}, \underline{\theta}), m_p^*(\bar{\theta}, \underline{\theta})) - \frac{\bar{\theta}\tilde{q}^2(m_a^*(\bar{\theta}, \underline{\theta}), m_p^*(\bar{\theta}, \underline{\theta}))}{2}$$

$$\geq \tilde{t}(\tilde{m}_a, m_p^*(\bar{\theta}, \underline{\theta})) - \underline{\theta}\tilde{q}(\tilde{m}_a, m_p^*(\bar{\theta}, \underline{\theta})) - \frac{\bar{\theta}\tilde{q}^2(\tilde{m}_a, m_p^*(\bar{\theta}, \underline{\theta}))}{2},$$

for all $\tilde{m}_a$ in $\mathcal{M}_a$.

Since the principal's utility function does not depend directly on θ, the pair of strategies $(m_a^*(\bar{\theta}, \underline{\theta}); (m_p^*(\bar{\theta}, \underline{\theta}))$ that implements the allocation $a^*(\bar{\theta}, \underline{\theta}) = (\hat{t}_2, \hat{q}^*)$ remains an equilibrium in state $(\underline{\theta}, \bar{\theta})$. Hence, there is no hope of finding a unique Nash implementation of the first-best outcome.

Let us now turn to a possible unique implementation using a three-stage extensive form mechanism and the more stringent concept of subgame-perfection.

The reader should be convinced that there is not too much problem in eliciting the preferences of the agent in states $(\underline{\theta}, \underline{\theta})$ and $(\bar{\theta}, \bar{\theta})$.[12] Hence, we will focus

---

[12]For instance, the states $(\underline{\theta}, \underline{\theta})$ and $(\bar{\theta}, \bar{\theta})$ can be revealed by an earlier stage with Nash implementation.

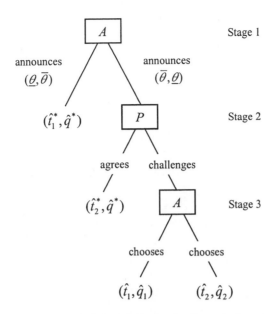

FIGURE 6.8: Subgame-Perfect Implementation

on a "reduced" extensive form that is enough to highlight the logic of subgame-perfect implementation. The objective of this extensive form is to have the agent truthfully reveal the state of nature when either $(\bar{\theta}, \underline{\theta})$ or $(\underline{\theta}, \bar{\theta})$ occurs.

In figure 6.8 we have represented such an extensive form.

The mechanism to be played in both states $(\underline{\theta}, \bar{\theta})$ and $(\bar{\theta}, \underline{\theta})$ is a three-stage game with the agent moving first and announcing whether $(\underline{\theta}, \bar{\theta})$ or $(\bar{\theta}, \underline{\theta})$ has been realized. If $(\underline{\theta}, \bar{\theta})$ is announced, the game ends with the allocation $(\hat{t}_1^*, \hat{q}^*)$. If $(\bar{\theta}, \underline{\theta})$ is announced, the principal may agree and then the game ends with the allocation $(\hat{t}_2^*, \hat{q}^*)$ or challenge. In the latter case, the agent has to choose between two possible out-of-equilibrium allocations $(\hat{t}_1, \hat{q}_1)$ and $(\hat{t}_2, \hat{q}_2)$. We have a greater flexibility with respect to Nash implementation, since now the agent has sometimes to choose between two allocations that are nonequilibrium ones instead of between an out-of-equilibrium one and an equilibrium one, as under Nash implementation. We want to use this flexibility to obtain $(\hat{t}_1^*, \hat{q}^*)$ in the state of nature $(\underline{\theta}, \bar{\theta})$ and $(\hat{t}_2^*, \hat{q}^*)$ in the state of nature $(\bar{\theta}, \underline{\theta})$. To do so, we are going to choose the allocations $(\hat{t}_1, \hat{q}_1)$ and $(\hat{t}_2, \hat{q}_2)$ in such a way that the agent prefers a different allocation in different states of the world.[13] Specifically, we choose them to have

$$\hat{t}_1 - \bar{\theta}\hat{q}_1 - \frac{\theta\hat{q}_1^2}{2} > \hat{t}_2 - \bar{\theta}\hat{q}_2 - \theta\frac{\hat{q}_2^2}{2} \tag{6.21}$$

[13]This pair of allocations is often called a *test-pair*.

and

$$\hat{t}_2 - \underline{\theta}\hat{q}_2 - \frac{\bar{\theta}\hat{q}_2^2}{2} > \hat{t}_1 - \underline{\theta}\hat{q}_1 - \frac{\bar{\theta}\hat{q}_1^2}{2}. \tag{6.22}$$

Then, since at stage 3 the agent chooses $(\hat{t}_1, \hat{q}_1)$ in state $(\bar{\theta}, \underline{\theta})$, to obtain $(t_2^*, \hat{q}^*)$ the principal should not be willing to challenge the agent's report at stage 2 of the game. This means that one should have

$$S(\hat{q}^*) - \hat{t}_2^* > S(\hat{q}_1) - \hat{t}_1. \tag{6.23}$$

Finally, the agent with type $(\bar{\theta}, \underline{\theta})$ should prefer to report truthfully that $(\bar{\theta}, \underline{\theta})$ has realized, i.e.:

$$\hat{t}_2^* - \bar{\theta}\hat{q}^* - \frac{\theta\hat{q}^{*2}}{2} > \hat{t}_1^* - \bar{\theta}\hat{q}_1^* - \frac{\theta\hat{q}_1^{*2}}{2}. \tag{6.24}$$

Now let us see how we can obtain $(\hat{t}_1^*, \hat{q}^*)$ in the state of nature $(\underline{\theta}, \bar{\theta})$. Since the agent chooses $(\hat{t}_2, \hat{q}_2)$ in state $(\underline{\theta}, \bar{\theta})$, the principal should be willing to challenge, i.e.,

$$S(\hat{q}_2) - \hat{t}_2 > S(\hat{q}^*) - \hat{t}_2^*. \tag{6.25}$$

Expecting this behavior by the principal, the agent should not be willing to announce $(\bar{\theta}, \underline{\theta})$ when the state of nature is $(\underline{\theta}, \bar{\theta})$. This means that the following inequality must also hold:

$$\hat{t}_1^* - \underline{\theta}\hat{q}^* - \frac{\bar{\theta}\hat{q}^{*2}}{2} > \hat{t}_2 - \underline{\theta}\hat{q}_2 - \frac{\bar{\theta}\hat{q}_2^2}{2}. \tag{6.26}$$

The remaining question is whether there exists a pair of contracts $(\hat{t}_1, \hat{q}_1)$ and $(\hat{t}_2, \hat{q}_2)$ that satisfy constraints (6.21) to (6.26). The response can be given graphically (figure 6.9). By definition, $(\hat{t}_1, \hat{q}_1)$ (resp. $(\hat{t}_2, \hat{q}_2)$) should be above (resp. below) the principal's indifference curve going through C^*. Note that for $q > \hat{q}^*$, the indifference curves of an agent with $(\underline{\theta}, \bar{\theta})$ have a greater slope than those of an agent with type $(\bar{\theta}, \underline{\theta})$. This helps to construct very easily the out-of-equilibrium allocations $(\hat{t}_1, \hat{q}_1)$ and $(\hat{t}_2, \hat{q}_2)$, as in figure 6.9.

> **Remark:** Subgame-perfect implementation is beautiful and attractive, but it should be noted that it has been sometimes criticized because it relies excessively on rationality. The kind of problem at hand can be illustrated with our example of figure 6.8. Indeed, when state $(\underline{\theta}, \bar{\theta})$ realizes and the principal has to decide to move at the second stage, he knows that the agent has already made a suboptimal move. Why should he still believe that the agent will behave optimally at stage 3, as needed by subgame-perfect implementation? ∎

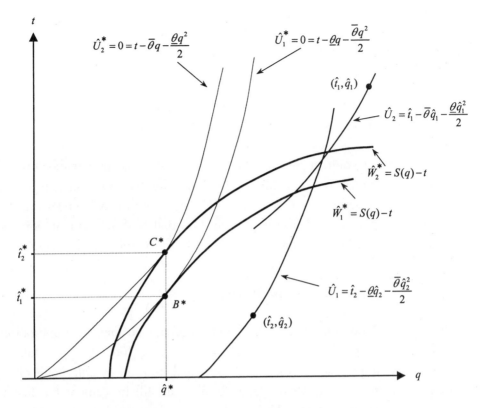

FIGURE 6.9: Subgame-Perfect Implementation

Moore and Repullo (1988) present a set of conditions ensuring subgame-perfect implementation in general environments, noticeably those with more than two agents. The construction is rather complex but close in spirit to our example. Abreu and Matsushima (1992) have developed the concept of *virtual-implementation* of an allocation rule. The idea is that the allocation rule may not be implemented with probability one but instead with very high probability. With this implementation concept, any allocation rule can be virtually implemented as a subgame-perfect equilibrium. ∎

6.5 Risk Aversion ★

The previous sections have discussed how various sorts of mechanisms may help to implement the first-best allocation rule when both the principal and the agent are risk neutral. The objective of this section is to discuss the potential of those mechanisms when either the principal or the agent is risk averse.

6.5.1 Risk-Averse Agent

When the agent is risk averse, signing no contract *ex ante* remains optimal if all the bargaining power is still left to the principal *ex post*. Indeed, *ex post* take-it-or-leave-it offers impose no risk on the agent, who is always maintained at the zero utility level.

An incentive contract performs badly, because there is now a trade-off between insurance and incentive compatibility. However, the Nash (and subgame-perfect) implementation performs rather well. It is straightforward to extend sections 6.3 and 6.4 to the case of a risk-averse agent to show that Nash implementation allows one to implement the first-best outcome with full insurance for the agent.[14]

6.5.2 Risk-Averse Principal

Clearly, signing no contract at the *ex ante* stage can no longer be optimal even if the principal has all of the bargaining power *ex post*. Indeed, *ex post* take-it-or-leave-it offers impose some risk on the principal from an *ex ante* point of view. However, an incentive contract $\{(\underline{t}, \underline{q}); (\bar{t}, \bar{q})\}$ can still implement the first-best, as we have seen in section 2.11.2. Making the agent residual claimant for the hierarchy's profit is again optimal in the case of nonverifiability. Of course, we still have to be sure that nonresponsiveness does not occur.

Finally, unique Nash implementation of the first-best outcome can also be obtained using a game form similar to that in figure 6.5. In our standard example, efficiency still requires that $\underline{q}^*$ and $\bar{q}^*$ are produced, such that $S'(\underline{q}^*) = \underline{\theta}$ and $S'(\bar{q}^*) = \bar{\theta}$. Providing insurance to the principal also requests that the principal gets the same payoff in each state of nature:

$$V = S(\underline{q}^*) - \underline{t}^* = S(\bar{q}^*) - \bar{t}^*. \tag{6.27}$$

Finally, the agent's *ex ante* participation constraint should also be binding:

$$v(\underline{t}^* - \underline{\theta}\underline{q}^*) + (1 - v)(\bar{t}^* - \bar{\theta}\bar{q}^*) = 0. \tag{6.28}$$

Since trade is more valuable in state $\underline{\theta}$ than in state $\bar{\theta}$, we have $\underline{W}^* = S(\underline{q}^*) - \underline{\theta}\underline{q}^* > S(\bar{q}^*) - \bar{\theta}\bar{q}^* = \bar{W}^*$. Solving (6.27) and (6.28) therefore yields $\underline{U}^* = \underline{t}^* - \underline{\theta}\underline{q}^* = (1 - v)(\underline{W}^* - \bar{W}^*) > 0$ and $\bar{U}^* = \bar{t}^* - \bar{\theta}\bar{q}^* = -v(\underline{W}^* - \bar{W}^*) < 0$.

---

[14]Indeed, in figure 6.6, we see that the agent makes zero profit in both states of nature and thus receives full insurance.

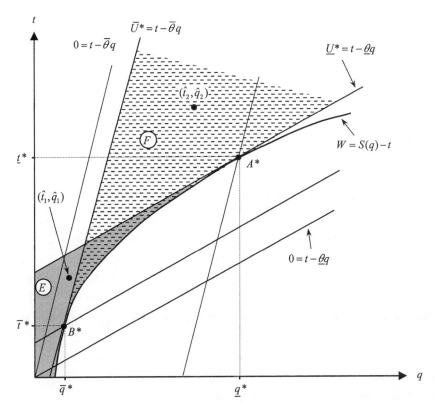

FIGURE 6.10: Unique Nash Implementation with Risk Aversion

In figure 6.10, we have represented the out of equilibrium contracts $(\hat{t}_1, \hat{q}_1)$ and $(\hat{t}_2, \hat{q}_2)$, which uniquely implement the first-best allocation rule. Proceeding as in Section 6.3, these contracts must again satisfy the following constraints:

$$\hat{t}_1 - \underline{\theta}\hat{q}_1 < \underline{t}^* - \underline{\theta}\underline{q}^*, \tag{6.29}$$

$$\hat{t}_1 - \bar{\theta}\hat{q}_1 > \underline{t}^* - \bar{\theta}\underline{q}^*, \tag{6.30}$$

$$S(\bar{q}^*) - \bar{t}^* > S(\hat{q}_1) - \hat{t}_1; \tag{6.31}$$

and

$$\hat{t}_2 - \bar{\theta}\hat{q}_2 < \bar{t}^* - \bar{\theta}\bar{q}^*, \tag{6.32}$$

$$\hat{t}_2 - \underline{\theta}\hat{q}_2 > \bar{t}^* - \underline{\theta}\bar{q}^*, \tag{6.33}$$

$$S(\underline{q}^*) - \underline{t}^* > S(\hat{q}_2) - \hat{t}_2. \tag{6.34}$$

We let the reader check that the set E (crossed area) (resp. F (dotted area)) of possible values of $(\hat{t}_1, \hat{q}_1)$ (resp. $(\hat{t}_2, \hat{q}_2)$) satisfying the constraints (6.29) to (6.31) (resp. (6.32) to (6.34)) can be represented as in figure 6.10. In particular, since the areas E and F now have a nonempty intersection, $(\hat{t}_1, \hat{q}_1)$ can be chosen equal to $(\hat{t}_2, \hat{q}_2)$. Risk aversion on the principal's side tends to simplify the mechanisms that can be used to implement the first-best.

The above construction may appear somewhat pointless, because *simple* incentive contracts $\{t(q)\}$ also achieve the first-best. However, it can be easily extended to common value environments where $S(\cdot)$ is also a function of θ, $S(q, \theta)$, and when incentive contracts may run into the difficulties of nonresponsiveness (see sections 2.10.2 and 2.11.1).

6.6 Concluding Remarks

The overall conclusion of this chapter is that the nonverifiability of the state of nature is not enough to create any transaction cost in contracting if a benevolent court of law is available and the trading partners are fully rational. Indeed, the principal can design games whose unique equilibria implement the first-best allocation despite the inability to directly condition contracts on the value of the state of nature.

Bounded rationality and/or limits in the commitment power or the benevolence of the court of law restrict the practical validity of the conclusions reached in this chapter even more than those obtained with adverse selection and moral hazard. This is because of the complexity of the mechanisms needed, which opens more opportunities for mistakes and manipulations.

However, assuming that only nonconditional contracts signed *ex ante* and followed by renegotiations are feasible is not satisfactory either, as the example of simple incentive contracts clearly shows. Finding a middle way with a fundamentalist approach requires proper modelling of bounded rationality and/or the court of law's behavior, which is not yet available. Various shortcuts have been proposed in the literature, such as considering only property rights on the use of the assets owned or imposing on contracting the inability to commit not to renegotiate. The analysis of these approaches,[15] although briefly sketched in chapter 9, is outside the scope of this volume.

---

[15] See the special issue of the *Review of Economics Studies* (January 1999)

7

Mixed Models ★

The pure models of chapter 2 for adverse selection, chapter 4 for moral hazard and chapter 6 for nonverifiability were highly stylized contracting settings. Each of those models aimed at capturing a *single* dimension of the incentive problems that may be faced by a principal at the time of designing the contract for his agent. In those chapters, the analysis of each of these respective paradigms has already provided a number of important insights that concern, on the one hand, the conflict (if any) between allocative efficiency and the distribution of the gains from trade and, on the other hand, the form of the optimal compensation schedule. Moreover, our investigation of more complex models than those of chapters 2 and 4 has also shown how the insights gleaned from these simple models carry over in more complex economic environments.[1]

In real world settings, contracts are rarely designed with the sole objective of solving one incentive problem. Most often, the principal's control of the agent requires that they deal simultaneously with both adverse selection and moral hazard, or with both the nonverifiability of the state of nature and moral hazard. In

---

[1] See chapter 3 for adverse selection and chapter 5 for moral hazard.

those complex environments, the most important question is, how do the agency costs due to the different paradigms interact? More precisely, we would like to assess whether the lessons from the pure models continue to hold in those more complex environments and, if they do not hold anymore, we would like to understand in which directions those lessons should be modified.

The aim of this chapter is not to give a complete overview of the huge and extremely heterogeneous literature that analyzes settings where several paradigms are useful to understand the economic problem at hand. Instead, we have tried to isolate three important lessons from those models. More specifically, we assess whether blending together more incentive problems increases or decreases allocative distortions. This simple criterion allows us indeed to clarify somewhat the rather noisy messages of these mixed models.[2]

Lesson 1: Adding the agency costs of the different paradigms may decrease allocative efficiency. First consider a model where the agent knows his type perfectly before contracting with the principal and performing a task on his behalf. For instance, as in chapter 2, an agent who is privately informed of his marginal cost of production may be supplying a good for the principal but may also exert some costly and nonobservable effort affecting the probability that an efficient trade takes place. Thus adverse selection occurs before moral hazard. With a risk-neutral agent protected by limited liability, we know from chapter 4 that the principal cannot costlessly structure the payments given to the agent for providing the moral hazard incentive. A limited liability rent must be given to the agent to induce effort provision. This rent plays the role of an added fixed cost from the principal's point of view. Inducing participation by the agent now becomes more difficult. The conflict between the participation and the adverse selection incentive constraints is thus exacerbated by moral hazard. This leads to possibly more shutdowns of types and to *greater allocative distortions* than in the absence of any moral hazard.

Insurance contracts are archetypal examples of contracts designed to solve simultaneously an adverse selection problem and a moral hazard problem. A risk-averse driver often has private information on how good a driver he is and also how safely he drives. To induce the high-risk agent to reveal his probability of accident, we saw in chapter 3 that the low-risk agent must receive less than full

---

[2]Of course, as we have seen in chapter 2, allocative efficiency is not the principal's criterion for evaluating different contracting environments. However, taking the principal's objective as a criterion would lead to a straightforward conclusion, because adding incentive problems always leads to a more (at least weakly) constrained problem from the principal's point of view.

insurance. Under pure moral hazard, both types of agents should instead receive incomplete insurance in order to induce them to exert safety care. When adverse selection takes place before moral hazard, the mere fact that the high-risk agent should now bear some risk to solve the moral hazard problem makes that agent's adverse selection rent more costly for the principal. This leads to more distortion for the low-risk agent, who now bears an even greater amount of risk than under pure adverse selection.

The general insight gleaned from these latter two models is that solving the moral hazard problem *ex post* leads the principal to introduce distortions in the agent's payoff that increase the cost of his adverse selection information rent. This leads to further allocative distortions and to a reduction in the expected gains from trade with respect to the case of pure adverse selection.

Lesson 2: Adding the agency costs of the different paradigms may improve allocative efficiency. Let us now consider the case where moral hazard takes place before adverse selection. For instance, an agent may carry out, on behalf of the principal, an effort that is privately known by the agent and stochastically affects the value of trade. The simplest way to do so is to merge the basic models of chapters 2 and 4. By choosing a nonobservable and costly effort, the agent increases the probability that a low marginal cost is realized. Contrary to chapter 4, we now assume that the random state of nature, i.e., how large the gains are from trade, is a piece of information that is privately learned by the agent. In such a context, the principal must offer a contract with a double objective in mind. On the one hand, the contract must provide the agent with enough incentives to exert effort at the *ex ante* stage. On the other hand, the contract must also induce the agent to reveal his private information *ex post*.

Of course, *ex ante* contracting has no cost for the principal if he deals with a risk-neutral agent. Both adverse selection and moral hazard can be solved costlessly by making the agent residual claimant for the value of trading with the principal, as we have seen in chapters 2 and 4. Hence, a second-best analysis arises only with risk aversion or limited liability. To fix ideas, we consider the case of a risk-neutral agent who is protected by limited liability. One of the main lessons of chapter 2 is that the agent should receive a higher rent when he is efficient in order to satisfy his adverse selection incentive compatibility constraint. It is precisely this rent differential that also helps the principal to incentivize the agent to exert effort. The rent necessary to solve the adverse selection problem may be either below or above the limited liability rent necessary to solve the moral hazard problem. Different regimes of optimal contracts can be found, depending on the parameters of the model. To solve the moral hazard problem, the principal might have to raise the agent's rent, and the principal does so by increasing the volume of trade. Then, the interplay between adverse selection and moral hazard improves allocative efficiency with respect to the case of pure adverse selection.

Lesson 3: Adding the agency costs of the different paradigms may have no new impact on allocative efficiency. We already know from the analysis in chapter 6 that the nonverifiability of the state of nature does not put any real constraint on the ability of the contractual partners to achieve the first-best by agreeing to contract, before the state of nature is realized, on a game form to be played *ex post*, i.e., once they both know which state of nature has been realized. In addition, we suppose that the agent can perform a nonobservable effort affecting the probability that an efficient trade takes place. If the state of nature were verifiable, this setting would be akin to a pure moral hazard model similar to chapter 4, and the principal and the agent would sign the pure moral hazard contract, which leads to an allocative distortion that is now well known. Once the nonverifiability of the state of nature is taken into account, the principal and the agent can agree, on top of this moral hazard contract, on a game form solving the nonverifiability constraint *ex post*, just as was done in chapter 6. We are then back to a standard pure moral hazard problem. The main point to stress here is that not all of the solutions to the nonverifiability problem perform equally well now. Indeed, we will show that Nash implementation strictly dominates both incentive contracts and *ex post* negotiations.

In section 7.1, we first analyze the case of adverse selection taking place before moral hazard. By means of an example, we show that solving the moral hazard problem exacerbates the allocative distortions due to adverse selection. This section also provides a version of the revelation principle, generalizing its applicability to models with both adverse selection and moral hazard. Lastly, we analyze *false moral hazard problems*, where the moral hazard and the adverse selection unknowns are blended together, in a deterministic way, into a single observation available for contracting. These models, which have been used extensively in the regulation and optimal taxation literatures, end up being pure adverse selection models. However, the interplay between moral hazard and adverse selection enriches considerably the interpretation of the models. In section 7.2, we change the timing above and focus on models where moral hazard takes place before adverse selection. We show that these models tend to reduce allocative inefficiency with respect to the case of pure adverse selection. Finally, in section 7.3 we analyze the case of moral hazard followed by the nonverifiabilty of the state of nature. Here we show that nonverifiability does not put a real constraint on contracting.

7.1 Adverse Selection Followed by Moral Hazard

In the standard moral hazard framework of chapter 4, it was first assumed that the agent had no private information of his own. In insurance markets, insurees often have some prior information about how risky they are before exerting any effort to prevent this risk. Similarly, in credit markets, a borrower may know the average return of his project before exerting any effort and sharing the resulting profits with a lender. Those examples illustrate how frequent adverse selection and moral hazard are intertwined. A general formulation of these mixed models, where adverse selection takes place before moral hazard, would be cumbersome to present. However, a few dimensions of the analysis can already be singled out by studying some examples.

7.1.1 Random Surplus and Screening

In the pure adverse selection framework of chapter 2, the principal was able to verify and contract on all the agent's actions. Of course, when moral hazard also occurs, this complete contractibility is no longer possible: some actions of the agent remain, by definition, under the agent's sole control.

Consider a situation where moral hazard affects the random benefit that the principal draws from his relationship with the agent. In the mixed model we analyze below, the principal already has a screening device at his disposal to start with. The random benefit $\tilde{S}(q)$ he gets from dealing with the agent depends indeed on an observable, the agent's production q, which can be used to screen the agent's type.

Let us thus assume that, with probability $\pi(e)$ (resp. $1 - \pi(e)$) the benefit of production obtained by the principal is $S_h(q)$ (resp. $S_l(q)$) with $S_h(q) > S_l(q)$, where the moral hazard variable e belongs to $\{0, 1\}$. Of course, we assume that $S_i(\cdot)$, for $i = h, l$, is increasing and strictly concave ($S_i' > 0$ and $S_i'' < 0$) and satisfies the Inada condition $S_i'(0) = \infty$. To motivate this random surplus model, one can think of effort as improving the quality of the product sold by the agent so that it generates a higher surplus. Of course, exerting effort will cost the agent a non-monetary disutility $\psi(e)$ with the usual normalizations $\psi(0) = 0$ and $\psi(1) = \psi$. Moreover, the agent produces at a constant marginal cost θ. As always, we assume that θ belongs to $\Theta = \{\underline{\theta}, \bar{\theta}\}$ with respective probabilities ν and $1 - \nu$. For simplicity, we also assume that the agent is risk neutral and protected by limited liability.

In this framework, the principal has two observables with which he can screen the agent's efficiency parameter; in fact, this is a special case of the multi-output

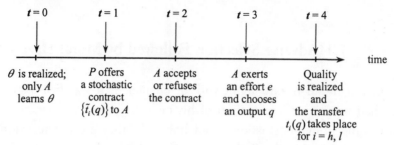

FIGURE 7.1: Timing of Contracting with Adverse Selection Followed by Moral Hazard

framework studied in section 2.10. These two observables are first, whether the good sold has a high or a low quality and second, the amount of this good that is actually produced. Hence, the contract offered to the agent is a priori stochastic; the transfer received by the agent depends on the realized quality of the good.

The timing of contracting with adverse selection being followed by moral hazard is illustrated in figure 7.1.

Typically, a direct revelation mechanism is thus a menu of triplets $\{(t_h(\tilde{\theta}),$ $t_l(\tilde{\theta}), q(\tilde{\theta}))\}_{\tilde{\theta} \in \Theta}$ stipulating the transfers t_h and t_l made to the agent depending on the quality of the good and an output q as functions of the agent's report on his type, $\tilde{\theta}$.[3] Moreover, we assume that contracting takes place at the interim stage (date $t = 1$), i.e., after the agent has learned his private information, but before the agent exerts effort.[4] In what follows, we also assume that the principal finds it valuable to always induce a high level of effort from both types of agent.[5] Using our usual notations, the efficient agent's adverse selection incentive constraint is written as:

$$\underline{U} = \pi_1 \underline{t}_h + (1 - \pi_1)\underline{t}_l - \underline{\theta}\underline{q} - \psi$$

$$\geq \max_{e \in \{0,1\}} \left\{ \pi(e)\bar{t}_h + (1 - \pi(e))\bar{t}_l - \underline{\theta}\bar{q} - \psi(e) \right\}, \tag{7.1}$$

with, in addition, the moral hazard incentive constraint

$$\underline{t}_h - \underline{t}_l \geq \frac{\psi}{\Delta\pi}, \tag{7.2}$$

so that the efficient agent exerts a positive effort.

---

[3] For the time being, we leave the question of whether the revelation principle applies in our framework unanswered and refer to section 7.1.2 below for a formal proof that shows that it does.

[4] Note that the agent must decide how much to produce before he knows what will be the quality of the good. Transfers are instead delayed until the quality of the good is learned. Thus, only transfers are stochastic.

[5] Hence, contrary to chapter 4, our focus is not on determining the conditions that ensure that the high effort level is second-best optimal.

Similarly, the inefficient agent's adverse selection incentive constraint becomes

$$\bar{U} = \pi_1 \bar{t}_h + (1 - \pi_1)\bar{t}_l - \bar{\theta}\bar{q} - \psi$$

$$\geq \max_{e \in \{0, 1\}} \pi(e)\underline{t}_h + (1 - \pi(e))\underline{t}_l - \bar{\theta}\underline{q} - \psi(e), \tag{7.3}$$

and his moral hazard incentive constraint is

$$\bar{t}_h - \bar{t}_l \geq \frac{\psi}{\Delta \pi}. \tag{7.4}$$

Since contracting takes place at the interim stage, the agent's participation constraints are written as:

$$\underline{U} \geq 0 \tag{7.5}$$

$$\bar{U} \geq 0. \tag{7.6}$$

Finally, the following limited liability constraints must be satisfied. For the efficient type [(7.7), (7.8)] and for the inefficient type [(7.9), (7.10)]:

$$\underline{u}_h = \underline{t}_h - \underline{\theta}q \geq 0, \tag{7.7}$$

$$\underline{u}_l = \underline{t}_l - \underline{\theta}q \geq 0, \tag{7.8}$$

$$\bar{u}_h = \bar{t}_h - \bar{\theta}\bar{q} \geq 0, \tag{7.9}$$

$$\bar{u}_l = \bar{t}_l - \bar{\theta}\bar{q} \geq 0. \tag{7.10}$$

The number of constraints that we are facing to solve this problem is already huge, and our first goal should be to get rid of some of them. A preliminary remark is useful to simplify the analysis significantly. Indeed, focusing on cases where the limited liability constraints are binding for both types, note that both types must be given the same transfer differential $t_h - t_l$ to exert effort at a minimal cost for the principal, namely $\bar{t}_h - \bar{t}_l = \underline{t}_h - \underline{t}_l = \frac{\psi}{\Delta \pi}$. Hence, at the optimum the incentive constraints (7.1) and (7.3) can be simplified to yield, respectively,

$$\underline{U} = \underline{u}_l + \frac{\pi_0 \psi}{\Delta \pi} \geq \bar{u}_l + \Delta\theta\bar{q} + \frac{\pi_0 \psi}{\Delta \pi} = \bar{U} + \Delta\theta\bar{q} \tag{7.11}$$

and

$$\bar{U} = \bar{u}_l + \frac{\pi_0 \psi}{\Delta \pi} \geq \underline{u}_l - \Delta\theta\underline{q} + \frac{\pi_0 \psi}{\Delta \pi} = \underline{U} - \Delta\theta\underline{q}. \tag{7.12}$$

We let the reader check that the only relevant constraints are the adverse selection incentive compatibility constraint of an efficient type (7.11) and the limited liability constraint of the inefficient type (7.10). When the expected payments to the agent $\pi_1 t_h + (1 - \pi_1)t_l$ and $\pi_1 \bar{t}_h + (1 - \pi_1)\bar{t}_l$ in both states of nature are replaced by, respectively, $\underline{U} + \underline{\theta}q + \psi$ and $\bar{U} + \bar{\theta}\bar{q} + \psi$, the principal's problem is then written as:

(P): $\qquad \max_{\{(q,\, \underline{u}_l);(\bar{q},\, \bar{u}_l)\}} \nu\left(\pi_1 S_h(\underline{q}) + (1 - \pi_1)S_l(\underline{q}) - \underline{\theta}\underline{q} - \underline{u}_l - \frac{\pi_0 \psi}{\Delta \pi} - \psi\right)$

$\qquad + (1 - \nu)\left(\pi_1 S_h(\bar{q}) + (1 - \pi_1)S_l(\bar{q}) - \bar{\theta}\bar{q} - \bar{u}_l - \frac{\pi_0 \psi}{\Delta \pi} - \psi\right)$

$$\text{subject to (7.10) and (7.11).}$$

This optimization leads immediately to $\underline{u}_l = \Delta\theta\bar{q} + \bar{u}_l$ and $\bar{u}_l = 0$. Hence, we can compute the rent of each type of agent as, respectively,

$$\underline{U} = \Delta\theta\bar{q} + \frac{\pi_0 \psi}{\Delta \pi}, \tag{7.13}$$

and

$$\bar{U} = \frac{\pi_0 \psi}{\Delta \pi}. \tag{7.14}$$

The reader will have recognized that these rents are precisely the information rents obtained under pure adverse selection ($\Delta\theta\bar{q}$ and 0 respectively, as in chapter 2), added up with the limited liability rent obtained under pure moral hazard ($\frac{\pi_0 \psi}{\Delta \pi}$, as in chapter 4). In this simple model with a risk-neutral agent protected by limited liability constraints, the agent's rent coming from the mixed model is simply obtained by adding up the respective rents due to adverse selection and moral hazard.

Solving for the optimal contract is now straightforward. The optimal outputs are obtained by equating expected marginal benefits and marginal virtual costs. For the efficient type, we find no output distortion as in a pure adverse selection model. Indeed, we have $q^{SB} = q^*$, where the first-best production now takes into account the random nature of quality and is defined by

$$\pi_1 S_h'(\underline{q}^*) + (1 - \pi_1)S_l'(\underline{q}^*) = \underline{\theta}. \tag{7.15}$$

For the inefficient type, we have instead

$$\pi_1 S_h'(\bar{q}^{SB}) + (1 - \pi_1)S_l'(\bar{q}^{SB}) = \bar{\theta} + \frac{\nu}{1 - \nu}\Delta\theta. \tag{7.16}$$

The production of the inefficient type is distorted downward below the first-best output $\bar{q}^*$ given by $\pi_1 S_h'(\bar{q}^*) + (1 - \pi_1)S_l'(\bar{q}^*) = \bar{\theta}$. As under pure adverse selection, this downward distortion helps to reduce the agent's information rent coming from his private information on θ.[6]

The reader might think that adding moral hazard in this model has no allocative impact on the distortion due to adverse selection, which is exactly the same as if effort was observable. This is not completely true. Indeed, the output $\bar{q}^{SB}$ is only the solution as long as shutdown of the least efficient type is not optimal. The no-shutdown condition is now written as

$$\nu\left(\pi_1 S_h(\underline{q}^*) + (1 - \pi_1)S_l(\underline{q}^*) - \underline{\theta}\underline{q}^* - \psi - \Delta\theta\bar{q}^{SB} - \frac{\pi_0\psi}{\Delta\pi}\right)$$

$$+ (1 - \nu)\left(\pi_1 S_h(\bar{q}^{SB}) + (1 - \pi_1)S_l(\bar{q}^{SB}) - \bar{\theta}\bar{q}^{SB} - \psi - \frac{\pi_0\psi}{\Delta\pi}\right)$$

$$> \nu\left(\pi_1 S_h(\underline{q}^*) + (1 - \pi_1)S_l(\underline{q}^*) - \underline{\theta}\underline{q}^* - \psi - \frac{\pi_0\psi}{\Delta\pi}\right). \qquad (7.17)$$

Simplifying, we find that the inefficient agent produces as long as the expected surplus he generates is greater than the sum of the adverse selection rent left to an efficient type and the limited liability rent left to the inefficient type. This condition is written as

$$\underbrace{(1 - \nu)\left(\pi_1 S_h(\bar{q}^{SB}) + (1 - \pi_1)S_l(\bar{q}^{SB}) - \bar{\theta}\bar{q}^{SB} - \psi\right)}_{\text{Expected surplus with a } \bar{\theta}\text{-type}} - \nu\underbrace{\Delta\theta\bar{q}^{SB}}_{\substack{\text{Adverse} \\ \text{selection} \\ \text{rent of the} \\ \underline{\theta}\text{-type}}} - (1 - \nu)\underbrace{\frac{\pi_0\psi}{\Delta\pi}}_{\substack{\text{Limited} \\ \text{liability} \\ \text{rent of} \\ \text{the } \bar{\theta}\text{-type}}} > 0.$$

With this condition, we see the role played by moral hazard in hardening the adverse selection problem. Inducing effort requires giving up a limited liability rent to the inefficient type. This rent plays exactly the same role as a *fixed cost* in a pure adverse selection framework (see section 2.6.3). It hardens the $\bar{\theta}$-agent's participation constraint and makes shutdown of the least efficient type more valuable for the principal. From this example, we can thus conclude that moral hazard hardens the adverse selection incentive problem. We state this as a general (but rather imprecise) proposition.

Proposition 7.1: *In mixed models with adverse selection before moral hazard, preventing moral hazard hardens the adverse selection problem, and allocative distortions are greater than under pure adverse selection.*

[6]Note that the Inada condition ensures that $\bar{q}^{SB}$ always remains positive.

📖 Laffont (1995) analyzes a related model of environmental regulation where $S_l(q) = S_h(q) - d(q)$ and $d(q)$ is an environmental damage. The added complexity of his model comes from the fact that the disutility of effort depends directly on the level of production. ∎

7.1.2 The Extended Revelation Principle

In section 7.1.1, we have studied a simple example, assuming a priori that the revelation principle holds in this context with both adverse selection and moral hazard. Now we will prove this principle, still using the basic structure of the model of section 7.1.1 for pedagogical purposes. The framework is nevertheless slightly more general, because we now allow the probability of having a high quality good to be a function of both the agent's effort e and his type θ. This added complexity turns out to be a useful intermediate step before analyzing the more complex model of the insurance market covered in section 7.1.3.

Just as in section 2.9, let us first consider a general *mechanism* in this context. As usual, a mechanism stipulates a message space $\mathcal{M}$ and an outcome function. Because the quality of the good is observed, that mechanism is a triplet $\{\tilde{t}_h(m), \tilde{t}_l(m), \tilde{q}(m)\}$ stipulating a transfer for each quality and an output level as functions of the agent's message m, which belongs to $\mathcal{M}$.

Our goal is to show a revelation principle in such a context. In order to do so, we must first describe the agent's behavior in front of any such mechanism. This description is more complex than in chapter 2. Indeed, given his type, the agent must now choose not only a message to be sent to the principal but also, given this message, what is the best effort that he should exert. Denoting by $m^*(\theta)$ and $e^*(\theta)$ the optimal message and effort,[7] we have

$$(m^*(\theta), e^*(\theta)) \in \arg\max_{(\tilde{m}, \tilde{e})} \pi(\theta, \tilde{e})\tilde{t}_h(\tilde{m}) + (1 - \pi(\theta, \tilde{e}))\tilde{t}_l(\tilde{m}) - \theta\tilde{q}(\tilde{m}) - \psi(\tilde{e})$$

for all θ in Θ, $\tilde{e}$ in $\{0, 1\}$, and $\tilde{m}$ in $\mathcal{M}$. (7.18)

Rewriting (7.18), we find

$$\pi(\theta, e^*(\theta))\tilde{t}_h(m^*(\theta)) + (1 - \pi(\theta, e^*(\theta)))\tilde{t}_l(m^*(\theta)) - \theta\tilde{q}(m^*(\theta)) - \psi(e^*(\theta))$$

$$\geq \pi(\theta, \tilde{e})\tilde{t}_h(\tilde{m}) + (1 - \pi(\theta, \tilde{e}))\tilde{t}_l(\tilde{m}) - \theta\tilde{q}(\tilde{m}) - \psi(\tilde{e})$$

for all θ in Θ, $\tilde{e}$ in $\{0, 1\}$ and $\tilde{m}$ in $\mathcal{M}$. (7.19)

[7]The optimal message and effort may not be unique. The revelation principle we outline in proposition 7.2 holds for any possible selection within these optimal choices. As the agent is indifferent between any of these selections, the one that maximizes the principal's payoff is selected.

Just as in section 2.9, let us construct a *direct revelation mechanism* $\{t_h(\tilde{\theta}), t_l(\tilde{\theta}), q(\tilde{\theta})\}$, as follows $t_h(\tilde{\theta}) = \tilde{t}_h(m^*(\tilde{\theta}))$, $t_l(\tilde{\theta}) = \tilde{t}_l(m^*(\tilde{\theta}))$, and $q(\tilde{\theta}) = \tilde{q}(m^*(\tilde{\theta}))$ for all $\tilde{\theta}$ in Θ. We can now state our version of the revelation principle.

Proposition 7.2: *There is no loss of generality in restricting the principal to offer a truthful direct revelation mechanism* $\{t_h(\tilde{\theta}), t_l(\tilde{\theta}), q(\tilde{\theta})\}_{\tilde{\theta} \in \Theta}$ *and to recommend a choice of effort* $e^*(\tilde{\theta})$. *With such a mechanism, the agent truthfully reveals his type to the principal and obeys the recommendation on the choice of effort.*

Proof: The proof is straightforward and follows almost the same path as that of proposition 2.2. Using (7.19) and the definition of the direct revelation mechanism $\{t_h(\tilde{\theta}), t_l(\tilde{\theta}), q(\tilde{\theta})\}$ associated with any mechanism $\{\tilde{t}_h(\tilde{m}), \tilde{t}_l(\tilde{m}), \tilde{q}(\tilde{m})\}$, we have

$$\pi(\theta, e^*(\theta))t_h(\theta) + (1 - \pi(\theta, e^*(\theta)))t_l(\theta) - \theta q(\theta) - \psi(e^*(\theta))$$

$$= \pi(\theta, e^*(\theta))\tilde{t}_h(m^*(\theta)) + (1 - \pi(\theta, e^*(\theta)))\tilde{t}_l(m^*(\theta)) - \theta\tilde{q}(m^*(\theta)) - \psi(e^*(\theta))$$

$$\geq \pi(\theta, \tilde{e})\tilde{t}_h(\tilde{m}) + (1 - \pi(\theta, \tilde{e}))\tilde{t}_l(\tilde{m}) - \theta\tilde{q}(\tilde{m}) - \psi(\tilde{e})$$

$$\text{for all } \theta \text{ in } \Theta, \tilde{e} \text{ in } \{0, 1\} \text{ and } \tilde{m} \text{ in } \mathcal{M}. \tag{7.20}$$

This latter inequality being true for all $\tilde{m}$, it is in particular true for $\tilde{m} = m^*(\tilde{\theta})$ for all $\tilde{\theta}$ in Θ. Hence, we have

$$\pi(\theta, e^*(\theta))t_h(\theta) + (1 - \pi(\theta, e^*(\theta)))t_l(\theta) - \theta q(\theta) - \psi(e^*(\theta))$$

$$\geq \pi(\theta, \tilde{e})t_h(\tilde{\theta}) + (1 - \pi(\theta, \tilde{e}))t_l(\tilde{\theta}) - \theta q(\tilde{\theta}) - \psi(\tilde{e}),$$

$$\text{for all pairs } (\theta, \tilde{\theta}) \text{ in } \Theta^2 \text{ and } \tilde{e} \text{ in } \{0, 1\}. \tag{7.21}$$

This latter constraint means that the agent with type θ prefers to reveal his type to the principal and obey his recommendation on what should be the level of effort. ∎

The revelation principle that we proved above has the same flavor as in a pure adverse selection framework. The logic is similar: the principal can always replicate the agent's choices by incorporating the agent's optimal message strategy into the initial contract he offers. However, on top of requesting that the agent sends a truthful message on his type, the principal also recommends now that the agent choose a particular level of effort.

Remark: Instead of insisting on the principal recommending a choice of effort to the agent, one could view this choice as being completely delegated and incorporated into the adverse selection problem in a

276 • Chapter 7

way that affects the different parties' utility functions. To see this point more precisely, let us define the agent's indirect utility function $U^I(\cdot)$ as

$$U^I(\theta, q, t_h, t_l) = \max_{e \in \{0, 1\}} \pi(\theta, e)t_h + (1 - \pi(\theta, e))t_l - \theta q - \psi(e).$$

(7.22)

The revelation principle can be directly applied at this stage to get the following pure adverse selection incentive compatibility constraints:

$$U^I(\theta, q(\theta), t_h(\theta), t_l(\theta)) \geq U^I(\theta, q(\tilde{\theta}), t_h(\tilde{\theta}), t_l(\tilde{\theta})),$$

$$\text{for all } (\theta, \tilde{\theta}) \text{ in } \Theta^2. \qquad (7.23)$$

The difficulty for the modeller comes from the fact that these incentive compatibility constraints may not be as easily ordered as those of the pure adverse selection models in chapters 2 and 3. The indirect utility function $U^I(\cdot)$ can fail to satisfy the Spence-Mirrlees property even in highly structured settings. ∎

Myerson (1982) developed the extended revelation principal above in a more abstract setting. He used the expression *obedience* to characterize the fact that the agent must follow the principal's instructions on his choice of effort. ∎

7.1.3 Insurance Contracts with Adverse Selection and Moral Hazard

Insurance contracts are good examples of contracts designed to solve simultaneously an adverse selection problem (how risky the agent is), and a moral hazard problem (how to induce enough safety care from the agent). We have already touched on the analysis of each of those two problems separately in chapters 3 and 4. This section is aimed at explaining how those two problems interact.

Remark In view of the analysis of section 7.1.1, with an insurance contract the principal now has only two instruments, namely different transfers depending on whether an accident occurs or not, to perform two tasks: incentivizing the agent to exert effort and inducing information revelation. This creates much of the complexity of this kind of model. ∎

Let us assume that a monopoly insurer, the principal, offers an insurance contract to agents having an initial wealth w. By having an accident, an agent incurs a monetary loss of d. There is a continuum of mass one of agents who differ *ex ante* according to their risk type θ. To make things simpler, we assume that, for each agent, θ belongs to $\Theta = \{\underline{\theta}, \bar{\theta}\}$ and that these types are independently drawn with respective probabilities[8] $1 - \nu$ and ν. Thus $\bar{\theta}$ (resp. $\underline{\theta}$) corresponds to a high (resp. low) risk for all levels of the moral hazard variable e. By exerting an effort e, an agent with type θ increases his probability $\pi(\theta, e)$ of not having an accident. We have thus $\pi_{\theta}(\theta, e) < 0$ and $\pi_e(\theta, e) > 0$ for all pairs (θ, e). Moreover, for technical reasons, we will assume that $\pi(\underline{\theta}, 0) > \pi(\bar{\theta}, 1)$.[9] Of course, the agent suffers from a disutility $\psi(e)$ when exerting an effort. As usual, we assume that effort belongs to $\{0, 1\}$, with $\psi(1) = \psi$ and $\psi(0) = 0$.

The insurance company requests a payment t_n from the agent when no accident occurs and gives a transfer t_a in the case of an accident. Its objective function is thus $V = \pi(\theta, e)t_n - (1 - \pi(\theta, e))t_a$. With these specifications, an agent with type θ who exerts effort e gets an expected utility $U = \pi(\theta, e)u(w - t_n) + (1 - \pi(\theta, e))u(w - d + t_a) - \psi(e)$, where $u(\cdot)$ is the agent's Von Neuman-Morgenstern utility function defined on monetary gains ($u' > 0$ and $u'' < 0$).

With our usual notations, a direct revelation mechanism writes as a pair $\{(\bar{t}_n, \bar{t}_a); (\underline{t}_n, \underline{t}_a)\}$.

Let us also assume that the damage d is large enough. The benefits of avoiding a damage are then so large that inducing the high level of effort is always optimal for the insurance company. When he exerts a high effort and truthfully reports his type to the principal, the high-risk agent gets an expected utility

$$\bar{U} = \pi(\bar{\theta}, 1)u(w - \bar{t}_n) + (1 - \pi(\bar{\theta}, 1))u(w - d + \bar{t}_a) - \psi. \quad (7.24)$$

Similarly, the low-risk agent gets

$$\underline{U} = \pi(\underline{\theta}, 1)u(w - \underline{t}_n) + (1 - \pi(\underline{\theta}, 1))u(w - d + \underline{t}_a) - \psi. \quad (7.25)$$

Inducing both types to participate in this contract requires that the following participation constraints are satisfied:

$$\bar{U} \geq \bar{U}_0 = \max_{e \in \{0, 1\}} \pi(\bar{\theta}, e)u(w) + (1 - \pi(\bar{\theta}, e))u(w - d) - \psi(e) \quad (7.26)$$

and

$$\underline{U} \geq \underline{U}_0 = \max_{e \in \{0, 1\}} \pi(\underline{\theta}, e)u(w) + (1 - \pi(\underline{\theta}, e))u(w - d) - \psi(e). \quad (7.27)$$

---

[8]Note that $\bar{\theta}$ now refers to the "good" type, i.e., that which will receive full insurance under pure adverse selection.

[9]This assumption simply means that the ranking between agents is strong.

To simplify the analysis, we also assume that

$$u(w) - u(w - d) \geq \max_{\theta \in \{\underline{\theta}, \bar{\theta}\}} \left(\frac{\psi}{\Delta \pi(\theta)} \right), \tag{7.28}$$

where $\Delta \pi(\theta) = \pi(\theta, 1) - \pi(\theta, 0)$. This assumption simply means that both types are willing to exert a positive effort in the absence of any insurance contract. In this case, the right-hand sides of (7.26) and (7.27) are respectively given by $\bar{U}_0 = \pi(\bar{\theta}, 1)u(w) + (1 - \pi(\bar{\theta}, 1))u(w - d) - \psi$ and $\underline{U}_0 = \pi(\underline{\theta}, 1)u(w) + (1 - \pi(\underline{\theta}, 1))u(w - d) - \psi$. Note that we have $\underline{U}_0 > \bar{U}_0$, because $\pi(\underline{\theta}, 1) > \pi(\bar{\theta}, 1)$ and $u(w) > u(w - d)$.

Because of moral hazard, inducing effort by both types calls for having the following moral hazard incentive constraints satisfied when agents report their types truthfully to the principal. For a high-risk agent, we get

$$u(w - \bar{t}_n) - u(w - d + \bar{t}_a) \geq \frac{\psi}{\Delta \pi(\bar{\theta})}. \tag{7.29}$$

For a low-risk agent, we have

$$u(w - \underline{t}_n) - u(w - d + \underline{t}_a) \geq \frac{\psi}{\Delta \pi(\underline{\theta})}. \tag{7.30}$$

Truthful revelation is obtained when the following adverse selection incentive constraints are satisfied: for the high-risk agent,

$$\bar{U} \geq \max_{e \in \{0, 1\}} \pi(\bar{\theta}, e)u(w - \underline{t}_n) + (1 - \pi(\bar{\theta}, e))u(w - d + \underline{t}_a) - \psi(e); \tag{7.31}$$

and for the low-risk agent,

$$\underline{U} \geq \max_{e \in \{0, 1\}} \pi(\underline{\theta}, e)u(w - \bar{t}_n) + (1 - \pi(\underline{\theta}, e))u(w - d + \bar{t}_a) - \psi(e). \tag{7.32}$$

> **Remark:** As for (7.1) and (7.3), the complexity of the latter two incentive constraints already shows some of the technical difficulties faced by the economist in modelling mixed environments. Indeed, when he considers deviating along the adverse selection dimension and not telling the truth to the principal anymore, the agent may also choose to change his supply of effort. Even if inducing a high effort is optimal for the principal when both types tell the truth, it is not necessary for the mechanism to require an agent to continue to exert this high effort if the agent lies about his type. Even in this simple environment, the right-hand sides of (7.31) and (7.32) are hard to describe, because the values of these maximands depend on how an agent with a given risk type changes his effort supply when he chooses different insurance contracts. ∎

To simplify this problem, let us assume that effort increases the probability that no accident occurs more when the agent is high risk than when he is low risk. This means that the following condition must be satisfied:

$$\Delta \pi(\underline{\theta}) < \Delta \pi(\bar{\theta}). \tag{7.33}$$

This condition ensures that the moral hazard incentive constraint for a high-risk type (7.29) is easier to satisfy than the one associated with a low-risk type (7.30). In this case, inducing effort from the low-risk agent requires a wedge between $u(w - \underline{t}_n)$ and $u(w - d + \underline{t}_a)$ that is large enough to ensure that a high-risk agent also prefers to exert a high effort, even when he lies and mimics a low-risk agent. Indeed, we have $u(w - \underline{t}_n) - u(w - d + \underline{t}_a) \geq \frac{\psi}{\Delta \pi(\underline{\theta})} > \frac{\psi}{\Delta \pi(\bar{\theta})}$. This condition greatly simplifies the writing of the adverse selection incentive constraint for the high-risk agent, which now becomes

$$\bar{U} \geq \pi(\bar{\theta}, 1)u(w - \underline{t}_n) + (1 - \pi(\bar{\theta}, 1))u(w - d + \underline{t}_a) - \psi.^{10} \tag{7.34}$$

Let us now introduce a new set of variables: $\bar{u}_a = u(w - d + \bar{t}_a)$, $\bar{u}_n = u(w - \bar{t}_n)$, $\underline{u}_a = u(w - d + \underline{t}_a)$, and $\underline{u}_n = u(w - \underline{t}_n)$. These new variables will help us describe the set of relevant constraints in a simpler way. As usual, we denote the inverse function of $u(\cdot)$ by $h = u^{-1}$. Using these new variables, the expected profit of the insurance company is written as

$$\nu(\pi(\bar{\theta}, 1)\bar{t}_n - (1 - \pi(\bar{\theta}, 1))\bar{t}_a) + (1 - \nu)(\pi(\underline{\theta}, 1)\underline{t}_n - (1 - \pi(\underline{\theta}, 1))\underline{t}_a). \tag{7.35}$$

Using that $\bar{t}_n = w - h(\bar{u}_n)$ (resp. $\underline{t}_n = w - h(\underline{u}_n)$) and $-\bar{t}_a = w - d - h(\bar{u}_a)$ (resp. $-\underline{t}_a = w - d - h(\underline{u}_a)$), we obtain

$$\nu[\pi(\bar{\theta}, 1)(w - h(\bar{u}_n)) + (1 - \pi(\bar{\theta}, 1))(w - d - h(\bar{u}_a))]$$
$$+ (1 - \nu)[\pi(\underline{\theta}, 1)(w - h(\underline{u}_n)) + (1 - \pi(\underline{\theta}, 1))(w - d - h(\underline{u}_a))]$$
$$= w - \nu[d(1 - \pi(\bar{\theta}, 1)) + \pi(\bar{\theta}, 1)h(\bar{u}_n) + (1 - \pi(\bar{\theta}, 1))h(\bar{u}_a)]$$
$$- (1 - \nu)[d(1 - \pi(\underline{\theta}, 1)) + \pi(\underline{\theta}, 1)h(\underline{u}_n) + (1 - \pi(\underline{\theta}, 1))h(\underline{u}_a)]. \tag{7.36}$$

The high-risk agent's adverse selection incentive constraint (7.34) now becomes

$$\pi(\bar{\theta}, 1)\bar{u}_n + (1 - \pi(\bar{\theta}, 1))\bar{u}_a \geq \pi(\bar{\theta}, 1)\underline{u}_n + (1 - \pi(\bar{\theta}, 1))\underline{u}_a. \tag{7.37}$$

---

[10] We focus as usual on the high-risk agent's incentive constraint.

The high-risk agent's moral hazard incentive constraint is

$$\bar{u}_n - \bar{u}_a \geq \frac{\psi}{\Delta\pi(\bar{\theta})}. \tag{7.38}$$

The low-risk agent's moral hazard incentive constraint is written as

$$\underline{u}_n - \underline{u}_a \geq \frac{\psi}{\Delta\pi(\underline{\theta})}. \tag{7.39}$$

Finally, the low-risk agent's participation constraint can be expressed as

$$\pi(\underline{\theta}, 1)\underline{u}_n + (1 - \pi(\underline{\theta}, 1))\underline{u}_a - \psi \geq \underline{U}_0. \tag{7.40}$$

Neglecting the other constraints, which will be checked only *ex post*, the insurance company's problem is written as

$$(P): \quad \max_{\{(\bar{u}_a, \bar{u}_n); (\underline{u}_a, \underline{u}_n)\}} w - \nu(d(1 - \pi(\bar{\theta}, 1)) + \pi(\bar{\theta}, 1)h(\bar{u}_n) + (1 - \pi(\bar{\theta}, 1))h(\bar{u}_a))$$

$$- (1 - \nu)(d(1 - \pi(\underline{\theta}, 1)) + \pi(\underline{\theta}, 1)h(\underline{u}_n) + (1 - \pi(\underline{\theta}, 1))h(\underline{u}_a))$$

subject to (7.37) to (7.40).

Before solving this problem it is useful to recall the main features of the optimal contracts found in the case of pure adverse selection and pure moral hazard.

In figure 7.2, we have represented the indifference curves of the high- and low-risk agents when they are forced to exert a positive effort, and this effort can be verified by a court of law. The indifference curve of the agent with a low probability of accident has a smaller slope than the indifference curve of an agent with a high probability of accident.

As we have shown in section 3.3.2, if θ were perfectly known by the principal the agent would receive the full insurance contracts A^* and B^*. Under pure adverse selection, however, the high-risk agent still receives full insurance at point B^{AS}, but the low-risk agent receives contract A^{AS} and is now imperfectly insured. Moving slightly away from A^* to A^{AS} entails only a second-order loss on the profit made by the principal with the low-risk agent, because the latter is then subject only to a small amount of risk. However, moving from A^* to A^{AS} also allows the principal to reduce the information rent of the high-risk agent to the first order.[11]

---

[11] See section 2.6.2 for a similar argument in the case of a rent-extraction efficiency trade-off.

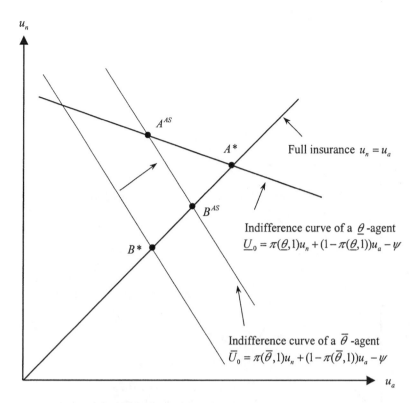

u_n

A^{AS}

$A*$

Full insurance $u_n = u_a$

B^{AS}

Indifference curve of a $\underline{\theta}$-agent
$\underline{U}_0 = \pi(\underline{\theta},1)u_n + (1-\pi(\underline{\theta},1))u_a - \psi$

$B*$

Indifference curve of a $\bar{\theta}$-agent
$\bar{U}_0 = \pi(\bar{\theta},1)u_n + (1-\pi(\bar{\theta},1))u_a - \psi$

u_a

FIGURE 7.2: Insurance Contracts: The Case of Pure Adverse Selection

Let us now turn to the case of pure moral hazard where effort is nonobservable but the agent's type is perfectly known to the insurance company. The indifference curves of the different types now have a kink where the agent is indifferent between exerting effort or not. Note that the assumption $\pi(\theta, 1) > \pi(\theta, 0)$ for each type θ implies that the indifference curve of each type has a smaller slope (in absolute value) when the agent exerts a positive effort than when he does not. Moreover, since we have assumed that $\pi(\underline{\theta}, 0) > \pi(\bar{\theta}, 1)$, the indifference curves of the two different types can only cross each other once.[12,13] The analysis of chapter 4 has shown us that the insurance company would like to offer contracts A^{MH} or B^{MH} to the agent, depending on his observable type, if the only issue was moral hazard. Each of these contracts is lying on an indifference curve where a given

---

[12]Remember that the agent's indifference curves have a kink with two portions that are straight lines with respective slopes $-\frac{(1-\pi(\theta,1))}{\pi(\theta,1)}$ above the incentive constraint $u_n = u_a + \frac{\psi}{\Delta\pi(\theta)}$, and $-\frac{(1-\pi(\theta,0))}{\pi(\theta,0)}$ below this incentive constraint. The assumption $\pi(\underline{\theta}, 0) > \pi(\bar{\theta}, 1)$ implies that the part of the low-risk agent's indifference curve below his incentive constraint has a smaller slope (in absolute terms) than the part of the high-risk agent's indifference curve above his incentive constraint.

[13]This single-crossing property plays the same role as the Spence-Mirrlees property in pure adverse selection problems. It will help to classify the agent's type by determining which type should attract the other one when there is asymmetric information on θ.

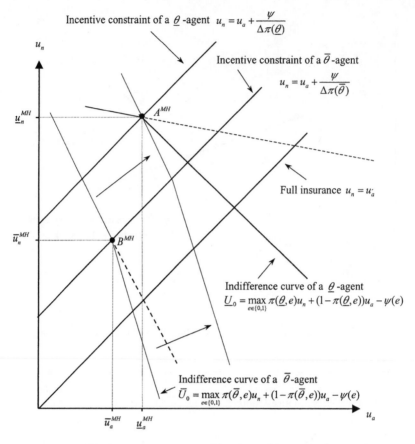

Incentive constraint of a $\underline{\theta}$-agent $u_n = u_a + \dfrac{\psi}{\Delta\pi(\underline{\theta})}$

u_n

Incentive constraint of a $\bar{\theta}$-agent

$u_n = u_a + \dfrac{\psi}{\Delta\pi(\bar{\theta})}$

$\underline{u}_n^{MH}$

A^{MH}

Full insurance $u_n = u_a'$

$\bar{u}_n^{MH}$

B^{MH}

Indifference curve of a $\underline{\theta}$-agent

$\underline{U}_0 = \max_{e\in\{0,1\}} \pi(\underline{\theta},e)u_n + (1-\pi(\underline{\theta},e))u_a - \psi(e)$

Indifference curve of a $\bar{\theta}$-agent

$\bar{U}_0 = \max_{e\in\{0,1\}} \pi(\bar{\theta},e)u_n + (1-\pi(\bar{\theta},e))u_a - \psi(e)$

$\bar{u}_a^{MH}$ $\underline{u}_a^{MH}$

u_a

FIGURE 7.3: Insurance Contracts: The Case of Pure Moral Hazard

type of agent is exactly indifferent between exerting effort or not. Of course, these contracts are above the $45°$ line to induce effort. Therefore, they provide only partial insurance to the agent, whatever his type (figure 7.3).

Under pure moral hazard, we could replicate the analysis of chapter 4, taking into account that an agent with type $\underline{\theta}$ has a nonzero reservation utility given by $\underline{U}_0$, to show that point A^{MH} corresponds to the *ex post* utility levels $\underline{u}_n^{MH} = \underline{U}_0 + \psi + \dfrac{(1-\pi(\underline{\theta},1))\psi}{\Delta\pi(\underline{\theta})}$ and $\underline{u}_a^{MH} = \underline{U}_0 + \psi - \dfrac{\pi(\underline{\theta},1)\psi}{\Delta\pi(\underline{\theta})}$. Similarly, taking into account that a $\bar{\theta}$-agent has a nonzero reservation utility given by $\bar{U}_0$, point B^{MH} corresponds to the *ex post* utility levels $\bar{u}_n^{MH} = \bar{U}_0 + \psi + \dfrac{(1-\pi(\bar{\theta},1))\psi}{\Delta\pi(\bar{\theta})}$ and $\bar{u}_a^{MH} = \bar{U}_0 + \psi - \dfrac{\pi(\bar{\theta},1)\psi}{\Delta\pi(\bar{\theta})}$.

Let us finally consider the more complex case entailing both moral hazard and adverse selection. Graphically, we see that the menu of contracts (A^{MH}, B^{MH}) is no longer incentive compatible. Following the logic of the case with pure adverse selection, the high-risk agent also would like to choose contract A^{MH} in order to increase his expected utility. The new level of utility that can be achieved by doing so is obtained by moving up the indifference curve of a $\bar{\theta}$-agent in a northeast direction until it reaches point A^{MH}.

More formally, the high-risk agent wants to mimic the low-risk one and exert a positive effort when

$$\pi(\bar{\theta}, 1)\underline{u}_n^{MH} + (1 - \pi(\bar{\theta}, 1))\underline{u}_a^{MH} - \psi = \underline{U}_0 - \frac{(\pi(\underline{\theta}, 1) - \pi(\bar{\theta}, 1))\psi}{\Delta\pi(\theta)}$$
$$> \pi(\bar{\theta}, 1)\bar{u}_n^{MH} + (1 - \pi(\bar{\theta}, 1))\bar{u}_a^{MH} - \psi$$
$$= \bar{U}_0.$$

This latter inequality is satisfied when

$$\underline{U}_0 - \bar{U}_0 = (\pi(\underline{\theta}, 1) - \pi(\bar{\theta}, 1))(u(w) - u(w - d))$$
$$> \frac{(\pi(\underline{\theta}, 1) - \pi(\bar{\theta}, 1))\psi}{\Delta\pi(\underline{\theta})}, \tag{7.41}$$

which is true when assumption (7.28) holds.

To prevent the high-risk agent from lying, the principal offers the pair of contracts (A^{SB}, B^{SB}) described in figure 7.4. Following the logic of the model with pure adverse selection, the contract A^{SB} offered to the low-risk agent entails more risk than under pure moral hazard to reduce the costly information rent of the high-risk type. Graphically, the indifference curve of a $\bar{\theta}$-agent crosses the indifference curve of a $\underline{\theta}$-agent at a point A^{SB} on the northwest of point A^{MH}. The high-risk agent is indifferent between contracts A^{SB} and B^{MH}, and the low-risk agent strictly prefers A^{SB} to B^{MH}. Contract A^{SB} entails imperfect insurance to induce this type to exert an effort. It corresponds to an expected utility greater than $\bar{U}_0$, to reward the high-risk agent for having revealed his information. Importantly, and contrary to the case of pure adverse selection, by moving from B^{MH} to B^{SB} the principal no longer suffers from a second-order loss in profit but instead suffers from a first-order loss. In order to solve the moral hazard, the low-risk agent must bear a strictly positive amount of risk. Hence, A^{MH} is no longer on the full insurance line but is now strictly above it. Starting from such a point, and increasing the risk to move towards A^{SB}, will thus create a first-order loss of profit for the insurance company.

Although A^{SB} lies strictly above the low-risk agent's moral hazard incentive constraint, it is nevertheless affected by moral hazard. Because of moral hazard, the high-risk agent must bear some risk. This risk affects the cost of his information rent from the principal's point of view and makes it more costly. This cost increase in turn has an impact on the risk borne by the low-risk agent to reduce this rent.

To see more precisely how the low-risk agent's risk is affected by the cost increase, note first that the participation constraint (7.26) is slack. Second, the

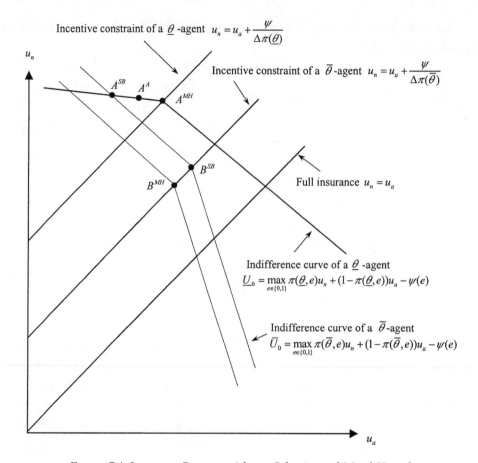

Incentive constraint of a $\underline{\theta}$-agent $u_n = u_a + \dfrac{\psi}{\Delta\pi(\underline{\theta})}$

Incentive constraint of a $\bar{\theta}$-agent $u_n = u_a + \dfrac{\psi}{\Delta\pi(\bar{\theta})}$

Full insurance $u_n = u_a$

Indifference curve of a $\underline{\theta}$-agent
$$\underline{U}_0 = \max_{e\in\{0,1\}} \pi(\underline{\theta},e)u_n + (1-\pi(\underline{\theta},e))u_a - \psi(e)$$

Indifference curve of a $\bar{\theta}$-agent
$$\bar{U}_0 = \max_{e\in\{0,1\}} \pi(\bar{\theta},e)u_n + (1-\pi(\bar{\theta},e))u_a - \psi(e)$$

FIGURE 7.4: Insurance Contracts: Adverse Selection and Moral Hazard

adverse selection incentive compatibility constraint (7.37), the moral hazard incentive constraint in (7.38), and the participation constraint of the low-risk agent (7.40) are all binding at the solution to (P). This yields the following expressions of the second-best utilities of each type of agent in each state of nature:

$$\underline{u}_n(\Delta u) = \underline{U}_0 + \psi + (1 - \pi(\underline{\theta},1))\Delta u \tag{7.42}$$

$$\underline{u}_a(\Delta u) = \underline{U}_0 + \psi - \pi(\underline{\theta},1)\Delta u \tag{7.43}$$

$$\bar{u}_n(\Delta u) = \underline{U}_0 + \psi + (1 - \pi(\bar{\theta},1))\dfrac{\psi}{\Delta\pi(\bar{\theta})} - (\pi(\underline{\theta},1) - \pi(\bar{\theta},1))\Delta u \tag{7.44}$$

$$\bar{u}_a(\Delta u) = \underline{U}_0 + \psi - \pi(\underline{\theta},1)\dfrac{\psi}{\Delta\pi(\bar{\theta})} - (\pi(\underline{\theta},1) - \pi(\bar{\theta},1))\Delta u, \tag{7.45}$$

where the dependence of those variables on $\Delta u = \underline{u}_n - \underline{u}_a$, the risk borne by the low-risk agent, is explicit.

Inserting these expressions into the principal's objective function yields a new problem, which depends only on Δu:

(P'): $\max_{\{\Delta u\}} w - v(d(1 - \pi(\bar{\theta}, 1)) + \pi(\bar{\theta}, 1)h(\bar{u}_n(\Delta u)) + (1 - \pi(\bar{\theta}, 1))h(\bar{u}_a(\Delta u)))$

$\qquad -(1 - v)(d(1 - \pi(\underline{\theta}, 1)) + \pi(\underline{\theta}, 1)h(\underline{u}_n(\Delta u)) + (1 - \pi(\underline{\theta}, 1))h(\underline{u}_a(\Delta u)))$

subject to

$$\Delta u \geq \frac{\psi}{\Delta \pi(\underline{\theta})}, \qquad (7.46)$$

where (7.46) is the low-risk agent's moral hazard incentive constraint.

We assume that the latter constraint is slack at the optimum, so that optimizing with respect to Δu yields the following first-order condition, which implicitly defines Δu^{SB} as

$$h'(\underline{u}_n^{SB}) - h'(\underline{u}_a^{SB}) = \left(\frac{v}{1-v}\right)\frac{(\pi(\underline{\theta}, 1) - \pi(\bar{\theta}, 1))}{\pi(\underline{\theta}, 1)(1 - \pi(\underline{\theta}, 1))}$$
$$\times \left[\pi(\bar{\theta}, 1)h'(\bar{u}_n^{SB}) + (1 - \pi(\bar{\theta}, 1))h'(\bar{u}_a^{SB})\right]. \qquad (7.47)$$

Because $\pi(\underline{\theta}, 1) > \pi(\bar{\theta}, 1)$, the right-hand side above is positive, and we conclude that $\underline{u}_n^{SB} - \underline{u}_a^{SB} = \Delta u^{SB} > 0$. Hence, the low-risk agent must bear some risk, as in the case of pure adverse selection.

We leave it to the reader to check that, to ensure that the moral hazard incentive constraint (7.46) is slack, a sufficient condition is that $\underline{u}_n(\frac{\psi}{\Delta\pi(\underline{\theta})})$, $\underline{u}_a(\frac{\psi}{\Delta\pi(\underline{\theta})})$, $\bar{u}_n(\frac{\psi}{\Delta\pi(\underline{\theta})})$, and $\bar{u}_a(\frac{\psi}{\Delta\pi(\underline{\theta})})$ satisfy

$$h'\left(\underline{u}_n\left(\frac{\psi}{\Delta\pi(\underline{\theta})}\right)\right) - h'\left(\underline{u}_a\left(\frac{\psi}{\Delta\pi(\underline{\theta})}\right)\right)$$
$$< \left(\frac{v}{1-v}\right)\frac{(\pi(\underline{\theta}, 1) - \pi(\bar{\theta}, 1))}{\pi(\underline{\theta}, 1)(1 - \pi(\underline{\theta}, 1))}$$
$$\times \left[\pi(\bar{\theta}, 1)h'\left(\bar{u}_n\left(\frac{\psi}{\Delta\pi(\underline{\theta})}\right)\right) + (1 - \pi(\bar{\theta}, 1))h'\left(\bar{u}_a\left(\frac{\psi}{\Delta\pi(\underline{\theta})}\right)\right)\right], \qquad (7.48)$$

where we note that $\underline{u}_n(\frac{\psi}{\Delta\pi(\underline{\theta})}) = \underline{u}_n^{MH}$ and $\underline{u}_a(\frac{\psi}{\Delta\pi(\underline{\theta})}) = \underline{u}_a^{MH}$.[14]

---

[14] If $h(u) = u + \frac{ru^2}{2}$ for $u \geq -\frac{1}{r}$ and $r > 0$, the condition (7.48) rewrites as

$$\frac{r\psi}{\Delta\pi(\underline{\theta})} < \left(\frac{v}{1-v}\right)\frac{(\pi(\underline{\theta}, 1) - \pi(\bar{\theta}, 1))}{\pi(\underline{\theta}, 1)(1 - \pi(\underline{\theta}, 1))}\left(1 + r\left(\underline{U}_0 + \psi - \frac{(\pi(\underline{\theta}, 1) - \pi(\bar{\theta}, 1))}{\Delta\pi(\underline{\theta})}\psi\right)\right),$$

and it holds if ψ is small enough.

Note that, when $h'(\cdot)$ is convex,[15] Jensen's inequality implies that the bracketed term on the right-hand side of (7.47) is greater than $h'(\pi(\bar{\theta}, 1)\bar{u}_n^{SB} + (1 - \pi(\bar{\theta}, 1))\bar{u}_a^{SB}) = h'(\underline{U}_0 + \psi - (\pi(\underline{\theta}, 1) - \pi(\bar{\theta}, 1))\Delta u^{SB})$. Hence, we have

$$h'(\underline{u}_n^{SB}) - h'(\underline{u}_a^{SB}) > \left(\frac{\nu}{1-\nu}\right)\frac{(\pi(\underline{\theta}, 1) - \pi(\bar{\theta}, 1))}{\pi(\underline{\theta}, 1)(1 - \pi(\underline{\theta}, 1))}$$
$$\times h'(\underline{U}_0 + \psi - (\pi(\underline{\theta}, 1) - \pi(\bar{\theta}, 1))\Delta u^{SB}). \quad (7.49)$$

Using the same techniques as in section 3.3.2, one can check that, with pure adverse selection, the insurance company would choose to let the low-risk agent bear a positive risk $\Delta u^{AS} = \underline{u}_n^{AS} - \underline{u}_a^{AS}$, such that

$$h'(\underline{u}_n^{AS}) - h'(\underline{u}_a^{AS}) = \left(\frac{\nu}{1-\nu}\right)\frac{(\pi(\underline{\theta}, 1) - \pi(\bar{\theta}, 1))}{\pi(\underline{\theta}, 1)(1 - \pi(\underline{\theta}, 1))}$$
$$\times h'(\underline{U}_0 + \psi - (\pi(\underline{\theta}, 1) - \pi(\bar{\theta}, 1))\Delta u^{AS}), \quad (7.50)$$

where $\underline{u}_n^{AS} = \underline{u}_n(\Delta u^{AS}) = \underline{U}_0 + \psi + (1 - \pi(\underline{\theta}, 1))\Delta u^{AS}$ and $\underline{u}_a^{AS} = \underline{u}_a(\Delta u^{AS}) = \underline{U}_0 + \psi - \pi(\underline{\theta}, 1)\Delta u^{AS}$.

Under pure adverse selection, the principal's objective function is concave with respect to Δu. Hence, the derivative of this objective function, which is proportional to

$$\left(\frac{\nu}{1-\nu}\right)\frac{(\pi(\underline{\theta}, 1) - \pi(\bar{\theta}, 1))}{\pi(\underline{\theta}, 1)(1 - \pi(\underline{\theta}, 1))}h'(\underline{U}_0 + \psi - (\pi(\underline{\theta}, 1) - \pi(\bar{\theta}, 1))\Delta u)$$
$$- h'(\underline{u}_n(\Delta u)) + h'(\underline{u}_a(\Delta u)),$$

is decreasing in Δu. Using (7.49) and (7.50), it can immediately be concluded that $\Delta u^{SB} > \Delta u^{AS}$.

With adverse selection and moral hazard, the risk borne by the low-risk agent is greater than with pure adverse selection. The intuition behind this result is straightforward. The high-risk agent must bear some risk to exert an effort, as can easily be seen by comparing $\bar{u}_n^{SB}$ and $\bar{u}_a^{SB}$. From the insurance company's point of view, dealing with a high-risk agent now costs $\pi(\bar{\theta}, 1)h(\bar{u}_n(\Delta u)) + (1 - \pi(\bar{\theta}, 1))h(\bar{u}_a(\Delta u))$. The marginal cost of decreasing the risk Δu borne by the low-risk agent is thus $-\bar{u}_n'(\Delta u)\pi(\bar{\theta}, 1)h'(\bar{u}_n(\Delta u)) - \bar{u}_a'(\Delta u)(1 - \pi(\bar{\theta}, 1))h'(\bar{u}_a(\Delta u))$. Taking into account the fact that $-\bar{u}_n'(\Delta u) = -\bar{u}_a'(\Delta u) = \pi(\underline{\theta}, 1) - \pi(\bar{\theta}, 1)$, this marginal cost is equal to $(\pi(\underline{\theta}, 1) - \pi(\bar{\theta}, 1))(\pi(\bar{\theta}, 1)h'(\bar{u}_n(\Delta u)) + (1 - \pi(\bar{\theta}, 1))h'(\bar{u}_a(\Delta u))$, which is greater than $(\pi(\underline{\theta}, 1) - \pi(\bar{\theta}, 1))h'(\pi(\bar{\theta}, 1)\bar{u}_n(\Delta u) +$

---

[15]This convexity is ensured when $p_u(x) < 3r_u(x)$, where $p_u(\cdot)$ and $r_u(\cdot)$ are respectively the coefficients of absolute prudence and absolute risk aversion of the agent. This latter condition is, for instance, satisfied when $u(\cdot)$ has constant absolute risk aversion.

$(1 - \pi(\bar{\theta}, 1))\bar{u}_a(\Delta u))$ when $h'(\cdot)$ is convex. Note that $(\pi(\underline{\theta}, 1) - \pi(\bar{\theta}, 1))h'(\underline{U}_0 + \psi - (\pi(\underline{\theta}, 1) - \pi(\bar{\theta}, 1))\Delta u)$ represents exactly the marginal cost of decreasing the risk borne by the low-risk agent under pure adverse selection. Hence, the randomness in the high-risk agent's payoff, which is implied by moral hazard, makes the insurance company less eager to decrease the risk borne by the low-risk agent even more than under pure adverse selection. Point A^{SB} lies on the north-west of A^{AS} on the indifference curve of the low-risk agent that corresponds to his expected utility without any insurance $\underline{U}_0$.

Putting together our findings here with those of section 7.1.1, we can finally conclude that the agency costs of adverse selection and moral hazard are not simply added together as in proposition 7.1 but may sometimes strongly reinforce each other.

7.1.4 Models with "False Moral Hazard"

Another important class of mixed models that has received much attention in the literature actually entails no randomness at all in the benefit obtained by the principal when dealing with the agent. The link between effort, types, and the contractual variable available to the principal is thus completely deterministic. The difficulty of such models comes only from the fact that the observation of this variable does not allow the principal to perfectly disentangle the type of the agent and his level of effort. Typically, q is the observable and $Q(\cdot)$ is a deterministic mapping between type and effort pairs into the set of feasible observables, so that we have $q = Q(\theta, e)$. Hence, given a target value of q, which can be imposed by the principal, and given the agent's type, effort is completely determined by the condition $e = E(\theta, q)$, where $E(\cdot)$ is implicitly defined by the identity $q = Q(\theta, E(\theta, q))$ for all θ in Θ and all q.

Those models can be classified under the name of *false moral hazard*, because the agent has no real freedom in choosing his effort level when he has decided how much to produce. This lack of freedom makes the analysis of these models closely related to the analysis of models with pure adverse selection that were seen in chapter 2. In order to illustrate false moral hazard, we present two models of procurement and optimal taxation that have been extensively used in the literature.

EXAMPLE 1: The Procurement Model

Let us assume that the principal requests only one unit of good (q in $\{0, 1\}$) from the agent, yielding a gross surplus S. The cost of producing this unit is assumed to be observable. Had we kept the usual specification $C(\theta, q) = \theta q$, with θ being distributed in $\Theta = \{\underline{\theta}, \bar{\theta}\}$ according to the common knowledge distribution $(\nu, 1 - \nu)$, the knowledge of $C = C(\theta, 1)$ would give to the principal complete information on θ.[16] To avoid this indirect finding of the efficiency parameter θ, let us assume that the cost of producing one unit of the good is not only related to the efficiency parameter θ but also to the agent's effort e in an additive manner: $C(\theta, e) = \theta - e$. By exerting effort e, the agent reduces the cost of producing the good. The point is that the observation of the cost $C = \theta - e$ is not enough to infer perfectly the agent's productivity parameter. Intuitively, an efficient agent $\underline{\theta}$ can exert an effort $e - \Delta\theta$ and still produce at the same cost as a less efficient agent $\bar{\theta}$ exerting also effort e.

Let us denote by t the transfer received by the agent. Since cost is observable, it is an accounting convention to have this transfer being net of cost. The principal's profit is written as $V = S - t - C$. The agent's utility becomes $U = t - \psi(e)$, where $\psi(\cdot)$ is the disutility of effort, such that $\psi' > 0$, $\psi'' > 0$ and $\psi''' > 0$.[17] Expressed only in terms of observables, the agent's utility can finally be written as $U = t - \psi(\theta - C)$.

The reader will have recognized a pure adverse selection model with the observable being the cost C. In this context, the revelation principle tells us that there is no loss of generality in restricting the principal to offer direct revelation mechanisms $\{(t(\tilde{\theta}), C(\tilde{\theta}))\}_{\tilde{\theta} \in \Theta}$, which are truth-telling.

With our usual notations, the following incentive constraints have to be satisfied:

$$\underline{U} = \underline{t} - \psi(\underline{\theta} - \underline{C}) \geq \bar{t} - \psi(\underline{\theta} - \bar{C}) = \bar{U} + \Phi(\bar{C}), \tag{7.51}$$

$$\bar{U} = \bar{t} - \psi(\bar{\theta} - \bar{C}) \geq \underline{t} - \psi(\bar{\theta} - \underline{C}) = \underline{U} - \Phi(\underline{C}), \tag{7.52}$$

where, from the assumptions made on ψ, $\Phi(C) = \psi(\bar{\theta} - C) - \psi(\underline{\theta} - C)$ is decreasing and convex in C. Also, the participation constraints are

$$\underline{U} \geq 0 \tag{7.53}$$

$$\bar{U} \geq 0. \tag{7.54}$$

Note that the indifference curves of both types in the space (t, C) satisfy the single-crossing property with those of the efficient type having a smaller slope. The reader will have recognized the Spence-Mirrlees property, which allows us to

---

[16] See section 9.6.2 for the case where C can also be contracted upon.
[17] The condition on the third-derivative of $\psi(\cdot)$ ensures that $\Phi(\cdot)$, defined below, is strictly convex and that stochastic mechanisms are never optimal. See section 2.13.

conclude that, at the optimal contract, the relevant binding constraints are (7.51) and (7.54). The principal's problem is thus written as

(P):
$$\max_{\{(\underline{U},\underline{C});(\overline{U},\overline{C})\}} S - \nu(\underline{C}+\psi(\underline{\theta}-\underline{C})+\underline{U}) - (1-\nu)(\overline{C}+\psi(\overline{\theta}-\overline{C})+\overline{U}),$$

subject to (7.51) and (7.54).

Both constraints above are binding at the optimum, and we have thus $\underline{U}^{SB} = \Phi(\overline{C}^{SB})$ and $\overline{U}^{SB} = 0$.

Optimizing with respect to the cost targets $\underline{C}$ and $\overline{C}$ amounts to optimizing with respect to the effort levels $\underline{e}$ and $\bar{e}$, which are indirectly requested from, respectively, an efficient type and an inefficient type once one has recognized that those cost targets and efforts are linked by the relationships $\underline{C} = \underline{\theta} - \underline{e}$ and $\overline{C} = \overline{\theta} - \bar{e}$. Expressing the principal's objective function in terms of efforts and taking into account that (7.51) and (7.54) are both binding at the optimum, the principal's problem becomes

(P'):
$$\max_{\{\underline{e},\bar{e}\}} S - \nu(\underline{\theta} - \underline{e} + \psi(\underline{e}) + \varphi(\bar{e})) - (1-\nu)(\overline{\theta} - \bar{e} + \psi(\bar{e})),$$

where $\varphi(e) = \psi(e) - \psi(e - \Delta\theta)$ is increasing and convex in e.

Optimizing with respect to $\underline{e}$ and $\bar{e}$ yields, respectively,

$$\psi'(\underline{e}^{SB}) = 1 \tag{7.55}$$

and

$$\psi'(\bar{e}^{SB}) = 1 - \frac{\nu}{1-\nu}\varphi'(\bar{e}^{SB}). \tag{7.56}$$

Note that under complete information, both types would be asked to exert the same first-best level of effort e^* such that the marginal disutility of effort equals the marginal cost reduction, i.e., $\psi'(e^*) = 1$. Under asymmetric information, only the most efficient type continues to exert this first-best level of effort. In order to reduce the costly information rent of this efficient type, the effort of the less efficient type is reduced below the first-best, and $\bar{e}^{SB} < e^*$.

These results are not surprising in light of the analysis presented in chapter 2. However, here the novelty comes from the interpretation of the model. Because the efficient agent is residual claimant for his effort, we will say that he is put on a *high-powered incentive scheme*, which is akin to a *fixed-fee contract*. The inefficient agent under-supplies effort because he is only partially residual claimant for his effort. We will say that he is instead put on a *low-powered incentive scheme*, which is closer to a *cost-plus contract*.

To better understand these denominations, let us assume that the principal offers a nonlinear contract $T(C)$, which is defined over all C in $[0, +\infty)$.

This mechanism should implement precisely the second-best allocation computed above, when the agent finds it optimal to exert effort $\underline{e}^{SB}$ and $\bar{e}^{SB}$. Assuming differentiability of the schedule $T(C)$ at the points $\underline{C}^{SB}$ and $\overline{C}^{SB}$, we must have $T'(\underline{C}^{SB}) = \psi'(\underline{\theta} - \underline{C}^{SB}) = \psi'(\underline{e}^{SB})$ and $T'(\overline{C}^{SB}) = \psi'(\overline{\theta} - \overline{C}^{SB}) = \psi'(\bar{e}^{SB})$.[18] Identifying with (7.55) and (7.56), we find that $T'(\underline{C}^{SB}) = 1$ and $T'(\overline{C}^{SB}) < 1$. This shows that only the efficient agent is given full incentives in cost reduction. The inefficient agent gets only a function of his marginal effort in cost reduction and thus under-provides effort.

Let us now turn to the shape of the nonlinear schedule $T(C)$. To get some ideas on this shape, it is useful to look at figure 7.5.

To ensure that the agent, whatever his type, chooses the second-best cost target computed by the principal, it is enough that the nonlinear transfer $T(C)$ be tangent to each indifference curve at points A and B. We may thus define $T(C)$ as

$$T(C) = \begin{cases} \underline{t}^{SB} - \psi'(e^*)(C - \underline{C}^*) & \text{for } C \leq \underline{C}^* = \underline{\theta} - e^*, \\ \psi(\underline{\theta} - C) + \Phi(\overline{C}^{SB}) & \text{for } C \text{ in } [\underline{C}^*, \overline{C}^{SB}], \\ \bar{t}^{SB} - \psi'(\bar{e}^{SB})(C - \overline{C}^{SB}) & \text{for } C \geq \overline{C}^{SB} = \overline{\theta} - \bar{e}^{SB}. \end{cases}$$

> **Remark:** In the case of a continuum of types, we will see in section 9.5.1 that the optimal contract can sometimes be implemented through a menu of linear contracts under rather weak assumptions. ∎

📖 This procurement model is due to Laffont and Tirole (1986, 1993), who have built a whole theory of regulation and procurement with elements of both moral hazard and adverse selection. Interesting issues arise in the case where output is no longer zero or one, as in this model. Indeed, on top of cost, output can then also be used as a screening variable. Depending on the exact mapping between cost, output, effort, and types, the pricing rule may or may not be distorted under asymmetric information. When it is not, Laffont and Tirole (1993) argue that there is a *dichotomy* between the pricing rule and the provision of incentives. Lazear (2000) uses a model with false moral hazard to analyze the relation between performance pay and productivity empirically. Lazear (2000) concludes: "workers respond to prices just as economic theory predicts." ∎

---

[18]We will see in figure 7.5 that this differentiability is not exactly satisfied. In this case, the first-order condition above is only true for the right-hand side derivative of $T(C)$ at $\overline{C}^{SB}$.

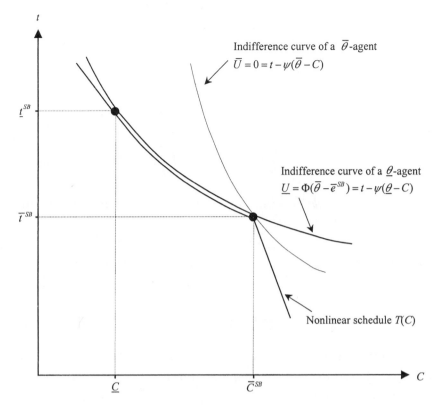

FIGURE 7.5: Implementation with a Nonlinear Schedule $T(C)$

EXAMPLE 2: The Income Taxation Model

Let us now return to the optimal redistribution model studied in section 3.7. One weakness of that model was the fact that the government was assumed to be unable to observe the actual income of each agent. Standard taxation models relax this somewhat unrealistic assumption. In order to still have a meaningful informational problem, we must now assume that each agent produces an amount $q = \theta e$ when his productivity parameter is θ (θ belongs to $\Theta = \{\underline{\theta}, \bar{\theta}\}$) with respective probabilities $1 - \nu$ and ν, and his effort e belongs to $[0, \bar{e}]$. Effort costs the agent a disutility $\psi(e)$ with $\psi' > 0$, $\psi'' > 0$ and $\psi''' > 0$ as before.

Normalizing the price of the production good at one, q also represents the agent's income, which is now assumed to be observable by the government. Note the similarity of this model with the procurement model above. Instead of being blended additively, type and effort are now blended multiplicatively into the observable that is available to the principal. When exerting effort e and paying a tax τ, the agent with productivity θ gets a utility $U = q - \tau - \psi(e)$, or, replacing effort as a function of the agent's type and his income, $U = q - \tau - \psi(\frac{q}{\theta})$. Again, the reader will have recognized that we are now back to a pure adverse selection model. In this context, a taxation mechanism can be viewed as a menu $\{(\bar{\tau}, \bar{q}); (\underline{\tau}, \underline{q})\}$, where

q is the agent's revenue and τ is the corresponding tax payment. The incentive compatibility constraints for this model are written as

$$\bar{U} = \bar{q} - \bar{\tau} - \psi\left(\frac{\bar{q}}{\theta}\right) \geq \underline{q} - \underline{\tau} - \psi\left(\frac{\underline{q}}{\theta}\right) = \underline{U} + \Phi(\underline{q}) \tag{7.57}$$

and

$$\underline{U} = \underline{q} - \underline{\tau} - \psi\left(\frac{\underline{q}}{\underline{\theta}}\right) \geq \bar{q} - \bar{\tau} - \psi\left(\frac{\bar{q}}{\underline{\theta}}\right) = \bar{U} - \Phi(\bar{q}), \tag{7.58}$$

where $\Phi(q) = \psi\left(\frac{q}{\underline{\theta}}\right) - \psi\left(\frac{q}{\bar{\theta}}\right)$ is increasing and convex in q from the assumptions made on $\psi(\cdot)$, $(\Phi' > 0, \Phi'' > 0)$.

On top of these incentive constraints, a taxation scheme is feasible if it satisfies the government budget constraint $\nu\bar{\tau} + (1 - \nu)\underline{\tau} \geq 0$.[19] Expressing taxes as a function of the rents $\bar{U}$ and $\underline{U}$ and efforts $\bar{e}$ and $\underline{e}$, this budget constraint becomes

$$\nu(\bar{\theta}\bar{e} - \psi(\bar{e})) + (1 - \nu)(\underline{\theta}\underline{e} - \psi(\underline{e})) \geq \nu\bar{U} + (1 - \nu)\underline{U}. \tag{7.59}$$

The government wants to maximize the social welfare function $\nu G(\bar{U}) + (1 - \nu)G(\underline{U})$, where $G(\cdot)$ is increasing and concave, $(G' > 0$ and $G'' < 0)$. The principal's problem is thus

(P): $$\max_{\{(\underline{U},\underline{e});(\bar{U},\bar{e})\}} \nu G(\bar{U}) + (1 - \nu)G(\underline{U}),$$

subject to (7.57) to (7.59).

We let the reader check that the relevant incentive constraint is, as usual, that of the most productive type $\bar{\theta}$. Denoting the multiplier of the budget constraint (7.59) by μ and the multiplier of the incentive constraint (7.57) by λ, we can write the Lagrangian of the problem as

$$L(\bar{U}, \underline{U}, \bar{e}, \underline{e}) = \nu G(\bar{U}) + (1 - \nu)G(\underline{U}) + \mu(\nu(\bar{\theta}\bar{e} - \psi(\bar{e}) - \bar{U})$$
$$+ (1 - \nu)(\underline{\theta}\underline{e} - \psi(\underline{e}) - \underline{U})) + \lambda(\bar{U} - \underline{U} - \varphi(\underline{e})) \tag{7.60}$$

where $\varphi(e) = \psi(e) - \psi\left(e\frac{\underline{\theta}}{\bar{\theta}}\right)$ is increasing and convex in e. Optimizing with respect to $\bar{U}$ and $\underline{U}$ yields, respectively,

$$\nu G'(\bar{U}^{SB}) = \mu\nu - \lambda, \tag{7.61}$$

$$(1 - \nu)G'(\underline{U}^{SB}) = \mu(1 - \nu) + \lambda. \tag{7.62}$$

---

[19] As in section 3.7, we normalize public expenditure to zero without a loss of generality.

Summing (7.61) and (7.62), we obtain

$$\mu = \nu G'(\overline{U}^{SB}) + (1 - \nu)G'(\underline{U}^{SB}) > 0, \tag{7.63}$$

and thus the budget constraint (7.59) is binding. Inserting this value of μ into (7.61), we get:

$$\lambda = \nu(1 - \nu)\big(G'(\underline{U}^{SB}) - G'(\overline{U}^{SB})\big). \tag{7.64}$$

Because $\overline{U}^{SB} > \underline{U}^{SB}$ is necessary to satisfy the incentive constraint (7.57), and because $G(\cdot)$ is concave, we have $\lambda > 0$. Hence, the incentive constraint (7.57) is also binding.

Optimizing with respect to efforts, we immediately find that

$$\psi'(\bar{e}^{SB}) = \bar{\theta} \tag{7.65}$$

and

$$\psi'(\underline{e}^{SB}) = \underline{\theta} - \frac{\nu(G'(\underline{U}^{SB}) - G'(\overline{U}^{SB}))}{\nu G'(\overline{U}^{SB}) + (1 - \nu)G'(\underline{U}^{SB})}\varphi'(\underline{e}^{SB}). \tag{7.66}$$

In the complete information framework, the government could perfectly redistribute wealth between both groups of agents to equalize their utilities. Moreover, the government could recommend to exert first-best efforts $\bar{e}^*$ and $\underline{e}^*$ such that the marginal disutility of effort of each type would equal his productivity, i.e., $\psi'(\bar{e}^*) = \bar{\theta}$ and $\psi'(\underline{e}^*) = \underline{\theta}$.

Under asymmetric information, only the most productive agent still exerts the first-best level of effort. Inducing information revelation calls for creating a positive wedge between the utilities of the high- and the low-productivity agents. Because the principal is adverse to inequality in the distribution of utilities, this risk is socially costly. To reduce this cost, the principal reduces the low-productivity agent's effort below its first-best value and $\underline{e}^{SB} < \underline{e}^*$.

Interestingly, it is worthwhile to recast these results in terms of the progressiveness or lack of progressiveness of the tax schedule. Indeed, as in the procurement model above, let us think of this optimal allocation as being implemented by a nonlinear income tax $\{\tau(q)\}$. When he faces this nonlinear tax, the high- (resp. low-) productivity agent will choose to exert the second best level of efforts $\bar{e}^{SB}$ and $\underline{e}^{SB}$, such that $\bar{\theta}(1 - \tau'(\bar{\theta}\bar{e}^{SB})) = \psi'(\bar{e}^{SB})$ and $\underline{\theta}(1 - \tau'(\underline{\theta}\underline{e}^{SB})) = \psi'(\underline{e}^{SB})$. Using (7.65) and (7.66), the marginal tax rates that concern each type are thus $\tau'(\bar{q}) = 0$ and $\tau'(\underline{q}) > 0$. Hence, the high-productivity agent is not taxed at the margin. The marginal tax rate at the top of the distribution is zero. The low-productivity agent instead has a positive marginal tax rate. The optimal taxation scheme is thus regressive at the margin, a surprising feature that has generated much debate in the optimal taxation literature.

> The basic model above is based on Diamond (1998a), who simplifies the initial framework of Mirrlees (1971) by restricting the analysis to quasi-linear utility functions. ∎

7.2 Moral Hazard Followed by Adverse Selection

Sometimes an agent undertakes an initial nonverifiable investment or performs an effort before producing any output for the principal. For instance, the agent can choose a costly technology that affects the distribution of his marginal cost of production. At the time of choosing whether to incur the nonverifiable investment or not, the agent is still uninformed on what will be the realization of his efficiency parameter *ex post*. If this efficiency parameter is privately known, we are now in a framework where moral hazard takes place *before* adverse selection.

7.2.1 The Model

We assume that the risk-neutral agent can change the stochastic nature of the production process by exerting a costly effort e, which belongs to $\{0, 1\}$. The disutility of effort is, as usual, normalized so that $\psi(0) = 0$ and $\psi(1) = \psi$. When exerting effort e, the agent induces a distribution of the productivity parameter θ on $\Theta = \{\underline{\theta}, \bar{\theta}\}$. With probability $\nu(e)$ (resp. $1 - \nu(e)$), the agent will be efficient (resp. inefficient); for the sake of simplicity, we denote $\nu(1) = \nu_1$, $\nu(0) = \nu_0$, and $\Delta\nu = \nu_1 - \nu_0$. To express the fact that exerting effort is valuable, we assume that effort increases the probability that the agent is efficient, i.e., $\Delta\nu > 0$.

If the efficiency parameter is θ, the agent who produces an output q and receives a transfer t from the principal gets a utility $U = t - \theta q - \psi(e)$. The principal has the usual utility function $V = S(q) - t$.

Through the contract he offers to the agent, the principal wants to control both the agent's effort and the agent's incentives to tell the truth on the state of nature that is realized *ex post*. The timing of contracting is described in figure 7.6.

In this mixed environment, the contract $\{t(q)\}$ must not only induce effort if the principal finds it sufficiently valuable, but it must also induce information revelation. Applying the revelation principle, there is no loss of generality in restricting the principal to offer a direct revelation mechanism $\{(\bar{t}, \bar{q}); (\underline{t}, \underline{q})\}$. Through this contract, the agent will be induced to reveal his private information on the state of nature θ.

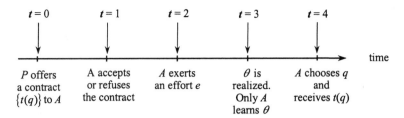

FIGURE 7.6: Timing of Contracting with Moral Hazard Followed by Adverse Selection

Of course, this contract is signed before the realization of the state of nature. Therefore, we are in a case of *ex ante* contracting similar to, albeit more complex than, those analyzed in section 2.11 and chapter 4.

7.2.2 No Limited Liability

To explain the new issues that arise with this type of mixed model, we start by analyzing the case of risk neutrality. We already know that the agent's risk neutrality calls for no allocative distortion either under pure moral hazard or under pure adverse selection. With pure adverse selection, as well as with pure moral hazard, the first-best outcome can be implemented by letting the agent be a residual claimant for the hierarchy's profit. One may wonder whether adding those two informational problems leads to any significant new problem.

Let us start by describing the first-best outcome. The first-best outputs equalize the marginal benefit and the marginal cost of production, so that $S'(\underline{q}^*) = \underline{\theta}$ and $S'(\bar{q}^*) = \bar{\theta}$. Denoting the first-best productive surplus in each state of nature by, respectively, $\underline{W}^* = S(\underline{q}^*) - \underline{\theta}\underline{q}^*$ and $\overline{W}^* = S(\bar{q}^*) - \bar{\theta}\bar{q}^*$, we find that inducing effort is socially optimal whenever:

$$\Delta\nu(\underline{W}^* - \overline{W}^*) > \psi. \tag{7.67}$$

We will assume that this last condition holds in what follows.

Let us now look at the case of moral hazard and adverse selection. Making the agent residual claimant still helps in this framework. Consider the following transfers $\underline{t}^* = S(\underline{q}^*) - T^*$ and $\bar{t}^* = S(\bar{q}^*) - T^*$, where the constant T^* will be fixed in the following.

First, we claim that the contract $\{(\underline{t}^*, \underline{q}^*); (\bar{t}^*, \bar{q}^*)\}$ induces information revelation by both types. Indeed, $\underline{t}^* - \underline{\theta}\underline{q}^* = S(\underline{q}^*) - \underline{\theta}\underline{q}^* - T^* > \bar{t}^* - \underline{\theta}\bar{q}^* = S(\bar{q}^*) - \underline{\theta}\bar{q}^* - T^*$ by the definition of $\underline{q}^*$, and $\bar{t}^* - \bar{\theta}\bar{q}^* = S(\bar{q}^*) - \bar{\theta}\bar{q}^* - T^* > \underline{t}^* - \bar{\theta}\underline{q}^* = S(\underline{q}^*) - \bar{\theta}\underline{q}^* - T^*$ by the definition of $\bar{q}^*$. Second, the contract $\{(\underline{t}^*, \underline{q}^*); (\bar{t}^*, \bar{q}^*)\}$ also induces effort. The agent's expected payoff from exerting effort is $\nu_1\underline{W}^* + (1 - \nu_1)\overline{W}^* - (\psi + T^*)$. It is greater than his expected payoff from not exerting effort, which is $\nu_0 \underline{W}^* + (1 - \nu_0)\overline{W}^* - T^*$ when (7.67) holds. Finally, the principal fixes the lump-sum payment T^* to reap all *ex ante* gains from trade with the agent, namely $T^* = \nu_1 \underline{W}^* + (1 - \nu_1)\overline{W}^* - \psi$. Hence, we can state proposition 7.3.

Proposition 7.3: *When moral hazard takes place before adverse selection and the agent is risk neutral, the first-best outcome can still be achieved by making the agent residual claimant for the hierarchy's profit.*

Note also that the contract, that makes the agent residual claimant for the hierarchy's profit also ensures the principal against any risk, because $S(\underline{q}^*) - \underline{t}^* = S(\bar{q}^*) - \bar{t}^* = T^*$. This contract also works perfectly well if the principal is risk averse.

7.2.3 Limited Liability and Output Inefficiency

Introducing the agent's risk aversion or protecting the risk-neutral agent with limited liability makes the implementation of the first-best outcome obtained above no longer possible. For clarification, let us assume that the agent is still risk neutral but is now protected by limited liability. Assuming that he has no asset to start with, the limited liability constraints in both states of nature are written as

$$\underline{U} = \underline{t} - \theta\underline{q} \geq 0 \tag{7.68}$$

and

$$\overline{U} = \bar{t} - \bar{\theta}\bar{q} \geq 0. \tag{7.69}$$

Moreover, inducing information revelation at date $t = 4$ through a direct revelation mechanism requires that we satisfy the following adverse selection incentive compatibility constraints:

$$\underline{U} \geq \overline{U} + \Delta\theta\bar{q} \tag{7.70}$$

and

$$\overline{U} \geq \underline{U} - \Delta\theta\underline{q}. \tag{7.71}$$

In our mixed environment, the rents $\underline{U}$ and $\overline{U}$ must also serve to induce effort. To induce effort as under complete information, the following moral hazard incentive constraint must now be satisfied:

$$\underline{U} - \overline{U} \geq \frac{\psi}{\Delta\nu}. \tag{7.72}$$

Finally, the agent accepts the contract at the *ex ante* stage when his *ex ante* participation constraint is satisfied

$$\nu_1 \underline{U} + (1 - \nu_1)\bar{U} - \psi \geq 0. \tag{7.73}$$

Still focusing on the case where it is always worth inducing the agent's effort, the principal's problem is

(P): $$\max_{\{(\underline{U},\underline{q});(\bar{U},\bar{q})\}} \nu_1(S(\underline{q}) - \underline{\theta}\underline{q} - \underline{U}) + (1 - \nu_1)(S(\bar{q}) - \bar{\theta}\bar{q} - \bar{U}),$$

subject to (7.68) to (7.73).

Depending on the respective importance of the moral hazard and adverse selection problems, the optimal contract may exhibit different properties. Some of the possible regimes of this optimal contract are summarized in the next proposition.[20]

Proposition 7.4: *With moral hazard followed by adverse selection, and with a risk-neutral agent protected by limited liability, the optimal contract has the following features:*

- *For $\frac{\psi}{\Delta\nu} \leq \Delta\theta\bar{q}^{SB}(\nu_1)$, (7.69) and (7.70) are both binding. Outputs are given by $\underline{q}^{SB} = q^*$ when $\underline{\theta}$ realizes and $\bar{q}^{SB} = \bar{q}^{SB}(\nu_1) < \bar{q}^*$ when $\bar{\theta}$ realizes with*

$$S'(\bar{q}^{SB}(\nu_1)) = \bar{\theta} + \frac{\nu_1}{1 - \nu_1}\Delta\theta. \tag{7.74}$$

- *For $\Delta\theta\bar{q}^{SB}(\nu_1) \leq \frac{\psi}{\Delta\nu} \leq \Delta\theta\bar{q}^*$, (7.69), (7.70), and (7.72) are all binding. The first-best output q^* is still requested when $\underline{\theta}$ realizes. Instead, production is distorted downward below the first-best when $\bar{\theta}$ realizes. We have $\bar{q}^{SB} < \bar{q}^*$ with*

$$\bar{q}^{SB} = \frac{\psi}{\Delta\theta\Delta\nu}. \tag{7.75}$$

- *For $\Delta\theta\bar{q}^* < \frac{\psi}{\Delta\nu} < \Delta\theta\underline{q}^*$, (7.69) and (7.72) are both binding. In both states of nature, the first-best outputs are implemented.*

To understand how those different regimes emerge, first note that solving the pure adverse selection problem requires the creation of a differential between the rents $\underline{U}$ and $\bar{U}$. This rent differential may be enough to induce effort when the corresponding disutility is small. In this case, moral hazard has no impact

---

[20]Working out the proof of this proposition is left to the reader.

and second-best distortions are completely driven by adverse selection. As effort becomes more costly, the pure adverse selection rent may no longer be enough to induce effort. When $\bar{\theta}$ realizes, the output must be distorted upward, with respect to the pure adverse selection distortion, to provide enough rent so that, *ex ante*, the agent wants to perform an effort. Finally, still increasing the disutility of effort, it is no longer worthwhile to make an output distortion. The principal prefers to maintain allocative efficiency in both states of nature and to sufficiently reward the agent in order to induce his effort. The design of the contract is then driven purely by moral hazard.

> **Remark:** The reader will have recognized the similarity of the analysis above with that made in section 3.3 when we analyzed type-dependent reservation values in pure adverse selection models. Indeed, one can view the design of incentives in this mixed model as a two-step procedure. The first step consists of the principal offering a reward when $\underline{\theta}$ is realized, that is large enough to induce effort provision at the *ex ante* stage. By doing so, the principal is committed to solving the moral hazard problem. Then, the second step consists of solving the adverse selection problem, that takes place *ex post*, and inducing information revelation. At this *ex post* stage, the principal may or may not be constrained by his previous commitment when he wants to extract the agent's private information on the state of nature which has been realized. ∎

To conclude, we stress that the main impact of the initial stage of moral hazard may be that it reduces allocative distortions and calls for greater information rents with respect to the case of pure adverse selection.

Proposition 7.5: *Mixed models with moral hazard followed by adverse selection tend to be characterized by less allocative distortions and greater information rents than those arising in models with pure adverse selection.*

7.3 Moral Hazard Followed by Nonverifiability

The last stage of our travel in the world of mixed models brings us to the analysis of models with both moral hazard and nonverifiability. We now assume that the agent first exerts a nonobservable effort that affects the realization of the state of nature, but this state of nature remains nonverifiable, even though its realization is common knowledge between the principal and the agent. The timing of contracting is thus exactly the same as in figure 7.6, except that, at date $t = 3$, the state of nature θ is now observed by both the principal and the agent.

If effort were observable, we would be in the case of models with pure non-verifiability of the state of nature θ. The analysis that we made in chapter 6 shows how the principal and the agent can then agree *ex ante*, i.e., at date $t = 0$, on a mechanism, possibly an extensive form game, which ensures that the first-best outcome is uniquely implemented *ex post* once the state of nature becomes known. How much of this result still holds when effort is not observable by the principal? The answer is quite unsurprising: the first-best can generally no longer be implemented, but the nonverifiability of the state of nature does not bring more distortion than what we find in a model with pure moral hazard and verifiability of the state of nature. In other words, an upper bound of what can be achieved by the principal in a mixed model with moral hazard and nonverifiability is obtained in the model with pure moral hazard, where the state of nature could be described *ex ante* and used to write the contract. Moreover, this upper bound is actually achieved.

To prove this result, let us consider the pure moral hazard model of section 4.4. Only the agent's effort cannot be verified. Assuming that the principal wants to induce a high effort from a risk-averse agent, we know that he must let the latter bear some risk. Still denoting the rents obtained by the agent in each state of nature by $\underline{U} = \underline{t} - \underline{\theta}\underline{q}$ and $\overline{U} = \overline{t} - \overline{\theta}\overline{q}$, the agent's moral hazard incentive compatibility constraint is written as

$$u(\underline{U}) - u(\overline{U}) \geq \frac{\psi}{\Delta\nu}. \tag{7.76}$$

The agent's participation constraint is

$$\nu_1 u(\underline{U}) + (1 - \nu_1)u(\overline{U}) - \psi \geq 0. \tag{7.77}$$

Under pure moral hazard, the principal's problem becomes

(P): $$\max_{\{(\underline{U},\underline{q});(\overline{U},\overline{q})\}} \nu_1(S(\underline{q}) - \underline{\theta}\underline{q} - \underline{U}) + (1 - \nu_1)(S(\overline{q}) - \overline{\theta}\overline{q} - \overline{U}),$$

subject to (7.76) and (7.77).

Repeating the analysis of section 4.4, we could easily prove that (7.76) and (7.77) are both binding. This yields the following expressions of the moral hazard *ex post* rents in each state of nature:

$$\underline{U}^{MH} = h\left(\psi + (1 - \nu_1)\frac{\psi}{\Delta\nu}\right) > 0 \tag{7.78}$$

and

$$\bar{U}^{MH} = h\left(\psi - v_1 \frac{\psi}{\Delta v}\right) < 0. \tag{7.79}$$

Moreover, the optimal outputs chosen by the principal in each state of nature are equal to their first-best values: q^* such that $S'(q^*) = \underline{\theta}$ when $\underline{\theta}$ realizes, and $\bar{q}^*$ such that $S'(\bar{q}^*) = \bar{\theta}$ when $\bar{\theta}$ instead realizes. Transfers in each state of nature are thus given by $\underline{t}^{MH} = \underline{\theta}q^* + \underline{U}^{MH}$ and $\bar{t}^{MH} = \bar{\theta}\bar{q}^* + \bar{U}^{MH}$.

Figure 7.7 describes these contracts by points A^{MH} and B^{MH}.

We now turn to the case where the state of nature θ is nonverifiable. Let us first consider how *ex post* negotiations perform in this environment. Assuming that the principal keeps all bargaining power at the *ex post* bargaining stage, the agent gets zero rent in each state of nature. Anticipating this, the agent has no incentive to exert effort at the *ex ante* stage. This is an instance of the *hold-up* problem that we will discuss more extensively in section 9.4.2. Signing an incentive compatible contract with a risk-averse agent at the *ex ante* stage implies some allocative inefficiency, even in the absence of moral hazard, as we know from section 2.11.2. Those inefficiencies can nevertheless be avoided if the agent and the principal

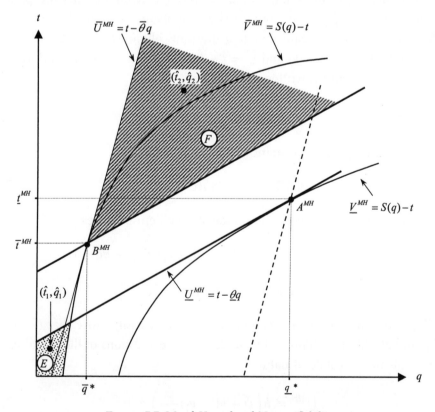

FIGURE 7.7: Moral Hazard and Nonverifiability

P's strategy

		$\underline{\theta}$	$\bar{\theta}$
A's strategy	$\underline{\theta}$	$(\underline{t}^{MH}, \underline{q}^*)$	$(\hat{t}_2, \hat{q}_2)$
	$\bar{\theta}$	$(\hat{t}_1, \hat{q}_1)$	$(\bar{t}^{MH}, \bar{q}^*)$

FIGURE 7.8: Nash Implementation in a Mixed Model

agree *ex ante* to play a mechanism *ex post*, where both report messages over the state of nature. To implement the pure moral hazard outcome (A^{MH}, B^{MH}), we will thus have to rely on Nash implementation, which now gets all of its strength.

Adopting the same notations as in chapter 6, the game form to be played in each state of nature is illustrated in figure 7.8.

The conditions for Nash implementation of the outcome with pure moral hazard are now easy to obtain.

To have a truthful Nash equilibrium in state $\underline{\theta}$, we should have

$$\underline{t}^{MH} - \underline{\theta}\underline{q}^* > \hat{t}_1 - \underline{\theta}\hat{q}_1, \tag{7.80}$$

$$S(\underline{q}^*) - \underline{t}^{MH} > S(\hat{q}_2) - \hat{t}_2. \tag{7.81}$$

Similarly, to have a truthful Nash equilibrium in state $\bar{\theta}$, we should have

$$\bar{t}^{MH} - \bar{\theta}\bar{q}^* > \hat{t}_2 - \bar{\theta}\hat{q}_2, \tag{7.82}$$

$$S(\bar{q}^*) - \bar{t}^{MH} > S(\hat{q}_1) - \hat{t}_1. \tag{7.83}$$

Finally, unique Nash implementation in both states of nature is obtained when

$$\bar{t}^{MH} - \underline{\theta}\bar{q}^* < \hat{t}_2 - \underline{\theta}\hat{q}_2 \tag{7.84}$$

and

$$\underline{t}^{MH} - \bar{\theta}\underline{q}^* < \hat{t}_1 - \bar{\theta}\hat{q}_1. \tag{7.85}$$

The possible values of $(\hat{t}_1, \hat{q}_1)$ (resp. $[\hat{t}_2, \hat{q}_2]$) satisfying the constraints (7.80), (7.83), and (7.85) (resp. (7.81), (7.82), and (7.84)) belong to set E (resp. F) in figure 7.7.

We leave it to the reader to check that those sets are nonempty and thus the moral hazard contract $(\underline{t}^{MH}, \underline{q}^*)$ and $(\bar{t}^{MH}, \bar{q}^*)$, appended with the out-of-equilibrium punishments $(\hat{t}_1, \hat{q}_1)$ and $(\hat{t}_2, \hat{q}_2)$, allows one to get rid of the nonverifiability constraint. Our conclusion is summarized in proposition 7.6.

Proposition 7.6: *Mixed models with moral hazard followed by nonverifiability of the state of nature do not entail more allocative distortions than those arising in models with pure moral hazard.*

The result above relies heavily on the ability of the agents to play a Nash mechanism *ex post*. Other forms of contracting or not contracting at all will entail significant losses of welfare, contrary to what happened in chapter 6.[21]

---

[21] See for instance section 9.4.

8 Dynamics under Full Commitment

Contracts are often repeated over time. Examples of such long-term relationships abound and span all areas of contract theory. Let us describe a few. The insurance contract of an agent entails bonuses and maluses that link his current coverage and risk premium to his past history of accidents. Labor contracts often continue to reward the past performances of an agent in the future, either in monetary terms or by means of promotions. Lastly, in many regulated sectors, regulatory contracts often stipulate the current price caps that apply to a given firm as a function of the past realizations of its costs.

In view of the analysis of the previous chapters, the general framework to understand those repeated contractual relationships must be one where the principal controls several activities performed by the agent at different points in time. In an adverse selection setting, the reader will probably have recognized the multi-output framework of section 2.10.3. Under moral hazard, the setting is akin to a multitask model along the lines of section 5.2. With respect to those general frameworks, the repeated contracting setting nevertheless has its own peculiarities that are worth studying. A few of these peculiarities are that the principal and the agent's utility functions are separable over time, that the information structures may change as time passes, and that the arrow of time introduces a natural asymmetry between today's and tomorrow's relationships.

Indeed, the analysis of long-term contractual relationships raises a number of new questions. How do the repeated contractual relationships compare with the one-shot relationships studied in previous chapters? How does the repetition of the relationship change the terms of the static trade-offs? How should we model changes in information structures? What are the benefits, if any, of long lasting relationships? Does the past history of the agent's performance play any role in current compensation, and if so, why? Are the implicit incentives provided by the desire of the agent to build a reputation vis-à-vis the labor market good disciplining devices?

To answer these questions, we remain in the general framework of this volume[1] and assume that the principal has the complete ability to *commit* to the contract he proposes to the agent. The principal designs the mechanism that is going to be played by the agent over time and sticks to its rules, no matter what happens during their relationship.[2]

Even though the information structures associated with moral hazard and adverse selection dynamic models may look somewhat different, they can nevertheless be classified within three broad categories that give rise to similar conclusions in both paradigms.

• **Permanent Shocks:** In an adverse selection setting, the agent's private information on the value of the trades that can be performed at different points of time may be constant over time. For instance, a regulated firm has a constant technology over the whole length of the regulated contract. A worker has a constant ability over the length of the labor contract. An insuree has a driving ability, i.e., a probability of having an accident, that does not change over his

---

[1] See chapters 2 and 4.

[2] In particular, commitment implies that the principal and the agent still continue to play the same mechanism no matter what information the principal may have learned during the first rounds of contracting. This assumption is an important one, because the endogenous changes in the information structures that may arise in a repeated relationship might open the door to valuable *renegotiations* as time passes. Even though these issues are particularly important for the understanding of enduring relationships, they are by and large beyond the scope of this volume and are relegated, by means of an example, to the beginning of chapter 9. Nevertheless, note that for some contractual settings that we analyze in this chapter, the assumption of commitment does not represent a restriction since the optimal long-term contract turns out to be *sequentially optimal*, i.e., recontracting from a given date on would not improve upon what is specified by the full commitment optimal contract.

entire life. In such a setting, the optimal long-term contract is obtained in a straightforward manner as *the replica of the one-shot optimal contract* described in chapter 2. Indeed, under the assumptions of separability of the principal's and the agent's utility functions between today's trades and tomorrow's trades, the intertemporal benefit of a given profile of trades and its intertemporal cost, including the informational cost, is obtained as the discounted sum of the per-period benefits and costs of the volumes of trade chosen in the different periods. Within each period, the optimal trade-off between rent extraction and allocative efficiency is similar to that in a one-shot static relationship. Thus, the optimal long-term contract is obtained as the replica of the optimal static contract.

Importantly, one way of implementing this long-term optimal contract is given by the dynamic version of the revelation principle under full commitment. With a direct mechanism, the principal requests that the agent reveals his type once and for all, before any trade takes place. The principal then commits to replicating the one-shot optimal contract in each period of their relationship.[3]

Because of these analogies between the optimal dynamic contract and a static optimal contract, these models have sometimes been grouped under the general terminology of *false dynamics*.

• **Correlated Shocks:** Still in an adverse selection setting, let us now turn to the more general case where the agent has private information on the values of trade with the principal in all periods and those values are correlated over time. For instance, the cost of producing a good for a seller may be the sum of two components, a permanent component linked to the production technology and a transient component linked to short-term shocks on the price of inputs. Similarly, because of learning by doing, a worker's ability may change over time but still with some correlation across periods. Those contractual settings are interesting because the mere realizations of the first-period volumes of trade convey some information about the future values of trade. The revelation principle still applies to these contractual relationships if one requests the agent to report any information he learns during the course of actions. In a direct revelation mechanism, the agent decides to report his type truthfully to the principal in any given period, knowing that the principal uses this information possibly to *update his beliefs* on the agent's

---

[3]Even if we do not develop the corresponding analysis in the present chapter, it is worth mentioning what would be the moral hazard counterpart to this model. Let us assume that the agent is performing a single effort in an initial period, and then the random stochastic production process associated with this effort is replicated over several periods. It becomes apparent that all that matters for the principal and the agent is the overall performance over the whole relationship. Hence, the optimal contract is again akin to an optimal static contract, where the stochastic returns of the agent's effort are simply the discounted sum of the per-period profits.

future types and may therefore specify different continuations of the long-term contract, depending on this latter report. This effect allows us to derive *dynamic incentive constraints* in a simple model with two periods and a risk-neutral agent. We then show how the principal should design the intertemporal contract by using earlier revelations of information in order to improve the terms of the rent extraction-efficiency trade-off in this dynamic setting.

It is interesting to observe the link between these latter models and the model of informative signals that improve contracting, which we already studied in section 2.14. In section 2.14, we analyzed how the principal may benefit from exogenous signals that are correlated with the agent's information to improve the terms of the rent extraction-efficiency trade-off in a static model. In dynamic relationships with correlated shocks, the past history of performances offers an endogenous signal that is correlated with the agent's current type. History-dependent contracts are useful to take into account the informativeness of earlier performances. As a corollary, the optimal long-term contract is *no longer* obtained as the replica of the one-shot optimal contract.

Again, it is worth pointing out the moral hazard counterpart to this model. Let us assume that the agent is performing a different effort at each date of his relationship with the principal but that the random stochastic productions at the different dates are correlated. In such a framework, it is a simple corollary of the Sufficient Statistic Theorem of section 4.6.1 that past performances should be used to compute current compensations.

The correlation of shocks also plays an important role in the emergence of implicit incentives in moral hazard environments. We analyze a model of career concerns, where the agent's current performance and ability affect the future rewards he may receive from the market. The agent's desire to build a reputation for being efficient provides incentives to exert effort but, of course, this disciplining device is only an imperfect substitute for explicit incentives contingent on performance.

• **Independent Shocks:** Let us now envision a case where there is no correlation across periods among the values of trade. For instance, an agent may be looking for insurance against independently distributed income shocks, or a seller may be subject to one-period independent shocks on his costs. In such a model, the past history of the agent's performances loses any informative role on the current values of trade. It does not mean that history plays no longer any role. Indeed, history may allow the principal to *smooth the cost of incentive compatibility over time*.

To stress this new effect, we develop a two-period simple moral hazard model in the context of an efficiency-insurance trade-off. The model is basically a twice-replica of that in chapter 4.[4] We derive the *dynamic incentive compatibility constraint* and optimize the principal's intertemporal objective function. We show that the optimal contract exhibits a *martingale property*, linking current compensations with future rewards and punishments. The source of this property comes from the desire of the principal to smooth the cost of incentive compatibility over time. We discuss how this smoothing can be somewhat perturbed if the agent can save part of his wealth or can end the relationship in any given period. Then, we develop an infinitely repeated version of the model to explore the intertemporal distribution of utilities achieved in the long run or the behavior of the contract as the discount factor goes to one. We show that agency problems disappear in the limit by means of a complete diversification of the risk borne by the agent in any given period.

Section 8.1 presents the dynamics of repeated adverse selection relationships for a two-period example. In this section we make various assumptions on the information structure and derive some of the conclusions stressed above. In section 8.1.4, we briefly discuss the full commitment assumption. section 8.2 deals with the case of repeated moral hazard, both in a two-period model with various contractual limits but also in an infinitely repeated setting. Here we provide the basic dynamic programming methods necessary to analyze such a setting. In section 8.3, we analyze implicit incentives in a moral hazard framework.

8.1 Repeated Adverse Selection

Consider the twice repetition of the model in chapter 2, where we can make various assumptions on the information structure and, in particular, on how it evolves over time. The goal of this section is to compare the optimal long-term contract with its static counterpart.

8.1.1 Perfect Correlation of Types and Risk Neutrality

Let us first start with the simplest case, where the adverse selection parameter θ in $\{\underline{\theta}, \bar{\theta}\}$ is the same in both periods. The principal's objective function writes now as $V = S(q_1) - t_1 + \delta(S(q_2) - t_2)$, where q_i (resp. t_i) is output (resp. transfer) at date $t = i$. The discount factor is $\delta \geq 0$, and we can allow it to be greater than one to represent cases where period 2 lasts much longer than period 1. The

---

[4]Similarly, the desire of the principal to smooth the cost of the incentive compatibility constraint would also be present in an adverse selection framework with *ex ante* contracting and risk aversion on the agent's side.

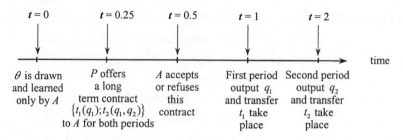

FIGURE 8.1: Timing of Contracting with Adverse Selection and Perfect Correlation

risk-neutral agent has the same discount factor as the principal and, because of perfect correlation of types between both periods, his objective function is written as $U = t_1 - \theta q_1 + \delta(t_2 - \theta q_2)$.

Note that the principal controls a pair of actions performed by the agent: the agent's productions at each date. Thus we are in a special case of the multi-output regulation studied in section 2.10, with the agent and the principal's objective functions being additively separable over the two periods.

The timing of contracting is described in figure 8.1.

With full generality, a long-term contract stipulates transfers and quantities in each period as a function of the whole past history of the game up to that period. In the case of two periods, this means that a typical long-term contract writes as a pair of nonlinear transfers $\{t_1(q_1); t_2(q_1, q_2)\}$ dependent, at each period, on the current as well as the past output realizations.

Since the principal can commit intertemporally, the revelation principle remains valid in this intertemporal framework, and the pair of nonlinear transfers described above can be replaced by a truthful direct revelation mechanism. With such a mechanism, the agent reports his type to the principal at a date $t = 0.75$, just before outputs and transfers for the first period are implemented. Moreover, because of risk neutrality, only the aggregate transfer $t = t_1 + \delta t_2$ matters when describing both the agent and the principal's utility functions. In this framework, a direct revelation mechanism is thus a pair of triplets $\{(\bar{t}, \bar{q}_1, \bar{q}_2); (\underline{t}, \underline{q}_1, \underline{q}_2)\}$, stipulating an aggregate transfer and an output target for each date according to the firm's report on the agent's type.

Denoting the efficient and the inefficient agents' information rents over both periods by, respectively, $\underline{U} = \underline{t} - \underline{\theta q}_1 - \delta \underline{\theta q}_2$ and $\bar{U} = \bar{t} - \bar{\theta} \bar{q}_1 - \delta \bar{\theta} \bar{q}_2$ the following incentive constraints must be satisfied:

$$\underline{U} \geq \bar{U} + \Delta\theta(\bar{q}_1 + \delta \bar{q}_2) \tag{8.1}$$

and

$$\bar{U} \geq \underline{U} - \Delta\theta(\underline{q}_1 + \delta \underline{q}_2). \tag{8.2}$$

The intertemporal participation constraints of both types are, respectively,

$$\underline{U} \geq 0 \tag{8.3}$$

and

$$\bar{U} \geq 0. \tag{8.4}$$

> **Remark:** Note that these participation constraints stipulate that only the agent's intertemporal rent must be positive. So, we assume momentarily that the agent commits to stay in the relationship once he has accepted the contract at date $t = 0.5$. In period 1, the agent can make a loss if it is covered by a gain in period 2, and vice versa. ∎

The principal's problem becomes

(P): $$\max_{\{(\underline{U}, \underline{q}_1, \underline{q}_2); (\bar{U}, \bar{q}_1, \bar{q}_2)\}} \nu(S(\underline{q}_1) - \underline{\theta} \underline{q}_1 + \delta(S(\underline{q}_2) - \underline{\theta} \underline{q}_2) - \underline{U})$$

$$+ (1 - \nu)(S(\bar{q}_1) - \bar{\theta} \bar{q}_1 + \delta(S(\bar{q}_2) - \bar{\theta} \bar{q}_2) - \bar{U}),$$

subject to (8.1) to (8.4).

Of course, the relevant constraints are, again, the efficient type's incentive constraint in (8.1) and the inefficient type's participation constraint in (8.4). For the optimal dynamic contract, only the efficient type gets a positive intertemporal rent, which is worth $\underline{U} = \Delta\theta(\bar{q}_1 + \delta\bar{q}_2)$, and the inefficient type's participation constraint is binding so that $\bar{U} = 0$. Inserting these expressions of the intertemporal rents into the principal's objective function and optimizing with respect to outputs, we immediately get the following proposition where we index this solution with a superscript D, meaning *dynamics*.

> **Proposition 8.1:** *With perfectly correlated types and a risk-neutral agent, the optimal long-term contract with full commitment for two periods is twice the repetition of the optimal static contract.*
>
> - *The constraints in (8.1) and (8.4) are the only binding ones.*
> - *The efficient agent produces efficiently in both periods $\underline{q}_1^D = \underline{q}_2^D = q^D = q^*$, such that $S'(q^*) = \underline{\theta}$.*
> - *The inefficient agent produces less than the first-best output in both periods $\bar{q}_1^D = \bar{q}_2^D = \bar{q}^D \leq \bar{q}^*$, such that:*
>
> $$S'(\bar{q}^D) = \bar{\theta} + \frac{\nu}{1 - \nu}\Delta\theta. \tag{8.5}$$
>
> *It is the same output as in the optimal static contract $\bar{q}^D = \bar{q}^{SB}$.*

• *Only the efficient agent gets a positive intertemporal rent* $\underline{U}^D = \Delta\theta(1+\delta)\bar{q}^D$.

Remark 1: Even if the optimal long-term contract implements the same outputs levels and the same intertemporal rents as the optimal static contract of chapter 2 repeated twice, some indeterminacy remains concerning the intertemporal distribution of these rents, because only the intertemporal transfers are pinned down by the binding constraints in (8.1) and (8.4). ∎

Remark 2: Let us instead assume that the principal offers the agent a contract covering both periods at the *ex ante* stage, i.e., before the agent learns his private information. Moreover, let us consider the case where the agent has an infinite degree of risk aversion below zero wealth and a positive degree above. In that case, the agent's intertemporal participation constraints in (8.3) and (8.4) should be replaced by a pair of participation constraints for each period, namely $\underline{U}_1 = \underline{t}_1 - \theta\underline{q}_1 \geq 0, \underline{U}_2 = \underline{t}_2 - \theta\underline{q}_2 \geq 0$ and $\bar{U}_1 = \bar{t}_1 - \bar{\theta}\bar{q}_1 \geq 0, \bar{U}_2 = \bar{t}_2 - \bar{\theta}\bar{q}_2 \geq 0$, respectively. Under these assumptions, the same result as in proposition 8.1 still holds. Moreover, because the agent has a positive rent in any given period, there is no need for him to commit to stay in the relationship. The agent never has the incentive to renege on the long-term contract offered by the principal. The main difference between the case of risk neutrality and interim contracting is that the intertemporal distribution of rents is now completely defined. The efficient type gets a positive rent in both periods $\underline{U}_i^D = \Delta\theta\bar{q}^D$, for $i = 1, 2$. The inefficient type instead gets zero in both periods. ∎

Remark 3: Of course, the optimal long-term contract would not be the twice replica of the one-shot optimal contract if either the agent's cost function or the principal's value functions were not separable over the two periods. ∎

Remark 4: Importantly, proposition 8.1 shows the importance of the principal's ability to commit. If the firm is inefficient, this fact is now common knowledge at the beginning of period 2. Still, the principal implements an inefficient contract with under-production. We come back to this commitment issue in section 8.1.4 below. ∎

 The dynamics of the optimal contract with full commitment was first analyzed in different settings by Roberts (1983) and Baron and Besanko

(1984b). At a more abstract level, the applicability of the revelation principle to a dynamic context (with possibly more complex information structures than those with perfect correlation) was demonstrated by Myerson (1986) and Forges (1986) (see Myerson 1991 for a review of the argument). ∎

8.1.2 Independent Types and Risk Neutrality

Let us now turn to the case where the agent's marginal cost in periods 1 and 2 are independently drawn from the same support $\Theta = \{\underline{\theta}, \bar{\theta}\}$, with identical probabilities ν and $1 - \nu$. The risk-neutral agent's utility is written as $U = t_1 - \theta_1 q_1 + \delta(t_2 - \theta_2 q_2)$, where θ_i is his marginal cost in period i.

We first assume that the principal offers a contract to the agent at the interim stage as described in figure 8.2.

Following the same logic as in section 8.1.1, it is intuitively clear that the optimal long-term contract with full commitment is obtained by putting together the optimal contract with interim contracting (see section 2.1) for the first period and the optimal contract with *ex ante* contracting (see section 2.11) for the second period. Indeed, at the time of signing the long-term contract with the principal, the risk-neutral agent does not know his second period type, and consequently adverse selection on this piece of information should be costless for the principal.

To see that, let us briefly describe the incentive compatibility and participation constraints for this case. At date $t = 2$, the following incentive constraints have to be specified:

$$\underline{U}_2(\tilde{\theta}_1) = \underline{t}_2(\tilde{\theta}_1) - \underline{\theta}\underline{q}_2(\tilde{\theta}_1) \geq \bar{t}_2(\tilde{\theta}_1) - \underline{\theta}\bar{q}_2(\tilde{\theta}_1) = \bar{U}_2(\tilde{\theta}_1) + \Delta\theta\bar{q}_2(\tilde{\theta}_1), \quad (8.6)$$

$$\bar{U}_2(\tilde{\theta}_1) = \bar{t}_2(\tilde{\theta}_1) - \bar{\theta}\bar{q}_2(\tilde{\theta}_1) \geq \underline{t}_2(\tilde{\theta}_1) - \bar{\theta}\underline{q}_2(\tilde{\theta}_1) = \underline{U}_2(\tilde{\theta}_1) - \Delta\theta\underline{q}_2(\tilde{\theta}_1), \quad (8.7)$$

where $\tilde{\theta}_1$ is the agent's first-period announcement on his type.

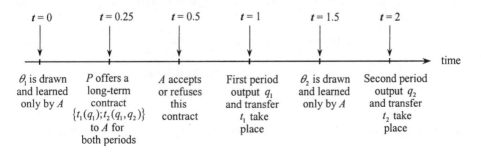

$t = 0$	$t = 0.25$	$t = 0.5$	$t = 1$	$t = 1.5$	$t = 2$
θ_1 is drawn and learned only by A	P offers a long-term contract $\{t_1(q_1); t_2(q_1, q_2)\}$ to A for both periods	A accepts or refuses this contract	First period output q_1 and transfer t_1 take place	θ_2 is drawn and learned only by A	Second period output q_2 and transfer t_2 take place

FIGURE 8.2: Timing with a Twice-Repeated Adverse Selection Problem and Independent Types

Let us also denote the first-period rents by $\underline{U}_1 = \underline{t}_1 - \underline{\theta}\underline{q}_1$ and $\overline{U}_1 = \overline{t}_1 - \overline{\theta}\overline{q}_1$. At date $t = 1$, given that the expected continuation rent for period 2 is $\nu\underline{U}_2(\tilde{\theta}_1) + (1 - \nu)\overline{U}_2(\tilde{\theta}_1)$, the incentive compatibility constraints are written as

$$\underline{U}_1 + \delta(\nu\underline{U}_2(\underline{\theta}) + (1 - \nu)\overline{U}_2(\underline{\theta}))$$
$$\geq \overline{U}_1 + \Delta\theta\overline{q}_1 + \delta(\nu\underline{U}_2(\overline{\theta}) + (1 - \nu)\overline{U}_2(\overline{\theta})), \tag{8.8}$$
$$\overline{U}_1 + \delta(\nu\underline{U}_2(\overline{\theta}) + (1 - \nu)\overline{U}_2(\overline{\theta}))$$
$$\geq \underline{U}_1 - \Delta\theta\underline{q}_1 + \delta(\nu\underline{U}_2(\underline{\theta}) + (1 - \nu)\overline{U}_2(\underline{\theta})). \tag{8.9}$$

The agent's intertemporal participation constraints are finally written as

$$\underline{U}_1 + \delta(\nu\underline{U}_2(\underline{\theta}) + (1 - \nu)\overline{U}_2(\underline{\theta})) \geq 0, \tag{8.10}$$
$$\overline{U}_1 + \delta(\nu\underline{U}_2(\overline{\theta}) + (1 - \nu)\overline{U}_2(\overline{\theta})) \geq 0. \tag{8.11}$$

Clearly (8.8) and (8.11) are both binding at the optimum of the principal's problem.[5] Using (8.11), the expected rents for period 2 are written, depending on the first report period, as

$$\delta(\nu\underline{U}_2(\overline{\theta}) + (1 - \nu)\overline{U}_2(\overline{\theta})) = -\overline{U}_1 \tag{8.12}$$

and

$$\delta(\nu\underline{U}_2(\underline{\theta}) + (1 - \nu)\overline{U}_2(\underline{\theta})) = \Delta\theta\overline{q}_1 - \underline{U}_1. \tag{8.13}$$

Then, following the logic of section 2.11, the following second period rents satisfy (8.6) and (8.7) without justifying any allocative distortion at date $t = 2$, i.e., $\overline{q}_2(\overline{\theta}) = \overline{q}_2(\underline{\theta}) = \overline{q}^*$ and $\underline{q}_2(\underline{\theta}) = \underline{q}_2(\overline{\theta}) = \underline{q}^*$:

$$\underline{U}_2(\overline{\theta}) = -\frac{\overline{U}_1}{\delta} + (1 - \nu)\Delta\theta\overline{q}^*, \tag{8.14}$$

$$\overline{U}_2(\overline{\theta}) = -\frac{\overline{U}_1}{\delta} - \nu\Delta\theta\overline{q}^*, \tag{8.15}$$

and

$$\underline{U}_2(\underline{\theta}) = \frac{1}{\delta}(\Delta\theta\overline{q}_1 - \underline{U}_1) + (1 - \nu)\Delta\theta\overline{q}^*, \tag{8.16}$$

$$\overline{U}_2(\underline{\theta}) = \frac{1}{\delta}(\Delta\theta\overline{q}_1 - \underline{U}_1) - \nu\Delta\theta\overline{q}^*. \tag{8.17}$$

Hence, the optimal outputs corresponding to the inefficient draws of types in both periods are such that $\overline{q}_1^D = \overline{q}^{SB}$ and $\overline{q}_2^D = \overline{q}^*$, respectively. The agent gets a positive rent only when he is efficient at date $t = 1$, and his expected intertemporal rent over both periods is $U^D = \nu\Delta\theta\overline{q}_1^D$. In summary, we get proposition 8.2.

---

[5]We leave it to the reader to check that (8.9) and (8.10) are both strictly satisfied.

Proposition 8.2: *With independent types and a risk-neutral agent, the optimal long-term contract for two periods with full commitment combines the optimal static contract written interim for period 1 and the optimal static contract written ex ante for period 2. In particular, the expected rent of the agent only equals the expectation of the agent's rent when he is efficient in period one and is worth $U^D = \nu \Delta \theta \bar{q}_1^D$.*

Remark: The same result would also be obtained if the risk-neutral agent could leave the relationship in period 2 if he does not get a positive expected rent in this period. In this case, the second period participation constraint

$$\nu \underline{U}_2(\tilde{\theta}_1) + (1 - \nu)\overline{U}_2(\tilde{\theta}_1) \geq 0, \tag{8.18}$$

for all $\tilde{\theta}_1 \in \Theta$, must be satisfied. It is then enough to fix $\overline{U}_1 = 0$ and $\underline{U}_1 = \Delta \theta \bar{q}^{SB}$ so that the right-hand sides of (8.12) and (8.13) are both equal to zero. ∎

8.1.3 Correlated Types and Infinite Risk Aversion ★

Let us generalize the previous information structure and turn now to the more general case where the agent's types are imperfectly correlated over time. We denote by ν_1 (resp. $1 - \nu_1$) the probability that the first period cost is $\underline{\theta}$ (resp. $\bar{\theta}$). Similarly, we denote the second period probabilities that the agent is efficient (resp. inefficient) by $\nu_2(\theta_1)$ (resp. $1 - \nu_2(\theta_1)$), following a cost realization θ_1 in the first period. A positive correlation between costs in both periods is obtained when $\nu_2(\underline{\theta}) > \nu_2(\bar{\theta})$.

Let us assume that the contract is offered *ex ante* and that the agent is infinitely risk averse below zero wealth in both periods or, alternatively, that the agent is risk-neutral and protected by limited liability. This imposes that the agent's payoff in any period must remain positive, whatever his type.[6]

The timing of the game is the same as in figure 8.2. In this framework, a direct revelation mechanism requires that the agent reports the new information in each period he has learned on his current type. Typically, a direct revelation mechanism is a four-uple $\{(t_1(\tilde{\theta}_1), q_1(\tilde{\theta}_1)); (t_2(\tilde{\theta}_1, \tilde{\theta}_2), q_2(\tilde{\theta}_1, \tilde{\theta}_2))\}$ for all pairs $(\tilde{\theta}_1, \tilde{\theta}_2)$ belonging to Θ^2, where $\tilde{\theta}_1$ (resp. $\tilde{\theta}_2$) is the date $t = 1$ (resp. date $t = 2$) announcement on his first-period (resp. second-period) type.

---

[6]The same constraints would be obtained if the contract were offered after the agent discovers θ_1 and if there were no commitment for a risk-neutral agent to stay in the relationship, i.e., if the agent could renege on the contract.

The important point to note here is that the first-period report can now be used by the principal to update his beliefs on the agent's second period type. This report can be viewed as an informative signal that is useful for improving second-period contracting. This idea is quite similar to that seen in section 2.14.1. The difference is that now the signal used by the principal to improve second-period contracting is not exogenously given by nature but comes from the first-period report $\tilde{\theta}_1$ of the agent on his type θ_1. Hence, this signal can be strategically manipulated by the agent in the first period in order to improve his second-period rent. This effect will thus affect the way we write intertemporal incentive constraints.

At date $t = 2$, following a first-period report $\tilde{\theta}_1$ made by the agent, the principal will choose outputs $\underline{q}_2(\tilde{\theta}_1)$ for the efficient type and $\bar{q}_2(\tilde{\theta}_1)$ for the inefficient type. The agent will also be proposed second-period rents $\overline{U}_2(\tilde{\theta}_1)$ and $\underline{U}_2(\tilde{\theta}_1)$. Of course, we have $\overline{U}_2(\tilde{\theta}_1) = \bar{t}_2(\tilde{\theta}_1) - \bar{\theta}\bar{q}_2(\tilde{\theta}_1)$ and $\underline{U}_2(\tilde{\theta}_1) = \underline{t}_2(\tilde{\theta}_1) - \underline{\theta}\underline{q}_2(\tilde{\theta}_1)$.

Because the agent is infinitely risk averse below zero wealth, his *ex post* participation constraint in period 2 is written as

$$\overline{U}_2(\tilde{\theta}_1) \geq 0 \tag{8.19}$$

and

$$\underline{U}_2(\tilde{\theta}_1) \geq 0, \quad \text{for all } \tilde{\theta}_1 \text{ in } \Theta. \tag{8.20}$$

Moreover, inducing information revelation by the agent in period 2 requires to satisfy the following incentive constraints:

$$\underline{U}_2(\tilde{\theta}_1) \geq \overline{U}_2(\tilde{\theta}_1) + \Delta\theta\bar{q}_2(\tilde{\theta}_1), \tag{8.21}$$

$$\overline{U}_2(\tilde{\theta}_1) \geq \underline{U}_2(\tilde{\theta}_1) - \Delta\theta\underline{q}_2(\tilde{\theta}_1), \quad \text{for all } \tilde{\theta}_1 \text{ in } \Theta. \tag{8.22}$$

Summing those two incentive constraints yields the usual monotonicity conditions $\bar{q}_2(\tilde{\theta}_1) \leq \underline{q}_2(\tilde{\theta}_1)$ for all $\tilde{\theta}_1$ in Θ.[7]

Because of full commitment, the second-period outputs $q_2(\tilde{\theta}_1)$ are decided at the time of the offering of the long term contract. Given these outputs, the continuation of the optimal contract for the second period calls for second-period rents that must solve, for any first-period announcement $\tilde{\theta}_1$, the following problem:

$(P(\tilde{\theta}_1))$: $$\max_{\{(\underline{U}_2(\tilde{\theta}_1), \overline{U}_2(\tilde{\theta}_1))\}} \nu_2(\tilde{\theta}_1)\left(S(\underline{q}_2(\tilde{\theta}_1)) - \underline{\theta}\underline{q}_2(\tilde{\theta}_1) - \underline{U}_2(\tilde{\theta}_1)\right)$$

$$+ (1 - \nu_2(\tilde{\theta}_1))\left(S(\bar{q}_2(\tilde{\theta}_1)) - \bar{\theta}\bar{q}_2(\tilde{\theta}_1) - \overline{U}_2(\tilde{\theta}_1)\right),$$

subject to (8.19) to (8.22).

---

[7]We will check *ex post* that these constraints are satisfied by the optimal second-period outputs.

(8.19) and (8.21) are both binding,[8] and the principal's second-period profit, denoted thereafter by $V_2(\tilde{\theta}_1, \underline{q}_2(\tilde{\theta}_1), \bar{q}_2(\tilde{\theta}_1))$, is written as a function of second-period outputs:

$$V_2\left(\tilde{\theta}_1, \underline{q}_2(\tilde{\theta}_1), \bar{q}_2(\tilde{\theta}_1)\right) = \nu_2(\tilde{\theta}_1)\left(S(\underline{q}_2(\tilde{\theta}_1)) - \underline{\theta}\underline{q}_2(\tilde{\theta}_1)\right)$$

$$+(1 - \nu_2(\tilde{\theta}_1))\left(S(\bar{q}_2(\tilde{\theta}_1)) - \bar{\theta}\bar{q}_2(\tilde{\theta}_1)\right)$$

$$-\nu_2(\tilde{\theta}_1)\Delta\theta\bar{q}_2(\tilde{\theta}_1). \tag{8.23}$$

Let us now go back to period 1. Knowing what will be the consequences of his first-period report $\tilde{\theta}_1$ on the principal's updated beliefs, the agent with a low first-period cost will truthfully reveal his type whenever the following intertemporal incentive constraint is satisfied:

$$\underline{U}_1 + \delta\nu_2(\underline{\theta})\Delta\theta\bar{q}_2(\underline{\theta}) \geq \bar{U}_1 + \Delta\theta\bar{q}_1 + \delta\nu_2(\underline{\theta})\Delta\theta\bar{q}_2(\bar{\theta}), \tag{8.24}$$

where $\underline{U}_1 = \underline{t}_1 - \underline{\theta}\underline{q}_1$ and $\bar{U}_1 = \bar{t}_1 - \bar{\theta}\bar{q}_1$ are the first-period rents. The terms $\delta\nu_2(\underline{\theta})\Delta\theta\bar{q}_2(\underline{\theta})$ and $\delta\nu_2(\underline{\theta})\Delta\theta\bar{q}_2(\bar{\theta})$ instead represent the discounted expected information rents that the agent can get in the second-period continuation of the contract if he reports, respectively, $\tilde{\theta}_1 = \underline{\theta}$ or $\tilde{\theta}_1 = \bar{\theta}$ to the principal at date $t = 1$, knowing that the probability that his second-period type is $\underline{\theta}$ is $\nu_2(\underline{\theta})$.

Similarly, the agent with a high first-period cost reveals truthfully when

$$\bar{U}_1 + \delta\nu_2(\bar{\theta})\Delta\theta\bar{q}_2(\bar{\theta}) \geq \underline{U}_1 - \Delta\theta\underline{q}_1 + \delta\nu_2(\bar{\theta})\Delta\theta\bar{q}_2(\underline{\theta}). \tag{8.25}$$

Summing (8.24) and (8.25) yields the following implementability condition:

$$\underline{q}_1 - \bar{q}_1 + \delta(\nu_2(\bar{\theta}) - \nu_2(\underline{\theta}))(\bar{q}_2(\bar{\theta}) - \bar{q}_2(\underline{\theta})) \geq 0.$$

Note that a positive correlation of types across periods implies that $\nu_2(\bar{\theta}) < \nu_2(\underline{\theta})$, and thus the implementability condition above is automatically satisfied when $\underline{q}_1 \geq \bar{q}_1$ in the first period and $\bar{q}_2(\bar{\theta}) \leq \bar{q}_2(\underline{\theta})$ in the second period. As usual, we will not address this condition but instead let the reader check *ex post* that it is indeed satisfied.

Again, infinite risk aversion below zero wealth requires that the *ex post* participation constraints for the first period

$$\underline{U}_1 \geq 0 \tag{8.26}$$

$$\bar{U}_1 \geq 0 \tag{8.27}$$

are both satisfied.

---

[8]The constraints (8.20) and (8.22) are slack at the optimum, as it can be checked ex post.

Taking into account the continuation payoffs $V_2(\tilde{\theta}_1; \underline{q}_2(\tilde{\theta}_1), \bar{q}_2(\tilde{\theta}_1))$ that the principal gets following a first-period announcement $\tilde{\theta}_1$, the principal's optimal long-term contract with full commitment is thus the solution to:

(P):
$$\max_{\{(\underline{q}_1, \underline{q}_2(\theta), \bar{q}_2(\theta), \underline{U}_1); (\bar{q}_1, \underline{q}_2(\bar{\theta}), \bar{q}_2(\bar{\theta}), \bar{U}_1)\}} \nu_1 \big(S(\underline{q}_1) - \underline{\theta}\underline{q}_1 - \underline{U}_1\big)$$

$$+ (1 - \nu_1)\big(S(\bar{q}_1) - \bar{\theta}\bar{q}_1 - \bar{U}_1\big)$$

$$+ \delta\big(\nu_1 V_2(\underline{\theta}, \underline{q}_2(\underline{\theta}), \bar{q}_2(\underline{\theta})) + (1 - \nu_1)V_2(\bar{\theta}, \underline{q}_2(\bar{\theta}), \bar{q}_2(\bar{\theta}))\big)$$

subject to (8.24) to (8.27).

The two relevant constraints are the incentive constraint (8.24) and the participation constraint in (8.27). Proposition 8.3 summarizes the dynamics of the optimal long-term contract.

> **Proposition 8.3:** *With a positive correlation of types and infinite risk aversion at zero wealth, the optimal long-term contract with full commitment entails, for δ small enough:*
>
> - *Constraints in (8.24) and (8.27) are the only binding constraints for δ small enough.*
> - *The agent always produces the first-best output $\underline{q}_1^D = \underline{q}_2^D(\underline{\theta}) = \underline{q}_2^D(\bar{\theta}) = q^*$ when he is efficient.*
> - *The agent generally produces below the first-best output when he is inefficient.*
>   *In period 1, the inefficient agent produces:*
>
> $$S'(\bar{q}_1^D) = \bar{\theta} + \frac{\nu_1}{1 - \nu_1}\Delta\theta. \qquad (8.28)$$
>
> *In period 2, following $\theta_1 = \bar{\theta}$, the inefficient agent produces:*
>
> $$S'(\bar{q}_2^D(\bar{\theta})) = \bar{\theta} + \left(\frac{\nu_2(\bar{\theta})}{1 - \nu_2(\bar{\theta})} + \frac{\nu_1\nu_2(\underline{\theta})}{(1 - \nu_1)(1 - \nu_2(\bar{\theta}))}\right)\Delta\theta, \qquad (8.29)$$
>
> *In period 2, following $\theta_1 = \underline{\theta}$, the inefficient agent produces the first-best output $\bar{q}_2^D(\underline{\theta}) = \bar{q}^*$. Hence, $\bar{q}_2^D(\bar{\theta}) < \bar{q}_2^D(\underline{\theta})$.*
> - *The agent's expected information rent over both periods is*
>
> $$U^D = \Delta\theta(\nu_1\bar{q}_1^D + \delta(\nu_1\nu_2(\underline{\theta}) + (1 - \nu_1)\nu_2(\bar{\theta}))\bar{q}_2^D(\bar{\theta})). \qquad (8.30)$$

To derive proposition 8.3 we have assumed that the first period participation constraint of the efficient type, i.e., $\underline{U}_1^D \geq 0$, was always strictly satisfied. Indeed, when, (8.24) and (8.27) are both binding, we have $\underline{U}_1^D = \Delta\theta\bar{q}_1^D - \delta\nu_2(\underline{\theta})\Delta\theta(\bar{q}_2^D(\underline{\theta}) -$

$\bar{q}_2^D(\bar{\theta}))$, and $\underline{U}_1^D$ is positive as long as the first-period rent $\Delta\theta\bar{q}_1^D$ is larger than the second-period expected rent differential $\delta v_2(\underline{\theta})\Delta\theta(\bar{q}_2^D(\underline{\theta}) - \bar{q}_2^D(\bar{\theta}))$, which is positive because $\bar{q}_2^D(\underline{\theta}) = \bar{q}^* > \bar{q}_2^D(\bar{\theta})$. This condition always holds for small enough δ. Then, for an agent who is efficient in the first period, the second-period expected rent can be recaptured in period 1, and the principal can afford an efficient production level $\bar{q}_2^D(\underline{\theta}) = \bar{q}^*$ for the inefficient type in period 2, following an announcement of $\underline{\theta}$ in period 1. However, for an inefficient agent who has no rent in period 1, this process is not possible. Hence, the principal requires some output distortion for an inefficient type in period 2 following the announcement of $\bar{\theta}$ in period 1.

Intuitively, distorting $\bar{q}_2^D(\bar{\theta})$ downward not only helps to reduce the second-period rent of the agent when he is efficient in period 2 following $\theta_1 = \bar{\theta}$, but it also helps to reduce the cost of the first-period incentive constraint (8.24). There are thus two reasons to distort this output downward, and the corresponding distortion is greater than for the optimal static contract that the principal would offer if his beliefs put a probability $v_2(\bar{\theta})$ on the agent being efficient. On the contrary, reducing $\bar{q}_2^D(\underline{\theta})$ helps to reduce the second-period rent of the agent when he is efficient in period 2 following $\theta_1 = \underline{\theta}$, but increasing $\bar{q}_2^D(\underline{\theta})$ also helps to reduce the cost of the first-period incentive constraint (8.24). These two effects compensate each other exactly so that there is no allocative distortion and $\bar{q}_2^D(\underline{\theta}) = \bar{q}^*$.

The main lesson of this section is that the past history of reports plays a role in determining the continuation of the optimal long term contract. Indeed, the principal can use these continuations to relax the cost of the first-period incentive compatibility constraint. In this section, the link between the past history of the agent's performances and the current production he is asked to produce comes from the intertemporal correlation of types and the informativeness of those past performances on future realizations of the efficiency parameter. We will see in section 8.2.4 how the past history of performances can also be useful to smooth the cost of a risk-averse agent's incentive compatibility constraint, even when shocks are identically distributed over time.[9]

> **Remark 1:** Note that the results of proposition 8.3 encompass both
> the case of independent draws and the case of perfectly correlated
> draws when the agent is infinitely risk averse below zero wealth in
> both periods. For independent draws, we have $v_2(\bar{\theta}) = v_2(\underline{\theta}) = v_1$,
> and we find that the second-period average marginal surplus with an
> inefficient type is equal to its first-period value: $E_{\tilde{\theta}_1}(S'(\bar{q}_2^D(\tilde{\theta}_1))) = \bar{\theta} +$

[9]We will then work in a moral hazard framework, but it should be clear that the lessons of the model carry over to the case of adverse selection analyzed in this section.

$\frac{\nu_1}{1-\nu_1}\Delta\theta$, where $E_{\tilde{\theta}_1}(\cdot)$ denotes the expectation operator with respect to $\tilde{\theta}_1$. In the case of perfectly correlated types, we have instead $\nu_2(\bar{\theta}) = 0$ and $\nu_2(\underline{\theta}) = 1$. Hence, as in section 8.1.1, the only second-period inefficient output produced with a positive probability is such that $S'(\bar{q}_2^D(\bar{\theta})) = \bar{\theta} + \frac{\nu_1}{1-\nu_1}\Delta\theta$, and thus $\bar{q}_2^D(\bar{\theta}) = \bar{q}_1^D$. Note that $\bar{q}_2(\underline{\theta}) = \bar{q}^*$ is now produced with zero probability. ∎

Remark 2: It is worth stressing again that the optimal contract found in proposition 8.3 uses the assumption of full commitment. Indeed, the production $\bar{q}_2^D(\bar{\theta})$ has been excessively distorted downwards to induce easier information revelation in period 1 and relax the intertemporal incentive constraint (8.25). When the second period comes, the first-period type has been revealed, and the principal does not have to distort as much the second-period output to induce a less costly revelation of types at this date. ∎

Baron and Besanko (1984b) derived optimal contracts with types correlated over time and full commitment of the principal. Laffont and Tirole (1996) provided an application of dynamic contracting models with adverse selection to characterize the optimal regulation of pollution rights. They also gave an interpretation of the optimal mechanisms in terms of markets with options. The case of types independently distributed has also been used in models of infinitely repeated relationships, starting with Townsend (1982), Green (1987), Phelan and Townsend (1991), Green and Oh (1991), Atkeson and Lucas (1992), Thomas and Worrall (1990), and Wang (1995). These authors are interested in deriving the properties of the long run distribution of the agent's utility and consumption, and sometimes draw some macroeconomic implications from the analysis of these distributions. Generally, the focus of this line of research is on the role of a long-term contract as a substitute to self- or co-insurance. These papers start with the assumption that the agent has a finite (and positive) degree of absolute risk aversion. They also assume that screening in a one-shot relationship is not feasible, because the principal has only one instrument to control the agent, namely the transfers (or the consumption) of the agent in a given period. In a long-term relationship, the specification of the continuation payoffs of the contracts is then the second crucial instrument needed to screen the agent. In section 8.2.6 below, we will analyze, for the case of infinitely repeated moral hazard, some of the recursive techniques used in this latter literature to characterize the optimal long-term contract. ∎

8.1.4 A Digression on Noncommitment ★

From the analysis above, it appears that the generalization of incentive theory to a dynamic context is straightforward, provided that the principal has the ability to commit. However, in the case where there is some correlation of types between both periods, the principal could use the information learned in the first period to propose a renegotiation of the initial long-term contract he has initially offered to improve the terms of the rent extraction-efficiency trade-off over the course of the contract. In other words, the optimal long-term contract with full commitment may fail to be *renegotiation-proof*. In section 2.12 we have already touched on this commitment issue in one-shot relationships, arguing that a simple, indirect mechanism can be a way around this commitment problem and that the possibility for renegotiating the contract comes partly as an artifact of the use of a direct revelation mechanism between the principal and the agent. In an intertemporal context, the commitment problem is much more of a concern. This concern arises because the course of actions leaves open dates for recontracting, and the information revelation is not an artifact of the modelling but corresponds to physical decisions. It is beyond the scope of this volume to solve for the optimal dynamic renegotiation-proof long-term contract. However, in section 9.4 we provide some preliminary formal analysis of the important trade-off between *ex post* efficiency and *ex ante* incentives, which arises when renegotiation is allowed.

8.2 Repeated Moral Hazard

Let us now move to repeated moral hazard relationship. The main goal of this section is to show how the past history of performances may help the principal to relax incentive compatibility constraints, even when there is no correlation between shocks in different periods.

8.2.1 The Model

We will come back to the moral hazard framework of chapter 4. For now, we assume that the relationship between the principal and the agent is repeated for two periods. The risk-averse agent has an intertemporal utility given by $U = u(t_1) - \psi(e_1) + \delta(u(t_2) - \psi(e_2))$, where t_i (resp. e_i) is the agent's transfer (resp. effort) at date i. Again, we assume that e_i belongs to $\{0, 1\}$, with disutilities normalized as usual because $\psi(1) = \psi$ and $\psi(0) = 0$. In each period, the agent's effort yields a

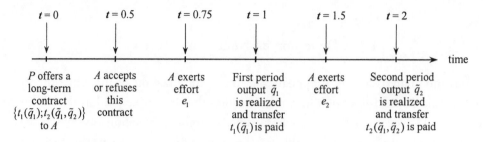

FIGURE 8.3: Timing with a Twice-Repeated Moral Hazard Problem

stochastic return $\tilde{q}_i = \bar{q}$ (resp. $\underline{q}$) with probability $\pi(e_i)$ (resp. $1 - \pi(e_i)$). We denote $\pi_0 = \pi(0)$, $\pi_1 = \pi(1)$, and $\Delta\pi = \pi_1 - \pi_0$. Stochastic returns are independently distributed over time, so that the past history of realizations does not yield any information on the current likelihood of a success or a failure of the production process. As usual, the principal is risk-neutral and has a separable utility function $V = S(q_1) - t_1 + \delta(S(q_2) - t_2)$.

In this two-period environment, the principal offers a long-term contract to the agent. In full generality, this contract involves transfers at each date that are contingent on the whole past history of outcomes. Typically, a long-term contract writes as $\{t_1(\tilde{q}_1); t_2(\tilde{q}_1, \tilde{q}_2)\}$, where $\tilde{q}_1$ and $\tilde{q}_2$ are output realizations in periods 1 and 2, respectively. Such a contract thus stipulates $2 + 2 \times 2 = 6$ possible transfers, depending on the realizations of outcomes. For simplicity of notation, we use $t_1(\bar{q}) = \bar{t}_1$ and $t_1(\underline{q}) = \underline{t}_1$ to denote the first-period transfers. Similarly, $\bar{t}_2(q_1)$ and $\underline{t}_2(q_1)$ denote transfers in the second period. As usual, the description of participation and incentive constraints is easier when one introduces the new variables $\bar{u}_1 = u(\bar{t}_1)$, $\underline{u}_1 = u(\underline{t}_1)$, $\bar{u}_2(q_1) = u(\bar{t}_2(q_1))$ and $\underline{u}_2(q_1) = u(\underline{t}_2(q_1))$.

For further references, the timing of contracting is shown in figure 8.3.

> **Remark:** The reader will have recognized the framework of a multitask moral hazard problem along the lines of that presented in chapter 5. There are two main differences. First, the sequentiality of actions that are now taken at two different dates implies that payments also take place at two different dates. Second, the separability of the agent's disutility of efforts over time will allow a somewhat simpler characterization of the optimal contract, as we will see below. ∎

8.2.2 The Optimal Long-Term Contract

We focus on the case where effort is extremely valuable for the principal, who always wants to implement a high level of effort in both periods. We can thus describe the second-period incentive constraints as

$$\bar{u}_2(q_1) - \underline{u}_2(q_1) \geq \frac{\psi}{\Delta\pi} \qquad \text{for all } q_1 \text{ in } \{\underline{q}, \bar{q}\}. \tag{8.31}$$

In full generality, these constraints obviously depend on the first-period level of output q_1, i.e., on the history of past performances.

Let us move backward. In period 1, the agent anticipates his future stream of random payoffs to evaluate the current benefit of exerting a first-period effort or not. The first-period incentive constraint is written as

$$\bar{u}_1 + \delta(\pi_1\bar{u}_2(\bar{q}) + (1 - \pi_1)\underline{u}_2(\bar{q})) - (\underline{u}_1 + \delta(\pi_1\bar{u}_2(\underline{q}) + (1 - \pi_1)\underline{u}_2(\underline{q}))) \geq \frac{\psi}{\Delta\pi}. \tag{8.32}$$

The terms $\bar{u}_1$ and $\underline{u}_1$ represent the current utility gains associated with the transfers received by the agent in period 1 depending on the realized production. The terms $\delta(\pi_1\bar{u}_2(\bar{q}) + (1 - \pi_1)\underline{u}_2(\bar{q}))$ and $\delta(\pi_1\bar{u}_2(\underline{q}) + (1 - \pi_1)\underline{u}_2(\underline{q}))$ represent the discounted expected utility gains associated with the transfers received by the agent in period 2 following each possible first-period output. Clearly, these continuation payoffs affect the first-period incentives to exert effort.

Finally, the agent accepts the long-term contract before $\tilde{q}_1$ and $\tilde{q}_2$ realize. His intertemporal participation constraint is written as

$$\pi_1\big(\bar{u}_1 + \delta(\pi_1\bar{u}_2(\bar{q}) + (1 - \pi_1)\underline{u}_2(\bar{q}))\big)$$
$$+ (1 - \pi_1)\big(\underline{u}_1 + \delta(\pi_1\bar{u}_2(\underline{q}) + (1 - \pi_1)\underline{u}_2(\underline{q}))\big) - (1 + \delta)\psi \geq 0. \tag{8.33}$$

Denoting the inverse function of the agent's utility function, again by $h = u^{-1}$, the problem that the principal must solve is

(P):
$$\max_{\{(\bar{u}_1, \underline{u}_1); (\bar{u}_2(\bar{q}), \underline{u}_2(\bar{q}), \bar{u}_2(\underline{q}), \underline{u}_2(\underline{q}))\}} \pi_1\Big(\overline{S} - h(\bar{u}_1) + \delta\big(\pi_1(\overline{S} - h(\bar{u}_2(\bar{q})))$$

$$+ (1 - \pi_1)(\underline{S} - h(\underline{u}_2(\bar{q})))\big)\Big)$$

$$+ (1 - \pi_1)\Big(\underline{S} - h(\underline{u}_1) + \delta\big(\pi_1(\overline{S} - h(\bar{u}_2(\underline{q}))) + (1 - \pi_1)(\underline{S} - h(\underline{u}_2(\underline{q})))\big)\Big)$$

subject to (8.31) to (8.34).

Solving this problem highlights the particular role played by the agent's continuation payoffs for the second period following the first-period realization q_1, namely $\pi_1\bar{u}_2(q_1) + (1 - \pi_1)\underline{u}_2(q_1) - \psi$. If the agent has been promised an expected second-period utility $u_2(q_1)$, the levels of utility $\bar{u}_2(q_1)$ and $\underline{u}_2(q_1)$ must satisfy the second-period participation constraints

$$\pi_1\bar{u}_2(q_1) + (1 - \pi_1)\underline{u}_2(q_1) - \psi \geq u_2(q_1), \qquad \text{for any } q_1. \tag{8.34}$$

It is important to look at (8.32) and (8.33) to observe that the first-period incentives to exert effort, and the decision whether to accept the long-term contract, depend on what occurs in the second period only through the values of the continuation payoffs $u_2(q_1)$. They do not depend on how the principal chooses $\bar{u}_2(q_1)$ and $\underline{u}_2(q_1)$. This flexibility only matters to provide the second-period incentives to exert effort.

Given the promise made by the principal (which is credible because of our assumption of full commitment) of a future utility $u_2(q_1)$ for the agent following a first-period output q_1, the continuation contract for the second period solves the problem below:

$$(P_2(q_1)): \qquad \max_{\{\bar{u}_2(q_1), \underline{u}_2(q_1)\}} \pi_1\big(\overline{S} - h(\bar{u}_2(q_1))\big) + (1 - \pi_1)\big(\underline{S} - h(\underline{u}_2(q_1))\big)$$

subject to (8.31) and (8.34).

We denote the value of problem $(P_2(q_1))$ by $V_2(u_2(q_1))$. This is the principal's second-period payoff, when he has promised a level of utility $u_2(q_1)$ to the agent.

This problem is almost the same as the static problem of chapter 4 (section 4.4), and its solution can be derived similarly. The only difference is that the agent receives the promise of a second-period utility $u_2(q_1)$ when the first-period output is q_1 instead of zero, as in the static model of chapter 4. Applying the same techniques as in chapter 4, it is straightforward to show that both constraints (8.31) and (8.34) are binding at the optimum. Hence, we can compute the second-period agent's payoffs in both states of nature as

$$\bar{u}_2^D(q_1) = \psi + u_2(q_1) + (1 - \pi_1)\frac{\psi}{\Delta\pi} \tag{8.35}$$

and

$$\underline{u}_2^D(q_1) = \psi + u_2(q_1) - \pi_1\frac{\psi}{\Delta\pi}, \qquad \text{for all } q_1 \text{ in } \{\underline{q}, \bar{q}\}, \tag{8.36}$$

where the superscript D means *dynamics*.

This yields the following expression of the second-best cost $C_2^{SB}(u_2(q_1))$ of implementing a high effort in period 2 following the promise of a second-period utility $u_2(q_1)$:

$$C_2^{SB}(u_2(q_1)) = \pi_1 h\left(\psi + u_2(q_1) + (1 - \pi_1)\frac{\psi}{\Delta\pi}\right)$$

$$+ (1 - \pi_1)h\left(\psi + u_2(q_1) - \frac{\pi_1\psi}{\Delta\pi}\right).^{10} \tag{8.37}$$

---

[10] We keep the superscript SB to be consistent with our notations of chapter 4.

Finally, the continuation value of the contract for the principal can be defined as

$$V_2(u_2(q_1)) = \pi_1 \overline{S} + (1 - \pi_1)\underline{S} - C_2^{SB}(u_2(q_1)). \tag{8.38}$$

For further references, note also that $V_2'(u_2(q_1)) = -C_2^{SB'}(u_2(q_1))$.

These optimal continuations of the contract for the second period being defined, we can now move backward to solve for the optimal long-term contract. Taking into account the expressions above, the principal's problem (P) can be rewritten as

$$(P'): \quad \max_{\{(\bar{u}_1, \underline{u}_1); (u_2(\bar{q}), u_2(\underline{q}))\}} \pi_1(\overline{S} - h(\bar{u}_1)) + (1 - \pi_1)(\underline{S} - h(\underline{u}_1))$$

$$+ \delta\big(\pi_1 V_2(u_2(\bar{q})) + (1 - \pi_1)V_2(u_2(\underline{q}))\big),$$

subject to

$$\bar{u}_1 + \delta u_2(\bar{q}) - (\underline{u}_1 + \delta u_2(\underline{q})) \geq \frac{\psi}{\Delta\pi}, \tag{8.39}$$

$$\pi_1(\bar{u}_1 + \delta u_2(\bar{q})) + (1 - \pi_1)(\underline{u}_1 + \delta u_2(\underline{q})) \geq \psi, \tag{8.40}$$

where (8.39) is the first-period incentive constraint and (8.40) the agent's intertemporal participation constraint. Both constraints are rewritten as functions of the expected continuation payoffs $u_2(\bar{q})$ and $u_2(\underline{q})$ that the agent will get in period 2 following each possible first-period output. Let us introduce the respective multipliers λ and μ. Note that (P') is a concave problem with linear constraints defining a nonempty constrained set for which the Kuhn and Tucker first-order conditions are necessary and sufficient to characterize optimality. Optimizing with respect to $\bar{u}_1$ and $\underline{u}_1$ yields, respectively,

$$\pi_1 h'(\bar{u}_1^D) = \lambda + \mu\pi_1, \tag{8.41}$$

$$(1 - \pi_1)h'(\underline{u}_1^D) = -\lambda + \mu(1 - \pi_1). \tag{8.42}$$

Summing those two equations, we obtain

$$\mu = \pi_1 h'(\bar{u}_1^D) + (1 - \pi_1)h'(\underline{u}_1^D) > 0, \tag{8.43}$$

and thus the agent's intertemporal participation constraint (8.40) is necessarily binding.

Also, from (8.41) and (8.42) we immediately get

$$\lambda = \pi_1(1 - \pi_1)(h'(\bar{u}_1^D) - h'(\underline{u}_1^D)). \tag{8.44}$$

Optimizing with respect to $u_2(\bar{q})$ and $u_2(\underline{q})$ yields

$$\pi_1 C_2^{SB'}(u_2^D(\bar{q})) = \lambda + \mu\pi_1, \tag{8.45}$$

$$(1 - \pi_1)C_2^{SB'}(u_2^D(\underline{q})) = -\lambda + \mu(1 - \pi_1). \tag{8.46}$$

Hence, we have another way of writing the multiplier λ:

$$\lambda = \pi_1(1 - \pi_1)\big(C_2^{SB'}(u_2^D(\bar{q})) - C_2^{SB'}(u_2^D(\underline{q}))\big). \tag{8.47}$$

Direct identifications of (8.41) with (8.45) and of (8.42) with (8.46) yield, respectively,

$$h'(\bar{u}_1^D) = C_2^{SB'}(u_2^D(\bar{q})) = \pi_1 h'(\bar{u}_2^D(\bar{q})) + (1 - \pi_1)h'(\underline{u}_2^D(\bar{q})) \tag{8.48}$$

and

$$h'(\underline{u}_1^D) = C_2^{SB'}(u_2^D(\underline{q})) = \pi_1 h'(\bar{u}_2^D(\underline{q})) + (1 - \pi_1)h'(\underline{u}_2^D(\underline{q})). \tag{8.49}$$

Those two equations show that the following *martingale property* must be satisfied at the optimum:

$$h'(u_1^D(q_1)) = \mathop{E}_{\tilde{q}_2}(h'(\tilde{u}_2^D(q_1))), \text{ for all } q_1 \text{ in } \{\underline{q}, \bar{q}\}, \tag{8.50}$$

where $E_{\tilde{q}_2}(\cdot)$ denotes the expectation operator with respect to the distribution of second-period output $\tilde{q}_2$ induced by a high effort at this date, and $\tilde{u}_2^D$ is the random value of second-period utilities.

This martingale property shows that the marginal cost of giving up some rewards to the agent in period 1 following any output q_1 must be equal to the marginal cost of giving up these rewards in the corresponding continuation of the contract. This property is rather important. It says that, because of the agent's risk aversion, the principal spreads the agent's rewards and punishments intertemporally to minimize the cost of implementing a high effort in period 1. To give all rewards and punishments necessary to induce effort in period 1 in this period only is clearly suboptimal. The principal prefers to smooth the burden of the incentive constraint between today and tomorrow.

Moreover, because $\lambda \geq 0$ and $C_2^{SB'}(\cdot)$ is increasing,[11] (8.47) implies that $u_2^D(\bar{q}) \geq u_2^D(\underline{q})$. But the equality is impossible, because from (8.48) and (8.49) it would be implied that $\bar{u}_1^D \leq \underline{u}_1^D$, and (8.39) would be violated. Since $u_2^D(\bar{q}) > u_2^D(\underline{q})$, we have necessarily $\lambda > 0$ from (8.47) and the agent intertemporal incentive constraint (8.39) is binding. Since we have $u_2^D(\bar{q}) > u_2^D(\underline{q})$ and $\bar{u}_1^D > \underline{u}_1^D$, the

---

[11]This monotonicity is obtained because $h(\cdot)$ is convex.

high first-period output is not only rewarded in period 1 but also in period 2. The optimal long-term contract with full commitment exhibits *memory*. Note that this memory property implies more generally that the first period payments and their expected continuations covary positively.

The main features of the optimal contract are summarized in proposition 8.4, which provides a useful benchmark with which we can assess the impact of various limitations that the principal may face in contracting with the agent in a long-term relationship.

Proposition 8.4: *With a twice-repeated moral hazard problem, the optimal long-term contract with full commitment exhibits memory, and the martingale property* $h'(u_1^D(q_1)) = E_{\tilde{q}_2}(h'(\tilde{u}_2^D(q_1)))$ *is satisfied.*

To get further insights on the structure of the agent's payments in a long-term relationship, let us come back to our usual quadratic example and assume that $h(u) = u + \frac{ru^2}{2}$ for some $r > 0$ and $u \geq \frac{-1}{r}$. The martingale property (8.50) immediately yields $u_1^D(q_1) = \pi_1 \bar{u}_2^D(q_1) + (1 - \pi_1)\underline{u}_2^D(q_1) = u_2(q_1) + \psi$, for all q_1 in $\{\underline{q}, \bar{q}\}$. Inserting those equalities into (8.39) and (8.40), which are binding yields, respectively, $\bar{u}_1^D - \underline{u}_1^D = \frac{\psi}{\Delta\pi(1+\delta)}$ and $\pi_1 \bar{u}_1^D + (1 - \pi_1)\underline{u}_1^D = \psi$.

Finally, the structure of the payments at each date can be fully derived as

$$\bar{u}_1^D = \psi + \frac{(1 - \pi_1)\psi}{\Delta\pi(1 + \delta)}, \tag{8.51}$$

$$\underline{u}_1^D = \psi - \frac{\pi_1\psi}{\Delta\pi(1 + \delta)}, \tag{8.52}$$

$$\bar{u}_2^D(\bar{q}) = \psi + \frac{(1 - \pi_1)\psi}{\Delta\pi(1 + \delta)} + \frac{(1 - \pi_1)\psi}{\Delta\pi}, \tag{8.53}$$

$$\underline{u}_2^D(\bar{q}) = \psi + \frac{(1 - \pi_1)\psi}{\Delta\pi(1 + \delta)} - \frac{\pi_1\psi}{\Delta\pi}, \tag{8.54}$$

$$\bar{u}_2^D(\underline{q}) = \psi - \frac{\pi_1\psi}{\Delta\pi(1 + \delta)} + \frac{(1 - \pi_1)\psi}{\Delta\pi}, \tag{8.55}$$

$$\underline{u}_2^D(\underline{q}) = \psi - \frac{\pi_1\psi}{\Delta\pi(1 + \delta)} - \frac{\pi_1\psi}{\Delta\pi}. \tag{8.56}$$

The values of these transfers immediately highlight two phenomena. First, compared with a static one-shot relationship, the first-period power of incentives needed to induce a first-period effort is lower. A factor $\frac{1}{1+\delta}$ strictly less than 1 reduces the risk borne by the agent during this first period in order to induce effort at this date. These formula are also useful for highlighting the fact that as the future matters more (δ large) the risk borne during the first period diminishes and more risk is shifted to the second period. Second, an early success (resp. failure) is translated into future compensations that are shifted upward (resp. downward). This captures the effect of the past history of performances on future compensations.

> Lambert (1983), Malcomson and Spinnewyn (1988), and Rogerson (1985b) all showed that the optimal long-term contract exhibits memory. Rey and Salanié (1990) showed how long-term contracts can generally be replaced by two-period short-term contracts in a framework with T periods. Chiappori et al. (1994) offered an interesting survey of the literature. ∎

8.2.3 Renegotiation-Proofness ★

Importantly, the recursive procedure that we have used in section 8.2.2 to compute the optimal long-term contract shows that it is in fact *sequentially optimal*. Given the promise $u_2(q_1)$ made by the principal following a first-period outcome q_1, there is no point in the principal offering a contract other than the continuation for the second period of the optimal long-term contract above. By definition, the optimal long-term contract is thus *renegotiation-proof*.

8.2.4 Reneging on the Contract ★

In the previous analysis, we have assumed that the agent commits himself to stay always in the relationship with the principal once he has accepted the long-term contract. The optimal contract with full commitment has only a single participation constraint. This contract forces the agent to stay in the relationship in period 2, even if his expected payoff for this period is negative. This is a rather strong assumption on the enforcement of a contract. Suppose now that the agent cannot commit himself to staying in a relationship if he gets less than his reservation value normalized at zero. To avoid any breach of contract, the continuation payoffs $u_2(q_1)$ following a first-period output q_1 must now satisfy the second-period participation, or *renegation-proofness*, constraints

$$u_2(q_1) \geq 0, \qquad \text{for all } q_1 \text{ in } \{\underline{q}, \bar{q}\}. \tag{8.57}$$

Considering the possibility of a breach of contract therefore puts more constraints on the principal's problem (P'). If the principal was unconstrained, he would like to decrease $u_2(\underline{q})$ and increase $u_2(\bar{q})$, because playing on future promises also helps to provide first-period incentives, as (8.40) has already shown us. However, diminishing $u_2(\underline{q})$ to its optimal value with no renegation on the contract conflicts with the second-period participation constraints (8.57). Indeed, using (8.55) and (8.56), we observe that the optimal long-term contract always violates the constraint (8.57), because $u_2^D(\underline{q}) = \pi_1 \bar{u}_2^D(\underline{q}) + (1 - \pi_1)\underline{u}_2^D(\underline{q}) - \psi = -\frac{\pi_1 \psi}{\Delta\pi(1+\delta)} < 0$. Hence, when the agent can walk away from the relationship in the second period, the constraint (8.57) must be binding following a low first-period output. The principal is then strongly limited in the second-period punishment he can inflict on the agent following this history of the game.

The optimal *renegation-proof contract* entails that (8.57) is binding for $q_1 = \underline{q}$. Following such a low first-period output, it should be clear that the continuation contract is the replica of the static contract found in chapter 4. Let us now derive the other components of the long-term contract, i.e., the levels of utilities in the first-period contract and in the second period following a high first-period continuation output $q_1 = \bar{q}$. The intertemporal incentive constraint is now written as

$$\bar{u}_1 + \delta u_2(\bar{q}) - \underline{u}_1 \geq \frac{\psi}{\Delta\pi}. \tag{8.58}$$

Similarly, the intertemporal participation constraint is obtained as

$$\pi_1(\bar{u}_1 + \delta u_2(\bar{q})) + (1 - \pi_1)\underline{u}_1 \geq \psi. \tag{8.59}$$

Taking into account the binding renegation-proofness constraint $u_2(\underline{q}) = 0$, the principal's problem can be rewritten as

(P): $\quad \max_{\{(\bar{u}_1,\underline{u}_1);u_2(\bar{q})\}} \pi_1\big(\bar{S} - h(\bar{u}_1) + \delta V_2(u_2(\bar{q}))\big) + (1 - \pi_1)\big(\underline{S} - h(\underline{u}_1) + \delta V_2(0)\big),$

subject to (8.58) and (8.59).

We index the solution to this problem with a superscript R meaning *renegation-proof*. Now we denote the respective multipliers of the two constraints (8.58) and (8.59) by λ and μ. The corresponding first-order conditions obtained by optimizing with respect to $\bar{u}_1$, $\underline{u}_1$, and $u_2(\bar{q})$ are written as

$$-\pi_1 h'(\bar{u}_1^R) + \lambda + \mu\pi_1 = 0, \tag{8.60}$$

$$-(1 - \pi_1)h'(\underline{u}_1^R) - \lambda + \mu(1 - \pi_1) = 0, \tag{8.61}$$

$$-\pi_1 C_2^{SB'}(u_2^R(\bar{q})) + \lambda + \mu\pi_1 = 0, \tag{8.62}$$

where $\bar{u}_1^R$ and $\underline{u}_2^R$ are the optimal payoffs in the first period, and $u_2^R(\bar{q})$ is the optimal continuation payoff following a high output in the first period.

Summing (8.60) and (8.61), we obtain $\mu = \pi_1 h'(\bar{u}_1^R) + (1 - \pi_1)h'(\underline{u}_1^R) > 0$, and the participation constraint (8.59) is again binding. Inserting this value of

μ into (8.60), we finally get $\lambda = \pi_1(1 - \pi_1)(h'(\bar{u}_1^R) - h'(\underline{u}_1^R))$. Using (8.60) and (8.62), we also obtain

$$h'(\bar{u}_1^R) = C_2^{SB'}(u_2^R(\bar{q})) = \pi_1 h'\left(\psi + u_2^R(\bar{q}) + \frac{(1 - \pi_1)\psi}{\Delta\pi}\right)$$

$$+ (1 - \pi_1)h'\left(\psi + u_2^R(\bar{q}) - \frac{\pi_1\psi}{\Delta\pi}\right). \tag{8.63}$$

This equation is again a martingale property, which now applies only following a first-period success. Smoothing the rewards for a first-period success between the two periods calls for equalizing the marginal cost of rewarding the agent in period 1 with its future expected value in period 2. Using the quadratic specification of $h(\cdot)$, the martingale property (8.63) is rewritten as

$$\bar{u}_1^R = u_2^R(\bar{q}) + \psi = \pi_1 \bar{u}_2^R(\bar{q}) + (1 - \pi_1)\underline{u}_2^R(\bar{q}). \tag{8.64}$$

As an exercise, we leave it to the reader to check that $\lambda > 0$.

Using (8.64) with the binding constraints (8.58) and (8.59) yields a linear system with three unknowns and three equations. Solving this system, we first obtain the following expressions of the agent's payoff in each state of nature:

$$\bar{u}_1^R = \psi + \frac{(1 - \pi_1)\psi}{\Delta\pi(1 + \delta)}, \tag{8.65}$$

$$\underline{u}_1^R = \psi - \frac{\pi_1\psi}{\Delta\pi}, \tag{8.66}$$

$$\bar{u}_2^R(\bar{q}) = \psi + \frac{(1 - \pi_1)\psi}{\Delta\pi(1 + \delta)} + \frac{(1 - \pi_1)\psi}{\Delta\pi}, \tag{8.67}$$

$$\underline{u}_2^R(\bar{q}) = \psi + \frac{(1 - \pi_1)\psi}{\Delta\pi(1 + \delta)} - \frac{\pi_1\psi}{\Delta\pi}. \tag{8.68}$$

Taking into account that $u_2^R(\underline{q}) = 0$, we also get

$$\bar{u}_2^R(\underline{q}) = \psi + \frac{(1 - \pi_1)\psi}{\Delta\pi} \tag{8.69}$$

and

$$\underline{u}_2^R(\underline{q}) = \psi - \frac{\pi_1\psi}{\Delta\pi}. \tag{8.70}$$

Comparing these expressions of the payoffs with those obtained when the agent cannot leave the relationship in period 2, we can state proposition 8.5.

Proposition 8.5: *Assuming that $h(\cdot)$ is quadratic with a twice-repeated moral hazard problem and a renegation-proofness constraint, the optimal long-term contract is the same as with full commitment, except for the payoffs corresponding to a low first-period output: $\underline{u}_1^R < \underline{u}_1^D$, $\bar{u}_2^R(\underline{q}) > \bar{u}_2^D(\underline{q})$, and $\underline{u}_2^R(\underline{q}) > \underline{u}_2^D(\underline{q})$.*

The renegation-proofness constraint (8.57) quite significantly affects the structure of the agent's payoffs following a low first-period output. However, the optimal long-term contract still exhibits memory and tracks the agent's performances over time, as with full commitment. An early success implies some greater rewards later on. Because the principal can no longer spread a punishment following a low first-period output $q_1 = \underline{q}$ between periods 1 and 2, all this punishment must be inflicted on the agent in the first-period.[12] Following such a low first-period output, the agent receives the optimal static contract in period 2, which corresponds to a zero participation constraint.

> One-sided lack of commitment was studied initially by Lambert (1983), who showed that the memory result still holds in this framework. Atkeson (1991) analyzed the infinitely repeated contractual model with one-sided commitment. Thomas and Worrall (1988) provided an analysis of the optimal long-term contract with two-sided lack of commitment in an infinitely repeated relationship without moral hazard. ∎

8.2.5 Saving

In the framework of section 8.2.2, we have assumed that the principal has the full ability to restrict the agent's access to the capital market. We have not allowed the agent either to save or to borrow. All the transfers received were immediately consumed. This seems a rather strong assumption, in particular, given the fact that the agent would like to save a positive amount in the first period, when he receives the second-best optimal long-term contract that we have described in proposition 8.4. To see this point, consider the impact of saving an amount s in the first period. The agent's expected utility is thus written as $u(t_1^D(q_1) - s) + \delta E_{\tilde{q}_2}(u(t_2^D(q_1, \tilde{q}_2) + (1 + R)s))$, where $E_{\tilde{q}_2}(\cdot)$ denotes the expectation operator with respect to the second-period production induced by a high effort. In a perfect

---

[12]With other utility functions, the principal may also be willing to increase the rewards offered to the agent in case of a success in order to restore efficient incentives. The renegation-proofness constraint along a path where the agent has performed poorly may also have an impact on a path where the agent has performed better.

credit market, the interest rate is $1 + R = \frac{1}{\delta}$. Marginally increasing s above zero improves the agent's intertemporal utility whenever

$$-u'(t_1^D(q_1)) + \mathop{E}_{\tilde{q}_2}\left(u'(t_2^D(q_1, \tilde{q}_2))\right) > 0. \tag{8.71}$$

Because the optimal contract satisfies the martingale property (8.50), we also have $\frac{1}{h'(u_1^D(q_1))} = \frac{1}{E_{\tilde{q}_2}(h'(\tilde{u}_2^D(q_1)))} < E_{\tilde{q}_2}(\frac{1}{h'(\tilde{u}_2^D(q_1))})$, where the last inequality is obtained by applying Jensen's inequality to the strictly convex function $\frac{1}{x}$. Finally, using $\frac{1}{h'(u_1^D(q_1))} = u'(t_1^D(q_1))$ and $\frac{1}{h'(\tilde{u}_2^D(q_1))} = u'(t_2^D(q_1, \tilde{q}_2))$, the strict inequality (8.71) holds, and a positive saving is thus optimal.

This positive saving perturbs the agent's incentives to exert effort in the second period. Indeed, because the second period transfers $t_2^D(q_1, \tilde{q}_2)$ are such that the second-period incentive constraints are binding, a positive saving that decreases the marginal utility of income makes the agent prefer a low effort. This calls for a careful reoptimization of the principal's problem.

More generally, when the saving made by the agent is nonobservable by the principal, it plays the role of another moral hazard variable that can only be indirectly controlled by the principal through the long-term contract they offer.

Let us now characterize some features of the optimal contract with saving. First, note that, given a first-period output q_1 and any long-term contract $\{\hat{t}_1(q_1); \hat{t}_2(q_1, q_2)\}$, the agent chooses to save an amount $s^*(q_1)$, such that it equalizes his marginal utilities of income in both periods:

$$u'(\hat{t}_1(q_1) - s^*(q_1)) = \mathop{E}_{\tilde{q}_2}\left(u'\left(\hat{t}_2(q_1, \tilde{q}_2) + \frac{1}{\delta}s^*(q_1)\right)\right), \quad \text{for all } q_1 \text{ in } \{\underline{q}, \bar{q}\}. [13] \tag{8.72}$$

In computing the expectation above, we have assumed that the agent anticipates that he will exert a high effort in period 2 so that the probability that $\tilde{q}_2$ is equal to $\bar{q}$ is π_1. Of course the choice of effort in the continuation is in fact endogenous and depends on how much the agent would like to save. We will come back to this issue below.

By shifting income from one period to the other, the agent is able to play on the incentive power of the long-term contract he receives from the principal. Now let us imagine that the principal replaces this initial contract by a new long-term contract $\{t_1(\bar{q}_1); t_2(\tilde{q}_1, \tilde{q}_2)\}$, which is designed to replicate the agent's choice and the final allocation of utilities that the latter gets in each state of nature. This new contract should thus satisfy $t_1(q_1) = \hat{t}_1(q_1) - s_1^*(q_1)$ for all q_1 in $\{\underline{q}, \bar{q}\}$ and

---

[13] When $s^*(q_1) < 0$, the agent is in fact borrowing from the capital market. Note that because the agent's objective function is strictly concave in s, saving is always deterministic.

$t_2(q_1, q_2) = \hat{t}_2(q_1, q_2) + \frac{1}{\delta}s_1^*(q_1)$ for all (q_1, q_2) in $\{\underline{q}, \bar{q}\}^2$. With this new contract, the marginal utilities of income are the same in both periods, because by definition

$$u'(t_1(q_1)) = \underset{\tilde{q}_2}{E}(u'(t_2(q_1, \tilde{q}_2))), \qquad \text{for all } q_1 \text{ in } \{\underline{q}, \bar{q}\}. \qquad (8.73)$$

The agent chooses neither to save nor to borrow. Moreover, the intertemporal costs of both contracts are the same for the principal, since

$$\hat{t}_1(q_1) + \delta\underset{\tilde{q}_2}{E}(\hat{t}_2(q_1, \tilde{q}_2)) = t_1(q_1) + s_1^*(q_1) + \delta\underset{\tilde{q}_2}{E}\left(t_2(q_1, \tilde{q}_2) - \frac{1}{\delta}s_1^*(q_1)\right)$$

$$= t_1(q_1) + \delta\underset{\tilde{q}_2}{E}(t_2(q_1, \tilde{q}_2)), \qquad \text{for all } q_1 \text{ in } \{\underline{q}, \bar{q}\}. \quad (8.74)$$

Hence, there is no loss of generality in restricting the principal to offer *saving-proof* long-term contracts.

The saving-proofness constraint, however, requires that the following martingale property, obtained from (8.73), be satisfied:

$$\frac{1}{h'(u_1(q_1))} = \underset{\tilde{q}_2}{E}\left(\frac{1}{h'(u_2(q_1, \tilde{q}_2))}\right), \qquad \text{for all } q_1 \text{ in } \{\underline{q}, \bar{q}\}. \qquad (8.75)$$

(8.75) significantly constrains the set of implementable allocations and raises the agency cost of implementing a high effort. The principal can no longer spread the future expected payoffs $u_2(\bar{q})$ and $u_2(\underline{q})$ as he would like in order to facilitate the first-period provision of incentives without inducing saving.

However, the martingale property (8.75) is not the only constraint on the principal's problem. Indeed, it would be the case if the stochastic production process in period 2 were completely exogenous. However, under moral hazard, the choice of effort and the stochastic production process in this second period are also endogenous—it depends, in a rather complex way, on how much the agent has saved in the first period and on the current contract. This means that, if the principal can be restricted to saving-proof long-term contracts on the equilibrium path, this restriction is no longer valid when the agent decides to change his first-period saving so that he prefers exerting a low effort in the second-period continuation. Given a long-term contract $\{t_1(q_1); t_2(q_1, q_2)\}$, which is saving-proof *on* the equilibrium path, the agent, by saving s_0 and exerting no effort in period 2, gets $u(t_1(q_1) - s_0) + \delta(\pi_0 u(t_2(q_1, \bar{q}) + \frac{s_0}{\delta}) + (1 - \pi_0)u(t_2(q_1, \underline{q}) + \frac{s_0}{\delta}))$.

To induce the agent to exert effort in period 2, the following incentive constraint must be satisfied by a saving-proof long-term contract:

$$u(t_1(q_1)) + \delta(\pi_1 u(t_2(q_1, \bar{q})) + (1 - \pi_1)u(t_2(q_1, \underline{q}))) - \delta\psi$$

$$\geq \underset{\{s_0\}}{\max} \; u(t_1(q_1) - s_0) + \delta\left(\pi_0 u\left(t_2(q_1, \bar{q}) + \frac{s_0}{\delta}\right) + (1 - \pi_0)u\left(t_2(q_1, \underline{q}) + \frac{s_0}{\delta}\right)\right).$$

$$(8.76)$$

Let us consider a second-period contract, such that $t_2(q_1, \bar{q}) > t_2(q_1, \underline{q})$ for any q_1 in $\{\underline{q}, \bar{q}\}$. It should be noted that s_0^*, defined as the maximizer of the right-hand side above, is such that

$$u'(t_1(q_1) - s_0^*) = \pi_0 u'\left(t_2(q_1, \bar{q}) + \frac{s_0^*}{\delta}\right) + (1 - \pi_0)u'\left(t_2(q_1, \underline{q}) + \frac{s_0^*}{\delta}\right)$$

$$> \pi_1 u'\left(t_2(q_1, \bar{q}) + \frac{s_0^*}{\delta}\right) + (1 - \pi_1)u'\left(t_2(q_1, \underline{q}) + \frac{s_0^*}{\delta}\right), \qquad (8.77)$$

since $u'(\cdot)$ is decreasing and $\pi_1 > \pi_0$. Using the fact that the agent's objective function is concave in s and maximized at zero saving when a positive effort is exerted in the second period, we can conclude that $s_0^* > 0$.

> **Remark:** It should be also noted that this double deviation along both the saving and the effort dimension introduces a positive slack into the second-period incentive constraint. Indeed, the right-hand side of (8.76) is strictly greater than what the agent can get by not saving at all and exerting no effort, namely $u(t_1(q_1)) + \delta \, (\pi_0 u(t_2(q_1, \bar{q}_2)) + (1 - \pi_0)u(t_2(q_1, \underline{q}_2)))$. Simplifying, we finally get
>
> $$u(t_2(q_1, \bar{q}_2)) - u(t_2(q_1, \underline{q}_2)) > \frac{\psi}{\Delta\pi}, \qquad \text{for any } q_1 \text{ in } \{\underline{q}, \bar{q}\}. \quad (8.78)$$
>
> This strict inequality implies that the optimal contract with full commitment is not sequentially optimal when saving is allowed. Indeed, the full commitment optimal contract requests that the second-period incentive constraint is slack, as shown on (8.78). However, once the decision of not saving has been made by the agent, and once the second period comes, the principal no longer has any reason to leave such a slack. The principal would like to renegotiate and offer a new contract such that second-period incentive constraints are binding. ∎

The general lesson of this section is that allowing saving and borrowing may significantly constrain what can be achieved by a long-term contract. Moreover, it introduces much complexity into the analysis.

The design of the optimal contract with saving and noncommitment is rather complex. Chiappori et al. (1994) provided some insights into the structure of the solution. Things are simpler with full commitment. Malcomson and Spinnewyn (1988) showed that the optimal long-term contract can be replicated by a sequence of optimal static contracts when the agent's saving decision can be controlled by the principal. Fudenberg, Holmström, and Milgrom (1990) obtained a similar result in the case where the agent has additively separable CARA preferences, where effort is counted in monetary terms, and where the production technology is common knowledge. They showed that the associated *one-period contract* corresponds to the optimal static contract offered to an agent with a lower degree of absolute risk aversion.   ∎

8.2.6 Infinitely Repeated Relationship

The two-period model is a highly stylized view of a long-term principal-agent relationship. Financial contracts, labor contracts, and tenancy contracts are most often enduring relationships lasting for a long period of time. Let us move now to an infinite horizon model extending the basic framework of section 8.2.2.[14] As we will see, the design of the optimal long-term contract still exhibits many of the features of our two-period example. The novelty is that the second period is no longer the end of the relationship. All periods are alike, and the principal faces a similar problem of control in each period. It is rather intuitive to see that the whole structure of the contract is now solved recursively. Given an initial promise of utility from any period on, the principal computes an optimal contract that stipulates not only the agent's current payments but also determines what are the utility levels that are promised from that period on, following each current realization of the production process. Then, the continuation of the optimal contract for the next period on is similar to the contract itself. Hence, the whole contract can be computed recursively.

The recursive structure of the optimal contract also implies that, at any given date, the contract depends on the whole history of past outcomes only through the utility level promised following such a history. This utility level can be viewed as a stochastic state variable that summarizes the past history of the agent's performances. Therefore, the optimal contract exhibits a *Markov property*.[15]

To describe better the optimal contract, let us denote the value function associated with the following dynamic programming problem by $V(\cdot)$:

(P): $$V(U) = \max_{\{u, \bar{u}, \bar{U}, \underline{U}\}} \pi_1(\bar{S} - h(\bar{u})) + (1 - \pi_1)(\underline{S} - h(\underline{u}))$$

$$+ \delta(\pi_1 V(\bar{U}) + (1 - \pi_1)V(\underline{U}))$$

[14]Hence, the principal can perfectly control the agent's access to the capital market.

[15]This feature of the optimal contract could be derived more rigorously; however, for the purpose of this volume, we content ourselves with the heuristic argument above.

subject to

$$\bar{u} + \delta\overline{U} - (\underline{u} + \delta\underline{U}) \geq \frac{\psi}{\Delta\pi}, \tag{8.79}$$

$$\pi_1(\bar{u} + \delta\overline{U}) + (1 - \pi_1)(\underline{u} + \delta\underline{U}) - \psi \geq U. \tag{8.80}$$

$V(U)$ is the value of the principal's problem (P) in an infinitely repeated relationship with moral hazard, assuming that the principal wants to induce a high effort in each period and promise an expected utility level U to the agent over the whole relationship.[16] Note that the principal must not only stipulate the current payments of the agent but also the levels of future utilities $\overline{U}$ and $\underline{U}$, which are promised in the continuation of the contract following the respective realizations of $\bar{q}$ and $\underline{q}$. The constraints (8.79) and (8.80) are, respectively, the incentive and participation constraints when an expected payoff U has been promised to the agent. These constraints make the role of these continuation payoffs explicit. Given that the principal has promised an expected level of utility U to the agent at a given period, he can get the expected payoff $V(U)$ from that period on. By offering the continuation payoffs $\underline{U}$ and $\overline{U}$ the principal knows, by the mere definition of the value function $V(\cdot)$, that he will get himself the continuation payoffs $V(\underline{U})$ and $V(\overline{U})$.

Let us denote the respective multipliers of the constraints (8.79) and (8.80) by λ and μ. Assuming the concavity of the value function $V(\cdot)$,[17] the optimizations with respect to $\overline{U}$ and $\underline{U}$ yield respectively

$$\pi_1 V'(\overline{U}(U)) + \lambda + \pi_1\mu = 0, \tag{8.81}$$

$$(1 - \pi_1)V'(\underline{U}(U)) - \lambda + (1 - \pi_1)\mu = 0, \tag{8.82}$$

where we make explicit the dependence of the solution on the level of promised utility U.

Summing these two equations, we obtain also

$$\mu = -E(V'(\tilde{U}(U))), \tag{8.83}$$

where $E(\cdot)$ is the expectation operator with respect to the distribution of current output induced by a high effort and $\tilde{U}(U)$ is the random continuation utility promised to the agent.

---

[16]Inducing a high effort may not be always second-best optimal under moral hazard. Indeed, it may be that, for some promised value U, the principal finds it optimal to induce zero effort in a given period. Implementing a high effort can always be viewed as an approximation of what is really optimal. However, the analysis of this section shows that this approximation already performs very well to come close to the first-best as the relationship is repeated often enough.

[17]See Stockey and Lucas (1989) for general conditions that ensure that a value function exists and is concave for a dynamic problem like (P).

Optimizing with respect to $\bar{u}$ and $\underline{u}$ also yields

$$\pi_1 h'(\bar{u}(U)) = \lambda + \pi_1 \mu, \tag{8.84}$$

$$(1 - \pi_1) h'(\underline{u}(U)) = -\lambda + (1 - \pi_1)\mu. \tag{8.85}$$

Summing these two equations, we finally get

$$\mu = E(h'(\tilde{u}(U))) > 0, \tag{8.86}$$

where $\tilde{u}(U)$ is the random current utility level. Hence, the participation constraint (8.80) is necessarily binding.

From (8.84) and (8.85), we also derive the following definition of λ:

$$\lambda = \pi_1(1 - \pi_1)\big(h'(\bar{u}(U)) - h'(\underline{u}(U))\big)$$

$$= \pi_1(1 - \pi_1)\big(V'(\underline{U}(U)) - V'(\overline{U}(U))\big). \tag{8.87}$$

Because $h(\cdot)$ is convex and $V(\cdot)$ is concave, (8.87) implies that $\overline{U}(U) \geq \underline{U}(U)$ if and only if $\bar{u}(U) \geq \underline{u}(U)$. To satisfy (8.79), it cannot be that $\bar{u}(U) \leq \underline{u}(U)$ and $\overline{U}(U) \leq \underline{U}(U)$ hold simultaneously. Hence, we necessarily have $\bar{u}(U) > \underline{u}(U)$ and $\overline{U}(U) > \underline{U}(U)$.

The economic interpretation of this condition is clear. In an infinitely repeated relationship, the optimal long-term contract again exhibits the *memory property*. A good performance today is not only rewarded today but also gives the agent a greater continuation payoff. The explanation is the same as in the two-period model of section 8.3.2. To smooth the agency costs of the relationship with the agent, the principal spreads the agent's rewards and punishments between the current period and its continuation, which now involves the whole future of their relationship.

Moreover, using the Envelope Theorem, we also have $V'(U) = -\mu$. Hence, the marginal value function satisfies the martingale property:

$$V'(U) = E(V'(\tilde{U}(U))). \tag{8.88}$$

This property characterizes how the principal intertemporally smoothes the agent's reward over time in such a way that one more unit of utility promised today costs him exactly what the principal gains from having less to promise tomorrow, following any realization of the output. This property generalizes what we have seen in section 8.2.2 to the case of an infinitely repeated relationship.

To make further progress toward the characterization of the optimal contract, we will assume that $h(u) = \frac{\exp(ru)-1}{r}$ for all u in $\mathbb{R}$.[18] This corresponds to a utility function $u(\cdot)$ that is given by $u(t) = \frac{1}{r}\ln(1 + rt)$, which is defined for all $t \geq t_{min} = -\frac{1}{r}$.[19]

This specification of the inverse utility function suggests that we should look for a value function of the kind $V(U) = \alpha - \frac{1}{\beta}\exp(\beta U + \gamma)$, where (α, β, γ) belongs to $\mathbb{R}^3$ with $\beta \geq 0$. Note that $V(\cdot)$ is then decreasing $(V'(U) = -\exp(\beta U + \gamma) \leq 0)$ and concave $(V''(U) = -\beta\exp(\beta U + \gamma) \leq 0)$.

Using (8.81) and (8.84), we immediately find that

$$-V'(\overline{U}(U)) = h'(\bar{u}(U)), \tag{8.89}$$

or to put it differently,

$$\exp(\beta\overline{U}(U) + \gamma) = \exp(r\bar{u}(U)). \tag{8.90}$$

Similarly, using (8.82) and (8.85), we obtain

$$-V'(\underline{U}(U)) = h'(\underline{u}(U)), \tag{8.91}$$

or

$$\exp(\beta\underline{U}(U) + \gamma) = \exp(r\underline{u}(U)). \tag{8.92}$$

The general discussion above has shown that the constraints (8.79) and (8.80) are both binding. This yields the following expressions of $\bar{u}(U)$ and $\underline{u}(U)$:

$$\bar{u}(U) = U + \psi + (1 - \pi_1)\frac{\psi}{\Delta\pi} - \delta\overline{U}(U) \tag{8.93}$$

and

$$\underline{u}(U) = U + \psi - \pi_1\frac{\psi}{\Delta\pi} - \delta\underline{U}(U). \tag{8.94}$$

Inserting those expressions into (8.90) and (8.92) yields, respectively,

$$\overline{U}(U) = \frac{r}{r\delta + \beta}\left(U + \psi + (1 - \pi_1)\frac{\psi}{\Delta\pi}\right) - \frac{\gamma}{r\delta + \beta} \tag{8.95}$$

---

[18]Note that $h(u) \approx u + \frac{ru^2}{2}$ when r is small enough. Hence, the quadratic model we have repeatedly used all over the book can be seen as a reasonable approximation of the exponential inverse utility function that we use here.

[19]Note that r is the agent's absolute risk aversion at zero: $-\frac{u''}{u'}(t)\Big|_{t=0} = r$.

and

$$\underline{U}(U) = \frac{r}{r\delta + \beta}\left(U + \psi - \pi_1 \frac{\psi}{\Delta\pi}\right) - \frac{\gamma}{r\delta + \beta}. \qquad (8.96)$$

With our specification for $h(\cdot)$, the martingale property (8.88) is rewritten as:

$$\exp(\beta U) = \pi_1 \exp(\beta \overline{U}(U)) + (1 - \pi_1)\exp(\beta \underline{U}(U)) \quad \text{for all } U. \qquad (8.97)$$

Inserting (8.95) and (8.96) into (8.97) and identifying the right-hand and left-hand sides for all values of U yields

$$1 = \frac{r}{r\delta + \beta}, \qquad (8.98)$$

and

$$\exp\left(\frac{\beta\gamma}{r\delta + \beta}\right) = \pi_1 \exp\left(\frac{\beta r}{r\delta + \beta}\left(\psi + (1 - \pi_1)\frac{\psi}{\Delta\pi}\right)\right)$$
$$+ (1 - \pi_1)\exp\left(\frac{\beta r}{r\delta + \beta}\left(\psi - \pi_1 \frac{\psi}{\Delta\pi}\right)\right). \qquad (8.99)$$

Finally, we get the following expressions of β and γ:

$$\beta = r(1 - \delta), \qquad (8.100)$$

$$\gamma = r\psi + \frac{1}{1 - \delta}\ln\left(\pi_1 \exp\left(r(1 - \delta)(1 - \pi_1)\frac{\psi}{\Delta\pi}\right)\right.$$
$$\left. + (1 - \pi_1)\exp\left(-r(1 - \delta)\pi_1 \frac{\psi}{\Delta\pi}\right)\right). \qquad (8.101)$$

These expressions yield the following laws of motion for the expected utility from any period on:

$$\overline{U}(U) = U + (1 - \pi_1)\frac{\psi}{\Delta\pi} - \frac{1}{r(1 - \delta)}\ln\left(\pi_1 \exp\left(r(1 - \delta)(1 - \pi_1)\frac{\psi}{\Delta\pi}\right)\right.$$
$$\left. + (1 - \pi_1)\exp\left(-r(1 - \delta)\pi_1 \frac{\psi}{\Delta\pi}\right)\right) \qquad (8.102)$$

and

$$\underline{U}(U) = U - \pi_1 \frac{\psi}{\Delta\pi} - \frac{1}{r(1 - \delta)}\ln\left(\pi_1 \exp\left(r(1 - \delta)(1 - \pi_1)\frac{\psi}{\Delta\pi}\right)\right.$$
$$\left. + (1 - \pi_1)\exp\left(-r(1 - \delta)\pi_1 \frac{\psi}{\Delta\pi}\right)\right). \qquad (8.103)$$

Moreover, the current payoffs are then obtained from (8.93), (8.94), (8.102), and (8.103) as

$$\bar{u}(U) = (1 - \delta)\left(U + \psi + (1 - \pi_1)\frac{\psi}{\Delta\pi}\right) + \frac{\delta\gamma}{r},\tag{8.104}$$

$$\underline{u}(U) = (1 - \delta)\left(U + \psi - \frac{\pi_1\psi}{\Delta\pi}\right) + \frac{\delta\gamma}{r}.\tag{8.105}$$

The laws of motion (8.102) and (8.103) are interesting, because they show that the optimal contract still exhibits the memory property in an infinitely repeated relationship. A success in any period moves up the agent's expected utility from this period on and $\bar{U}(U) > U$. A failure moves it down, $\underline{U}(U) < U$. However, the upward shift is smaller than the downward shift, which creates a tendency for expected utility to move downward, as we will discuss below.

Note that as δ goes to one, the following Taylor approximation holds:

$$\bar{U}(U) = U + (1 - \pi_1)\frac{\psi}{\Delta\pi} - r(1 - \delta)\pi_1(1 - \pi_1)\frac{\psi^2}{2(\Delta\pi)^2}\tag{8.106}$$

and

$$\underline{U}(U) = U - \pi_1\frac{\psi}{\Delta\pi} - r(1 - \delta)\pi_1(1 - \pi_1)\frac{\psi^2}{2(\Delta\pi)^2}.\tag{8.107}$$

As δ goes to one, whatever his degree of risk aversion, the agent behaves almost as a risk-neutral agent being incentivized by a reward (in utility terms)$(1 - \pi_1)\frac{\psi}{\Delta\pi}$ following a success and a punishment $-\pi_1\frac{\psi}{\Delta\pi}$ following a failure. This already suggests that the agency cost may not be too important when the future is not discounted too much.

To find the behavior of the value function as δ goes to one, let us now determine the last parameter α. Using the definition of $V(\cdot)$, we have

$$V(U) = \pi_1\bar{S} + (1 - \pi_1)\underline{S} + \frac{1}{r} - \frac{\pi_1\exp(r\bar{u}(U)) + (1 - \pi_1)\exp(r\underline{u}(U))}{r}$$

$$+ \delta(\pi_1 V(\bar{U}(U)) + (1 - \pi_1)V(\underline{U}(U))),\tag{8.108}$$

where $(\bar{u}(U), \underline{u}(U))$ are given by (8.104) and (8.105) and $(\bar{U}(U), \underline{U}(U))$ are given by (8.102) and (8.103). Inserting these latter expressions in (8.108) and simplifying yields, after some tedious computations,

$$\alpha = \frac{1}{1 - \delta}\left(\pi_1\bar{S} + (1 - \pi_1)\underline{S} + \frac{1}{r}\right).\tag{8.109}$$

Finally, the value function is written as

$$V(U) = \frac{1}{1-\delta}\left(\pi_1\overline{S} + (1-\pi_1)\underline{S} + \frac{1}{r}\right) - \frac{1}{r(1-\delta)}\exp(r(1-\delta)U + \gamma).$$

$$(8.110)$$

Normalizing the length of the period by $1 - \delta$, the *per-period* value function is written as

$$\overline{V}(U) = (1-\delta)V(U) = \pi_1\overline{S} + (1-\pi_1)\underline{S} - \frac{(\exp(r(1-\delta)U + \gamma) - 1)}{r}.$$

$$(8.111)$$

When δ converges to one, γ converges towards $r\psi$ and the per-period value function uniformly converges on all compact intervals of U toward

$$W_1^* = \pi_1\overline{S} + (1-\pi_1)\underline{S} - h(\psi), \qquad (8.112)$$

which is the first-best profit of the principal inducing a positive effort.

Proposition 8.6: *As δ goes to one, the principal's per-period expected profit in an infinitely repeated relationship with moral hazard converges towards its first-best value.*

The intuition for this result is straightforward. Recall from chapter 4 that the source of inefficiency in a static moral hazard problem is the fact that the principal must let the risk-averse agent bear some risk. The principal benefits from the repetition of the game, because he can spread the agent's rewards and punishments over time and let the agent only bear a small fraction of the risk associated with his current effort in any given period. This risk is proportional to the *length* of the period $1 - \delta$. When δ is close to one, the risk borne by the agent in each period is thus made arbitrarily close to zero, as can be seen easily by computing the difference $\bar{u}(U) - \underline{u}(U) = \frac{\beta}{r}(\overline{U}(U) - \underline{U}(U)) = (1-\delta)\frac{\psi}{\Delta\pi}$, which converges towards 0 as δ goes to 1. Therefore, the cost of moral hazard in a given period almost disappears, and the first-best level of profit is achieved when δ is close enough to one.

Another interpretation of this result should be stressed. As the contractual relationship is repeated, the risk-averse agent is subject to many independent risks that arise at different points in time. The principal structures the intertemporal contract of the agent to let him become *perfectly diversified*. As a result of this complete diversification, the agent is almost risk-neutral, and the first-best outcome can be obtained just as in a static model with risk neutrality. In this sense, one can say that the infinitely repeated relationship is a good substitute to self-insurance if the relationship is repeated often enough.

Finally, it is interesting to characterize how the distribution of utilities that the agent gets after i periods evolves. Given that (8.102) and (8.103) both hold, the utility $\tilde{U}_i$, which is promised to the agent from any date $t = i$ on, is such that $\tilde{U}_i = E_{\tilde{q}_{i+1}}(\tilde{U}_{i+1}) + \rho$, where $E_{\tilde{q}_{i+1}}$ denotes the expectations of the output at date $t = i+1$ when the agent exerts a positive effort in this period and $\rho = \frac{1}{r(1-\delta)} \ln(\pi_1 \exp(r(1 - \delta)(1 - \pi_1)\frac{\psi}{\Delta\pi}) + (1 - \pi_1) \exp(-r(1 - \delta)\pi_1 \frac{\psi}{\Delta\pi}))$ is strictly positive. Using the Law of Iterated Expectations, we get $E_{\tilde{q}_i}(\tilde{U}_i) = E_{\tilde{q}_i}(E_{\tilde{q}_{i+1}}(\tilde{U}_{i+1})) + \rho = E_{(\tilde{q}_i, \tilde{q}_{i+1})}(\tilde{U}_{i+1}) + \rho$. Proceeding recursively, we finally obtain $U_0 = E_{\tilde{q}_1}(\tilde{U}_1) + \rho = E_{h_i}(\tilde{U}_i) + i\rho$, where $U_0 = 0$ is the agent's reservation utility at the start of the relationship and $h_i = (\tilde{q}_i, \tilde{q}_{i-1}, \dots, \tilde{q}_1)$ is the whole history of past outcomes up to date $t = i$. In particular, we have

$$\underset{h_i}{E}(\tilde{U}_i) = -i\rho, \tag{8.113}$$

which converges towards minus infinity as i goes to infinity. The expected utility of the agent from any period on decreases linearly over time, pushing the agent into regions where continuation payoffs are very likely to be negative. The assumption that the agent cannot leave the relationship is thus crucial for the result where the first-best outcome can be approximatively implemented as δ goes to one.

This property is also useful when computing the whole distribution of expected utilities $\tilde{U}_i$ from any period i on. The laws of motion are given by (8.102) and (8.103). Figure 8.4 below explains how this distribution evolves over time.

It is straightforward to observe that the future expected utility $U(h_i)$ following any history h_i depends only on the number of high outcomes $\tilde{q}$ that have been realized up to date $t = i$. Assuming n realizations of $\tilde{q}$ in a given history h_i, we have $U(h_i) = U_i(n) = n(\frac{(1 - \pi_1)\psi}{\Delta\pi}) + (i - n)(\frac{-\pi_1\psi}{\Delta\pi}) - i\rho$, where $\frac{(1 - \pi_1)\psi}{\Delta\pi}$ is the agent's reward when a high output realizes and $\frac{-\pi_1\psi}{\Delta\pi}$ is his punishment following a low output. Note that the probability that such a history with n high outcomes up to period i takes place is $\binom{i}{n} \pi_1^n (1 - \pi_1)^{i-n}$, i.e., the probability of n successes in an i-Bernoulli trial.

It is also interesting to note that the distribution of $\tilde{U}_i + i\rho$ converges in law toward a normal distribution. From a direct application of the Central Limit Theorem we have indeed

$$\frac{\tilde{U}_i + i\rho}{\frac{\psi}{\Delta\pi}\sqrt{\pi_1(1 - \pi_1)}} \underset{\text{Law}}{\longrightarrow} N(0, 1),$$

where $N(0, 1)$ is a normal distribution with zero mean and unit variance. This convergence suggests that the utility levels promised to the agent from any date on are unlikely to diverge too much away from the downward drift as the relationship becomes infinitely long.

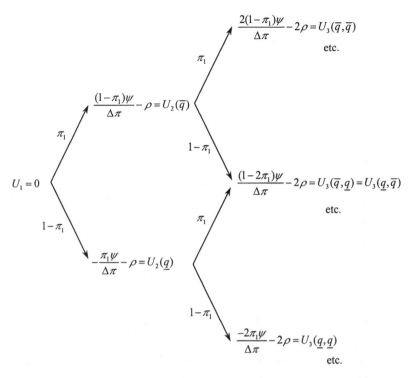

FIGURE 8.4: Distribution of Future Expected Utilities up to Period 3

The structure of the incentive scheme is also easily obtained from the structure of the utilities. If there have been n successes up to date $t = i$, the incentive scheme is such that

$$\bar{t}_i(n) = h\left(\psi + (1 - \delta)\left(\frac{(1 - \pi_1)\psi}{\Delta\pi} + U_i(n)\right) + \delta\rho\right) \qquad (8.114)$$

and

$$\underline{t}_i(n) = h\left(\psi + (1 - \delta)\left(\frac{-\pi_1\psi}{\Delta\pi} + U_i(n)\right) + \delta\rho\right). \qquad (8.115)$$

As the number of periods increases, the downward drift of utility toward minus infinity implies that transfers get closer and closer to their lowest possible bound $t_{min} = -\frac{1}{r}$.

Spear and Srivastava (1987) were the first to state the infinitely repeated moral hazard problem as a recursive problem. Using the first-order approach, they focused on the case of a continuum of possible levels of effort and found many difficulties in the characterization of the optimal contract. They also proved the Markov property of the optimal contract. At a more abstract level, repeated principal-agent relationships are examples of repeated games with strategies based on public information, namely the history of past performances. The earlier contributions to the repeated principal-agent literature were precisely cast in a theoretic game setting. Rubinstein (1979) showed that the first-best effort can also be implemented when agents do not discount the future by the use of so-called *review strategies*. Such a strategy punishes the agent's deviations when he no longer exerts the first-best level of effort if those deviations are *statistically* detectable. Radner (1985) also used review strategies in the case of discounting. These latter papers were not interested in computing the optimal dynamic contract, but they already showed that a repeated relationship could alleviate much of the agency problem. Radner, Maskin, and Myerson (1986) provided an example (involving team production, not a single agent) such that efficiency is lost even when the common discount factor δ goes to one. The general theory of repeated games with public information is due to Fudenberg, Levine, and Maskin (1994). They derived sufficient conditions on the information structure to ensure first-best implementation when δ goes to one. They devoted a whole section to the case of principal-agent models and compared their approach, which was based on dynamic programming, with that used by Radner (1985), Rubinstein (1979), and Rubinstein and Yaari (1983). In the context of insurance against income shocks, i.e., in an adverse selection context, Green (1987), Thomas and Worrall (1990), Atkeson and Lucas (1992), and Phelan (1994) have computed explicit expressions for the value function for some specifications of preferences.   ∎

8.3 Constraints on Transfers: The Role of Implicit Incentives

In section 4.7, we reported the Fama (1980) argument according to which the labor market acts as an incentive instrument and provides managers with incentives to exert optimal effort levels. Indeed, managers want to influence the perception that the market has on their productivity. According to this argument, this desire for good reputation should induce them to perform efficiently and therefore explicit monetary incentives might not be needed. Of course, this argument requires a dynamic model with both a moral hazard ingredient and a signaling ingredient, because the labor market tries to infer the managers' abilities from their past performances.

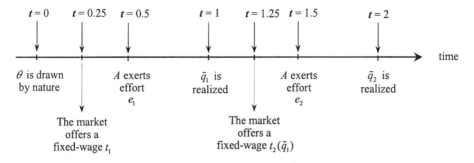

FIGURE 8.5: Timing with Implicit Incentives

Let us sketch such a model. The risk-neutral agent may be of two possible types (or abilities) θ in $\Theta = \{\underline{\theta}, \bar{\theta}\}$, with respective probabilities $1 - \nu$ and ν. For simplicity, we assume that $\bar{\theta} = 1$ and thus $1 > \underline{\theta}$.

There are two periods $t = 1$ and $t = 2$ and no discounting. The agent's output in each period q_i may take two possible values $\underline{q}$ and $\bar{q}$ with respective probabilities $\theta\pi(e_i)$ and $1 - \theta\pi(e_i)$, where e_i is the agent's effort in period i. These outputs yield, respectively, the benefits $\bar{S}$ and $\underline{S}$ to the principal employing the agent in any period. As usual, we denote $\Delta S = \bar{S} - \underline{S}$. The agent's effort e_i may be either 0 or 1 with the usual normalization $\psi(1) = \psi$ and $\psi(0) = 0$.

We assume that there is perfect competition between alternative principals to attract the agent in period 2. Moreover, a first important assumption of the model is that neither the manager nor the principals are informed of the ability of the manager. A second important assumption is that the principals cannot write contracts conditional on the production level. The idea here is that the production level is observable but not contractible. Accordingly, the first-period wage is a fixed wage t_1 while the second-period (fixed) wage can depend on past observation $t_2(q_1)$.

The timing of the model is the one shown in figure 8.5.

Let us start with a benchmark—the case where the agent's effort in each period is observable but his ability remains unknown for both the market and the agent. In this case, the agent exerts a high effort in the first period when

$$(\nu + \underline{\theta}(1 - \nu))\Delta\pi\Delta S \geq \psi. \tag{8.116}$$

This formula is the traditional first-best comparison between the benefit of exerting effort and its cost.[20] However, the information on the agent's productivity is still incomplete, and this criterion must be applied to the average productivity of the agent.

---

[20]See the condition (4.9), for instance.

> **Remark:** Note that the first-best outcome can still be achieved if the principal cannot observe effort but can use explicit incentives with a wage linked to the agent's performance. Indeed, making the risk-neutral agent residual claimant for the profit of the organization achieves the first-best outcome.[21] ∎

Suppose now that effort is nonobservable. We solve the game backward. At date $t = 1.5$, the agent does not exert any effort, $e_2 = 0$, because the labor market offers only a fixed wage independent of the realization of q_2.

Because of perfect competition among principals, in period 2 the fixed-wage $t_2(q_1)$ is such that

$$t_2(q_1) = (v_{\hat{e}}(q_1) + \underline{\theta}(1 - v_{\hat{e}}(q_1)))\pi_0 \overline{S}$$

$$+ (1 - (v_{\hat{e}}(q_1) + \underline{\theta}(1 - v_{\hat{e}}(q_1)))\pi_0)\underline{S}, \qquad (8.117)$$

where $v_{\hat{e}}(q_1)$ is the posterior belief held by the market on the agent's ability after the first-period output has been observed. We make these posterior beliefs explicitly dependent on $\hat{e}$, the market's conjecture about the first-period effort.

It is easy to compute this posterior belief by using Bayes' rule. If the labor market expects that the agent exerts a high effort $\hat{e} = 1$ in the first period, these posterior beliefs are written respectively, as

$$v_1(\bar{q}) = \frac{v\pi_1}{v\pi_1 + (1 - v)\underline{\theta}\pi_1} \qquad (8.118)$$

and

$$v_1(\underline{q}) = \frac{v(1 - \pi_1)}{v(1 - \pi_1) + (1 - v)(1 - \underline{\theta}\pi_1)}.^{22} \qquad (8.119)$$

The agent's incentive constraint that needs to be satisfied in order to induce a high effort in the first period is finally written as

$$(v + (1 - v)\underline{\theta})\Delta\pi(t_2(\bar{q}) - t_2(\underline{q})) \geq \psi. \qquad (8.120)$$

Using (8.117) to (8.119), this condition is rewritten as

$$(v + (1 - v)\underline{\theta})(v_1(\bar{q}) - v_1(\underline{q}))(1 - \theta)\pi_0\Delta\pi\Delta S \geq \psi. \qquad (8.121)$$

---

[21] See section 4.3.
[22] It is easy to check that $v(\bar{q}) > v(\underline{q})$ when $\theta < 1$.

The comparison of (8.116) and (8.121) is straightforward. The term $(v(\bar{q}) - v(\underline{q}))(1 - \theta)\pi_0$ is strictly lower than one, and thus (8.121) is a more stringent condition than (8.116). It is thus harder to incentivize the agent through his desire to build a reputation vis-à-vis the labor market than if he can receive explicit monetary incentives.

Proposition 8.7: *Implicit incentives can only be imperfect substitutes for the explicit monetary incentives obtained with a wage linked to performance.*

Remark: When (8.121) holds, the rational expectation equilibrium we have isolated induces the agent to exert effort, because the market expects this effort and rewards the agent accordingly. It is easy to see that there may exist another rational expectation equilibrium where the market anticipates the fact that the agent exerts no effort and offers second-period wages that fail to incentivize the agent in the first period.

To ensure that such an equilibrium with a low effort exists, it must be that

$$(v + (1 - v)\underline{\theta})(v_0(\bar{q}) - v_0(\underline{q}))(1 - \underline{\theta})\pi_0 \Delta\pi \Delta S < \psi, \qquad (8.122)$$

where $v_0(\bar{q})$ and $v_0(\underline{q})$ are respectively given by

$$v_0(\bar{q}) = \frac{v\pi_0}{v\pi_0 + (1 - v)\underline{\theta}\pi_0} = v_1(\bar{q}) \qquad (8.123)$$

and

$$v_0(\underline{q}) = \frac{v(1 - \pi_0)}{v(1 - \pi_0) + (1 - v)(1 - \underline{\theta}\pi_0)} > v_1(\underline{q}). \qquad (8.124)$$

Hence, $v_0(\bar{q}) - v_0(\underline{q}) < v_1(\bar{q}) - v_1(\underline{q})$, and one can find parameter values of ΔS and ψ, such that (8.121) and (8.122) both hold simultaneously.

This multiplicity of equilibria points to another reason why implicit incentives fail to replace efficiently explicit incentives. ∎

Holmström (1999a) was the first paper to formalize career concerns. Contrary to our model, he assumes a continuum of effort levels, a continuum of performances, a continuum of abilities both normally distributed, and an infinitely repeated relationship. The agent's observable output writes as $y = \theta + e + \varepsilon$, where θ is ability, e is effort, and ε is some noise.[23] He first shows that the agent's effort in the unique rational expectation equilibrium is declining over time. As time passes, the agent's ability gets better known by the market and the agent can no longer affect the perception of the market on his ability by exerting effort. To avoid this phenomenon, Holmström assumes that ability varies over time but with some positive correlation. Dewatripont, Jewitt, and Tirole (1999a) compare various information structures with implicit incentive schemes. Dewatripont, Jewitt, and Tirole (1999b) also propose applications of this framework to incentives in the public sector and stress the existence of multiple equilibria. Gibbons and Murphy (1992) analyze the interplay between explicit and implicit incentives and provide some empirical background on the career concern model. Other nice applications of the implicit incentives paradigm are McLeod and Malcomson (1988b) and Meyer and Vickers (1997) for multiagent organizations. Gibbons (1997) provides an overview of the literature. ∎

---

[23]Note that effort is a perfect substitute for ability.

9   Limits and Extensions

The goal of this concluding chapter is to point out a number of possible extensions of the basic paradigms developed in the preceding chapters. All of these chapters, even though they deal with different kinds of agency costs, have a number of key assumptions in common. These assumptions are

- the absence of private information for the principal,
- the existence of a costless and benevolent court of law that enforces contracts,
- the ability of players to commit to the contract they have signed,
- the signing of the contract taking place before the partners perform any specific investment that is valuable for their relationship,
- the availability of a whole range of verifiable observables that can be used in a contract as screening devices,
- the complete rationality of all players, and
- the exogeneity of the information structures.

We devote one full section to each of those assumptions. Each section is aimed at showing how the standard analysis can be extended in order to relax that assumption. Often these extensions are not the only ones possible. Our purpose is not to be exhaustive and definitive in our treatment of each of the possible perturbations of the basic paradigms. Instead, we view these extensions as indicative of the possible routes that can be pursued beyond the sometimes stringent assumptions made in the previous chapters.

• **Informed principal:** Throughout this book, we have assumed that the principal was never more informed than his agent. In some instances, this assumption is unrealistic. The government may want to elicit the consumer's preferences for a public good, but the government certainly has a better knowledge of the cost of producing this good than taxpayers. In general, mechanism design by an informed principal raises issues difficult to take into account, such as the informational leakage that takes place when the principal already knows his information at the time that he offers a contract to the agent. Those issues are largely outside the scope of the present chapter. However, in section 9.1, we illustrate, using a very simple model of *ex ante* contracting, the role played by the principal's incentive constraint to justify a new allocative inefficiency.

• **Imperfection of the judicial system and limited enforcement:** Implicit in our whole analysis throughout this volume is the fact that a benevolent court of law can costlessly *enforce* the contract signed by the principal and his agent. The lack of perfect ability to enforce contracts would be without any consequence if none of the contractual partners was actually willing to renege on the contractual agreement. However, that cannot be the case if the optimal contract calls for punishing the agent in some states of nature.[1] To ensure the contract enforceability, the court must first be able to verify that an agent has disobeyed the agreed clauses of the contract. Second, the court must also be able to impose punishments on the agent in order to ensure his compliance. Of course, this enforcement system itself is not perfect. Using the judicial system to enforce the contract is obviously costly, and the punishments that can be imposed on the agent are most often limited by the agent's own liabilities. In section 9.2 we present a simple model with adverse selection and *ex ante* contracting that shows that the contractual partners can, without loss of generality, be restricted to offer *enforcement-proof* mechanisms. Under *ex ante* contracting and with a risk-neutral agent, we show how the distortions imposed by an imperfect enforcement can be parameterized by the enforcement technology of the judicial system and the agent's liabilities.

---

[1] Remember that under *ex ante* contracting with either adverse selection (section 2.11.2) or moral hazard (section 4.4) it is optimal to use such punishments.

• **Limits on commitment and renegotiation:** A related point concerns the *lack of commitment* of the agents to the contract. If the judicial system was perfect, it could certainly ensure that the validity of any long-term contract extends over its whole length of duration. However, the judicial system is not perfect. Partners to the contract often renegotiate the terms of the contract if some Pareto-improving new agreement becomes feasible during the course of action. The analysis of chapters 2, 4, and 8 has already shown us how the optimal contract under full commitment requires that the parties to the contract commit themselves to some *ex post* inefficiency in order to ensure *ex ante* optimality.[2] *Ex post*, a Pareto-improving *renegotiation* may be valuable for the contractual partners. Anticipating this renegotiation, agents take actions in the earlier periods of the relationship that reduce *ex ante* optimality. There is a trade-off between *ex post* efficiency and *ex ante* incentives. Therefore, renegotiation puts constraints on any long-term contract. Without loss of generality, the principal can restrict himself to renegotiation-proof contracts. Taking into account a renegotiation-proofness constraint, in section 9.3 we analyze the optimal two-period renegotiation-proof contract, restricting ourselves to deterministic mechanisms. We show that the common discount factor of the agent and the principal plays an important role in determining whether the full separation of types takes place in the initial round of the relationship or a pooling allocation is preferred by the principal.

• **Limits on commitment and the hold-up problem:** In the standard moral hazard paradigm of chapter 4 and in some of the mixed models of chapter 7, the agent's effort is fully anticipated by the principal at the time of contracting. The principal can commit to a set of rewards and punishments that are both necessary to incentivize the agent and to compensate him for his effort. We can instead envision a less perfect contractual setting where the principal and the agent cannot write any contract before the agent performs some specific investment that improves the value of trade. In this mixed model, the principal has no ability to promise any reward to the agent for inducing his costly investment. This lack of commitment may reduce the agent's incentives to invest with respect to the case of full commitment: an instance of *contractual opportunism*. This hold-up problem is analyzed in section 9.4.

• **Limits on the complexity of contracts:** When deriving optimal contracts in various environments, we have put no actual limit on the complexity of the feasible contracts. In most real world settings, contracts take the form of simple linear arrangements. In the absence of any significant and manageable breakthrough in modelling the cost of writing various contingencies in a contract, theorists have

---

[2]See sections 2.12, 4.9, and 8.1.4 for discussions of these trade-offs between *ex ante* and *ex post* optimality.

derived those simple contracts from optimality in highly structured environments. We review two results of the literature that derive optimal linear contracts in section 9.5. First, under adverse selection and with a continuum of possible types, the optimal contract can sometimes be implemented through a *menu of linear contracts*. Second, under moral hazard, some assumptions on the agent's utility function and the observability of his performances may also lead to the optimality of *a single linear contract*.

• **Limits on the verifiability of actions:** In an adverse selection framework, the principal may sometimes be limited in his ability to screen the agent. For instance, the principal might only be interested in buying one unit of goods produced by the agent. Using quantity as a screening variable is not possible. Following the insight of Spence (1973, 1974), the principal and the agent may look for other *screening devices* to avoid the allocative inefficiency associated with such a pooling mechanism. One such signaling device can be for the agent to exert an observable and verifiable effort, the cost of which is correlated with the agent's type. In this chapter we develop a simple model showing how useful these screening devices can be.

A related question concerns the choice among alternative screening instruments when using any of these instruments is costly for the principal. To illustrate this issue in a simple model, we explore when the agent's contract should be based on his input and when it should be based on his output. Section 9.6 deals with these two topics related to the endogenous determination of the principal's screening ability.

• **Limits on rational behavior:** The whole principal-agent relationship has been developed in a framework where agents are fully rational maximizers. There is no doubt that consumers facing the complex nonlinear prices offered by a seller may find difficulties in signing for one or the other of the proposed options. In this case, the agent may fail to optimize within those options and exhibit some irrational behavior. There are lots of possible ways to model a boundedly rational behavior. In section 9.7, we describe two particular ways of modelling bounded rationality that are amenable to slight modifications of the complete contracting framework used throughout the book. In the first way the agent may make some small errors in deciding which contract he should choose within the menu that he receives from the principal. In the second way the agent is not a global optimizer and only compares nearby contracts before making his choice in a menu. Finally, we also touch upon the consequence of introducing communication costs in the realm of incentive theory.

• **Endogenous information structures:** Very recently, a new class of models has been developed to relax the somewhat strong assumption made by incentive theory that information structures are exogenously given to the agents. We present such a model in section 9.8 and show that the standard lessons from incentive theory may require some revisions when information structures are endogenous.

9.1 Informed Principal ⋆

In the basic framework of chapter 2, we have assumed that the uninformed party has all the bargaining power and makes a contractual offer to the privately informed agent. In the case of common value, i.e., where the principal's utility function depends on the state of nature ($V = S(q, \theta) - t$), let us now flip the roles of these two players and assume that the privately informed player makes the contractual offer. To avoid the difficult issues of signaling,[3] we assume that the informed principal makes his contractual offer before he learns the state of nature θ. The timing of this *ex ante* contracting is shown in figure 9.1.

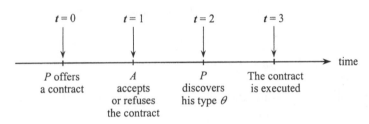

FIGURE 9.1: Timing of *Ex Ante* Contracting with an Informed Principal

The principal now has a utility function $V = S(q, \theta) - t$ for which we assume that the Spence-Mirrlees property $S_{q\theta}(q, \theta) < 0$ is satisfied. The agent gets a payoff $U = u(t - \theta q)$, where $u(\cdot)$ is some increasing and strictly concave utility function ($u' > 0$, $u'' < 0$ with $u(0) = 0$). As usual, θ belongs to $\Theta = \{\underline{\theta}, \bar{\theta}\}$ with respective probabilities ν and $1 - \nu$.

According to the revelation principle, there is no loss of generality in restricting the principal to offer direct revelation mechanisms of the kind $\{(\bar{t}, \bar{q}); (\underline{t}, \underline{q})\}$. For further references, we denote the principal's information rents in both states of nature by $\underline{V} = S(\underline{q}, \underline{\theta}) - \underline{t}$ and $\bar{V} = S(\bar{q}, \bar{\theta}) - \bar{t}$. As usual, we can replace the menu of contracts $\{(\bar{t}, \bar{q}); (\underline{t}, \underline{q})\}$ by the menu of rent-output pairs $\{(\bar{V}, \bar{q}); (\underline{V}, \underline{q})\}$ to perform the optimization of the principal's problem.

---

[3]In doing so we bypass a major difficulty of the informed principal models. However, the analysis of signaling is clearly outside the scope of this volume, because it requires that we manipulate the notion of perfect Bayesian equilibrium. Nevertheless, in remark 1 of this chapter we will touch upon the link between our results that follow and those obtained with signaling models.

The principal being informed of his type *ex post*, any contract that he offers at the *ex ante* stage must satisfy the following incentive constraints of the principal:

$$\underline{V} \geq \overline{V} + \Phi(\bar{q}), \tag{9.1}$$

$$\overline{V} \geq \underline{V} - \Phi(\underline{q}), \tag{9.2}$$

where $\Phi(q) = S(q, \underline{\theta}) - S(q, \bar{\theta})$. Because of the assumptions made on $S(\cdot)$, $\Phi(\cdot)$ is an increasing function of q. Summing these two incentive constraints and using that $\Phi'(\cdot) > 0$, we obtain the monotonicity condition

$$\underline{q} \geq \bar{q}. \tag{9.3}$$

Moreover, because the contract is offered at the *ex ante* stage, the risk-averse agent's *ex ante* participation constraint is written as

$$\nu u(\underline{t} - \underline{\theta}\underline{q}) + (1 - \nu)u(\bar{t} - \bar{\theta}\bar{q}) \geq 0. \tag{9.4}$$

Expressing transfers as functions of the principal's information rents $\underline{V}$ and $\overline{V}$, we obtain

$$\nu u(S(\underline{q}, \underline{\theta}) - \underline{\theta}\underline{q} - \underline{V}) + (1 - \nu)u(S(\bar{q}, \bar{\theta}) - \bar{\theta}\bar{q} - \overline{V}) \geq 0. \tag{9.5}$$

In what follows, we can neglect the principal's *ex ante* participation constraint, because the principal has all the bargaining power at the *ex ante* stage when the contract is offered. The principal's problem can be written as

$$(P): \qquad \max_{\{(\underline{V}, \underline{q}); (\overline{V}, \bar{q})\}} \quad \nu\underline{V} + (1 - \nu)\overline{V}$$

subject to (9.1), (9.2), and (9.5).

Indeed, the principal must maximize his *ex ante* payoff subject to the agent's participation constraint and to his own incentive constraints, ensuring that *ex post*, i.e., once he has learned the state of nature, he will truthfully reveal this state of nature.

Symmetric Information

As a benchmark, let us ignore for a while the incentive constraints (9.1) and (9.2) and solve for the optimal contract under symmetric information. This contract requests efficient production for both types, i.e., $\underline{q}^*$ and $\bar{q}^*$, such that $S_q(\underline{q}^*, \underline{\theta}) = \underline{\theta}$ and $S_q(\bar{q}^*, \bar{\theta}) = \bar{\theta}$. Moreover, this contract provides full insurance to the risk-averse agent. Formally, we must have

$$0 = S(\underline{q}^*, \underline{\theta}) - \underline{\theta}\underline{q}^* - \underline{V}^* = S(\bar{q}^*, \bar{\theta}) - \bar{\theta}\bar{q}^* - \overline{V}^*. \tag{9.6}$$

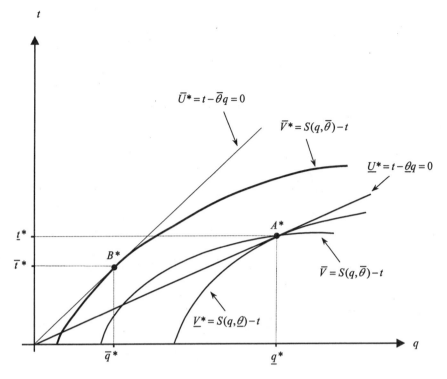

FIGURE 9.2: First-Best Contracts with an Informed Principal

The Spence-Mirrlees property $S_{q\theta} < 0$ ensures that the monotonicity condition always holds for the first-best outputs, i.e., $\underline{q}^* > \bar{q}^*$. In order to make the problem interesting, we assume that the incentive constraint (9.2) is not satisfied by the first-best allocation. Using (9.6), this occurs if $\bar{V}^* - \underline{V}^* = S(\bar{q}^*, \bar{\theta}) - \bar{\theta}\bar{q}^* - (S(\underline{q}^*, \bar{\theta}) - \bar{\theta}\underline{q}^*) < -S(\underline{q}^*, \underline{\theta}) + S(\underline{q}^*, \bar{\theta}) = -\Phi(\underline{q}^*)$, which holds if

$$S(\bar{q}^*, \bar{\theta}) - \bar{\theta}\bar{q}^* < S(\underline{q}^*, \bar{\theta}) - \underline{\theta}\underline{q}^*. \tag{9.7}$$

We have represented the optimal first-best contracts A^* and B^*, offered in the states of nature $\underline{\theta}$ and $\bar{\theta}$, respectively, in figure 9.2. Note that the Spence-Mirrlees property $S_{q\theta} < 0$ ensures that the indifference curve of the $\bar{\theta}$-type crosses the indifference curve of the $\underline{\theta}$-type only once and then has a lower slope, as in figure 9.2. A higher level of utility is obtained when the isoutility curve moves in the southeast direction.

Asymmetric Information

Let us move now to the case of asymmetric information, where only P knows the value of θ. By moving from B^* to A^* when state $\bar{\theta}$ realizes, the principal can increase his expected profit. On the contrary, the principal never wants to offer B^* when he should offer A^* in state $\underline{\theta}$.

The previous analysis suggests that (9.2) is the relevant incentive constraint in problem (P) when (9.7) holds. Denoting the multipliers of (9.2) and (9.5), by λ and μ, respectively, and optimizing with respect to $\underline{V}$ and $\overline{V}$ yields

$$\nu - \lambda - \mu\nu u'\left(S(\underline{q}^{IP}, \underline{\theta}) - \underline{\theta}\underline{q}^{IP} - \underline{V}^{IP}\right) = 0, \tag{9.8}$$

$$1 - \nu + \lambda - \mu(1 - \nu)u'\left(S(\bar{q}^{IP}, \bar{\theta}) - \bar{\theta}\bar{q}^{IP} - \overline{V}^{IP}\right) = 0, \tag{9.9}$$

where the index IP means *informed principal*.

Summing these two equations, we obtain

$$\mu = \frac{1}{\nu u'(\underline{U}^{IP}) + (1 - \nu)u'(\overline{U}^{IP})} > 0, \tag{9.10}$$

where $\underline{U}^{IP} = S(\underline{q}^{IP}, \underline{\theta}) - \underline{\theta}\underline{q}^{IP} - \underline{V}^{IP}$ and $\overline{U}^{IP} = S(\bar{q}^{IP}, \bar{\theta}) - \bar{\theta}\bar{q}^{IP} - \overline{V}^{IP}$ are the agent's payoffs in the different states of nature. Hence (9.5) is necessarily binding at the optimum.

Lastly, we have

$$\lambda = \frac{\nu(1 - \nu)(u'(\overline{U}^{IP}) - u'(\underline{U}^{IP}))}{\nu u'(\underline{U}^{IP}) + (1 - \nu)u'(\overline{U}^{IP})}. \tag{9.11}$$

Because $u(\cdot)$ is concave, λ is positive if and only if $\overline{U}^{IP} < \underline{U}^{IP}$.[4]

Optimizing (P) with respect to outputs yields the second-best outputs, which are such that $\bar{q}^{IP} = \bar{q}^*$, and

$$S_q(\underline{q}^{IP}, \underline{\theta}) = \underline{\theta} - \frac{\lambda\Phi'(\underline{q}^{IP})}{\nu\mu u'(\underline{U}^{IP})}. \tag{9.12}$$

We can summarize our findings in proposition 9.1.

Proposition 9.1: *Assume that the agent is strictly risk averse and that the informed principal makes the contractual offer at the* ex ante *stage. Then, the optimal contract entails the following:*

- *Both the principal's incentive constraint in state $\bar{\theta}$ (9.2) and the agent's* ex ante *participation constraint (9.5) are binding.*
- *No output distortion for the production that is obtained when $\bar{\theta}$ realizes $\bar{q}^* = \bar{q}^{IP}$.*

---

[4]To ensure that $\lambda > 0$, we must check that $\overline{U}^{IP} < 0 < \underline{U}^{IP}$, or equivalently that $S(\underline{q}^{IP}, \underline{\theta}) - \underline{\theta}\underline{q}^{IP} - \underline{V}^{IP} > S(\bar{q}^*, \bar{\theta}) - \bar{\theta}\bar{q}^* - \overline{V}^{IP}$. This yields the condition $S(\bar{q}^{IP}, \bar{\theta}) - \underline{\theta}\underline{q}^{IP} > S(\bar{q}^*, \bar{\theta}) - \bar{\theta}\bar{q}^*$. This condition means that the indifference curve of the principal in state $\bar{\theta}$, which is going through B^*, is above that of the principal going through point C, as can be seen in figure 9.3b. Since C is below A^{IP}, which yields the same utility as B^{IP}, which is itself below B^*, we get the result.

- *An upward distortion for the production that is obtained when $\underline{\theta}$ realizes $\underline{q}^{IP} > \underline{q}^*$, where*

$$S_q(\underline{q}^{IP}, \underline{\theta}) = \underline{\theta} - \frac{(1-\nu)(u'(\overline{U}^{IP}) - u'(\underline{U}^{IP}))\Phi'(\underline{q}^{IP})}{u'(\underline{U}^{IP})}. \qquad (9.13)$$

To understand the results of proposition 9.1, note that the principal's incentive constraint (9.2) in state $\overline{\theta}$ is more easily satisfied when $\overline{V}$ increases, $\underline{V}$ decreases and q increases with respect to the symmetric information optimal contract. Since only the incentive constraint (9.2) is binding, there is no need to distort the production when state $\overline{\theta}$ realizes. Under complete information, full insurance of the risk-averse agent requires zero profit for the agent in each state of nature. Under asymmetric information, the agent now receives a negative (resp. positive) payoff when $\overline{\theta}$ (resp. $\underline{\theta}$) is realized. Doing so increases (resp. decreases) the informed principal's payoff $\overline{V}$ (resp. $\underline{V}$).

These results are represented graphically in figures 9.3a and 9.3b. Keeping the same outputs as under symmetric information but decreasing (resp. increasing) the

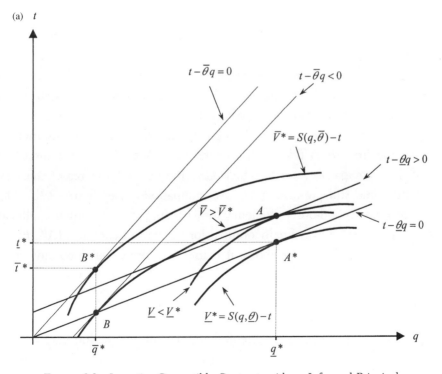

FIGURE 9.3a: Incentive Compatible Contracts with an Informed Principal

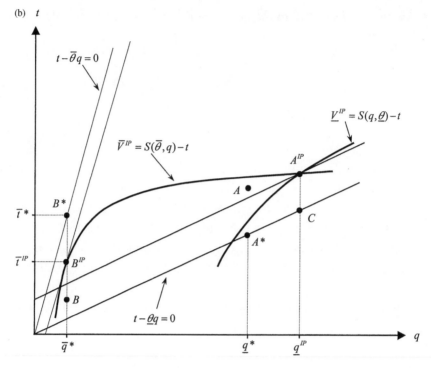

FIGURE 9.3b: Second-Best Contracts with an Informed Principal

principal's payoff when $\underline{\theta}$ (resp. $\bar{\theta}$) realizes, the principal could offer the incentive compatible menu of contracts (A, B).

This menu is incentive compatible because the principal is indifferent between contracts A and B in state $\bar{\theta}$ and strictly prefers A to B in state $\underline{\theta}$. However, this menu imposes too much risk on the agent, who gets a negative payoff when $\underline{\theta}$ occurs and a positive payoff when $\bar{\theta}$ realizes instead. Slightly increasing $\bar{t}$, i.e., moving from B to B^{IP}, while moving from A to A^{IP} on the indifference curve of the principal in state $\bar{\theta}$, which goes through B^{IP}, decreases this risk to the first-order and still preserves incentive compatibility (see figure 9.3b). Doing so only creates a second-order efficiency loss, because $\bar{q}^*$ is maximizing allocative efficiency. This distortion is finally optimal for the pair of contracts (A^{IP}, B^{IP}).

Starting from the analysis above, it is useful to stress two important limiting cases.

Risk Neutrality
Let us assume that the agent is risk neutral and has utility function $u(x) = x$ for all n. Then $u'(x) = 1$ for all x, and (9.11) suggests that $\lambda = 0$. Indeed, with risk neutrality, the first-best outcome can still be implemented by the informed principal.

To see that, consider the following information rents of the principal:

$$\underline{V}^* = v(S(\underline{q}^*, \underline{\theta}) - \underline{\theta}\underline{q}^*) + (1 - v)(S(\bar{q}^*, \bar{\theta}) - \bar{\theta}\bar{q}^*) + (1 - v)\Phi(\underline{q}^*), \quad (9.14)$$

$$\bar{V}^* = v(S(\underline{q}^*, \underline{\theta}) - \underline{\theta}\underline{q}^*) + (1 - v)(S(\bar{q}^*, \bar{\theta}) - \bar{\theta}\bar{q}^*) - v\Phi(\underline{q}^*). \quad (9.15)$$

It is easy to check that (9.1), (9.2), and (9.5) are all satisfied by these information rents of the principal. As a result, the principal's incentive constraints do not conflict with the agent's participation constraint when contracting takes place *ex ante* and the agent is risk neutral. Juxtaposing this insight with the result of section 2.11.1, we can conclude that *ex ante* contracting never entails any allocative inefficiency when both agents are risk neutral, whatever the allocation of bargaining power at the *ex ante* contracting stage.

Infinite Risk Aversion

Let us now assume that the agent is infinitely risk averse below zero wealth and risk neutral above. The *ex ante* participation constraint (9.5) is now replaced by a pair of *ex post* participation constraints, one for each state of nature:

$$\underline{U} = S(\underline{q}, \underline{\theta}) - \underline{\theta}\underline{q} - \underline{V} \geq 0, \quad (9.16)$$

$$\bar{U} = S(\bar{q}, \bar{\theta}) - \bar{\theta}\bar{q} - \bar{V} \geq 0. \quad (9.17)$$

Obviously those two constraints are binding at the optimum of the principal's problem. Inserting the expressions $\underline{V}$ and $\bar{V}$, which are obtained when (9.16) and (9.17) are binding, into the principal's objective leads to the reduced form of the principal's problem:

$$(P'): \qquad \max_{\{(\underline{q}, \bar{q})\}} v(S(\underline{q}, \underline{\theta}) - \underline{\theta}\underline{q}) + (1 - v)(S(\bar{q}, \bar{\theta}) - \bar{\theta}\bar{q}),$$

subject to

$$S(\bar{q}, \bar{\theta}) - \bar{\theta}\bar{q} \geq S(\underline{q}, \bar{\theta}) - \underline{\theta}\underline{q}. \quad (9.18)$$

(9.18) is the principal's incentive constraint when $\bar{\theta}$ is realized, i.e., (9.2) when $\underline{V}$ and $\bar{V}$ have been replaced by their expressions obtained when (9.16) and (9.17) are binding.[5]

The solution to this problem is easy to obtain. There is no output distortion when $\bar{\theta}$ is realized, and again $\bar{q}^{IP} = \bar{q}^*$. Alternatively, there is an output distortion when $\underline{\theta}$ is realized. Since (9.7) holds, and since $S(\underline{q}, \bar{\theta}) - \underline{\theta}\underline{q}$ is decreasing over

---

[5]We will let the reader check that (9.1) is written as $S(\underline{q}, \underline{\theta}) - \underline{\theta}\underline{q} > S(\bar{q}, \underline{\theta}) - \bar{\theta}\bar{q}$ and that it holds strictly for the second-best outputs $(\underline{q}^{IP}, \bar{q}^*)$.

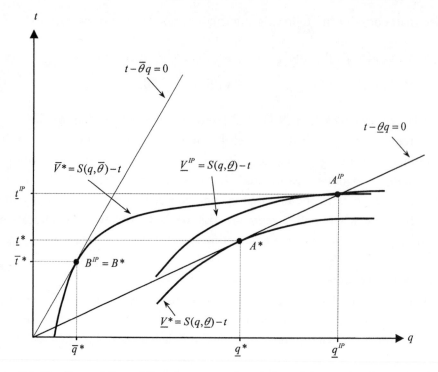

FIGURE 9.4: First-Best and Second-Best Contracts with an Informed Principal and an Infinitely Risk-Averse Agent

the interval $[q^*, +\infty)$,[6] the incentive constraint is satisfied for a whole interval of outputs q in $[\underline{q}^{IP}, +\infty)$, where $\underline{q}^{IP}$ is defined as

$$S(\bar{q}^*, \bar{\theta}) - \bar{\theta}\bar{q}^* = S(\underline{q}^{IP}, \bar{\theta}) - \underline{\theta}\underline{q}^{IP}. \tag{9.19}$$

We can easily check that $\underline{q}^{IP} > \underline{q}^*$. Because $\underline{q}^{IP} > \underline{q}^*$, allocative efficiency is maximized over the interval of incentive compatible outputs by picking $\underline{q}^{IP}$.

   This distortion is represented graphically in figure 9.4, where we see that the full information contracts A^* and B^* lie on the zero-profit lines of the agent for each possible realization of the state of nature. For these contracts, the zero-profit lines are tangent to the principal's indifference curves in each state of nature. Under asymmetric information, the inefficient principal still receives the allocation B^*. The efficient principal instead over-consumes the good and chooses contract A^{IP}. The corresponding output lies at the intersection between the principal's first-best indifference curve in state $\bar{\theta}$ and the agent's zero-profit line when $\underline{\theta}$ realizes. This allocation ensures incentive compatibility, because the principal strictly

---

[6]Indeed, $S_q(q, \bar{\theta}) - \underline{\theta} < S_q(q, \underline{\theta}) - \underline{\theta} < 0$ for $q \geq \underline{q}^*$, where the first inequality comes from $S_{q\theta} < 0$ and the second inequality comes from the fact that $S(q, \underline{\theta}) - \underline{\theta}q$ is strictly concave in q and maximized for $q = \underline{q}^*$.

prefers A^{IP} to B^* in state $\underline{\theta}$ and is indifferent between those two allocations in state $\bar{\theta}$. Moreover, $\underline{q}^{IP}$ is the output closest to $\underline{q}^*$ on the zero-profit line of the agent in state $\underline{\theta}$, such that the principal's incentive compatibility constraint in state $\bar{\theta}$ remains satisfied.

> **Remark 1:** The reader who is knowledgeable in the theory of signaling will probably have recognized the similarity between the second-best outcome obtained above with the so-called *least-costly separating equilibrium* of signaling games. Indeed, let us consider the following game. First, the principal learns the state of nature θ, second, he chooses a "capacity of consumption" q, and third, a competitive market of sellers, the "agent," offers the good to the principal up to his consumption capacity. One can show that this game has different classes of perfect Bayesian equilibria: pooling equilibria where the principal chooses the same capacity in each state of nature and separating equilibria where those capacities are different. Separating equilibria thus reveals the private information learned by the principal to the competitive market. We leave it to the reader to check that those latter equilibria entail over-investment in capacity by the efficient type in order to credibly commit to signal his type to the market.[7] Moreover, the Cho-Kreps *intuitive criterion* selects the *least-costly separating allocation* from among these equilibria, which is precisely the allocation that is obtained when the principal chooses $\bar{q}^{IP}$ in state $\bar{\theta}$, exactly as under *ex ante* contracting (Cho and Kreps, 1987). In our model, the inefficiency of some equilibria of the signaling game can be overcome by writing an *ex ante* contract. However, not all inefficiency disappears even in this case, because incentive compatibility must be preserved. ∎

> **Remark 2:** The allocative inefficiency obtained above is strongly linked to the assumption of common values. Suppose instead that θ does not enter into the agent's utility function, which is thus written as $U = t - q$ for $t - q \geq 0$, $-\infty$ otherwise. Then, it is easy to check that $\underline{t}^* = \underline{q}^*$ and $\bar{t} = \bar{q}^*$ implement the first-best productions. To have inefficiency, we must be in a common value environment. ∎

---

[7]The analogy with a Spencian model of the labor market is straightforward, and the method of resolution used in standard textbooks such as Mas-Colell, Whinston, and Green (1995, chap. 13) can be used to derive these signaling equilibria.

The literature on informed principals is relatively thin but complex. Myerson (1983) and Maskin and Tirole (1990, 1992) are interested in models with *ex post* contracting, i.e., models where the principal offers the contract to the agent once he already knows the state of nature. These models belong to the realm of signaling theory. Maskin and Tirole (1990) offer a noncooperative analysis of the game with private values. They show that the principal's private information had no value in the case of quasi-linear utility functions. With risk aversion, they also show that the perfect Bayesian equilibria of the game are obtained as Walrasian equilibria in an exchange economy among the different types of principal. Maskin and Tirole (1992) analyze a game with common values and show that the perfect Bayesian equilibria of this game could be easily obtained as contracts giving higher payoffs to each type of principal than what they get in the least costly separating allocation.[8] Taking a cooperative perspective, Myerson (1983) shows an *inscrutability principle*, arguing that the principal could always build the revelation of the agent's type into the mechanism itself. He goes on, presenting various concepts of solution, some of them being rather cooperative. Stoughton and Talmor (1990) compare the signaling and the screening distortions in a model of transfer pricing. Finally, Beaudry (1994) analyzes a mixed model where the principal privately knows the distribution of outcomes that the agent may generate by exerting a nonobservable effort. He shows that an informed principal may be willing to leave a rent to his agent, even if the latter is risk neutral, just to signal his information on the technology. Interesting applications of the informed principal framework also arise in the industrial organization literature. In Aghion and Bolton (1987), for instance, a supplier/principal wants to signal a low probability of entry to his buyer/agent by specifying inefficient damages for breach of the exclusive contract. See also Aghion and Hermalin (1990) and Spier (1992) for related arguments. ∎

9.2 Limits to Enforcement

In this volume, we have assumed that the judicial system is perfect and benevolent, and consequently can enforce any contract without cost. Implicit behind this

---

[8]This allocation is often called the Rothschild-Stiglitz-Wilson allocation (see Rothschild and Stiglitz 1976, and Wilson 1977).

enforcement is the use of penalties that prevent both partners from breaching the contract. We now briefly discuss a model of imperfect contractual enforcement.

Consider the model in section 2.11.1 with adverse selection, risk neutrality, and *ex ante* contracting, i.e., the principal offers a contract before the risk-neutral agent discovers its private information. We know that the first-best is then implementable. However, the *ex post* utility level of the agent is negative when $\bar{\theta}$ realizes. For example, for the contract that makes the efficient agent's incentive constraint binding,[9] the inefficient agent's payoff is $\bar{U}^* = \bar{t}^* - \bar{\theta}\bar{q}^* = -\nu\Delta\theta\bar{q}^* < 0$. The inefficient agent may be tempted to renege on the contract proposed by the principal to avoid this negative payoff.

Let us first assume that the judicial system is so inefficient that the principal can never enforce a contract with such a negative payoff. Anticipating this fact, the principal reverts to *self-enforcing* contracts, which are such that both *ex post* participation constraints $\underline{U} = \underline{t} - \underline{\theta}\underline{q} \geq 0$ and $\bar{U} = \bar{t} - \bar{\theta}\bar{q} \geq 0$ are satisfied. In this case, we are in exactly the same situation as if the agent knew his private information at the time of signing the contract. The optimal self-enforcing contract is thus identical to the contract characterized in section 2.6.

The expected loss L^{SB} incurred by the principal because of the complete absence of enforcement can be easily computed as

$$
\begin{aligned}
L^{SB} &= \left(\nu(S(\underline{q}^*) - \underline{\theta}\underline{q}^*) + (1 - \nu)(S(\bar{q}^*) - \bar{\theta}\bar{q}^*)\right) \\
&\quad - \left(\nu(S(\underline{q}^*) - \underline{\theta}\underline{q}^* - \Delta\theta\bar{q}^{SB}) + (1 - \nu)(S(\bar{q}^{SB}) - \bar{\theta}\bar{q}^{SB})\right) \\
&= \underbrace{\nu\Delta\theta\bar{q}^{SB}}_{\text{Rent Loss}} + (1 - \nu)\underbrace{\left((S(\bar{q}^*) - \bar{\theta}\bar{q}^*) - (S(\bar{q}^{SB}) - \bar{\theta}\bar{q}^{SB})\right)}_{\text{Efficiency Loss}} .
\end{aligned}
\tag{9.20}
$$

The expected loss associated with the complete absence of a judicial system that is enforcing contracts is thus composed of two terms: first, the information rent needed to elicit information when the agent's *ex post* participation constraints must be satisfied; and second, the corresponding allocative inefficiency when $\bar{\theta}$ realizes.

Let us now analyze the case where the judicial system can enforce any contract stipulating a negative payoff with some probability p and at a cost $c(p)$. We assume that the cost of enforcement is increasing and convex: $c(0) = 0, c' \geq 0$ (with the Inada conditions $c'(0) = 0$ and $c'(1) = +\infty$), and $c'' > 0$.

A mechanism is *enforcement-proof* if the inefficient agent always finds it optimal to comply and prefers taking the promised rent $\bar{U}$ rather than refusing to produce. If he refuses to comply, the court nevertheless enforces the contract with

---

[9]This contract is the one which maximizes the payoff in the state of nature $\bar{\theta}$.

probability p and imposes a penalty P on the agent.[10] The *enforcement-proofness* constraint is thus written as

$$\bar{U} \geq p(\bar{U} - P) \tag{9.21}$$

or, putting it differently, as

$$\bar{U} \geq -\frac{pP}{1-p}. \tag{9.22}$$

As in our analysis of auditing models made in section 3.6, the monetary punishment P can be either endogenous or exogenous. In the first case, P is bounded above by the value of the agent's assets l plus the latter's information rent

$$P \leq \bar{U} + l. \tag{9.23}$$

In the case of exogenous punishments, P is only bounded by the value of the agent's assets,

$$P \leq l. \tag{9.24}$$

We will focus on exogenous punishments in what follows. When the principal chooses to implement an enforcement-proof mechanism, he solves the following program:

(P): $$\max_{\{(\bar{U},\bar{q});(\underline{U},\underline{q});p\}} \nu\big(S(\underline{q}) - \underline{\theta}\underline{q} - \underline{U}\big) + (1-\nu)\big(S(\bar{q}) - \bar{\theta}\bar{q} - \bar{U} - c(p)\big),$$

subject to (9.22), (9.24), and[11]

$$\underline{U} \geq \bar{U} + \Delta\theta\bar{q}, \tag{9.25}$$

$$\nu\underline{U} + (1-\nu)\bar{U} \geq 0. \tag{9.26}$$

First, note that the principal incurs the cost of the judicial system. Specifically, we assume that the principal pays an amount $(1-\nu)c(p)$ to maintain a judicial system of quality p. Second, the principal's objective function takes into account the fact that the contract is always enforced on the equilibrium path when it is enforcement-proof. Hence, the punishment P is only used as an out-of-equilibrium

---

[10] In fact, only the inefficient agent is willing to renege on the contract, because the efficient agent always gets a positive payoff. Hence, the court and the principal know the agent's type when the latter refuses to enforce the contract.

[11] We neglect the inefficient agent's incentive constraint, which is satisfied, as it can be easily checked *ex post*.

threat to force the inefficient agent's compliance. Of course, the maximal punishment principle already seen in section 3.6 still applies in this context, and the constraint (9.24) is binding at the optimum.

> **Remark 3:** The reader will have noticed that the previous model is somewhat similar to the models of audit discussed in section 3.6. The only difference comes from the role played by the probability of enforcement p. Instead of being used to relax an incentive constraint as the probability of audit does, a greater probability of enforcement relaxes a participation constraint. ∎

It is beyond the scope of this section to analyze all possible regimes that may arise at the optimum. However, note that (9.22) is binding when

$$\nu \Delta \theta \bar{q} > \frac{p}{1-p} l. \tag{9.27}$$

In this case, the agent's information rents in the states of nature $\underline{\theta}$ and $\bar{\theta}$ are respectively given by $\underline{U} = \Delta \theta \bar{q} - \frac{p}{1-p} l$ and $\overline{U} = -\frac{p}{1-p} l$. Inserting those expressions into the principal's objective function and optimizing with respect to $\underline{q}$ and $\bar{q}$ leads to the following expressions of the optimal outputs: $\underline{q}^{EP} = q^*$ and $\bar{q}^{EP} = \bar{q}^{SB}$, where the superscript EP means *enforcement-proof*. These outputs are thus exactly the same as in the case of self-enforcing contracts seen above.

Omitting terms that do not depend on p, the principal finds the optimal probability of enforcement as a solution to the following problem:

(P'):
$$\max_{\{p\}} \frac{pl}{1-p} - (1-\nu)c(p).$$

This objective function is strictly concave with respect to p when $c(\cdot)$ is sufficiently convex. Hence, its maximum is obtained for p^{EP} such that $0 < p^{EP} < 1$, and the value of the maximand is strictly positive, i.e., $\frac{p^{EP} l}{1-p^{EP}} - (1-\nu)c(p^{EP}) > 0$.

The judicial system therefore commits to an optimal probability of enforcement p^{EP}, which is the unique solution to

$$\frac{l}{(1-\nu)(1-p^{EP})^2} = c'(p^{EP}). \tag{9.28}$$

Note also that the probability of enforcement p^{EP} increases with the liability of the agent l when $c(\cdot)$ is sufficiently convex.

Of course, the pair $(\bar{q}^{EP}, p^{EP})$ is really the solution we are looking for when the condition (9.27) holds for p^{EP}, as defined in (9.28). In particular, this condition holds when the marginal cost of enforcing contracts is large enough so that p^{EP} is close enough to zero.

With the optimal enforcement-proof mechanism, the principal obtains an expected payoff:

$$V^{EP} = \nu(S(\underline{q}^*) - \underline{\theta}\underline{q}^*) + (1 - \nu)(S(\bar{q}^{SB}) - \bar{\theta}\bar{q}^{SB}) - \nu\Delta\theta\bar{q}^{SB}$$

$$- (1 - \nu)c(p^{EP}) + \frac{p^{EP}l}{1 - p^{EP}}. \tag{9.29}$$

Compared with the full enforcement outcome, the expected loss L^{EP} incurred by the principal when the judicial system ensures a random enforcement of the contract is written as

$$L^{EP} = L^{SB} - \left\{ \frac{p^{EP}l}{1 - p^{EP}} - (1 - \nu)c(p^{EP}) \right\}. \tag{9.30}$$

The bracketed term is always strictly positive, and therefore $L^{EP} < L^{SB}$. Hence, the principal always finds it optimal to use an enforcement-proof mechanism involving the threat of some random intervention by the judge. Because p^{SB} is strictly positive, the principal does strictly better with an enforcement-proof mechanism than what he can get by writing a self-enforcing contract. Note in particular that the information rent obtained by the inefficient type remains negative, just as in the case of full enforcement.

We summarize this section in proposition 9.2.

Proposition 9.2: *There is no loss of generality in using enforcement-proof contracts. The judicial system is not used on the equilibrium path, but the mere possibility that it could be used improves* ex ante *contracting.*

Laffont and Meleu (2000) analyzed a model similar to the one that we have just presented, but they allowed for endogenous punishments and possibly fixed costs of enforcement. In particular, they observed that self-enforcing contracts may be optimal because of the fixed cost of using the judicial system. Fafchamps and Minten (1999) showed empirically that contracts used in less developed countries (LDC) are designed for low exposure to the breach of contracts. Indeed, low liabilities call for a reduction in the probability of using the judicial system. Krasa and Villamil (2000) analyzed the issue of costly enforcement in the case of financial contracts. ∎

9.3 Dynamics and Limited Commitment

In an intertemporal framework, what is needed for the optimal dynamic contract to be credible is not only the ability of the contractual partners to commit to a contract, but the stronger assumption that those two contractual partners also have the ability to commit not to renegotiate their initial agreement. The assumption that economic agents have the ability to commit not to renegotiate is an extreme assumption about the perfection of the judicial system. Clearly, weakening the assumption that the court of law is perfect implies that, as we know in practice, it is very difficult and often impossible to commit not to renegotiate.

Starting with Dewatripont (1986), the literature has explored the implications of this institutional "imperfection" that corresponds to the agents' inability to commit not to renegotiate. Moving away from the framework of full commitment raises numerous issues, such as how should we model the renegotiation game,[12] how do agents update their beliefs dynamically, and finally how can we characterize implementable allocations.

Below we sketch the nature of the difficulty due to an imperfect commitment in repeated adverse selection models. Take the two-period model of section 8.1.1 and assume now that the principal cannot commit not to renegotiate the long-term agreement he has signed with the agent. The agent knows that any information he might reveal in the first period of the relationship will be fully used by the principal in the second period if a renegotiation is feasible. We assume that the principal still has all the bargaining power at the renegotiation stage, which takes place before the second period output is realized. Let us thus envision two possible classes of renegotiation-proof contracts[13] that give rise to two different classes of implementable allocations.

Separating Contracts

Suppose that, in period 1, the agent behaves differently when $\theta = \underline{\theta}$ then when $\theta = \bar{\theta}$, as is requested by the full commitment optimal contract. The first-period action signals the agent's type perfectly to the principal. The principal is therefore informed of the agent's type when period 2 comes. In particular, if the agent is a $\bar{\theta}$-type, the principal would like to raise allocative efficiency in period 2 by increasing the second-period output while still maintaining the second-period rent, which was promised in the optimal long-term contract with full commitment to the $\underline{\theta}$-type. However, raising allocative efficiency *ex post* has a drawback on the first-period incentives. Indeed, the efficient agent is no longer indifferent between telling the truth or not in the first period. Instead, he would like to lie in order to benefit from the higher rent promised in period 2. Raising *ex post* efficiency

[12]In chapter 6 the reader has seen instances of contracting environments where the allocation of bargaining power may change during the relationship. The same issue arises when one allows for renegotiation.

[13]There is, in the same spirit as in the revelation principle, no loss for the principal to restrict himself to renegotiation-proof contracts. A renegotiation-proofness principle holds in this context.

through the renegotiation procedure hardens first-period incentives. Offering a first-period contract that fully separates both types facilitates information learning in the organization and improves the value of recontracting in period 2. However, this information learning may be quite costly for the principal from a first-period point of view, because he must further compensate the efficient agent for an early revelation of his type. Such a fully separating allocation is robust to the possibility of renegotiation, i.e., is *renegotiation-proof*, if, conditional upon the information learned after the choice of output made in period 1, the principal cannot propose a Pareto-improving second-period contract to the agent.

Let us denote with a subscript i the contract offered at date $t = i$. If the first-period contract fully separates both types, the second-period outputs are efficient in both states of nature[14] and are thus (with our usual notations) given by q^* and $\bar{q}^*$, depending on the agent's type. The efficient agent's intertemporal incentive constraint, which must be satisfied to induce information revelation in period 1, is finally written as

$$\underline{U} \geq \bar{U} + \Delta\theta(\bar{q}_1 + \delta\bar{q}^*), \tag{9.31}$$

where $\Delta\theta\bar{q}_1$ (resp. $\delta\Delta\theta\bar{q}^*$) is the first- (resp. second-) period benefit of a $\underline{\theta}$-agent mimicking the $\bar{\theta}$-agent.

The inefficient agent's intertemporal participation constraint is written as

$$\bar{U} \geq 0. \tag{9.32}$$

With such a separating contract, the principal promises to the efficient (resp. inefficient) agent that he will get a rent $\Delta\theta\bar{q}^*$ (resp. 0) in period 2. Given this initial commitment, coupled with the fact that the principal is fully informed of the agent's type at the renegotiation stage, the principal cannot further raise the second-period *ex post* efficiency, because it is already maximized with outputs q^* and $\bar{q}^*$. Hence, this type of long-term separating contract is clearly renegotiation-proof.

Within the class of contracts that are fully separating and renegotiation-proof, the principal finds the optimal one as a solution to the following problem:

(P^S):
$$\max_{\{(\underline{q}_1, \underline{U}); (\bar{q}_1, \bar{U})\}} \nu\left(S(\underline{q}_1) - \underline{\theta}\underline{q}_1 + \delta(S(q^*) - \underline{\theta}q^*) - \underline{U}\right)$$

$$+ (1 - \nu)\left(S(\bar{q}_1) - \bar{\theta}\bar{q}_1 + \delta(S(\bar{q}^*) - \bar{\theta}\bar{q}^*) - \bar{U}\right),$$

subject to (9.31) and (9.32).

---

[14]Indeed, renegotiation takes place under complete information and leads to an efficient outcome.

We index the solution to this problem with a superscript *RPS*, which means *renegotiation-proof and separating*.

We leave it to the reader to check that (9.31) and (9.32) are the only two binding constraints of the problem above. Optimizing with respect to outputs, we find that the optimal fully separating contract entails no allocative distortion for the efficient type in both periods $\underline{q}_1^{RPS} = q^*$. On the contrary, it entails a downward distortion in the first period only for the inefficient type, i.e., $\bar{q}_1^{RPS} = \bar{q}^{SB} < \bar{q}^* = \bar{q}_2^{RPS}$, where as usual $S'(\bar{q}^{SB}) = \bar{\theta} + \frac{\nu}{1-\nu}\Delta\theta$.

Let us denote by $V(\underline{q}, \bar{q})$ the principal's profit when he implements a pair of outputs $(\underline{q}, \bar{q})$ in a one-period static relationship at minimal cost. We know from chapter 2 that the following equality holds:

$$V(\underline{q}, \bar{q}) = \nu(S(\underline{q}) - \underline{\theta}\underline{q}) + (1 - \nu)\left(S(\bar{q}) - \bar{\theta}\bar{q} - \frac{\nu}{1-\nu}\Delta\theta\bar{q}\right). \tag{9.33}$$

It is easy to check that the intertemporal profit achieved with the optimal fully separating contract can be written as

$$V^S = V(\underline{q}^*, \bar{q}^{SB}) + \delta V(\underline{q}^*, \bar{q}^*). \tag{9.34}$$

Pooling Contracts

Suppose instead that, in period 1, the agent chooses the same behavior, whatever his type θ. In this case, the principal learns nothing from the first-period action. The continuation contract for period 2 should thus be equal to the optimal static contract, conditional on the prior beliefs $(\nu, 1 - \nu)$ since beliefs are unchanged. This contract is well known from chapter 2. Now we index the optimal contract with a superscript *RPP*, which means *renegotiation-proof and pooling*.

First, note that the second-period outputs $\underline{q}_2^{RPP}$ and $\bar{q}_2^{RPP}$ are defined by $\underline{q}_2^{RPP} = q^*$ and $\bar{q}_2^{RPP} = \bar{q}^{SB}$. With a first-period single contract (t, q), which induces full pooling between both types in the first period, the intertemporal incentive constraint of the efficient agent is written as

$$\underline{U} \geq \bar{U} + \Delta\theta(q + \delta\bar{q}^{SB}), \tag{9.35}$$

where $\Delta\theta q$ (resp. $\delta\Delta\theta\bar{q}^{SB}$) is the first- (resp. second-) period benefit of a $\underline{\theta}$-agent from mimicking a $\bar{\theta}$-agent.

The principal's problem, which consists of finding the best long-term contract that induces full pooling in the first period, is then

$(P^P):$
$$\max_{\{(q,\underline{U},\bar{U})\}} \nu\left(S(q) - \underline{\theta}q + \delta(S(\underline{q}^*) - \underline{\theta}\underline{q}^*) - \underline{U}\right)$$
$$+ (1 - \nu)\left(S(q) - \bar{\theta}q + \delta(S(\bar{q}^{SB}) - \bar{\theta}\bar{q}^{SB}) - \bar{U}\right),$$

subject to (9.35) and (9.32).

Again, those latter two constraints are binding at the optimum, and we find that $q_1^{RPP} = \bar{q}^*$. The second-period contract is the optimal static contract computed with prior beliefs, therefore it is obviously renegotiation-proof, i.e., optimal in period 2 given the common knowledge information structure at that date.

The principal's intertemporal profit with a pooling contract now becomes

$$V^P = V(\bar{q}^*, \bar{q}^*) + \delta V(\underline{q}^*, \bar{q}^{SB}). \tag{9.36}$$

By definition of the optimal static contract, we have

$$\max(V(\bar{q}^*, \bar{q}^*), V(\underline{q}^*, \bar{q}^*)) \le V(\underline{q}^*, \bar{q}^{SB}). \tag{9.37}$$

The comparison of V^P and V^S is now immediate.

Proposition 9.3: *There exists $\delta_0 > 0$ such that the principal prefers to offer a separating and renegotiation-proof contract rather than a renegotiation-proof pooling contract if and only if $0 \le \delta \le \delta_0$. We have*

$$\delta_0 = \frac{V(\underline{q}^*, \bar{q}^{SB}) - V(\bar{q}^*, \bar{q}^*)}{V(\underline{q}^*, \bar{q}^{SB}) - V(\underline{q}^*, \bar{q}^*)}. \tag{9.38}$$

This proposition illustrates the basic trade-off faced by the principal under renegotiation. When the future does not count much (δ small), the principal can afford full revelation in the first period without having too much (in discounted terms) to offer for the second period. The separating long-term contract dominates. When the future matters much more (δ large[15]), the principal would like to commit in a renegotiation-proof way so that he can offer the full commitment static solution in the second period. The principal can do so at almost no cost (again in discounted terms) by offering a pooling contract in the first period, because this first period does not count too much. The pooling long-term contract dominates.

> **Remark 1:** The last proposition also provides some insights about the optimal speed of information revelation in the hierarchy, namely the fraction of efficient types who reveal themselves in the first period. This speed is a decreasing function of the discount factor. ∎

---

[15]We consider that δ can be larger than one in order to capture the idea that the second period is much longer than the first period.

Remark 2: The previous analysis has focused on two simple classes of renegotiation-proof mechanisms: fully separating and fully pooling contracts. More generally, it is optimal for the principal to offer a *menu of contracts* in period 1, which induces the efficient agent to randomize between the long-term contract intended for the efficient agent and the long-term contract intended for the inefficient one. The $\bar{\theta}$-agent chooses the latter contract with probability one. Therefore, when the principal observes the agent choosing the contract intended for the efficient agent, he knows that it is the efficient agent who made this choice for sure. When he observes the agent choosing the contract intended for the inefficient agent, the principal is still unsure of the agent's type. Both types of agents may have taken this contract. The principal must *update* his beliefs about the agent's type from the equilibrium strategies of the agent, and he offers the optimal menu of contracts in period 2 conditional on his new beliefs. For an equilibrium to hold, mixing is crucial. The efficient agent must be indifferent between the first-period rent he gets if he reveals his type in period 1, and the sum of the rent he gets in period 1 by mimicking the $\bar{\theta}$-type and of the rent he gets in period 2 by choosing its best element within the menu offered. Inducing randomization by the $\underline{\theta}$-agent is the only way available to "indirectly commit" to leave a rent to the $\underline{\theta}$-agent in period 2. Indeed, leaving a rent in period 2 is *ex post* optimal for a principal who suffers from asymmetric information about the agent's type. As the reader may have guessed from the discussion above, a careful analysis of the optimal contract with renegotiation requires a complex notion of equilibrium involving both dynamic considerations and asymmetric information: the perfect Bayesian equilibrium.[16] ∎

Dewatripont (1989) analyzed long-term renegotiation-proof labor contracts in a T-period environment. The focus was on the choice between separating and pooling mechanisms. Dewatripont (1986) and Hart and Tirole (1988) provided proofs of the *Renegotiation-Proofness Principle*, which allowed the modeller to restrict the principal to offer *renegotiation-proof* long-term contracts. Hart and Tirole (1988) also studied a T-period environment with the quantities traded restricted to $\{0, 1\}$. The main achievement of the paper was to provide an analysis of the process by which information is gradually revealed over time. Laffont and Tirole (1990b) offered

---

[16]The same holds for short-term contracts (one-period commitment).

a complete analysis of the two-period model with randomized strategies and unrestricted quantities. Rey and Salanié (1996) discussed the conditions under which the optimal long-term contract over T periods can be replicated by a sequence of two-period short-term contracts. Bester and Strausz (2001) extended the revelation principle in this context and showed that there is no loss of generality in looking at first-period mechanisms stipulating as many transfers and outputs as the cardinality of the type space even if the agent's first-period strategies are not fully revealing. Crémer (1995) and Dewatripont and Maskin (1995) all analyzed the role of the information structure as a commitment to harden the renegotiation-proofness constraint. ∎

9.4 The Hold-Up Problem

Let us now consider a setting where the agent has to make some initial investment before dealing with the principal. The motivation for this contractual setting is that the agent and the principal can only meet each other after the agent's investment has been made. Such situations are likely to occur in market environments where the trading relationships are only short term.

9.4.1 Nonverifiability and Contracting

Let us return to the mixed model of section 7.3 with the only difference being that effort is chosen by the agent before contracting, as described by the timing of figure 9.5.

The risk-neutral agent may exert his binary effort e at date $t = 1$ to improve the probability that the good state of nature $\underline{\theta}$ realizes. We denote those probabilities by $v(1) = v_1$ and $v(0) = v_0$. $\Delta v = v_1 - v_0 > 0$ is the increase in the probability of having an efficient type when the agent makes a high effort.

In the *hold-up* problem, the principal cannot commit to reward the agent *ex ante* for his nonobservable effort. *Ex post* (i.e., at date $t = 1$), when the principal

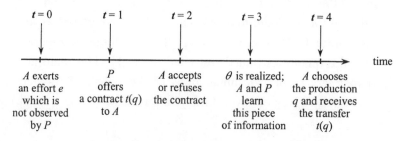

FIGURE 9.5: Timing of the Hold-Up Problem

offers the contract, the agent's effort has already been sunk. The principal has now lost his role as Stackelberg leader in the design of incentives for effort, and so we must look for a Nash equilibrium between the principal and the agent. The principal offers a contract anticipating a particular choice of effort made by the agent. The agent chooses an effort level anticipating the contract he will receive from the principal.

Suppose first that the principal can offer to play a game as in chapter 6. For each value of the effort level $\hat{e}$ chosen by the agent at date $t = 0$, the principal can implement the first-best (conditional on $\hat{e}$) in Nash (or subgame perfect, if needed) equilibrium. From section 7.3, we know that the agent always obtains a zero utility level. Anticipating this, the agent exert no effort at date 0.

We will now describe two modelling options that enable the principal to mitigate the hold-up problem. The first option, which has been the focus of most of the literature, is to assume that contracts cannot be signed[17] at date $t = 1$ and that bargaining between the traders occurs after date $t = 3$, when they have both learned the state of nature θ. The second option is to assume that only the agent is informed about the state of nature before date $t = 1$, so that asymmetric information exists at date $t = 1$, and to maintain the assumption that incentive contracts can be offered at date $t = 1$. In both cases, the principal is obliged to give up a rent to the agent, which indirectly provides the agent with some incentives for effort at date $t = 0$ and mitigates the hold-up problem.

9.4.2 Nonverifiability and Bargaining

Taking the Nash bargaining solution with equal weights to compute their final payoffs, we find that the agent's *ex ante* expected utility writes as $\frac{1}{2}(\nu(e)\underline{W}^* + (1 - \nu(e))\overline{W}^*) - \psi(e)$, where, as usual, $\underline{W}^* = S(\underline{q}^*) - \underline{\theta}\underline{q}^*$ and $\overline{W}^* = S(\bar{q}^*) - \bar{\theta}\bar{q}^*$ denote the first-best gains from trade in each state of nature. Hence, the agent invests if and only if

$$\frac{\Delta\nu}{2}(\underline{W}^* - \overline{W}^*) \geq \psi. \tag{9.39}$$

---

[17]The lack of contract is justified by the assumption that the state of nature is hard to describe in advance, i.e., at the time where the specific investment of the agent should be made (see Hart 1995, pp. 25–26 for an extensive discussion of the hold-up problem). Contracts can only be written once the trading partners have a better idea of the distribution of the states of nature that the agent's investment induces. Note, however, that the agent must anticipate his expected payoff as a function of his effort level in order to choose this effort level.

The first-best condition that ensures that exerting an effort is optimal is $\Delta v(\underline{W}^* - \overline{W}^*) > \psi$. The condition (9.39) may no longer hold when $\frac{\Delta v}{2}(\underline{W}^* - \overline{W}^*) < \psi < \Delta v(\underline{W}^* - \overline{W}^*)$. In this case there is underinvestment, and the hold-up problem prevents efficiency.

Of course, this result can be generalized to other allocations of the bargaining power as long as the agent does not have all the bargaining power *ex post*.

Proposition 9.4: *Assume that the state of nature is nonverifiable and that the agent has only a limited bargaining power in the negotiation over the ex post gains from trade; then an under-investment may occur.*

The intuition behind this proposition is straightforward. Since the agent only receives half of the *ex post* gains from trade, he has only half of the social incentives to exert effort at the ex ante stage. Underprovision of effort follows.[18]

> **Remark:** Simple solutions to this hold-up problem can be found by the contractual partners. First, the *ex post* bargaining power could be fully allocated to the agent, making him residual claimant for the social return to investment. Of course, this solution may not be optimal if the principal also has to invest in the relationship[19] or if the agent is risk-averse, because he would then bear too much risk. Second, let us assume that the principal and the agent can agree *ex ante* on an *ex post* allocation (t_0, q_0), which stipulates the status quo payoffs of both the agent and the principal in the *ex post* bargaining taking place when θ has realized. This contract is relatively simple to write since it stipulates only one transfer and an output. Moreover, we assume that the principal keeps all the bargaining power in the *ex post* bargaining stage. Therefore, he must solve the following problem:
>
> $(P):$ $$\max_{\{(q,\,t)\}} S(q) - t$$
>
> subject to
>
> $$t - \theta q \geq t_0 - \theta q_0, \tag{9.40}$$

---

[18]On this point, see also Grout (1984).

[19]This kind of model requires that both the principal and the agent exert a nonverifiable investment at the *ex ante* stage. They fall in the realm of double moral hazard incentive problems, which are outside the scope of this volume.

where (9.40) is the agent's participation constraint, which is obviously binding at the optimum because the principal wants to reduce the agent's transfer as much as possible.

Since there is complete information *ex post*, the efficient production levels q^* and $\bar{q}^*$ are chosen by the principal depending upon which state of nature is realized. The agent's expected payoff is written as $t_0 - (\nu(e)\underline{\theta} + (1 - \nu(e))\bar{\theta})q_0 - \psi(e)$ when he exerts effort e. The agent exerts a positive effort when q_0 is fixed, so that $\Delta\nu\Delta\theta q_0 = \psi$. The status quo output q_0 therefore defines the agent's marginal incentives to invest. Then, t_0 can be adjusted so that the agent's expected utility is zero, i.e., $t_0 = (\nu_1\underline{\theta} + (1 - \nu_1)\bar{\theta})q_0 + \psi$. The principal's expected payoff becomes $\nu_1\underline{W}^* + (1 - \nu_1)\overline{W}^* - \psi$, exactly as in a world of complete contracts.[20]   ∎

This very nice solution to the hold-up problem is due to Chung (1991). Various other solutions have been found in the incomplete contracts literature. See Tirole (1999) for an exhaustive survey of this literature. Another way to solve the hold-up problem, at least partially, that is well developed in the literature is to allocate property rights. The analysis of this literature is beyond the scope of the present volume, but a few general ideas are worth stressing here. The general framework to analyze the role of property rights on the assets is due to Grossman and Hart (1986) and Hart and Moore (1990) (see also Hart 1995). Property rights are usually incomplete contracts. Indeed, property rights define what can be obtained by the agents in the status quo of the *ex post* Nash bargaining over the gains from trade. In general, the literature envisions double moral-hazard problems, where both the buyer and the seller must perform a specific investment in the relationship and compares the performances of various ownership structures. A major result of this literature is that complementary assets should be owned by the same person (see Hart 1995). Maskin and Tirole (1999) provide conditions such that allocating property rights implements the optimal contract.   ∎

9.4.3 Adverse Selection

Let us assume now that the agent is informed about θ before date $t = 1$, when the principal offers him an incentive contract.

---

[20]Since the principal is residual claimant for the social surplus, this procedure would also induce him to invest efficiently if he could affect the probability $\nu_1(e_p)$ by some costly effort e_p. Hence, this procedure works better than simply allocating all the bargaining power to the agent.

Let us denote by ν_e the conjecture of the principal over the probability that type $\underline{\theta}$ realizes. Using the results of chapter 2, the *best-response* of the principal is thus characterized by an output distortion (for the inefficient type only) $\bar{q}(\nu_e)$, which is defined by

$$S'(\bar{q}(\nu_e)) = \bar{\theta} + \frac{\nu_e}{1 - \nu_e} \Delta\theta, \tag{9.41}$$

and a positive information rent (for the efficient type only) given by $\underline{U}(\nu_e) = \Delta\theta\bar{q}(\nu_e)$. Note that $\bar{q}(\nu_e)$ and $\underline{U}(\nu_e)$ are both decreasing with ν_e.

Anticipating such a contract, and more specifically the rent $\Delta\theta\bar{q}^e$ he will get when he turns out to be efficient, the agent invests in increasing this probability according to the following best response $e = 1$ if $\Delta\nu\Delta\theta\bar{q}^e > \psi$, $e = 0$ if $\Delta\nu\Delta\theta\bar{q}^e < \psi$, and e in $\{0, 1\}$ if $\Delta\nu\Delta\theta\bar{q}^e = \psi$.

Putting together the principal and the agent's best responses yields the following characterization of the Nash equilibrium contract and effort in this framework without any commitment.

Proposition 9.5: *Assume that the principal cannot commit to a contract before the agent exerts effort. Then, the equilibrium allocation is characterized as follows:*

- *If $\Delta\theta\bar{q}(\nu_1) > \frac{\psi}{\Delta\nu}$, the agent exerts a positive effort and $\bar{q}(\nu_1)$ is chosen by the principal.*
- *If $\Delta\theta\bar{q}(\nu_0) < \frac{\psi}{\Delta\nu}$, the agent does not exert any effort and $\bar{q}(\nu_0)$ is chosen by the principal.*
- *If $\Delta\theta\bar{q}(\nu_1) \leq \frac{\psi}{\Delta\nu} \leq \Delta\theta\bar{q}(\nu_0)$, the agent randomizes between exerting effort or not with respective probabilities ε and $1 - \varepsilon$. We have $\nu_e = \varepsilon\nu_1 + (1 - \varepsilon)\nu_0$ and $\Delta\theta\bar{q}(\nu_e) = \frac{\psi}{\Delta\nu}$.*

When $\frac{\psi}{\Delta\nu} \geq \Delta\theta\bar{q}(\nu_1)$, underinvestment occurs with respect to the case with full commitment that we have already discussed in section 7.2.3.[21] Again, the logic underlying this result is simple. The agent only receives a share (his information rent) of the overall surplus of production which occurs in period 4; hence he may not have enough incentives to exert effort.

Riordan (1990) used the hold-up model under adverse selection as an ingredient of a theory of vertical integration. Laffont and Tirole (1993, chap. 1) analyzed how cost-reimbursement rules must be adapted to

---

[21] Recall that in this section we made the assumption that the principal's benefit from inducing a high effort was large enough.

protect the specific investment of regulated firms. Schmidt (1996) used the underinvestment model presented in this section to build a theory of privatization. In this theory, the cost of public ownership is the inability of the state to reward a specific investment made at the *ex ante* stage by the public utility.

∎

9.5 Limits to the Complexity of Contracts ★

In most of this book, we have deliberately chosen to emphasize simple models, where shocks are discretely distributed both in the case of adverse selection and moral hazard. However, the analysis in appendices 3.1 and 4.2 also suggests that optimal contracts may have very complex shapes in the richer case where those shocks are continuously distributed. This complexity has often been viewed as a failure of contract theory to capture the simplicity of real world contracting environments. We now illustrate in this section how incentive theory can be reconciled with this observed simplicity, provided that the contractual environment is sufficiently structured.

9.5.1 Menu of Linear Contracts under Adverse Selection

Let us reconsider the optimal contract obtained in appendix 3.1, in the case of a continuum of types distributed according to the cumulative distribution $F(\cdot)$ with density $f(\cdot)$ on the interval $[\underline{\theta}, \bar{\theta}]$. Let us slightly generalize the framework of that appendix and also assume that the agent has a cost function $\theta c(q)$ where $c' > 0$ and $c'' > 0$ with the Inada condition $c'(0) = 0$. This extension is straightforward and we leave it unsolved as an exercise for the reader. The optimal second-best production levels $q^{SB}(\theta)$ under asymmetric information are characterized by

$$S'(q^{SB}(\theta)) = \left(\theta + \frac{F(\theta)}{f(\theta)}\right) c'(q^{SB}(\theta)).^{22} \qquad (9.42)$$

When the monotone hazard rate property is satisfied, namely $\frac{d}{d\theta}\left(\frac{F(\theta)}{f(\theta)}\right) \geq 0$, the schedule of output $q^{SB}(\theta)$ is invertible. Let $\theta^{SB}(q)$ be its inverse function. The transfer $t^{SB}(\theta)$ paid to the agent is such that

$$t^{SB}(\theta) - \theta c(q^{SB}(\theta)) = \int_{\theta}^{\bar{\theta}} c(q^{SB}(x)) \, dx, \qquad (9.43)$$

where the right-hand side above is θ-type's information rent $U(\theta)$.

---

[22]The Inada condition on $c(\cdot)$ ensures that $q^{SB}(\theta)$ is always positive, even when we assume that $S'' = 0$ as we do later in this section.

Instead of using the truthful direct revelation mechanism $\{(t^{SB}(\theta), q^{SB}(\theta))\}$, the principal could give up any communication with the agent and let him choose an output directly, within a nonlinear schedule $T^{SB}(q)$. This procedure is basically the reverse of the revelation principle; it is sometimes called the taxation principle.[23] To reconstruct the indirect mechanism $T^{SB}(q)$ from the direct mechanism $\{(t^{SB}(\theta), q^{SB}(\theta))\}$ is rather easy. Indeed, we must have $T^{SB}(q) = t^{SB}(\theta^{SB}(q))$.

When he faces the nonlinear payment $T^{SB}(q)$, the agent replicates the same choice of output as with the direct revelation mechanism $\{(t^{SB}(\theta), q^{SB}(\theta))\}$. Indeed, we have $\dot{T}^{SB}(q) = \dot{t}^{SB}(\theta^{SB}(q))\dot{\theta}^{SB}(q)$, and thus

$$\dot{T}^{SB}(q^{SB}(\theta)) = \frac{\dot{t}^{SB}(\theta)}{\dot{q}^{SB}(\theta)}, \qquad \text{for any } \theta \text{ in } [\underline{\theta}, \bar{\theta}]. \tag{9.44}$$

Differentiating (9.43) with respect to θ immediately yields $\dot{t}^{SB}(\theta) = \theta c'(q^{SB}(\theta))\dot{q}^{SB}(\theta)$.[24] Inserting it into (9.44), we obtain

$$\dot{T}^{SB}(q^{SB}(\theta)) = \theta c'(q^{SB}(\theta)), \tag{9.45}$$

which is precisely the first-order condition of the agent's problem when he chooses an output within the nonlinear schedule $T^{SB}(\cdot)$.

It is important that the agent's choice can be implemented with a nonlinear payment $T^{SB}(\cdot)$. However, in practice, one often observes menus of linear contracts to choose from. This is the case, for instance, in the relationship between regulatory agencies and regulated firms or the relationship between a buyer and a seller.[25]

To obtain an implementation of the second-best outcome with a menu of linear contracts, we need to be able to replace the nonlinear schedule $T^{SB}(q)$ by the menu of its tangents. The slope of the tangent at a given point $q^{SB}(\theta)$ is the same as that of $T^{SB}(q)$ at this point. Hence, the type θ agent's marginal incentives to deviate away from $q^{SB}(\theta)$ are the same with both mechanisms. Moreover, the tangent also has the same value as $T^{SB}(q)$ at $q^{SB}(\theta)$. Hence, the nonlinear schedule $T^{SB}(\cdot)$ and its menu of tangents provide the agent with the same information rent. This equivalence is nevertheless only possible when $T^{SB}(q)$ is in fact *convex*. Figure 9.6 represents this case.

[23] See Guesnerie (1995) and Rochet (1985).
[24] The reader will have recognized the first-order condition associated with the fact that truth-telling is an optimal strategy for the agent with type θ when he faces the truthful direct revelation mechanism $\{(t^{SB}(\theta), q^{SB}(\theta))\}$.
[25] Wilson (1993) argues that a menu with very few linear contracts can almost replicate the performances of a more complex nonlinear price.

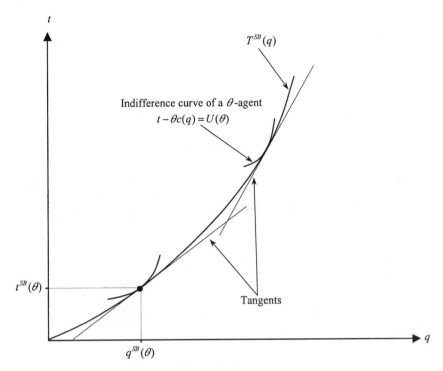

FIGURE 9.6: Convexity of the Nonlinear Schedule $T^{SB}(q)$

Let us thus derive the conditions ensuring this convexity. Differentiating (9.45), we obtain

$$\ddot{T}^{SB}(q^{SB}(\theta)) = \frac{c'(q^{SB}(\theta))}{\dot{q}^{SB}(\theta)} + \theta c''(q^{SB}(\theta)), \qquad (9.46)$$

where $\dot{q}^{SB}(\theta)$ is obtained by differentiating (9.42) with respect to θ. Now we find that

$$\frac{\dot{q}^{SB}(\theta)}{c'(q^{SB}(\theta))} = \frac{1 + \frac{d}{d\theta}\left(\frac{F(\theta)}{f(\theta)}\right)}{S''(q^{SB}(\theta)) - \frac{c''(q^{SB}(\theta))S'(q^{SB}(\theta))}{c'(q^{SB}(\theta))}}. \qquad (9.47)$$

Inserting this latter expression into (9.46), we get

$$\ddot{T}^{SB}(q^{SB}(\theta)) = c''(q^{SB}(\theta))\left(\theta + \frac{\frac{S''(q^{SB}(\theta))}{c''(q^{SB}(\theta))} - \left(\theta + \frac{F(\theta)}{f(\theta)}\right)}{1 + \frac{d}{d\theta}\left(\frac{F(\theta)}{f(\theta)}\right)}\right)$$

$$= \frac{c''(q^{SB}(\theta))}{\left(1 + \frac{d}{d\theta}\left(\frac{F(\theta)}{f(\theta)}\right)\right)}\left(\theta\frac{d}{d\theta}\left(\frac{F(\theta)}{f(\theta)}\right) - \frac{F(\theta)}{f(\theta)} + \frac{S''(q^{SB}(\theta))}{c''(q^{SB}(\theta))}\right). \qquad (9.48)$$

Now we obtain proposition 9.6.

Proposition 9.6: *Assume that $\frac{F(\theta)}{\theta f(\theta)}$ is increasing with θ and that $S''(q) = 0$ for all q. Then, $T^{SB}(\cdot)$ is convex and can be implemented with the menu of its tangents.*

Indeed, let us now consider the menu of tangents to $T^{SB}(\cdot)$. The equation of the tangent $T(\cdot, q_0)$ to $T^{SB}(\cdot)$ at a point q_0 can be obtained as

$$T(q, q_0) = T^{SB}(q_0) + \dot{T}^{SB}(q_0)(q - q_0). \tag{9.49}$$

Facing the family of linear contracts $\{T(\cdot, q_0)\}$, the agent has now to choose which tangent is its most preferred one and what output to produce according to that contract. Therefore, the agent solves

(P):
$$\max_{\{(q, q_0)\}} T(q, q_0) - \theta c(q).$$

Substituting $T(q, q_0)$ with its expression coming from (9.49), the first-order conditions for this problem are, respectively,

$$\dot{T}^{SB}(q_0) = \theta c'(q) \tag{9.50}$$

and

$$\ddot{T}^{SB}(q_0)(q - q_0) = 0. \tag{9.51}$$

If these necessary conditions are also sufficient, the agent with type θ chooses $q = q_0 = q^{SB}(\theta)$. The sufficiency of (9.50) and (9.51) is guaranteed when $T(q, q_0) - \theta c(q)$ is concave in (q, q_0). Computing the corresponding Hessian H of second-order derivatives at the point $(q^{SB}(\theta), q^{SB}(\theta))$ yields

$$H = \begin{pmatrix} -\theta c''(q^{SB}(\theta)) & \ddot{T}^{SB}(q^{SB}(\theta)) \\ \ddot{T}^{SB}(q^{SB}(\theta)) & -\ddot{T}^{SB}(q^{SB}(\theta)) \end{pmatrix}. \tag{9.52}$$

This Hessian is strictly definite-negative when $\ddot{T}^{SB}(q^{SB}(\theta)) > 0$ (i.e., if $T^{SB}(\cdot)$ is convex as already assumed) and $\ddot{T}^{SB}(q^{SB}(\theta))(\theta c''(q^{SB}(\theta)) - \ddot{T}^{SB}(q^{SB}(\theta))) > 0$, but the latter condition is satisfied, as can easily be seen by using (9.46).

> **Remark:** Note that if the principal observes only a random signal of q, say $q + \tilde{\varepsilon}$, where $\tilde{\varepsilon}$ is a random variable with zero mean ($E(\tilde{\varepsilon}) = 0$), the menu of linear contracts still implements the same allocation. Indeed, the random variable $\tilde{\varepsilon}$ disappears in the incentive problem of the risk-neutral agent by the linearity of the expectation operator. Hence, the menu of linear contracts is robust to the addition of some noise. ∎

The implementation of the optimal contract with the menu of its tangents has been extensively used in the field of regulation by Laffont and Tirole (1986, 1993) and Rogerson (1987). Caillaud, Guesnerie, and Rey (1992) survey various extensions of these results and in particular its robustness when the observation of production is noisy. On this latter point, see also Melumad and Reichelstein (1989). ∎

9.5.2 Linear Sharing Rules and Moral Hazard

Moral hazard environments can also have enough structure to let the linearity of contracts emerge at the optimum. To see that, we now consider a twice-repeated version of the model of section 5.3.2 without discounting. Thus the agent has a utility function $U = u(t - \psi(e))$, which is defined over monetary gains, and the disutility of effort is counted in monetary terms. We assume constant risk aversion, so that $u(x) = -\exp(-rx)$ for some $r > 0$. Note that $u(0) = -1$. We denote the outcome of the stochastic production function in period i by q_i. These realizations are independently distributed over time. In each period, the agent can exert a binary effort e in $\{0, 1\}$ with a monetary cost normalized so that $\psi(1) = \psi$ and $\psi(0) = 0$. We assume that only the whole history of outputs can be used by the principal to remunerate the agent. Given a history (q_1, q_2), the agent receives a transfer $t(q_1, q_2)$ only at date $t = 3$ (see figure 9.7 for a timing of the game after the offer of the contract by the principal and its acceptance by the agent). Because there are two possible outputs in each period, the number of possible histories, and thus the number of final transfers $t(q_1, q_2)$, is $2 \times 2 = 4$.

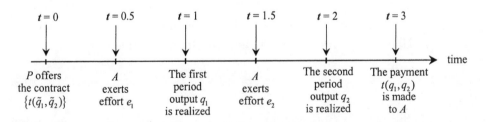

FIGURE 9.7: Timing of the Contractual Game.

The logic underlying this model is that the principal can only incentivize the agent at the end of the working period (date $t = 3$), but the agent has to choose an effort at dates $t = 0.5$ and $t = 1.5$.[26]

---

[26]Note the difference with the repeated moral hazard problem of section 8.3, where a monetary transfer is also given at the end of date 1, once the first-period output has already been observed.

Let us denote the agent's value function from date $t = 0.5$ on by U_1, i.e., his expected payoff if he exerts a positive effort in each period. We have

$$U_1 = \underset{(\tilde{q}_1, \tilde{q}_2)}{E} (u(t(\tilde{q}_1, \tilde{q}_2) - 2\psi)), \qquad (9.53)$$

where $E_{(\tilde{q}_1, \tilde{q}_2)}(\cdot)$ denotes the expectation operator with respect to the distribution of histories induced by the agent exerting a high effort in both periods. Note that with the agent's disutility of effort being counted as a monetary term, one must subtract the total cost of efforts along the whole history to evaluate the net monetary gain of the agent.

Using that $u(x) = -\exp(-rx)$ and the Law of Iterated Expectations, we obtain

$$U_1 = \exp(r\psi)\underset{\tilde{q}_1}{E}(U_2(\tilde{q}_1)), \qquad (9.54)$$

where $U_2(q_1) = E_{\tilde{q}_2}(u(t(q_1, \tilde{q}_2) - \psi))$ is actually the agent's value function from exerting a positive effort in period 2 following an output q_1 at date $t = 1$.

Using the certainty equivalents (denoted by $w_2(q_1)$) of the random continuation monetary gains $t(q_1, \tilde{q}_2) - \psi$, we can in fact rewrite $U_2(q_1) = u(w_2(q_1))$. Hence, inserting this into (9.54), we obtain $U_1 = E_{\tilde{q}_1}(u(w_2(\tilde{q}_1) - \psi))$.

Inducing effort at date $t = 0.5$ requires that the following incentive constraint be satisfied:

$$U_1 = -\pi_1 \exp(-r(w_2(\bar{q}) - \psi)) - (1 - \pi_1) \exp(-r(w_2(\underline{q}) - \psi))$$
$$\geq -\pi_0 \exp(-rw_2(\bar{q})) - (1 - \pi_0) \exp(-rw_2(\underline{q})). \qquad (9.55)$$

Similarly, inducing participation from date $t = 0.5$ on requires that the agent gets more utility than by refusing to work and obtaining a zero wealth certainty equivalent. Hence, the agent's participation constraint is written as

$$U_1 \geq -1. \qquad (9.56)$$

From the analysis of section 5.3.2, the pair of certainty equivalents $\{(w_2(\bar{q}), w_2(\underline{q}))\}$ belongs to the set of incentive feasible transfer pairs $\{(\bar{t}, \underline{t})\}$ that induce effort and participation, with the agent being given a zero wealth outside opportunity in the static model of section 5.3.2. Let us denote by $F(0)$ the set of incentive feasible transfers defined by the constraints in (5.83) and (5.84). We have thus $w_2(\bar{q}) = \bar{t}_1$ and $w_2(\underline{q}) = \underline{t}_1$ for some pair $(\bar{t}_1, \underline{t}_1)$, which belongs to $F(0)$.

Let us now move to date $t = 1.5$. Following a first-period output q_1, the agent knows then that he will receive the certainty equivalent $w_2(q_1)$. Hence, the following participation constraint is satisfied: $U_2(q_1) = -\exp(-rw_2(q_1))$. To induce effort at date $t = 1.5$ following a first-period output q_1, it must be that the following incentive constraints (which are dependent on q_1) are also satisfied:

$$U_2(q_1) = -\pi_1 \exp(-r(t(q_1, \bar{q}) - \psi)) - (1 - \pi_1) \exp(-r(t(q_1, \underline{q}) - \psi))$$

$$\geq -\pi_0 \exp(-rt(q_1, \bar{q})) - (1 - \pi_0) \exp(-rt(q_1, \underline{q})). \tag{9.57}$$

Immediate observation shows that the pair of transfers $\{(t(q_1, \bar{q}), t(q_1, \underline{q}))\}$ must belong to the set of incentive feasible transfers inducing effort and participation in the static model of section 5.3.2 when the agent has an outside opportunity leaving him a wealth certainty equivalent $w_2(q_1)$.

From remark 2 in section 5.3.2, we know that we can write those transfers as $t(q_1, \bar{q}) = w_2(q_1) + \bar{t}_2$, and $t(q_1, \underline{q}) = w_2(q_1) + \underline{t}_2$, where the pair $\{(\bar{t}_2, \underline{t}_2)\}$ belongs, as $\{(w_2(\bar{q}), w_2(\underline{q}))\}$, to $F(0)$. Hence, the overall transfers $t(\tilde{q}_1, \tilde{q}_2)$ are the *sum* of two contracts belonging to $F(0)$. This property constitutes a significant reduction of the space of useful contracts.

Using the fact that shocks in each period are independently distributed, the principal's problem now becomes:

(P): $\displaystyle\max_{\{(\bar{t}_1, \underline{t}_1); (\bar{t}_2, \underline{t}_2)\}} \pi_1^2 (2\bar{S} - \bar{t}_1 - \bar{t}_2) + \pi_1(1 - \pi_1)(2\bar{S} + 2\underline{S} - \bar{t}_1 - \underline{t}_1 - \bar{t}_2 - \underline{t}_2)$

$$+ (1 - \pi_1)^2 (2\underline{S} - \underline{t}_1 - \underline{t}_2)$$

subject to $\{(\bar{t}_i, \underline{t}_i)\}$ in $F(0)$ for $i = 1, 2$.

It is apparent that the optimal solution to this problem is the twice replica of the solution $(\bar{t}^{SB}, \underline{t}^{SB})$ to the static problem discussed in section 5.3.2. We immediately obtain the linearity of the optimal schedule.

Proposition 9.7: *The optimal sharing rule $t^{SB}(\tilde{q}_1, \tilde{q}_2)$ is linear in the number of successes or failures of the production process. We have:* $t^{SB}(\bar{q}, \bar{q}) = 2\bar{t}^{SB}$, $t^{SB}(\bar{q}, \underline{q}) = t^{SB}(\underline{q}, \bar{q}) = \bar{t}^{SB} + \underline{t}^{SB}$, *and* $t^{SB}(\underline{q}, \underline{q}) = 2\underline{t}^{SB}$.

This result obviously generalizes to $T \geq 2$ periods and more than two outcomes. Understanding this linearity result requires us to return to the main features of the solution to the static problem of section 5.3.2. The CARA specification for the agent's utility function implies the absence of any wealth effect. The wage as well as the cost of effort in period 1 (which is counted in monetary terms) are sunk from the point of view of period 2 and have no impact on the incentive pressure that is then needed to induce effort. This incentive pressure is exactly the same as in a static one-shot moral hazard problem. Therefore, the principal views periods 1 and 2 as equivalent, in terms of both the stochastic processes generating output in each period and the incentive pressure needed to induce effort. The principal offers the same contract in each period, and the overall sharing rule, based only on the whole history of outputs up to date $t = 2$, is linear in the number of successes and failures.

Assume now that there are $T \geq 2$ periods. Then, following the same logic as above, the transfer associated with n successes and $T - n$ failures only depends on the total production and not on the dates at which these successes and failures take place. More precisely, when we denote the common value of these transfers by $t^{SB}(\cdot)$ we get $t^{SB}(n\bar{q} + (T - n)\underline{q}) = n\bar{t}^{SB} + (T - n)\underline{t}^{SB}$, where n is the number of successes. When we denote by X the aggregate output in the T-Bernoulli trials, where at each date $\bar{q}$ is obtained with probability π_1 and $\underline{q}$ is obtained with probability $1 - \pi_1$, we have $X = n\bar{q} + (T - n)\underline{q}$ and

$$t^{SB}(X) = \underbrace{T\left(\underline{t}^{SB} - \underline{q}\left(\frac{\bar{t}^{SB} - \underline{t}^{SB}}{\bar{q} - \underline{q}}\right)\right)}_{\text{Fixed-Fee}} + \underbrace{\left(\frac{\bar{t}^{SB} - \underline{t}^{SB}}{\bar{q} - \underline{q}}\right)X}_{\text{Marginal Incentives}}. \qquad (9.58)$$

This relationship shows that the sharing rule between the principal and the agent is linear in X. However, in the analysis above, the fixed-fee in (9.58) becomes infinitely large as T goes to infinity. Holmström and Milgrom (1987) solved this difficulty by using a continuous time model where in each period the agent controls the drift of a Brownian process. Typically, on an infinitesimal interval of time $[t, t + dt]$, the aggregate output $q(t)$ up to date t jumps up only by a term proportional to the effort performed during the interval of length dt plus some noise. More precisely, $q(t + dt) - q(t) - edt$ is the sum of dt independently and identically distributed random variables with a mean of zero. The aggregate output is a unidimensional Brownian motion that follows the stochastic differential equation

$$dq = edt + \sigma^2 dB, \qquad (9.59)$$

where B is a unidimensional Brownian motion with unit variance, and e is the agent's effort on the interval $[t, t + dt]$.[27]

In the continuous time model presented here, the principal can only use the overall aggregate output $q(1) = q$ at the end of a $[0, 1]$ interval of time to incentivize the agent. Note that (9.59) holds on all intervals $[t, t + dt]$ and that the principal offers the same incentive pressure on each of those infinitesimal intervals so that effort is constant over time. Hence, the aggregate output $q(1)$ is a normal variable with mean e and variance σ^2. Holmström and Milgrom (1987, 321) show that the optimal contract is a linear contract $t(q) = a + bq$. Then, the agent's final

---

[27] Dixit and Pyndick (1994) provide a nice introduction to Brownian motions and stochastic calculus for economists.

wealth is also a normal variable with mean $a + be$ and variance $b^2\sigma^2$. Because the agent has constant absolute risk aversion, his certainty equivalent income w_e is such that

$$\exp(-rw_e) = \int_{-\infty}^{+\infty} \exp(-r(a + bq - \psi(e))) \frac{\exp\left(-\frac{(q-e)^2}{2\sigma^2}\right)}{\sqrt{2\pi\sigma^2}}\, dq,$$

where $\exp(-\frac{(q-e)^2}{2\sigma^2})/\sqrt{2\pi\sigma^2}$ is the density of the normal distribution with mean e and variance σ^2. We easily find that[28]

$$w_e = a + be - \psi(e) - \frac{rb^2\sigma^2}{2}. \tag{9.60}$$

When the agent's disutility of effort is quadratic, i.e., $\psi(e) = \frac{e^2}{2}$, the sufficient and necessary condition for the optimal choice of effort is $e = b$. The fixed-fee a can be set so that the agent's certainty equivalent income is zero and thus $a = (r\sigma^2 - 1)\frac{e^2}{2}$.

The risk-neutral principal's expected payoff can be computed as

$$\int_{-\infty}^{+\infty} (q - t(q)) \frac{\exp\left(-\frac{(q-e)^2}{2\sigma^2}\right)}{\sqrt{2\pi\sigma^2}}\, dq = (1 - b)e - a. \tag{9.61}$$

The principal's problem is thus written in a reduced form as follows:

$(P):$
$$\max_{\{b,a,e\}} (1 - b)e - a,$$

subject to

$$b = e \text{ and } a = (r\sigma^2 - 1)\frac{e^2}{2}.$$

Replacing b and a with their values as functions of e, the principal's problem can be reduced to

$(P'):$
$$\max_{\{e\}} e - \frac{e^2}{2}(1 + r\sigma^2).$$

---

[28]To compute this certainty equivalent, we use the identity

$$\int_{-\infty}^{+\infty} \exp\left(-\alpha x - \frac{x^2}{2\sigma^2}\right) \frac{dx}{\sqrt{2\pi\sigma^2}} = \exp\left(\frac{\sigma^2\alpha^2}{2}\right),$$

for any α.

Optimizing, we easily find the second-best effort e^{SB}:

$$e^{SB} = \frac{1}{1 + r\sigma^2} < 1 = e^{FB}, \tag{9.62}$$

where e^{FB} is the first-best level of effort.

It is interesting to note that, as the index of absolute risk aversion increases, the second-best effort is further distorted downward. Similarly, as the output becomes a less informative measure of the agent's effort, i.e., as σ^2 increases, this effort is also reduced. These insights were already highlighted by our basic model in chapter 4.[29]

The Holmström and Milgrom (1987) model can be extended to the case of a multidimensional Brownian process that corresponds to the case where the agent's output is multidimensional and to the case of a multidimensional effort as we show below. Schättler and Sung (1993) showed that a time-dependent technology calls for the optimal contract to be nonlinear. Sung (1995) showed that the optimal contract can still be linear when the agent controls the variance of the stochastic process. Hellwig and Schmidt (1997) proposed further links between the discrete and the continuous time model. Lastly, Bolton and Harris (1997) generalized the Brownian motion. Diamond (1998b) proposed a static model with limited liability, risk neutrality and three possible outcomes; linearity emerges because the agent has a rich set of choices in the distribution of these outcomes. More generally, it is also worth stressing that the linearity of contracts may be imposed when the principal must prevent arbitrage or resale among his agents. ∎

Once the Holmström-Milgrom framework is accepted, i.e., the CARA utility function, the Brownian motion of output whose drift is affected by effort, transfers depending only on the final aggregate output, the analysis is made very easy because contracts can be taken to be linear, and these linear contracts can be developed in many directions. Below we give an example of an interesting use of the model.

A Multitask Illustration

The model above with a CARA utility function and a normal distribution of the performance is also useful when analyzing multitask agency models. To see that, let us assume that the agent exerts a vector of effort $e = \begin{pmatrix} e_1 \\ e_2 \end{pmatrix}$ for the principal. The disutility of effort is written as $\psi(e)$, where $\psi(\cdot)$ is convex. To make things simpler we will assume that $\psi(\cdot)$ is a quadratic form, and we will write $\psi(e) = \frac{1}{2}e'\psi e$ for

---

[29]See section 4.4.

some semidefinite positive and symmetric matrix

$$\psi = \begin{pmatrix} \psi_{11} & \psi_{12} \\ \psi_{12} & \psi_{22} \end{pmatrix}.$$

We denote $\Phi = \psi^{-1}$ as the inverse matrix that is also symmetric. Contrary to the model of section 5.2.3, the disutility of effort is counted in monetary terms. Each of these efforts affects the mean of a random variable $\tilde{q}_i$ in the following manner:

$$\tilde{q}_i = e_i + \tilde{\varepsilon}_i, \tag{9.63}$$

where $\tilde{\varepsilon}_i$ is a random variable. We will denote the vector of performances by $q = \begin{pmatrix} q_1 \\ q_2 \end{pmatrix}$. The vector of random variable $\tilde{\varepsilon} = \begin{pmatrix} \tilde{\varepsilon}_1 \\ \tilde{\varepsilon}_2 \end{pmatrix}$ is normally distributed with a zero mean and a covariance matrix given by

$$\Sigma = \begin{pmatrix} \sigma_1^2 & \sigma_{12} \\ \sigma_{12} & \sigma_2^2 \end{pmatrix}.$$

Let us thus write the optimal linear contract offered by the principal as $t(q_1, q_2) = a + b_1 q_1 + b_2 q_2$ or, using the inner product,

$$t(q) = a + b'q. \tag{9.64}$$

With this type of linear contract, the agent gets a certainty equivalent income w_e such that

$$\exp(-rw_e) = \int_{-\infty}^{+\infty} \exp\left(-r\left(a + b'q - \frac{1}{2}e'\psi e\right) - \frac{1}{2}(q - e)'\Sigma^{-1}(q - e)\right)$$

$$\times \frac{dq}{(2\pi \det \Sigma)^{1/2}}. \tag{9.65}$$

Using the moment generating function,[30] we find that

$$w_e = a + b'e - \frac{1}{2}e'\psi e - \frac{r}{2}b'\Sigma b. \tag{9.66}$$

Optimizing (9.66) with respect to e yields the agent's response to any linear contract. We obtain the following incentive constraints:

$$b = \psi e. \tag{9.67}$$

---

[30]The moment generating function of a random variable $\tilde{x}$ is $M_{\tilde{x}}(s) = \int_{-\infty}^{+\infty} \exp(sx)dF(x)$, where $F(\cdot)$ is the distribution of x. Standard results in statistics show that, for a multivariate, normally distributed random variable such that $x \sim N(\mu, \Sigma)$, the moment generating function writes as $M_{\tilde{x}}(s) = \exp\left(s'\mu + \frac{1}{2}s'\Sigma s\right)$. We apply this formula to get (9.66).

This yields the following expression of the certainty equivalent income of the agent:

$$w_e = a - \frac{r}{2}b'\Sigma b + \frac{1}{2}b'\Phi b. \tag{9.68}$$

Of course, this certainty equivalent income must be positive in order to provide the agent with at least his outside opportunity.

The risk-neutral principal benefits from the sum of the performances on each particular task. The principal's expected payoff is written as

$$\int_{-\infty}^{+\infty} (q_1 + q_2 - t(q_1, q_2)) \exp\left(-\frac{1}{2}(q-e)'\Sigma^{-1}(q-e)\right) \frac{dq}{2\pi(\det \Sigma)^{1/2}}. \tag{9.69}$$

Expressing this term, we find an expected payoff for the principal of $(\mathbb{1}' - b')e - a$, where $\mathbb{1}' = (1, 1)$ is the line vector having all of its components equal to one.

We can finally write the principal's problem as:

(P): $$\max_{\{b,a,e\}} (\mathbb{1}' - b')e - a$$

subject to (9.67) and (9.68).

Of course, these two constraints are binding at the optimum, and we can rewrite the principal's problem in reduced form as

(P'): $$\max_{\{b\}} \mathbb{1}'\Phi b - \frac{r}{2}b'\Sigma b - \frac{1}{2}b'\Phi b.$$

This problem is concave in b, and the second-best vector of optimal marginal incentives is obtained as a solution to

$$b^{SB} = (Id + r\Sigma\psi)^{-1} \mathbb{1}, \tag{9.70}$$

where

$$Id = \begin{pmatrix} 1 & 0 \\ 0 & 1 \end{pmatrix}$$

is the identity matrix.

The matrix $\Sigma\psi$, which is computed from the technology and the informativeness of the different signals, plays a significant role in determining the second-best marginal incentives and the optimal effort.[31] This matrix measures the discrepancy between second-best and first-best incentives.

---

[31] See Holmström and Milgrom (1991) for further details.

As an example, let us assume that efforts are imperfect substitutes, with $\psi_{11} = \psi_{22} = 1 > \psi_{12}$, and off-diagonal terms of Σ are all equal to zero. Then, the values of the marginal incentives are given by

$$b_1^{SB} = \frac{1 + r\sigma_2^2(1 - \psi_{12})}{1 + r(\sigma_1^2 + \sigma_2^2) + r^2\sigma_1^2\sigma_2^2(1 - \psi_{12}^2)}, \tag{9.71}$$

$$b_2^{SB} = \frac{1 + r\sigma_1^2(1 - \psi_{12})}{1 + r(\sigma_1^2 + \sigma_2^2) + r^2\sigma_1^2\sigma_2^2(1 - \psi_{12}^2)}. \tag{9.72}$$

Assume for instance that $\sigma_2 = \infty$ to capture the fact that the performance $\tilde{q}_2$ may not be observable at all by the principal. Then we have

$$b_1^{SB} = \frac{1 - \psi_{12}}{1 + r\sigma_1^2(1 - \psi_{12}^2)}, \tag{9.73}$$

$$b_2^{SB} = 0. \tag{9.74}$$

It becomes impossible to reward the hardly observable task $\tilde{q}_2$, and so all incentive pressure is put on the first task.[32] This points to the complementarity between rewarding different substitute tasks in a second-best environment that we already stressed in the bare-bones model of section 5.2.5. On this, see also Holmström and Milgrom (1994).

9.6 Limits in the Action Space ★

Let us now come back to an adverse selection context. Our goal in this section is to understand how one can possibly endogenize the action space used to contract with the agent.

9.6.1 Extending the Action Space

We start with a highly stylized model of procurement between a principal (the buyer) and an agent (the seller). We assume that the agent's marginal cost θ belongs to $\Theta = \{\underline{\theta}, \bar{\theta}\}$ with respective probabilities ν and $1 - \nu$. Let us also suppose that the principal desires only one unit of the good and has a valuation S for this unit. In this setting, the only screening variable available is the set of types with whom the principal wants to contract. If the price of the unit is $\underline{\theta}$, only the efficient agent produces and the principal gets $\nu(S - \underline{\theta})$. If the price is instead $\bar{\theta}$, both types

---

[32] In the extreme case where tasks are perfect substitutes, i.e., where $\psi_{12} = 1$, $b_1^{SB} = 0$, and the first task also becomes impossible to incentivize.

of agent produce and the principal gets instead $v(S - \underline{\theta}) + (1 - v)(S - \bar{\theta}) - v\Delta\theta$. Having both types producing is thus optimal when $v(S - \underline{\theta}) < v(S - \underline{\theta}) + (1 - v)(S - \bar{\theta}) - v\Delta\theta$, i.e., when

$$S - \bar{\theta} > v(S - \underline{\theta}). \tag{9.75}$$

When (9.75) holds, there is no screening between both types.[33]

Let us now consider the case where the seller can signal his type θ through the choice of a positive quality s. One can think of this quality as some after-sales services offered by the seller to the buyer.[34] To produce a signal with quality s, the seller must incur a cost $c(s, \theta) = \frac{s^2}{2\theta}$ for $s \geq 0$. For the sake of the proof, we will also assume that there exists an upper bound, $s_{\max}$, on s.

Note that the technologically inefficient agent produces a high-quality signal more easily than the efficient one, because $c_{s\theta}(s, \theta) = -\frac{s}{\theta^2} < 0$.[35] This Spence-Mirrlees property has the opposite sign of that obtained by taking cross-derivatives with respect to type and production.[36]

In this context, the signaling stage can be incorporated into the contract. A direct revelation mechanism stipulates a transfer $t(\tilde{\theta})$ and a quality $s(\tilde{\theta})$ as a function of the agent's announcement of their type. A truthful direct revelation mechanism is thus a pair $\{(\underline{t}, \underline{s}); (\bar{t}, \bar{s})\}$, which satisfies the incentive constraints

$$\underline{U} = \underline{t} - \underline{\theta} - \frac{\underline{s}^2}{2\underline{\theta}} \geq \bar{U} + \Delta\theta + \frac{\bar{s}^2}{2\bar{\theta}} - \frac{\bar{s}^2}{2\underline{\theta}}, \tag{9.76}$$

$$\bar{U} = \bar{t} - \bar{\theta} - \frac{\bar{s}^2}{2\bar{\theta}} \geq \underline{U} - \Delta\theta + \frac{\underline{s}^2}{2\underline{\theta}} - \frac{\underline{s}^2}{2\bar{\theta}}, \tag{9.77}$$

and the standard participation constraints

$$\underline{U} \geq 0, \tag{9.78}$$

$$\bar{U} \geq 0. \tag{9.79}$$

By adding the incentive constraints (9.76) and (9.77), we obtain the implementability condition

$$\bar{s} \geq \underline{s}. \tag{9.80}$$

---

[33] The reader will have recognized a condition similar to the one obtained in section 2.6.3, when we analyzed the issue of shutdown.

[34] To simplify the analysis, we assume that quality is not valued by the consumer.

[35] Implicit here is the idea that agents who produce efficiently have more difficulty providing after-sales services.

[36] This new feature of the agent's preferences may introduce the possibility of countervailing incentives. However, we will choose parameter values below so that this case does not arise.

We will focus on the case where (9.76) and (9.79) remain the two binding constraints, despite the fact that $c_{s\theta} < 0$. This will be the case as long as $\Delta\theta > \frac{\bar{s}^2}{2}(\frac{1}{\underline{\theta}} - \frac{1}{\bar{\theta}})$ or $\bar{s} \leq (2\underline{\theta}\bar{\theta})^{\frac{1}{2}}$.[37] In this case, the principal's problem becomes

$$(P): \quad \max_{\{(\underline{s},\underline{U});(\bar{s},\bar{U})\}} \nu\left(S - \underline{\theta} - \frac{\underline{s}^2}{2\underline{\theta}} - \underline{U}\right) + (1 - \nu)\left(S - \bar{\theta} - \frac{\bar{s}^2}{2\bar{\theta}} - \bar{U}\right),$$

subject to (9.76) and (9.79).

These two constraints are binding at the optimum, and the principal's problem is rewritten as

$$(P'): \quad \max_{\{\underline{s},\bar{s}\}} \nu\left(S - \underline{\theta} - \Delta\theta - \frac{\underline{s}^2}{2\underline{\theta}} + \frac{\bar{s}^2\Delta\theta}{2\underline{\theta}\bar{\theta}}\right) + (1 - \nu)\left(S - \bar{\theta} - \frac{\bar{s}^2}{2\bar{\theta}}\right).$$

The objective function is strictly concave in $\underline{s}$ and maximized at $\underline{s}^{SB} = 0$. Things are rather different for $\bar{s}$. Two cases must be distinguished. For $\nu\bar{\theta} < \underline{\theta}$, the objective function is also concave in $\bar{s}$ and maximized at $\bar{s}^{SB} = 0$. The signal is not used, and the decision to have both types producing is taken with the criterion (9.75).

For $\nu\bar{\theta} > \underline{\theta}$, the objective function is now convex and increasing in $\bar{s}$. It is thus maximized for

$$\bar{s}^{SB} = s_{\max}. \tag{9.81}$$

In this case, the benefit of inducing a positive signal by the inefficient agent to relax the efficient agent's incentive constraint in (9.76) exceeds the physical cost of the signal.

The condition for having both types producing the good now becomes

$$S - \bar{\theta} + \frac{s_{\max}^2}{2\bar{\theta}\underline{\theta}}(\nu\bar{\theta} - \underline{\theta}) > \nu(S - \underline{\theta}), \tag{9.82}$$

which is easier to satisfy than (9.75), because $\nu\bar{\theta} - \underline{\theta} > 0$.

To conclude, the costly signal reduces the informational gap between the principal and his agent; it may be used to induce more production than in its absence, and therefore it increases efficiency.

Spence (1974) was the first to use this idea to elicit agents' productivities from their education level in his Signaling Theory. Maggi and Rodriguez-Clare (1995b) presented a model that is closely related to the one shown here. In their model, the principal can observe, on top of output,

---

[37] We will assume that $s_{\max} \leq (2\bar{\theta}\underline{\theta})^{1/2}$ to avoid countervailing incentives.

a noisy signal $\theta + s$ on the agent's marginal cost. This signal is provided to improve incentives. However, the agent manipulates this observable by playing on the noise s at a cost. Countervailing incentives may arise from the fact that the Spence-Mirrlees property may no longer be satisfied. ∎

9.6.2 Costly Action Space

When a principal-agent problem is defined, some variables are assumed to be verifiable, and contracts can be conditioned on those variables. For example, in our canonical models of chapters 2 and 4 it is assumed that the production level is contractible because it is observable and verifiable by a court of law. However, observability and verifiability are generally costly, and one may have the choice of observing and verifying more or less variables. In our basic adverse selection model, we have potentially two observables, the production level q and the *ex post* cost $C = C(q, \theta)$. Suppose that there is a fixed cost of observing either q or C. If both C and q are observed by the principal, he can perfectly infer the value of θ and achieve the first-best. This outcome is assumed to be too costly because of these fixed costs. In our canonical model, we have assumed that q is observed but that C is not observed. In this case, an information rent must be given up to the agent, and this calls for a distortion in the inefficient type's production level.

On the contrary, if C is observed and not q, let $q = Q(\theta, C)$ be the solution in q of the equation $C = C(\theta, q)$. Then the principal's problem is written as:

(P): $\quad \max_{\{(\underline{C},\underline{t});(\bar{C},\bar{t})\}} \nu(S(Q(\underline{\theta}, \underline{C})) - \underline{t}) + (1 - \nu)(S(Q(\bar{\theta}, \bar{C})) - \bar{t}),$

subject to

$$\underline{t} - \underline{C} \geq \bar{t} - \bar{C}, \tag{9.83}$$

$$\bar{t} - \bar{C} \geq \underline{t} - \underline{C}, \tag{9.84}$$

$$\underline{t} - \underline{C} \geq 0, \tag{9.85}$$

$$\bar{t} - \bar{C} \geq 0. \tag{9.86}$$

The incentive constraints (9.83) and (9.84) imply $\underline{t} - \underline{C} = \bar{t} - \bar{C}$. Both participation constraints are also binding, and the problem reduces to

(P'): $\quad \max_{\{\underline{C}, \bar{C}\}} \nu(S(Q(\underline{\theta}, \underline{C})) - \underline{C}) + (1 - \nu)(S(Q(\bar{\theta}, \bar{C})) - \bar{C}).$

The corresponding first-order conditions of this problem are

$$S'(q) \cdot Q_C(\underline{\theta}, \underline{C}) = 1, \tag{9.87}$$

$$S'(\bar{q}) \cdot Q_C(\bar{\theta}, \overline{C}) = 1. \tag{9.88}$$

Taking into account that $Q_C(\theta, C) = \frac{1}{C_q(q,\theta)}$, we find that the optimal outputs $\underline{q}^*$ and $\bar{q}^*$ are efficient

$$S'(\underline{q}^*) = C_q(\underline{q}^*, \underline{\theta}), \tag{9.89}$$

$$S'(\bar{q}^*) = C_q(\bar{q}^*, \bar{\theta}). \tag{9.90}$$

The principal can thus implement the first-best outputs without giving up any rent. Indeed, observing costs makes it possible to adjust the transfers in order to leave no rent. However, in this case the agent is indifferent between telling the truth and not telling the truth and, as usual, we break this indifference by assuming that he reveals the truth to the principal.

This is a spectacular example, where the choice of the right observable enables the principal to achieve the first-best outcome. However, note that the costs of observing q or C have a priori no reason to be identical.

The literature has studied the comparison of regulation by the output or regulation by the input more generally (see Maskin and Riley 1985, Crampes 1986, Khalil and Lawarrée 1995, and Bontemps and Bourgeon 2000). The levels of information rent are affected by the choice of the contractible variables. ∎

9.7 Limits to Rational Behavior

Even though incentive theory has been developed under the standard assumption that all players are rational, it can take into account whatever bounded rationality assumption one may wish to choose.[38] However, there is an infinity of possible theories of bounded rationality and, in each case, the modeller must derive specific optimal contracts. Let us consider a few examples that allow us to introduce bounded rationality without perturbing the basic lessons of incentive theory too much.

9.7.1 Trembling-Hand Behavior

Let us come back to the canonical model of chapter 2. We will assume that the agent is *ex ante* rational when he accepts the contract but makes a mistake with

---

[38]In what follows, we restrict the principal to offer a menu of contracts having the same dimensionality as the number of types.

some probability when he chooses the contract *ex post*. *Ex ante* rationality implies that the agent anticipates the impact of these future errors on his expected utility at the time of acceptance.

This possibility of an *ex post* irrational behavior only matters for the efficient type when the size of the mistakes is small enough. Recall that, in the standard solution to chapter 2, only the efficient type is indifferent between taking his contract and taking the contract of the inefficient type. The inefficient agent strictly prefers his contract and will continue to do so as long as mistakes are small enough.

Let us denote by ε the error term in the efficient agent's choice. The latter agent chooses the contract $(\underline{t}, \underline{q})$ when

$$\underline{U} \geq \bar{U} + \Delta\theta\bar{q} + \varepsilon, \tag{9.91}$$

i.e., with probability $G(\underline{U} - \bar{U} - \Delta\theta\bar{q})$, where $G(\cdot)$ is the cumulative distribution of ε on some centered interval $[-\bar{\varepsilon}, \bar{\varepsilon}]$. The density of this random variable is denoted by $g(\cdot)$ with $g(0) > 0$. Moreover, we will assume that the monotone hazard rate property $\frac{d}{d\varepsilon}\left(\frac{G(\varepsilon)}{g(\varepsilon)}\right) > 0$ is satisfied. When $\bar{\varepsilon}$ is less than $\Delta\theta\underline{q}$, the inefficient agent does not make any error and chooses the right contract with probability one. His acceptance is thus ensured when

$$\bar{U} \geq 0.^{39} \tag{9.92}$$

The principal's problem then becomes

(P):
$$\max_{\{(\bar{U},\bar{q});(\underline{U},\underline{q})\}} \nu G(\underline{U} - \bar{U} - \Delta\theta\bar{q})(S(\underline{q}) - \underline{\theta}\underline{q} - \underline{U})$$

$$+ \left(1 - \nu G(\underline{U} - \bar{U} - \Delta\theta\bar{q})\right)(S(\bar{q}) - \bar{\theta}\bar{q} - \bar{U}),$$

subject to (9.92).

Introducing $\hat{\varepsilon}$ as the greatest value of ε such that the efficient type's incentive constraint (9.91) is binding, this problem is rewritten

(P'):
$$\max_{\{(\hat{\varepsilon},\bar{q},\underline{q})\}} \nu G(\hat{\varepsilon})(S(\underline{q}) - \underline{\theta}\underline{q} - \Delta\theta\bar{q} - \hat{\varepsilon}) + (1 - \nu G(\hat{\varepsilon}))(S(\bar{q}) - \bar{\theta}\bar{q}),$$

since (9.92) is necessarily binding at the optimum.

---

[39] The efficient agent's participation constraint is instead

$$G(\underline{U} - \bar{U} - \Delta\theta\bar{q})\underline{U} + (1 - G(\underline{U} - \bar{U} - \Delta\theta\bar{q}))(\bar{U} + \Delta\theta\bar{q}) \geq 0.$$

Again, when $\bar{\varepsilon}$ is small enough this participation constraint is strictly satisfied and can be omitted in the analysis.

We index the optimal contract by a superscript BR, meaning *bounded ratio-nality*.

Proposition 9.8: *With a trembling-hand behavior, the optimal contract entails no output distortion for the efficient type, $q^{BR} = q^*$, and a downward distortion for the inefficient type, $\bar{q}^{BR} < \bar{q}^*$, such that*

$$S'(\bar{q}^{BR}) = \bar{\theta} + \frac{\nu G(\hat{\varepsilon}^{BR})}{1 - \nu G(\hat{\varepsilon}^{BR})} \Delta\theta, \qquad (9.93)$$

where $\hat{\varepsilon}^{BR}$ is given by

$$S(\underline{q}^*) - \underline{\theta}\underline{q}^* - (S(\bar{q}^{BR}) - \underline{\theta}\bar{q}^{BR}) = \hat{\varepsilon}^{BR} + \frac{G(\hat{\varepsilon}^{BR})}{g(\hat{\varepsilon}^{BR})}. \qquad (9.94)$$

Because $\bar{q}^{BR} < q^*$, the left-hand side of (9.94) is strictly positive. This left-hand side is the difference between the first-best surplus and what would be obtained if the efficient agent had made a mistake and taken the contract of an inefficient one. Since $G(\cdot)$ satisfies the monotone hazard rate property, $\varepsilon + \frac{G}{g}(\varepsilon)$ is increasing and $\hat{\varepsilon}^{BR}$ is uniquely defined. For an interior solution such that $G(\hat{\varepsilon}^{BR}) < 1$, everything happens as if the efficient type was less likely. The rent differential $\Delta\theta\bar{q}$ given up to the efficient agent is less costly than in a model with no mistake. Hence, $\bar{q}^{BR} > \bar{q}^{SB}$, and the output distortion is less important than without the mistake.

> **Remark:** The reader will have recognized the similarity of this section with the model of section 3.4. There, random decisions did not affect the efficient type's incentive constraint, but instead they affected the inefficient type's participation constraint. ∎

9.7.2 Satisficing Behavior

Consider a three-type example along the lines of section 3.1 with a general cost function $C(q, \theta)$. The incentive constraints of the three types are written respectively as

$$\underline{t} - C(\underline{q}, \underline{\theta}) \geq \hat{t} - C(\hat{q}, \underline{\theta}) \qquad (9.95)$$

$$\geq \bar{t} - C(\bar{q}, \underline{\theta}) \qquad (9.96)$$

$$\hat{t} - C(\hat{q}, \hat{\theta}) \geq \underline{t} - C(\underline{q}, \hat{\theta}) \qquad (9.97)$$

$$\geq \bar{t} - C(\bar{q}, \hat{\theta}) \qquad (9.98)$$

$$\bar{t} - C(\bar{q}, \bar{\theta}) \geq \hat{t} - C(\hat{q}, \bar{\theta}) \tag{9.99}$$

$$\geq \underline{t} - C(\underline{q}, \bar{\theta}). \tag{9.100}$$

Suppose that the agent has a *satisficing behavior* and only looks at the nearby contracts, which are ordered as $\{(\underline{t}, \underline{q}); (\hat{t}, \hat{q}); (\bar{t}, \bar{q})\}$. Starting from an initial contract choice that may be suboptimal, the agent moves to another contract choice if the nearby contract yields a higher payoff.

Then it is immediately apparent that, if the Spence-Mirrlees property is satisfied, the agent will discover the optimal contract for him, and, neglecting temporary misallocations, the theory can proceed as if the agent was fully rational.[40] Indeed, whatever his initial choice in the menu, he will move in the right direction in this set.

For example, let us take the case where $C(q, \theta) = \theta q$. If the agent has type $\bar{\theta}$ and starts from the contract $(\underline{t}, \underline{q})$, he moves to $(\hat{t}, \hat{q})$ if and only if $\hat{t} - \bar{\theta}\hat{q} \geq \underline{t} - \bar{\theta}\underline{q}$, which can be rewritten as $\hat{t} - \hat{\theta}\hat{q} \geq \underline{t} - \hat{\theta}\underline{q} + \Delta\theta(\hat{q} - \underline{q})$. This last inequality holds, because both $\hat{q} \leq \underline{q}$ and the $\hat{\theta}$-incentive compatibility constraint $\hat{t} - \hat{\theta}\hat{q} \geq \underline{t} - \hat{\theta}\underline{q}$ are satisfied. In a second step of the tâtonnement process, the $\bar{\theta}$-agent will move to contract $(\bar{t}, \bar{q})$, because by the incentive compatibility of the contract the following inequality $\bar{t} - \bar{\theta}\bar{q} \geq \hat{t} - \bar{\theta}\hat{q}$ holds.

However, if the Spence-Mirrlees property is not satisfied, the agent may get stuck at a nonoptimal contract at some point in the tâtonnement process. The principal might then want to take those potential inefficiencies into account (which depend on the starting choices) when structuring a menu. In an extreme case, he might choose a single bunching contract that gives up screening but avoids these temporary inefficiencies.

There are many examples where an approach that takes the agent's bounded rationality into account could be fruitful. An obvious case is when the choice is made by a group of agents (a family, a firm, or an organization) that does not reach an efficient collective decision mechanism.

9.7.3 Costly Communication and Complexity

The complexity of information places some limits on the possibility of its full communication and utilization. Costs of transmission, storage, and information processing are among the factors that could cause a principal to limit the potential for information flows between the agent and himself.

---

[40]We assume here for simplicity that the principal cannot change the menu of contracts he has offered during the discrete-time "tâtonnement" of the agent.

An earlier trend in the mechanism design literature dealt with the size of communication spaces needed to implement a particular allocation while ignoring incentive constraints (see Mount and Reiter 1974, and Hurwicz 1977, among others). The analysis of the interaction of incentive and communication constraints is a difficult topic. Green and Laffont (1986a; 1987) introduced data compression technics and dimensionality restrictions in adverse selection environments. See also Reichelstein and Reiter (1988). Green and Laffont (1986b) analyzed how exogenous constraints on communication may invalidate the revelation principle. Legros and Newman (1999) analyzed incentive problems where agents have to secure their communication channels with the principal. For multiagent settings, see the work of Melumad, Mookherjee, and Reichelstein (1997) and the references therein. Various papers also explicitly introduced the cost of including multiple contingencies in contracts (see Dye 1985, Allen and Gale 1992, and Anderlini and Felli 2000 for a recent synthesis).

9.8 Endogenous Information Structures ★

One often heard criticism of incentive theory is that it takes information structures as given. A more complete view of organizational design should account for the endogeneity of these information structures. To investigate these new issues, we now assume that the agent does not know his type a priori but can decide or not to acquire information about his type at a cost c. Results depend on the precise, extensive form of the game representing the sequence of events and, in particular, on when information is acquired. We outline the timing in figure 9.8.

Note that, at date $t = 6$, the agent reveals the information he has learned, if any. The principal can decide to offer contracts that induce or do not induce information gathering by the agent, at a strictly positive cost c.

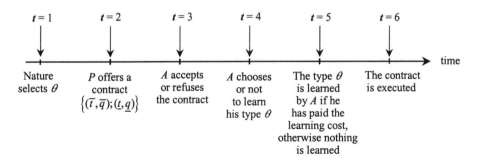

$t = 1$	$t = 2$	$t = 3$	$t = 4$	$t = 5$	$t = 6$
Nature selects θ	P offers a contract $\{(\bar{t},\bar{q});(\underline{t},\underline{q})\}$	A accepts or refuses the contract	A chooses or not to learn his type θ	The type θ is learned by A if he has paid the learning cost, otherwise nothing is learned	The contract is executed

FIGURE 9.8: Timing of the Contractual Game with Endogenous Information Structures

If the principal was not delegating the tasks of production and information gathering, he would choose to invest in information gathering when

$$v(S(\underline{q}^*) - \underline{\theta}\underline{q}^*) + (1 - v)(S(\bar{q}^*) - \bar{\theta}\bar{q}^*) - c \geq \max_{q}\{S(q) - E(\theta)q\}, \qquad (9.101)$$

where $E(\theta) = v\underline{\theta} + (1 - v)\bar{\theta}$.

To implement this outcome with delegation, the principal can offer a non-linear schedule $t(q) = S(q) - T^*$. With such a schedule, the risk-neutral agent is made residual claimant for the hierarchy's profit. When choosing to become informed, the agent produces $\underline{q}^*$ and $\bar{q}^*$ in the different states of nature. Information gathering thus occurs whenever

$$v(S(\underline{q}^*) - \underline{\theta}\underline{q}^*) + (1 - v)(S(\bar{q}^*) - \bar{\theta}\bar{q}^*) - T^* - c \geq \max_{q}\{S(q) - E(\theta)q\} - T^*, \quad (9.102)$$

which is equivalent to (9.101).

Finally, when (9.101) holds, the principal fixes T^* to reap all *ex ante* gains from trade and $T^* = v(S(\underline{q}^*) - \underline{\theta}\underline{q}^*) + (1 - v)(S(\bar{q}^*) - \bar{\theta}\bar{q}^*) - c$.

Let us now envision the case where the risk-neutral agent has limited liability so that making him residual claimant for the firm's profit is impossible.

We denote a direct revelation mechanism by $\{(\bar{t}, \bar{q}); (\underline{t}, \underline{q})\}$. The usual incentive constraints,

$$\underline{U} \geq \bar{U} + \Delta\theta\bar{q} \qquad (9.103)$$

and

$$\bar{U} \geq \underline{U} - \Delta\theta\underline{q}, \qquad (9.104)$$

should hold when the agent decides to learn information.

The following *ex post* participation constraints must also be satisfied:

$$\underline{U} \geq 0, \qquad (9.105)$$

$$\bar{U} \geq 0. \qquad (9.106)$$

Moreover, the agent must choose to participate at the *ex ante* stage, i.e., the following participation constraint must be satisfied:

$$v\underline{U} + (1 - v)\bar{U} - c \geq 0. \qquad (9.107)$$

The agent decides to acquire information when

$$\nu\underline{U} + (1 - \nu)\overline{U} - c \geq \max\{\underline{t} - E(\theta)\underline{q}, \overline{t} - E(\theta)\overline{q}\}, \tag{9.108}$$

or, expressing the right-hand side as a function of $\underline{U}$ and $\overline{U}$,

$$\nu\underline{U} + (1 - \nu)\overline{U} - c \geq \max\{\underline{U} - (1 - \nu)\Delta\theta\underline{q}, \overline{U} + \nu\Delta\theta\overline{q}\}. \tag{9.109}$$

One can rewrite this latter inequality as a pair of inequalities,

$$\underline{U} - \overline{U} \geq \Delta\theta\overline{q} + \frac{c}{\nu} \tag{9.110}$$

and

$$\overline{U} - \underline{U} \geq -\Delta\theta\underline{q} + \frac{c}{1 - \nu}. \tag{9.111}$$

The set of possible values of $\underline{U}$ and $\overline{U}$ satisfying (9.110) and (9.111) is nonempty when

$$\nu(1 - \nu)\Delta\theta(\underline{q} - \overline{q}) \geq c. \tag{9.112}$$

When he wants to induce information gathering, the principal's problem is thus:

(P) $$\max_{\{(\underline{U},\underline{q});(\overline{U},\overline{q})\}} \nu(S(\underline{q}) - \underline{\theta}\underline{q} - \underline{U}) + (1 - \nu)(S(\overline{q}) - \overline{\theta}\overline{q} - \overline{U}),$$

subject to (9.103) to (9.106) and (9.110) to (9.112).

First neglecting the implementability condition (9.112) and the *ex ante* participation constraint (9.107), which turns out to be satisfied at the optimum, the binding constraints are (9.106) and (9.110), which is more costly than (9.103). The optimal outputs are thus $\underline{q}^{IG} = q^*$ and $\overline{q}^{IG} = \overline{q}^{SB}$, where the superscript *IG* means *information gathering*. Outputs are thus equal to their second-best levels as long as the implementability condition in (9.112) holds, i.e.,

$$\nu(1 - \nu)\Delta\theta(q^* - \overline{q}^{SB}) > c. \tag{9.113}$$

As c increases, the latter constraint becomes binding in order to induce information gathering, and both outputs are distorted away from their second-best values without information gathering.

If the principal does not induce information gathering, satisfying the *ex post* participation constraint of the agent requires $t = \overline{\theta}q$, and the optimal output chosen by the principal is $\overline{q}^*$. This yields an expected payoff $V^0 = S(\overline{q}^*) - \overline{\theta}\overline{q}^*$.

In the first regime, where (9.113) holds, the principal wants to induce information gathering when

$$V^{IG} = \nu(S(\underline{q}^*) - \underline{\theta}\underline{q}^*) + (1 - \nu)(S(\bar{q}^{SB}) - \bar{\theta}\bar{q}^{SB}) - \nu\Delta\theta q^{SB} - c > V^0. \quad (9.114)$$

Of course, this inequality holds when c is small enough.

Crémer, Khalil, and Rochet (1998) offered a similar analysis when the agent accepts or rejects the contract after the information gathering stage and there is a continuum of possible types. They also reviewed the recent literature. Kessler (1998) analyzed a similar model with only two types. Lewis and Sappington (1991, 1993, 1997), Crémer and Khalil (1992), and Mezzetti and Tsoulouhas (2000) also presented models where information gathering takes place before the signing of the contract.

References

Abreu, D., and H. Matsushima. (1992). "Virtual Implementation in Iteratively Undominated Strategies: Complete Information." *Econometrica* 56: 1259–1281.

Aghion, P., and P. Bolton. (1987). "Contracts as a Barrier to Entry." *American Economic Review* 77: 388–401.

Aghion, P., and B. Hermalin. (1990). "Legal Restrictions on Private Contracts Can Enhance Efficiency." *Journal of Law, Economics and Organization* 6: 381–409.

Aghion, P., and J. Tirole. (1997). "Formal and Real Authority in Organizations." *Journal of Political Economy* 105: 1–29.

Akerlof, G. (1970). "The Market for 'Lemons': Quality Uncertainty and the Market Mechanism." *Quarterly Journal of Economics* 84: 488–500.

Allen, F. (1983). "Credit Rationing and Payment Incentives." *Review of Economic Studies* 50: 639–646.

Allen, F., and D. Gale. (1992). "Measurement Distortion and Missing Contingencies in Optimal Contracts." *Economic Theory* 2: 1–26.

Aloi, E. (1997). "First-Order Approach to the Principal-Agent Problems: A Generalization." *The Geneva Papers on Risk and Insurance Theory* 22: 59–65.

Anderlini, L., and L. Felli. (2000). "Bounded Rationality and Incomplete Contracts." Mimeo. London School of Economics.

Anderson, E. (1985). "The Saleperson as Outside Agent or Employee: A Transaction Cost Perspective." *Management Science* 4: 234–254.

Anderson, E., and D. Schmittlein. (1984). "Integration of the Sales Force: An Empirical Investigation." *Rand Journal of Economics* 15: 385–395.

Araujo, A., and H. Moreira. (2000). "Adverse Selection Problems without the Spence-Mirrlees Condition." Mimeo. IMPA, Rio de Janeiro.

———. (2001). "A General Lagrangian Approach for Non-Concave Moral Hazard Problems." Journal of Mathematical Economics 35: 1–16.

Armstrong, M. (1996). "Multiproduct Nonlinear Pricing." Econometrica 64: 51–76.

———. (1999). "Price Discrimination by a Many-Product Firm." Review of Economic Studies 66: 151–168.

Armstrong, M., and J. C. Rochet. (1999). "Multidimensional Screening: A User's Guide." European Economics Review 43: 959–979.

Arnott, R., and J. Stiglitz. (1988). "Randomization with Asymmetric Information." Rand Journal of Economics 19: 344–362.

Arrow, K. (1951). Social Choice and Individual Values. New York: Wiley.

———. (1963a). "Research in Management Controls: A Critical Synthesis." In Management Controls: New Directions in Basic Research, eds. C. Bonini, R. Jaediche, and H. Wagner, pp. 317–327. New York: McGraw-Hill.

———. (1963b). "Uncertainty and the Welfare Economics of Medical Care." American Economic Review 53: 91–96.

———. (1975). "Vertical Integration and Communication." Bell Journal of Economics 6: 173–183.

Arrow, K., and T. Scitovsky. (1969). Readings in Welfare Economics. Homewood, Ontario: R. Irwin, Inc.

Aspremont, C. d', and L. A. Gérard-Varet. (1979). "Incentives and Incomplete Information." Journal of Public Economics 11: 25–45.

Atkeson, A. (1991). "International Lending with Moral Hazard and Risk of Repudiation." Econometrica 59: 1069–1089.

Atkeson, A., and R. Lucas. (1992). "On Efficient Distribution with Private Information." Review of Economic Studies 59: 427–453.

Atkinson, A., and J. Stiglitz. (1980). Lectures in Public Economics. New York: McGraw-Hill.

Averch, H., and L. L. Johnson. (1962). "Behavior of the Firm under Regulatory Constraint." American Economic Review 52: 1053–1069.

Babbage, C. (1835). On the Economy of Machinery and Manufactures. London: Charles Knight.

———. (1989). The Works of Charles Babbage. London: William Pickering.

Bagnoli, M., and T. Bergstrom. (1989). "Log-Concave Probability and Its Applications." CREST WP # 89-23, University of Michigan.

Baker, G. (1992). "Incentive Contracts and Performance Measurement." Journal of Political Economy 100: 598–614.

Bardhan, P. (1991). The Economic Theory of Agrarian Institutions. Oxford: Clarendon Press.

Barnard, C. (1938). The Functions of the Executive. Cambridge: Harvard University Press.

Baron, D., and D. Besanko. (1984a). "Regulation, Asymmetric Information, and Auditing." Rand Journal of Economics 15: 447–470.

———. (1984b). "Regulation and Information in a Continuing Relationship." Information Economics and Policy 1: 267–302.

Baron, D., and R. Myerson. (1982). "Regulating a Monopolist with Unknown Costs." Econometrica 50: 911–930.

Beaudry, P. (1994). "Why an Informed Principal May Leave Rents to an Agent." International Economic Review 35: 821–832.

Beaudry P., and M. Poitevin. (1993). "Signalling and Renegotiation in Contractual Relationships." Econometrica 61: 745–782.

———. (1994). "The Commitment Value of Contracts under Dynamic Renegotiation." Rand Journal of Economics 25: 501–517.

Berliner, J. (1976). Innovation in Soviet Industry. Cambridge: MIT Press.

Bester, H., and S. Strausz. (2001). "Contracting with Imperfect Commitment and the Revelation Principle: The Single Agent Case." *Econometrica* 69: 1077–1078.

Biglaiser, G., and C. Mezzetti. (1993). "Principals Competing for an Agent in Presence of Adverse Selection and Moral Hazard." *Journal of Economic Theory* 61: 302–330.

Biglaiser, G., and C. Mezzetti. (2000). "Incentive Auctions and Information Revelation." *Rand Journal of Economics* 31: 145–164.

Black, D. (1948). "On the Rationale of Group Decision Making." *Journal of Political Economy* 56: 23–34.

Blackwell, D. (1951). "Comparison of Experiments." *Proceedings of the Second Berkeley Symposium on Mathematics, Statistics and Probability*, pp. 93–102. Berkeley: University of California Press.

———. (1953). "Equivalent Comparison of Experiments." *Annals of Mathematical Statistics* 24: 267–272.

Boiteux, M. (1956). "Sur la gestion des monopoles naturels astreints à l'équilibre budgétaire." *Econometrica* 24: 22–40.

Bolton, E., and D. Scharfstein. (1990). "A Theory of Predation Based on Agency Problems in Financial Contracting." *American Economic Review* 80: 93–106.

Bolton, P., and C. Harris. (1997). "The Continuous-Time Principal-Agent Problem: First-Best Risk-Sharing Contracts and their Decentralization." Mimeo. Oxford University.

Bontemps, P., and J. M. Bourgeon. (2000). "Creating Countervailing Incentives through the Choice of Instrument." *Journal of Public Economics* 76: 181–202.

Borda, J. C. de. (1781). Mémoire sur les Elections au Scrutin. *Histoire de l'Académie Royale des Sciences*. Imprimerie Royale, Paris.

Border, D., and J. Sobel. (1987). "Samourai Accountant: A Theory of Auditing and Plunder." *Review of Economic Studies* 54: 525–540.

Bowen, H. (1943). "The Interpretation of Voting in the Allocation of Economic Resources." *Quarterly Journal of Economics* 58: 27–48.

Boyer, M., and J. J. Laffont, (2000). "Competition and the Reform of Incentives in the Public Sector." Mimeo. Forthcoming in *Journal of Public Economics*.

Brainard, L., and D. Martimort. (1996). "Strategic Trade Policy for Uninformed Policy-Makers." *Journal or International Economics* 42: 33–65.

Braverman, A., and J. Stiglitz. (1982). "Sharecropping and the Interlinking of Agrarian Markets." *American Economic Review* 72: 695–715.

Brown, M., S. H. Chiang, S. Ghosh, and E. Wolfstetter. (1986). "A New Class of Sufficient Conditions for the First-Order Approach to Principal-Agent Problems." *Economic Letters* 21: 1–6.

Caillaud, B., R. Guesnerie, and P. Rey. (1992). "Noisy Observation in Adverse Selection Models." *Review of Economic Studies* 59: 596–615.

Capen, E. C., R. V. Clapp, and W. M. Campbell. (1971). "Competitive Bidding in High-Risk Situations." *Journal of Petroleum Technology* 23: 641–653.

Carmichael, L. (1985). "Can Unemployment Be Involuntary?" *American Economic Review* 75: 1213–1214.

Champsaur, P., and J. C. Rochet. (1989). "Multiproduct Duopolists." *Econometrica* 57: 533–557.

Chari, V. (1983). "Involuntary Unemployment and Implicit Contracts." *Quarterly Journal of Economics (Supplement)* 98: 107–122.

Che, Y. K., and I. Gale. (2000). "The Optimal Mechanism for Selling to Budget-Constrained Consumers." *Journal of Economic Theory* 92: 198–233.

Chiappori, P. A., and B. Salanié. (2000). "Testing Contract Theory: A Survey of some Recent Works." Mimeo. University of Chicago.

Chiappori, P. A., I. Macho, P. Rey, and B. Salanié. (1994). "Repeated Moral Hazard: The Role of Memory, Commitment, and the Access to Credit Markets." *European Economic Review* 38: 1527–1555.

Cho, I. K., and D. Kreps. (1987). "Signaling Games and Stable Equilibria." *Quarterly Journal of Economics* 102: 179–221.

Chung, T. (1991). "Incomplete Contracts, Specific Investments, and Risk-Sharing." *Review of Economic Studies* 58: 1031–1042.

Clarke, E. (1971). "Multipart Pricing of Public Goods." *Public Choice* 11: 17–33.

Crampes, C. (1986). "Des Instruments pour le Contrôle des Entreprises Publiques." *Revue Economique* 37: 757–781.

Crémer, J. (1995). "Arm's-Length Relationships." *Quarterly Journal of Economics* 110: 275–295.

Crémer, J., and F. Khalil. (1992). "Gathering Information before Signing a Contract." *European Economic Review* 38: 675–682.

Crémer, J., F. Khalil, and J. C. Rochet. (1998). "Strategic Information Gathering before a Contract is Offered." *Journal of Economic Theory* 81: 163–200.

Crémer, J., and R. McLean. (1988). "Full Extraction of the Surplus in Bayesian and Dominant Strategy Auctions." *Econometrica* 56: 1247–1258.

Dasgupta, P., and E. Maskin. (1986). "The Existence of Equilibrium in Discontinuous Economic Games: 2 Applications." *Review of Economic Studies* 46: 27–42.

Dasgupta, P., P. Hammond, and E. Maskin. (1979). "The Implementation of Social Choice Rules: Some General Results on Incentive Compatibility." *Review of Economic Studies* 46: 185–216.

Demougin, D., and C. Fluet. (1999). "Monitoring vs. Incentives: Substitutes or Complements?" Mimeo. UQAM.

Demsetz, H. (1967). "Towards a Theory of Property Rights." *American Economic Review* 57: 347–359.

Demski, J., and D. Sappington. (1984). "Optimal Incentive Contracts with Multiple Agents." *Journal of Economic Theory* 33: 152–171.

Dewatripont, M. (1986). "Renegotiation and Information Revelation over Time in Optimal Labor Contracts." In *On the Theory of Commitment with Applications to the Labor Market*, Ph.D. Dissertation. Harvard University.

———. (1989). "Renegotiation and Information Revelation over Times: The Case of Optimal Labor Contracts." *Quarterly Journal of Economics* 104: 489–620.

Dewatripont, M., I. Jewitt, and J. Tirole. (1999a). "The Economics of Career Concerns, Part I: Comparing Information Structures." *Review of Economic Studies* 66: 183–198.

———. (1999b). "The Economics of Career Concerns, Part II: Application to Missions and Accountability of Government Agencies." *Review of Economic Studies* 66: 199–217.

Dewatripont, M., and E. Maskin. (1995). "Contractual Contingencies and Renegotiation." *Rand Journal of Economics* 76: 704–719.

Diamond, P. (1998a). "Optimal Income Taxation: An Example with a U-Shaped Pattern of Optimal Marginal Tax Rates." *American Economic Review* 88: 83–95.

———. (1998b). "Managerial Incentives: On the Near-Optimality of Optimal Compensation." *Journal of Political Economy* 106: 931–957.

Dickerson, O. (1959). *Health Insurance*. Homewood, Ontario: Richard D. Irwin, Inc.

Dixit, A., and R. Pindyck. (1994). *Investment under Uncertainty*. Princeton: Princeton University Press.

Drèze J., and D. de la Vallée Poussin. (1971). "A Tâtonnement Process for Public Goods." *Review of Economic Studies* 38: 133–150.

Dummett, M., and R. Farquharson. (1961). "Stability in Voting." *Econometrica* 29: 33–43.

Dupuit, J. (1844). "De la Mesure de l'utilité des Travaux Publics." *Annales des Ponts et Chaussées*, Paris, eds. Scientifiques et Medicales Elsevier.

Dutta, B., and A. Sen. (1991). "A Necessary and Sufficient Condition for Two-person Nash-Implementation." *Review of Economic Studies* 58: 121–128.

Dye, R. (1985). "Costly Contract Contingencies." *International Economic Review* 26: 233–250.

Eaton, J., and M. Gersovitz. (1981). "Debt with Potential Reputation: Theoretical and Empirical Analysis." *Review of Economic Studies* 48: 289–309.

Edgeworth, F. Y. (1897). "The Pure Theory of Taxation." *Economic Journal* 46–70: 223–38, 550–71.

———. (1913). "Contributions to the Theory of Railways I–IV." *Economic Journal* 21–23.

Eswaran, M., and A. Kotwal. (1985). "A Theory of Contractual Choice in Agriculture." *American Economic Review* 75: 352–367.

Fafchamps, M., and B. Minten. (1999). "Property Rights in a Flea Market Economy." Mimeo. Center for the Study of African Economies, University of Oxford.

Fama, E. (1980). "Agency Problem and the Theory of the Firm." *Journal of Political Economy* 88: 288–307.

Faulkner, E. J. (1960). *Health Insurance*. New York: McGraw-Hill.

Feenstra, R., and T. Lewis. (1991). "Negotiated Trade Restrictions with Private Political Pressure." *Quarterly Journal of Economics* 56: 1287–1307.

Foley, D. (1967). "Resource Allocation and the Public Sector." *Yale Economic Essays* 7: 45–98.

Forges, F. (1986). "An Approach to Communication Equilibrium." *Econometrica* 54: 1375–85.

Freixas, X., and J. J. Laffont. (1990). "Optimal Banking Contracts." In *Essays in Honor of Edmond Malinvaud, Vol. 2, Macroeconomics*, ed. P. Champsaur et al. Cambridge: MIT Press.

Freixas, X., and J. C. Rochet. (1999). *Microeconomics of Banking*. Cambridge: MIT Press.

Friedman, M. (1956). "A Competitive Bidding Strategy." *Operations Research* 4: 104–112.

Fudenberg, D., B. Holmström, and P. Milgrom. (1990). "Short-Term Contracts and Long-Term Agency Relationship." *Journal of Economic Theory* 51: 1–31.

Fudenberg, D., and J. Tirole. (1990). "Moral Hazard and Renegotiation in Agency Contracts." *Econometrica* 58: 1279–1320.

———. (1991). *Game Theory*. Cambridge: MIT Press.

Fudenberg, D., D. Levine, and E. Maskin. (1994). "The Folk Theorem with Imperfect Public Information." *Econometrica* 62: 997–1040.

Gabor, A. (1955). "A Note on Block-Tariffs." *Review of Economic Studies* 23: 32–41.

Gale, D., and M. Hellwig. (1985). "Incentive-Compatible Debt Contracts: The One-Period Problem." *Review of Economic Studies* 52: 647–663.

———. (1989). "Repudiation and Renegotiation: The Case of Sovereign Debt." *International Economic Review* 30: 3–31.

Gibbard, A. (1973). "Manipulation of Voting Schemes: A General Result." *Econometrica* 41: 587–601.

Gibbons, R. (1997). "Incentives and Careers in Organizations." *Advances in Economics and Econometrics: Theory and Applications, 7th World Congress*, eds. D. Kreps and K. Wallis, pp. 1–37. Cambridge: Cambridge University Press.

Gibbons, R., and K. Murphy. (1992). "Optimal Incentive Contracts in the Presence of Career Concerns: Theory and Evidence." *Journal of Political Economy* 100: 468–505.

Gjesdal, F. (1982). "Information and Incentives: The Agency Information Problem." *Review of Economic Studies* 49: 373–390.

Goldman, M. H., Leland, H., and D. Sibley. (1984). "Optimal Nonuniform Pricing." *Review of Economic Studies* 51: 305–320.

Good, I. J. (1952). "Rational Decisions." *Journal of the Royal Economic Society* B. 14: 1, 105–115.

Green, E. (1987). "Lending and the Smoothing of Uninsurable Income." In *Contractual Arrangements for Intertemporal Trade*. eds. E. Prescott and N. Wallace. Minnesota University Press, Minnesota.

Green, E., and S. N. Oh. (1991). "Contracts, Constraints and Consumption." *Review of Economic Studies* 58: 883–899.

Green, J., and C. Kahn. (1983). "Wage-Employment Contracts." *Quarterly Journal of Economics* 98, supplement: 173–188.

Green, J., and J. J. Laffont. (1977). "Characterization of Satisfactory Mechanisms for the Revelation of Preferences for Public Goods." *Econometrica* 45: 427–438.

———. (1979). *Incentives in Public Decision Making*. Amsterdam: North-Holland.

———. (1986a). "Incentive Theory with Data Compression." *Essays in Honor of K. J. Arrow, Vol. 3*, eds. W. Heller, R. Starr and D. Starrett. Cambridge: Cambridge University Press.

———. (1986b). "Partially Verifiable Information and Mechanism Design." *Review of Economic Studies* 53: 447–456.

———. (1987). "Limited Communication and Incentive Compatibility." *Information, Incentives and Economic Mechanisms*, eds. T. Groves, R. Radner, and S. Reiter. Minneapolis: University of Minnesota Press.

———. (1992). "Renegotiation and the Form of Efficient Contracts." *Annales d'Economie et de Statistique* 25/26: 123–150.

Green, J., and N. Stockey. (1983). "A Comparison of Tournaments and Contracts." *Journal of Political Economy* 91: 349–364.

Grossman, S., and O. Hart. (1983). "An Analysis of the Principal-Agent Problem." *Econometrica* 51: 7–45.

———. (1986). "The Costs and Benefits of Ownership: A Theory of Vertical and Lateral Integration." *Journal of Political Economy* 94: 691–719.

Grout, P. (1984). "Investment and Wages in the Absence of Binding Contracts: A Nash Bargaining Approach." *Econometrica* 52: 449–460.

Groves, T. (1973). "Incentives in Teams." *Econometrica* 41: 617–631.

Groves, T., and M. Loeb. (1975). "Incentives and Public Inputs." *Journal of Public Economics* 4: 311–326.

Guesnerie, R., and J. J. Laffont. (1979). "Taxing Price Makers." *Journal of Economic Theory* 19: 423–455.

———. (1984). "A Complete Solution to a Class of Principal-Agent Problems with an Application to the Control of a Self-Managed Firm." *Journal of Public Economics* 25: 329–369.

Guesnerie, R. (1995). *A Contribution to the Pure Theory of Taxation*. Cambridge: Cambridge University Press.

Harris, M., and A. Raviv. (1979). "Optimal Incentive Contracts with Imperfect Information." *Journal of Economic Theory* 20: 231–259.

———. (1992). "Financial Contracting Theory." *Advances in Economic Theory, 6th World Congress*, ed. J. J. Laffont, pp. 64–150. Cambridge University Press.

Harsanyi, J. (1955). "Cardinal Welfare, Individualistic Ethics, and Interpersonal Comparisons of Utility." *Journal of Political Economy* 63: 309–321.

———. (1967, 1968). "Games of Incomplete Information Played by Bayesian Players." *Management Science* 14: 159–82, 320–34, 486–502.

Hart, O. (1983b). "Optimal Labour Contracts under Asymmetric Information: An Introduction." *Review of Economic Studies* 50: 3–35.

———. (1995). *Firms Contracts and Financial Structure*. Oxford: Oxford University Press.

Hart, O., and B. Holmström. (1987). "The Theory of Contracts." *Advances in Economic Theory: 5th World Congress*, ed. T. Bewley. Cambridge: Cambridge University Press.

Hart, O., and J. Moore. (1990). "Property Rights and the Theory of the Firm." *Journal of Political Economy* 98: 1119–1158.

Hart, O., and J. Tirole. (1988). "Contract Renegotiation and Coasian Dynamics." *Review of Economic Studies* 55: 509–540.

Heady, E. (1947). "Economics of Farm Leasing System." *Journal of Farm Economics* 29: 659–678.

Heal, G. (1973). *The Theory of Economic Planning*. Amsterdam: North Holland.

Hellwig, M. (1987). "Some Recent Developments in the Theory of Competition in Markets with Adverse Selection." *European Economic Review* 31: 319–325.

Hellwig, M., and K. Schmidt. (1997). "Discrete-Time Approximations of the Holmström-Milgrom Brownian Motion Model of Intertemporal Incentive Problems." Mimeo. University of Munich.

Helpman, E., and J. J. Laffont. (1975). "On Moral Hazard in General Equilibrium Theory." *Journal of Economic Theory* 15: 8–23.

Hermalin, B., and M. Katz. (1991). "Moral Hazard and Verifiability: The Effects of Renegotiation in Agency." *Econometrica* 59: 1735–1754.

Hill, D. H. (1960). "The Economic Incentive Provided by Sampling Inspection." *Applied Statistics* 2: 69–81.

Holmström, B. (1979). "Moral Hazard and Observability." *Bell Journal of Economics* 10: 74–91.

———. (1999a). "Managerial Incentive Problems: A Dynamic Perspective." *Review of Economic Studies* 66: 169–182.

———. (1999b). "The Firm as a Subeconomy." *Journal of Law, Economics and Organization* 15: 74–103.

Holmström, B., and P. Milgrom. (1987). "Aggregation and Linearity in the Provision of Intertemporal Incentives." *Econometrica* 55: 303–328.

———. (1991). "Multi-Task Principal Agent Analysis: Incentive Contracts, Asset Ownership, and Job Design." *Journal of Law, Economics, and Organization* 7: 42–52.

———. (1994). "The Firm as an Incentive System." *American Economic Review* 84: 972–991.

Holmström, B., and J. Tirole. (1988). "The Theory of the Firm." In *Handbook of Industrial Organization, Vol. 1*, eds. R. Schmalensee and R. Willig. Amsterdam: North-Holland.

———. (1994). "Financial Intermediation, Loanable Funds, and the Real Sector." *Journal of Political Economy* 112: 663–692.

Hotelling, H. (1939). "The Relation of Prices to Marginal Costs in an Optimum System." *Econometrica* 7: 151–155.

Hume, D. A. (1740). *Treatise of Human Nature*. Oxford: Oxford University Press.

Hurwicz, L. (1960). "Optimality and Informational Efficiency in Resource Allocation Processes." *Mathematical Methods in the Social Sciences*, eds. Arrow, K., S. Karlin, and P. Suppes. Stanford: Stanford University Press.

———. (1977). "On the Dimensional Requirements of Informationally Decentralized Pareto Satisfactory Adjustment Processes." In *Studies in Resource Allocation Processes*, eds. K. J. Arrow and L. Hurwicz. Cambridge: Cambridge University Press.

Innes, R. (1990). "Limited Liabilities and Incentive Contracting with *ex ante* Action Choices." *Journal of Economic Theory* 52: 45–67.

Jensen, M. (1986). "Agency Costs of Free-Cash Flow, Corporate Finance and Takeovers." *American Economic Review* 76: 323–329.

Jensen, M., and W. Meckling. (1976). "The Theory of the Firm, Managerial Behavior, Agency Costs and Ownership Structure." *Journal of Financial Economics* 3: 305–360.

Jensen, M., and K. Murphy. (1990). "Performance Pay and Top Management Incentives." *Journal of Political Economy* 98: 225–264.

Jeon, D. S., and J. J. Laffont. (1999). "The Efficient Mechanism for Downsizing the Public Sector." *The World Bank Economic Review* 13: 67–88.

Jewitt, I. (1988). "Justifying the First-Order Approach to Principal-Agent Problems." *Econometrica* 56: 1177–1190.

———. (2000). "Information and Principal-Agent Problems." Mimeo. Oxford University.

Johnson, G. (1950). "Resource Allocation and Share Contracts." *Journal of Political Economy* 58: 111–123.

Jullien, B. (2000). "Participation Constraint in Adverse-Selection Models." *Journal of Economic Theory* 93: 1–47.

Kahn, C. (1985). "Optimal Severance Pay with Incomplete Information." *Journal of Political Economy* 93: 435–451.

Kamien, M., and N. Schwartz. (1981). *Dynamic Optimization*. New York: North-Holland.

Keren, M. (1972). "On the Tautness of Plans." *Review of Economic Studies* 39: 469–486.

Kessler, A. (1998). "The Value of Ignorance." *Rand Journal of Economics* 29: 339–354.

Khalil, F. (1997). "Auditing without Commitment." *Rand Journal of Economics* 28: 629–640.

Khalil, F., and J. Lawarrée. (1995). "Input versus Output Monitoring: Who is the Residual Claimant?" *Journal of Economic Theory* 66: 139–157.

Kim, S.K. (1995). "Efficiency and Information System in an Agency Model." *Econometrica* 63: 89–102.

Knight, F. (1921). *Risk, Uncertainty and Profit*. Boston: Houghton.

Kowalick, T. (1976). "Oscar Lange." In *Problems of the Planned Economy*, eds. J. Eatwell, M. Milgate, and P. Neuman. New York: Norton.

Krasa, S., and A. Villamil. (2000). "Optimal Contract When Enforcement is a Decision Variable." *Econometrica* 68: 119–134.

Lacker, J. M., and J. A. Weinberg. (1989). "Optimal Contracts under Costly State Verification." *Journal of Political Economy* 97: 1345–1363.

Laffont, J. J. (1985). "Incitations dans les procédures de planification." *Annales de l'INSEE* 58: 3–36.

———. (1995). "Regulation, Moral Hazard and Insurance of Environmental Risks." *Journal of Public Economics* 58: 319–336.

Laffont, J. J., and E. Maskin. (1980). "A Differential Approach to Dominant Strategy Mechanisms." *Econometrica* 48: 1507–1520.

Laffont, J. J., E. Maskin, and J. C. Rochet. (1987). "Optimal Nonlinear Pricing with Two Characteristics." In *Information, Incentives, and Economic Mechanism*, eds. T. Groves, R. Radner, and S. Reiter. Minneapolis: University of Minnesota Press.

Laffont, J. J., and M. Matoussi. (1995). "Moral Hazard, Financial Constraints and Sharecropping in El Oulja." *Review of Economic Studies* 62: 381–399.

Laffont, J. J., and M. Meleu. (2000). "Enforcement of Contracts with Adverse Selection in LDCs." Mimeo. IDEI, Toulouse.

Laffont, J. J., and R. Rochet. (1998). "Regulation of a Risk Averse Firm." *Games and Economic Behavior* 25: 149–173.

Laffont, J. J., and J. Tirole. (1986). "Using Cost Observation to Regulate Firms." *Journal of Political Economy* 94: 614–641.

———. (1990a). "Bypass and Creamskimming." *American Economic Review* 80: 1042–1061.

———. (1990b). "Adverse Selection and Renegotiation in Procurement." *Review of Economic Studies* 57: 597–626.

———. (1993). A *Theory of Incentives in Procurement and Regulation*. Cambridge: MIT Press.

———. (1996). "Pollution Permits and Compliance Strategies." *Journal of Public Economics* 62: 85–125.

Lambert, R. (1983). "Long-Term Contracts and Moral Hazard." *Bell Journal of Economics* 14: 255–275.

Lange, O. (1936). "On the Economic Theory of Socialism: Part I." *Review of Economic Studies* 4: 53–71.

Lange, O. (1967). "The Computer and the Market." In *Socialism, Capitalism and Economic Growth, Essays presented to M. Dobb*, ed. C. H. Feinstein, Cambridge: Cambridge University Press.

Launhardt, W. (1885). "Mathematische Begründung der Volkswirtschaftslehre." Leipzig: B. G. Teubner.

Lazear, E. (2000). "Performance Pay and Productivity." *American Economic Review* 90: 1346–1361.

Leeman, W. (1970). "Bonus Formulae and Soviet Management." *Southern Economic Journal* 36: 434–445.

Legros, P., and A. Newman. (1999). "Interference, Contracts and Authority with Insecure Communication." Mimeo. ULB, Ecare Bruxelles.

Leibenstein, H. (1966). "Allocative Efficiency Versus 'X-Efficiency.'" *American Economic Review* 56: 392–415.

Lerner, P. P. (1934). "The Concept of Monopoly and the Measurement of Monopoly Power." *Review of Economic Studies* 2: 157–175.

LeRoy, S., and L. Singell. (1987). "Knight on Risk and Uncertainty." *Journal of Political Economy* 95: 394–406.

Lewis, T., and D. Sappington. (1989). "Countervailing Incentives in Agency Problems." *Journal of Economic Theory* 49: 294–313.

———. (1991). "All or Nothing Information Control." *Economic Letters* 37: 111–113.

———. (1993). "Ignorance in Agency Problems." *Journal of Economic Theory* 61: 169–183.

———. (1995). "Optimal Capital Structure in Agency Relationships." *Rand Journal of Economics* 26: 343–361.

———. (1997). "Information Management in Incentive Problems." *Journal of Political Economy* 105: 796–821.

———. (2000). "Contracting with Wealth-Constrained Agents." *International Economic Review* 41: 743–768.

———. (2001). "Optimal Contracting with Private Knowledge of Wealth and Ability." *Review of Economic Studies* 68: 21–44.

Loeb, M., and W. Magat. (1979). "A Decentralized Method of Utility Regulation." *Journal of Law and Economics* 22: 399–404.

Lollivier, S., and J. C. Rochet. (1983). "Bunching and Second-Order Conditions: A Note on Optimal Tax Theory." *Journal of Economic Theory* 31: 392–400.

Ma, C. T. (1994). "Renegotiation and Optimality in Agency Contracts." *Review of Economic Studies* 61: 109–130.

Maggi, G., and A. Rodriguez-Clare. (1995a). "On Countervailing Incentives." *Journal of Economic Theory* 66: 238–263.

———. (1995b). "Costly Distortion of Information in Agency Problems." *Rand Journal of Economics* 26(4): 675–689.

Malcomson, J., and F. Spinnewyn. (1988). "The Multiperiod Principal-Agent Problem." *Review of Economic Studies* 55: 391–408.

Marschak, J. (1955). "Elements for a Theory of Teams." *Management Science* 1: 127–137.

Marschak, J., and R. Radner. (1972). *Economic Theory of Teams*. New Haven: Yale University Press.

Mas-Colell, A., M. Whinston, and J. Green. (1995). *Microeconomic Theory*. Oxford: Oxford University Press.

Maskin, E. (1977). "Nash Equilibrium and Welfare Optimality," Mimeo.

Maskin, E. (1999). "Nash Equilibrium and Welfare Optimality." *Review of Economic Studies* 66: 23–38.

Maskin, E., and J. Riley. (1984). "Monopoly with Incomplete Information." *Rand Journal of Economics* 15: 171–196.

———. (1985). "Input vs. Output Incentive Schemes." *Journal of Public Economics* 28: 1–23.

Maskin, E., and J. Tirole. (1990). "The Principal-Agent Relationship with an Informed Principal, I: Private Values." *Econometrica* 58: 379–410.

———. (1992). "The Principal-Agent Relationship with an Informed Principal, II: Common Values." *Econometrica* 60: 1–42.

———. (1999). "Two Remarks on the Property Rights Literature." *Review of Economic Studies* 66: 139–149.

Matthews, S. (1995). "Renegotiation of Sales Contracts." *Econometrica* 63: 567–591.

Matthews, S., and J. Moore. (1987). "Monopoly Provision of Quality and Warranties: An Exploration in the Theory of Multidimensional Screening." *Econometrica* 55: 441–467.

McAfee, P., and J. McMillan. (1988). "Multidimensional Incentive Compatibility and Mechanism Design." *Journal of Economic Theory* 46: 335–354.

McCarthy, J. (1956). "Measures of the Value of Information." *Proc. Nat. Acad. Sciences* 42: 654–655.

McLeod, W. B. and J. Malcomson. (1987). "Involuntary Unemployment in Dynamic Contract Equilibria." *European Economic Review* 31: 427–435.

———. (1988a). "Implicit Contracts, Incentive Compatibility, and Involuntary Unemployment." *Econometrica* 57: 447–480.

———. (1988b). "Reputation and Hierarchy in Dynamic Models of Employment." *Journal of Political Economy* 96: 832–854.

Melumad, N., D. Mookherjee, and S. Reichelstein. (1997). "Contract Complexity, Incentives and the Value of Delegation." *Journal of Economics and Management Strategies* 6: 257–289.

Melumad, N., and S. Reichelstein. (1989). "Value of Communication in Agencies." *Journal of Economic Theory* 47: 334–368.

Meyer, M., and J. Vickers. (1997). "Performance Comparisons and Dynamic Incentives." *Journal of Political Economy* 105: 547–581.

Mezzetti, C., and T. Tsoulouhas. (2000). "Gathering Information before Signing a Contract with a Privately Informed Principal." *International Journal of Industrial Organization* 18: 667–689.

Milgrom, P. (1981). "Good News and Bad News: Representation Theorems and Application." *Bell Journal of Economics* 12: 380–391.

Milgrom, P., and I. Segal. (2000). "Envelope Theorems for Arbitrary Choice Sets." Mimeo. Stanford University.

Milgrom, P., and R. Weber. (1982). "A Theory of Auctions and Competitive Bidding." *Econometrica* 50: 1089–1122.

Mirrlees, J. (1971). "An Exploration in the Theory of Optimal Income Taxation." *Review of Economic Studies* 38: 175–208.

———. (1975). "The Theory of Moral Hazard and Unobservable Behavior: Part. I." Mimeo. Oxford University.

———. (1999). "The Theory of Moral Hazard with Unobservable Behavior: Part I." *Review of Economic Studies* 66: 3–22.

Modigliani, F., and M. M. Miller. (1958). "The Cost of Capital, Corporation Finance, and the Theory of Investment." *American Economic Review* 48, 261–297.

Mookherjee, D. (1984). "Optimal Incentive Schemes with Many Agents." *Review of Economic Studies* 51: 433–446.

Mookherjee, D., and I. P'ng, (1989). "Optimal Auditing, Insurance and Redistribution." *Quarterly Journal of Economics* 104: 399–415.

Moore, J. (1985). "Optimal Labour Contracts When Workers Have a Variety of Privately Observed Reservation Wages." *Review of Economic Studies* 52: 37–67.

Moore, J., and R. Repullo. (1988). "Subgame-Perfect Implementation." *Econometrica* 56: 1191–1220.

———. (1990). "Nash Implementation: A Full Characterization." *Econometrica* 28: 1083–1099.

Mount, K., and S. Reiter. (1974). "The Informational Size of Message Spaces." *Journal of Economic Theory* 8: 161–192.

Mussa, M., and S. Rosen. (1978). "Monopoly and Product Quality." *Journal of Economic Theory* 18: 301–317.

Muthoo, A. (1999). *Bargaining Theory with Applications.* Cambridge: Cambridge University Press.

Myerson, R. (1979). "Incentive Compatibility and the Bargaining Problem." *Econometrica* 47: 61–73.

———. (1981). "Optimal Auction Design." *Mathematics of Operations Research* 6: 58–63.

———. (1982). "Optimal Coordination Mechanisms in Generalized Principal-Agent Models." *Journal of Mathematical Economics* 10: 67–81.

———. (1983). "Mechanism Design by an Informed Principal." *Econometrica* 51: 1767–1798.

———. (1986). "Multistage Games with Communication." *Econometrica* 54: 323–358.

――――. (1991). *Game Theory: Analysis of Conflict*. Cambridge: Harvard University Press.

Myles, G. (1997). *Public Economics*. Cambridge: Cambridge University Press.

Nalebuff, B., and J. Stiglitz. (1983). "Prizes and Incentives: Towards a General Theory of Compensation." *Bell Journal of Economics* 14: 21–43.

Oi, W. Y. (1971). "A Disneyland Dilemma: Two Part Tariffs for a Mickey Mouse Monopoly." *Quarterly Journal of Economics* 85: 77–96.

Osborne, M. J., and A. Rubinstein. (1994). *A Course in Game Theory*. Cambridge: MIT Press.

Page, F. (1987). "The Existence of Optimal Contracts in the Principal-Agent Model." *Journal of Mathematical Economics* 16: 157–167.

Park, E. S. (1995). "Incentive Contracting with Limited Liability." *Journal of Economics and Management Strategy* 4: 477–490.

Pauly, M. V. (1968). "The Economics of Moral Hazard." *Quarterly Journal of Economics* 88: 44–62.

――――. (1974). "Overinsurance and Public Provision of Insurance: The Roles of Moral Hazard and Adverse Selection." *Quarterly Journal of Economics* 88: 44–62.

Phelan, C. (1994). "Incentives and Aggregate Shocks." *Review of Economic Studies* 61: 681–700.

Phelan, C., and R. Townsend. (1991). "Computing Multi-Period, Information Constrained Optima." *Review of Economic Studies* 58: 853–881.

Pigou, A. C. (1920). *The Economics of Welfare*. London: MacMillan.

Prendergast, C. (1999). "The Provision of Incentives in Firms." *Journal of Economic Literature* 37: 7–63.

Radner, R. (1985). "Repeated Principal-Agent Games with Discounting." *Econometrica* 53: 1173–1198.

Radner, R., E. Maskin, and R. Myerson. (1986). "An Example of a Repeated Partnership Game with Discounting and with Uniformly Inefficient Equilibria." *Review of Economic Studies* 53: 59–70.

Ramsey, F. (1927). "A Contribution to the Theory of Taxation." *Economic Journal* 37: 47–61.

Reichelstein, S., and S. Reiter. (1988). "Game Forms with Minimal Message Spaces." *Econometrica* 56: 661–692.

Reinganum, J., and L. Wilde. (1985). "Income Tax Compliance in a Principal-Agent Framework." *Journal of Public Economics* 26: 1–18.

Rey, P., and B. Salanié. (1990). "Long-Term, Short-Term and Renegotiation: On the Value of Commitment in Contracting." *Econometrica* 58: 597–619.

――――. (1996). "On the Value of Commitment with Asymmetric Information." *Econometrica* 64: 1395–1414.

Riley, J. (1979). "Informational Equilibrium." *Econometrica* 47: 331–359.

Riordan, M. (1990). "What is Vertical Integration." In *The Firm as a Nexus of Treaties*, ed. M. Aoki et al. London: Sage.

Riordan, M., and D. Sappington. (1988). "Optimal Contracts with Public Ex Post Information." *Journal of Economic Theory* 45, 189–199.

Roberts, K. (1983). "Long Term Contracts." Mimeo. University of Warwick.

Rochet, J. C. (1984). "Monopoly Regulation with Two Dimensional Uncertainty." Mimeo. Université Paris IX.

――――. (1985). "The Taxation Principle and Multi-Time Hamilton-Jacoby Equations." *Journal of Mathematical Economics* 14: 113–128.

Rochet, J. C., and P. Choné. (1998). "Ironing, Sweeping, and Multidimensional Screening." *Econometrica* 66: 783–826.

Rochet, J. C., and L. Stole. (2000). "Nonlinear Pricing with Random Participation." Forthcoming in *Review of Economic Studies*.

Rogerson, W. (1985a). "The First-Order Approach to Principal-Agent Problems." *Econometrica* 53: 1357–1368.

Rogerson, W. (1985b). "Repeated Moral Hazard." *Econometrica* 58: 597–619.

———. (1987). "On the Optimality of Linear Contracts." Mimeo. Northwestern University.

Rosenthal, R. and A. Weiss. (1984). "Mixed-Strategy Equilibrium in a Market with Asymmetric Information." *Review of Economic Studies*, 51: 333–42.

Ross, S. (1973). "The Economic Theory of Agency: The Principal's Problem." *American Economic Review* 63: 134–139.

Rothkopf, P. (1969). "A Model of Rational Competitive Bidding." *Management Science* 15: 774–777.

Rothschild, M., and J. Stiglitz. (1976). "Equilibrium in Competitive Insurance Markets." *Quarterly Journal of Economics* 93: 541–562.

Rubinstein, A. (1979). "Offenses That May Have Been Committed by Accident—An Optimal Policy of Retribution." In *Applied Game Theory*, eds. S. Brams, A. Shotter, and G. Schwodiauer, pp. 406–413.

———. (1982). "Perfect Equilibrium in a Bargaining Model." *Econometrica* 50: 97–109.

Rubinstein, A., and M. Yaari. (1983). "Insurance and Moral Hazard." *Journal of Economic Theory* 14: 441–452.

Saha, B. (2001). "Red Tape, Incentive Bribe and the Provision of Subsidy." *Journal of Development Economics* 65: 113–34.

Saint-Paul, G. (1996). *Dual Labor Markets*. Cambridge: MIT Press.

Salanié, B. (1990). "Sélection adverse et aversion pour le risque." *Annales d'Economie et Statistique* 18: 131–150.

Salop, S. (1979). "A Model of the Natural Rate of Unemployment." *American Economic Review* 69: 117–125.

Sappington, D. (1983). "Limited Liability Contracts Between Principal and Agent." *Journal of Economic Theory* 29: 1–21.

Satterthwaite, M. (1975). "Strategy-Proofness and Arrow's Conditions: Existence and Correspondence Theorems for Voting Procedures and Social Welfare Functions." *Journal of Economic Theory* 10: 187–217.

Savage, L. J. (1971). "Elicitation of Personal Probabilities and Expectations." *Journal of the American Statistical Association* 66: 783–801.

Scharfstein, D. (1988a). "Product Market Competition and Managerial Slack." *Rand Journal of Economics* 19: 147–155.

———. (1988b). "The Disciplinary Role of Takeovers." *Review of Economic Studies* 55: 185–200.

Schättler, H., and J. Sung. (1993). "The First-Order Approach to the Continuous Time Principal-Agent Problem with Exponential Utility." *Journal of Economic Theory* 61: 331–371.

Schmidt, K. (1996). "The Costs and Benefits of Privatization." *Journal of Law, Economics and Organization* 12: 1–24.

———. (1997). "Managerial Incentives and Product Market Competition." *Review of Economic Studies* 64: 191–214.

Schultze, C. (1969). "The Role of Incentives, Penalties, and Rewards in Attaining Effective Policy." In *The Analysis and Evaluation of Public Expenditures: The PPB System, Vol. 1,* Joint Economic Committee Compendium, 91st Congress, 1st Session.

Schumpeter, J. (1954). *History of Economic Analysis*. Oxford: Oxford University Press.

Schickele, R. (1941). "Effect of Tenure Systems on Agriculture Efficiency." *Journal of Farm Economics* 23: 187–207.

Scotchmer, S. (1987). "Audit Classes and Tax Enforcement Policy." *American Economic Review* 77: 129–136.

Shapiro, C., and J. Stiglitz. (1984). "Equilibrium Unemployment as a Worker Discipline Device." *American Economic Review* 74: 433–444.

Shavell, S. (1979). "On Moral Hazard and Insurance." *Quarterly Journal of Economics* 93: 541–562.

Sibley, D. and P. Srinagesh (1997). "Multiproduct Nonlinear Pricing with Multiple Taste Characteristics," *Rand Journal of Economics* 28: 684–707.

Sidgwick, H. (1883). *Method of Ethics*. London: MacMillan.

Simon, H. (1951). "A Formal Theory of the Employment Relationship." *Econometrica* 19: 293–305.

Sinclair-Desgagné, B. (1994). "The First-Order Approach to Multi-Signal Principal-Agent Problems." *Econometrica* 62: 459–466.

Smith, A. (1776). *The Wealth of Nations*. New York: The Modern Library.

Solow, R. (1979). "Another Possible Source of Wage Rigidity." *Journal of Macroeconomics* 1: 79–82.

Spear, S., and S. Srivastava. (1987). "On Repeated Moral Hazard with Discounting." *Review of Economic Studies* 54: 599–617.

Spence, M. (1973). "Job Market Signaling." *Quarterly Journal of Economics* 87: 355–74.

———. (1974). *Market Signaling: Informational Transfer in Hiring and Related Processes*. Cambridge: Harvard University Press.

———. (1977). "Nonlinear Prices and Welfare." *Journal of Public Economics* 8: 1–18.

Spence, M., and R. Zeckhauser. (1971). "Insurance Information, and Individual Action." *American Economic Review* 61: 380–387.

Spier, K. (1992). "Incomplete Contracts and Signaling." *Rand Journal of Economics* 23: 432–443.

Stiglitz, J. (1974). "Incentives and Risk Sharing in Sharecropping." *Review of Economic Studies* 41: 219–255.

———. (1977). "Monopoly Non Linear Pricing and Imperfect Information: The Insurance Market." *Review of Economic Studies* 44: 407–430.

———. (1987). "Pareto Efficient and Optimal Taxation and the New Welfare Economics." In *Handbook of Public Economics*, eds. A. Auerbach and M. Feldstein. Amsterdam: Elsevier Science Publishers BV.

Stiglitz, J., and A. Weiss, (1983). "Incentive Effects of Terminations: Applications to the Credit and Labor Markets." *American Economic Review* 73: 912–925.

Stockey, N., and R. Lucas. (1989). *Recursive Methods in Economic Dynamics*. Cambridge: Harvard University Press.

Stole, L. (1995). "Nonlinear Pricing and Oligopoly." *Journal of Economics and Management Strategy* 4: 529–562.

Stoughton, N., and E. Talmor. (1990). "Screening vs. Signaling in Transfer Pricing." Mimeo. UC-Irvine and Tel-Aviv University.

Sung, J. (1995). "Linearity with Project Selection and Controllable Diffusion Rate in Continuous-Time Principal-Agent Problem." *Rand Journal of Economics* 26: 270–743.

Thiele, H., and A. Wambach. (1999). "Wealth Effects in the Principal-Agent Model." *Journal of Economic Theory* 89: 247–260.

Thomas, J., and T. Worrall. (1988). "Self-Enforcing Wage Contracts." *Review of Economic Studies* 55: 541–554.

———. (1990). "Income Fluctuations and Asymmetric Information: An Example of a Repeated Principal-Agent Problem." *Journal of Economic Theory* 51: 367–390.

Tirole, J. (1988). *The Theory of Industrial Organization*. Cambridge: MIT Press.

———. (1999). "Incomplete Contracts: Where Do We Stand?" *Econometrica* 67: 741–782.

Townsend, R. (1978). "Optimal Contracts and Competitive Markets with Costly State Verification." *Journal of Economic Theory* 21: 417–425.

———. (1982). "Optimal Multi-period Contracts, and the Gain from Enduring Relationship under Private Information." *Journal of Political Economy* 90: 1166–1186.

Varian, H. (1988). "Price Discrimination." In *Handbook of Industrial Organization*, eds. R. Schmalensee and R. Willig. Amsterdam: North Holland.

———. (1992). *Microeconomic Analysis*. New York: W.W. Norton.

Vickrey, W. (1945). "Measuring Marginal Utility by Reactions to Risk." *Econometrica* 13: 319–333.

Vickrey, W. (1960). "Utility, Strategy, and Social Decision Rules." *Quarterly Journal of Economics* 74: 507–535.

———. (1961). "Counterspeculation, Auctions, and Sealed Tenders." *Journal of Finance* 16: 8–37.

Von Neumann, J., and R. Morgenstern (1944). *Theory of Games and Economic Behavior.* Princeton: Princeton University Press.

Walras, L. (1897). "L'Etat et les chemins de fer." *Revue du Droit Public et de la Science Politique,* reprinted in August et Léon Walras Œuvres Economiques Complètes, Vol. X, Economica, 1992. Paris.

Wambach, A. (1999). "Renegotiation Before Contract Execution." Mimeo. Munich University.

Wang, C. (1995). "Dynamic Insurance with Private Information and Balanced Budget." *Review of Economic Studies* 62: 577–598.

Weitzman, M. L. (1974). "Prices versus Quantities." *Review of Economic Studies* 41: 479–491.

———. (1976). "The New Soviet Incentive Model." *The Bell Journal of Economics* 7: 251–257.

Wesson, J. (1972). "On the Distribution of Personal Incomes." *Review of Economic Studies* 39: 77–86.

Whittle, P. (1954). "Optimum Preventive Sampling." *Journal of Operat. Res. So. Am.* 2: 197.

Wicksell, K. (1896). *Finanztheoretische Untersuchungen und das Steuerwesen Schwedens.* Jena, Germany: Gustav Fischer Verlagsbuchhandlung.

Williamson, O. (1975). *Markets and Hierarchies.* New York: The Free Press.

———. (1985). *The Economic Institutions of Capitalism.* New York: The Free Press.

Williamson, S. (1987). "Costly Monitoring, Loan Contracts and Equilibrium Rationing." *Quarterly Journal of Economics* 52: 135–146.

Wilson, C. (1977). "A Model of Insurance Markets with Incomplete Information." *Journal of Economic Theory* 16: 167–207.

Wilson, R. (1967). "Competitive Bidding with Asymmetric Information." *Management Science* 13: 816–820.

———. (1968). "The Theory of Syndicates." *Econometrica* 36: 119–132.

———. (1969). "Competitive Bidding with Disparate Information." *Management Science* 15: 446–448.

———. (1977). "A Bidding Model for Perfect Competition." *Review of Economic Studies* 44: 511–518.

———. (1993). *Nonlinear Pricing.* Oxford: Oxford University Press.

Zeckhauser, R. (1970). "Medical Insurance: A Case Study of the Trade-Off Between Risk Spreading and Appropriate Incentives." *Journal of Economic Theory* 2: 10–26.

Author Index

Subject Index

absolute risk aversion, 382–84
action space; cost of, 390–91; limits in, 387–91
actions, verifiability of, 350
adverse selection, 3–6, 19, 28–30; constraints and, 82–144; correlations, 95–96; hold-up problem and, 373–75; moral hazard and, 267–302; repetition of, 307–19
adverse selection canonical model, 31
agency costs, 266–68
agency model, 29
aggregate effort, 203
aggregate performances, 217–18
agrarian contracts, 219–23
agricultural contracts, 7–11
allocation rules, 49–50; monotonicity of, 242, 254–56
allocations, 30, 31, 40, 66
allocative distortions, 5, 266
allocative efficiency, 5, 29, 40; agency costs and, 266–68; improving, 267–68; increase in, 43; lack of, 47
Arrow-Debreu theory, 4
assets, ownership of, 224–26
asymmetric common value model, 27
asymmetric information, 4, 5, 25, 30, 33, 40; financial markets and, 75; informed principal and, 353–56; marginal costs and, 48; multidimensional, 93–100;

optimal contract under, 41–43; theory of, 46–48; unions and, 76–81
asymmetric tasks, 215–17, 238–39
auctions, 8, 27
audit mechanisms, 121–30
audit technology, 122
auditing, 84–85

bang-bang incentives, 223
Baron-Myerson model, 105, 109
Bayes' rule, 70, 344
Bayesian equilibrium, 5, 30, 51, 359, 360, 369
Bayesian-Nash equilibrium, 5, 27, 51
behavior, 2, 391–94
benchmarking, 167
bidimensional asymmetric information, 94–95, 100
binding participation constraints, 229–30
Blackwell's condition, 170–72
bounded rationality, 393
Brownian motion, 382, 384
budget constraints, 85, 233
bunching contracts, 38, 83, 89–90, 140–42
bypass technology, 106–7

CARA (constant absolute risk aversion), 230–32, 382–84
Central Limit Theorem, 340